PROBLEMS IN
POLITICAL ECONOMY
An Urban Perspective

PROBLEMS IN
POLITICAL ECONOMY
An Urban Perspective

Edited and with Introductions by
DAVID M. GORDON

D.C. HEATH AND COMPANY
Lexington, Massachusetts

TO MY PARENTS

ACKNOWLEDGMENTS

This book grew out of a course I gave at Yale in the fall of 1969 on "The Economics of Urban Problems." Though large, the course allowed me a good deal of contact with my students. As we tried to communicate about this particular set of domestic problems, I became increasingly aware of our mutual dissatisfaction with standard curricular fare. We rarely found materials to feed our more and more radical curiosities. The students had difficulty understanding the similarities and differences among radical, liberal, and conservative analyses of the kinds of problems we were discussing, and I had trouble developing those comparisons. Often we complained to each other about the sterility of conventional economics.

Especially for their humanity, engagement, and concern, my most important debt is owed to those many students with whom I shared my initial frustrations. I also want to express my debts and thanks to several others:

Samuel Bowles, Joseph Persky, and Michael Reich, all of whom gave me important suggestions on potential readings;

Staff members of the College Division of D. C. Heath who prompted me to prepare the book, aided in the development of the manuscript, assisted me in securing permissions, and coordinated the production of the book;

Kay Larson, who offered many valuable suggestions for revision of the preliminary manuscript; and

Diana Gordon, who made helpful criticisms of all of my own contributions to the volume.

D. M. G.

CONTENTS

3 Education

4 Poverty

5 Crime

6 Health

7 Housing

8 Transportation

9 Environment

GENERAL INTRODUCTION

George Kennan once found the perfect simile for America's style of response to new political problems. He was describing United States reaction to its involvement in World War I.[1]

I sometimes wonder whether . . . a democracy is not uncomfortably similar to one of those prehistoric monsters with a body as long as this room and a brain the size of a pin: he lies there in his comfortable primeval mud and pays little attention to his environment; he is slow to wrath—in fact, you practically have to whack his tail off to make him aware that his interests are being disturbed; but, once he grasps this, he lays about him with such blind determination that he not only destroys his adversary but largely wrecks his native habitat.

In the same way that the United States suddenly awoke to the European conflict more than fifty years ago, it dramatically uncovered an "urban crisis" in the 1960's. The country had ignored urban problems for years while it contained Communism. But the crisis of events clobbered us over the head. Riots, crime, poverty, congestion, slums, pollution—they all assaulted our slumber.

Tyrannosaurically, the democracy declared war on its urban problems. A barrage of reports and programs boomed from the Washington cannons. Whenever we turned around, another commission professed its wisdom or another agency declared its plans. For wisdom, we read reports from the Kerner Commission on riots, the Eisenhower Commission on violence, the Kaiser Commission on urban housing, the Douglas Commission on urban problems, the Heineman Commission on income maintenance programs, the Crime Commission, and the Commission on hunger. The Ribicoff subcommittee met through 17 volumes of hearings on the "federal role in urban affairs." City officials competed for press coverage with escalating estimates of the billions it would take to solve their local problems.

For action, we watched Great Society programs proliferate like stepchildren of the New Deal. Almost randomly permuting numbers and letters, planners coined scores of new names for their projects. MDTA, NYC, CEP, and CAMPS, to pick a few, would solve our manpower problems. ESEA Title I would help the schools. Armed with 221D-3, we would rebuild the city slums. And HUD, DOT, and OEO would form a domestic Joint Chiefs of Staff, directing the battles for the capital.

By the end of the decade, the government's frantic response to crisis had indeed wrecked the "habitat." Slums were leveled but new housing rarely replaced the old. Promises abounded but performance lagged. Their expectations raised, many citizens reacted bitterly to program failures. Many others, a not so silent and quite angry majority, complained they had been ignored in the rush of the decade. One remembered that triumphant American general after the battle of Hue in South Vietnam: "We had to destroy the city in order to save it."

---

[1] George Kennan, *American Diplomacy* (N.Y.: New American Library, 1952), p. 59.

Finally, nearly as suddenly, after the swirl and gunshot, the country tried to forget the crisis. From under the rubble, a new Administration proclaimed a new calm. In effect, the democracy reclined again in the primeval mud. Describing the mood in Washington in 1970, Richard Sennett wrote: "Now, during the current ascendancy of the 'hardheaded realists,' conservatives in both the Administration and Congress have concluded that the cure for the diseases of previous liberal action programs is 'pragmatic' inaction. . . . [Men] of various motives have come to believe in the idea of 'benign neglect'. . . ."[2]

The problems, of course, remained. One set of responses had failed to solve them. Another, more conservative reflex had chosen to ignore them. The only advantage of the quiet was that we finally had time to reflect on the validity of these public analyses. I have prepared this book of readings to contribute to that reflection. The urban crisis persists, however deeply we've buried our heads, and I would argue that neither liberal nor conservative analysis understands its basic source.

PROBLEMS IN POLITICAL ECONOMY

The problems of the urban crisis constitute only a few of the important social problems confronting the United States as the 1970's begin. And the reigning liberal and conservative responses to the crisis comprise only two of several general analytic views of social problems. In analyzing any of the problems facing this country, one can view them from a wide variety of academic disciplines and from a number of contrasting analytic and normative perspectives.

Central to the understanding of all of those problems are the tools of "political economy"— tools which help us understand how economic, political, and social institutions determine the allocation of scarce economic resources and goods; through those allocative patterns, social problems are defined and emerge. Three principal analytic and normative perspectives are typically applied to understand the political economy of those problems in the United States— radical, liberal, and conservative views of society. Each of these three basic perspectives tends to interpret the sources of the problems differently, and each tends to suggest varying solutions.

In general and somewhat indirectly, I have hoped with this book of readings to exemplify and crystallize the nature of conflict among these three analytic perspectives, and through that crystallization to help clarify some basic issues about the nature of the American political economy. I have chosen to concentrate on the problems of the urban crisis as examples because that concentration permits an indispensable detail of discussion, because so much confusion has plagued the public discussion of these problems, and because the liberal and conservative perspectives have had such direct influence on the evolution of public policies toward their solution.

I have chosen to emphasize the radical analysis of the problems with which this book deals, because that analysis has generally been neglected in public discussion and because I think the radical perspective provides the only valid framework within which to understand their origins, manifestations, and potential solutions. Other books are available which thoroughly outline the liberal and conservative approaches. I have intended in this book to suggest a framework within which we can compare perspectives, and, redressing historic neglect, to outline the radical analysis of urban problems as fully as possible. Within much too narrow covers, the arguments in this book could never be conclusive. I can only hope that this book will begin to suggest some ways to ask questions about our political economy, and second, to reveal the fundamental importance of the radical view.

To encompass the urban crisis, I have chosen eight critical urban problems which seemed to dominate the substance and tone of the crisis during the 1960's: the urban problems of employment, education, poverty, crime, health, housing, transportation, and environment. These are not our only serious domestic problems, nor are they the only problems with special severity in urban areas. As Americans responded to urban problems in the previous decade, however, these eight seemed to dominate public attention.

Public concern with these problems often focused exclusively on their virulence in central-

---

[2] Richard Sennett, "Survival of the Fattest," *New York Review of Books*, August 13, 1970.

city ghettos, especially black slums in the North. In this book, too, I have paid special attention to conditions in those ghettos. I have done so not because I think the problems exist only there, nor even because I think ghetto conditions demand the most urgent government action. Rather, I have tried to confront public perceptions of urban problems in terms of the public's own definitions, in order most cogently to suggest a radical explanation of those problems. My interest, it should be clear, involves debate about analysis, not about definition.

A radical analysis of such social problems involves the application of a radical "paradigm" or general set of theories about society. The application of that paradigm requires three stages of argument. First, one argues that the dynamics of the mode of production in capitalist societies tend to produce certain kinds of dominant class and institutional structures. Second, one contends that the nature of those classes and institutions—manifest in different ways in different social settings—"explains" a particular set of social problems, that those problems can be seen as inevitable consequences of the institutions. Third, one concludes that the problems cannot be "solved" without fundamental changes in those institutions, and that it would require a radically different mode of production to allow the necessary institutional change.

THE SCOPE AND STRUCTURE OF THE BOOK

It would require many volumes adequately to compare perspectives on the urban crisis and to cover all three stages of the radical analysis. In the space available, I have been able to pursue only part of the task. In order most directly to fulfill the general purposes of this book, I have found it convenient to concentrate on the second of the three stages of the radical analysis, on the argument that these problems derive from the basic institutions of our capitalist society. The general radical paradigm has been developed elsewhere, but it has not been extensively *applied* to this particular set of problems. And perhaps more clearly than any others, these problems dramatically illustrate the differences among perspectives and the usefulness of the radical view.

The most explicit and direct purpose of this book, in short, is *to present eight specific urban problems as inevitable consequences of the American class and institutional structure.*

To fulfill that objective, I have organized the readings and introductions on three different levels.

1. To understand the application of a general analytic perspective, one must obviously understand something about the general contours of that perspective. Further, to make some decisions about its relative validity, one must understand something about other interpretations of the same reality. As Thomas Kuhn has written, "To be accepted as a paradigm, a theory must seem better than its competitors. . . ."[3]

The book begins at this general level in Chapter One. The chapter is intended to acquaint the reader briefly with the three principal views about society: the radical perspective applied throughout this book, the liberal perspective ascendant during the 1960's, and the conservative perspective dominant in Washington in the early '70s. The chapter's readings and introductions outline the basic analytic hypotheses of those perspectives, their respective theories of the State, and their most pervasive normative predispositions. Because the perspectives have been discussed at great length in other works, the chapter covers them somewhat cursorily.

2. The next eight chapters analyze the separate problems. To make the boundaries of the analysis clear, I have devoted some space in each chapter to a summary of definitions and magnitudes. The Introductions begin with a summary of facts and figures, and each set of readings begins with a cluster of selections on Impressions, Definitions, and Magnitudes. In each of those initial groups of readings, I have included one piece of journalism evoking a qualitative impression of the problem; it seemed important to glimpse the problems in human terms before dissecting them analytically. Not all of the readings in these sections are by radicals. I have chosen selections which discussed the dimensions of each problem in the clearest way; often, those definitions have been presented by analysts with quite different opinions from my own.

3. Finally, each chapter contains a basic core of analytic discussion. My Introductions summarize the general structure of the radical argument, sketching the application of the paradigm to the respective problems. Necessarily, the nature of the application varies from case to case.

[3] Thomas Kuhn, *The Structure of Scientific Revolutions* (Chicago: Phoenix paperbacks, 1964), p. 17.

Further, the Introductions note some important differences between the radical interpretations on the one hand and the liberal and conservative analyses on the other—again to permit some comparison of the relative validity of the three perspectives. The readings then elaborate important points of the radical analysis. Sometimes I have either lacked space or have not been able to find readings amplifying each step of the radical argument. One should therefore read the Introductions first, to understand the general outline of the analysis, and then explore the separate readings within that general framework.

Ironically, some of the readings supporting the radical analysis have not been written by radicals. In some cases, it seemed to me that a single point of the general argument had been stated most clearly by someone of different general persuasion. I have noted those instances in the separate chapters. Also, I have sometimes included readings which apply the liberal or conservative analyses further to underscore the differences between those and the radical perspectives. Each Introduction carefully clarifies the purpose of the separate selections.

I have concluded each chapter with a bibliography of additional readings. Though not as detailed as they might be, the bibliographies offer relatively extensive additional references on each problem. I have organized the bibliographies in each chapter by subject, and have arranged the suggestions in order of their difficulty or specificity. I have also added brief annotations if the titles did not seem self-explanatory.

In three of the chapters—on employment, education, and health—I have added a selection suggesting a vision of how the problem might be "solved" in a completely different institutional context. In most cases, one needs little imagination to envision a solution to the problem; in the case of crime, for instance, one simply seeks a society without any. In these three instances, however, it seemed to me useful to illustrate the human dimensions of possible solutions to the problem.

Further, in some cases, I have added an Editor's Supplement to the readings to summarize some indispensable facts or arguments where I could not find an appropriate selection.

Finally, it seems important to note that I have not been able, either in Introductions or with readings, thoroughly to explore the important *interconnections* among these eight problems. Each problem is directly related to the other seven, and they all have mutual causes and effects, but there has been such limited space that I have been forced to outline analyses of each problem quite separately from the others. Because of those space limitations, and because of the impossibility of sketching interconnections, I fear that the outlines of the radical analysis in the separate chapters may seem slightly exaggerated and one-dimensional. In this preface of cautions and explanations, I feel the need especially to urge the importance of trying to use the book as an implicit guide to the critical and proliferating connections among social problems like these. Above all else, the radical analysis stresses that each problem derives jointly from some mutual structural sources, and that each problem tends inevitably to reinforce the others.

THE USES AND LIMITATIONS OF THE BOOK

This book of readings, typically, has been intended primarily for use in college curricula, although I hope it will be read by others outside the college setting. I have not designed it for use in any particular course because I suspect it could be helpful in four different kinds of courses.

One could use it best, probably, in an introductory course on urban problems, either an economics or an interdisciplinary course. Ideally, it should be used in conjunction with other books which detail the liberal and conservative analyses of these same problems. Fortunately, some very recent books provide an excellent expression of those other perspectives; they would be perfect complements to this book. Edward Banfield's book, *The Unheavenly City*, provides a coherent and vigorous articulation of the conservative view.[4] And three recent books are available to elaborate the liberal perspective. Dick Netzer's *Economics and Urban Problems* offers a single author's rather consistent application of the views of conventional economic analysis.[5] And two collections of readings provide intelligent discussions of most of the problems included in this book. An excellent collection of essays edited by James Q. Wilson, *The Metropolitan*

[4] (Boston: Little, Brown, 1970).
[5] (N.Y.: Basic Books, 1970).

Enigma, originally published in 1968, has been revised for a recent paperback edition.[6] A slightly less coherent collection, edited by Daniel P. Moynihan, *Toward a National Urban Policy,* was also published last year.[7]

The limitation of this volume for an interdisciplinary course on urban problems is that the reading selections concentrate on the economic aspects of these problems. This economic emphasis reflects my own background, and it also obviously derives from the central argument of radical analysis—that the economic mode of production determines the basic structure of social and economic conditions. It does mean, however, that courses more interested in the sociological or political elements of urban problems might need to develop additional materials.

A second principal use for the book could come in an introductory course in radical economic analysis. This volume of readings would provide a very useful illustration of the ways in which the general radical paradigm can be applied to specific problems.

Third, the book might be helpful in conventional introductory economics courses. More and more, such courses have tried to illustrate the relevance of orthodox economic theory to important social problems. The problems discussed in this book are current and critical; without question, they pose an extremely difficult test of the relevance of orthodox tools.

The book might also be helpful in another kind of course, a traditional exploration of "urban economics." Here the book would be limited to use as an introduction to the reality of problems which urban economic theory tries to interpret. It could not possibly serve as a core text. Its usefulness to such courses would be limited for two reasons. First, traditional urban economics courses rely on the standard analytic tools of orthodox economic theory; this volume of readings draws on a paradigm which disputes the validity of those tools. Second, I have excluded discussion of two issues which have traditionally dominated the field of urban economics: the economic development of cities and local public finance. I have not included the former because it does not effectively constitute a critical problem we care very much about solving. (Understanding the patterns and forces of urban economic development helps us to understand the problems in this book, but the consequences of those patterns flow through the problems included here; they do not develop a separate life of their own.) And I have not included the subject of local public finance because including it would have confused the nature of the analysis in this book. The crisis of local public finance is that cities no longer have any money to mount their own programs to solve their own problems. The implication of the radical analysis is that local governments could not solve the problems even if they had the money, for they would neither attempt to nor be able to change the basic class and institutional structure of society.

Nonetheless, despite all those limitations, I think that the book would provide a very provocative introduction to the kinds of problems discussed in conventional courses on urban economics.

A POLITICAL DISCLAIMER

The arguments in this book suggest that we must radically change the structure of all our institutions before we can effectively solve any of our problems in urban areas. It argues, in effect, that this country needs a revolution to solve its urban crisis. I should make it absolutely clear, however, that the book does not in any way offer insights on the best political means for achieving that revolution. Discussion of that political issue has filled volumes before and will obviously fill more to come. I have not had space in this volume to add to the debate.

My aim has been merely to contribute to the clarity of our thinking about a group of social problems. Before any of us can effectively debate political strategies for solving those problems, we must be absolutely clearheaded about their origins. Eldridge Cleaver once put the tactical debates in their proper context. "We go back to basic principles," he wrote, "and we say that in order for this situation to be salvaged, we need sane people in this country; we need sane black people and we need sane white people."[8] Shedding our illusions, restoring our sanity, we can begin to act with intelligence and compassion.

---

[6] (Cambridge: Harvard University Press, 1968), and (Garden City: Doubleday, 1970).
[7] (N.Y.: Basic Books, 1970).
[8] *Post-Prison Writings and Speeches of Eldridge Cleaver,* ed. by Robert Scheer (N.Y.: McGraw-Hill Ramparts Book), p. 117.

1 General Perspectives...
Radical, Liberal, Conservative

Editor's Introduction

"Normal science" means research firmly based upon one or more past scientific achievements, achievements that some particular scientific community acknowledges for a time as supplying the foundation for its further practice. . . . [Textbooks codifying these achievements] served for a time to define the legitimate problems and methods of a research field for succeeding generations of practitioners. . . . Their achievement was sufficiently unprecedented to attract an enduring group of adherents away from competing modes of scientific activity. Simultaneously, it was sufficiently open-ended to leave all sorts of problems for the redefined group of practitioners to resolve.

Achievements that share these two characteristics I shall . . . refer to as "paradigms." . . . In the absence of a paradigm or some candidate for paradigm, all of the facts that could possibly pertain to the development of a given science are likely to seem equally relevant. . . . To be accepted as a paradigm, a theory must seem better than its competitors. . . .

—Thomas S. Kuhn
The Structure of Scientific Revolutions[1]

When asked whether or not we are Marxist, our position is the same as that of a physicist or a biologist when asked if he is a "Newtonian" or if he is a "Pasteurian."

There are truths so evident, so much a part of people's knowledge, that it is now useless to discuss them. One ought to be "Marxist" with the same naturalness with which one is "Newtonian" in physics, or "Pasteurian" in biology, considering that if facts determine new concepts, these new concepts will never divest themselves of that portion of truth possessed by the older concepts they have outdated. . . .

The advances in social and political science, as in other fields, belong to a long historical process whose links are connecting, adding up, molding and constantly perfecting themselves.

—Ernesto "Che" Guevara
"Notes for the Study of the Ideology of the Cuban Revolution"[2]

With readings and introductions, this book seeks to present a radical analysis of some critical urban problems in the United States. The analyses of these separate problems derive from a general radical view of society, from a radical "paradigm" or basic conception of social reality.[3] Like many other "paradigms" in the social sciences, the radical perspective involves some general analytic and philosophical assumptions about the nature of individuals and their relations

---

[1] (Chicago: University of Chicago Press, 1962), pp. 10, 15, 17.
[2] *Studies on the Left*, Vol. 1, No. 3, 1960.
[3] Kuhn's book, from which the first opening quotation was taken, provides a brilliant discussion of the role of paradigms in defining the terms of research in the natural sciences. He speaks some in the book about research in the social sciences. For one interesting discussion of the application of Kuhn's insights to the social sciences and especially to economics, see Paul Sweezy, "Toward a Critique of Economics," *The Review of Radical Political Economics*, Spring, 1970.

1

in society. One cannot begin to appreciate the implications of succeeding chapters in this book without first understanding the structure of the radical "paradigm" and its differences from other important social perspectives. I have tried in this introductory chapter to provide the barest skeleton of background for the specific analyses which follow.

I have concentrated on three general social perspectives: radical, liberal, and conservative. One can reasonably argue (and radicals often do) that liberal and conservative views of society do not differ fundamentally, but rather that they represent opposite extremes on a continuum of qualitatively similar definitions of social reality.[4] (The views' similarities are discussed further in the concluding remarks of this introduction.) I have chosen to treat them separately in this chapter because their views on the role of the State differ so strongly. In analyzing urban problems, one must pay special attention to varying positions on the potential of government solutions to those problems. A paradigm's postulates about the State therefore assume critical importance.[5]

This chapter focuses on three particular elements of these general perspectives. First, I have tried very briefly to outline the paradigms' basic analytic hypotheses about social reality, their "positive" preconceptions about the ways in which individuals relate to each other in a social context. Second, I have tried to sketch their views of the State, of its role in present societies and the role it ought to play in any society. Third, I have suggested a few important elements of their "normative" assumptions and values, their criticisms of current societies and their visions of an "ideal" society. I do not intend that this book should provide elaborate arguments about the "best" kind of society.[6] But I do not believe that analyses of society can be completely objective, free somehow of all normative judgments. With Gunnar Myrdal, I believe that "every study of a social problem, however limited in scope, is and must be determined by valuations. A 'disinterested' social science has never existed and, for logical reasons, can never exist."[7] In order to understand the radical analysis of social problems and its differences with other views of those problems, one must necessarily isolate the kinds of normative predispositions that different analysts have carried with them into their work.

In this Introduction, I have discussed the radical view in the first section and the liberal and conservative perspectives in the second section. In a third section, I have briefly described the six selections which follow. Two readings represent each paradigm; of the two, the first amplifies the paradigm's general approach to social problems, while the second outlines its postulates about the State.

I have tried to avoid arguments at this stage of the book about the relative validity of the three perspectives. Although I feel strongly that the radical view provides the clearest understanding of reality and that its normative vision is most compelling, I have tried to abstain from criticisms of the two other views in this Introduction. I agree with Paul Sweezy about the appropriate basis for choosing among alternative paradigms: "It seems to me that from a scientific point of view the question of choosing between . . . approaches . . . can be answered quite simply. Which more accurately reflects the fundamental characteristics of social reality which is under analysis?"[8] Since the specific analyses in the succeeding chapters deal much more directly with reality than the abstractions of this Introduction, I have saved my comments, criticisms, and preferences about the perspectives until then.

THE RADICAL VIEW

A modern radical analysis of society draws from but does not depend exclusively on the seminal nineteenth-century work of Karl Marx. Marx's analysis of society made original theoreti-

---

[4] Many radicals certainly view the liberal and conservative views as qualitatively similar expressions of a basic orthodox analysis. Furthermore, there is some confusion over the terminology, since modern conservatism derives directly from classical nineteenth-century English "liberalism."

[5] For perhaps the strongest recent statement of these differences, see Milton Friedman, *Capitalism and Freedom* (Chicago: University of Chicago Press, 1962), *passim*, and the selection from the book below.

[6] Obviously I think such discussions are quintessentially important. I simply think that they should be conducted at length, in detail, and with considerable subtlety. I have not had enough space in this book to allow such discussion.

[7] Gunnar Myrdal, *Objectivity in Social Research* (N.Y.: Pantheon Books, 1969), p. 55.

[8] "Toward a Critique of Economics," *op. cit.*, p. 2.

cal contributions on both substantive and methodological levels. In his methodological discussions, he insisted that general theories or analytic views of society cannot remain aloof from the course of history, somehow eternally fixed above the evolutions and revolutions of society below. As society changes, so must theories about its nature change. Analysis of society should reflect a dynamic synthesis of theory and reality.[9]

Thoroughly in agreement, modern radicals no longer dwell exclusively on textual exegeses of Marx's writings. As Ernest Mandel puts it, radical economic analysis "endeavours to start from the empirical data of the science of today in order to examine whether or not the essence of Marx's economic propositions remains valid."[10] In sketching the basic features of a radical analysis of American society, I have built from recent radical writings more than from Marx, and from recent historical events more than from the events which Marx perceived.[11]

The underlying analytic framework of the radical "paradigm" involves five basic clusters of hypotheses about society.

1. The analysis argues that the structure and evolution of any society depend principally on the society's dominant mode of economic production. Because basic modes of production differ, capitalist societies differ fundamentally from feudal societies, for instance, and from socialist societies.[12] "By mode of production [Marx] did not refer merely to the state of technique—to what he termed the state of the productive forces—but to the way in which the means of production were owned and to the social relations between men which resulted from their connections with the process of production."[13] As Robert Tucker further elaborates, "In every instance . . . the mode of productive activity has been the definitive fact of the social epoch, the determinant of the character of society in all of its superstructural expressions: political, legal, intellectual, [and] religious. . . ."[14]

2. The most important and most distinctive feature of the mode of production in capitalist societies is its organization of labor by means of the wage-contract.

Thus Capitalism was not simply a system of production for the market—a system of commodity-production as Marx termed it—but a system under which labour-power had 'itself become a commodity' and was bought and sold on the market like any other object of exchange. Its historical prerequisite was the concentration of ownership of the means of production in the hands of a class, consisting of only a minor section of society, and the consequential emergence of a propertyless class for whom the sale of their labour-power was their only source of livelihood. Productive activity was furnished, accordingly, by the latter, not by virtue of legal compulsion, but on the basis of a wage-contract.[15]

Recent anthropological evidence has made clear that this basic organization of work and labor originated historically with capitalist societies, that antecedent societies organized work in different ways. Writing about this singular characteristic of production in capitalist societies, Marx himself said, "Without it there is no capital, no bourgeoisie, no bourgeois society."[16]

3. The analysis isolates two other important features of capitalist societies—the private

---

[9] Indeed, Marx's major criticism of orthodox classical political economists was that they tried to abstract from historical change, that they attempted, in his words, "to blot out all historical differences." ("Introduction to the Critique of Political Economy," in David Horowitz, ed., *Marx and Modern Economics* [N.Y.: Monthly Review Press, 1968], p. 45. For the best presentation of Marx's methodological views, see this article.)

[10] Ernest Mandel, *Marxist Economic Theory* (N.Y.: Monthly Review Press, 1969), Vol. I, p. 17.

[11] The two best recent discussions, in addition to Mandel, *ibid.*, are Paul Baran and Paul Sweezy, *Monopoly Capital* (N.Y.: Monthly Review Press, 1966), and André Gorz, *Strategy for Labor* (Boston: Beacon Press, 1967).

[12] Marx presented this basic argument most eloquently in Marx and Friedrich Engels, *The Communist Manifesto* (N.Y.: International Publishers, 1948), first published in 1848.

[13] Maurice Dobb, *Studies in the Development of Capitalism* (N.Y.: International Publishers, 1963), rev. ed., p. 7.

[14] Tucker, *The Marxian Revolutionary Idea* (N.Y.: W. W. Norton, 1969), p. 15.

[15] Dobb, *op. cit.*, p. 7.

[16] Marx, *The Class Struggles in France 1848-1850* (N.Y.: International Publishers, n.d.), p. 42. For quite convincing evidence on earlier societies, see the anthropological discussions in Mandel, *op. cit.*, and some of the essays of Karl Polanyi in George Dalton, ed., *Primitive, Archaic, and Modern Economies: Essays of Karl Polanyi* (Garden City: Doubleday, 1968), especially "The Self-Regulating Market and the Fictitious Commodities: Land, Labor and Money."

ownership of capital and the dominance of impersonal "markets" in which goods and productive factors are exchanged for money.[17] It contends that these two features combine to produce the central dynamic force in capitalist societies, the unceasing attempt by owners of capital to increase continuously their absolute and relative share of capital by nearly any means.[18] The forces of competition among capitalists, whether among small independent shopkeepers or corporate giants, inevitably force owners of capital to protect themselves against their competitors by producing more goods and accumulating more and more profit.[19] As Mandel puts it, "The capitalist mode of production thus becomes the first mode of production in the history of mankind the essential aim of which appears to be *unlimited increase in production.* . . ."[20] Because this dominates the priorities of the society, as Edwards and MacEwan put it in their selection below, "Human needs become subordinated to the needs of the market and to capital expansion."[21]

4. Given the specific historical circumstances in which capitalism first appeared in Western societies, this consuming drive for capital accumulation has produced enormous increases in aggregate social production and wealth. Once begun, these increases in productive capacity tend to reinforce themselves, with each major technological innovation leading inevitably to another. Spurred by the continuing competition among capitalists for markets and profits, this process of productive-capacity-increase creates a dynamic momentum all its own.[22]

These enormous increases in productive capacity and in social wealth create two principal and related contradictions in capitalist societies with fundamental impact on the evolution of those societies.

a. First, they build on and lead to what Mandel calls the "objective socialisation of production."[23] Men no longer work individually, producing for their own needs. The division of labor under capitalism inevitably effects a complete *interdependence* among men as producers. "The work of each is indispensable to the survival of all, so that each can survive only thanks to the work of thousands and thousands of other men."[24]

But at the same time, capitalism depends on and enforces a totally private, frequently ruthless competition among men. Capitalists must compete with capitalists, workers with workers, through every phase of social activity. Brought into "objective" relationships of social cooperation in production, men are induced subjectively to fight against those cooperative ties. White workers learn to hate black workers, for instance, even though they are thrown together in working situations. The juxtaposition of these two basic dynamics in capitalist societies becomes fundamentally contradictory; they feed upon each other to determine many of the characteristics of capitalist institutions.[25]

---

[17] There were impersonal markets and private ownership of capital before capitalism, but they never so thoroughly defined any other economic systems. See Mandel, *op. cit.,* Chapters One through Four.

[18] There is some disagreement in the radical literature about the importance of the form of original appropriation. Many Marxists have argued that capitalists originally acquired their capital almost exclusively through robbery and piracy. This argument was originally stated most strongly by Proudhon in *What Is Property? An Inquiry Into the Principles of Right and Government,* written in 1840. Other radicals acknowledge that some original capital, as orthodox economists claim, was acquired by thrift, patience, calculation, and entrepreneurial energy. For a balancing of the two views, see Mandel, *op. cit.* In any case, everyone agrees that capitalists continue inevitably to produce more and try to enlarge their share of capital *once* they have acquired their original store.

[19] For the best recent discussions of the dynamics of this competition among corporate giants, see Baran and Sweezy, *Monopoly Capital, op. cit.,* and, from a liberal's point of view, J. K. Galbraith, *The New Industrial State* (Boston: Houghton Mifflin, 1967).

[20] *Marxist Economic Theory, op. cit.,* p. 133. (Emphasis Mandel's.)

[21] See section II of their article reprinted below.

[22] For a brilliant discussion of the dynamics of this technological side of capitalist societies, see Jacques Ellul, *Technological Society* (N.Y.: Knopf, 1964). Ellul is in fact not a Marxist; he attributes to the unique nature of technological change the same kind of determining force and power that radicals attribute to the mode of capitalist production.

[23] *Marxist Economic Theory, op. cit.,* p. 170.

[24] *Loc. cit.*

[25] This argument is difficult to formulate but its importance cannot possibly be underestimated. The contradiction's effects pervade capitalist societies. For instance, workers become increasingly cooperative (in this objective sense) in bureaucratic organizations, in which everyone works jointly on the "products" of the bureaucracy. But the nature of capitalist institutions cannot permit an equality of cooperation, for that would undercut the class divisions from which capitalists derive their power. So all kinds of new,

b. In similar ways, these vast increases in productive capacity establish for the first time in history the fundamental irrationality of class conflict in society. Class conflicts have always existed, but they seemed rather inevitable in pre-capitalist societies. With the very early pre-capitalist development of social cooperation in production and with primitive technological innovations, individual men first became capable of producing more with their own labor than was necessary to sustain their own existence—to feed, house, and clothe them and their families. In primitive societies, the village and tribal communities sometimes used this emergent "surplus product" communally, cooperatively reducing all of their working times and increasing all of their opportunities for leisure. But pre-capitalist forms of production did not generate very large surplus products, certainly not enough to allow all members of a society to share in very much leisure. Inevitably, some members of society sought to free themselves from work altogether. At different stages of social and economic development and in different ways, some men in societies gained control over the labor of others, providing for themselves by living off the surplus product of those whose labor they controlled. Chieftains lived off the product of their slaves, for instance, while the slaves worked long enough to provide both for themselves and for their rulers. Class conflict grew out of that appropriation of "surplus product."[26] As Mandel puts it, "The producers have never accepted as normal or natural that the surplus product of their labour should be seized by the possessing classes, who thus obtain a monopoly of leisure and culture. . . . The history of mankind is nothing but a long succession of class struggles."[27]

Finally, with capitalist society, the struggles of producers to reclaim some of their surplus product *could* cease. Society begins to produce enough so that *everyone* in society could acquire opportunities for considerable leisure activities. Mandel explains this development clearly:[28]

It is the capitalist mode of production that, by the extraordinary advance of the productive forces which it makes possible, creates for the first time in history the economic conditions needed for the abolition of class society altogether. The social surplus product would suffice to reduce extensively the working time of all men, which would ensure an advance of culture that would enable functions of accumulation (and management) to be exercised by the whole of society.

But capitalism depends on the private ownership of property and the ability of owners of capital constantly to (try to) accumulate more and more of "surplus product." Some members of society continue to obtain enormous shares of wealth and leisure, while others continue to support both themselves and others with their labor. Class conflicts inevitably continue in capitalist societies.[29] The facts that society now produces enough so that everyone could share adequately in wealth and leisure—without some receiving disproportionate shares—and that class conflicts could therefore potentially cease render those conflicts all the more irrational.[30]

relatively artificial distinctions develop within the bureaucratic organization to permit objectively cooperative work but to maintain sharp distinctions among workers. Job titles are refined to establish distinct job hierarchies, offices become badges to status, innumerable "ports-of-entry" develop to stratify the work force by initial job level and educational attainment. For more on this example, see the Introduction to the chapter on employment.

[26] This discussion draws heavily on Mandel, *op. cit.*, pp. 170–177. Mandel provides plentiful examples of very early class conflicts.

[27] *Ibid.*, p. 175.

[28] *Ibid.*, p. 177.

[29] It has been an essential argument of orthodox liberal and conservative critiques of Marxism that class conflicts have disappeared in advanced capitalist economies like the United States. These arguments emphasize the "happiness" of relatively affluent blue-collar workers. They ignore, first of all, the obvious bloodiness of the fight for union recognition and workers' rights in the United States between 1870 and 1940. And they tend to neglect the extent to which class conflict has been successfully diffused by capitalist institutions into many conflicts among many classes. On this point, see the piece by Edwards and MacEwan below. For general discussion, see T. B. Bottomore, *Classes in Modern Society* (N.Y.: Random House, 1966).

[30] This argument obviously provides a historical background for an observation often made about the recent struggle by blacks for freedom and equality in the United States. It has often been noted that their movement gained its strength at least partly from the phenomenon of "relative deprivation": from the increasingly striking gap between black standards of living and white standards of living in the midst of affluence. Blacks see the goods on television, and tend increasingly to demand them as the goods seem more attractive. For several statements of this argument, see Kenneth Clark and Talcott Parsons, eds., *The Negro American* (Boston: Houghton Mifflin, 1967).

5. Finally, these basic forces defining and driving capitalist societies produce a constantly changing set of basic social institutions. These institutions largely determine the nature and content of daily life in capitalist societies, as well as the ways in which the basic forces driving capitalist societies are manifested. MacEwan and Edwards isolate five "system-defining" institutions in capitalist societies; these institutions, in turn, determine the nature of other important institutions. The "system-defining" institutions are:[31]

. . . the market in labor, in which labor is treated as a commodity and allocated on the basis of the highest bidder; control of the work process by those who own and control capital, including the concomitant loss of control by the worker over his activities during the hours of work; the legal relations of ownership, by which income distribution is determined through payments to owners for the use of their productive factors; homo economicus, *the system of personality traits characteristic of and functional to capitalism, including especially the system of individual gain incentives; and the ideology which abstracts and organizes 'reality' in such a way as to justify and facilitate the operation of the other institutions.*

Given these primary institutions, the analysis involves three basic hypotheses about them: first, that the nature and structure of these institutions directly determine the nature of social relations in society; second, that these institutions determine the distribution of power among groups and individuals and therefore determine the specific historical resolutions of class conflicts; and third, that the most important institutions ultimately benefit those directly included in or associated with the capitalist class. Louis Althusser summarizes this set of hypotheses precisely:[32]

They reveal the basic notion that the contradiction between Capital and Labor is never simple, but always specified by the historically concrete forms and circumstances in which it is exercised. *It is specified by the forms of the superstructure (the State, the dominant ideology, religion, politically organized movements, etc.); specified by the internal and external historical situation which determines it as on the one hand a function of the* national past . . . *and on the other as functions of the* existing world context.

In their selection below, Edwards and MacEwan discuss the ways in which the basic institutions of capitalism "specify" the general tendencies of capitalist societies, especially in the United States.

The radical view of the State follows clearly from these basic postulates. Since it is discussed quite completely in the pieces by Sweezy and by Edwards and MacEwan which follow, this view can be summarized very briefly here. The State, in the radical view, operates ultimately to serve the interests of the controlling class in a class society. Since the "capitalist class" fundamentally controls capitalist societies, the State functions in those societies to serve that class. It does so either directly, by providing services only to members of that class, or indirectly, by helping preserve the system of institutions which support and maintain the power of that class. In the United States, government subsidy of defense firms provides a clear example of the former, while government support of and control over an educational system which fundamentally supports the "system-defining" institutions illustrates the latter.[33]

Given this basic perspective, the radical analysis of specific social problems flows quite directly. A radical argues that specific social problems represent the inevitable consequences of the structure of capitalist institutions. Edwards and MacEwan, in the selection below, provide many examples of this kind of analysis of general problems in the United States, glancing briefly, for instance, at alienation, inequality, racism, and imperialism. The chapters which follow this introduction provide examples of this analysis at a more specific level, examining eight separate problems associated with the "urban crisis" of the 1960's in the United States. In each of those chapters, I have attempted to use introductions and readings to provide a specific illustra-

---

[31] See section II of their article below.

[32] "Contradiction and Overdetermination," in Carl Oglesby, ed., *The New Left Reader* (N.Y.: Grove Press, 1969), p. 73. (Emphasis Althusser's.) In the United States, obviously, the specification is dominated by large corporations, racial tension, affluence, our liberal ideology, the power of the state, its international role, and so on.

[33] Edwards and MacEwan discuss these and other examples at greater length in their selection below.

tion of this basic view. In different ways, each chapter argues that the problem with which it is concerned has flowed inevitably from the specific manifestation of capitalism and the specific evolution of capitalist institutions in the United States. The conclusions of the separate chapters follow precisely: *One cannot expect the problems to disappear unless the basic institutions themselves change.* And one cannot expect changes in these fundamental institutions unless the needs of capitalists change, or unless those classes in conflict with capitalists become strong enough to force such change.[34]

Some of the flavor of those specific chapters depends heavily on the normative elements of the radical perspective, on its criticisms of capitalist societies and its vision of a "better" society.

Radicals criticize capitalist society essentially because it evolves irrationally. Its basic mode of production and the structures of its institutions create conflicts which do not need to exist. In the language of economics, it forces "trade-offs" that are not necessary. Fundamentally, radicals argue, capitalism forces a conflict between the aggregate wealth of society (and obviously the enormous wealth of some individuals) and the freedom of most individuals. In another, truly democratic, humanist and socialist society, radicals argue, conditions could be forged in which increases in aggregate social wealth complemented the personal freedom of all individuals.[35] Edwards and MacEwan mention some of the other unnecessary conflicts created (or sustained) by capitalist societies: "income growth versus a meaningful work environment, employment versus stable prices, private versus social costs, public versus private consumption, and income versus leisure."[36] Other conflicts can be specified, but the criticisms gain force in the context of the radical vision of a "better" society.[37]

It should be emphasized in discussing the radical vision that many modern radicals, though socialist, do not view most modern socialist countries with great approval. To many Western radicals, the purposes and the realities of the socialist revolution in Cuba provide the closest manifest approximation to their ideals. Che Guevara, in many ways a more important ideologue of that revolution than Fidel Castro, has often expressed those ideals most eloquently.[38]

[34] Classically, the union movement in Western capitalist societies had the effect not only of improving conditions for many workers but also of changing many aspects of the basic work-place institutions and power relationships.

[35] Liberal and conservative ideologies argue the opposite, of course; they contend that capitalist societies provide maximum freedom and that socialist countries infringe on personal liberties. For extremely illuminating discussions of these normative issues, see Robert Wolff, *The Poverty of Liberalism* (Boston: Beacon Press, 1968), and Herbert Gintis, "Neo-Classical Welfare Economics and Individual Development," Occasional Paper No. 3, Union for Radical Political Economics, July, 1970 (URPE, P.O. Box 287, Cambridge, Mass. 02138). The classic defense of capitalist modes of production is that they are at least more efficient than other modes, therefore justifying some of their other problems. This may not even be true. Seymour Melman has described an extremely interesting study he made, for instance, of the relative efficiency (in purely capitalist or industrial terms) of conventional firms and cooperatively organized firms in Israel. The former, conventional firms predominate in Israel, but there are many communally owned firms in the *kibbutzim*. Melman quite carefully selected pairs of firms for comparative purposes, and found quite uniformly that the cooperative enterprises were more efficient (in terms of return to investment, labor and capital productivity) than the managerially administered enterprises in almost every instance and on nearly every dimension of comparison. His explanation, of course, was that the workers in the cooperative enterprises were much more highly motivated and that the firms required much less administrative superstructure. Seymour Melman, "Industrial Efficiency Under Managerial vs. Cooperative Decision-making: A Comparative Study of Manufacturing Enterprises in Israel," in *Studies in Comparative Economic Development* (Beverly Hills: Sage, 1969), also reprinted in *Review of Radical Political Economics*, Spring, 1970.

[36] See section II of their article below.

[37] For more on these "irrationalities" and conflicts, see especially Mandel, *op. cit.*, Gorz, *op. cit.*, and Herbert Marcuse, *One Dimensional Man* (Boston: Beacon, 1966). Some radicals obviously also criticize capitalist societies because they are unjust. Robert Tucker has argued very forcefully that Marx himself refused to criticize capitalism on these grounds. Marx felt that justice was purely situational, that values are defined exclusively within the context of a specific economic system and its institutions. Tucker concludes his argument that this was Marx's view: "Each mode of production has its own mode of distribution and its own form of equity, and it is meaningless to pass judgment on it from some other point of view." *The Marxian Revolutionary Idea, op. cit.*, p. 46. In any case, most radicals would agree that the irrationality of capitalism provides a sufficient basis for rejecting it on a normative level.

[38] For discussions of most of the following points, see Mandel, *op. cit.*, Oglesby, ed., *The New Left Reader, op. cit.*, and John Gerassi, ed., *Venceremos: The Speeches and Writings of Che Guevara* (N.Y.: Simon and Schuster, 1968).

Radicals envision an "ideal" society in which man could be free to develop himself as a human being and could at the same time cooperate socially with his fellowmen to help all men develop their potential. They argue that man could be free in democratic, humanist socialist societies, in contrast to his condition in capitalist societies, in the following ways:

—He could be free from the "whip of hunger," as Max Weber called it. Society would provide him with the necessities of life, all of them free. He would not be tied in sustaining himself to the income he received from the sale of his labor power.[39]

—He could be free from exploitation by more powerful classes. Socialist societies would consciously pursue a true equality among all, placing equality far above economic growth as a priority.[40]

—He could be free from the personal pressures and anxieties engendered by basically competitive relationships with other men. He would not have to compete for more income, better housing or more leisure, for all would be provided equally according to need.[41]

—He would be free, ultimately, from the tyranny of the perpetual division of labor. Through education and technology, radicals hope to reduce the amount of specialized labor necessary to produce social wealth so that all men have the chance to develop themselves through leisure as creative workers in widely varying pursuits.[42]

—He could be free to develop his individuality. Contrary to claims for capitalist society, radicals argue that capitalist society (and most current socialist societies) sacrifice human individuality to the standardized requirements of the production process. Radicals insist on establishing the highest priority for the development of humans as individuals.[43]

—He could be free to contribute positively to the welfare of fellow members of his community. In capitalism, radicals argue, man is forced to compete with others. In a socialist society with new institutions, he could be free to build together with others.

Guevara tries to contrast the condition of man in pre-revolutionary capitalist Cuba with his condition in the society toward which the revolution in Cuba is building. Under capitalism, he writes, society is "a dispersed force, divisible in thousands of fractions shot into space like the fragments of a grenade, trying by any and all means, in a fierce struggle with their equals, to achieve a position that would give them support in the face of an uncertain future."[44]

In building toward a truly communist society, Guevara says,[45]

Man begins to free his thought from the bothersome fact that presupposed the need to satisfy his animal needs by working. He begins to see himself portrayed in his work and to understand its human magnitude through the created object, through the work carried out. This no longer involves leaving a part of his being in the form of labor power sold, which no longer belongs to him; rather it signifies an emanation from himself, a contribution to the life of society in which he is reflected, the fulfillment of his social duty.

We are doing everything possible to give work this new category of social duty and to join it to the development of technology, on the one hand, which will provide the conditions

---

[39] Cuba has indeed begun to provide most basic consumer commodities free. See the piece by Zeitlin in the chapter on employment below.

[40] Although, as footnote 35 illustrates above, there may not necessarily be a conflict between the two objectives. See the piece by Zeitlin for a discussion of productivity in revolutionary Cuba.

[41] Guevara emphasizes that a spirit of cooperation does not somehow spontaneously appear in the first minute of a socialist society. He writes: "The flaws of the past are translated into the present in the individual consciousness and constant efforts must be made to eradicate them. The process is twofold: On the one hand society acts upon the individual by means of direct and indirect education; while on the other hand the individual undergoes a conscious phase of self-education." "Man and Socialism in Cuba," in Gerassi, ed., *op. cit.*, p. 390.

[42] Mandel, in Chapter 17 of *Marxist Economic Theory,* provides a very useful discussion of this point. "Nobody is *born* a street-sweeper, a welder, or a labourer," Mandel argues. "Vocational guidance endeavours at most to make use of *certain* callings in order to adapt man as rationally as possible to the needs of production . . ." in capitalist societies. Mandel, *ibid.*, p. 680. (Emphasis Mandel's.)

[43] Guevara strongly criticizes most modern socialist countries on these grounds, for instance. To avoid that pitfall, he argues, "Society must become a huge school." Men must learn an entirely new set of values and this becomes possible only in the context of an entirely new set of institutions. "Man and Socialism in Cuba," *op. cit.*, p. 391.

[44] *Ibid.*, p. 399.

[45] *Ibid.*, pp. 394, 400.

for greater freedom, and to voluntary work on the other, based on the Marxist concept that man truly achieves his full human condition when he produces without being compelled by the physical necessity of selling himself as a commodity.

We will make the twenty-first-century man. . . .

THE LIBERAL AND CONSERVATIVE VIEWS

This section will treat its subject perspectives quite briefly. I hope to summarize these paradigms only for comparative purposes. In the separate chapters which follow, I do not present the liberal and conservative analyses in detail. It seems necessary in this introductory chapter simply to provide some general reference points for later discussions.

I will summarize the basic points of the liberal and conservative analyses together, for they begin with the same fundamental hypotheses about social reality. I will discuss their views of the State separately, and their normative predispositions separately, for the two perspectives differ most widely on those levels. I rely primarily on the readings in this chapter to provide the full flavor of each view.

The liberal perspective has never been quite so clearly formulated as the other two paradigms. It has evolved gradually in the Western world, growing from and through historical experience, rather than springing from the coherent ideas and writings of a single scholar, as the radical perspective does from the works of Marx. Befitting its pragmatic orientations, it has been molded especially by its applications in public policy. Its underlying logical structure has not so often been formulated logically and coherently as it has been suggested or evoked in its specific applications. In some ways, the clearest presentation of liberal postulates about the economy is available in Paul Samuelson's classic introductory textbook, *Economics*.[46] A reasonably clear statement of the liberal's hypotheses about politics and the State can be found in many books presenting the "pluralist" view of democracy in the United States.[47] In some ways, the most precise illustration of the liberal perspective as it has molded public policy and ideology in the United States is presented in a very difficult book written during the 1950's by Robert Dahl and Charles Lindblom, *Politics, Economics and Welfare*.[48]

Conservative analysis has, on the other hand, grown from quite specific historical roots and has received rather precise recent formulation. It springs from classical English liberalism of the nineteenth century, and especially from the work of the English philosopher John Stuart Mill.[49] It has been quite forcefully presented by the modern American economist Milton Friedman, especially in his recent book, *Capitalism and Freedom*.[50] And, directly serving the comparative purposes of this book, conservative analysis has been consistently applied to most of the urban problems discussed below in a very recent book by Edward Banfield, *The Unheavenly City*.[51] Since I have included *both* the conclusion to Banfield's book (to evoke the general approach of the perspective) *and* Friedman's arguments about the role of the State in the readings below, I can be especially brief in these introductory summaries of the perspective.

Both liberal and conservative analyses of social problems begin from an underlying view of the society, formulated most rigorously in orthodox economic analysis.[52] This underlying view abstracts from the specific social relations and institutions of a society, taking the existing system of institutions for granted. It then builds from some basic postulates about the behavior of in-

[46] Now in its 8th edition from McGraw-Hill.
[47] Perhaps the best such discussion is Arnold Rose, *The Power Structure: Political Process in America* (N.Y.: Oxford University Press, 1968).
[48] (N.Y.: Harper Torchbooks, 1965). For an interesting history of liberalism in America, see Louis Hartz, *The Liberal Tradition in America* (N.Y.: Harcourt, Brace & World, 1955).
[49] Wolff, in *The Poverty of Liberalism, op. cit.*, has some especially interesting discussions of Mill and modern conservative and liberal philosophies.
[50] (Chicago: University of Chicago Press, 1962).
[51] (Boston: Little, Brown, 1970). The similarities of Banfield's and Friedman's views are not coincidental. Banfield acknowledges his debts to and agreements with Friedman often in his book.
[52] The use of the term "orthodox economic analysis" is not intended normatively or pejoratively. It is often used to refer to the dominant traditions in economic theory, extending back to the nineteenth century, preoccupied with marginal analysis at the micro-economic level and with Keynesianism at the macro-economic level. For the best discussion of the tradition, see Mark Blaug, *Economic Theory in Retrospect* (Homewood, Ill.: Irwin, 1962).

dividual decision-making units—like households, workers, or firms—and the ways in which they adjust to the given institutional framework. The analysis postulates specifically that individual units act rationally and are free rationally to maximize their welfare subject to the simplest of constraints. For example, it presumes that consumers are free to choose whatever goods will maximize their welfare, subject to the simple constraint that their expenses not exceed their income. The analysis does not explore the ways in which institutions predetermine the range of goods from which individuals can choose.[53] In political analysis, it tends to imply that voters are free to choose rationally among wide varieties of public alternatives—whether candidates in elections or government programs through representatives.[54] From that beginning, the postulates imply a simple conclusion: final decisions made by individuals accurately reflect their real preferences, about cars or congressmen, for instance, without regard to the institutional context in which those choices are made. The postulates tend also to imply that nearly an infinite number of decisions is possible.

In terms of aggregate social behavior, the liberal and conservative analysis assumes that individual actions combine (or "aggregate," in the technical terms of economics) to produce stable, harmonious social equilibria.[55] This basic postulate involves three separate elements. First, it implies that there is such a thing as an equilibrium in social terms—a conjunction of social forces and relations such that movements from it will tend to produce counter-movements reestablishing the equilibrium. This basic notion dominates economics, where the concept of equilibrium pervades orthodox analysis; sociology, especially in modern applications of "structural-functional" analysis; and much of political science, with its emphases on the stability of political systems. Second, the notion of equilibrium implies that society is relatively free from conflict, that individuals acting privately and independently are capable of combining socially to produce social situations with which few are basically discontented, from which few would like to move.[56] And third, it tends to imply, more dynamically, that changes in society come gradually, moving slowly from one harmonious equilibrium to the next.[57]

Given those basic postulates, the two perspectives begin to diverge. Each admits that social problems or difficulties occasionally develop. Each perspective admits, for instance, that the market produces an income distribution in which some earn too little to live, and that, therefore, some way should be found to assist the poorest in society. And each insists that problems develop from minor imperfections in the basic social mechanisms, principally from inadequate information or shortsightedness among individuals.[58] *But* the two perspectives differ sharply on what should be done about such problems.

And this difference draws essentially from their respective analyses of the State. In the liberal view, the State in a modern democracy adequately reflects individual wishes through group representatives. The government is justified in acting, essentially, because it incorporates the preferences of all individuals and because it seeks to advance the interests of all individuals.[59]

[53] J. K. Galbraith has always insisted on this point in his books without reference to radical analysis or a radical critique of these views. See, for instance, *The New Industrial State, op. cit.*

[54] This is especially true of the discussion in conventional economic theory of "public goods" and "public benefits." For the briefest flavor of these discussions, see Otto Eckstein, *Public Finance* (Englewood Cliffs, N.J.: Prentice-Hall, 1966), or for a more technical discussion, Richard Musgrave, *The Theory of Public Finance* (N.Y.: McGraw-Hill, 1959).

[55] This tradition extends all the way back to Adam Smith's seminal notion of an "invisible hand" in *The Wealth of Nations* (1776).

[56] Indeed, much of orthodox economic analysis is concerned with arguing that these equilibria represent "optimal" situations, from which it would be impossible to move without the decrease in some individuals' welfare exceeding the gain in others' welfare. For an introduction to these notions, see Samuelson, *Economics, op. cit.*

[57] This is almost a methodological necessity of the analyses. In order to ensure that the behavior of individual units in a social setting can be adequately and rigorously studied, one must presume that the social setting itself does not change very much in the course of study.

[58] See the Introduction to the chapter on transportation below for a good example.

[59] This contention has dominated an interesting series of conflicts between two schools of political analysis in this country. On the one hand, "pluralists" have argued the liberal view that the government represents everyone. On the other hand, following the original contribution of C. Wright Mills, radicals have argued that a "power elite," dominated by the capitalist class, has controlled the government, ensuring that it represents the interests almost exclusively of that class. For a recent summary of the pluralist view, see Rose, *The Power Structure, op. cit.* For the "power elite" argument, see Mills, *The Power Elite* (N.Y.:

In the liberal analysis, there are three principal kinds of government action which society both prefers and requires. First, the government should redistribute income.[60] Second, the government should act when private market mechanisms cannot satisfy consumer preferences effectively.[61] Third, the government should act to provide certain goods that the market mechanism is incapable of providing, like national defense. Armed with these principles, the liberal perspective has motivated and justified a vast increase in government responsibilities in the United States during the twentieth century. Programs have developed to overcome market inefficiencies in housing, for instance, from public construction of low-cost housing to public provision of financial subsidies for those too poor to afford decent housing.

In the conservative view, the role of the State should be much more limited. Conservatives tend to have greater faith than liberals in the efficiency and optimality of the private market mechanism, and to have greater fear than liberals of both government inefficiency and government infringement on personal liberties. Friedman elaborates these points clearly below.

Despite these differences, however, the two perspectives agree on one central disagreement with the radical view of the State. In neither the liberal nor the conservative perspective does the State serve the interests only of one class, as radicals argue. To conservatives it can barely serve anyone's interest, and to liberals it can effectively serve the interests of all.

The liberal and conservative perspectives also differ sharply with each other on normative grounds, although the differences seem more precisely disagreements of temperament than of basic principle. Conservatives tend to place the highest priority on individual freedom and social order, while liberals tend to place their highest priority on individual equality and social justice.[62] Liberals seem more willing to countenance both rapid social change and extensive government involvement in the private sector. Both differ completely from the radical perspective in one important respect: each tends to regard capitalism as the "best" economic mode of production because it affords, they argue, the maximum possible economic wealth and the maximum feasible individual freedom. Each perspective envisions as its "ideal" society a perfectly functioning capitalist democracy. Each imagines that we can come extremely close to that ideal without major changes in current capitalist institutions (although conservatives would certainly prefer a much less powerful government than we have in the United States). These normative views thoroughly inform their specific analyses of the problems discussed in succeeding chapters.

THE READINGS

Two selections elaborate the arguments of each perspective, the first evoking its general approach to social problems and the second presenting its theory of the State.

The pieces by Edwards and MacEwan and by Sweezy represent the radical view. Edwards and MacEwan provide a superb discussion of the radical argument that basic social and economic institutions determine the structure and evolution of social problems. Although their article does not concentrate on urban problems in particular, it illustrates the application of the radical analysis to a wide variety of problems. They clearly intend that the analysis would be applied in precisely the same way to the specific set of urban problems discussed in this book. The selection from Paul Sweezy's book provides a straightforward exposition of the radical view of the State, contrasting that theory with the liberal view. Sweezy's book was published originally in 1942, although this selection comes from a later revised version. The book belongs to a slightly

Oxford University Press, 1956), and G. William Domhoff, *Who Rules America?* (Englewood Cliffs, N.J.: Prentice-Hall, 1967). For a collection of essays from both sides, see Domhoff and Hoyt Ballards, eds., *C. Wright Mills and the Power Elite* (Boston: Beacon, 1968).

[60] The argument presumes that the final pattern of redistribution will reflect aggregate social preferences (and therefore all individual preferences) about the shape of the income distribution.

[61] The classic example of this in economics is the example of pollution from a chimney stack. A firm does not have to consider the "social costs" of soot from the chimney (costs to others of cleaning clothes, for instance). It bases its production solely on its private, internal costs. Theoretically, if it were forced to pay the social costs too, it would produce less or install machinery to eliminate the pollution. Thus, the analysis justifies government intervention in the form of a pollution tax or pollution-abatement incentive. For a summary and criticism of this traditional argument, see E. J. Mishan, *The Costs of Economic Growth* (N.Y.: Praeger, 1967). See also the chapter on the environment below.

[62] On all of these values and their precise philosophic foundations, see Wolff, *The Poverty of Liberalism, op. cit.*

earlier era of radical analysis, much more dominated by an exegesis of Marx's views, and seems stylistically rooted in that earlier school of radical argument. But it provides the clearest statement of this view of the State.

The selections by Moynihan and by Heller represent the liberal view. Unlike the other four pieces in this chapter, these two do not seek to expound a general approach; as the previous section of the Introduction noted, the liberal view is rarely formulated in a rigorous way. Rather, these two pieces *illustrate* the principal perspectives of the liberal view. Moynihan's article provides ample evidence of the liberal tendency to regard social problems as imperfections requiring varieties of ameliorative government action. Notably, in his concentration on urban problems, Moynihan speaks almost entirely of *procedural* changes in the social equilibrium, particularly in the processes of government. Like most liberals, he presumes that technical and procedural efficiency can help perfect the social machine. Heller's piece also illustrates rather than expounds. His discussion of the potential role of the State clearly manifests the liberal view that government officials have a choice among a nearly infinite variety of social outcomes and that, despite the technical problems involved in such choices, government actions will accurately reflect the will of all the people.

The selections from the books by Banfield and Friedman represent the conservative view with such striking vigor that they require little explanation. Banfield's discussion of urban problems—the conclusion of his fascinating book on the "urban crisis"—quite clearly manifests the general conservative approach to such problems. He argues against government action, and he contends that the problems are not anywhere as serious as we believe them to be. Friedman presents the conservative view of the State more precisely, trying rather rigorously to establish some very narrow boundaries beyond which the government should not interfere with the private market mechanism and the freedom of individual citizens.

A RADICAL APPROACH TO ECONOMICS

Richard C. Edwards, Arthur MacEwan, and the Staff of Social Sciences 125, Harvard University

The first of two selections representing the general radical perspective, this article argues that important social problems in a capitalist society derive inevitably from the basic structure of capitalist institutions. Although the selection does not concentrate specifically on urban problems, it illustrates the application of radical analysis to a wide variety of social problems. The authors clearly intend that the analysis would be applied in the same way to the more specific set of issues discussed in this book.

The article is reprinted here almost in its entirety from the *American Economic Review*, May, 1970. That article was a revised version of a longer discussion based on a course taught at Harvard University called "The Capitalist Economy: Conflict and Power." Edwards and MacEwan wrote the article as an expression of the ideas of the course's entire staff, which met weekly to work out the course approach and the ideas reflected here. Other members of the staff involved in these discussions were Keith Aufhauser, Peter Bohmer, Roger Bohmer, Samuel Bowles, Herbert Gintis, Carl Gotsch, Stephan Michelson, Ralph Pochoda, Patricia Quick, Michael Reich, and Thomas Weisskopf.

Edwards is currently completing work on his doctorate in economics at Harvard. MacEwan is an assistant professor of economics at Harvard.

I. INTRODUCTION

The purpose of this paper is to outline a radical approach to economics and to suggest how several important social problems might be dealt with in that framework. . . .

Orthodox economic analysis . . . is based upon an acceptance of the *status quo* in social relations. Microanalysis presupposes the individualistic ownership and decision-making systems typical of capitalist societies, and in this narrow context the pecuniary behavior of firms and individuals is examined. In macroanalysis, when the aggregate operations of these individual units are the subject matter, attention is focused on the fiscal and monetary adjustments necessary to keep the system smoothly functioning. All in all, the curriculum of modern economics is one of philosophic marginalism: existing social relations are taken as a datum and the problem is one of administering the system by adjustments around the edges.

SOURCE: *Richard Edwards and Arthur MacEwan, "A Radical Approach to Economics,"* American Economic Review, *Papers and Proceedings* (1970).

The marginalist approach is useful only if, accepting the basic institutions of capitalism, one is primarily concerned with its administration. If one questions the virtue of capitalism as a system, then the basic social relations and the institutions of the system themselves must be subjected to analysis. A new approach is necessary.

The old approach—that which accepts capitalism and is in general the basis of present economics curricula—cannot deal with the problems of modern society. All that the curricula say about the war in Vietnam is how it can be financed more efficiently. The very existence of imperialism is denied. Racism, it is taught, has its origins in personal preferences, and the poverty of blacks and others is "explained" in terms of their low productivity. The destruction of the environment enters the curricula only as an aside when the existence of "externalities" is pointed out as limiting the theory. The subjugation of women, the meaninglessness of work activities, and the alienation of workers are topics which do not enter the curricula at all. Socialist alternatives and the process of revolution are examined only in terms of the value system of a capitalist environment. . . .

In Sections II and III we lay out a basic substantive argument for a radical approach to economics, which can be summarized as follows. We begin with an analysis of the fundamental capitalist institutions. These institutions function so as to limit the range of social outcomes available; we show how the social problems mentioned above (income inequality, alienation, imperialism, and so forth) are directly attributable to the operation of these institutions. But the basic institutions also confer power differentially, favoring those who already benefit from the economic system. Therefore, of the limited social outcomes potentially available, there is a tendency to choose those outcomes least conducive to a decent society. We discuss (in Section III) how this power is exercised, particularly through the state, in the service of class interests. . . .

II. CONFLICT, POWER, AND INSTITUTIONS

The problems we have cited as providing the motivation for a new economics curriculum—imperialism, inequality, alienation, racism, etc.—directly involve economic conflicts; that is, in each case there are social groups with contradictory economic interests. Conflicts are decided through the exercise of power and through the operations of institutions. More precisely, power—the ability of groups or individuals to resolve conflicts in their favor—is not exercised in a vacuum; rather it is always exercised within a well-defined environment of economic institutions which place strict limitations on its scope of operation.

For example, in the determination of wages in a capitalist society, the institutional environment narrowly confines the scope in which collective bargaining, a process involving power, takes place. First, the bargaining is predicated on the assumption that the struggle is one over distribution of "excess profits"; that is, over what is left after all the "costs" of production ("normal" profits and socially unnecessary expenditures such as advertising, as well as socially necessary costs) have been subtracted from total revenues. In the context of capitalism, the size of these costs is nonnegotiable. Indeed, in the context of capitalism, it would likely be

against the interests of the workers involved to cut into these costs because doing so might force the firm out of business. Second, once a negotiated agreement regarding wages has been reached, it can often be vitiated by price increases. Thus, both before and after its operation, power in the bargaining situation is severely constrained by the institutions of the system.

One hypothesis which lies at the core of a radical approach to economics is that basic economic institutions to a large extent determine the nature of social relations and the outcomes of social conflict processes; that is, social decision making is largely organized and effected through the basic economic institutions. This hypothesis involves two questions. First, to what extent do institutions directly determine social relations and the outcomes of social conflict processes? Second, to what extent is the distribution of power among groups and individuals determined by the structure of institutions?

In considering the role of capitalist institutions, we emphasize as basic (that is, system-defining) institutions the following:[1] the market in labor, in which labor is treated as a commodity and allocated on the basis of the highest bidder; control of the work process by those who own and control capital,[2] including the concomitant loss of control by the worker over his activities during the hours of work; the legal relations of ownership, by which income distribution is determined through payments to owners for the use of their productive factors; *homo economicus*, the system of personality traits characteristic of and functional to capitalism, including especially the system of individual gain incentives; and the ideology which abstracts and organizes "reality" in such a way as to justify and facilitate the operation of the other institutions.

These institutions create several of the social problems we have mentioned: income inequality, alienation, destruction of the environment, and imperialism. Furthermore,

[1] See Polanyi in Dalton [14], [15] [37] for discussions of the operation of capitalist institutions and their development.
[2] While "owners" and "controllers" are not necessarily the same persons, as a group they define the goals of the capitalist firm to be profit maximization; on this point see Baran and Sweezy [3] and Solow [52] who counter Galbraith [21]. All we require here is that firms "approximately" maximize profits, or that they do so in the "long run."

racism and the subjugation of women become functional in a society organized by these institutions. The arguments we shall suggest next are intended to make explicit the links between the operation of capitalist institutions and these problems.

The consequences of capitalist institutions:

Income inequality. Tendencies toward inequality are an integral part of the functioning of capitalist institutions. Consider first the consequences of a market in labor. In order to insure that the vast majority of workers will sell their labor power on the market, it is important that workers not have the option to work for themselves; that is, it is necessary that workers own no factors of production other than their own labor [38, VIII] [49]. As a result, capital ownership must be concentrated in the hands of a relatively small number of nonworkers. Furthermore, as long as material rewards are the main motivation for work, the incentive structure required to induce workers to acquire and apply productive skills must be characterized by significant inequalities in labor earnings.[3]

The capitalist's side of the production process makes similar demands. First, substantial reward differences are needed in order to induce entrepreneurs to perform their social functions as innovators, production organizers, and risk-takers. Second, given economies of scale in production (either technological or those deriving simply from market power, etc.) and given the institutional association between capital ownership and control of the productive process, concentration of ownership necessarily develops.

Finally, profit maximization leads to a rapid rate of technological change. In a market setting, the capacity to exploit profitable innovations depends on the ability to raise the necessary capital. Once inequalities begin to develop (or given historic inequalities), this ability is unequally distributed. As a result, the rewards of technological change, which are often considerable, tend to be distributed to those who are already at the top of the income distribution, lending a further tendency away from equality [50]. The above tendencies of technological progress operate even in the absence of biases which directly reduce the labor share of income in the choice of capital- or labor-saving technology. In a society with more or less competitive factor markets but with collective control by capitalists over research and development, it can easily be shown that the selection of the pattern of technological progress will be to the disadvantage of labor.

These tendencies toward inequality derive directly from the fundamental institutions. We would not argue, however, that the distribution of income is entirely determined by the operation of capitalist institutions. Income determination is—perhaps above all else—a struggle. One of the principal aspects of this struggle is the effort by groups to increase the prices of the factors they own. Thus, the income struggle can be viewed as a class struggle, where classes are defined in terms of their relation to the means of production.

Alienation. The leisure-labor dichotomy characteristic of neoclassical economic analysis reflects an acceptance of the notion that in general, labor or work activities will be nonfulfilling drudgery undertaken to secure an income, and that creative activities leading to individual development must necessarily be nonwork ("leisure") activities. There is considerable anthropological evidence that this division of life is historically specific to labor-market societies, and that productive activities have not always been separated from creative, developmental ones [14, pp. 19–25].

Within capitalist society, the capitalist's control of the work process means that the workers—that is, those who sell their labor on a market—do not determine the technological or social organization of the work process; likewise, they do not determine what product will be produced or what the product will be used for. Thus, the worker is separated or alienated from both his work activities and his product. Likewise, since labor power cannot be separated from the laborer himself, control by the capitalist of the worker's labor carries with it control of the worker's life during the work day.[4]

---

[3] Inequalities in conjunction with personal material incentives exist in some socialist societies as well as in capitalist societies. Meade [41] explains the dual role of prices in a market economy, pointing out that prices which lead to efficient allocation may yield a very undesirable income distribution.

[4] Marx [39] provides the classical statement of the process of alienation. Readings based on the more modern situation include [22] [12] [6] [28] [20].

Under these circumstances, work activities are in general neither creative nor self-developmental.[5] The worker has no intrinsic interest in either his direct activities or their goal, and motivation must then take the form of working for the extrinsic incentive of wages. As pointed out above, for wage incentives to be effective, considerable inequality (and therefore considerable reward for working properly) must exist.

But solving the problem of motivation in an alienated work environment is not left to wages (and the requisite wage inequality) alone. In modern capitalist societies, the United States in particular, the educational system serves the function of preparing workers for the conditions of their employment. The educational system disciplines the work force.

Most people on the job find little use for those cognitive abilities acquired in school, other than the most elementary ones (the "three R's"), or, insofar as they do, they could just as well have learned these abilities on the job. On the other hand, coming on time, following directions and learning to respect authority, learning to work for external incentives (grades), and budgeting time are modes of behavior, affective traits, which the school instills and the job requires. Thus the schools prepare, by experience, their students to function effectively in an alienated environment.[6]

[5] More generally, insofar as a trade-off exists between the quality of the work process and maximum profits, in capitalist society the former will always be sacrificed to the latter. This situation is illustrated graphically below. Of course, in a society where workers' preferences dominated, the transformation locus might look very different, due both to a different motivational orientation of workers and conscious development of new technologies consonant with higher quality work.

[6] . . . Useful readings concerning the function of schools include [24] [48] [27] [19]. It should be noted that what has been said about alienation and education in the capitalist environment could

The consequences of alienation are obviously very great. When the organization and purpose of one's major life role—i.e., work—are externally controlled and motivated, that role and life itself tend to become meaningless. Character development and self-expression are distorted and stifled by the work environment and achieve only stunted realization through nonwork activities. Cynicism—towards oneself, towards others, and towards society—tends to be the result.

The worker's alienation can be viewed as a fragmentation of his existence: his working hours are not controlled (arranged, organized, or motivated) by him and are therefore fragmented from the rest of his existence. His family, his recreation, his intellectual activity are not integrated with work activity which dominates his life.[7] Furthermore, even his work activities are fragmented: capitalist production drives towards a technology with an ever finer division of labor, so the worker cannot even participate in production of a complete product.

Alienation is not a "cost" to workers which can be recouped through a higher supply price of labor. In the first place, workers are not able to extract higher wages as "compensation" because there are few if any meaningful nonalienating alternatives available to them; that is, alienation is pervasive throughout the capitalist economy. Furthermore, insofar as a variety of work conditions does exist, stratification of labor markets insures that persons in alienating work environments have only similar environments as alterna-

also be true in other modern, highly bureaucratized and organized societies. Thus, while the elimination of capitalism is a necessary condition for the elimination of this problem, it is not a sufficient condition. On the personality requirements of bureaucracy, see [22] [42].

[7] On the issue of fragmentation of life, see readings listed in the preceding footnote as well as Polanyi in [14] and [29, especially pp. 243–68].

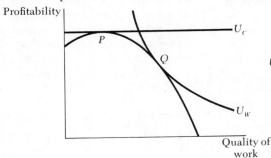

Profitability

P

Q

U_c

U_c: Capitalists' preferences
U_w: Workers' preferences
 P: Capitalists' equilibrium
 Q: Workers' equilibrium

U_w

Quality of work

tives (a bureaucrat typically does not have the option of becoming a doctor). Also, the lack of creative, self-developmental work activities insures that workers will not demand such a work environment: their preferences (like everyone else's) are molded by their environment, and the absence of nonalienating alternatives allows workers no basis on which to change their preferences.

Destruction of the environment. Capitalism is usually credited—by Marx, Schumpeter, and many others—as being a system which attains maximum output expansion from a given resource base. Markets and *homo economicus* prove to be powerful tools for organizing an economy towards growth. The ideology of capitalism, in turn, places high value on the rise of material output.

The acceptance of aggregate output per se as an indicator of welfare, however, would be at best a questionable procedure. The prices at which aggregate output is valued are reflections of the existing distribution of income and the preferences engendered by the system. They therefore cannot be endowed with any objective welfare meaning. Furthermore, the very process of output expansion has consequences outside of the market which are detrimental to social welfare.

The capitalist growth process has historically involved the fracture of community. This process takes many forms, including current phenomena: traditional, nonalienating work processes are destroyed by competition with modern industry; agricultural communities are decimated by the introduction of new technology; cities grow and decay depending upon the vagaries of the market; urban inhabitants experience anomie because their communities are functionally fragmented. Community is not a good which can be produced for market sale.

Because the capitalist controls the work process and his goal is profit maximization, there will be no tendency to minimize costs which fall on others. Indeed, for any given level of costs, there will be an effort to maximize the share of costs borne by others. These extramarket costs take the form of fracture of the community, water and air pollution, congestion, "urban sprawl," etc.— a general destruction of the environment which cannot be viewed as a secondary issue but one of dominant importance in the society. Furthermore, capitalists' efforts to choose technology and to organize production so as to minimize their own, but not social, costs insures that the importance of the problem increases over time. (The rich are often able to protect themselves from pollution, by zoning for example.) Thus the rise in concern regarding problems of pollution is in no way surprising, nor should it be surprising that anti-pollution groups make headway only when the problems become severe. To halt the destruction of the environment, it would be necessary to restrict seriously the operation of basic capitalist institutions. Thus human needs become subordinated to the needs of the market and to capital expansion.

Imperialism. Subordination of human needs to the needs of capital expansion has been a pervasive characteristic of capitalist growth, and this process has been carried out, not only domestically, but also on an international scale. The geographic spread of capitalism derives from the operations of its basic institutions. First, the individual gain rationale of capitalism leads constantly in search of new sources of profits. For the firm, continued well-being depends upon finding new, profitable uses for its previously accrued profits. Second, the opportunities for assuring the availability of such investment opportunities are greater, the greater is the geographic scope of the system.

The spreading of the system has been a characteristic of capitalism throughout its history. It has involved breaking down the restrictions on the operation of the market, on the capitalist control of the work process, and on the system of individual gain. Earlier, the problem was one of creating nations and then spheres of influence. Today, when one capitalist nation has become dominant, the problem is one of integrating an international capitalist system. This integration means at a minimum that the nefarious aspects of capitalism—inequality, alienation, destruction of environment—are spread, or, insofar as they already exist, they are maintained. However, because this integration takes place under the dominance of the business interests of an advanced capitalist nation, the output expansion capacity of capitalism is not necessarily transmitted to the poorer countries. First, simply the operation of comparative advantage which operates in an integrated capitalist system would inhibit industrialization and growth in poor countries.

Second, the monopolistic conditions of business in the United States allow even less opportunity for development in poor countries. Because of its power, which operates both within and outside the market, U.S. business (or business from other advanced capitalist nations) is able to preempt investment opportunities and inhibit the development of a historically progressive industrial bourgeoisie in the poor countries. Finally, the interests of international capital require the maintenance of a "favorable investment climate" and so the state power of advanced countries is used to prevent radical political and social change in poor countries.[8]

Racism. Racism in the United States can be seen as functionally supportive of the interests of capital. In our discussion of alienation, we asserted that the segmentation and stratification of the labor force is one mechanism by which labor is prevented from obtaining a higher wage for undertaking less desirable jobs. Black people clearly comprise one of the most oppressed segments of the labor force in the United States. They are restricted to the most undesirable jobs and they are paid the lowest wages.

It is often alleged that white workers benefit from racism and that the losers are the capitalists who are prevented by racism from hiring blacks. Such an allegation is true, if at all, only in the static sense when total labor income is fixed. The division of the labor force by race, however, weakens the position of workers as a group, and their share of income is consequently reduced. Demands by white workers are attenuated by the threat of being replaced by workers from the black labor pool.[9]

Furthermore, antagonisms of white workers are directed by racism towards blacks rather than towards employers; that is, institutionalized racism dilutes awareness of class divisions. When the animosity of white workers is directed against blacks, the white workers see themselves as having a stake in the system—they are not at the bottom.

The subjugation of women. The segmentation of the labor force, of course, involves many divisions other than race. Extensive division by "skill" and education categories is of obvious importance. The division by sex and the concomitant subjugation of women pervade the entire society. In this paper we will only point out that there are many parallels to racism, and the points we have made above, especially those regarding the functional role of stratification in allowing low wages to be paid for undesirable work, are again relevant. Indeed, for most of their labor, namely, housework, women receive no wages as such and have very little choice in the matter [46] [5].

Summary. In this section we have suggested arguments regarding the relationship between important social problems and the institutions of a capitalist society. We believe that the general analysis forms a basic component in a radical approach to economics. The points we would like to emphasize in summary are the following:

1. The negative characteristics which we have ascribed to capitalism are completely compatible with successful, rapid expansion of output. Indeed, it is in the very process of yielding a maximum output (maximum profit) situation that the institutions of capitalism yield income inequality and alienation, for example. Thus, the analysis is only in small part based upon the occurrence of business cycles, unemployment, etc. In essence, the critique is fully applicable when the capitalist economy is in boom. And however one may value output versus other variables which contribute to welfare, it seems obvious that the greater the output, the less valuable it is relative to the other variables. Thus a capitalist society becomes increasingly less tolerable.

2. The core institutions of capitalism interact in such a way as to determine social relations and circumscribe the outcomes of conflict situations. First, these institutions work in a parallel fashion to produce a class society. Reliance on individual gain incentives, capitalist control of the production process, and the legal relations of ownership insure that capitalist development will produce division into classes. Second, the core institutions are highly interdependent in that they sustain and facilitate the opera-

[8] Useful references putting forth the radical analysis of imperialism include [56] [36] [18] [2] [32]. On the history of U.S. imperialism, see [31] [61] [47].

[9] Michael Reich, in his investigation of the relationship between racism and class divisions, has found that racial inequality between blacks and whites (as measured by the difference between white and nonwhite median incomes) is significantly and positively related to class inequality among whites (as measured by the Gini coefficient for white incomes). See [53, Chap. VII and *passim*].

tion of each other; the functional interrelations are such that severe alteration of any one is incompatible with maintaining the others.

3. The acceptance of capitalist institutions carries with it certain constraints on the functioning of the society. These constraints usually take the form of conflicts between alternative social needs. For example, the trade-off between output growth and income equality exists within the context of capitalism. The trade-off is created by the functional requisites of the institutions. But we can easily imagine a society in which such a trade-off would not exist. Such would be the case if men worked because they cared for and felt on equal terms with the entire community rather than if they worked for direct personal gain. Other examples of such generally accepted trade-offs, which are artifacts of capitalism, include income growth versus a meaningful work environment, employment versus stable prices, private versus social costs, public versus private consumption, and income versus leisure.

4. The core capitalist institutions tend to subordinate other institutions to serve their needs. We have illustrated with the case of education (other examples would be the family and religion) how other institutions serve the needs of the economy. In this sense, capitalism may be characterized as an "economic society."

There are, of course, limits to the extent to which capitalist institutions shape society, and a curriculum based only on the argument to this point would certainly be deficient. Thus, we now turn to a consideration of the exercise of power—in particular, the role of the state—in the context of capitalist institutions.

III. THE EXERCISE OF POWER

Class divisions in capitalist society. As we have noted, the development and operation of capitalist institutions divides society into classes. First, class division is a prerequisite for the effective organization of the institutions: most of the population must be reduced to worker status while simultaneously a capitalist elite is created and its existence justified. Second, the basic institutions function so as to augment the wealth, power, and privilege of that elite.

The analysis of economic institutions

which leads to these conclusions provides a basis for examining the exercise of power— the ability of groups to resolve the outcomes of social conflict processes in their own favor. First, the analysis provides the working hypothesis that economic organization is the basis of power. Second, the analysis emphasizes that the different classes have conflicting interests with regard to the maintenance of the existing social relations. Together, these statements would lead us to hypothesize that power in a capitalist society is dominated by the capitalist class, and since social conflict may lead to instability in the institutions themselves, the class exercises power primarily to maintain the institutions which function in its favor. The intervention of power—to deflect political threats, depoliticize class conflict, and so forth—assures the smooth functioning of capitalism.[10]

The operation of ruling class power—the state. An example of the interaction between the operation of institutions and the exercise of power is provided by the recent history of welfare programs. As we have pointed out in Section II, an unequal income distribution results from the functioning of the labor market, the system of individual gain incentives, and the linking of income to ownership and sale of productive factors. There are, however, several secondary forces which exacerbate inequality, and the reality of capitalism

[10] While we argue that power is dominated by the capitalist class, that is not to say that it monopolizes power or that its rule is unrestricted. Furthermore, capitalists need not monopolize decision-making positions nor must they operate according to an articulated schema in order to be dominant. The existence of an ideology which favors capitalist interests and a sufficiently pervasive common set of objective self-interests among capitalists serves to assure that decisions will be in their favor. It is in this sense that we can identify the capitalist class as a ruling class. The dichotomous division of society into workers and capitalists obviously involves a simplification. Other groups (e.g., highly paid professionals, land-owning farmers, etc.) exist who cannot be identified directly with either class. However, we use the term "worker" broadly to identify all who sell their labor power on a market and therefore the class categories extend to most of the population. Furthermore, our preceding analysis of capitalist institutions and our analysis below of the exercise of power lead us to the conclusion that these are the most important groups to study for understanding social change. On the American ruling class, see [54, Chap. 9] [45] [16]; on the nature of classes, see [57] [8] [4].

is even worse than the model. First, there are many family units which own no salable labor or other factors of production: the sick, the aged, the disabled. Second, there are those who own labor power but who are discriminated against in the labor market: blacks, other non-whites, and women. Third, income inequalities are exacerbated by unequal access to activities through which labor quality is "improved" (e.g., schooling and apprenticeship). Fourth, unemployment is always present in a capitalist system, and its incidence falls heaviest on the groups already at the bottom of the income ladder.[11]

This situation poses a threat to capitalism. Those affected have no stake in maintaining the system and become unruly. The preservation of capitalism requires that the misery of poverty be alleviated, or at least that something be done about its appearance. Yet an attack on the basic causes of the problem, the functioning of the basic economic institutions, is ruled out. For example, an adequate welfare program would interfere with work incentives; it would conflict with the principle that income is a payment for productive factors. Therefore, political power is focused on the secondary factors and symptoms, but the basic processes remain unaffected. Old age pension programs are established; equal opportunity employment regulations are legislated; manpower training programs are set up; unemployment compensation schemes are developed. Even if such programs were successful on their own terms, they could eliminate only the most severe aspects of inequality and poverty. In fact, most of these programs fail to achieve their own modest objectives.

Opposition to system-preserving welfare programs derives not only from their conflict with the institutions. Often, interest groups within the capitalist class or powerful professional groups are hurt by welfare legislation. Thus, the A.M.A. battles against medical care; housing developers oppose public housing programs and city planning; the automobile companies work to keep public transit facilities inadequate; textile employers subvert equal employment opportunity legislation. These are cases where class interests and self-interest seem to conflict. While the ruling class as a whole would benefit by

establishing an ameliorative program and thereby securing its position, some of its members would be hurt. Thus because ruling-class solidarity (see below) is at least as important for the preservation of that system as is preventing disruption by the poor, inadequate welfare programs are the outcome.

Welfare programs are but one example of ruling-class functioning—taking action, compromising within itself, absorbing discontent—carried out through the state. Other revealing examples are public education, tariff policies, financing of research programs, agriculture and transportation subsidies, and the structure of taxation. We believe that these operations of the state are best understood if the state is viewed as basically operating in the interests of the capitalist class.[12]

The priorities of the state. If, as according to our hypothesis, the state is dominated by the capitalist class, then the operations of the state should reflect the needs of the capitalist class. In modern capitalist states, when the basic institutions have been thoroughly established, the maintenance and preservation of these institutions upon which the structure of class and privilege depends is of the greatest importance to the capitalist class. The uninhibited operation of the economic institutions will continue to bestow power, wealth, and prestige upon the capitalists. They do not need the state to enhance their position, only to assure it.

The system-preserving function of the state is evident in several areas. A continued threat to capitalism has been the failure of the economy autonomously to generate adequate aggregate demand. This failure has brought recurring crises with substantial unemployment. In spite of once seemingly inviolable ideological objections to the contrary, the state has assumed the function of demand regulator. Such regulation does not eliminate unemployment, but simply reduces it to levels which are not system threatening.

A second system-preserving function of the state has been its decisive role in obfuscation and suppression of class conflict. This is accomplished through suppressing system-threatening groups (e.g., the Wobblies, Black Panthers), by deflecting their demands for structural changes into accept-

[11] Miller [44] provides a good description of these secondary forces. For a left critique of Miller, see [30].

[12] Sweezy [55, Chap. 13] provides a good statement of this view of the state. The classic argument is provided by Lenin [33, especially Part I] [34].

able material demands (e.g., labor union economism, black capitalism), or through ameliorative programs. If we may modify the jargon of public finance, state actions such as suppression or amelioration may be viewed as "class goods." When the challenge posed by workers becomes severe, no single capitalist can protect himself. Were he to give concessions to his workers, his competitive position would be endangered. To employ private armies has been possible but highly inefficient. Thus, action by the capitalists as a class is necessary.

The enormous military establishment provides another example of system-preserving state operations; as such, it performs a dual function. First, it provides the rationale for huge expenditures which serve to maintain aggregate demand without threatening the security or position of any group in the ruling class. For example, social welfare measures often do threaten such groups. Second, as the capitalist system becomes increasingly an international system, the military directly protects the far-flung parts of that system [3].

The response of the state to changes in the process of production which require more highly developed labor, illustrates a second priority of the state; namely, the creation of new institutions. The rise of mass education in the United States has occurred in response to the need by industry for a skilled work force.[13] Because workers are not tied to particular employment, individual capitalists cannot invest in the general training of workers and expect to appropriate the returns. Thus, capitalists turn to the state to provide a skilled work force. When education is handled by the state and portrayed as social welfare, it is paid for by general tax revenue rather than by the capitalists themselves [35, Chap. 3] [51] [43] [9] [60].

The structure of the educational system betrays its class-oriented genesis. Mass education in the United States covers a vast quality range, and a positive association has been established between parents' incomes or class and the quality of public education which children receive. If, as seems reasonable, the benefits of education are correlated with the quality of that education, then the class bias of U.S. education is obvious. Thus the educational system operates to reinforce the class bias of the core economic institutions.[14]

There is a further aspect of the educational function which reveals its class bias; namely, its role in transmitting ideology. Students are taught a view of society which justifies the *status quo* and which poses efforts for change as unnecessary or futile.

The primacy of the roles of the state in preserving the system and in developing new institutions to meet changing circumstances should not obscure the fact that the state also intervenes directly in the economy to benefit immediate interests of capitalists. The most significant realm—in quantitative terms —where the state intervenes is in military and space spending, which we discussed above.[15]

Another example of direct intervention, one which illustrates the case particularly well, is the government's relation to the agricultural sector. The general picture of what has happened in agriculture is well known. Wages in agriculture have remained low and unemployment high. Subsistence farmers have been unable to survive. The rural poor have been forced into the urban ghettos, supplying the low-cost labor force for industrial expansion. All the while, large farm-

---

[13] See, for example, [11] [13, pp. 23–57].

[14] The relationship between inequalities in schooling and inequalities in the total income distribution may be expressed as follows. Let Y represent individual income, K represent earnings from capital, and L represent earnings from labor. If we let the variance of Y over the mean Y represent our measure of income inequality, it can easily be seen that

$$\frac{\text{var } Y}{\overline{Y}} = \left(\frac{\overline{K}}{Y}\right)\frac{\text{var } K}{K} + \left(\frac{\overline{L}}{Y}\right)\frac{\text{var } L}{\overline{L}} + \frac{2 \text{ covar } (K, L)}{Y}.$$

On the plausible assumption that most of the inequalities in labor earnings are due to inequalities in skills, education, and the general socialization process, we see that inequalities in schooling may contribute to income inequality, even where school inequalities are not associated with inequalities in capital ownership. However, note that the last term on the right-hand side of the above expression represents the contribution to total income inequality of the degree to which inequalities in capital earnings are associated with inequalities in labor earnings. Given the social class inequalities of our educational system, we expect the covariance term to be positive.

[15] For a documentation of the subsidies provided to military contractors, see [59] and Joint Economic Committee [58].

ers have received subsidies, price supports, and protection [1].

Furthermore, the very process which creates the agricultural problem is exacerbated by government programs. Government expenditure on agricultural research and extension has played a significant role in raising agricultural productivity at a more rapid rate than general productivity and has thereby contributed to the mass-dislocation of rural workers and subsistence farmers. Those statistical studies which are available confirm casual empiricism: the overall impact of the government in its agricultural programs has been to increase inequality within the agricultural sector [7] [10].

The point is, however, not only that the process has worked toward increasing inequality but that it is the large owners of property—of the agricultural means of production—who benefit. Their benefit is derived directly from the programs which have been developed for "helping agriculture." Payment for unused land is of no help to rural laborers. Price supports for marketable surplus are of no help to subsistence farmers. Government subsidies for capital-augmenting technical change have the same class bias.

Military spending, agricultural subsidies, and other such programs provide ample ammunition for the muckraker. However, in terms of their importance in the overall operations of the state, we believe they are not of highest priority. Their position is behind the system-preserving and secondary-institutions-creating roles of the state. Nonetheless, when studied as a group, these actions of the state which directly enhance the privilege of the capitalist class reveal the basic character of the state in a capitalist society and provide a useful starting point for the analysis of power.[16]

Cohesion of the ruling class. The term "ruling class" may evoke the image of a small, conspiratorial group which coldly calculates the oppression of the poor and its own gain. The actual functioning of the capitalist ruling class in the United States cannot, however, be well understood in such terms.

---

[16] It would be consistent with this theory if the state were to take some actions which, in terms of their direct impact, increased income equality, provided these actions could be interpreted as serving the stability of the system. Lenin [33] analyzes the ten-hour day legislation in these terms.

A class operates as a class in a number of ways. First, the class can be conscious of itself as a group with common objective interests, and can function cohesively on the basis of that consciousness. Second, the class can hold in common a value system or ideology which justifies the class's position and serves as a guide to action. Third, the class can coalesce on specific issues which serve the interests of some of its members if the favor is returned when the special interests of other members are at issue.

In general, it is difficult to distinguish which of these three mechanisms is at work at any given time. In the case of the United States, all three mechanisms operate. For example, elite schools, class-segregated neighborhoods, and social clubs tend to instill in ruling-class members a sense of identity and of their separateness from the rest of society. Thus, they become aware of their special stake in the *status quo* social relations and consciously work for the stability of the system. Obviously, if aware of their own position and if working toward a common goal, the members of the ruling class need not "conspire" to assure behavior in their common interest.

On the other hand, the very strong capitalist ideology in the United States tends to make class consciousness per se less important. A set of values that justify the position of the capitalist class, the basic institutions of capitalism, and the *status quo* in general provide a guide to action. Indeed, the prevalence of the capitalist ideology not only assures common action by members of the capitalist class but means that others will cooperate to serve capitalist interests above their own. This is the case, for example, when white workers accept racism and reject a working-class consciousness.

On many issues, logrolling furthers the class interest. This occurs when each group within the capitalist class structures its own policies so that they do not come into conflict with other groups within the class, expecting (and receiving) such cooperation in return.

These mechanisms which tie a class together should not be confused with the objective identity of the class itself. The capitalist class in the United States is a ruling class. The degree to which it has consciousness, a strong ideology, and internal cooperation determines how successfully it can rule.[17]

1. Sidney Baldwin, *Poverty and Politics* (North Carolina Press, 1964).
2. Paul A. Baran, *The Political Economy of Growth* (Monthly Review Press, 1957).
3. Paul A. Baran and Paul M. Sweezy, *Monopoly Capital* (Monthly Review Press, 1966).
4. Reinhard Bendix and Seymour Martin Lipset, *Class Status and Power* (The Free Press, 1966).
5. Margaret Benston, "The Political Economy of Women's Liberation," *Monthly Rev.*, Sept., 1969.
6. Robert Blauner, *Alienation and Freedom* (Univ. of Chicago Press, 1964).
7. James Bonnen, "The Distribution of Benefits from Selected U.S. Farm Programs," *Rural Poverty in the United States* (National Advisory Commission on Rural Poverty, May, 1968).
8. T. B. Bottomore, *Classes in Modern Society* (Random House, 1966).
9. Samuel Bowles, "Towards an Educational Production Function," . . . in W. Lee Hansen, ed., *Education, Income, and Human Capital* (N.B.E.R., 1970).
10. David Boyne, "Changes in the Income Distribution in Agriculture," *J. of Farm Econ.*, Dec., 1965.
11. Frank Tracy Carleton, *Economic Influences upon Educational Progress in the United States, 1820–50* (Univ. of Wisconsin Press, 1908).
12. Ely Chinoy, *Automobile Workers and the American Dream* (Beacon Press, 1965).
13. Lawrence A. Cremin, *The Transformation of the School* (Vintage Books, 1964).
14. George Dalton, ed., *Primitive, Archaic, and Modern Economies: Essays of Karl Polanyi* (Doubleday and Co., 1968).
15. Maurice Dobb, *Studies in the Development of Capitalism* (International Publishers, 1963).
16. G. William Domhoff, *Who Rules America?* (Prentice-Hall, Inc., 1967).
17. Robert Dreeben, *On What Is Learned in School* (Addison-Wesley Pub. Co., 1968).
18. Andre Gundèr Frank, *Capitalism and Underdevelopment in Latin America* (Monthly Review Press, 1967).
19. Edgar Z. Friedenberg, *Coming of Age in America* (Random House, 1963).
20. Erich Fromm, "Individual and Social Origins of Neurosis," *American Soc. Rev.*, June, 1944.
21. John K. Galbraith, *The New Industrial State* (Houghton Mifflin Co., 1967).
22. Hans Gerth and C. W. Mills, eds., *From Max Weber: Essays in Sociology* (Oxford Univ. Press, 1958).
23. Herbert M. Gintis, "Alienation and Power: Towards a Radical Welfare Economics" (unpublished Ph.D. dissertation, Harvard, 1969).
24. ———, "New Working Class and Revolutionary Youth," . . . *Socialist Revolution* [May–June, 1970].
25. Paul Goodman, *Like a Conquered Province* (Random House, 1968).
26. Ernesto Guevara, "Notes for the Study of the Ideology of the Cuban Revolution," *Studies on the Left*, Vol. 1, No. 3, 1960.
27. Alex Inkeles, "Social Structure and the Socialization of Competence," *Harvard Educa. Rev.*, June, 1966.
28. Eric and Mary Josephson, eds., *Man Alone* (Dell Pub. Co., 1962).
29. Kenneth Keniston, *The Uncommitted* (Dell Pub. Co., 1960).
30. Gabriel Kolko, "On Blaming the Poor for Poverty," *New Politics*, Vol. 3, No. 2, 1965.
31. Walter LaFeber, *The New Empire* (Cornell Univ. Press, 1963).
32. V. I. Lenin, *Imperialism, the Highest Stage of Capitalism* (first published 1917) (International Publishers, 1939).
33. ———, *State and Revolution* (first published 1918) (International Publishers, 1939).
34. ———, "The State" (lecture delivered at Sverdlov University, July 11, 1919), *V. I. Lenin Collected Works*, Vol. 29 (Moscow: Progress Publishers, 1965).
35. Henry M. Levin, *et al.*, *Schools and Inequality* (Urban Coalition, 1969).
36. Harry Magdoff, *The Age of Imperialism* (Monthly Review Press, 1969).
37. Ernest Mandel, *Marxist Economic Theory*

[17] Readers of this paper may well ask to what extent we consider our approach Marxist. The following quotation seems relevant:

". . . When asked whether or not we are Marxist, our position is the same as that of a physicist or a biologist when asked if he is a 'Newtonian' or if he is a 'Pasteurian.'

"There are truths so evident, so much a part of people's knowledge, that it is now useless to discuss them. One ought to be 'Marxist' with the same naturalness with which one is 'Newtonian' in physics, or 'Pasteurian' in biology, considering that if facts determine new concepts, these new concepts will never divest themselves of that portion of truth possessed by the older concepts they have outdated. Such is the case, for example, of Einsteinian relativity or Planck's 'quantum' theory with respect to the discoveries of Newton; they take nothing at all away from the greatness of the learned Englishman. Thanks to Newton, physics was able to advance until it had achieved new concepts in space. The learned Englishman provided the necessary steppingstones for them.

"The advances in social and political science, as in other fields, belong to a long historical process whose links are connecting, adding up, molding and constantly perfecting themselves. . . .

"The merit of Marx is that he suddenly produces a qualitative change in the history of social thought. He interprets history, understands its dynamic, predicts the future, but in addition to predicting it (which would satisfy his scientific obligation) he expresses a revolutionary concept: the world must not only be interpreted, it must be transformed." The statement is by Ernesto "Che" Guevara [26].

(2 vols. Pearce, Brian, trans.) (Monthly Review Press, 1968).

38. Karl Marx, *Capital* (3 vols.; first English edition, 1887) (International Publishers, 1967).

39. ———, *Economic and Philosophic Manuscripts of 1844* (International Publishers, 1964).

40. Karl Marx and Frederick Engels, *The Communist Manifesto* (first published 1848) (International Publishers, 1948).

41. J. E. Meade, *Efficiency, Equality and the Ownership of Property* (Harvard Univ. Press, 1965).

42. Robert K. Merton, ed., *Reader in Bureaucracy* (The Free Press, 1952).

43. Stephan Michelson, "School Resources and Equal Protection," *Inequality in Education,* Dec., 1969.

44. Herman P. Miller, *Rich Man Poor Man* (New American Library, 1964).

45. C. Wright Mills, *The Power Elite* (Oxford Univ. Press, 1956).

46. Juliet Mitchell, "Women: The Longest Revolution," *New Left Rev.,* Nov.-Dec., 1966. (Available as a pamphlet from New England Free Press, Boston, Mass.)

47. Scott Nearing and Joseph Freeman, *Dollar Diplomacy* (Monthly Review Press, 1966).

48. Talcott Parsons, "The School Class as a Social System: Some of Its Functions in American Society," *Harvard Educa. Rev.,* Fall, 1959).

49. Karl Polanyi, *The Great Transformation* (Beacon Press, 1957).

50. Joseph A. Schumpeter, *The Theory of Economic Development* (Oxford Univ. Press, 1951).

51. Patricia C. Sexton, *Education and Income* (Viking Press, 1961).

52. Robert Solow, "The New Industrial State or Son of Affluence," *Public Interest,* Spring, 1968.

53. Sterling D. Spero and Abram L. Harris, *The Black Worker* (Atheneum, 1968).

54. Paul M. Sweezy, *The Present as History* (Monthly Review Press, 1953).

55. ———, *The Theory of Capitalist Development* (Monthly Review Press, 1942).

56. Paul M. Sweezy and Harry Magdoff, "The Multinational Corporation," *Monthly Rev.* (2 parts), Oct., Nov., 1969.

57. E. P. Thompson, *The Making of the English Working Class* (Random House, 1963).

58. U.S. Congress, Joint Economic Committee, Subcommittee on Economy in Government, "The Economics of Military Procurement" (U.S. Government Printing Office, Washington, D.C., 1969).

59. Murray L. Weidenbaum, "Arms and the American Economy: A Domestic Convergence Hypothesis," *A.E.R.,* May, 1968.

60. Randall Weiss, "The Effects of Education on the Earnings of Blacks and Whites" [*Review of Economics and Statistics,* May, 1970].

61. William A. Williams, *The Great Evasion* (Quadrangle Books, 1964).

THE RADICAL THEORY OF THE STATE

Paul Sweezy

This selection from Sweezy's book, *The Theory of Capitalist Development,* exposits the basic radical view of the State and its role in class society. The excerpt comes from a longer chapter on the State in the revised version of Sweezy's book, which was originally published in 1942. In contrast to liberal views, the radical theory argues that the State serves the interest of the dominant class in society. It does this both by providing services directly to members of that class and by helping stabilize the institutional system within which that class flourishes.

Sweezy has been a leading Marxist economist in the United States since the 1930's, when he received his Ph.D. in economics from Harvard. He has written widely, co-authored the much more recent radical book *Monopoly Capital* (with Paul Baran), and co-edits the radical journal *The Monthly Review.*

SOURCE: *Reprinted by permission of Monthly Review Press, 116 W. 14th Street, New York, N.Y. Copyright © 1942 by Paul M. Sweezy.*

THE PRIMARY FUNCTION OF THE STATE

There is a tendency on the part of modern liberal theorists to interpret the state as an institution established in the interests of society as a whole for the purpose of mediating and reconciling the antagonisms to which social existence inevitably gives rise. This is a theory which avoids the pitfalls of political metaphysics and which serves to integrate in a tolerably satisfactory fashion a considerable body of observed fact. It contains, however, one basic shortcoming, the recognition of which leads to a theory essentially Marxian in its orientation. A critique of what may be called the class-mediation conception of the state is, therefore, perhaps the best way of introducing the Marxian theory.[1]

The class-mediation theory assumes, usually implicitly, that the underlying class structure, or what comes to the same thing, the system of property relations is an immutable datum, in this respect like the order of nature itself. It then proceeds to ask what arrangements the various classes will make to get along with each other, and finds that an institution for mediating their conflicting interests is the logical and necessary answer. To this institution powers for maintaining order and settling quarrels are granted. In the real world what is called the state is identified as the counterpart of this theoretical construction.

The weakness of this theory is not difficult to discover. It lies in the assumption of an immutable and, so to speak, self-maintaining class structure of society. The superficiality of this assumption is indicated by the most cursory study of history.[2] The fact is that many forms of property relations with their concomitant class structures have come and gone in the past, and there is no reason to assume that they will not continue to do so in the future. The class structure of society is no part of the natural order of things; it is the product of past social development, and it will change in the course of future social development.

Once this is recognized it becomes clear that the liberal theory goes wrong in the manner in which it initially poses the problem. We cannot ask: Given a certain class structure, how will the various classes, with their divergent and often conflicting interests, manage to get along together? We must ask: How did a particular class structure come into being and by what means is its continued existence guaranteed? As soon as an attempt is made to answer this question, it appears that the state has a function in society which is prior to and more fundamental than any which present-day liberals attribute to it. Let us examine this more closely.

A given set of property relations serves to define and demarcate the class structure of society. From any set of property relations one class or classes (the owners) reap material advantages; other classes (the owned and the non-owners) suffer material disadvantages. A special institution capable and willing to use force to whatever degree is required is an essential to the maintenance of such a set of property relations. Investigation shows that the state possesses this characteristic to the fullest degree, and that no other institution is or can be allowed to compete with it in this respect. This is usually expressed by saying that the state, and the state alone, exercises sovereignty over all those subject to its jurisdiction. It is, therefore, not difficult to identify the state as the guarantor of a given set of property relations.

If now we ask where the state comes from, the answer is that it is the product of a long and arduous struggle in which the class which occupies what is for the time the key positions in the process of production gets the upper hand over its rivals and fashions a state which will enforce that set of property relations which is in its own interest. In other words any particular state is the child of the class or classes in society which benefit from the particular set of property relations which it is the state's obligation

[1] Among the most important Marxist writings on the state the following may be mentioned: Engels, *The Origin of the Family, Private Property and the State*, particularly Ch. IX; Lenin, *The State and Revolution*; Rosa Luxemburg, 'Sozialreform oder Revolution?' *Gesammelte Werke*, Vol. III. An English translation of the latter work is available (*Reform or Revolution?*, Three Arrows Press, N.Y., 1937), but it is unfortunately not a very satisfactory one. A reasonably adequate survey of a large body of Marxist literature on the state is contained in S. H. M. Chang, *The Marxian Theory of the State* (1931).

[2] Many theorists recognize this up to a point, but they believe that what was true of past societies is not true of modern society. In other words, capitalism is regarded as the final end-product of social evolution.

to enforce. A moment's reflection will carry the conviction that it could hardly be otherwise. As soon as we have dropped the historically untenable assumption that the class structure of society is in some way natural or self-enforcing, it is clear that any other outcome would lack the prerequisites of stability. If the disadvantaged classes were in possession of state power, they would attempt to use it to establish a social order more favorable to their own interests, while a sharing of state power among the various classes would merely shift the locale of conflict to the state itself.

That such conflicts within the state, corresponding to fundamental class struggles outside, have taken place in certain transitional historical periods is not denied. During those long periods, however, when a certain social order enjoys a relatively continuous and stable existence, the state power must be monopolized by the class or classes which are the chief beneficiaries.

As against the class-mediation theory of the state, we have here the underlying idea of what has been called the class-domination theory. The former takes the existence of a certain class structure for granted and sees in the state an institution for reconciling the conflicting interests of the various classes; the latter, on the other hand, recognizes that classes are the product of historical development and sees in the state an instrument in the hands of the ruling classes for enforcing and guaranteeing the stability of the class structure itself.

It is important to realize that, so far as capitalist society is concerned, 'class domination' and 'the protection of private property' are virtually synonymous expressions. Hence when we say with Engels that the highest purpose of the state is the protection of private property,[3] we are also saying that the state is an instrument of class domination. This is doubtless insufficiently realized by critics of the Marxian theory who tend to see in the notion of class domination something darker and more sinister than 'mere' protection of private property. In other words they tend to look upon class domination as something reprehensible and the protection of private property as something meritorious. Consequently, it does not occur to them to

[3] *Origin of the Family, Private Property and the State*, Kerr, ed., p. 130.

identify the two ideas. Frequently, no doubt, this is because they have in mind not capitalist property, but rather private property as it would be in a simple commodity-producing society where each producer owns and works with his own means of production. Under such conditions there are no classes at all and hence no class domination. Under capitalist relations, however, property has an altogether different significance, and its protection is easily shown to be identical with the preservation of class dominance. Capitalist private property does not consist in things —things exist independently of their ownership—but in a social relation between people. Property confers upon its owners freedom from labor and the disposal over the labor of others, and this is the essence of all social domination whatever form it may assume. It follows that the protection of property is fundamentally the assurance of social domination to owners over non-owners. And this, in turn, is precisely what is meant by class domination, which it is the primary function of the state to uphold.

The recognition that the defense of private property is the first duty of the state is the decisive factor in determining the attitude of genuine Marxist socialism towards the state. 'The theory of the Communists,' Marx and Engels wrote in the *Communist Manifesto*, 'can be summed up in the single sentence: Abolition of private property.' Since the state is first and foremost the protector of private property, it follows that the realization of this end cannot be achieved without a head-on collision between the forces of socialism and the state power.[4]

THE STATE AS AN ECONOMIC INSTRUMENT

The fact that the first concern of the state is to protect the continued existence and stability of a given form of society does not mean that it performs no other functions of economic importance. On the contrary, the

[4] The treatment of the relation between the state and property has of necessity been extremely sketchy. In order to avoid misunderstanding, the following note should be added. The idea that the state is an organization for the maintenance of private property was by no means an invention of Marx and Engels. On the contrary, it constituted the cornerstone of the whole previous development of political thought from the breakdown of feudalism and the origins of the modern state.

state has always been a very significant factor in the functioning of the economy within the framework of the system of property relations which it guarantees. This principle is generally implicitly recognized by Marxist writers whenever they analyse the operation of an actual economic system, but it has received little attention in discussions of the theory of the state. The reason for this is not difficult to discover. The theory of the state has usually been investigated with the problem of transition from one form of society to another in the foreground; in other words, what we have called the primary function of the state has been the subject of analysis. Lenin's *State and Revolution*—the title clearly indicates the center of interest —set a precedent which has been widely followed. Consequently, the theory of the state as an economic instrument has been neglected, though evidently for our purposes it is necessary to have some idea of the essentials of Marx's thinking on the subject.

Fortunately Marx, in his chapter on the length of the working day,[5] provides a compact and lucid analysis of the role of the state in relation to one very important problem of capitalist economy. By examining this chapter in some detail we can deduce the guiding principles of Marxist teaching on the role of the state within the framework of capitalist property relations.

The rate of surplus value, one of the key variables in Marx's system of theoretical economics, depends on three factors: the productivity of labor, the length of the work-

Bodin, Hobbes, Locke, Rousseau, Adam Smith, Kant, and Hegel—to mention but a few outstanding thinkers of the period before Marx—clearly recognized this central function of the state. They believed private property to be the necessary condition for the full development of human potentialities, the *sine qua non* of genuine freedom. Marx and Engels added that freedom based on private property is freedom for an exploiting class, and that freedom for *all* presupposes the abolition of private property, that is to say the achievement of a classless society. Nevertheless, Marx and Engels did not forget that the realization of a classless society (abolition of private property) is possible only on the basis of certain definite historical conditions; without the enormous increase in the productivity of labor which capitalism had brought about, a classless society would be no more than an empty Utopia.

[5] *Capital* I, Chapter x. [Ed.: Sweezy's citations refer to the three-volume edition of *Capital* published by Charles Kerr and Company, Chicago, 1933.]

ing day and prevailing subsistence standards. It is therefore a matter of importance to discover the determinants of the length of the working day. This is clearly not a question of economic law in any narrow sense. As Marx put it,

Apart from extremely elastic bounds, the nature of exchange of commodities itself imposes no limits to the working day, no limit to surplus labor. The capitalist maintains his rights as a purchaser when he tries to make the working day as long as possible . . . . On the other hand . . . the laborer maintains his right as a seller when he wishes to reduce the working day to one of definite normal duration. There is here, therefore, an antinomy, right against right, both equally bearing the seal of the law of exchanges. Between equal rights force decides. Hence it is that in the history of capitalist production, the determination of what is a working day presents itself as the result of a struggle, a struggle between collective capital, i.e. the class of capitalists, and collective labor, i.e. the working class.[6]

After describing certain forms, both precapitalist and capitalist, of exploitation involving the duration of the working day, Marx examines 'The Struggle for a Normal Working Day' in the historical development of English capitalism. The first phase of this struggle resulted in 'Compulsory Laws for the Extension of the Working Day from the Middle of the 14th to the End of the 17th Century.'[7] Employers, straining to create a trained and disciplined proletariat out of the available pre-capitalist material, were frequently obliged to resort to the state for assistance. Laws extending the length of the working day were the result. For a long time, however, the extension of the working day was a very slow and gradual process. It was not until the rapid growth of the factory system in the second half of the eighteenth century that there began that process of prolonging hours of work which culminated in the notorious conditions of the early nineteenth century:

After capital had taken centuries in extending the working day to its normal maximum length, and then beyond this to

[6] *Ibid.*, p. 259.
[7] Chapter x, Section 5.

the limit of the natural day of 12 hours, there followed on the birth of machinism and modern industry in the last third of the 18th century a violent encroachment like that of an avalanche in its intensity and extent . . . . As soon as the working class, stunned at first by the noise and turmoil of the new system of production, recovered in some measure its senses its resistance began.[8]

The beginnings of working-class resistance ushered in the second phase of the development: 'Compulsory Limitation by Law of the Working Time, The English Factory Acts, 1833 to 1864.'[9] In a series of sharp political struggles, the workers were able to wring one concession after another from their opponents. These concessions took the form of laws limiting hours of work for ever wider categories of labor, until by 1860 the principle of limitation of the working day was so firmly established that it could no longer be challenged. Thereafter progress pursued a smoother course.

The limitation of the working day was not simply a question of concessions by the ruling class in the face of a revolutionary threat, though this was undoubtedly the main factor. At least two other considerations of importance have to be taken into account. Marx noted that,

Apart from the working class movement that daily grew more threatening, the limiting of factory labor was dictated by the same necessity which spread guano over the English fields. The same blind eagerness for plunder that in the one case exhausted the soil had, in the other, torn up by the roots the living forces of the nation.[10]

Moreover, the question of factory legislation entered into the final phase of the struggle for political mastery between the landed aristocracy and the industrial capitalists:

However much the individual manufacturer might give the rein to his old lust for gain, the spokesmen and political leaders of the manufacturing class ordered a change in front and of speech toward the workpeople. They had entered upon the contest for the repeal of the Corn Laws

and needed the workers to help them to victory. They promised, therefore, not only a double-sized loaf of bread, but the enactment of the Ten Hours Bill in the Free Trade millennium . . .[11]

And after repeal of the Corn Laws had gone through, the workers 'found allies in the Tories panting for revenge.'[12] Thus factory legislation derived a certain amount of support from both sides to the great struggle over free trade.

Finally Marx concluded his treatment of the working day with the following statement:

For 'protection' against 'the serpent of their agonies' the laborers must put their heads together and, as a class, compel the passing of a law, an all-powerful social barrier that shall prevent the very workers from selling, by voluntary contract with capital, themselves and their families into slavery and death. In place of the pompous catalogue of the 'inalienable rights of man' comes the modest Magna Charta of a legally limited working day, which shall make clear 'when the time which the worker sells is ended, and when his own begins.' Quantum mutatus ab illo![13]

What general conclusions can be deduced from Marx's discussion of the working day? The principle of most general bearing was stated by Engels. Answering the charge that historical materialism neglects the political element in historical change, Engels cited the chapter on the working day 'where legislation, which is surely a political act, has such a trenchant effect' and concluded that 'force (that is, state power) is also an economic power' and hence is by no means excluded from the causal factors in historical change.[14] Once this has been established, it is necessary to ask under what circumstances and in whose interest the economic power of the state will be brought into action. On both points the analysis of the working day is instructive.

First, the state power is invoked to solve problems which are posed by the economic development of the particular form of society under consideration, in this case capi-

[8] Capital I, pp. 304–5.
[9] Chapter x, Section 6.
[10] Capital I, pp. 263–4.
[11] Ibid., pp. 308–9.
[12] Ibid., p. 311.
[13] Ibid., p. 330.
[14] Letter from Engels to Conrad Schmidt, 27 October 1890. Selected Correspondence, p. 484.

talism. In the earlier period a shortage of labor power, in the later period over-exploitation of the laboring population were the subjects of state action. In each case the solution of the problem required state intervention. Many familiar examples of a similar character readily come to mind.

Second, we should naturally expect that the state power under capitalism would be used first and foremost in the interests of the capitalist class since the state is dedicated to the preservation of the structure of capitalism and must therefore be staffed by those who fully accept the postulates and objectives of this form of society. This is unquestionably true, but it is not inconsistent to say that state action may run counter to the immediate economic interests of some or even all of the capitalists provided only that the overriding aim of preserving the system intact is promoted. The legal limitation of the working day is a classic example of state action of this sort. The intensity of class antagonism engendered by over-exploitation of the labor force was such that it became imperative for the capitalist class to make concessions even at the cost of immediate economic advantages.[15] For the sake of preserving domes-

tic peace and tranquility, blunting the edge of class antagonisms, and ultimately avoiding the dangers of violent revolution, the capitalist class is always prepared to make concessions through the medium of state action. It may, of course, happen that the occasion for the concessions is an actual materialization of the threat of revolution.[16] In this case their purpose is to restore peace and order so that production and accumulation can once again go forward uninterruptedly.

Let us summarize the principles underlying the use of the state as an economic instrument within the framework of capitalism. In the first place, the state comes into action in the economic sphere in order to solve problems which are posed by the development of capitalism. In the second place, where the interests of the capitalist class are concerned, there is a strong predisposition to use the state power freely. And, finally, the state may be used to make concessions to the working class provided that the consequences of not doing so are sufficiently dangerous to the stability and functioning of the system as a whole.

[15] This example makes clear the concession character of state action favoring the working class, since it could not possibly be maintained that the workers had a share in state power in England at the time the main factory acts were passed. In this connection it is sufficient to recall that the

Reform Act of 1832 contained high property qualifications for voting and it was not until 1867 that the franchise was next extended. By this time the most important victories in the struggle for factory legislation had already been won.
[16] For example, Marx remarked that in France, 'the February [1848] revolution was necessary to bring into the world the 12 hours' law.' *Capital* I, p. 328.

TOWARD A NATIONAL URBAN POLICY
Daniel P. Moynihan

Moynihan's essay, only slightly shortened from its original version, provides an interesting illustration of the general liberal perspective. Although Moynihan is not concerned with formulating that general view, his discussion of urban problems clearly manifests some important features of the liberal approach to social problems. He regards urban problems as imperfections in a basically decent society. He suggests wide varieties of government actions to help solve those problems since, like most liberals, he believes in active

SOURCE: *Extract of Chapter 1 of* Toward a National Urban Policy *edited by Daniel P. Moynihan.*

government involvement in or stimulus to the private sector. And he concentrates on proposals which would seek to improve the technical efficiency of government and the private sector. He would not seek to change the substance of basic social or economic institutions.

This essay appeared originally as an introduction to a collection of short essays on various urban problems; the book was also called *Toward a National Urban Policy*. Most of the essays were written by important members of a generally liberal intellectual "establishment," and Moynihan tends to reflect the tenor of many of those specific expressions of the liberal perspective.

Moynihan has recently served as a liberal member of President Nixon's White House staff, counseling the President on urban affairs, and as secretary to the President's Urban Affairs Council. During his stay in the White House, he was on leave from Harvard University, where he was a professor of education and director of the Harvard-MIT Joint Center for Urban Studies.

The United States does not now have an urban policy. The idea that there might be such a policy is new; so also is the Urban Affairs Council, established by President Nixon on January 23, 1969, as the first official act of his administration, to "advise and assist" with respect to urban affairs, specifically "in the development of a national urban policy, having regard both to immediate and to long-range concerns, and to priorities among them."

The central circumstance, as stated, is that America is an urban nation, and has been one for half a century.

This is not to say that most Americans live in large cities. They do not. In 1960 only 9.8 percent of the population lived in cities populated by one million or more inhabitants. In fact, 98 percent of the units of local government have fewer than 50,000 persons. In terms of the 1960 census only somewhat more than a quarter of congressmen represented districts in which a majority of residents lived in central city areas. The 1970 census will show that the majority of Americans in metropolitan areas in fact live in suburbs, while a great many more live in urban settlements of quite modest size. But they are not the less urban for that reason, providing conditions of living and problems of government profoundly different from that of the agricultural, small-town past.

The essentials of the present urban crisis are simple enough to relate. Until about World War II the growth of the city, as Otto Eckstein argues, was "a logical, economic development." At least it was such in the northeastern quadrant of the United States, where most urban troubles are supposed to exist. The political jurisdiction of the city more or less defined the area of intensive economic development which more or less defined the area of intensive settlement. Thereafter economic incentives and social desires combined to produce a fractionating process which made it ever more difficult to collect enough power in any one place to provide the rudiments of effective government. As a result of or as a part of this process, the central area ceased to grow and began to decline. The core began to rot. This most primitive analogue began to suggest to us that in some way life itself was in decline.

Two special circumstances compounded this problem. First, the extraordinary migration of the rural Southern Negro to the northern city. Second, a postwar population explosion (90 million babies were born between 1946 and 1968) which placed immense pressures on municipal services, and drove many whites to the suburbs seeking relief. (Both these influences are now attenuating somewhat, but their effects will be present for at least several decades, and indeed a new baby boom may be in the offing.) As a result the problems of economic stagnation of the central city became desperately exacerbated by those of racial tension. In the course of the 1960's tension turned into open racial strife.

City governments began to respond to the onset of economic obsolescence and social rigidity a generation or more ago, but quickly found their fiscal resources strained near to the limit. State governments became involved, and much the same process ensued. Starting in the postwar period, the federal government itself became increasingly caught up with urban problems. In recent years resources on a fairly considerable scale have flowed from Washington to the cities of the land and will clearly continue.

However, in the evolution of a national urban policy, more is involved than merely the question of national goals and the provision of resources with which to attain them. Too many programs have produced too few results simply to accept a more or less straightforward extrapolation of past and present practices into an oversized but familiar future.

The question of method has become as salient as that of goals themselves. As yet the federal government, no more than state or local government, has not found an effective incentive system—comparable to profit in private enterprise, prestige in intellectual activity, rank in military organization —whereby to shape the forces at work in urban areas in such a way that urban goals— whatever they may be—are in fact attained. This search· for incentives, and the realization that present procedures such as categorical grant-in-aid programs do not seem to provide sufficiently powerful ones, must accompany and suffuse the effort to establish goals as such. We must seek not just policy, but policy allied to a vigorous strategy for obtaining results from it.

Finally, the federal establishment must develop a much heightened sensitivity to its "hidden" urban policies. There is hardly a department or agency of the national government whose programs do not in some way have important consequences for the life of cities, and those who live in them. Frequently—one is tempted to say normally!— the political appointees and career executives concerned do not see themselves as involved with, much less responsible for the urban consequences of their programs and policies. They are, to their minds, simply building highways, guaranteeing mortgages, advancing agriculture, or whatever. No one has made clear to them that they are simultaneously redistributing employment opportunities, segregating neighborhoods, or desegregating them, depopulating the countryside and filling up the slums, and so forth: all of these things are second and third order consequences of nominally unrelated programs. Already this institutional naïveté has become cause for suspicion; in the future it simply must not be tolerated. Indeed, in the future, a primary mark of competence in

a federal official should be the ability to see the interconnections between programs immediately at hand, and the urban problems that pervade the larger society.

THE FUNDAMENTS OF URBAN POLICY

It having long been established that with respect to general codes of behavior eleven precepts are too many, and nine too few, ten points of urban policy may be set forth, scaled roughly to correspond to a combined measure of urgency and importance.

1. The poverty and social isolation of minority groups in central cities is the single most serious problem of the American city today. It must be attacked with urgency, with a greater commitment of resources than has heretofore been the case, and with programs designed especially for this purpose.

The 1960's have seen enormous economic advances among minority groups, especially Negroes. Outside the South, 37 percent of Negro families earn $8,000 per year or more, that being approximately the national median income. In cities in the largest metropolitan areas, 20 percent of Negro families in 1967 reported family incomes of $10,000 or over. The earnings of young married black couples are approaching parity with whites.

Nonetheless, certain forms of social disorganization and dependency appear to be increasing among the urban poor. Recently, Conrad Taueber, Associate Director of the Bureau of the Census, reported that in the largest metropolitan areas—those with one million or more inhabitants—"the number of black families with a woman as head increased by 83 percent since 1960; the number of black families with a man as head increased by only 15 percent during the same period." Disorganization, isolation, and discrimination seemingly have led to violence, and this violence has in turn been increasingly politicized by those seeking a "confrontation" with "white" society. Urban policy must have as its first goal the transformation of the urban lower class into a stable community based on dependable and adequate income flows, social equality, and social mobility. Efforts to improve the conditions of life in the present caste-created slums must never take precedence over efforts to enable the slum population to disperse throughout the metropolitan areas involved. Urban policy accepts the reality of ethnic neighborhoods based on choice, but asserts that the active intervention of government is called for to enable free choice to include integrated living as the normal option.

It is impossible to comprehend the situation of the black urban poor without first seeing that they have experienced not merely a major migration in the past generation, but also that they now live in a state almost of demographic siege as a result of population growth. The dependency ratio, in terms of children per thousand adult males, for blacks is nearly twice that for whites, and the gap widened sharply in the 1960's.

CHILDREN PER 1000 ADULT MALES

	1960	1966
White	1,365	1,406
Negro	1,922	2,216

It is this factor, surely, that accounts for much of the present distress of the black urban slums. At the same time, it is fairly clear that the sharp escalation in the number of births that characterized the past twenty-five years has more or less come to an end. The number of Negro females under age five is exactly the number aged five to nine. Thus the 1980's will see a slackening of the present severe demands on the earning power of adult Negroes, and also on the public institutions that provide services for children. But for the decade immediately ahead, those demands will continue to rise—especially for central city blacks, whose median age is a little more than ten years below that for whites—and will clearly have a priority claim on public resources.

1967 NEGRO FEMALE POPULATION

Age	Number
Under 5	1,443,000
5 to 9	1,443,000
10 to 14	1,298,000
15 to 19	1,102,000
20 to 24	840,000

2. Economic and social forces in urban areas are not self-balancing. Imbalances in industry, transportation, housing, social services and similar elements of urban life frequently tend to become more rather than less pronounced, and this tendency is often abetted by public policies. The concept of urban balance may be tentatively set forth: a social condition in which forces tending to produce imbalance induce counterforces that simultaneously admit change while maintaining equilibrium. It must be the constant object of federal officials whose programs affect urban areas—and there are few whose do not—to seek such equilibrium.

The evidence is considerable that many federal programs have induced sharp imbalances in the "ecology" of urban areas—the highway program, for example, is frequently charged with this, and there is wide agreement that other, specifically city-oriented programs such as urban renewal, have frequently accomplished just the opposite of their nominal objectives. The reasons are increasingly evident. Cities are complex social systems. Interventions that, intentionally or not, affect one component of the system almost invariably affect second, third, and fourth components as well, and these in turn affect the first component, often in ways quite opposite to the direction of the initial intervention. Most federal urban programs have assumed fairly simple cause and effect relationships which do not exist in the complex real world. Moreover, they have typically been based on "common sense" rather than research in an area where common sense can be notoriously misleading. In the words of Jay W. Forrester, "With a high degree of confidence we can say that the intuitive solution to the problems of complex social systems will be wrong most of the time."

This doubtless is true, but it need not be a traumatizing truth. As Lee Rainwater, Harvard professor of sociology and a contributor to this volume, argues, the logic of multivariate analysis and experience with it suggest that some components of a complex system are always vastly more important than others, so that when (if) these are accurately identified, a process of analysis that begins with the assertion of chaos can in fact end by producing quite concise and purposeful social strategies.

3. At least part of the relative ineffectiveness of the efforts of urban government to respond to urban problems derives from the fragmented and obsolescent structure of urban government itself. The federal government should constantly encourage and provide incentives for the reorganization of local government in response to the reality of metropolitan conditions. The objective of the federal government should be that local government be stronger and more effective, more visible, accessible, and meaningful to local inhabitants. To this end the federal government should discourage the creation of paragovernments designed to deal with special problems by evading or avoiding the jurisdiction of established local authorities, and should encourage effective decentralization.

Although the quality of local government, especially in large cities, has been seen to improve of late, there appears to have been a decline in the vitality of local political systems, and an almost total disappearance of serious effort to reorganize metropolitan areas into new and more rational governmental jurisdictions. Federal efforts to recreate ethnic, neighborhood-based community organizations, as in the poverty program, or to induce metropolitan area planning, as in various urban development programs, have had a measure of success, but nothing like that hoped for. The middle-class norm of "participation" has diffused downward and outward, so that federal urban programs now routinely require citizen participation in the planning process and beyond, yet somehow this does not seem to have led to more competent communities. In some instances it appears rather to have escalated the level of stalemate.

It may be we have not been entirely candid with ourselves in this area. Citizen participation, as Elliott A. Krause has pointed out, is in practice a "bureaucratic ideology," a device whereby public officials induce non-public individuals to act in a way the officials desire. Although the putative object may be, indeed almost always is, to improve the lot of the citizen, it is not settled that the actual consequences are anything like that. The ways of the officials, of course, are often not those of the elected representatives of the people, and the citizens may become a rope in the tug of war between bureaucrat and representative. Especially in a federal system, citizen participation easily becomes a device whereby the far-off federal bureaucracy acquires a weapon with which to battle the elected officials of local government. Whatever the nominal intent, the normal outcome is federal support for those who would diminish the legitimacy of local government. But it is not clear that the federal purposes are typically advanced through this process. To the contrary, an all-round diminishment, rather than enhancement of energies seems to occur.

(This would appear especially true when citizen participation has in effect meant putting citizens on the payroll. However much they may continue to protest, the protest acquires a certain hollow ring. Something like this has surely happened to groups seeking to influence public opinion on matters of public policy when the groups have been openly or covertly supported by the federal government. This is a new practice in American democracy. It began in the field of foreign affairs, and has now spread to the domestic area. To a quite astonishing degree it will be found that those groups which nominally are pressing for social change and development in the poverty field, for example, are in fact subsidized by federal funds. This occurs in protean ways—research grants, training contracts, or whatever—and is done with the best of intentions. But, again, with what results is far from clear. Can this development, for example, account for the curious fact that there seems to be so much protest in the streets of the nation, but so little, as it were, in its legislatures? Is it the case, in other words, that the process of public subsidy is subtly debilitating?)

Whatever the truth of this judgment, it is nevertheless clear that a national urban policy must look first to the vitality of the elected governments of the urban areas, and must seek to increase their capacity for independent, effective, and creative action. This suggests an effort to find some way out of the present fragmentation, and a certain restraint in the creation of federally financed "competitive governments."

Nathan Glazer has made the useful observation that in London and Tokyo comprehensive metropolitan government is combined with a complex system of "sub-governments"—the London Boroughs—representing units of 200,000–250,000 persons.

These are "real" governments, with important powers in areas such as education, welfare, and housing. In England, at all events, they are governed through an electoral system involving the national political parties in essentially their national postures. (Indeed, the boroughs make up the basic units of the parties' urban structure.) It may well be there is need for social interventions of this kind in the great American cities, especially with respect to power over matters such as welfare, education, and housing which are now subject to intense debates concerning local control. The demand for local control is altogether to be welcomed. In some degree it can be seen to arise from the bureaucratic barbarities of the highway programs of the 1950's, for example. But in the largest degree it reflects the processes of democracy catching up with the content of contemporary government. As government more and more involves itself in matters that very much touch on the lives of individual citizens, those individuals seek a greater voice in the programs concerned. In the hands of ideologues or dimwits, this demand can lead to an utter paralysis of government. It has already done so in dozens of urban development situations. But approached with a measure of sensitivity—and patience—it can lead to a considerable revitalization of urban government.

4. A primary object of federal urban policy must be to restore the fiscal vitality of urban government, with the particular object of ensuring that local governments normally have enough resources on hand or available to make local initiative in public affairs a reality.

For all the rise in actual amounts, federal aid to state and local government has increased only from 12 percent of state-local revenue in 1958 to 17 percent in 1967. Increasingly, state and local governments that try to meet their responsibilities lurch from one fiscal crisis to another. In such circumstances, the capacity for creative local government becomes least in precisely those jurisdictions where it might most be expected. As much as any other single factor, this condition may be judged to account for the malaise of city government, and especially for the reluctance of the more self-sufficient suburbs to associate themselves with the nearly bankrupt central cities. Surviving from one fiscal deadline to another, the central cities commonly adopt policies which only compound their ultimate difficulties. Yet their options are so few. As James Q. Wilson writes, "The great bulk of any city's budget is, in effect, a fixed charge the mayor is powerless to alter more than trivially." The basic equation, as it were, of American political economy is that for each 1 percent increase in the Gross National Product (GNP) the income of the federal government increases 1.5 percent while the normal income of city governments rises .5 to .75 at most. Hence both a clear opportunity and a no less manifest necessity exist for the federal government to adopt as a deliberate policy an increase in its aid to urban governments. This should be done in part through revenue sharing, and in part through an increase in categorical assistance, hopefully in much more consolidated forms than now exist, and through credit assistance.

It may not be expected that this process will occur rapidly. The prospects for an enormous "peace and growth dividend" to follow the cessation of hostilities in Vietnam are far less bright than they were painted. But the fact is that the Gross National Product grows at better than a billion dollars a week, and we can afford the government we need. This means, among our very first priorities, an increase in the resources available to city governments.

A clear opportunity exists for the federal government to adopt as a deliberate policy an increase in its aid to state and local governments in the aftermath of the Vietnam war. Much analysis is in order, but in approximate terms it may be argued that the present proportion of aid should be about doubled, with the immediate objective that the federal government contribution constitute one-third of state and local revenue.

5. Federal urban policy should seek to equalize the provision of public services as among different jurisdictions in metropolitan areas.

Although the standard depiction of the (black) residents of central cities as grossly deprived with respect to schools and other social services, when compared with their suburban (white) neighbors, requires endless qualification, the essential truth is that life for the well-to-do is better than life for the poor, and that these populations tend to be separated by artificial government boundaries within metropolitan areas. (The people in between may live on either side of the boundaries, and are typically overlooked altogether.)

As a minimum, federal policy should seek a dollar-for-dollar equivalence in the provision of social services having most to do with economic and social opportunity. This includes, at the top of the list, public education and public safety. (Obviously there will always be some relatively small jurisdictions—e.g., the Scarsdale school system—that spend a great deal more than others, but there can be national or regional norms and no central city should be forced to operate below them.)

Beyond the provision of equal resources lies the troubled and elusive question of equal results. Should equality of educational opportunity extend to equality of educational achievement (as between one group of children and another)? Should equality of police protection extend to equality of criminal victimization? That is to say, should there be not only as many police, but also as few crimes in one area of the city as in another? These are hardly simple questions, but as they are increasingly posed it is increasingly evident that we shall have to try to find answers.

The area of housing is one of special and immediate urgency. In America, housing is not regarded as a public utility (and a scarce one!) as it is in many of the industrial democracies of Europe, but there can hardly be any remaining doubt that the strong and regular production of housing is very nearly a public necessity. We shall not solve the problem of racial isolation without it. Housing must not only be open, *it must be available*. The process of filtration out from dense center city slums can only take place if the housing perimeter, as it were, is sufficiently porous. For too long now the production of housing has been a function not of the need for housing as such, but rather of the need to increase or decrease the money supply, or whatever. Somehow a greater regularity of effective demand must be provided the housing industry, and its level of production must be increased.

6. The federal government must assert a specific interest in the movement of people, displaced by technology or driven by poverty, from rural to urban areas, and also in the movement from densely populated central cities to suburban areas.

Much of the present urban crisis derives from the almost total absence of any provision for an orderly movement of persons off the countryside and into the city. The federal government made extraordinary, and extraordinarily successful, efforts to provide for the resettlement of Hungarian refugees in the 1950's and Cuban refugees in the 1960's. But almost nothing has been done for Americans driven from their homes by forces no less imperious.

Rural to urban migration has not stopped, and will not for some time. Increasingly, it is possible to predict where it will occur, and in what time sequence. In 1968, for example, testing of mechanical tobacco harvesting began on the East Coast and the first mechanical grape pickers were used on the West Coast. Hence, it is possible to prepare for it, both by training of those who leave, and providing for them where they arrive. Doubtless the United States will remain a nation of exceptionally mobile persons, but the completely unassisted processes of the past need not continue with respect to the migration of impoverished rural populations. There are increasing indications that the dramatic movement of Negro Americans to central city areas may be slackening, and that a countermovement to surrounding suburban areas may have begun. This process is to be encouraged in every way, especially by the maintenance of a flexible and open housing market.

But it remains the case that in the next thirty years we shall add one hundred million persons to our population. Knowing that, it is impossible to have no policy with respect to where they will be located. To let nature take its course is a policy. To consider what might be best for all concerned and to seek to provide it is surely a more acceptable goal.

7. State government has an indispensable role in the management of urban affairs, and must be supported and encouraged by the federal government in the performance of this role.

This fact, being all but self-evident, tends

to be overlooked. The trend of recent legislative measures, almost invariably prompted by executive initiatives, has been to establish a direct federal-city relationship. States have been bypassed, and doubtless some have used this as an excuse to avoid their responsibilities of providing the legal and governmental conditions under which urban problems can be effectively confronted.

It has, of course, been a tradition of social reform in America that city government is bad and that, if anything, state government is worse. This is neither true as a generalization nor useful as a principle. But on the other hand, by and large, state governments, with an occasional exception such as New York, have not involved themselves with urban problems, and are readily enough seen by mayors as the real enemy. But this helps neither. States must become involved. City governments, without exception, are creatures of state governments. City boundaries, jurisdictions, and powers are given and taken away by state governments. It is surely time the federal establishment sought to lend a sense of coherence and a measure of progressivism to this fundamental process.

The role of state government in urban affairs cannot easily be overlooked: it is more typically ignored on political or ideological grounds. By contrast, it is relatively easy to overlook county government, and possibly an even more serious mistake to do so. In a steadily increasing number of metropolitan areas, the county, rather than the original core city, has become the only unit of government that makes any geographical sense. That is to say, the only unit whose boundaries contain most or all of the actual urban settlement. The powers of county government have typically lagged well behind its potential, but it may also be noted that in the few—the very few—instances of urban reorganization to take place since World War II, county government has assumed a principal, even primary role in the new arrangement.

8. The federal government must develop and put into practice far more effective incentive systems than now exist whereby state and local governments and private interests can be led to achieve the goals of federal programs.

The typical federal grant-in-aid program provides its recipients with an immediate reward for promising to work toward some specified goal—raising the educational achievement of minority children, providing medical care for the poor, cleaning up the air, reviving the downtown business district —but almost no reward for actually achieving such goals, and rarely any punishment for failing to do so.

It is by now widely agreed that what federal grant-in-aid programs mostly reward is dissimulation. By and large the approach of the federal government to most urban problems is to provide local institutions with money in the hope they will perform but with no very powerful incentives to do so.

There is a growing consensus that the federal government should provide market competition for public programs, or devise ways to imitate market conditions. In particular, it is increasingly agreed that federal aid should be given directly to the consumers of the programs concerned—individuals included—thus enabling them to choose among competing suppliers of the goods or services that the program is designed to provide.

Probably no single development would more enliven and energize the role of government in urban affairs than a move from the monopoly service strategy of the grant-in-aid programs to a market strategy of providing the most reward to those suppliers that survive competition.

In this precise sense, it is evident that federal programs designed to assist those city-dwelling groups that are least well off, least mobile, and least able to fend for themselves must in many areas move beyond a *services* strategy to an approach that provides inducements to move from a dependent and deficient status to one of independence and sufficiency. Essentially, this is an *income* strategy, based fundamentally on the provision of incentives to increase the earnings and to expand the property base of the poorest groups.

Urban policy should in general be directed toward raising the level of political activity and concentrating it in the electoral process. It is nonetheless possible and useful to be alert for areas of intense but unproductive political conflict and to devise ways to avoid such conflict through market strategies. Thus conflicts over "control" of public education systems have frequently of late taken on the aspect of disputes over control of a monopoly, a sole source of a needed good. Clearly some of the ferocity that ensues can be avoided through free choice arrangements that, in effect, eliminate monopoly control.

If we move in this direction, difficult "minimum standard" regulation problems will almost certainly arise, and must be anticipated. No arrangement meets every need, and a good deal of change is primarily to be justified on grounds that certain systems need change for its own sake. For example, small school districts, controlled by locally elected boards, may be just the thing for New York City. However, in Phoenix, Arizona, where they have just that, consolidation and centralization would appear to be the desire of educational reformers. But either way, a measure of market competition can surely improve the provision of public services, much as it has proved an efficient way to obtain various public paraphernalia, from bolt action rifles to lunar landing vehicles.

Here, as elsewhere, it is essential to pursue and to identify the formerly hidden urban policies of government. These are nowhere more central to the issue than in the matter of incentives. Thus for better than half a century now, city governments with the encouragement of state and federal authorities have been seeking to direct urban investment and development in accordance with principles embodied in zoning codes, and not infrequently in accord with precise city plans. However, during this same time the tax laws have provided the utmost incentive to pursue just the opposite objectives of those incorporated in the codes and the plans. It has, for example, been estimated that returns from land speculation based on zoning code changes on average incur half the tax load of returns from investment in physical improvements. Inevitably, energy and capital have diverted away from pursuing the plan, toward subverting it. It avails little for government to deplore the evasion of its purposes in such areas. Government has in fact established two sets of purposes, and provided vastly greater inducements to pursue the implicit rather than the avowed ones. Until public authorities, and the public itself, learn to be much more alert to these situations, and far more open in discussing and managing them, we must expect the present pattern of self-defeating contradictions to continue.

9. The federal government must provide more and better information concerning urban affairs, and should sponsor extensive and sustained research into urban problems.

Much of the social progress of recent years derives from the increasing quality and quantity of government-generated statistics and government-supported research. However, there is general agreement that the time is at hand when a general consolidation is in order, bringing a measure of symmetry to the now widely dispersed (and somewhat uneven) data-collecting and research-supporting activities of the federal government. Such consolidation should not be limited to urban problems, but it must surely include attention to urban questions.

The federal government should, in particular, recognize that most of the issues that appear most critical just now do so in large measure because they are so little understood. This is perhaps especially so with respect to issues of minority group education, but generally applies to all the truly difficult and elusive issues of the moment. More and better inquiry is called for. In particular, the federal government must begin to sponsor longitudinal research designed to follow individual and communal development over long periods of time.

It should also consider providing demographic and economic projections for political subdivisions as a routine service, much as the weather and the economy are forecast. (Thus, Karl Taueber has shown how seemingly unrelated policies of local governments can increase the degree of racial and economic differentiation between political jurisdictions, especially between central cities and suburbs.)

Similarly, the extraordinary inquiry into the education system begun by the U.S. Office of Education under the direction of James S. Coleman should somehow be established on a continuing basis. It is now perfectly clear that little is known about the processes whereby publicly provided resources affect educational outcomes. The great mass of those involved in education, and of that portion of the public which interests itself in educational matters, continue undisturbed in the old beliefs. But the bases of their beliefs are already thoroughly undermined and the whole structure is likely to collapse in a panic of disillusion and despair unless something like new knowledge is developed to replace the old. Here again, longitudinal inquiries are essential. And here also, it should be insisted that however little the new understandings may have diffused beyond the academic research centers in which they originated, the American public is accustomed to the idea that understandings do change and, especially in the field of education, is quite open to experimentation and innovation.

Much of the methodology of social science originated in clinical psychology, and perhaps for that reason tends to be deficiency-oriented. Social scientists raise social problems, the study of which can become a social problem in its own right if it is never balanced by the identification and analysis of social successes. We are not an unsuccessful country. To the contrary, few societies work as hard at their problems, solve as many, and in the process stumble on more unexpected and fulsome opportunities. The cry of the decent householder who asks why the profession (and the news media which increasingly follow the profession) must be ever preoccupied with juvenile delinquency and never with "juvenile decency" deserves to be heard. Social science, like medical science, has been preoccupied with pathology, with pain. A measure of inquiry into the sources of health and pleasure is overdue, and is properly a subject of federal support.

10. The federal government, by its own example, and by incentives, should seek the development of a far heightened sense of the finite resources of the natural environment, and the fundamental importance of aesthetics in successful urban growth.

The process of "uglification" may first have developed in Europe, but as with much else, the technological breakthroughs have taken place in the United States. American cities have grown to be as ugly as they are, not as a consequence of the failure of design so much as of the success of a certain interaction of economic, technological, and cultural forces. It is economically efficient to exploit the natural resources of land, air, and water by technological means which the culture does not reject, even though the result is an increasingly despoiled, debilitated, and now even dangerous urban environment.

It is not clear how this is to change, and so the matter which the twenty-second century, say, will almost certainly see as having been the primary urban issue of the twentieth century, is ranked last in the public priorities of the moment. But there are signs that the culture is changing, that the frontier sense of a natural environment of unlimited resources, all but impervious to human harm, is being replaced by an acute awareness that serious, possibly irreparable harm is being done to the environment, and that somehow the process must be reversed. This could lead to a new, nonexploitive technology, and thence to a new structure of economic incentives.

The federal establishment is showing signs that this cultural change is affecting its actions, and so do state and city governments. But the process needs to be raised to the level of a conscious pursuit of policy. The quality of the urban environment, a measure deriving from a humane and understanding use of the natural resources, together with the creative use of design in architecture and in the distribution of activities and people must become a proclaimed concern of government. And here the federal government can lead. It must seek out its hidden policies. The design of public housing projects, for example, surely has had the consequence of manipulating the lives of those who inhabit them. By and large the federal government set the conditions which have determined the disastrous designs of the past two decades. It is thus responsible for the results, and should force itself to realize that. And it must be acutely aware of the force of its own example. If scientists (as we are told) in the Manhattan Project were prepared to dismiss the problem of long-lived radioactive wastes as one that could be solved merely by ocean dumping, there are few grounds for amazement that business executives in Detroit for so long manufactured automobiles that emitted poison gases into the atmosphere. Both patterns of decision evolved from the primacy of economic concerns in the context of the exploitation of the natural environment in ways the culture did not forbid. There are, however, increasing signs that we are beginning to change in this respect. We may before long evolve into a society in which the understanding of and concern about environmental pollution, and the general uglification of American life, will be both culturally vibrant and politically potent.

Social peace is the primary objective of social policy. To the extent that this derives from a shared sense of the value and significance of the public places and aesthetic value of the city, the federal government has a direct interest in encouraging such qualities.

Daniel J. Elazar has observed that while Americans have been willing to become urbanized, they have adamantly resisted becoming citified. Yet a measure of this process is needed. There are not half a dozen cities in America whose disappearance would, apart from the inconvenience, cause any real regret. But to lose one of those half-dozen would plunge much of the nation and almost all the immediate inhabitants into genuine grief. Something of value in our lives would have been lost, and we would know it. The difference between those cities that would be missed and those that would not be resides fundamentally in the combination of architectural beauty, social amenity, and cultural vigor that so sets them apart. It has ever been such. To create such a city and to preserve it was the great ideal of the Greek civilization, and it may yet become ours as we step back ever so cautiously from the worship of the nation state with its barbarous modernity and impotent might. We might well consider the claims for a different life asserted in the oath of the Athenian city-state:

We will ever strive for the ideals and sacred things of the city, both alone and with many;
We will unceasingly seek to quicken the sense of public duty;
We will revere and obey the city's laws;
We will transmit this city not only not less, but greater, better and more beautiful than it was transmitted to us.

REFLECTIONS ON PUBLIC EXPENDITURE THEORY
Walter W. Heller

This selection reflects several important features of the liberal theory of the State, although it does not seek rigorously to formulate that theory. It illustrates the general theory especially in its emphasis on the nearly infinite number of options open to the government and in its belief that the State can represent all groups in society rather than the interests of only one class. As Heller puts it, the liberal view expects that the government can achieve "any combination of Government services, income redistribution, and economic redistribution and economic stability we set our sights on." All this regardless of the structure of economic institutions and the relative power of competing groups.

The selection comes from a slightly longer piece included in *Private Wants and Public Needs*. It offers a simple and discursive expression of the basic theory of public expenditure dominating liberal economic thought in this country, more rigorously formulated in Richard Musgrave, *The Theory of Public Finance*.

A leading liberal academic economist, Heller teaches at the University of Minnesota. He served as chairman of the Council of Economic Advisers under President John F. Kennedy, playing a leading role in the establishment of "The New Economics" as a dominant strain in government economic policy.

SOURCE: *Reprinted from* Private Wants and Public Needs, *edited with an introduction by Edmund S. Phelps, Yale University. By permission of W. W.* Norton & Company, Inc. Copyright © 1965, 1962, by W. W. Norton & Company, Inc.

What does the economist have to offer a perplexed public and its policymaking representatives on the theory of Government functions as they effect the budget? The cynic's offhand answer, "not much," may be close to the mark if one demands definitive rules of thumb for determining the precise scope of Government functions and level of Government expenditures. But if, instead, the demand is for economic guidelines to aid the budgetary decisionmaker (1) in blending rationally the service, stabilization, and income-transfer functions of Government, (2) in identifying those deficiencies in the private-market mechanism which call for Government budgetary action or, more broadly, those activities where Government use or control of resources promises greater returns than private use or control, and (3) in selecting the most efficient means of carrying out Government functions and activities (whether by Government production, contracts with private producers, transfer payments, loans, guaranties, tax concessions, and so forth)—if this is the nature of the demands on him, the economist is prepared to make a modest offering now and to work along lines that promise a greater contribution in the future.

In a sense, this paper is a progress report designed to show where the economist can already offer some useful counsel, to indicate some of the lines along which promising work is being done, and to suggest certain limitations or constraints within which the economic criteria for dividing resources between public and private use must be applied.

A BASIC FRAMEWORK

As a first step in the search for economic guideposts, we need to disentangle, classify, and define the basic objectives and functions of Government that shape its budgetary decisions. Fortunately, Prof. Richard A. Musgrave has developed a conceptual framework for this task in his "multiple theory of budget determination."[1]

The component functions of the budget as he brings them into focus are: (1) The service, or want-satisfying, function: to provide for the satisfaction of those individual wants which the market mechanism cannot satisfy effectively (e.g., education and conservation) or is incapable of satisfying (e.g., defense and justice); (2) the income-transfer or distributional function: to make those corrections in the existing income distribution (by size, by occupational groups, by geographical area, etc.) which society desires; and (3) the stabilization function: to join with monetary policy and other measures to raise or lower the level of aggregate demand so as to maintain full employment and avoid inflation. The first function is of dominant interest [here] and the succeeding sections of the paper return to it. But several general implications of the Musgrave system as a whole deserve attention before turning to specifics.

Musgrave's formulation helps unclutter our thinking on the component parts of the budget decision. It drives home the significant point that our decisions on how much and what kind of want-satisfying services to provide by Government budgets need not be tied to our demands on the budget for correction of either the existing patterns of income distribution or the level of aggregate demand. If we prefer, we can have a small budget for services (financed by taxes levied on the benefit principle) combined with a big budget for redistributive transfers of income (financed by taxes levied on the ability principle), or vice versa; and either combination can be coupled with either a deficit to stimulate demand and employment or a surplus to reduce demand and check inflation. In this respect, it is reminiscent of Samuelson's "daring doctrine" that by appropriate fiscal-monetary policy "a community can have full employment, can at the same time have the rate of capital formation it wants, and can accomplish all this compatibly with the degree of income-redistributing taxation it ethically desires."[2] Musgrave, in turn, points the way to achieving any combination of Government services, income redistribution, and economic redistribution, and economic stability we set our sights on. . . .

---

[1] See, for example, "A Multiple Theory of Budget Determination," *Finanzarchiv* 1957, vol. 13, no. 3, pp. 333–343, and the relevant chapters of his treatise, *The Theory of Public Finance* (New York: McGraw-Hill, 1959).

[2] Paul A. Samuelson, "The New Look in Tax and Fiscal Policy," in *Federal Tax Policy for Economic Growth and Stability*, Joint Committee on the Economic Report, Washington, November 9, 1955, p. 234.

ECONOMIC DETERMINANTS OF THE PROPER SPHERE OF GOVERNMENT ACTIVITY

Given a framework for straight thinking about budget functions, the economist is brought face to face with two questions that come closer to the central problem of the proper sphere of Government activity. First, where competitive bidding via the pricing mechanism is inapplicable, how are the preferences of voters for governmental services to be revealed, measured, and appropriately financed? Second, waiving the question of measurement of preferences, where would the line between public and private control over resources be drawn if economic efficiency were the only criterion to be implied?

On the first question, insofar as it relates to individual preferences for public goods, economists have agreed on the nature and difficulty of the problem, have made some intriguing suggestions as to its solution, and have concluded that it is next to insoluble. The key difficulty is that the voting process, unlike the pricing process, does not force the consumer of public goods to show his hand. The essence of preference measurement is the showing of how much of one good or service the consumer is willing to forgo as the price of acquiring another. But the amount of a public good or service (say, of defense, police protection, or schooling) available to the voter is independent of the amount he pays in taxes or the intensity of his demand for it.[3] Unless and until we devise a reliable and reasonably accurate method of detecting specific voter preferences in some detail, our definition of the proper sphere of government activity will have to rely chiefly on the informed judgment and perception of those whom we vote into legislative and executive office.[4]

This being the case, the economist's task is to contribute what he can to this informed judgment and perception. In effect, the economist's job becomes one of telling the voters and their representatives what their preferences as to governmental activities would be if they were guided by the principle of economic efficiency. In doing so, the economist is not proposing that decisions as to what kinds of activities should be assigned to government—what wants should be satisfied and resources should be redirected through government action—should be made on economic grounds alone. He is fully aware that values such as those of political and economic freedom play a vital role in these decisions. But he can perform the valuable service of identifying those deficiencies in the market mechanism and those inherent economic characteristics of government which make it economically advantageous to have certain services provided by government rather than by private initiative. In other words he can show where government intervention in resource allocation and use promises a greater return per unit of input than untrammeled private use.

The economist recognizes, of course, that there are areas in which he is necessarily mute, or at least should not speak unless spoken to. These are the areas of pure public goods, whose benefits are clearly indivisible and nonmarketable, and no amount of economic wisdom can determine the appropriate levels of output and expenditure.[5] In the realm of defense, for example, one successful Russian earth satellite or intercontinental ballistics missile will (and should) outweigh 10,000 economists in determining the appropriate level of expenditures. At most, the economist stands ready to offer analysis and judgments as to the critical levels of defense expenditures beyond which they threaten serious inflation in the absence of drastic tax action or curtailment of civilian programs, or, given that action, threaten impairment of producer incentives and essential civilian programs.

A much more fruitful activity for the

---

[3] For an illuminating exploration of ways and means to get at a more valid and clear-cut expression of voter preferences for government services, see the pioneering work by Howard R. Bowen, *Toward Social Economy*, New York, 1948, especially ch. 18, "Collective Choice." In this chapter Bowen explores both voting and polling techniques for ascertaining those individual tastes and preferences which cannot find expression in, or be measured by, the market mechanism.

[4] Insofar as voter wants in the public sphere go beyond individualistic preferences to general welfare choices . . . the problem changes form, but the desirability of sharper definition of voter preferences remains undiminished.

[5] No attempt is made here to define a public good. Samuelson (in "The Pure Theory of Public Expenditures," *The Review of Economics and Statistics*, November 1954, vol. 36, p. 387) has defined "collective consumption goods" as those in which one individual's consumption of the good leads to no diminution of any other individual's consumption of that good. . . .

economist is to demonstrate the economic advantage offered by government intervention, budgetary and otherwise, in those intermediate service areas where benefits are at least partially divisible and marketable. A number of economists have made useful contributions on this front.[6] In what situations does economic logic point to government intervention to correct the market mechanism's allocation of resources in the interests of greater efficiency in their use?

1. Where there are important third-party benefits [usually known as neighborhood effects, external effects, or externalities] which accrue to others than the direct beneficiary of the service, as in the case of education, disease prevention, police and fire protection, the market price and demand schedules underestimate the marginal and total social benefits provided by the service in question. By and large, the direct beneficiaries are the only ones who enter the private market as buyers, with the result that the services would be undervalued, underpriced, and underproduced unless Government entered the transaction. Government is the instrument for representing the third-party beneficiaries and correcting the deficiency of the market place (though this is not to deny that private religious and philanthropic organizations, for example, also represent third-party beneficiaries and operate on budget rather than market principles).

2. Just as there may be indirect benefits not reflected in market demand, there may be indirect costs inflicted on society which do not enter the private producer's costs and therefore do not influence market supply. Classic examples are the costs of smog, water pollution, denuding of forests, and the like. In these areas, private output will exceed the optimum level unless government corrects the situation either by regulation or by a combination of expenditure and charge-backs to the private producers involved.

3. Where a service is best provided, for technical reasons, as a monopoly (e.g., postal service, electricity, railroad transportation), the Government is expected to step in either by regulation or operation to avoid costly duplication and improve the quality of service. Ideally, its function would also be to guide prices toward levels consistent with optimum output. Involved here is the problem of the decreasing cost industry, where efficient plant size is so large relative to total demand that average cost decreases as output increases, and the market solution of the output and price problem will not result in best use of the productive assets. To push production to a point representing an ideal use of resources may require, if not Government operation, a subsidy financed out of tax revenues.

4. Government may enjoy some advantages in production or distribution which make it an inherently more efficient producer of certain services. Here, the classic case is highways, streets, and sidewalks. By providing them free to all comers, Government effects substantial savings in costs of distribution since it does not have to meter the service and charge a price for each specific use. In this category we might also fit projects, such as the initial development of atomic energy, which involve such great risks and huge accumulations of capital that the private market does not have the financial tools to cope with them.

ALTERNATIVE MEANS OF CARRYING OUT GOVERNMENT FUNCTIONS

Given the decisions as to the appropriate sphere of Government activity (on the basis not merely of considerations of greatest economic gain but also of value preferences), there remains the problem of choice among alternative methods to implement these decisions, to achieve given aims and satisfy expressed public wants. This choice will affect the budget in different ways. It may increase expenditures, decrease revenues, establish contingent liabilities, or perhaps have no effect on the budget at all (except for a small amount of administrative expenses involved in the supervisory and regulatory activities). Since the operational question is not merely what functions and activities Government should carry out, but what budgetary principles and expenditure levels these lead to, the

[6] See, for example, O. H. Brownlee and E. D. Allen, *Economics of Public Finance*, second edition, New York, 1954, ch. 10, "The Role of Government Expenditure." See also Max F. Millikan, "Objectives for Economic Policy in a Democracy" (especially pp. 62–68), and Robert Dahl and Charles E. Lindblom, "Variation in Public Expenditure," both in *Income Stabilization for a Developing Democracy*, Max F. Millikan, editor, New Haven, 1953.

problem of implementation must be included in any applied theory of public expenditures.

Here, the economist's role is to determine the most efficient method of providing the service or otherwise influencing resource allocation. He is concerned with minimizing costs, i.e., achieving the stated objective with a minimum expenditure of resources. Needless to say, other considerations will also influence the selection among alternative means, as even a brief consideration of the types of choices involved in the implementation process will make clear.

What are these choices? Take first the case of direct satisfaction of individuals' public wants. Should the Government produce the desired public goods or obtain them from private industry by purchase or contract? To accomplish redistributive ends, should the Government provide transfers in cash or transfers in kind?[7] Should Government rely on public production of educational services, or should it consider private production combined with earmarked transfers of purchasing power to parents? Thus far, the choices all involve direct budgetary expenditures, the level of which differs, at least marginally, depending on the relative efficiency of the method chosen. But in making his choice, the policymaker must consider not merely the direct costs of providing the service but whether one method involves more or less disturbance of private market incentives and patterns of production than another, whether it involves more or less interference with individual freedom (which is largely a function of the extent of Government expenditures and intervention but certainly in part also a function of the form of that intervention), and so on.

Another set of choices may take the item off of the expenditure side of the budget entirely, or leave it there only contingently. Should such subsidies as those to promote oil and gas exploration, stimulate foreign investment, expand the merchant marine, promote low-cost housing, and increase the flow of strategic minerals take the form of (1)

outright subsidies or above-market-price purchase programs, (2) Government loan programs, (3) Government guaranties, or (4) tax concessions? The choice will clearly involve quite different impacts on Government expenditures.

In many of these cases, the economist can be helpful with his efficiency criterion. But one would be naive to think that efficiency alone dictates the choice. The economist may show that a direct subsidy could stimulate a given amount of private direct investment abroad or a given amount of exploration for oil and gas, with a much smaller cost to the budget than is implicitly required in the tax concession method of achieving the same end. Yet, the costlier tax concession method may be preferred for two simple reasons: (1) it is virtually self-administering, involving no administrative hierarchy to substitute its authority for relatively free private decisions, and (2) it does not involve an increase in the expenditure side of the budget, a fact which has certain attractions to the Executive and Congress.

As yet, no clear boundary lines have been drawn among the various forms of Government intervention to mark off those that properly belong within the scope of public expenditure theory. But this illustrative review of the various choices makes clear that some forms of Government activity which are not reflected in expenditures at all (tax concessions) or only contingently (guaranties) are an integral part of such expenditure theory. In fact, there may be a stronger case for embracing these in expenditure theory than many Government activities which require budgetary outlays but are conducted on the pricing principle, i.e., Government enterprise activities.

Economists are conducting some provocative inquiries into questions of alternative methods of carrying out Government programs in areas where the answers had heretofore been taken for granted. For example, the transfer of schooling to a private production and Government transfer payment basis has been urged by Professor Milton Friedman as a more efficient means of providing the desired service.[8] . . . Once fairly conclusive findings are devised as to the methods most likely to minimize costs, there remains

---

[7] One involves so-called resource-using (also called factor-purchase or exhaustive) Government expenditures, i.e., payments in exchange for current goods and services rendered, with direct control of resources remaining in public hands. The other involves transfer payments, i.e., payments made without any provision of current goods and services in return, with direct control over resources passing into private hands.

[8] See Milton Friedman, "The Role of Government in Education," in *Economics and the Public Interest,* Robert A. Solo, editor, New Brunswick,

the vital task of blending these findings with the nonmonetary values that would be gained or lost in the process of transferring from public to private production.

SOME CONSTRAINTS ON THE APPLICATION OF SPECIFIC ECONOMIC CRITERIA

Repeatedly in this discussion, the note has been sounded that, in determining the level of Government activity, the policymaker cannot live by economics alone. More particularly, we need to guard against setting up our economic guides solely in terms of those considerations which lend themselves to sharp economic analysis and definition. In other words, the role of both economic and noneconomic constraints must be given full weight.

The former include a host of considerations relating particularly to economic motivation in Government versus private undertakings. Government may, for example, have a decided edge in the efficiency of distribution or be able to achieve a better balancing of social costs and social benefits in a variety of fields. Yet, there may be important offsets to these economic advantages in terms of (1) bureaucracy, (2) lack of the profit criterion to gage the results of Government activities, and (3) undesigned or unintended (presumably adverse) economic effects of taxation.[9]

The latter factor, in particular the fact

1955, pp. 123–144. In his prescription, Friedman would, of course, have Government regulate the private schools to the extent of insuring that they meet certain minimum standards in their programs and facilities.

[9] These less sharply defined economic effects have to be balanced, of course, against comparable and perhaps offsetting drawbacks in the market mechanism. For an exploration of some of these factors, both in the private and the public sphere, see Robert A. Dahl and Charles E. Lindblom, *Politics, Economics, and Welfare,* New York, 1953, especially pt. V. See also C. Lowell Harriss, "Government Spending: Issues of Theory and Practices," *Public Finance,* vol. 12, 1957, pp. 7–19.

that tax financing of public services involves breaking the link between an individual's cost of a given service and his benefit from it, may involve important offsets to economic advantages otherwise gained by Government expenditure. Thus far, to be sure, no dire consequences of the disincentive effects of taxation have been firmly proved, but changes in the form of private economic activity to minimize taxes are certainly a cost that must be weighed when netting out the balance of economic advantage in Government versus private performance of services.

Beyond the economic factors, one encounters an even more basic and less manageable constraint, namely that of freedom of choice. Thus, it is quite conceivable that following the kinds of economic criteria discussed earlier in the paper would take us considerably farther in the direction of Government spending and control over resource allocation than we would wish to go in terms of possible impairment of economic and political freedom. This consideration enters importantly not merely in decisions as to the proper range of Government activity but also in choosing among alternative methods of providing Government services.

This is not to imply that all value considerations run counter to the expansion of the Government sector of our economy. Such expansion may serve a number of social values, such as greater equality of income and opportunity, a more acceptable social environment, and so on.[10]

To get all of these considerations into the decision-making equation on private versus public provision of a particular service, or on the choice among alternative forms of providing the service, requires a wisdom which goes well beyond the field of economics. Perhaps this explains why so few economists enter politics.

[10] This type of consideration is examined in William Vickrey, "An Exchange of Questions Between Economics and Philosophy," in *Goals of Economic Life,* edited by A. Dudley Ward, New York, 1953, pp. 148–177. See also Max F. Millikan, *op. cit.*

THE UNHEAVENLY CITY
Edward C. Banfield

The following selection illustrates the general conservative approach to the problems discussed in this book of readings. It comprises the concluding chapter of Banfield's recent book on urban problems (by the same title). Banfield's book represents an exact conservative counterpart to the focus of this book; in it, Banfield quite carefully outlines a conservative analysis of almost all of the problems discussed in succeeding chapters in this volume. In the concluding chapter reprinted below, Banfield summarizes the important points of his book.

The author is Henry Lee Shattuck Professor of Urban Government at Harvard University. He has written many books on urban politics and problems, including *City Politics* (with James Q. Wilson).

It is probable that at this time we are about to make great changes in our social system. The world is ripe for such changes and if they are not made in the direction of greater social liberality, the direction forward, they will almost of necessity be made in the direction backward, of a terrible social niggardliness. We all know which of those directions we want. But it is not enough to want it, not even enough to work for it—we must want it and work for it with intelligence. Which means that we must be aware of the dangers which lie in our most generous wishes.

—Lionel Trilling[1]

It is impossible to avoid the conclusion that the serious problems of the cities will continue to exist in something like their present form for another twenty years at least. Even on the most favorable assumptions we shall have large concentrations of the poor and the unskilled, and—what, to repeat, is by no means the same thing—the lower class in the central cities and the larger, older suburbs. The outward movement of industry and commerce is bound to continue, leaving ever-larger parts of the inner city blighted or semi-abandoned. Even if we could afford to throw the existing cities away and build new ones from scratch, matters would not be essentially different, for the people who moved into the new cities would take the same old problems with them. Eventually, the present problems of the cities

SOURCE: *From* The Unheavenly City *by Edward C. Banfield, by permission of Little, Brown & Co. Copyright © 1968, 1970, by Edward C. Banfield.*

[1] *The Liberal Imagination* (Garden City, N.Y.: Anchor Books, 1953), pp. 214–215.

will disappear or dwindle into relative unimportance; they will not, however, be "solved" by programs of the sort now being undertaken or contemplated. On the contrary, the tendency of these programs will be to prolong the problems and perhaps even make them worse.

For the most part, the problems in question have arisen from and are inseparably connected with developments that almost everyone welcomes: the growth and spread of affluence has enabled millions of people to move from congested cities to new and more spacious homes in the suburbs; the availability of a large stock of relatively good housing in the central cities and older suburbs has enabled the Negro to escape the semislavery of the rural South and, a century late, to move into industrial society; better public health measures and facilities have cut the deathrate of the lower class; the war and postwar baby boom has left the city with more adolescents and youths than ever before; and a widespread and general movement upward on the class-cultural scale has made poverty, squalor, ignorance, and brutality—conditions that have always and everywhere been regarded as inevitable in the nature of things—appear as anomalies that should be removed entirely and at once.

What stands in the way of dealing effectively with these problems (insofar as their nature admits of their being dealt with) is mainly the virtues of the American political system and of the American character. It is because governmental power is widely distributed that organized interests are so often able to veto measures that would benefit large numbers of people. It is the generous and public-regarding impulses of voters and taxpayers that impel them to support measures—for example, the minimum wage and compulsory high school attendance—the ultimate effect of which is to make the poor poorer and more demoralized. Our devotion to the doctrine that all men are created equal discourages any explicit recognition of class-cultural differences and leads to "democratic" —and often misleading—formulations of problems: for example, poverty as lack of income and material resources (something external to the individual) rather than as inability or unwillingness to take account of the future or to control impulses (something internal). Sympathy for the oppressed, indignation at the oppressor, and a wish to make amends for wrongs done by one's ancestors lead to a misrepresentation of the Negro as the near-helpless victim of "white racism." Faith in the perfectibility of man and confidence that good intentions together with strenuous exertions will hasten his progress onward and upward lead to bold programs that promise to do what no one knows how to do and what perhaps cannot be done, and therefore ends in frustration, loss of mutual respect and trust, anger, and even coercion.

Even granting that in general the effect of government programs is to exacerbate the problems of the cities, it might perhaps be argued that they have a symbolic value that is more than redeeming. What economist Kenneth Boulding has said of national parks —that we seem to need them "as we seem to need a useless dome on the capitol, as a symbol of national identity and of that mutuality of concern and interest without which government would be naked coercion"[2] —may possibly apply as well to Freedom

Budgets, domestic Marshall Plans, and other such concoctions. That government programs do not succeed in reducing welfare dependency, preventing crime, and so on, is a rather minor objection to them if in fact without them the feeling that the society is "not worth saving" would be widespread. One would hope, however, that other and better means—a useless dome on the capitol, for example—would serve the symbolic need well enough. Moreover, there is an evident danger that the failure of urban programs to contribute to the attainment of our objectives will make them symbols not of national identity and mutual concern, but rather of national divisiveness, confusion, and unwisdom.

That government cannot solve the problems of the cities and is likely to make them worse by trying does not necessarily mean that calamity impends. Powerful accidental (by which is meant nongovernmental and, more generally, nonorganizational) forces are at work that tend to alleviate and even to eliminate the problems. Hard as it may be for a nation of inveterate problem-solvers to believe, social problems sometimes disappear in the normal course of events.

One powerful accidental force at work is economic growth. Because capital tends to increase by geometric progression, a rich country becomes exceedingly rich in the space of a few years. If Americans in the future take no more of their income in the form of leisure than they do now, the national income should increase from $713 billion in 1968 to $2,628 billion in the year 2000. If there has meanwhile been no great amount of immigration by people who are slow to adapt to the ways of industrial society, the end of urban poverty, in the sense of hardship, will be at hand even if the pattern of income distribution remains substantially unchanged.

A second such force is demographic change. The presence of large numbers of adolescent boys is (along with the presence of a large lower class) mainly responsible for school, job, crime, and disorder problems. This troublesome part of the population is now increasing at an extraordinary rapid rate (in the ten years ending in 1975 the number of males aged 15 to 24 will increase from 15,540,000 to an estimated 20,296,000). The increase will almost stop before long,

[2] Kenneth Boulding, book review in the *Journal of Business* (January 1963): 121.

however (in 1985 there will be about 21,107,000 males in this age group), and the proportion of boys and young men in the population will be smaller than it is now. A decline in the relative importance of the young male part of the population will do more to relieve strain on city institutions, it is safe to say, than even the most "massive" of government programs.

A third such force—perhaps the most important of all—is the process of middle- and upper-class-ification. For the reasons that were given in Chapter 10 [of *The Unheavenly City*], it does not seem likely that the lower class will be absorbed into the culture of the larger society. With this important exception, however, there will no doubt continue to be a general upward movement all along the class-cultural scale. This will mean a softening of manners, better performance in schools, less violence (but not necessarily less nonviolent crime and disorder), and a reduction in racial prejudice and discrimination.

The decline of prejudice and discrimination should proceed with gathering momentum because of the operation of what Gunnar Myrdal, in *An American Dilemma*, called "the principle of cumulation."

White prejudice and discrimination keep the Negro low in standards of living, health, education, manners and morals. This, in turn, gives support to white prejudice. White prejudice and Negro standards thus mutually "cause" each other. . . . Such a static "accommodation" is, however, entirely accidental. If either of the factors changes, this will cause a change in the other factor, too, and start a process of interaction where the change in one factor will continuously be supported by the reaction of the other factor.[3]

It is impossible to judge how much effect these accidental forces will have on the lower class. As was pointed out in Chapter 10, it makes a great deal of difference how much of the present-orientedness of that class is cognitive, how much situational, and how much volitional, but this is a question for which answers do not exist at present. If, as many social scientists want to believe, present-orientedness is mainly or even entirely situational, rapid economic growth may before long offer the lower class the incentives —especially job opportunities—needed to bring its members into normal culture. On the other hand, increasing affluence may have a contrary effect: overgenerous welfare programs may destroy more incentives to look ahead and provide for the future than improved job and other opportunities can provide. For this and other reasons that have already been discussed, an increase in the absolute (if not the relative) size of the lower class is by no means out of the question. Unless the increase were very large, however, it would not necessarily lead to a radical worsening of the situation or precipitate a crisis in the life of the nation.

Although the *objective* situation does not warrant the alarmist tone of much that is said and written about the city, the *subjective* one may. However much the accidental forces may reduce the *real* importance of the problems that have been under discussion, they may have no impact on their *seeming* importance. Indeed, this is likely to grow, for some of the very same factors that improve the objective situation also raise people's standards and expectations, thus leaving the subjective situation no better—and perhaps even worse—than it was to begin with. What people *think* a situation is may (as sociologist Robert K. Merton has pointed out) become an integral part of that situation, and therefore a factor in its subsequent development. A false public definition of the situation may, as Merton says, evoke new behavior that makes the originally false definition come true, thus perpetuating a "reign of error."[4] In short, wrong public definitions of urban problems may lead to behavior that will make matters worse despite the ameliorating influence of the accidental forces.

This possibility is most painfully apparent in the case of the Negro. That racial prejudice has long been declining and may be expected to continue to decline at an accelerating rate counts for little if the Negro *thinks* that white racism is as pervasive as ever; that his opportunities to improve his position by acquiring skills are at last fairly good counts for little if he *thinks* that "massive" government welfare, housing, and other programs—and *only* these—can help

[3] Gunnar Myrdal, *An American Dilemma* (New York: Harper, 1944), pp. 75–76.

[4] Robert K. Merton, *Social Theory and Social Structure* (New York: The Free Press, 1949), p. 181.

him. If he misperceives the situation in these ways, he is likely to do things that are counterproductive (for example, to cut himself off from "white" schools, jobs, and politics and to enter the fantasy world of black separatism). Such a course, if carried far enough, may validate his original (false) hypothesis —that is, he may become in fact as dependent upon government programs as he (wrongly) supposed himself to be and may revive the fact of white prejudice by giving it some objective grounds to feed upon.

Nothing could be so tragic and ironic as the acceptance of a false public definition of the situation that proves to be a self-fulfilling prophecy of racial hatred. Even if nonracial factors had not in recent years superseded the racial ones as the Negro's main handicap, it would be well to pretend that they had, for a self-fulfilling prophecy of the unimportance of racial factors would be as great a blessing as its opposite would be a curse.

Except as they create, or reinforce, counterproductive public definitions of problems and thereby encourage a "reign of error," wrong governmental measures are not likely to lead to catastrophe or even to any very significant worsening of the situation. Most wrong measures will lead to nothing worse than some additional waste and delay, usually a trivial amount. (One gets a sense of how unimportant even "important" governmental actions may be from one economist's estimate that the elimination of monopoly in the United States in 1929 would have raised income by no more than 1/13 of 1 percent, and from the estimate of another that benefits attributable to better resource allocation by virtue of the Common Market would also be much less than 1 percent.)[5] The governmental measures having the largest effect upon the city since the turn of the century are probably subsidization of truck and automobile transportation and subsidization of home ownership for the well-off; these measures certainly hastened the departure of the white middle class from the central city and, *a fortiori*, the entry of the poor—especially the black poor—on a large scale, but they did not significantly change the pattern of metropolitan growth; this was determined by accidental forces—the demographic, technological, economic, and class-cultural imperatives described in Chapters 2 and 3 [of Banfield's book].

Although it is easy to exaggerate the importance, either for good or ill, of the measures that government has adopted or might adopt, there does appear to be a danger to the good health of the society in the tendency of the public to define so many situations as "critical problems"—a definition that implies (1) that "solutions" exist or can be found and (2) that unless they are found and applied at once, disaster will befall. The import of what has been said in this book is that although there are many difficulties to be coped with, dilemmas to be faced, and afflictions to be endured, there are very few problems that can be solved; it is also that although much is seriously wrong with the city, no disaster impends unless it be one that results from public misconceptions that are in the nature of self-fulfilling prophecies.

Insofar as delusory and counterproductive public definitions of the situation arise from biases that lie deep within the culture (for example, from the impulse to DO SOMETHING! and to DO GOOD!), they are likely to persist in the face of all experience. To exhort the upper classes to display more of the quality that Trilling calls moral realism would be to offer a problem-begging "solution," since the very want of moral realism that constitutes the problem would prevent their recognizing the need of it.

The biases of the culture limit the range of possibilities, but they do not determine fully how the public will define the situation. This definition is in large part the result of a process of opinion formation that goes on within a relatively small world of officials, leaders of civic associations and other interest groups, journalists, and social scientists, especially economists; from this small world opinion is passed on to the public-at-large through the mass media, books, classroom instruction, campaign oratory, after-dinner speeches, and so on. Needless to say, a vast amount of misinformation, prejudice, and illogic enters into the process of opinion formation. (The agony of the cities, someone has remarked, is what the network executive and his fellow-commuters on the Long Island Railroad see out the window as they make their agonized way to and from their offices in Manhattan.) Within the past decade or two, developments have occurred that could

[5] Harvey Leibenstein, "Allocative Efficiency vs. 'X-Efficiency,'" *American Economic Review,* 56 (June 1966): 392–393.

make for a more realistic view of the urban situation—for example, the number of technically trained persons working on urban problems has increased greatly, their resources for gathering and manipulating data and the analytical apparatus that they can bring to bear upon policy questions are much improved, and what they have to say is taken much more seriously by politicians and administrators and therefore also by journalists. It would not be surprising if the conventional wisdom were to be very much revised in the next decade or two as a consequence of these developments. Turnover within the small world of opinion-makers is rapid, and the young newcomers in that world tend to be open to new ideas and even in search of them. Because communication within the small world and between it and the public-at-large is excellent, a new definition of the situation, once formulated, could catch on very quickly.

It would be pleasant to be able to end this discussion on that relatively optimistic note. Unfortunately, another side to the matter requires mention. Technically trained persons have their own characteristic biases, and if their view of the city is different from that of the commuter on the Long Island Railroad it is not necessarily more realistic. Moreover, as the technician comes to play a more important part in policy-making he is bound to come more and more under the discipline of large organizations, especially foundations and government agencies, whose maintenance and enhancement depends in some way upon the elaboration of an alarmist, or at any rate expansionist, public definition of the situation. That young newcomers to the small world of opinion-makers tend to be open to new ideas is not altogether reassuring either, for they may tend to accept new ideas *just because* they are new. To the pessimist, the prospect is that a new conventional wisdom about the problems of the city, the product of many millions of dollars' expenditure on research, cast in the language of systems analysis and the computer, will only compound the existing confusion. The optimist, however, will see reason to believe that facts, rational analysis, and deliberation about the nature of the public interest will play a somewhat larger part than hitherto in the formation of both opinion and policy.

THE ROLE OF GOVERNMENT IN A FREE SOCIETY

Milton Friedman

This selection quite rigorously exposits the conservative theory of the State. In it, Friedman argues strongly against active government intervention in the private market system. His positions derive in important ways from the views of classic nineteenth-century English "liberalism," from the views of philosophers like John Stuart Mill. (He uses the word "liberal" in that classical sense.)

The selection is Chapter II of Friedman's book *Capitalism and Freedom*. Throughout that book, the author offers a variety of arguments reflecting conservative economic views of economy and society. His book is perhaps the most important recent exposition of such views.

Friedman teaches economics at the University of Chicago, is one of the most widely respected technical economists in the United States, and also writes a regular column on economics for *Newsweek*.

SOURCE: *Milton Friedman, "The Role of Government in a Free Society," from Friedman,* Capitalism and Freedom. *Copyright © 1962 by The* University of Chicago. *All rights reserved. Published in 1962.*

A common objection to totalitarian societies is that they regard the end as justifying the means. Taken literally, this objection is clearly illogical. If the end does not justify the means, what does? But this easy answer does not dispose of the objection; it simply shows that the objection is not well put. To deny that the end justifies the means is indirectly to assert that the end in question is not the ultimate end, that the ultimate end is itself the use of the proper means. Desirable or not, any end that can be attained only by the use of bad means must give way to the more basic end of the use of acceptable means.

To the liberal, the appropriate means are free discussion and voluntary co-operation, which implies that any form of coercion is inappropriate. The ideal is unanimity among responsible individuals achieved on the basis of free and full discussion. This is another way of expressing the goal of freedom emphasized in the preceding chapter.

From this standpoint, the role of the market, as already noted, is that it permits unanimity without conformity; that it is a system of effectively proportional representation. On the other hand, the characteristic feature of action through explicitly political channels is that it tends to require or to enforce substantial conformity. The typical issue must be decided "yes" or "no"; at most, provision can be made for a fairly limited number of alternatives. Even the use of proportional representation in its explicitly political form does not alter this conclusion. The number of separate groups that can in fact be represented is narrowly limited, enormously so by comparison with the proportional representation of the market. More important, the fact that the final outcome generally must be a law applicable to all groups, rather than separate legislative enactments for each "party" represented, means that proportional representation in its political version, far from permitting unanimity without conformity, tends toward ineffectiveness and fragmentation. It thereby operates to destroy any consensus on which unanimity with conformity can rest.

There are clearly some matters with respect to which effective proportional representation is impossible. I cannot get the amount of national defense I want and you, a different amount. With respect to such indivisible matters we can discuss, and argue, and vote. But having decided, we must conform. It is precisely the existence of such indivisible matters—protection of the individual and the nation from coercion are clearly the most basic—that prevents exclusive reliance on individual action through the market. If we are to use some of our resources for such indivisible items, we must employ political channels to reconcile differences.

The use of political channels, while inevitable, tends to strain the social cohesion essential for a stable society. The strain is least if agreement for joint action need be reached only on a limited range of issues on which people in any event have common views. Every extension of the range of issues for which explicit agreement is sought strains further the delicate threads that hold society together. If it goes so far as to touch an issue on which men feel deeply yet differently, it may well disrupt the society. Fundamental differences in basic values can seldom if ever be resolved at the ballot box; ultimately they can only be decided, though not resolved, by conflict. The religious and civil wars of history are a bloody testament to this judgment.

The widespread use of the market reduces the strain on the social fabric by rendering conformity unnecessary with respect to any activities it encompasses. The wider the range of activities covered by the market, the fewer are the issues on which explicitly political decisions are required and hence on which it is necessary to achieve agreement. In turn, the fewer the issues on which agreement is necessary, the greater is the likelihood of getting agreement while maintaining a free society.

Unanimity is, of course, an ideal. In practice, we can afford neither the time nor the effort that would be required to achieve complete unanimity on every issue. We must perforce accept something less. We are thus led to accept majority rule in one form or another as an expedient. That majority rule is an expedient rather than itself a basic principle is clearly shown by the fact that our willingness to resort to majority rule, and the size of the majority we require, themselves depend on the seriousness of the issue involved. If the matter is of little moment and the minority has no strong feelings about being overruled, a bare plurality will suffice. On the other hand, if the minority feels strongly about the issue involved, even a bare majority will not do. Few of us would be willing to have issues of free speech, for example, decided by a bare majority. Our legal structure is full of such distinctions among kinds of issues that require different kinds of majorities. At the extreme are those issues embodied in the Constitution. These are the principles that are so important that we are willing to make minimal concessions to expediency. Something like essential consensus was achieved initially in accepting them, and we require something like essential consensus for a change in them.

The self-denying ordinance to refrain from majority rule on certain kinds of issues that is embodied in our Constitution and in similar written or unwritten constitutions elsewhere, and the specific provisions in these constitutions or their equivalents prohibiting coercion of individuals, are themselves to be regarded as reached by free discussion and as reflecting essential unanimity about means.

I turn now to consider more specifically, though still in very broad terms, what the areas are that cannot be handled through the market at all, or can be handled only at so great a cost that the use of political channels may be preferable.

GOVERNMENT AS RULE-MAKER AND UMPIRE

It is important to distinguish the day-to-day activities of people from the general customary and legal framework within which these take place. The day-to-day activities are like the actions of the participants in a game when they are playing it; the framework, like the rules of the game they play. And just as a good game requires acceptance by the players both of the rules and of the umpire to interpret and enforce them, so a good society requires that its members agree on the general conditions that will govern relations among them, on some means of arbitrating different interpretations of these conditions, and on some device for enforcing compliance with the generally accepted rules. As in games, so also in society, most of the general conditions are the unintended outcome of custom, accepted unthinkingly. At most, we consider explicitly only minor modifications in them, though the cumulative effect of a series of minor modifications may be a drastic alteration in the character of the game or of the society. In both games and

society also, no set of rules can prevail unless most participants most of the time conform to them without external sanctions; unless, that is, there is a broad underlying social consensus. But we cannot rely on custom or on this consensus alone to interpret and to enforce the rules; we need an umpire. These then are the basic roles of government in a free society: to provide a means whereby we can modify the rules, to mediate differences among us on the meaning of the rules, and to enforce compliance with the rules on the part of those few who would not otherwise play the game.

The need for government in these respects arises because absolute freedom is impossible. However attractive anarchy may be as a philosophy, it is not feasible in a world of imperfect men. Men's freedoms can conflict, and when they do, one man's freedom must be limited to preserve another's—as a Supreme Court Justice once put it, "My freedom to move my fist must be limited by the proximity of your chin."

The major problem in deciding the appropriate activities of government is how to resolve such conflicts among the freedoms of different individuals. In some cases, the answer is easy. There is little difficulty in attaining near unanimity to the proposition that one man's freedom to murder his neighbor must be sacrificed to preserve the freedom of the other man to live. In other cases, the answer is difficult. In the economic area, a major problem arises in respect of the conflict between freedom to combine and freedom to compete. What meaning is to be attributed to "free" as modifying "enterprise"? In the United States, "free" has been understood to mean that anyone is free to set up an enterprise, which means that existing enterprises are not free to keep out competitors except by selling a better product at the same price or the same product at a lower price. In the continental tradition, on the other hand, the meaning has generally been that enterprises are free to do what they want, including the fixing of prices, division of markets, and the adoption of other techniques to keep out potential competitors. Perhaps the most difficult specific problem in this area arises with respect to combinations among laborers, where the problem of freedom to combine and freedom to compete is particularly acute.

A still more basic economic area in which

the answer is both difficult and important is the definition of property rights. The notion of property, as it has developed over centuries and as it is embodied in our legal codes, has become so much a part of us that we tend to take it for granted, and fail to recognize the extent to which just what constitutes property and what rights the ownership of property confers are complex social creations rather than self-evident propositions. Does my having title to land, for example, and my freedom to use my property as I wish, permit me to deny to someone else the right to fly over my land in his airplane? Or does his right to use his airplane take precedence? Or does this depend on how high he flies? Or how much noise he makes? Does voluntary exchange require that he pay me for the privilege of flying over my land? Or that I must pay him to refrain from flying over it? The mere mention of royalties, copyrights, patents; shares of stock in corporations; riparian rights, and the like, may perhaps emphasize the role of generally accepted social rules in the very definition of property. It may suggest also that, in many cases, the existence of a well specified and generally accepted definition of property is far more important than just what the definition is.

Another economic area that raises particularly difficult problems is the monetary system. Government responsibility for the monetary system has long been recognized. It is explicitly provided for in the constitutional provision which gives Congress the power "to coin money, regulate the value thereof, and of foreign coin." There is probably no other area of economic activity with respect to which government action has been so uniformly accepted. This habitual and by now almost unthinking acceptance of governmental responsibility makes thorough understanding of the grounds for such responsibility all the more necessary, since it enhances the danger that the scope of government will spread from activities that are, to those that are not, appropriate in a free society, from providing a monetary framework to determining the allocation of resources among individuals. We shall discuss this problem in detail in chapter iii.

In summary, the organization of economic activity through voluntary exchange presumes that we have provided, through government, for the maintenance of law and order to precent coercion of one individual by another, the enforcement of contracts voluntarily entered into, the definition of the meaning of property rights, the interpretation and enforcement of such rights, and the provision of a monetary framework.

ACTION THROUGH GOVERNMENT ON GROUNDS OF TECHNICAL MONOPOLY AND NEIGHBORHOOD EFFECTS

The role of government just considered is to do something that the market cannot do for itself, namely, to determine, arbitrate, and enforce the rules of the game. We may also want to do through government some things that might conceivably be done through the market but that technical or similar conditions render it difficult to do in that way. These all reduce to cases in which strictly voluntary exchange is either exceedingly costly or practically impossible. There are two general classes of such cases: monopoly and similar market imperfections, and neighborhood effects.

Exchange is truly voluntary only when nearly equivalent alternatives exist. Monopoly implies the absence of alternatives and thereby inhibits effective freedom of exchange. In practice, monopoly frequently, if not generally, arises from government support or from collusive agreements among individuals. With respect to these, the problem is either to avoid governmental fostering of monopoly or to stimulate the effective enforcement of rules such as those embodied in our anti-trust laws. However, monopoly may also arise because it is technically efficient to have a single producer or enterprise. I venture to suggest that such cases are more limited than is supposed but they unquestionably do arise. A simple example is perhaps the provision of telephone services within a community. I shall refer to such cases as "technical" monopoly.

When technical conditions make a monopoly the natural outcome of competitive market forces, there are only three alternatives that seem available: private monopoly, public monopoly, or public regulation. All three are bad so we must choose among evils. Henry Simons, observing public regulation of monopoly in the United States, found the results so distasteful that he concluded public monopoly would be a lesser evil. Walter

Eucken, a noted German liberal, observing public monopoly in German railroads, found the results so distasteful that he concluded public regulation would be a lesser evil. Having learned from both, I reluctantly conclude that, if tolerable, private monopoly may be the least of the evils.

If society were static so that the conditions which give rise to a technical monopoly were sure to remain, I would have little confidence in this solution. In a rapidly changing society, however, the conditions making for technical monopoly frequently change and I suspect that both public regulation and public monopoly are likely to be less responsive to such changes in conditions, to be less readily capable of elimination, than private monopoly.

Railroads in the United States are an excellent example. A large degree of monopoly in railroads was perhaps inevitable on technical grounds in the nineteenth century. This was the justification for the Interstate Commerce Commission. But conditions have changed. The emergence of road and air transport has reduced the monopoly element in railroads to negligible proportions. Yet we have not eliminated the ICC. On the contrary, the ICC, which started out as an agency to protect the public from exploitation by the railroads, has become an agency to protect railroads from competition by trucks and other means of transport, and more recently even to protect existing truck companies from competition by new entrants. Similarly, in England, when the railroads were nationalized, trucking was at first brought into the state monopoly. If railroads had never been subjected to regulation in the United States, it is nearly certain that by now transportation, including railroads, would be a highly competitive industry with little or no remaining monopoly elements.

The choice between the evils of private monopoly, public monopoly, and public regulation cannot, however, be made once and for all, independently of the factual circumstances. If the technical monopoly is of a service or commodity that is regarded as essential and if its monopoly power is sizable, even the short-run effects of private unregulated monopoly may not be tolerable, and either public regulation or ownership may be a lesser evil.

Technical monopoly may on occasion justify a *de facto* public monopoly. It cannot by itself justify a public monopoly achieved by making it illegal for anyone else to compete. For example, there is no way to justify our present public monopoly of the post office. It may be argued that the carrying of mail is a technical monopoly and that a government monopoly is the least of evils. Along these lines, one could perhaps justify a government post office but not the present law, which makes it illegal for anybody else to carry mail. If the delivery of mail is a technical monopoly, no one will be able to succeed in competition with the government. If it is not, there is no reason why the government should be engaged in it. The only way to find out is to leave other people free to enter.

The historical reason why we have a post office monopoly is because the Pony Express did such a good job of carrying the mail across the continent that, when the government introduced transcontinental service, it couldn't compete effectively and lost money. The result was a law making it illegal for anybody else to carry the mail. That is why the Adams Express Company is an investment trust today instead of an operating company. I conjecture that if entry into the mail-carrying business were open to all, there would be a large number of firms entering it and this archaic industry would become revolutionized in short order.

A second general class of cases in which strictly voluntary exchange is impossible arises when actions of individuals have effects on other individuals for which it is not feasible to charge or recompense them. This is the problem of "neighborhod effects." An obvious example is the pollution of a stream. The man who pollutes a stream is in effect forcing others to exchange good water for bad. These others might be willing to make the exchange at a price. But it is not feasible for them, acting individually, to avoid the exchange or to enforce appropriate compensation.

A less obvious example is the provision of highways. In this case, it is technically possible to identify and hence charge individuals for their use of the roads and so to have private operation. However, for general access roads, involving many points of entry and exit, the costs of collection would be extremely high if a charge were to be made for the specific services received by each individual, because of the necessity of establishing toll booths or the equivalent at all entrances. The gasoline tax is a much cheaper method of charging individuals roughly in proportion to their use of the roads. This method, however, is one in which the particular payment cannot be identified closely with the particular use. Hence, it is hardly feasible to have private enterprise provide the service and collect the charge without establishing extensive private monopoly.

These considerations do not apply to long-distance turnpikes with high density of traffic and limited access. For these, the costs of collection are small and in many cases are now being paid, and there are often numerous alternatives, so that there is no serious monopoly problem. Hence, there is every reason why these should be privately owned and operated. If so owned and operated, the enterprise running the highway should receive the gasoline taxes paid on account of travel on it.

Parks are an interesting example because they illustrate the difference between cases that can and cases that cannot be justified by neighborhood effects, and because almost everyone at first sight regards the conduct of National Parks as obviously a valid function of government. In fact, however, neighborhood effects may justify a city park; they do not justify a national park, like Yellowstone National Park or the Grand Canyon. What is the fundamental difference between the two? For the city park, it is extremely difficult to identify the people who benefit from it and to charge them for the benefits which they receive. If there is a park in the middle of the city, the houses on all sides get the benefit of the open space, and people who walk through it or by it also benefit. To maintain toll collectors at the gates or to impose annual charges per window overlooking the park would be very expensive and difficult. The entrances to a national park like Yellowstone, on the other hand, are few; most of the people who come stay for a considerable period of time and it is perfectly feasible to set up toll gates and collect admission charges. This is indeed now done, though the charges do not cover the whole costs. If the public wants this kind of an activity enough to pay for it, private enterprises will have every incentive to provide such parks. And, of course, there are many private enterprises of this nature now in existence. I cannot myself conjure up any

neighborhood effects or important monopoly effects that would justify governmental activity in this area.

Considerations like those I have treated under the heading of neighborhood effects have been used to rationalize almost every conceivable intervention. In many instances, however, this rationalization is special pleading rather than a legitimate application of the concept of neighborhood effects. Neighborhood effects cut both ways. They can be a reason for limiting the activities of government as well as for expanding them. Neighborhood effects impede voluntary exchange because it is difficult to identify the effects on third parties and to measure their magnitude; but this difficulty is present in governmental activity as well. It is hard to know when neighborhood effects are sufficiently large to justify particular costs in overcoming them and even harder to distribute the costs in an appropriate fashion. Consequently, when government engages in activities to overcome neighborhood effects, it will in part introduce an additional set of neighborhood effects by failing to charge or to compensate individuals properly. Whether the original or the new neighborhood effects are the more serious can only be judged by the facts of the individual case, and even then, only very approximately. Furthermore, the use of government to overcome neighborhood effects itself has an extremely important neighborhood effect which is unrelated to the particular occasion for government action. Every act of government intervention limits the area of individual freedom directly and threatens the preservation of freedom indirectly for reasons elaborated in the first chapter.

Our principles offer no hard and fast line how far it is appropriate to use government to accomplish jointly what it is difficult or impossible for us to accomplish separately through strictly voluntary exchange. In any particular case of proposed intervention, we must make up a balance sheet, listing separately the advantages and disadvantages. Our principles tell us what items to put on the one side and what items on the other and they give us some basis for attaching importance to the different items. In particular, we shall always want to enter on the liability side of any proposed government intervention, its neighborhood effect in threatening freedom, and give this effect considerable weight. Just how much weight to give to it, as to other items, depends upon the circumstances. If, for example, existing government intervention is minor, we shall attach a smaller weight to the negative effects of additional government intervention. This is an important reason why many earlier liberals, like Henry Simons, writing at a time when government was small by today's standards, were willing to have government undertake activities that today's liberals would not accept now that government has become so overgrown.

ACTION THROUGH GOVERNMENT ON PATERNALISTIC GROUNDS

Freedom is a tenable objective only for responsible individuals. We do not believe in freedom for madmen or children. The necessity of drawing a line between responsible individuals and others is inescapable, yet it means that there is an essential ambiguity in our ultimate objective of freedom. Paternalism is inescapable for those whom we designate as not responsible.

The clearest case, perhaps, is that of madmen. We are willing neither to permit them freedom nor to shoot them. It would be nice if we could rely on voluntary activities of individuals to house and care for the madmen. But I think we cannot rule out the possibility that such charitable activities will be inadequate, if only because of the neighborhood effect involved in the fact that I benefit if another man contributes to the care of the insane. For this reason, we may be willing to arrange for their care through government.

Children offer a more difficult case. The ultimate operative unit in our society is the family, not the individual. Yet the acceptance of the family as the unit rests in considerable part on expediency rather than principle. We believe that parents are generally best able to protect their children and to provide for their development into responsible individuals for whom freedom is appropriate. But we do not believe in the freedom of parents to do what they will with other people. The children are responsible individuals in embryo, and a believer in freedom believes in protecting their ultimate rights.

To put this in a different and what may seem a more callous way, children are at one and the same time consumer goods and potentially responsible members of society.

The freedom of individuals to use their economic resources as they want includes the freedom to use them to have children—to buy, as it were, the services of children as a particular form of consumption. But once this choice is exercised, the children have a value in and of themselves and have a freedom of their own that is not simply an extension of the freedom of the parents.

The paternalistic ground for governmental activity is in many ways the most troublesome to a liberal; for it involves the acceptance of a principle—that some shall decide for others—which he finds objectionable in most applications and which he rightly regards as a hallmark of his chief intellectual opponents, the proponents of collectivism in one or another of its guises, whether it be communism, socialism, or a welfare state. Yet there is no use pretending that problems are simpler than in fact they are. There is no avoiding the need for some measure of paternalism. As Dicey wrote in 1914 about an act for the protection of mental defectives, "The Mental Deficiency Act is the first step along a path on which no sane man can decline to enter, but which, if too far pursued, will bring statesmen across difficulties hard to meet without considerable interference with individual liberty."[1] There is no formula that can tell us where to stop. We must rely on our fallible judgment and, having reached a judgment, on our ability to persuade our fellow men that it is a correct judgment, or their ability to persuade us to modify our views. We must put our faith, here as elsewhere, in a consensus reached by imperfect and biased men through free discussion and trial and error.

CONCLUSION

A government which maintained law and order, defined property rights, served as a means whereby we could modify property rights and other rules of the economic game, adjudicated disputes about the interpretation of the rules, enforced contracts, promoted competition, provided a monetary framework, engaged in activities to counter technical monopolies and to overcome neighborhood effects widely regarded as sufficiently

[1] A. V. Dicey, *Lectures on the Relation between Law and Public Opinion in England during the Nineteenth Century* (2d ed.; London: Macmillan & Co., 1914), p. li.

important to justify government intervention, and which supplemented private charity and the private family in protecting the irresponsible, whether madman or child—such a government would clearly have important functions to perform. The consistent liberal is not an anarchist.

Yet it is also true that such a government would have clearly limited functions and would refrain from a host of activities that are now undertaken by federal and state governments in the United States, and their counterparts in other Western countries. Succeeding chapters will deal in some detail with some of these activities, and a few have been discussed above, but it may help to give a sense of proportion about the role that a liberal would assign government simply to list, in closing this chapter, some activities currently undertaken by government in the U.S., that cannot, so far as I can see, validly be justified in terms of the principles outlined above:

1. Parity price support programs for agriculture.

2. Tariffs on imports or restrictions on exports, such as current oil import quotas, sugar quotas, etc.

3. Governmental control of output, such as through the farm program, or through prorationing of oil as is done by the Texas Railroad Commission.

4. Rent control, such as is still practiced in New York, or more general price and wage controls such as were imposed during and just after World War II.

5. Legal minimum wage rates, or legal maximum prices, such as the legal maximum of zero on the rate of interest that can be paid on demand deposits by commercial banks, or the legally fixed maximum rates that can be paid on savings and time deposits.

6. Detailed regulation of industries, such as the regulation of transportation by the Interstate Commerce Commission. This had some justification on technical monopoly grounds when initially introduced for railroads; it has none now for any means of transport. Another example is detailed regulation of banking.

7. A similar example, but one which deserves special mention because of its implicit censorship and violation of free speech, is the control of radio and television by the Federal Communications Commission.

8. Present social security programs, especially the old-age and retirement programs compelling people in effect (a) to spend a specified fraction of their income on the purchase of retirement annuity, (b) to buy the annuity from a publicly operated enterprise.

9. Licensure provisions in various cities and states which restrict particular enterprises or occupations or professions to people who have a license, where the license is more than a receipt for a tax which anyone who wishes to enter the activity may pay.

10. So-called "public-housing" and the host of other subsidy programs directed at fostering residential construction such as F.H.A. and V.A. guarantee of mortgage, and the like.

11. Conscription to man the military services in peacetime. The appropriate free market arrangement is volunteer military forces; which is to say, hiring men ·to serve. There is no justification for not paying whatever price is necessary to attract the required number of men. Present arrangements are inequitable and arbitrary, seriously interfere with the freedom of young men to shape their lives, and probably are even more costly than the market alternative. (Universal military training to provide a reserve for war time is a different problem and may be justified on liberal grounds.)

12. National parks, as noted above.

13. The legal prohibition on the carrying of mail for profit.

14. Publicly owned and operated toll roads, as noted above.

This list is far from comprehensive.

2 Employment

Editor's Introduction

We mold men to jobs, not jobs to men.
> —Corporate personnel officer[1]

*I told him that the reason I wasn't too sure if I wanted the job was because
they weren't paying enough money, and plus I was looking for a job with a
future. I don't want to work where I can see I wasn't going to make no kind
of progress or build myself up with no kind of background or nothing.*
> —19-year-old black high school
> graduate[2]

The millions of workers in the United States are burdened by different kinds of employment problems—with varying symptoms and causes. It could hardly be otherwise. As Elliot Liebow has put it, "The centrality of work . . . is not new to human experience."[3] Employment dominates the ways we spend our time, the ways we earn our living and the contributions we make to the world. Although I have chosen to discuss the problems of only one group of American workers in this chapter—the underemployed—I do not intend to imply that all other groups of workers are free from such characteristic fates as exploitation on the job or severe alienation. I have hoped to illustrate the ways in which employment problems derive from the basic structure of capitalist institutions. The analysis could easily be transposed to other equally important labor market issues, problems or groups.[4]

I have concentrated in this chapter on the problem of "underemployment" in the United States, especially as that problem was perceived and defined by the American public in the late 1960's. In the public view, the problem of underemployment seemed most entrenched and complicated in Northern central city ghettos, particularly among black ghetto workers. Many policies and programs arose throughout the sixties to help solve ghetto employment problems. Despite their obviously benign intentions, none of them seemed to do any good. By the end of the decade, Congress was beginning to wonder if federal programs should be continued at all; according to one newspaper report in early 1970, "Friends as well as foes agree that only a small proportion of the 6.4 million persons who were in the programs have really been helped."[5] Private corporations which had rushed into special training programs for "disadvantaged" workers were also backing off; many believed that they "had acted too impulsively" and that training ghetto workers "was not something they were very good at."[6]

This chapter indicates that such failures should have been expected. As Chapter One made clear, the radical analysis of problems like underemployment views them as inevitable consequences of the basic set of institutions dominating capitalist societies like the United States. The manpower programs of the 1960's did not seek to change the structure of those institutions and were therefore likely to have marginal effects. In presenting the outline of that

---

[1] Quoted in Peter Doeringer and Michael Piore, *Internal Labor Markets and Manpower Analysis* (Lexington, Mass.: D. C. Heath, 1971), Chapter Five.

[2] Quoted in Herb Goro, *The Block* (N.Y.: Random House, 1970), p. 143.

[3] Elliot Liebow, "No Man Can Live with the Terrible Knowledge that He Is Not Needed," *New York Times Magazine,* April 5, 1970, p. 29.

[4] Some of the dimensions of transposition are suggested in the piece by Edwards and MacEwan above, in the chapter on general perspectives.

[5] *The New York Times,* February 20, 1970, p. 20.

[6] *The New York Times,* March 1, 1970, p. 42.

argument in this introduction, I have divided the discussion into four sections: first, the definition of urban underemployment; second, a summary of the liberal and conservative analyses of those problems; third, an elaboration of the radical analysis of ghetto employment problems; and finally, an introduction to the purpose and contents of the reading selections which follow.

PROBLEM DEFINITIONS AND MAGNITUDES

As the public became more concerned about employment problems in central-city ghettos during the 1960's, it revised its basic definitions of labor market disadvantage. Earlier, public policy had sought to help the "unemployed"—those who wanted to work but could not find a job. Those who were employed seemed satisfied, at least, and those who were not looking for work seemed incapable of working for health or family reasons. The unemployment rate seemed a perfectly adequate measure of the severity of employment problems.[7] But several developments during the decade forced attention on a new set of problems. Greater prosperity had solved the employment problems of many workers who had formerly been unemployed.[8] The civil rights movement and ghetto riots had focused concern on the difficulties of blacks, especially those in the central cities.[9] And the continuing evolution and frequent failure of manpower programs produced new impressions of success and failure which affected objectives and priorities.[10]

By the end of the decade, analysts and government officials tended to use the concept of "underemployment" to evoke the new set of problems with which they had become preoccupied. The concept encompassed those who were unemployed, those who were working full time at very low wages, those who wanted to work full time but could find only part-time work, those who wanted to work but had dropped out of the labor force, and those who seemed so unattached to primary labor market institutions that they were often missed by the surveys upon which employment statistics were based.[11] The concept intended to reflect the problems of a large group of disadvantaged workers, often described as "secondary workers" or the "underclass," who were frequently able to find work but earned low wages, worked intermittently and could rarely hope for occupational advancement. While *unemployment* rates, measured by traditional statistical categories, were often around 8 or 9 percent in central-city ghettos by the end of the decade, *underemployment* rates soared as high as 30 to 35 percent.[12]

The three defining characteristics of "underemployed" workers were their low wages, their low skill levels, and their rather random, frequently unpredictable patterns of work.[13] Each of these characteristics reinforced the others, joining to form a self-perpetuating cycle of underemployment. If a worker earned low wages, for instance, he was often likely to quit his job—to search for higher-paying work, to hustle on the "illegitimate" job market, or to collect relief. This would gradually establish a fairly fixed pattern of unstable employment. The record of instability would often prevent the worker from qualifying for jobs in which employers consider stability important, and in which increasing job tenure leads to the acquisition of significant skills on the job. Missing those opportunities to acquire skills on the job would make the worker undesirable to any but the lowest-wage employers. The employee would be back where he began, and the pattern of job instability would be perpetuated.

---

[7] Unemployment is defined as the percentage of the total labor force which is not employed. The labor force includes those who are employed and those who say they are looking for work. Those who are neither employed nor looking for work are considered "not in the labor force." For further discussion of these categories and their historical justification, see Seymour Wolfbein, *Employment and Unemployment in the United States* (N.Y.: Science Research Associates, 1964).

[8] During the 1960's, for instance, the unemployment rate had dropped from nearly 7 percent to roughly 3.5 percent before it began to rise again in 1969.

[9] The "Riot Commission Report" crystallized many of these influences. See *The Report of the National Advisory Commission on Civil Disorders* (N.Y.: Bantam, 1968).

[10] For a discussion of these programs, see Sar Levitan and Garth Mangum, *Federal Training and Work Programs in the Sixties* (Ann Arbor: Inst. of Labor and Industrial Relations, 1969).

[11] For a discussion of the first use of this concept and its statistical embodiment, see *The Manpower Report of the President, 1967* (Washington: U.S. Government Printing Office, 1967), pp. 74–75.

[12] *Ibid.*, p. 75.

[13] For perhaps the best impressionistic account of these characteristics and their interactions, see Elliot Liebow, *Tally's Corner* (Boston: Little, Brown, 1967).

This evolving concern with underemployment involved several important changes in traditional perceptions of the labor market. First, more and more attention was directed toward the problem of job stability; varieties of evidence suggested that one of the dominant differences between the poor and the non-poor was the randomness and instability of work histories among the poor.[14] Second, many analysts began to focus more clearly on the ways in which we define "skills" and "disadvantage." Should we emphasize years of schooling, general labor market experience, specific vocational skills, poor reading ability, all or none of the above? Referring to these various dimensions of labor market skills, Anthony Pascal has concluded, "We know exceedingly little about their relative importance."[15] Third, most traditional assumptions about worker motivation crumbled. One could no longer presume that all male workers inevitably preferred work under almost any conditions to all other pastimes. Fourth, more and more emphasis has been placed on the structure and characteristics of jobs available in the labor market, reflecting an erosion of previous preoccupations with the "supply" characteristics of workers. Analysts became increasingly aware of the manifold ways in which job characteristics determined worker characteristics. Fifth, policy paid increasing attention to the effects of extra-labor market institutions on labor market problems, particularly the effects of housing segregation. And finally, the discussion of underemployment became permeated with a concern for the causes and effects of labor market discrimination, not only against racial minorities but also against women and teenagers.[16]

LIBERAL AND CONSERVATIVE VIEWS

The public policies developed to respond to this new set of perceptions followed directly from conventional analyses of employment problems. As is true with many other problems in this book, liberal and conservative perspectives agree on underlying analytic assumptions but tend to differ on policy prescriptions. In this section, I have first summarized the analytic assumptions and then described the policy differences.

The analyses begin from basic orthodox economic analysis and its postulates about the distribution of income from labor. According to those postulates, a worker's wages in the labor market tend to equal his marginal product in competitive equilibrium.[17] Those with high marginal productivities will earn relatively high incomes, while those with low productivities will earn less. According to a recent reformulation of these basic theories, a worker's wages can be viewed as a return on the amount of money invested in his training, or, as the new perspective puts it, a return to investment in "human capital."[18] Human capital analysis emphasizes that educational investments while workers are in school and firm investments in on-the-job training are analytically comparable, for each represents a capital investment designed to increase a worker's productivity. If some workers have low productivities, the analysis assumes that either they or society think that returns to investments in their productivities would be too low to warrant the expenditure. If some jobs do not provide on-the-job training, the analysis implies that employers would not find it profitable to invest in worker training in those economic circumstances.[19]

The implications of this kind of analysis for underemployment are clear. Lester Thurow puts

[14] For some discussion of this evidence, see Lester Thurow, *Poverty and Discrimination* (Washington: Brookings, 1969), Chapter Five.

[15] Pascal, "Manpower Training and Jobs," in Pascal, ed., *Cities in Trouble: Agenda for Urban Research* (Santa Monica: RAND Corporation, 1968), p. 68.

[16] Ironically, by the end of the decade, the "minority" groups were no longer in the minority. White males between 25 and 64, the basic "primary" group in the labor force, had fallen to exactly 50 percent of the total labor force by 1970; women, blacks, and teenagers had all increased their relative proportions since World War II. See *The Monthly Labor Review*, any issue, for statistics on labor force composition.

[17] One can begin reading about these theories at the beginning, with the discussion on income distribution in Paul Samuelson, *Economics* (N.Y.: McGraw-Hill, 1970).

[18] For a basic statement of human capital analysis, see Gary Becker, *Human Capital* (N.Y.: NBER, 1964), or Becker, *Human Capital and the Personal Distribution of Income* (Ann Arbor: University of Michigan Press, 1967).

[19] For an application of these concepts to the specific problems discussed in this chapter, see Thurow, *Poverty and Discrimination, op. cit.*

it simply: "If an individual's income is too low, his productivity is too low. His income can be increased only if his productivity can be raised."[20]

Within that analytic framework, liberal and conservative policy prescriptions diverge. Conservatives emphasize two basic points. First, they argue that individuals have many opportunities to raise their own productivities. They can stay in school, work steadily, and stay on jobs long enough to learn new skills. If some individuals have low productivities, they are primarily to blame for their own disadvantages. Second, they argue that individual opportunities to work in the labor market are seriously distorted by government intervention in that market, and that we should try to minimize government involvement with market institutions. In particular, conservatives have argued that minimum wage laws have produced high unemployment among those with low productivities, and particularly among young workers. According to this argument, employers could afford to hire low-skilled workers only at wages below currently legislated minimum wage floors. With the establishment of minimum wage laws, they must try to hire more highly skilled workers, and low-skilled workers cannot find employment.[21] This kind of argument obviously manifests the conservative emphasis on the virtues of the private market mechanism and the deleterious effects of government intervention.

Liberals present fundamentally different policy arguments. They contend that wide varieties of social, economic, and institutional factors explain the low skills of many workers, that the individuals are not necessarily to blame. They further argue that it is the government which can most easily stimulate efforts to raise individual productivities to permit increased individual incomes. Once workers become more productive, the liberals believe, the self-perpetuating cycle of interaction among wages, productivity, and stability would end. If workers increased their skill levels, they would find job opportunities in which they would find it more attractive to stay on the job. The higher wages on those jobs would induce stability, and the stability would in turn increase worker productivity through on-the-job experience and training. Given these increases in productivity, wages would increase more, further increasing stability. And so on.

These contentions helped stimulate most of the innovations in manpower programs during the 1960's. Wide varieties of public efforts were designed to stimulate training: institutional vocational training; financial incentives to firms to provide more on-the-job training to disadvantaged workers; job referral services to steer workers toward the most stable job opportunities; various programs to improve worker motivation and stability; and additional programs to open up new job opportunities for disadvantaged workers.[22]

Sharing many of the same basic analytic assumptions underlying these programs, the more conservative Nixon Administration did not move to change these programs when it assumed power at the end of the decade. Befitting its more conservative suspicions about the potential of government programs, it intended simply to slow down the pace of innovation, hopefully improving coordination and management of all the different programs.[23]

THE RADICAL VIEW

A radical analysis of underemployment begins with the same description of reality. It simply explains that reality in entirely different ways.

In general terms, echoing the discussion in Chapter One, the radical analysis views such problems as inevitable consequences of basic capitalist institutions. Those institutions serve the interests of the dominant capitalist class and define the status of workers in the labor market. In contrast to orthodox postulates about the process of income determination and distribution, the radical analysis offers a very different view of wage and status determination.

In the radical analysis, there are two stages in the determination and distribution of income. First, a complex set of social, economic, and technological forces determine a given worker's

[20] *Ibid.,* p. 26.
[21] Edward Banfield summarizes these arguments in simple fashion in his *The Unheavenly City* (Boston: Little, Brown, 1970).
[22] The list of programs is too long to cover here. See Levitan and Mangum, *Federal Training and Work Programs in the Sixties, op. cit.*
[23] For a discussion of the Administration's position, see *The New York Times,* February 20, 1970, and the various *Manpower Reports of the President* since Nixon became President.

total productivity; this can vary with the worker's skills and the characteristics of the job in which he works. Then, the relative power of employers and employees determines the share of the worker's total product paid to the worker in wages. He receives some of the product as wages and the employer receives the rest as "surplus value." The worker's final wage thus depends *both* on his productivity *and* on the relative power of the class or group with which he is identified. Employers seek constantly either to increase or to maintain their relative share of total product. At the same time, they hope to provide workers enough return so that the working class does not revolt in response to its oppression or impoverishment. Ernest Mandel summarizes these general propositions.[24]

In fact, it is not the absolute level of wages that matters to capital. . . . What matters to capital is the possibility of extracting more surplus labour, more unpaid labour, more surplus value, more profit from its workers. The growth in the productivity of labour, which makes possible the growth of relative surplus value, implies the possibility of a slow rise in real wages . . . on condition that the equivalent of these increased real wages is produced in an ever shorter period of time, i.e. that wages rise less quickly than productivity. . . .

The rise in real wages does not follow automatically from the rise in the productivity of labour. The latter only creates the possibility of such a rise, within the capitalist framework, provided profit is not threatened. For this potential increase to become actual, two interlinked conditions are needed: a favourable evolution of 'relations of strength in the labour market' . . . and effective organization . . . of the wage workers which enables them to abolish competition among themselves and so to take advantage of these 'favourable market conditions.'

Over time in capitalist societies, workers are drawn together in large work places and, as Marx and Engels predicted, are increasingly likely to perceive their common interests and unite around those interests to demand a larger share of total product and better working conditions.[25] In societies based on democratic traditions, the capitalist class cannot easily suppress those worker demands. Instead, the capitalist class is likely to seek to promote class divisions *within* the working class in order to weaken the unity of worker protest. The more labor is internally divided and competes among its separate strata, the less unified it will be in its demands of employers.[26] It will always be in the interests of employers to promote or preserve such intra-class stratifications.

These general propositions are intended to apply to any capitalist economy. Their specific manifestations will vary from country to country and from time to time, depending on the relative stage of economic development of different societies and on their peculiar historical traditions. As Chapter One explained, these characteristic patterns are "specified" by the unique features of individual economies. To understand the implications of these basic propositions for ghetto underemployment in the United States, it is necessary to examine the specific structure and history of labor market institutions in this country.

Traditionally, employers have been able to extract surplus value quite easily from the least powerful and most disadvantaged workers in American society because those workers have been inclined to acquiesce in their disadvantaged status in the labor market. They have often been patient with the conditions of their work. They or their children have frequently been able to build from this patience, staying on jobs or in school long enough to acquire more skills and higher status. Their perseverance has helped stabilize the system of labor market institutions. And it has also helped individual workers advance themselves, because—as all economists have increasingly recognized—on-the-job experience and training constitute important determinants of total skills and productivity.

It is no longer true, I would argue, that the most disadvantaged workers in the labor market

---

[24] Mandel, *Marxist Economic Theory* (N.Y.: Monthly Review Press, 1969), p. 145. The general argument draws from the references cited in Chapter One as basic sources for recent radical views.
[25] They made this argument first in *The Communist Manifesto* (N.Y.: International Publishers, 1948).
[26] This obviously has implications for interpretations of trade union history in the United States. The craft unions were clearly more acceptable to employers than the industrial unions because the former tended to promote stratification.

are willing to stay on their jobs long enough to acquire better skills and higher incomes. The underlying patience, docility and dedication which characterized lower-class workers in this country has begun to dissolve.

To elaborate, I suspect that there has been a qualitative change in the attitudes of disadvantaged workers about their status and their work. Traditionally, disadvantaged workers in this country have been recent migrants (from Europe or from the South); they have been willing to work patiently at menial work because those jobs offered higher wages, better working conditions, or better prospects than jobs in their previous social settings. The act of migration had fostered a basic optimism about their or their children's prospects. But a new generation of Northern-born ghetto workers has now entered the labor force, starting at the lowest rungs of the occupational ladder. They have not migrated and cannot build from that hopeful act. I have called this the "promised land" effect, after Claude Brown's book *Manchild in the Promised Land*. Brown compares the attitudes of black migrants from the South with those of blacks born, raised, and initiated in Northern ghettos:[27]

> Going to New York was good-bye to the cotton fields, good-bye to "Massa Charlie,"
> good-bye to the chain gang, and, most of all, good-bye to those sunup-to-sundown working
> hours. . . .
> Before the soreness of the cotton fields had left Mama's back, her knees were getting sore
> from scrubbing "Goldberg's" floor. Nevertheless, she was better off; she had gone from the
> fire into the frying pan.
> The children of these disillusioned colored pioneers inherited the total lot of their parents
> —the disappointments, the anger. To add to their misery, they had little hope of deliverance.
> For where does one run to when he's already in the promised land?

Without "hope of deliverance," these workers are looking at their jobs more realistically than previously disadvantaged workers. They find that they both earn low wages and have few chances for rising occupationally. In the sectors of the labor market to which they seem limited, it does not matter if they move in and out of jobs or the labor force, because it appears that neither their skills nor their work histories affect their chances for better jobs. And so, it seems to them to make little difference if they continue in school or work diligently on the job. They place little value in work, they often earn more by "hustling" and they assume that rewards in the labor market do not correspond to their merit or abilities. In these sectors of the labor market, indeed, their perceptions seem accurate. As Liebow points out,[28]

> Both the employee and employer are contemptuous of the [secondary] job. The employee
> shows his contempt by his reluctance to accept it or keep it, the employer by paying less
> than is required to support a family. . . . With few exceptions, jobs filled by the streetcorner
> men are at the bottom of the employment ladder in every respect, from wage level to prestige.

Older workers, with different histories and different time horizons, were apparently willing to tolerate those jobs. Younger workers in the ghetto, it now appears, will not.[29]

Given those attitudes, it seems clear that training programs will not work for ghetto workers —regardless of their subtlety and sophistication—unless the programs manifestly guarantee entirely different kinds of job opportunities to those workers. Many younger workers are no longer interested in training themselves if training permits a barely improved job with barely higher wages and inconsequential opportunities for training and advancement on the job. These workers clearly want jobs in the "primary" labor market, jobs which pay decent wages, and jobs which offer opportunities for rapid and guaranteed promotion. To the extent that many of these younger workers are black, they obviously insist on equal opportunities with whites for

[27] *Manchild in the Promised Land* (N.Y.: Macmillan, 1965), pp. 7–8.
[28] *Tally's Corner, op. cit.*, p. 58.
[29] Their refusals have obviously also become more feasible with the increasing prevalence of extra-labor market income opportunities—through crime or public assistance. One doesn't actually know whether illegitimate opportunities have become more available, although one assumes they have with increasing urbanization. Public assistance has obviously become more prevalent and remunerative, especially in important Northern states like New York and California.

landing those jobs. All the varieties of government programs which offer them less than this end up offering them nothing.[30]

In a long interview with Herb Goro for *The Block,* a 19-year-old black high school graduate clearly expressed most of these attitudes:[31]

I want a respectable job—clean. I was explaining it to my counselor why I wanted a job in the hospital, he came out and—bang, out of his mouth—he came out and said, "Why don't you get a job with the Sanitation Department? Why don't you be a delivery boy or something like that?" You know. I told him, I said, "Why do you think I went to school twelve years, to become a delivery boy? You must be kidding!" He said, "You want a job, right?" I said, "Well, if that's the case I don't need no job. I was doing pretty good without that before, you know." . . . You see, my thing was that being I was black and he was white, he just didn't want me to get in a clean hospital or decent place to work. He wanted me to work out there in the Sanitation Department where people could laugh at me, you know, and say, well, "He's a Sanitation man, he's got to sweep the streets. He got a high school diploma and he's sweeping the streets. He's just a fool"—you know, like that. . . .

I'm concerned about respect, that's what I'm concerned about. And I'm concerned about a job with respect and salary. . . . I mean I make more than $1.50 shooting dice. . . .

I'm not going to lower my pride to be no type of porter. And I'll always be like that. Long as I live. I rather starve than be somebody's porter. Just like they said, when you take a man's pride, Jim, you might rather take the man, too. . . . Even if the job was a hundred fifty dollars. I'm not going to be nobody's porter.

Given those demands, our potential for solving underemployment among ghetto workers depends fundamentally on the capacity of programs for opening large numbers of "primary" jobs and guaranteeing opportunities in those jobs for disadvantaged workers. According to the radical analysis, this is becoming increasingly impossible in the American economy. For a variety of critical historical reasons, the labor market is becoming increasingly segmented, avenues for internal job mobility are being restricted, and discrimination against demographically defined classes of workers has grown functionally more important. I have briefly developed these arguments in the following three sections.

1. As the American economy has changed, some of the traditional ways in which social and economic institutions have preserved the strength of the capitalist class and the weaknesses of workers have eroded. With these erosions, it has become increasingly important, from the point of view of the capitalist class, that institutions change in such a way that new mechanisms for class stratification can develop. I have summarized four kinds of trends tending to dissolve traditional class divisions in this section, and have linked them in the third section with other trends to sketch the kinds of institutional changes they have tended to produce.

In traditional manufacturing industries, class divisions were exemplified and even established by the nature of the production process. Workers used their hands and their bodies, while management used their heads. With the historical shift from manufacturing to service industries and from blue-collar to white-collar occupations in those industries, the production process no longer so uniquely establishes class divisions.[32] Both "labor" and management often work in the same kinds of conditions, and the nature of their work no longer so clearly divides them.

As the country has become more urbanized and as steady streams of foreign (and Southern) migrants have poured into the cities, some traditional class divisions have become less important. The distinctions between rural and urban workers, between foreign- and domestic-born workers, or between foreign-language and English-speaking workers have become less important. The nature of urban society, with its interactions and chaos, has tended to allow and perhaps even to promote a greater mobility within the working class.[33]

[30] For some general conclusions on the failures of government training programs, see Lester Thurow, "Raising Incomes through Manpower Training Programs," in Pascal, ed., *Contributions to the Analysis of Urban Problems* (Santa Monica: RAND Corporation, 1968).

[31] Quoted in Goro, *The Block, op. cit.,* p. 156.

[32] For a useful summary of most of these trends, see Victor Fuchs, *The Service Economy* (N.Y.: NBER, 1969).

[33] Daniel P. Moynihan and Nathan Glazer have illustrated some of these phenomena for New York City in *Beyond the Melting Pot* (Cambridge: MIT Press, 1970), rev. ed.

To the extent that many traditional manufacturing occupations were governed by a piece-work wage system, employers did not have to worry about the clarity of incentives to workers. If a worker did more on his job, he would earn more.[34] With the switch to bureaucratic modes of production, an individual's contribution to output has become relatively less distinguishable from that of other workers; wage incentives become that much less effective. One response has undoubtedly been to substitute status incentives for monetary incentives, permitting those who work better to rise within the firm. *But,* the advent of mobility also carries with it a certain erosion of previous status distinctions and suggests the need for new stratification mechanisms.[35]

With technological change, there is always a danger of increasingly high unemployment.[36] Also, new technology sometimes creates new skill requirements which general institutional education can often meet better than specific on-the-job training. Both of these trends make it convenient for employers to increase the (often arbitrary) general education requirements they impose as hiring standards for jobs of constant skills. Encouraging the labor force to stay in school through higher levels serves a dual purpose. It cuts down the amount of time any potential worker will spend in the labor force and therefore reduces the potential size of the pool of unemployed. It also imposes on the general public the costs of certain kinds of training, freeing private firms of those costs. *But,* the longer most workers remain in school, the less effective are traditional stratifications between those with no schooling and those with some. It becomes necessary either to adjust relative educational distinctions upward (establishing college as a new boundary between groups of workers, for instance), or to devise new forms of distinction on the job or within labor market institutions (to replace previous distinctions created by education).[37]

2. A second set of trends in the American economy has been equally important. The relationships between wages and manifest labor skills have undoubtedly become hazier over time. In traditional manufacturing activities, a worker's contribution to output was usually quite clear; especially in piece-work operations, the worker could be paid according to how many pieces he finished. The shift to larger, more bureaucratic, more service-oriented modes of production has had two important related effects, each undermining the clarity of those relationships.

As production processes have become more technologically complex, as components of the processes have become more interdependent, as organizations have become larger and more bureaucratic, it seems likely that a worker's "productivity" to the firm has grown increasingly dependent on the amount of time he spends with that specific firm. Traditionally, especially in piece-work processes, a worker performed many separate operations but did not have to know anything about the rest of the firm's operations. In assembly-line manufacturing processes, a worker's specific tasks become more menial—he must watch one gauge or turn one screw—but he must become increasingly knowledgeable about the entire operation in the firm. If he spots a defect in the product, for instance, he is most valuable to the firm if he knows exactly the position of the operation producing the defect. Most clearly, workers in white-collar bureaucracies often perform extremely menial tasks. They stamp forms, or answer one kind of telephone call, or type one kind of letter. Their value to the firm depends increasingly on the subtlety of their knowledge of the firm's operations. If a form doesn't come across their desks on schedule, they must know where to look for it. If a secretary needs to arrange a meeting on quick notice, she must know where to find the participants. Those kinds of "skills" depend entirely on simple tenure within the firm, on a basic familiarity with the nuances of the firm's operations. As a result, productivity depends increasingly on specific job tenure, and decreasingly on specifiable

---

[34] For a discussion of some of these important historical features of the wage system, see Mandel, *Marxist Economic Theory, op. cit.,* pp. 149–150; and Maurice Dobb, *Wages* (Cambridge, Eng.: Cambridge University Press, 1956), rev. ed.

[35] Incentive problems developed in blue-collar work as well, with the switch from piece-work to assembly-line production. Thus, employers became involved in efforts like the famous Hawthorne Experiments, in which Western Electric experimented with subtle environmental changes in the plant (like wall-paint and background music) to test for increases in productivity. See some of the essays in Daniel Bell, *The End of Ideology* (N.Y.: Collier Books, 1962), rev. ed.

[36] This echoes Marx's original argument that institutional changes evolve around variations in the size of the "industrial reserve army." See Marx, *Das Kapital,* or Mandel, *Marxist Economic Theory.*

[37] Both of these responses have been dramatically evident in the United States. For a general discussion of the relationship between the educational system and labor market institutions, see Florence Howe and Paul Lauter, "The Schools Are Rigged for Failure," *New York Review of Books,* June 20, 1970.

"skills." Potential job stability becomes an increasingly important criterion to employers as they search for potential workers.[38]

With these trends, it becomes increasingly difficult for a firm to devise tests to measure a worker's potential productivity. If a worker is required to shovel dirt, an employer can test his brute strength. If an assembler must use his hands with dexterity, an employer can test his skill by asking him to fit round pegs in round holes. If a secretary must do nothing more than type letters, an employer can test her spelling and typing abilities. But when an employee's potential contribution to the firm will depend ultimately on how long he stays with the firm, it becomes extremely difficult to test for that "skill." Psychological tests are probably too insensitive to differentiate potential stability among broad classes of workers. It becomes increasingly likely that employers will rely on superficial characteristics as approximate predictors of potential job stability. If it has been generally true in the past that blacks, women, and teenagers stay on the job less predictably than prime-age white males, an employer will be increasingly likely to discriminate against the former groups. This kind of discrimination has been called statistical discrimination.[39]

3. These first two general phenomena—the several erosions of traditional stratification mechanisms and the increasing importance of on-the-job stability as a component of productivity—have combined to have the following general effects on the American labor market.

—The functional economic importance to employers of discrimination by race, age, and sex has undoubtedly grown more important over time, for three reasons. First, as employers have had to rely increasingly on statistical discrimination, they have undoubtedly found it easiest to discriminate by race, age, and sex. These characteristics can hardly be disguised by workers very easily, and basic social and economic institutions have both tolerated discrimination against these workers and legitimized greater employment instability within these groups. Second, mobility within and the bargaining strength of the "primary" group of prime-age white male workers has probably increased, for many of the reasons cited above. For employers to continue to maintain or increase their share of total product, it has become increasingly important to heighten distinctions against "secondary" groups, thereby weakening the power of these lower-class workers and increasing the potential surplus employers can take from them. Third, as these three secondary groups have comprised an increasingly large proportion of the American labor force, it has become increasingly *possible* for employers to maintain their relative share of product by relying on discrimination against these groups; a constant measure of exploitation produces absolutely larger amounts of surplus as the exploited group increases in size.

—It has probably become more and more necessary for employers to create relatively meaningless and arbitrary status distinctions and class divisions on the job and within the production process, for three reasons. First, the necessity of devising new incentives to replace piece-work and wage bonus incentives has probably established the importance of nonmonetary incentives like larger desks, more important sounding titles, or offices with windows. Each of these new modes of incentive establishes new divisions within the work force. Second, the several erosions of traditional mechanisms determining class stratification have increased the importance of on-the-job stratification. Now employers determine status not by class origin but by job title, office size, and position in the hierarchy. Third, to promote stability, employers find it easiest to give the illusion of mobility by creating trees of artificial job positions which workers can climb, branch by meaningless branch.

—In those "primary" jobs where potential worker stability has become most important to employers, the attractiveness of the jobs has become increasingly colored by their nonmonetary fringe benefits; wages measure less and less of a job's attractiveness. (If a firm rewards stability by wage increases, then employers jeopardize their share of total product.) Thus, one has seen

---

[38] One can refer to two fascinating illustrations of these phenomena. First, Elinor Langer has described all of these developments as manifest in the organization of work in the telephone company; see her brilliant series of articles in *The New York Review of Books* during March, 1970. Second, Michel Crozier found in his classic study of bureaucracy in France that those employees in a large government bureaucracy who had the longest experience in that organization were also the most productive (to a statistically significant degree). Crozier, *The Bureaucratic Phenomenon* (Chicago: Phoenix Books, 1964), p. 21n.

[39] See the selection by Piore in this chapter.

historically in the United States an increasing proliferation of seniority structures, non-vested pension rights, deferred fringe benefits, and so on.

—The prominence of job characteristics in determining relative income among workers has undoubtedly grown in importance as job structures have tended increasingly to dominate relative opportunities among workers for skill acquisition. The more that skills must be developed within specific job situations, the more the structure and distribution of those situations tends to affect the distribution of skills among workers. Abstract individual abilities (like reasoning or reading abilities) become less and less important in determining or explaining variations in labor market status and income.

It would be possible considerably to extend this list of important trends and effects.[40] These examples illustrate the general argument well enough. A simple summary of the argument follows quite directly. Numerous important historical changes in the American labor market have created an increasingly segmented labor market in which the distribution of individual status and income has become more and more dominated by superficial characteristics like race, age, and sex on the one hand, and by circumstantial access to opportunities for highly stratified job mobility, training, and experience on the other. Denied those opportunities for reasons of increasing functional importance to employers, ghetto blacks will continue their marginal attachment to the labor market, impatiently rejecting traditional kinds of lower-class jobs. Reinforced by this historically determined interaction of objective institutional forces and subjective worker preferences, the cycle of underemployment follows its course. The objective and subjective conditions are rooted too solidly in reality for marginal government programs to have an effect. Only some fundamental changes in the entire structure of labor market institutions in this country could break the vicious circle.

THE READINGS

The arguments in the preceding sections have covered much ground, so I have chosen readings selectively to illustrate these general points. A first group of readings provides some short but fundamental impressions and definitions of ghetto employment problems. The brief vignette from Liebow's book, *Tally's Corner*, evokes the nature of frustration among disadvantaged workers with their *relative* (rather than absolute) status. The selections from the "Riot Commission Report" and from a Bureau of Labor Statistics report provide some basic definitions and figures defining the problem of ghetto underemployment. Though dry, the statistics sketch a depressing picture of poverty, instability, and disadvantage.

A second group of readings establishes the contours of theoretical disagreement between conventional and radical perspectives on these problems. The selection by Richard Leftwich elaborates the basic orthodox theory of the distribution of income from labor, discussing the determinants of marginal productivity as it varies among workers. The selection by Lester Thurow argues the empirical importance of these theoretical concepts, attempting to measure the extent and direction of differences among workers in marginal productivities. In contrast, five selections provide pieces of the alternative radical explanation of labor market status and income. The selection by Michael Piore discusses the kinds of historically important economic factors which have tended to divide the labor market into distinct and discontinuous sectors, between which it becomes increasingly difficult for workers to move. For heuristic purposes, Piore makes the argument in terms of two markets, a "primary" and a "secondary" market.[41] The piece by Harold Baron and Bennett Hymer, excerpted from a longer article, concentrates on the institutional forces which produce labor market segmentation; in their piece, they speak of the segmentation between "white" and "black" sectors. Barry Bluestone discusses the kinds of economic factors which have concentrated so many jobs in the "low-wage" sector and have made it increasingly difficult for the poor to earn more than a minimum wage. In the next article, Michael Reich argues the functional importance of racism in the labor market, suggesting that blacks cannot hope to equalize their employment opportunities without fundamental

---

[40] I have extended and elaborated all of these arguments in my doctoral dissertation, "Class, Productivity and the Ghetto," Department of Economics, Harvard University, 1971, unpublished.
[41] Piore is not a radical in the terms of this book, but his selection provides the best available discussion of the economic forces creating specific segmentations in the labor market.

changes in the structure of labor market institutions. Marilyn Power Goldberg presents the same kinds of arguments about discrimination against women.

A third group of readings illustrates the basically misguided intentions of liberal/conservative policies and programs. The three articles can be viewed within a slightly larger context. Liberal proposals to solve ghetto underemployment have been summarized, for instance, by the report of the National Advisory Commission on Civil Disorders.[42] (This summary has *not* been included in the readings.) The report urged special emphasis on

1. coordination of existing programs, improved recruitment, and better job information;
2. programs for "motivating the hard-core unemployed";
3. special new public training efforts;
4. special new private training efforts; and
5. increased investment in ghetto areas and increased aid for small businessmen in those areas.

I have included reading selections illustrating the irrelevance of three of those five emphases. First, the piece by David Wellman makes clear that programs cannot "motivate" young ghetto workers without fundamentally changing the structure of employment opportunities available to them. As the preceding section argued, their perceptions of those opportunities are much too accurate for them to change simply because we want them to change. Second, the selection by Jules Cohn places in context all our recent efforts to develop subtle incentives to private employers for on-the-job training of the disadvantaged. Manpower policy has assumed that the failures of many such programs have derived from their lack of sensitivity to the needs of disadvantaged workers. In his review of recent efforts, Cohn shows that the success of such programs depends on basic economic forces rather than on psychological subtleties. If firms need skilled workers, they find ways to train them; if they don't, they don't. If economic conditions tend to undercut such efforts, one can hardly fight those economic imperatives with moral suasion.[43] And third, Barry Bluestone provides an important perspective on the potential importance of ghetto economic development, or "black capitalism," as it has been called. He argues that fundamental structural changes in the economy would have to occur before "black capitalism" could make much difference in the lives of ghetto workers.

Although I have not covered the other two policy directions urged by the Commission on Civil Disorders, one should have little illusion about their potential effectiveness. There is already sufficient evidence available to warrant some pessimistic conclusions about those two strands of policy.[44]

Finally, it seemed necessary to include one more reading. The radical argument implies that ghetto employment problems derive fundamentally from basic capitalist institutions. This implies that a different set of institutions would produce qualitatively different sets of employment conditions. As Chapter One noted, many radicals admire the ways in which socialism has been applied in Cuba since the Castro revolution. The piece by Maurice Zeitlin provides some extremely important information about the structure of the labor market in Cuba and the effect of basic priorities and institutions on worker conditions. Quite clearly, from Zeitlin's article, the Cubans have placed equality, worker participation, and the quality of working conditions above other priorities valued in capitalist societies, like efficiency and growth. Although the Cuban effort has not been without its problems, it seems to have succeeded in establishing much greater equality among *all* workers, a much more meaningful involvement by workers in all the decisions affecting their work, and a much more humane set of working conditions. These achievements would have been impossible in a capitalist society.

---

[42] *Report of the National Advisory Commission on Civil Disorders, op. cit.,* pp. 413–424.

[43] Cohn, like Piore, is not a radical, but his article provides the most extensive discussion of these very recent programs.

[44] On the futility of labor market coordination, recruitment, and information, for instance, see Penny Feldman, David Gordon, Michael Reich, Peter Doeringer and Michael Piore, *Low-Income Labor Markets and Urban Manpower Programs* (Washington: U.S. Department of Labor, forthcoming), a study of several programs with such objectives in Boston, Mass. And for an example of the ways in which special public training programs worked, see the selections on the Job Corps camp run by Litton Industries in David Horowitz and Reese Ehrlich, "Litton Industries: Proving Poverty Pays," *Ramparts,* December 14–28, 1968.

TALLY'S JOB

Elliot Liebow

This very simple little anecdote comes from the chapter on "Men and Jobs" in Liebow's classic study of streetcorner life in the ghetto, *Tally's Corner*. Tally's attitude about his job—a regular, relatively well-paying, semiskilled job—reflects increasingly strong feelings among disadvantaged workers in this country about relative occupational status and prestige. It also illustrates the extraordinary importance of employment in establishing the tenor of workers' lives.

Tally and I were in the Carry-out. It was summer, Tally's peak earning season as a cement finisher, a semiskilled job a cut or so above that of the unskilled laborer. His take-home pay during these weeks was well over a hundred dollars—"a lot of bread." But for Tally, who no longer had a family to support, bread was not enough.

"You know that boy came in last night? That Black Moozlem? That's what I ought to be doing. I ought to be in his place."

"What do you mean?"

"Dressed nice, going to [night] school, got a good job."

"He's no better off than you, Tally. You make more than he does."

"It's not the money. [Pause] It's position, I guess. He's got position. When he finish school he gonna be a supervisor. People respect him. . . . Thinking about people with position and education gives me a feeling right here [pressing his fingers into the pit of his stomach]."

"You're educated, too. You have a skill, a trade. You're a cement finisher. You can make a building, pour a sidewalk."

"That's different. Look, can anybody do what you're doing? Can anybody just come up and do your job? Well, in one week I can teach you cement finishing.

SOURCE: From Tally's Corner *by Elliot Liebow, by permission of Little, Brown & Co. Copyright © 1967 by Little, Brown & Company (Inc.).*

You won't be as good as me 'cause you won't have the experience but you'll be a cement finisher. That's what I mean. Anybody can do what I'm doing and that's what gives me this feeling. [Long pause] Suppose I like this girl. I go over to her house and I meet her father. He starts talking about what he done today. He talks about operating on somebody and sewing them up and about surgery. I know he's a doctor 'cause of the way he talks. Then she starts talking about what she did. Maybe she's a boss or a supervisor. Maybe she's a lawyer and her father says to me, 'And what do you do, Mr. Jackson?' [Pause] You remember at the courthouse, Lonny's trial? You and the lawyer was talking in the hall? You remember? I just stood there listening. I didn't say a word. You know why? 'Cause I didn't even know what you was talking about. That's happened to me a lot."

"Hell, you're nothing special. That happens to everybody. Nobody knows everything. One man is a doctor, so he talks about surgery. Another man is a teacher, so he talks about books. But doctors and teachers don't know anything about concrete. You're a cement finisher and that's your specialty."

"Maybe so, but when was the last time you saw anybody standing around talking about concrete?"

GHETTO UNEMPLOYMENT AND UNDEREMPLOYMENT

The National Advisory Commission on Civil Disorders

This brief selection from the influential Riot Commission Report provides some useful basic definitions and figures describing employment problems in urban ghettos, especially among disadvantaged black workers. It emphasizes the importance of moving beyond "unemployment" as a simple measure of employment problems.

THE CRITICAL SIGNIFICANCE OF EMPLOYMENT

The capacity to obtain and hold a "good job" is the traditional test of participation in American society. Steady employment with adequate compensation provides both purchasing power and social status. It develops the capabilities, confidence, and self-esteem an individual needs to be a responsible citizen and provides a basis for a stable family life. As Daniel P. Moynihan has written:

The principal measure of progress toward equality will be that of employment. It is the primary source of individual or group identity. In America what you do is what you are: to do nothing is to be nothing; to do little is to be little. The equations are implacable and blunt, and ruthlessly public.

For the Negro American it is already, and will continue to be, the master problem. It is the measure of white bona fides. It is the measure of Negro competence, and also of the competence of American society. Most importantly, the linkage between problems of employment and the range of social pathology that afflicts the Negro community is unmistakable. Employment not only controls the present for the Negro American but, in a most profound way, it is creating the future as well.

For residents of disadvantaged Negro neighborhoods, obtaining good jobs is vastly more difficult than for most workers in so-

ciety. For decades, social, economic, and psychological disadvantages surrounding the urban Negro poor have impaired their work capacities and opportunities. The result is a "cycle of failure"—the employment disabilities of one generation breed those of the next.

NEGRO UNEMPLOYMENT

Unemployment rates among Negroes have declined from a postwar high of 12.6 percent in 1958 to 8.2 percent in 1967. Among married Negro men, the unemployment rate for 1967 was down to 3.2 percent.

Notwithstanding this decline, unemployment rates for Negroes are still double those for whites in every category, including married men, as they have been throughout the postwar period. Moreover, since 1954, even during the current unprecedented period of sustained economic growth, unemployment among Negroes has been continuously above the 6.0 percent "recession" level widely regarded as a sign of serious economic weakness when prevalent for the entire work force.

While the Negro unemployment rate remains high in relation to the white rate, the number of additional jobs needed to lower this to the level of white unemployment is surprisingly small. In 1967, approximately 3.0 million persons were unemployed during an average week, of whom about 638,000, or 21 percent, were nonwhites. When corrected for undercounting, total nonwhite unemployment was approximately 712,000 or 8 percent of the nonwhite labor force. To reduce the unemployment rate to 3.4 percent, the rate prevalent among whites, jobs must be found for 57.5 percent of these unemployed persons. This amounts to nearly 409,000 jobs, or about 28 percent of the net number of new jobs added to the economy in the year 1967 alone and only slightly more than ½ of 1 percent of all jobs in the United States in 1967.

THE LOW-STATUS AND LOW-PAYING NATURE OF MANY NEGRO JOBS

Even more important perhaps than unemployment is the related problem of the undesirable nature of many jobs open to Negroes. Negro workers are concentrated in the lowest-skilled and lowest-paying occupations. These jobs often involve substandard wages, great instability and uncertainty of tenure, extremely low status in the eyes of both employer and employee, little or no chance for meaningful advancement, and unpleasant or exhausting duties. Negro men in particular are more than twice as likely as whites to be in unskilled or service jobs which pay far less than most:

This concentration in the least desirable jobs can be viewed another way by calculating the changes which would occur if Negro men were employed in various occupations in the same proportions as the male labor force as a whole (not solely the white labor force).

Thus, upgrading the employment of Negro men to make their occupational distribution identical with that of the labor force as a whole would have an immense impact upon the nature of their occupations. About 1.3 million nonwhite men—or 28 percent of those employed in 1966—would move up the employment ladder into one of the higher-status and higher-paying categories. The effect of such a shift upon the incomes of Negro men would be very great. Using the 1966 job distribution, the shift indicated above would produce about $4.8 billion more earned income for nonwhite men alone if they received the 1965 median income in each occupation. This would be a rise of approximately 30 percent in the earnings actually received by all nonwhite men in 1965 (not counting any sources of

Type of Occupation	Percentage of Male Workers in Each Type of Occupation —1966		Median Earnings of All Male Civilians in Each Occupation —1965
	White	Nonwhite	
Professional, technical, managerial	27%	9%	$7,603[1]
Clerical and sales	14	9	$5,532[1]
Craftsmen and foremen	20	12	$6,270
Operatives	20	27	$5,046
Service workers	6	16	$3,436
Non-farm laborers	6	20	$2,410
Farmers and farm workers	7	8	$1,699[1]

[1] Average of two categories from normal Census Bureau categories as combined in data presented in The Social and Economic Conditions of Negroes in the United States (BLS #332).

Type of Occupation	Number of Male Nonwhite Workers—1966			
	As Actually Distributed[2]	If Distributed the Same as All Male Workers	Difference	
			No.	Percent
Professional, technical, managerial	415,000	1,173,000	+758,000	+183%
Clerical and sales	415,000	628,000	+213,000	+51%
Craftsmen and foremen	553,000	894,000	+341,000	+62%
Operatives	1,244,000	964,000	−280,000	−23%
Service workers	737,000	326,000	−411,000	−56%
Non-farm laborers	922,000	340,000	−582,000	−63%
Farmers and farm workers	369,000	330,000	−39,000	−11%

[2] Estimates based upon percentages set forth in BLS #332, page 41.

income other than wages and salaries). . . .

This conclusion underlines the difficulty of really improving the economic status of Negro men. It is far easier to create new jobs than either to create new jobs with relatively high status and earning power, or to upgrade existing employed or partly-employed workers into such better-quality employment. Yet only such upgrading will eliminate the fundamental basis of poverty and deprivation among Negro families.

Access to good-quality jobs clearly affects the willingness of Negro men actively to seek work. In cities with the largest percentage of Negroes in skilled and semi-skilled jobs, Negro men participate in the labor force to the same extent as, or greater than, white men. Conversely, where most Negro men were heavily concentrated in menial jobs, they participated less in the labor force than white men.

Even given similar employment, Negro workers with the same education as white workers are paid less. This disparity doubtless results to some extent from inferior training in segregated schools, and also from the fact that large numbers of Negroes are only now entering certain occupations for the first time. However, the differentials are so large and so universal at all educational levels that they clearly reflect the patterns of discrimination which characterize hiring and promotion practices in many segments of the economy. For example, in 1966 among persons who had completed high school, the

median income of Negroes was only 73 percent that of whites. Even among persons with an eighth-grade education, Negro median income was only 80 percent of white median income.

At the same time, a higher proportion of Negro women than white women participates in the labor force at nearly all ages except 16 to 19. For instance, in 1966, 55 percent of nonwhite women from 25 to 34 years of age were employed, compared to only 38 percent of white women in the same age group. The fact that almost half of all adult Negro women work reflects the fact that so many Negro males have unsteady and low-paying jobs. Yet even though Negro women are often better able to find work than Negro men, the unemployment rate among adult nonwhite women (20 years old and over) in 1967 was 7.3 percent, compared to the 4.3 percent rate among adult nonwhite men.

Unemployment rates are, of course, much higher among teenagers, both Negro and white, than among adults; in fact about one-third of all unemployed Negroes in 1967 were between 16 and 19 years old. During the first nine months of 1967, the unemployment rate among nonwhite teenagers was 26.5 percent; for whites, it was 10.6 percent. About 219,300 nonwhite teenagers were unemployed.[3] About 58,300 were still in school but were actively looking for jobs.

[3] After adjusting for Census Bureau undercounting.

EMPLOYMENT PROBLEMS IN SIX GHETTOS
Bureau of Labor Statistics

This government report provides the most recent description available of the dimensions and distributions of employment problems in urban ghettos. It provides more recent numbers than those in the preceding selection, and it also emphasizes the important variations in the nature of underemployment among different ghettos around the country. It underscores the importance of focusing clearly on the very specific manifestations of general problems, of recognizing the varying effects of specific labor market institutions and histories.

SOURCE: *U.S. Department of Labor, Bureau of Labor Statistics, "Employment Situation in Poverty Areas of Six Cities, July 1968–June 1969."* *Urban Employment Survey, BLS Report No. 370, October, 1969.*

For most Americans, 1969 was a year of relative economic well being. Employment was at record levels, and the unemployment rate was near post-Korean War lows. However, a large segment of our population was not sharing in this prosperity. In the Concentrated Employment Program (CEP)[1] areas of six major U.S. cities, many of the mainly black and Spanish-American residents were plagued by high unemployment rates and low weekly earnings and annual incomes. They were also concentrated in less desirable occupations—a large proportion worked in service and nonfarm laborer jobs that are often seasonal and provide only intermittent work. In addition, many CEP area residents were not even seeking work because of poor health or discouragement over their job-finding prospects. In each of the target areas, the proportion of persons with employment problems was much greater than for persons in the Nation as a whole.

This report, which sheds new light on the employment problems of people in poverty areas, presents the first detailed results of the Urban Employment Survey (UES). The survey was conducted by the U.S. Bureau of the Census for the Bureau of Labor Statistics with the cooperation and financing of the Labor Department's Manpower Administration. It provides information on the employment status, work experience, earnings, income, and educational attainment of persons living in each of the CEP areas of six large U.S. cities—Atlanta, Chicago, Detroit, Houston, Los Angeles, and New York City.[2] The data refer to the twelve-month period, July 1968 through June 1969. Releases on the employment situation in each of these areas have also been prepared by the regional offices of the Bureau of Labor Statistics and are available on request from the Bureau.

[1] Concentrated Employment Program areas are target poverty areas in which the Department of Labor has combined separate manpower programs in order to concentrate the effects of these programs in specific neighborhoods. Since the boundaries of the CEP areas were made for administrative and program purposes, the areas are not entirely homogeneous in relation to one another; comparisons and conclusions concerning area differences should be made with caution.

[2] The six areas will be referred to interchangeably as CEP, UES, poverty, or target areas in this report.

POPULATION

Approximately 815,000 men and women 16 years and over resided in the six poverty areas surveyed during the July 1968–June 1969 period. The New York City survey area also includes similar neighborhoods outside the CEP areas. It made up nearly half of this target population (389,000). In addition, the survey covered 117,000 persons in Chicago, 98,000 in Detroit, 82,000 in Houston, 68,000 in Los Angeles, and 60,000 in Atlanta.

The poverty areas included in the UES were specifically chosen to obtain information on employment and other characteristics of residents with diverse racial and national origin backgrounds. About 70 percent of the area residents were Negro; the remainder were about equally divided between Spanish Americans and other white persons.

The race/ethnic composition of the population in each of the areas differed considerably. Three of the areas included significant proportions of persons of Spanish-American descent. Nearly half the residents of the Los Angeles UES area and about one-fifth of the Houston area population were of Mexican descent; nearly one-fifth of the UES population in New York City was Puerto Rican. The balance of the population in those three areas was predominantly Negro. In the remaining three areas, Negroes composed three-fourths or more of the population.

LABOR FORCE PARTICIPATION

Adult men residing in the UES poverty areas generally were less likely to be working or seeking work than men living in other areas. These rates reflected in part the less favorable job situation for poverty residents. Although male labor force participation rates varied substantially among the six areas, they were generally lower than for men in the Nation as a whole and more in line with that for the Nation's Negro men. Among both adult men and women, participation rates were higher in the Atlanta, Chicago, and Houston survey areas than in Detroit, Los Angeles, and New York City.

Among those who were not in the labor force (neither working nor looking for work), there was a large pool of "potential" workers. Nearly 30 percent of the men and women in the Atlanta and Chicago target areas who were not in the labor force indicated that they wanted a job "now." In the remaining survey areas, the proportion was somewhat lower—around 24 percent. Nevertheless, in each of the survey areas the proportion of nonparticipants who indicated that they wanted a job was higher than for persons in the Nation as a whole; again, the proportions were in line with that for the Nation's Negro workers.

Although large proportions of the men and women out of the labor force indicated their desire for a job, the vast majority of these persons had compelling reasons for their nonparticipation in the labor force. In each of the target areas, at least three-quarters of the reasons given by men for being out of the labor force were related to retirement, old age, school attendance, or health reasons. Health reasons were cited most frequently in the Atlanta, Detroit, and New York City target areas. Lack of skill, education, or experience was also reported as reasons for nonparticipation by men who wanted a job. These factors were most frequently cited in Atlanta, where the proportion was twice as high as in the entire Nation.

Family responsibilities was the major reason that women in the target areas who wanted a job were out of the labor force, although in Atlanta health reasons were cited just as frequently. In the New York and Chicago target areas, family responsibilities was the reason given by two out of five women who wanted a job and were not in the labor force. In addition, significant proportions of women in the Atlanta, Detroit, and Houston target areas (11 to 12 percent) were not in the labor force because they felt they lacked the requisite skills, experience, or education.

EMPLOYMENT

Employed persons in UES areas were more likely to have part-time jobs than the Nation's jobholders, but the incidence of part-time work varied significantly from area to area. Part-time work was particularly prevalent in Atlanta, where more than one out of four persons were employed less than 35 hours weekly, considerably greater than the proportion in the New York City or Chicago target areas. In the United States as a whole, only about one out of five white and one out of four Negro workers are employed part time.

Most of those who were working part time during the survey week did so voluntarily; others wanted but could not find full-time jobs and thus were on short workweeks for economic reasons such as slack work, material shortages, and repairs to plant and equipment. In five of the areas, the proportions ranged from 15 to 20 percent, slightly above that for all workers in the country. However, involuntary part-time work was less common in the New York City area, where only 12 percent of those working part time were on short workweeks for economic reasons.

Adult workers residing in the target areas were more likely to be concentrated in low paying, low status occupations than the Nation's workers. However, the proportion of survey area residents working in less desirable jobs was about the same as for the Nation's Negro workers.

A large proportion of adult men (particularly Negro men) was employed in nonfarm laborer or service jobs (many of which are low skilled) during the survey period. The problem was greatest in Atlanta and Houston, where more than one out of three employed Negro men held these low skill jobs. In the remaining target areas, a slightly smaller proportion was employed in these occupations, about the same proportion as for the Nation's Negro men.

White men (many of whom were Spanish American) in these areas were also disproportionately employed in low skill occupations although less so than Negro men. The proportion of white men holding jobs in these occupations was about one out of four in Detroit, Houston, and New York City and one out of five in Los Angeles. In Atlanta, only one out of eight white men held such jobs, much the same proportion as the Nation's white workers.

On the other hand, working men in these areas were less likely to be employed in white-collar professional or managerial jobs. Compared with about 30 percent of the employed men in the United States, only seven to fifteen percent of the white men and about half that proportion of Negro men in the target areas had professional or managerial jobs. New York, Detroit, and Atlanta had much higher proportions of white workers in these jobs while Los Angeles and New York had the highest proportions of Negro men employed in white-collar positions.

Adult women in the target areas were also more likely to be working in less desirable occupations than women in the Nation as a whole. For example, about two out of three Negro women in the Atlanta and Houston target area worked in the service occupations (mostly private household work). In the Chicago survey area, the proportion was relatively low, and it was about two out of five in the remaining three target areas. About one out of three in Detroit and Houston were employed as domestics and in other service jobs, but only one out of eight white women in the Los Angeles and New York City target areas (where a large proportion were Mexican American or Puerto Rican) held these low paying jobs.

UNEMPLOYMENT

During the 12-month period, unemployment rates for workers in the target areas were two to three times as great as the rate for workers in the Nation as a whole (3.4 percent). Except for workers in the New York City target area, the overall jobless rate in each of these areas was significantly greater even than that for the Nation's Negro workers (6.5 percent).

There were substantial differences in jobless rates among residents of the UES areas. The rate was highest in the Detroit survey area (12.2 percent),[3] followed by a very high rate in the Los Angeles area (10.3 percent). Unemployment rates were about 8½ percent for workers in the Atlanta, Houston, and Chicago target areas. The jobless rate was lowest for New York City target area workers although still twice that of the Nation's workers.

Negro workers had higher jobless rates than white CEP area residents in each of the survey areas except New York City. Jobless rates were especially high for Negroes in Los Angeles (15.2 percent) and Detroit (13.5 percent). Nevertheless, the unemployment rate for white workers (many of whom

are Spanish American) was also very high, about twice that of white workers in the Nation. It ranged from 5.5 to 9 percent in the five areas which include significant numbers of white persons.[4] Negro jobless rates ranged from 1.5 to 2.5 times those of white workers in the target areas, compared with a 2-to-1 ratio in the Nation as a whole.

As is true for the entire country, teenage workers make up a disproportionate share of total unemployment in the UES areas. During the period, from one out of four teenagers in New York City to more than one out of three in the Detroit survey area were jobless. These are close to the jobless proportion for Negro teenagers in the country—about one out of four. In contrast, about one out of eight of the Nation's white teenage workers are unemployed.

Unemployment usually has more serious economic implications for adult workers, many of whom are family breadwinners. Jobless rates for adult men living in these survey areas were especially high in Los Angeles and Detroit, where between 6 and 7 percent were unemployed, twice the rate for all Negroes and three times that for all workers in the United States. The lower rates for adult men in Atlanta and Houston were nearer to that of Negroes in the Nation..

Among adult women, a significant proportion of whom are family heads, the rate in five of the six areas was also two to three times higher than for women in the Nation. The rate was highest (12.5 percent) in the Detroit area. New York City had the lowest rate (5.4 percent), about in line with comparable Negro rates in the U.S. The jobless rate ranged from about 7.5 to 9.5 percent in the remaining areas, all above the rate for Negroes in the Nation as a whole.

WORK EXPERIENCE

In addition to the labor force status of persons during the survey week, another gauge of the magnitude of employment problems faced by residents of the UES areas is their work experience over a full year. This concept measures the total number of persons who worked or looked for work at any time during the year, rather than the total

[3] The high unemployment rate in the Detroit survey area may, in part, reflect the effects of model changeover in the automobile industry. Workers on temporary layoff (less than 30 days) are counted as unemployed.

[4] Data on white persons in the Chicago survey area [are] not included, as whites represent only 4 percent of the target population. The sampling error on these data is quite large.

number employed or unemployed during a particular week.

UES area residents were much more likely to have experienced some unemployment during the year than workers in other areas. In the Detroit area in particular, about one out of every three workers, twice the proportion as in the New York City survey area, were jobless at some time during the year. The proportion who had some unemployment was nearer one in four in the remaining areas, only slightly above that for Negro workers in the Nation during 1968, but still twice the proportion for the entire Nation's work force.

Another indication of the dimension of unemployment in these target areas is the proportion of unemployed workers who sought a job at some time during the year, but who were unable to find any employment. There was some variation among the six areas, with the proportion ranging from about 16 percent in the Chicago and New York City target areas to 22 percent in Los Angeles. In each area the proportions of whites and Negroes experiencing unemployment were significantly higher than the proportions in the Nation as a whole.

Although workers in the poverty areas were more likely to be unemployed during the year than workers in the entire country, those who were unemployed at some time throughout the year did not experience substantially longer duration of joblessness than workers in the Nation as a whole. The proportion of the jobless with long term unemployment—15 weeks or more—was lowest in Atlanta and Chicago (18 percent) and highest in Los Angeles and New York City (27 percent). In each of the survey areas, jobless adult men were more likely to have experienced 15 weeks or more of unemployment during the year than other age/sex groups.

Notwithstanding this high degree of joblessness in the target areas, eight out of ten adult men in each of the areas except Detroit worked at some time during the year, roughly similar to the proportion for the Nation's workers during 1968. The proportion was about 75 percent in the Detroit survey area.

Most UES workers were employed year round and full time. A low of 58 percent of adult men in Detroit worked 50 to 52 weeks at full-time jobs compared with a high of 76 percent in the New York City and Chicago

survey areas. In the U.S. as a whole, more than 70 percent of adult men worked 50 to 52 weeks at full-time jobs.

WEEKLY EARNINGS

Weekly earnings data, particularly in two UES areas, graphically illustrate the degree to which many of the workers in these poverty areas are underpaid. A large proportion of the full-time workers in the UES areas earned less than $65 a week, the weekly equivalent of the current Federal minimum wage. The proportion was especially high in Houston and Atlanta, more than 25 percent of all full-time workers, whereas in Chicago, Detroit, Los Angeles and New York, from 8 to 14 percent of full-time workers reported weekly pay of less than $65.

Median weekly earnings for full-time workers in the target areas even more deeply reflected the area-to-area disparity. Average weekly earnings were substantially lower in the Atlanta ($81) and Houston ($83) areas than in the other four areas. New York City ($94) was the only other area in which workers averaged less than $100. In the Detroit, Los Angeles, and Chicago target areas, the average for full-time workers was over $100, ranging up to $120 in Detroit. In each of the areas, women earned considerably less than men. In Atlanta and in Houston, Negroes earned less than whites; in Detroit and New York, earnings for white and Negro workers were about the same; in Los Angeles, however, Negro workers earned more than whites (mainly Mexican-Americans).

Median earnings for men who were household heads were considerably higher than for women who headed households. Weekly earnings for men 20 to 64 years old who were household heads ranged from $102 in Atlanta to $140 in Detroit; for adult women —who head about 40 percent of the UES households—earnings varied from $56 in Los Angeles to $86 in Chicago. This differential was evident in each of the areas and particularly sharp in Detroit and Houston, where women who headed households earned only a little more than half the weekly pay of men.

Although large proportions of UES area workers received these low earnings, there was a significant proportion of the employed persons in each area who had substantial weekly earnings. In Detroit, where overall earnings were highest, about 30 percent of the full-time workers earned $150 or more weekly. However, in the Atlanta, Houston and New York City survey areas, only about 10 percent of the workers with full-time jobs averaged this much.

ANNUAL FAMILY INCOME

The labor force experience and earnings of individuals are not complete or sufficient measures of a family's economic health. Nor is having a job a guarantee of financial independence for many families. A more comprehensive measure of family economic well-being is the level of annual family income.[5]

Despite significant differences among the UES areas, average incomes of families in all six areas were sharply lower than for families in the Nation as a whole. However, they generally conformed closely to those for urban Negro families in the United States. The median income of families (two or more persons) was highest in the Chicago target area ($7,200), followed by Detroit ($6,300), Los Angeles ($6,200), New York City ($5,500), Houston ($5,200), and Atlanta ($4,900). These levels are in sharp contrast to the $8,600 median income received by all of the Nation's families in 1968. The income levels for UES area families, a large proportion of whom are Negro, more closely approximate the average income level of all Negro families in large central cities—$6,600. White families in the United States averaged about $8,900 in 1968; those in large central cities averaged $9,300.

Inter-area differences in levels of annual income can be placed more clearly in perspective, however, by considering variations that exist in living costs in these areas. The Bureau of Labor Statistics has recently issued cost of living benchmarks for carefully defined families of four persons in different financial circumstances in 39 areas.[6]

These data show that the cost of a "low" annual budget for a family of four persons in the target areas was estimated at from $5,500 to $6,300 in the spring of 1967. It is significant that among the cities included in

the Survey, the BLS budget estimate was lowest in Atlanta and Houston, two of the three cities in which average family income was lowest for poverty area residents. However, further comparison of the budget and the income rankings show some differences. For example, of the six cities, the highest cost for a "low" annual budget was in Los Angeles. Yet average incomes for UES area residents in that city ranked near the midpoint of the six areas. Nevertheless, the data do suggest some correlation between the level of income and the cost of living in the areas being surveyed. It should be noted, however, that the "low" budget figures are for four person families for the spring of 1967; price levels have risen substantially since that time.

The proportion of target area families with very low or "poverty level" incomes varied sharply from area to area and between Negro and white families. In Atlanta and in Houston, one out of three Negro families in these two areas had this level of income, a proportion well above that for families in the other target areas. Conversely, only about one out of five Negro families in Atlanta and Houston reported incomes of $8,000 or more annually compared to at least one out of three for both white and Negro families in all the remaining areas except New York City, where just over one out of four had this level of family income.

EDUCATIONAL ATTAINMENT

One factor which contributes to the high jobless levels and low earnings of residents of the CEP areas is their generally low level of educational attainment. Except for Negroes in the New York and Los Angeles target areas and whites in the Detroit survey areas, fewer than 40 percent of the workers in each survey area had completed four years of high school or more. Half of the Los Angeles Negro and Chicago white workers had completed at least a high school education. In all of the areas, the proportion completing a high school education was substantially less than among the Nation's workers, although it was more in line with that of Negro workers nationwide.

In the Houston (10.7 years), Los Angeles (12.0 years), and New York (11.0 years) survey areas, Negro workers had completed more schooling than did their white counterparts (9.0, 9.6, and 10.2 years respectively).

[5] Includes incomes from all sources: earnings, welfare payments, rents, social security, and other sources.
[6] Bulletin 1570, *Three Standards of Urban Living*, Bureau of Labor Statistics, U.S. Department of Labor.

However, in these areas, the white population has a high proportion of Puerto Ricans and Mexican Americans, some of whom are relatively recent arrivals to the United States and have language difficulties. Among the Spanish Americans, attainment levels were much lower in the Houston poverty area (7.6 percent) than in either Los Angeles or New York (about 9.1 years).

In each of the UES survey areas, adult women workers (25 years and over) were better educated than their male counterparts. The largest differences were noted in Chicago, Atlanta, and Detroit where about 30 percent more women than men had at least high school educations. In the Nation as a whole, only a slightly higher proportion of adult women than men had completed that amount of education.

ENTIRE CITY FINDINGS— DETROIT AND ATLANTA

Although the primary focus of the UES is on the CEP areas of the cities, the survey has also developed some information on the employment situation in the whole of Atlanta and Detroit. These data permit comparisons of the target area findings with similar information for persons residing in other neighborhoods in these two cities and should provide additional insights and perspective to the target area findings.[7] Some of the highlights from these data are presented in this section. (More detailed information may be found in the BLS reports for Atlanta and Detroit which are available from the Bureau.)

In terms of unemployment, educational attainment, weekly earnings, and annual income, Detroit target area residents (who made up about 10 percent of the city's population) were much worse off than those living in the whole city. The unemployment rate for CEP area workers was 12.2 percent, nearly twice that for all workers in the city.[8]

In addition, one out of three workers in the poverty areas compared with one out of four in the entire city experienced unemployment at some time during the year. The higher incidence of joblessness among target area residents is directly related to their lower levels of educational attainment. Only 37 percent of the workers living in the program area had completed high school compared with 56 percent of those in the city as a whole.

The employment problems of Detroit CEP area residents were clearly reflected in their weekly earnings and annual income. Average weekly earnings for full-time workers in the target area stood at $120—$21 less than that for all workers in the city. There was also a substantial difference in the level of family income. Detroit target area families averaged only $6,300 in the year prior to the survey compared with nearly $9,000 for families in the entire city. Looking at this income variation in a different way, the proportion of families in the CEP area that had annual incomes below the "poverty line" (less than $3,500 annually) was twice that in the city as a whole (13 percent).

In Atlanta, target-area residents made up about 20 percent of the city's population and had more serious employment and related problems than their counterparts in the city. Differences in the unemployment rates were not as great as in Detroit, but there was a wider variation in weekly earnings. The jobless rate for residents of the target area was 8.6 percent, more than one and a half times that for all workers in the city. Poverty area workers in Atlanta were also much less likely to have completed high school than workers in the entire city, 35 and 59 percent, respectively.

Full-time workers in the program area averaged $81 weekly—$25 less than workers in the city. In addition, annual family incomes were much less in the CEP area than in the city, $4,900 and $7,600, respectively. About three out of ten target area families received less than $3,500 annually compared to less than two out of ten families in the entire city.

SUMMARY

These first findings of the UES illustrate clearly that residents of the CEP areas of six

---

[7] Data for Detroit and Atlanta central cities should be interpreted with caution, since the balance of Atlanta and Detroit, i.e., the areas outside the UES areas, also include some poverty neighborhoods.

[8] Figures on the city of Detroit available from the Urban Employment Survey may differ somewhat from similar data collected in the Current Population Survey and reported in "Unemployment in 20 Large Urban Areas," *Employment and Earnings and Monthly Report on the Labor Force,* March 1969, pages 5–18. Variations result from differences in sample size, questionnaire design,

interviewer procedures, and methods of estimation.

of the Nation's largest cities were not sharing equally in the prosperity that was being enjoyed by most of the Nation's workers. Workers in these target areas were much more likely to be unemployed than workers in the Nation as a whole and even when employed were more likely to work part time and part year and to have jobs in lower paying, less desirable occupations. In addition, they and their families had to get by with lower earnings and smaller incomes than their counterparts in the Nation as a whole.

The survey results further highlight the fact, however, that there are many variations in employment and economic well-being among the areas. This concluding section briefly summarizes the situation for each area and provides an indication of the relative severity of the different measures of employment problems.

In the Detroit target area, employment problems were particularly severe. The proportion of workers who were unemployed was substantially higher than in the other areas. In addition, the proportion of employed household heads who were working part time for reasons beyond their control was relatively high. On the other hand, both weekly earnings and family income in the Detroit area were high relative to the other UES areas, although still well below the Detroit city and U.S. averages.

The most serious problem for residents of the Los Angeles target area also was very high unemployment. An average of more than one out of ten workers in the area was jobless during the July 1968–June 1969 period, about three times the proportion for workers in the Nation as a whole and sig-

nificantly greater than that for the Nation's Negro workers. Average annual income for families in Los Angeles was near the midpoint relative to the other poverty areas, and a large proportion of the families had poverty level earnings.

In Atlanta and Houston, a major problem for CEP area residents was especially low levels of weekly earnings and family income. Average weekly earnings for full-time workers, at about $80, were lower than in the other target areas. Similarly, annual incomes of families residing in Atlanta and Houston, at about $5,000, were not only much lower than for families living in the other CEP areas but also significantly less than the average income of urban Negro families in the United States in 1968. Unemployment rates in these two areas, at 8.5 percent, were substantially higher than for workers in the Nation as a whole and for the Nation's Negro workers. There was also a very high proportion of employed persons working in low skill, less desirable jobs.

In the New York City and Chicago target areas, no single indicator of employment problems could be singled out relative to the other four areas. However, the proportion of workers who were unemployed or in low paying jobs was still very high compared with persons living in other neighborhoods in the country. Furthermore, in New York, weekly earnings for male full-time workers were relatively low and the difference in earnings for adult men and women was not as substantial as in the other areas. The median family income in the New York poverty area was also very low, only moderately above the levels in Atlanta and Houston.

PERSONAL INCOME AND MARGINAL PRODUCTIVITY

Richard H. Leftwich

This selection comes from a standard economics textbook. It elaborates the basic orthodox analysis of the distribution of income, arguing that incomes reflect the marginal productivities of workers. This basic analytic perspective informs most government efforts to improve the skills of the poor. It also clearly illustrates the basic satisfaction of liberal and conservative analyses with the capitalist system. Leftwich concludes, "Redistribution of resources can be accomplished within the framework of the price system and the free enterprise economy."

Leftwich is a professor of economics at Oklahoma State University.

INDIVIDUAL INCOME DETERMINATION

The generally accepted principles of individual income determination and of income distribution are provided by marginal productivity theory. These principles have been met in previous chapters [of Leftwich's book], but we shall draw them together and summarize them in this section. A distinction will be made among conditions of pure competition, both in product markets and in resource markets—monopoly in product markets, and monopsony in resource markets. First we shall note certain criticisms levied against marginal productivity theory; then we shall discuss its role in the determination of individual incomes.

Criticisms of Marginal Productivity Theory

Marginal productivity theory is sometimes criticized on two counts. In the first place, some refuse to accept it because they believe it attempts to justify or approve the existing income distribution—and they do not like the existing distribution. However, observation of how a free enterprise economy does in fact distribute income in no sense consti-

SOURCE: *From Chapter 16 of* The Price System and Resource Allocation, *Third Edition, by Richard H. Leftwich. Copyright © 1955, 1960, by Richard H. Leftwich. Copyright © 1966 by Holt, Rinehart and Winston, Inc. Reprinted by permission of Holt, Rinehart and Winston, Inc.*

tutes justification or approval of that distribution. If marginal productivity principles furnish the best available explanation of income determination and income distribution in a free enterprise economy, we should understand their operations whether or not we like their results. A clear understanding of how distribution occurs necessarily precedes any intelligent modification of it.

The second criticism is more serious. Some maintain that marginal productivity is not an adequate basis for income determination and distribution theory—that there is no close correlation between the remunerations received by resource owners and the values of marginal product or the marginal revenue products of the resources which they own. If these critics are correct, and can produce the evidence substantiating their criticisms, then marginal productivity must go by the board—as must most of the rest of the marginal analysis of economic activity. To date the necessary evidence has not been forthcoming and marginal productivity continues to occupy the center of distribution theory.

Income Determination

The principles of income determination where pure competition prevails, both in product markets and in resource markets, were developed in [another] chapter. The owner of a given resource is paid a price per unit for the units employed equal to the value of marginal product of the resource. However, the price of the resource is not determined by any single employer or by any single resource owner. It is determined by the interactions of all buyers and all sellers in the market for the resource.

If for some reason the price of a resource should be less than the value of its marginal product, a shortage will occur. Employers want more of it at that price than resource owners are willing to place on the market. Employers, bidding against each other for the available supply, will drive the price up until the shortage disappears and each is hiring (or buying) that quantity of the resource at which its value of marginal product equals its price.

A price high enough to create a surplus of the resource will set forces in motion to eliminate the surplus. Employers take only those quantities sufficient to equate its value of marginal product to its price. Resource owners undercut each other's prices to secure employment for their unemployed units. As price drops, employment expands. The undercutting continues until employers are willing to take the quantities that resource owners want to place on the market.

Where some degree of monopoly[1] exists in product markets, the foregoing principles will be altered to some extent. Monopolistic firms employ those quantities of the resource at which its marginal revenue product is equal to its price. Thus the price per unit received by owners of the resource is less than its value of marginal product, and the resource is exploited monopolistically.

Some degree of monopsony in the purchase of a given resource will cause it to be paid still less than its marginal revenue product. The monopsonist, faced with a resource supply curve sloping upward to the right, employs that quantity of the resource at which its marginal revenue product is equal to its marginal resource cost. Marginal resource is greater than the price paid for the resource. Monopsonistic exploitation of the resource occurs to the extent that its marginal revenue product exceeds its price. If the resource purchaser is also a monopolist, marginal revenue product of the resource in turn will be less than its value of marginal product, and the resource will be exploited monopolistically as well as monopsonistically.

. . . [A]n individual's income per unit of time is the sum of the amounts earned per unit of time by the various resources which he owns. If he owns a single kind of resource, his income will be equal to the number of units placed in employment multiplied by the price per unit which he receives for it. If he owns several kinds of resources, the income from each can be computed in the same manner. These can be totaled to determine his entire income. . . .

CAUSES OF INCOME DIFFERENCES

With reference to the determinants of individual[2] incomes, it becomes clear that differences in incomes arise from two basic sources: (1) differences in the kinds and quantities of resources owned by different individuals, and (2) differences in prices paid in different employments for units of any given resource. The former are the more fundamental. The latter arise from various types of interference with the price system in the performance of its functions and from any resource immobility which may occur. . . .

In this section we shall consider, first, differences in kinds and quantities of labor resources owned by different individuals. Next, differences in capital resources owned will be discussed. Last, we shall examine the effects on income distribution of certain interferences with the price mechanism. [Ed.: The last section, on "interferences with the price mechanism," has been deleted for reasons of space. It makes use of the same kinds of analysis and assumptions as the first two sections.]

Differences in Labor Resources Owned

The labor classification of resources is composed of many different kinds and qualities of labor. These have one common characteristic—they are human. Any single kind of labor is a combination or complex of both inherited and acquired characteristics. The acquired part of a man's labor power is sometimes referred to as human capital; however, separation of innate ability from the results of investment in the human agent, if

---

[1] Again we use the term to refer to all cases in which the firm faces a downward sloping product demand curve. They include cases of pure monopoly, oligopoly, and monopolistic competition.

[2] The term *individual* will be used throughout the rest of the chapter to refer to a spending unit regardless of its size or composition.

we were able to accomplish it, would be of little value to us.

Labor can be subclassified horizontally and vertically into many largely separate resource groups. Vertical subclassification involves grading workers according to skill levels from the lowest kind of undifferentiated manual labor to the highest professional levels. Horizontal subclassification divides workers of a certain skill level into the various occupations requiring that particular degree of skill. An example would be the division of skilled construction workers into groups—carpenters, bricklayers, plumbers, and the like. Vertical mobility of labor refers to the possibility of moving upward through the vertical skill levels. Horizontal mobility means the ability to move sideways among groups at a particular skill level.

Horizontal differences in labor resources. At any specific horizontal level, individuals may receive different incomes because of differences in demand and supply conditions for the kinds of labor which they own. A large demand for a certain kind of labor relative to the supply of it available will make its marginal revenue product and its price high. On the same skill level, a small demand for another kind of labor relative to the supply available will make its marginal revenue product and its price low. The difference in prices tends to cause differences in incomes for owners of the two kinds of labor. Suppose, for example, that initially bricklayers and carpenters earn approximately equal incomes. A shift in consumer tastes occurs from wood construction to brick construction in residential units. The incomes of bricklayers will increase while those of carpenters will decrease because of the altered conditions of demand for them. Over a long period of time horizontal mobility between the two groups tends to decrease the income differences thus arising.

Quantitative differences in the amount of work performed by individuals owning the same kind of labor resource may lead to income differences. Some occupations afford considerable leeway for individual choice of the number of hours to be worked per week or per month. Examples include independent professional men such as physicians, lawyers, and certified public accountants, along with independent proprietors such as farmers, plumbing contractors, and garage owners. In other occupations, hours of work are beyond the control of the individual. Yet in different employments of the same resource, differences in age, physical endurance, institutional restrictions, custom, and so on, can lead to differences in hours worked and to income differences among owners of the resource.

Within a particular labor resource group, qualitative differences or differences in the abilities of the owners of the resource often create income differences. Wide variations occur in public evaluation of different dentists, or physicians, or lawyers, or automobile mechanics. Consequently, within any one group, variations in prices paid for services and in quantities of services which can be sold to the public will lead to income differences. Usually a correlation exists between the ages of the members of a resource group and their incomes. Quality tends to improve with accumulated experience. Data reported by Friedman and Kuznets suggest, for example, that incomes of physicians tend to be highest between the tenth and twenty-fifth years of practice, and incomes of lawyers tend to be highest between the twentieth and thirty-fifth years of practice.[3]

Vertical differences in labor resources. The different vertical strata themselves represent differences in labor resources owned and give rise to major labor income differences. Entry into high-level occupations such as the professions or the ranks of business executives is much more difficult than is entry into manual occupations. The relative scarcity of labor at top levels results from two basic factors. First, individuals with the physical and mental characteristics necessary for performance of high-level work are limited in number. Second, given the necessary physical and mental characteristics, many lack the opportunities for training and the necessary environment for movement into high-level positions. Thus limited vertical mobility keeps resource supplies low relative to demands for them at the top levels and it keeps resource supplies abundant relative to demands for them at the low levels.

Differences in labor resources owned because of differences in innate physical and mental characteristics of individuals are accidents of birth. The individual has nothing to

[3] Milton Friedman and Simon Kuznets, *Income from Independent Professional Practice* (New York: National Bureau of Economic Research, 1945), pp. 237–260.

do with choosing them. Nevertheless they account partly for restricted vertical mobility and for income differences. The opportunities of moving toward top positions and relatively large incomes are considerably enhanced by the inheritance of a strong physical constitution and a superior intellect; however, these by no means ensure that individuals so endowed will make the most of their opportunities.

Opportunities for training tend to be more widely available to individuals born into wealthy families than to those born into families in the lower-income groups. Some of the higher-paying professions require long and expensive university training programs —often beyond the reach of the latter groups. The medical profession is a case in point. However, the advantages that the wealthy have should not be overemphasized. Every day we see individuals who have had the initial ability, the drive, and the determination necessary to overcome economic obstacles thrown in the way of vertical mobility.

Differences in social inheritance constitute another cause of differences in labor resources owned. These will be closely correlated with differences in material inheritance. Frequently, individuals born on the wrong side of the tracks face family and community attitudes that sharply curtail their opportunities and their desires for vertical mobility. Others, more fortunately situated, acquire the training necessary to be highly productive and to obtain large incomes because it is expected of them by the social groups in which they move. Their social position alone, apart from the training induced by it, may be quite effective in facilitating vertical mobility.

Differences in Capital Resources Owned

In addition to inequalities in labor incomes, large differences occur in individual incomes from differences in capital ownership. Different individuals own varying quantities of capital—corporation or other business assets, farm land, oil wells, and property of various other forms. We shall examine the fundamental causes of inequalities in capital holdings.

Material inheritance. Differences in the amounts of capital inherited or received as gifts by different individuals create large differences in incomes. The institution of private property on which free enterprise rests usually is coupled with inheritance laws allowing large holdings of accumulated property rights to be passed on from generation to generation. The individual fortunate enough to have selected a wealthy father inherits large capital holdings, his resources contribute much to the productive process, and he is rewarded accordingly. The son of the southern sharecropper, who may be of equal innate intelligence, inherits no capital, contributes less to the productive process, and receives correspondingly a lower income.

Fortuitous circumstances. Chance, luck, or other fortuitous circumstances beyond the control of individuals constitute a further cause of differences in capital holdings. The discovery of oil, uranium, or gold on an otherwise mediocre piece of land brings about a large appreciation in its value or its ability to yield income to its owner. Unforeseen shifts in consumer demand increase the values of certain capital holdings while decreasing the values of others. National emergencies such as war lead to changes in valuations of particular kinds of property and, hence, to differential incomes from capital. Dalton cites an example of the stockholders in a concern which made mourning weeds. As the casualty lists grew during World War I, their capital holdings appreciated in value.[4] Fortuitous circumstances can work in reverse, also, but even so their effects operate to create differences in the ownership of capital.

Propensities to accumulate. Differing psychological propensities to accumulate and differing abilities to accumulate lead to differences in capital ownership among individuals. On the psychological side a number of factors influence the will to accumulate. Stories circulate of individuals determined to make a fortune before attainment of a certain age. Accumulation sometimes occurs for purposes of security and luxury in later life. It sometimes occurs from the desire to make one's children secure. The power and the prestige accompanying wealth provide the motivating force in some cases. To others, accumulation and manipulation of capital holdings is a gigantic game—the activity involved is fascinating to them. Whatever the motives, some individuals have them and others do not. In some instances the will to

[4] Hugh Dalton, *The Inequality of Incomes* (London: Routledge & Kegan Paul, Ltd., 1925), p. 273.

accumulate may be negative and the opposite of accumulation occurs.

The ability of an individual to accumulate depends largely upon his original holdings of both labor resources and capital resources. The higher the original income the easier saving and accumulation tend to be. The individual possessing much initially in the way of labor resources is likely to accumulate capital with his income from labor—he invests in stocks and bonds, real estate, a cattle ranch, or other property. Or the individual possessing substantial quantities of capital initially—and the ability to manage it—receives an income sufficient to allow saving and investment in additional capital. In the process of accumulation, labor resources and capital resources of an individual augment each other in providing the income from which further accumulation can be accomplished. . . .

A GREATER MEASURE OF EQUALITY

For various reasons—economic, ethical, and social—many people favor some mitigation of income differences. The causes of differences should furnish the clues for measures leading toward their mitigation—if movement toward greater equality is thought by society to be desirable. Thus equalizing measures may be (and are) attempted via the price system or they may be (and are) attempted through redistribution of resources among resource owners. We shall consider each of these in turn.

Via Administered Prices

Equalizing measures attempted via the price system are likely to miss their mark except in monopsonistic cases. Where competitive and monopolistic conditions prevail in product markets and where competitive conditions prevail in the purchase of a given resource, the equilibrium price of the resource tends to be equal to its value of marginal product or its marginal revenue product, as the case may be. Additionally, the resource tends to be so allocated that its price is the same in its alternative employments. Successful administered price increases are likely to result in unemployment and malallocation of the resource and this in turn contributes toward greater rather than smaller income differences. As we have observed before, administered resource prices in monopsony cases can offset monopsonistic exploitation of a resource by increasing both its price and its level of employment.

Via Redistribution of Resources

The major part of any movement toward greater income equality must consist of redistribution of resources among resource owners, since here is the major cause of income differences. Redistributive measures can take two forms: (1) redistribution of labor resources, and (2) redistribution of capital resources.

Labor resources. Labor resources can be redistributed through measures designed to increase vertical mobility. Greater vertical mobility will increase labor supplies in the top vocational levels and decrease labor supplies in the lower levels. Greater supplies at the top will decrease values of marginal product or marginal revenue products and consequently will reduce the top incomes. Smaller supplies at the lower levels will increase values of marginal product or marginal revenue products, thereby increasing incomes at the lower occupational levels. The transfers from lower to higher occupations will mitigate income differences and will increase net national product in the process.

At least three methods of increasing vertical mobility can be suggested. First, there are possibilities of providing greater equality in educational and training opportunities for capable individuals. Second, to the extent that differences in capital ownership are reduced, greater equality in the economic opportunities for development of high-grade labor resources will tend to occur. Third, measures may be taken to reduce those barriers to entry established by associations of resource owners in many skilled occupations.[5]

Measures to increase horizontal mobility also can serve to decrease income differences. These include the operation of employment exchanges, perhaps some subsidization of movement, vocational guidance, adult education and retraining programs, and other mea-

[5] An example of such a barrier is provided by the professional association which controls licensing standards when prospective entrants must be licensed in order to practice the profession.

sures of a similar nature. The argument here is really one for better allocation of labor resources, both among alternative jobs within a given labor resource category, and among the labor resource categories themselves. Greater horizontal mobility, as well as greater vertical mobility, will increase net national product at the same time that it decreases income differences.

Capital resources. Redistribution of capital resources meets considerable opposition in a free enterprise economy. Many vociferous advocates of movement toward greater income equality will protest vigorously measures designed to redistribute capital ownership—and these are the measures which will contribute most toward that objective. The opposition centers around the rights of private property ownership and stems from a strong presumption that the right to own property includes the right to accumulate it and to pass it on to one's heirs.

Nevertheless, if income differences are to be mitigated, some means of providing greater equality in capital accumulation and capital holdings among individuals must be employed. The economy's system of taxation may move in this direction. In the United States, for example, the personal income tax, the capital gains tax, and estate and gift taxes—both federal and state—already operate in an equalizing manner.

The personal income tax by its progressive nature serves to reduce income differences directly and in so doing it reduces differences in abilities to accumulate capital. But the personal income tax alone cannot be expected to eliminate those differences without seriously impairing incentives for efficient employment of resources and for reallocation of resources from less productive to more productive employments.

The capital gains tax constitutes either a loophole for escaping a part of the personal income tax, or a plug for a loophole in the personal income tax, depending upon one's definition of income. The capital gains tax is applied to realized appreciation and depreciation in the value of capital assets. Those who can convert a part of their income from capital resources into the form of capital gains have that part of their remuneration taxed as capital gains at a rate ordinarily below the personal income tax rate. For them the capital gains tax provides a loophole through which personal income taxes can be escaped. On the other hand, if certain capital gains would escape taxation altogether under the personal income tax, but are covered by the capital gains tax, the latter can be considered a supplement to the personal income tax. In either case the capital gains tax allows some remuneration from capital resources to be taxed at rates below the personal income tax rates and, if differences in opportunities to accumulate capital are to be mitigated, it must be revised to prevent individuals from taking undue advantage of its lower rates.

Estate and gift taxes will play the major roles in any tax system designed to reduce differences in capital ownership. The estate taxes in such a system would border on the confiscatory side above some maximum amount in order to prevent the transmission of accumulated capital resources from generation to generation. Gift taxes would operate largely to plug estate tax loopholes. They would be designed to prevent transmission of estates by means of gifts from the original owner to heirs prior to the death of the original owner.

Redistribution and the price system. Redistribution of labor resource and capital resource holdings can be accomplished within the framework of the price system and the free enterprise economic system if movement toward greater income equality is thought by society to be desirable. Redistribution measures such as those sketched out above need not seriously affect the operation of the price mechanism. In fact, the price mechanism can act as a positive force assisting the measures to reach the desired objectives. Some of the fundamental measures—educational opportunities, progressive income taxes, gift and estate taxes—are already in existence, although their effectiveness could be increased greatly. Redistribution measures can be thought of as rules of the free enterprise game—along with a stable monetary system, monopoly control measures, and other rules of economic conduct.

SUMMARY

Individual claims to net national product depend upon individual incomes; thus, the theory of product distribution is really the theory of income distribution. Marginal productivity theory provides the generally accepted principles of income determination and income distribution. Resource owners tend to be remunerated according to the marginal revenue products of the resources which they own except in cases where resources are purchased monopsonistically.

Incomes are unequally distributed among spending units in the United States. Income differences stem from three basic sources: (1) differences in labor resources owned, (2) differences in capital resources owned, and (3) restrictions placed on the operation of the price mechanism. With regard to labor resources, different individuals own different kinds of labor at the same general skill level. These we call horizontal differences in labor resources. Different individuals also own different kinds of labor graded vertically from undifferentiated manual labor to the top-level professions. Differences in capital resources owned result from differences in material inheritance, fortuitous circumstances, and differences in propensities to accumulate. Administered prices for a given resource often lead to unemployment or malallocation of some units of the resource and hence to differences in incomes among owners of the resource. The case of monopsony provides an exception. Under monopsony, administered resource prices can offset monopsonistic exploitation of the resources involved.

Attacks on income differences, if society desires to mitigate those differences, should be made by way of redistribution of resources among resource owners. Attacks made by way of administered prices are not likely to accomplish the task. Redistribution of labor resources can be accomplished through measures designed to increase both horizontal and vertical mobility. These will in turn increase net national product. The tax system offers the means of effecting redistribution of capital resources. Estate and gift taxes will bear the major burden of redistribution and should be supplemented by adequate personal income and capital gains taxes. Redistribution of resources can be accomplished within the framework of the price system and the free enterprise economy.

POVERTY AND HUMAN CAPITAL

Lester C. Thurow

This selection is taken from Thurow's recent book *Poverty and Discrimination.* Thurow applies the general analytic perspective of orthodox economics to the problems of this chapter. He argues that incomes reflect marginal productivities (or "human capital" invested in workers). He outlines the separate components of productivity and assesses the relative importance of each component in effecting low incomes among disadvantaged workers in this country.

The selection is taken from Chapter Five of Thurow's book. It excludes a very technical empirical section in which Thurow applies the theoretical concepts discussed in the first part of the chapter. His section on "Implications" is based on those excluded empirical results.

Thurow is a professor of economics at Massachusetts Institute of Technology.

Human capital (the skills and knowledge of the individual) is one of the key determinants of the distribution of income. In-

SOURCE: *Lester C. Thurow,* Poverty and Discrimination. *Copyright © 1969 by The Brookings Institution, 1775 Massachusetts Avenue, N.W., Washington, D.C. 20036.*

dividuals with little education, training, and skills have low marginal productivities and earn low incomes. With very little human capital, they earn poverty incomes. Blacks who have less capital than whites earn less.

This being the case, more investment in human capital should help increase incomes.

What might be called the productivity approach to the elimination of poverty and low Negro income is thus aimed at improving the quantity and distribution of human capital.[1] As a first step, the factors which create human capital need to be more clearly defined and quantified. To make the concept of human capital operational, it is necessary to specify the factors which cause increases in income and thus in human capital.

INCOME, EDUCATION, AND EXPERIENCE

With education serving as a proxy for human capital, the skeleton of the problem is revealed in Figure 1. The distribution of income is much more diffuse than that of education. There are many more people with low incomes than with low educational attainment. If the distribution of education determined the distribution of income, there should be a greater number of individuals concentrated in the center of the income range. Other factors such as the distribution of intelligence, energy, or health may affect income distribution, but the figure shows that the same problem exists with respect to intelligence (IQ): the distribution of income is again less concentrated. The large number of people in the lower tail of the income distribution cannot be explained by the distribution either of education or of intelligence, except in terms of a most peculiar cross-distribution.[2] The elderly and disabled can

[1] Because of the many noneconomic benefits of education, the investment or human capital approach should not dominate either private or social planning for education and training. The human capital approach is justified, however, when education and training are being narrowly evaluated as instruments for improving the distribution of income. Here the only aim is to change income flows. Actual evaluations of education programs must consider benefits other than changes in the income distribution, but such benefits are beyond the sphere of interest of this book.
[2] Some people would have to be poor because of low intelligence and other people because of low education levels. If there were no overlap between the bottom parts of the intelligence and education distributions, there could be two independent causes of poverty to be added together. This still would not produce enough people in the bottom of the income distribution, but it is a step in the right direction. For this to be true, however, those with little education would have to be those with higher IQs; this is contrary to the usual assumption that those with the highest IQ have the most education. Education may also be a substitute for

explain part; and interrelationships between intelligence and education can explain why there are some with very high incomes and others with very low ones. However, to isolate the factors which determine the distribution of income, it is necessary to go beyond the distribution of education or intelligence.

In practice, observed income flows are used to measure indirectly the value of an individual's human capital. People with higher incomes are assumed to have more capital. Consequently, the distribution of capital determines the distribution of earnings. Since this explanation is true by definition, it does not provide much insight into the causes of the distribution of earnings. The factors which create human capital still must be specified.

One procedure is to isolate all of the factors which cause differences in observed earnings and call them human capital. Another procedure is to narrow the definition, with only some of the factors termed human capital. The problem then is to determine the amount of the observed changes caused by these factors.

In this book, the narrow definition is used: human capital is acquired through formal education and on-the-job experience. The latter covers a wide range of activities; a major part of its value comes from formal and informal training programs. Another part comes from general knowledge of how a particular business is run: where and when to report; what to do in case of emergency; familiarity with a particular group of jobs. All of these are factors that lead to higher productivities and are part of a man's total capital of skills and knowledge.

The value of human capital can be divided into price and quantity components. Education and on-the-job experience provide the principal means for increasing the quantity or quality of an individual's capital. Migration, improvements in information, and the elimination of market imperfections, such as prejudice, are the chief instruments to raise the price for existing capital. Although the price factor would not exist in perfect markets where all were paid equal amounts for the use of identical skills, in imperfect markets it is an important element in valuing human capital.

IQ, but this hypothesis would lead to a more nearly equal income distribution than that given by the distribution of either IQ or education.

FIGURE I
DISTRIBUTION OF INCOME, EDUCATION, AND INTELLIGENCE (IQ) OF MALES TWENTY-FIVE YEARS OF AGE AND OVER IN 1965

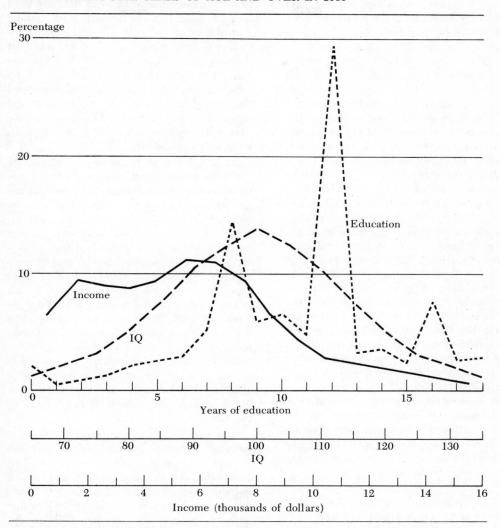

SOURCES: Income data from U.S. Bureau of the Census, *Current Population Reports,* Series P-60, No. 51 "Income in 1965 of Families and Persons in the United States" (1967), p. 34; education data estimated from U.S. Bureau of the Census, *Statistical Abstract of the United States: 1967,* p. 113; IQ data from David Wechsler, *Wechsler Adult Intelligence Scale Manual* (Psychological Corp., 1955), p. 20.

While price and quantity effects are theoretically distinguishable, in practice the distinction is blurred by using observed income flows as an indirect measure. Price and quantity effects are lumped together as changes in value. In most cases this is not a serious problem, since both the individual and society are interested in raising the value of human capital. Real investment is usually necessary to alter either price or quantity. The basic problem is finding that investment which will earn the greatest return. It may be one to increase the quantity or one to raise the price.

The use of income flows as a gauge requires that efforts to measure the specific effects of one factor must make explicit allowance for the impacts of all other factors. For example, since innate ability (whatever it is and however it is measured) and education levels are probably linked, each of them contributes to the incomes associated with higher levels of education. If some correction is not made for ability, observed income flows will overstate the actual returns to education.

Similarly, since on-the-job training and education are associated,[3] the returns to more education will be overstated if the effects of training are not considered; and since training programs have associated costs as well as benefits, the error is compounded in calculations of net returns to education. The benefits from training are included in the returns, but the costs have not been added to the education costs. In the case of ability, clearly there are no associated costs to be deducted.

Various efforts have been made to separate the returns to education from results attributable to ability.[4] Less effort has been made to solve the problems presented by on-the-job training, which is not surprising. Practically no direct information is available on either its amount or its costs. The informal aspects of much of the training mean that there is no practical method of obtaining direct information. A great deal of it is acquired in the course of work and does not result from deliberate programs. Costs are involved, but they are difficult to estimate.

The problem presented by on-the-job experience goes beyond that presented by ability in another way. Since by definition innate ability cannot be altered, society and individuals want to know the returns to increasing education, a variable which can be altered. On-the-job experience and training also can be altered. It is important to know what *combination* of education and training yields the greatest net return.

COMPLEMENTARITIES BETWEEN EDUCATION AND EXPERIENCE

The standard technique for isolating the returns to any one factor, such as education,

[3] According to Jacob Mincer, on-the-job training in 1958 accounted for 54 percent of the total training costs of those with a college education, 46 percent for those with a high school education, and 69 percent for those with an elementary education. "On-the-Job Training: Costs, Returns, and Some Implications" (paper presented before the Exploratory Conference on Capital Investment in Human Beings, New York City, Dec. 1–2, 1961, sponsored by the Universities-National Bureau Committee for Economic Research), *Journal of Political Economy,* Vol. 70 (October 1962: Supplement), p. 55.
[4] See Giora Hanoch, "An Economic Analysis of Earnings and Schooling," *Journal of Human Resources,* Vol. 2 (Summer 1967), pp. 310–29.

has been to hold all other explanatory factors constant and to note the remaining differences in observed income flows. Either regression techniques or detailed data are used to hold those factors constant. Both assume that the effect of each of the explanatory factors is independent of all others and that their separate effects are additive. Thus, the amount of experience is assumed to have no influence on the returns to education, and the returns to increasing both education and experience are assumed to be equal to the sum of the separate returns to increasing each variable independently.

In fact, however, many of the explanatory variables which affect income flows are not independent but complementary. Returns are not additive but multiplicative. This may be clearly seen in on-the-job experience and education. The returns from experience depend partially on the trainee's level of formal education. Low education levels make some types of training impossible and other types expensive, but as the levels rise, training costs fall and the variety of training which can be given expands. These complementarities also work in the opposite direction. Most jobs require some knowledge which is peculiar to the job and is not or cannot be acquired in school. Without this experience, education is of little value. Education and experience combined yield larger benefits than the sum of the two.

The same kinds of complementarities can be seen between human capital and the amount of physical capital used by a worker. Education and training are of little value without physical capital with which to work, but physical capital is also of little value without the necessary human skills to operate it efficiently. Most training is designed to teach labor to operate some piece of mechanical equipment. Thus the returns to either physical capital or training depend on the quality of the other.

There are two main sources of complementarities. Those that are technological occur when the skills and knowledge acquired in school are complementary to those acquired in training. Price complementarities occur when market imperfections are reduced in the process of acquiring education and training: a black might receive a larger income if higher levels of education and training allowed him to move into occupations where less discrimination existed.

The degree of complementarity differs. In some jobs there is little; in others, education and training are rigidly linked together. A priori reasoning leads to the conclusion that complementarities are important, and the data presented below confirm this conclusion.

Ignoring complementarities leads to biased estimates of the returns to increasing education. Holding training levels constant while observing the returns to education may provide a valid estimate of the returns within each training level, but it provides a distorted view of the general returns, part of which arises from shifting training levels as well as from moving up the income ladder within each level. To estimate the returns while holding the level of training constant is to seriously underestimate the actual returns to education.[5]

Individuals receive formal and informal training while they are at work. The effect of one year of work experience on the value of an individual's human capital varies according to the amount of training received or the impact of work experience on the price of existing capital. While one year of work yields everyone one year of experience, the returns from that experience—the income flows produced by it—may be very different. If observed income flows are higher, the value of human capital has increased, as a result of increases either in the quantity of human capital or its price. If there are no price effects, income flows depend on the amount of skills and knowledge received. Thus the returns to a year of work experience can be used as a surrogate variable to measure the returns to investment in on-the-job training. If labor training markets are in equilibrium, the rates of return on training will be equal for all formal and informal training projects; in this case different returns to experience would reflect different amounts of investment in on-the-job training, since equal investments would earn equal returns. If labor training markets are not in equilibrium this will not be true, but the returns to experience still indicate the pattern of gross benefits from training. The function simply measures the gross returns to a year of work experience. . . .

[5] This is equivalent to holding occupations constant while studying the returns to education. Many of the returns occur by moving across occupations rather than within occupations.

IMPLICATIONS

Private decisions will not lead to the socially desired distribution of human capital. Since an optimal income distribution does not exist, the purchases of human capital must be less than optimal. If the market for human capital is imperfect and there are social benefits from human capital investment, the distortions are even larger. Imperfect knowledge, a less than optimal income distribution, and imperfections in the capital lending markets all lead to private investment decisions that result in an ever widening distribution of human capital. If public investment in human capital is shortchanging the poor and the racial minorities, the problem is simply compounded. If equalizing the Negro and white income distributions and eliminating the lower tail of the income distribution are important, the distribution of investment in human capital must be altered by public policies.

As will be pointed out in the next chapter, education and on-the-job experience do not completely explain the distribution of earnings, but they are important ingredients. These two factors explain a major proportion of observed income flows. Although the problems of poverty and low Negro incomes cannot be solved by programs to alter either the quantity, quality, or price of human capital, they can be significantly reduced by such programs.

The existence of strong complementarities means that the returns from programs designed to improve education, on-the-job experience, or shift coefficients* are heavily dependent on what is happening simultaneously to each of the other variables. Increasing education will have little effect on incomes if individuals work in areas with low shift coefficients and little training. Conversely, education will have a large impact

* [Ed.: In Thurow's empirical equation for estimating the returns to education and labor force experience, the "shift coefficient" was included to measure the other characteristics of a job which tended to affect the returns to those two components of human capital. If two workers with equal amounts of education and experience worked in jobs with unequal amounts of physical capital, the worker with more physical capital around him would probably get a higher return to his "human capital." The shift coefficient measures that phenomenon; those with higher shift coefficients work in situations, for instance, with more physical capital.]

on incomes if the individuals work in areas with ample training and high shift coefficients. The same complementarities affect the returns to programs designed to alter either experience or shift coefficients. If the other factors are unchanged, the returns to any one program will be very low. This means that education programs, training programs, and efforts to move individuals into areas with high shift coefficients must be coordinated. The combination of policies which will produce the greatest income changes at the least cost cannot be determined abstractly. The present positions of the individuals to be aided must be determined. Only then can the marginal benefits and costs be determined.

Given the general characteristics of the poor, large returns could be earned by remedial programs designed to raise everyone in the labor force to at least eighth grade standards of literacy. The social benefits from such a program are large, but from a narrow economic point of view also, the benefits are also large. The marginal income flows from raising education levels in this range are great and the complementarities with on-the-job experience programs are very important. Without this level of education, training has little payoff. Unless an individual possesses an eighth grade literacy standard, he is under a very severe competitive handicap, and as general education levels rise this handicap will grow. Since most individuals in this low range are beyond the normal school age, efforts to bring the working population up to this standard must focus on adult education programs. This is precisely the area where the least effort has been made in educational programs for the poor. Concentrating on children might eliminate poverty in the long run, but the long run is intolerably long. Something must be done for those who are going to be in the labor force for the next thirty years.

For Negroes, however, the principal need is for more on-the-job experience. It is true that education plays a vital role in eliminating the differences between the income distributions for whites and Negroes. Negroes receive less education, and part of the observed differences in the economic returns to education for Negroes is caused by differences in the quality of the education that is provided. Nevertheless, a large fraction of the difference between white and black incomes is explained by differences in the returns to on-the-job experience, from which blacks receive much less value. . . . Unless this defect can be corrected, education programs will have little impact on the incomes of blacks in the United States.

THE DUAL LABOR MARKET: THEORY AND IMPLICATIONS

Michael Piore

Piore discusses the importance of understanding segmentations in the labor market. Although not intended as part of the more general radical analysis, Piore's selection clearly illustrates some of the important economic forces postulated by that analysis as determinants of labor market stratification. Like more radical writers, Piore argues that the stratifications pose almost insurmountable barriers to individual movements between sectors. He differs with orthodox analysis in arguing that workers' income and status do not reflect their productivity in uniform ways throughout the economy; at least in the "secondary" market, incomes bear little relationship to productivity.

SOURCE: *Reprinted from Michael J. Piore, "Jobs and Training," in Beer, Barringer, eds., The State* and the Poor, *by permission of the publisher. Copyright © 1970 by Winthrop Publishers, Inc.*

The selection comes from a longer paper originally written for a faculty seminar sponsored by the Kennedy School of Government at Harvard University. The papers were later reprinted in a book edited by Beer and Barringer, *The State and the Poor*. The rest of Piore's essay applies his general comments here to some local labor markets in Massachusetts.

Piore is an associate professor of economics at Massachusetts Institute of Technology. With Peter Doeringer, he has written *Internal Labor Markets and Manpower Analysis*.

The central tenet of the analysis [in Piore's paper] is that the role of employment and of the disposition of manpower in the perpetuation of poverty is best understood in terms of a dual labor market. One sector of that market, which I have termed elsewhere the primary market,[1] offers jobs which possess several of the following traits: high wages, good working conditions, employment stability and job security, equity and due process in the administration of work rules, and chances for advancement. The other, or secondary sector, has jobs which, relative to those in the primary sector, are decidedly less attractive. They tend to involve low wages, poor working conditions, considerable variability in employment, harsh and often arbitrary discipline, and little opportunity to advance. The poor are confined to the secondary labor market. The elimination of poverty requires that they gain access to primary employment.

The factors which generate the dual market structure and confine the poor to the secondary sector are complex. At some injustice to that complexity, they may be summarized as follows: First, the most important characteristic distinguishing jobs in the primary sector from those in the secondary sector appears to be the behavioral requirements which they impose upon the work force, particularly that of employment stability. Insofar as secondary workers are barred from primary jobs by real qualifications, it is generally their inability to show up for work regularly and on time. Secondary employers are far more tolerant of lateness and absenteeism, and many secondary jobs are of such short duration that these do not matter. Work skills, which receive considerable emphasis in most discussions of poverty and employ-

ment, do not appear a major barrier to primary employment (although, because regularity and punctuality are important to successful learning in school and on the job, such behavioral traits tend to be highly correlated with skills).

Second, certain workers who possess the behavioral traits required to operate efficiently in primary jobs are trapped in the secondary market because their superficial characteristics resemble those of secondary workers. This occurs because employment decisions are generally made on the basis of a few readily (and hence inexpensively) assessed traits such as race, demeanor, accent, educational attainment, test scores, and the like. Such traits tend to be statistically correlated with job performance but not necessarily (and probably not usually) causally related to it. Hence, a number of candidates who are rejected because they do not possess these traits are actually qualified for the job. Exclusion on this basis may be termed *statistical discrimination*. In addition to statistical discrimination, workers are also excluded from primary employment by discrimination *pure and simple*.

Discrimination of any kind enlarges the captive labor force in the secondary sector, and thus lowers the wages which secondary employers must pay to fill their jobs. This gives to such employers an economic stake in its perpetuation. Since it limits the supply of labor in the primary sector and raises the wages of workers who have access to jobs there, primary workers also have a stake in discrimination. Discrimination pure and simple is not generally of economic value to primary employers since it forces them to pay higher wages without obtaining corresponding economic gains. In statistical discrimination, however, the higher wages are compensated by the reduced cost of screening job candidates, and the interest of secondary employers and primary workers in

[1] See Michael J. Piore, "Public and Private Responsibilities in On-The-Job Training of Disadvantaged Workers," Massachusetts Institute of Technology, Department of Economics Working Paper No. 23, June 1968.

such discrimination is shared by primary employers as well.

Third, the distinction between primary and secondary jobs is not, apparently, technologically determinate. A portion—perhaps a substantial proportion—of the work in the economy can be organized for either stable or unstable workers. Work normally performed in the primary sector is sometimes shifted to the secondary sector through subcontracting, temporary help services, recycling of new employees through probationary periods and the like. Nor is the primary-secondary distinction necessarily associated with a given enterprise. Some enterprises, most of whose jobs possess the character of primary employment and are filled with stable, committed workers, have subsections or departments with inferior job opportunities accommodated to an unstable work force. Secondary employers generally have a few, and some have a large number, of primary jobs. Nonetheless, despite a certain degree of elasticity in the distribution of work between the primary and secondary sectors, shifts in the distribution generally involve changes in the techniques of production and management and in the institutional structure and procedures of the enterprises in which the work is performed. The investment necessary to effect these changes acts to strengthen resistance to anti-poverty efforts.

Fourth, the behavioral traits associated with the secondary sector are reinforced by the process of working in secondary jobs and living among others whose life-style is accommodated to that type of employment. Hence, even individuals who are forced into the secondary sector initially by discrimination tend, over time, to develop the traits predominant among secondary workers. Thus, for example, by working in a world where employment is intermittent and erratic, one tends to lose habits of regularity and punctuality. Similarly, when reward and punishment in the work place are continually based upon personal relationships between worker and supervisor, workers forget how to operate within the impersonal, institutional grievance procedures of the primary sector and when they do gain access to primary jobs, are frustrated by the failure of the system to respond on a personal basis and their own inability to make it respond on an institutional basis.

Finally, income sources alternative to employment among the poor, especially public assistance and illicit activity, tend to be more compatible with secondary than with primary employment. The public assistance system discourages full-time work, and forces those on welfare into jobs which are either part time or which pay income in cash which will not be reported to the social worker or can be quickly dropped or delayed when the social worker discovers them or seems in danger of doing so. The relationship between social worker and client builds upon the personal relationship which operates in the secondary sector rather than the institutional mechanisms which tend to operate in the primary sector. Illegitimate activity also tends to follow the intermittent work pattern prevalent in secondary employment, and the attractions of such activity, as well as life patterns and role models it presents to those not themselves involved but associating with people who are, foster behavioral traits antagonistic to primary employment.

The central implications of the dual market interpretations of poverty are that the poor do participate in the economy; that it is the manner of their participation, not the question of participation per se, which constitutes the manpower problem of the poor; and that their current mode of participation is ultimately a response to a series of pressures—economic, social, and technical—playing upon individuals and labor market institutions. This suggests that a distinction can be drawn between policies designed to alleviate the pressures which generate the dual market structure in the first place, and those which attempt to attack the problem by moving individuals from secondary to primary employment directly. The latter policies operate against the prevailing pressures but leave the forces which generate them intact. The next section of the paper draws heavily upon this distinction. The thrust of the argument in that section is that, in concentrating upon training, counseling, and placement services for the poor, manpower policy has overemphasized direct approaches and that more weight should be placed upon policies which affect the environment in which employment decisions are made and the pressures which it generates. Among such policies, we include anti-discrimination policy, occupational licensing reform, the structure of public assistance, and the legal distinctions between legitimate and illegitimate activity. [Ed.: This section has not been included.]

A further implication to be drawn from the analysis of the dual labor market is that, because the poor do participate in the economy, there are certain groups interested in that participation and the way in which it occurs. Policies directed at the movement of the poor out of the secondary market and into primary employment work against the interests of these groups and, for that reason, are in danger of being subverted by them. This is one of the major reasons for concentrating upon indirect approaches, for these are not susceptible to the same kind of subversion and in fact, because they alleviate the pressures generating the dual market structure, they reduce the resistance to policies that move directly against that structure. The dangers to which existing institutions subject programs designed to move the poor directly out of the secondary market are twofold: The new institutions created by these programs can be rejected by the prevailing economic system and isolated off to one side. A program, for example, would then recruit workers into training which provides skills little utilized in either the secondary or the primary market. Alternatively, the new institutions may be captured by the prevailing economic system and used to facilitate its operation. Examples of programs subverted in this way are the neighborhood employment offices which recruit secondary workers for secondary jobs, and training provided in primary employment to workers who would have gotten it anyway in establishments that otherwise would have financed it themselves. The central problem in the design of direct approaches to manpower programs is to organize them in such a way that they can resist this twofold threat of rejection, on the one hand, and capture, on the other. . . .

While these conclusions follow directly from the dual market interpretation of the poverty problem, they are not uniquely dependent upon it. The dual labor market is one of a class of theoretical constructs which views poverty in the United States in terms of a dichotomy in the economic and social structure. Such a dichotomy is implicit in the concept of a "culture of poverty" and in the expression of public policy goals associated with poverty in terms of an income cut off. Most such views of poverty entertain the idea that the dichotomy is a product of forces endogenous to the economy (or, more broadly, the society as a whole).[2] It follows that attempts to eliminate poverty will tend to run counter to the natural operation of the economy; that they will be resisted by existing institutions and are in jeopardy of rejection. To say all this is perhaps to say little more than that, if poverty were easy to eliminate, it woudn't be around in the first place. But it does, at least, point to the task of equipping the institution which works with the poor to withstand the rejection pressures as a central problem in the program design.

What the dual labor market interpretation implies which is not implicit in dichotomous interpretations in general is that the poor are not only separated from the non-poor in the negative sense of exclusion from activities and institutions to which the non-poor have access, they are also separated from the non-poor in the positive sense that they have economic value where they are and hence that there are groups interested, not only in resisting the elimination of poverty, but in actively seeking its perpetuation. It is this which makes new institutions created to work with the poor in the labor market subject to the threat of capture as well as the threat of rejection.

The major alternative to the dual labor market interpretation as a foundation for manpower policy is one that associates poverty with either the inability to find work or with full-time work at low wages. This interpretation of poverty would emphasize the high incidence of unemployment among the poor and their relatively low rates of labor force participation, on the one hand, and the number of people employed full time, full year at low-paying jobs, on the other. It should be noted that many upon whom this interpretation focuses attention, but the dual labor market emphasis ignores, are incapable of productive employment in any realistic sense and, hence, their poverty is beyond reach of manpower policy. This group includes, for example, large numbers of aged; people with serious physical handicaps; major mental and emotional disorders;

[2] The alternative to this view is one in which poverty is defined in relation to a continuum: there is no great chasm to bridge and a marginal movement of individuals within the existing system will meet the public policy objective.

and small children in families headed by these individuals. A small proportion of the people in these groups can be helped to work: there is a series of programs designed to do this; we did not investigate them. The dual market interpretation implies that much of the remainder of what appears statistically to be an unemployment problem results from the attempt to classify and interpret the experience of the secondary market in a set of statistical categories derived from a model of the primary labor market. Thus, for example, measured unemployment and labor force participation rates in poor neighborhoods are distorted by numbers of individuals who are frictionally unemployed because of the instability of jobs, unwilling to work continuous five-day weeks, working illegal or quasi-illegal jobs, supported by family members not classified as such by the survey, and the like. The second group of poor which the dual labor market interpretation tends to slight (the full-time, full-year, but low-wage workers) could not be separately identified for Massachusetts. This number is large nationally, but, we would like to argue, probably concentrated in the South and in rural areas.

The dual labor market provides quite a convincing interpretation of the realities of the black urban ghetto labor markets. The combination of high measured unemployment rates and bitter complaints of narrow employment opportunity, on the one hand, with high turnover rates and persistent employer complaints of labor shortage cannot be reconciled with a conventional unemployment interpretation but are readily comprehended with a two-sector model in which the sectors are distinguished by the relative stability of jobs and workers. Such a model is also consistent with autobiographical and sociological descriptions of urban ghetto life. In Massachusetts, it certainly constitutes an accurate diagnosis of black and Puerto Rican poverty in the city of Boston. How far beyond these ghetto communities the applicability of the model extends is a moot question. Some attempt to assess its limits was made for the present study. Within Boston, it was generally felt by those working in manpower programs that the model is somewhat less applicable to the white ethnic poor than to the black poor. It appears that a larger proportion of the white ethnic poor are simply locked into low-wage jobs which do not possess the combination of debilitating characteristics typical of low-paying black employment. On the other hand, many of these ethnic white workers do not think of themselves as poor and resent efforts to treat them as such.

THE DYNAMICS OF THE DUAL LABOR MARKET

Harold M. Baron and Bennett Hymer

This selection discusses the institutional "specification" of labor market segmentation in a local community. Like Piore's preceding piece, it illustrates the radical argument that basic economic institutions have effected important separations among sectors in the economy. Whereas Piore writes of "primary" and "secondary" markets, Baron and Hymer postulate white and black sectors. Their intentions are the same, nonetheless, for each article criticizes the simplistic view of orthodox analysis and its abstractions from the determinant effects of institutions.

The selection comes from a long article called "The Negro Worker in the

SOURCE: From "The Negro Worker in the Chicago Labor Movement" by Harold M. Baron and Bennett Hymer, as included in the book The Negro and the American Labor Movement edited by Julius Jacobson. Copyright © 1968 by Julius Jacobson. Reprinted by permission of Doubleday & Company, Inc.

Chicago Labor Market." A section on "De Facto Barriers" has been deleted from this discussion; it details the effect of extra-labor market institutions on the preservation of the dual labor market structure.

The authors are both members of the Research Department of the Chicago Urban League. Baron is director of that department.

The types of disparities between white and Negro workers which were described in the first part of the paper have been permanent features of the Chicago labor market since World War I. Prior to the war Chicago had only a small Negro population, largely employed in menial- and personal-service-type occupations. During a tight wartime labor market, aggravated by the cessation of European immigration, many employers began to recruit Negro labor from the South to fill manpower shortages. It was at this point of time that Negroes formed a sizable and distinct ethnic group in the Chicago labor force.

For the majority of Negroes coming to Chicago from the South, their point of entry into the labor market was at the bottom of the occupational hierarchy. Both rural work backgrounds and the emergence of discriminatory policies prevented their movement into higher-skilled and better-paying occupations. Soon after, the racial occupation lines that were emerging became permanently frozen.

Since 1920 there has been only a small change in the status of the Negro worker relative to that of the white worker. While both groups have improved their employment conditions—higher wages, more leisure—Negroes have not been able to catch up and close the gaps in income, occupation, and training. A comparison between Negro and white immigrants to the city further illustrates the inability of the Negro worker to eliminate these disparities. White immigrants in one or two generations were able to disperse throughout society and the economy of the Northern city. Negroes, on the other hand, one hundred years after emancipation and following almost three generations of intensive migration to the North, are still confined to certain sectors of the labor market.

A constantly increasing proportion of the Negro population in Chicago has been born and reared in the North. If Negroes operated only under the same handicaps that European immigrants did, we would expect to find a closing of the gap as the percentage of second and third generations of Northern Negroes increased. Instead, we find that the disparities have become fixed features of the overall socioeconomic structure. Neither urbanization nor substantial increases in the level of Negro educational attainment have eradicated the disparities in income and occupations between whites and Negroes. In other words, just as the large city has confined Negroes to residential ghettos and segregated schools, so has it locked them into definite (and inferior) sectors of the labor market.

To date, no satisfactory explanation has been offered for the perpetuation of Negroes' second-class status in the Northern city. Instead, comprehension of the Negro worker's position in the Northern labor market has been obscured by the myths inherited from America's racial history. In accounting for the Negro's status in the Northern city, Americans have substituted a continuation of Southern economic folklore for fact. Explanations tend to be deduction from myths instead of cold analysis of the urban status quo. . . .

The racial folklore of the Negro worker's experience in the Northern labor market can now be replaced with a more sophisticated analysis. By utilizing recent findings in the study of Northern race relations and urban labor markets, the disparities between white and Negro workers can be related to institutional factors within the large urban labor market—the existence of barriers that divide the labor market into distinct compartments based upon race.

For expository purposes a blueprint of the typical Northern labor market will be drawn. Although the main point of reference is Chicago, the model is highly applicable to other urban labor markets having a sizable Negro labor force. Basically, the blueprint consists of three generalizations describing the way in which the Chicago labor market generates differences based upon race. These generalizations are:

1. The labor market is divided into two racial components—a sector for the deployment of white labor and a sector for the deployment of Negro labor. Each sector has its own separate institutions and mechanisms for the recruitment, training, and allocation of jobs and workers. Firms are cognizant of this division and have different perceptions of the two labor forces when they shop for labor.

2. The Negro labor force has served as a pool of surplus labor used to fill shortages of white labor that occur during war years or periods of rapid economic growth. A large segment of the Negro labor force has been frozen into positions that are regarded as traditionally Negro jobs. These jobs are usually marginal and low paying; they require little skill or formal training; they often involve physical hazards; they frequently offer only seasonal or cyclical employment; and they are frequently in stagnant or declining industries.

3. Northern *de facto* segregation, in general, is maintained by a complex of interrelated and mutually supportive institutions whose combined effect is greater than the sum of the effects of each institution considered singularly. The racial distinctions and differentiations created in any one institutional area operate as effective barriers supporting the segregation and status differentiation that occurs in other institutions. The division of the labor market into a Negro sector and a white sector is made more effective by the existence of the barriers in non-labor-market institutions. These barriers feed back to limit the Negro worker's access in many areas of the labor market.

RACIAL DUALISM IN THE URBAN LABOR MARKET

The racially dual labor markets found in Northern cities have their origins in the earlier system of Southern slavery and rural peonage.[1] However, if the Negro's subordi-nate position in the North were merely a historical atavism from his Southern past, it would be expected that race would lose its significance as a social and economic category with the passage of time. Instead, we find that the Negro's second-class status has been effectively institutionalized in the Northern city—far removed from Southern rural conditions.

The marked and systematic disparities that exist between whites and Negroes in regard to income, employment, occupation, and labor-force participation offer *prima facie* evidence that a dual racial labor market exists. The two distinct and enduring patterns of employment characteristics that have been described cannot be explained in terms of a single homogeneous market. The description of these disparities, however, documents the dualism at only a general level of observation.

In more specific terms, a racially dual labor market means that there exists a primary metropolitan labor market in which firms recruit white workers and in which white workers look for jobs; side by side with the major market, there exists a smaller labor sector in which Negroes are recruited and in which Negroes look for employment.[2] For each sector there are separate demand and supply forces determining the allocation of jobs to workers and workers to jobs. Over time, this dualism is characterized by a transfer of jobs from the white sector to the Negro sector as the economy develops and as the Negro labor force expands in absolute and relative numbers.[3]

To understand the perpetuation of the Negro's second-class status, it is necessary to examine the mechanisms by which the labor market and in a broader sense the general socioeconomic structure have distributed jobs between whites and Negroes. The conception of a division of the labor market along

[1] Both these systems can be considered as forms of social and economic segregation, which made possible the exploitation of the Negro labor force by the Southern landed ruling class. The division of the labor force also enabled many Southern manufacturers to practice wage discrimination, i.e. to pay Negroes less than whites for similar work and to pay Southern whites lower wages than Northern whites.

[2] In the Chicago area Negro workers comprise one seventh of the total labor force.

[3] It should be noted that the generalization concerning the dual labor market is made at a high level of abstraction and that there are obvious exceptions at the level of particulars. The need here is to comprehend the process, and comprehension requires some degree of abstraction.

racial lines in a city such as Chicago is an important factor in understanding how racial differences have been systematically maintained.

The racial divisions in the Chicago labor market are visible in many dimensions—by industry, by occupation, by geographic area, by firms, and by departments within firms. In general, Negro workers tend to be hired by certain industries and by particular firms wthin those industries. Some firms have absolute racial barriers in hiring, with Negroes being completely excluded. Within all industries and even in government employment there is unmistakable evidence of occupational ceilings for Negroes. Within single establishments that hire both whites and nonwhites, Negro workers are usually placed in particular job classifications and production units. A good rule of thumb is that the lower the pay or the more disagreeable and dirty the job, the greater the chance of finding a high proportion of Negroes.

Racial concentration by industry in Chicago is shown in the fact that 20 percent of employed Negro males work for federal, state, or local government as compared to only 6 percent of employed white males. Six percent of Negro males are in the primary metal industry as compared to 3 percent of white males. At the other extreme, 1.5 percent of white males are in the banking and finance industry as compared to only 0.2 percent of Negro males. The existence of limited entry for Negroes can also be found in manufacturing—for example, 6 percent of all white men are employed in the nonelectrical machinery industry while only 2 percent of all Negro men are in that field.

While an examination of broad industrial classifications indicates certain tendencies toward racial dualism in the labor market, the pattern becomes much more distinct when individual firms and occupations within an industry are considered. A recent survey based on a sample of firms from the membership of the Chicago Association of Commerce and Industry makes this point strongly by showing the percentage of firms in the Chicago labor market that do not employ nonwhites. Seven out of every ten small firms, one out of every five medium-sized firms, and one out of every thirteen large firms do not hire nonwhites. Construction, transportation and utilities, and finance and insurance

are the *most segregated* industries. Those small firms that employ any nonwhites tend to have labor forces with a very high proportion of nonwhite workers. While nonwhites account for 10.4 percent of total employment by small firms, they are confined to 30.9 percent of the universe of small firms.

Employment of some nonwhites by a firm does not necessarily mean that it has an integrated work force. Within a firm, racial segregation can take place on the basis of production units, branch operation, or occupational classification. Table 1 offers conclusive proof of this point. For each major occupation it shows the percentage of employees working for firms that have no nonwhites in that particular occupational classification. It stands out clearly that within individual firms, four occupations—professional, managerial, sales, and craftsmen—tend to exclude nonwhites. In the case of professionals and managers Table 1 understates the segregation of Negroes, as a high proportion of the nonwhites in these classifications are Orientals.

In some firms that are integrated by occupation, departments within that occupational group may be divided along racial lines. Negroes are especially segregated into hot, dirty departments like foundries and heat-treating shops. Sometimes within the same operation there will be occupational segregation in which the laborers are Negro and the machine operators are white, or in other cases the machine operators are Negro and the higher-paid mechanics are white. A plant might have an integrated semiskilled work force, but it will almost invariably have segregation of its craftsmen and lower-level supervisory employees, even though most of these jobs are filled by within plant recruitment. In general, the lower the position on the occupational scale, the greater the chance that there will be integration for a particular job classification. . . .

In response to this segregated job pattern in the total labor market, Negroes and whites have developed separate patterns of job seeking. Whites do not seek employment with firms that they identify as being totally in the Negro labor market, nor do they seek jobs that they identify as being Negro jobs. In firms which have integration among their unskilled or semiskilled workers, it is the whites in these categories who operate with the expectation that they will be chosen for

TABLE 1

PROPORTION OF EMPLOYMENT
SEGREGATION BY OCCUPATIONAL
GROUPS AND COLOR

Occupation	Percent Segregated (nonwhite)
Professional	43.3%
Managers	75.1
Clerical Workers	27.3
Sales Workers	54.7
Craftsmen, Skilled	66.2
Semiskilled	11.5
Service Workers	8.0
Laborers	11.0

SOURCE: Chicago Association of Commerce and Industry, *Manpower Survey, 1964*, p. 16, Table 11.

on-the-job training or considered for promotion.

Negroes, on the other hand, shop in what they consider to be the Negro labor market. Firms are identified as employing Negroes, e.g. in Chicago certain mail-order houses and the Post Office; or jobs, such as laborer or foundry work, are identified as being Negro jobs. The Negro job seeker expects automatic rebuff outside the identified Negro labor market, and he accordingly limits his shopping to the places where he feels that he has some chance of success. Not surprisingly, most jobs in the white labor market are never sought by Negroes.

These segregated job-seeking patterns are reinforced by several practices. Many firms fill vacancies by word of mouth to friends and relatives of employees, thus recruiting from the same racial groups as their present labor force. Labor-market intermediaries—the Illinois State Employment Service, some five hundred private employment agencies, and vocational counselors—tend to operate on the basis of the dual labor market. Negro youngsters in school are encouraged to seek careers in occupations that are traditionally Negro jobs. Nonwhite job seekers are counseled to apply for positions within the Negro labor market. Both public and private employment services, in spite of legal prohibitions, tend to respect the racial lines of the labor market in their referrals.

SURPLUS LABOR SUPPLY

The concept of dualism is a convenient way of describing a major feature of North-

ern race relations in the area of employment —the segregation and division of the white and Negro labor forces. To understand further the operation of urban labor markets where there is a sizable Negro labor force, it is necessary to describe the processes of how Negroes advance occupationally and how certain jobs are either kept from or allocated only to the Negro labor force.

Our second generalization, i.e. the surplus labor pool, shows that the Negro labor force has served as an excess supply of labor utilized for jobs that whites have recently vacated, or for jobs where there are shortages of white labor, or for jobs that have become traditionally Negro jobs. According to this generalization, the Negro labor force can be broken down into three distinct groups:

1. A Negro *service sector* selling goods and services to the Negro community.
2. A *standard sector* regularly employed by major white-controlled firms or institutions, including government;
3. A *surplus labor factor* that is without work or tenuously employed in low-paying, marginal jobs.

By the Negro service sector we refer to Negroes self-employed or employed by firms, either white or Negro owned, which service the Negro community. In the case of professional services, such as medical or legal, the persons within this sector are usually well paid. At the other extreme are small neighborhood retail establishments providing only a subsistence income to their proprietors. In general, the size of the service sector is dependent upon the amount of money that Negroes have available for consumption expenditures.

By the standard sector of the Negro labor force we refer to workers regularly employed in firms and institutions that supply goods and services to the total economy. Annual earnings in this sector are well above the subsistence level and in many cases are comparable to those for whites. Jobs in this sector are either with major employers or with firms that are competitive with the major companies. Within this standard sector Negro workers are often segregated by firm and within firms by job classification or production unit. The size of this sector is generally determined by the extent to which past or present labor shortages have allowed the entry of Negro workers into areas where previously just whites were hired. Currently, approximately half the Negro labor force is in this category.

The surplus sector of the Negro labor jobs consists of workers occupied in traditional Negro jobs outside the standard sector and workers who are unemployed or are out of the labor force, or are in marginal jobs. Workers in the surplus sector who have jobs occupy positions that are at the very bottom of the occupational ladder. These jobs are low paying, involve dirty and unsafe work, are often of short duration, and have little advancement potential. Many of these jobs are assigned to the Negro labor force only as the white labor force advances into higher occupations. Traditional Negro jobs like bootblacks, car washers, busboys, washroom attendants, porters, and servants are positions that through custom have gradually formed an area of employment exclusively for Negroes, or other minority groups, regardless of employment conditions elsewhere in the labor market.

Table 2 provides estimates for each of these sectors of the Negro labor force for 1959. Because earlier data were not available, changes in the relative and absolute sizes of each sector cannot be measured.

Many workers in the surplus sector are dependent upon some form of public aid for their incomes. In Chicago approximately one fourth of all Negroes receive some form

TABLE 2
ESTIMATES OF THE SECTORS OF THE NEGRO LABOR SUPPLY IN CHICAGO METROPOLITAN AREA BY SEX, 1959

	Male	Female
Standard Sector	125,000	57,000
Negro Service Sector	20,000	15,000
Surplus Sector	80,000	53,000
Total	225,000	125,000

of public assistance. All persons in this sector have low incomes, close to or at a subsistence level, that cover only the basic necessities. For all members of this sector, both those with and those without work, the level of subsistence income is primarily established outside the labor market by the political determination of welfare payments. The level of welfare payments serves as an effective minimum income. The size of this sector has

generally been dependent upon the degree of unemployment in the general labor market and, in earlier years, upon the amount of white immigration.

The concept of the surplus labor supply can also be viewed as a dynamic process occurring over time. Usually some Negro workers are moving from the surplus sector into the standard sector. This movement is often accelerated in periods of rapid economic growth when tight labor markets help break down many discriminatory barriers. Many firms will begin to shop in the Negro labor market when they are confronted by a shortage of white labor. In Illinois these positions are often in declining industries that are losing their labor force to the growth industries.[4] Sometimes this movement reverses itself. For example, many Negroes in the Chicago meat-packing industry were forced back into the surplus sector when displaced from their jobs at the time the packinghouses left Chicago. But usually the breakthroughs in employment that occur are irreversible partly because of social custom, and partly because of seniority and other forms of job security.

In the last twenty-five years the number of Negro workers who have left the Negro surplus labor sector has increased considerably. However, the Negro labor force is still growing today, primarily through the entry of indigenous teen-agers and secondarily through the migration of Southerners. In the face of this growing labor force the expansion in employment opportunities for Negroes has not been sufficient either to have eliminated or to have reduced substantially the size of the surplus labor pool. Negro teen-agers are frequently trapped in the surplus labor sector because of the inadequate preparation they receive in inferior, segregated schools like those in Chicago. Negro workers displaced from Southern agriculture are even worse off as the gap between the requirements necessary for industrial employment and unskilled Southern rural labor has widened over time.

The concepts of the dual labor market and the surplus labor supply can be more closely related by considering their more general usage. Social scientists who specialize in the study of underdeveloped countries

[4] Dale Hiestand, Economic Growth and Employment Opportunities for Minorities (New York, 1964), 87.

point out that these economies are usually composed of two clearly identifiable sectors: an advanced industrialized sector using modern technology and skilled labor, and a subsistence peasant sector, using very little machinery and containing a large unskilled labor force that has high rates of unemployment and underemployment. We find a parallel in the urban labor market that we have been examining. Here, there is a white labor force which, for the most part, uses modern technology and contains a large percentage of skilled and highly skilled workers; then there is a Negro labor force which, to a large extent, is unskilled and employed in jobs either located in declining industries or providing only marginal types of employment. In fact, the surplus sector of the Negro labor force forms a type of urban peasantry comparable in certain aspects to the subsistence sector in underdeveloped economies. Since this supply of labor is outside the general economy and workers in it live at a subsistence income, they can easily be attracted into regular employment in large numbers without forcing wages to rise.

That racial dualism exists in most urban labor markets and that the Negro labor force has served as a surplus labor pool may explain why unemployment rates in the U.S. have been above those tolerated by workers in the Western European countries.[5] In the U.S. the unemployment rate for Negroes is almost always double that for whites, if not higher, and a much greater proportion of the Negro labor force is concentrated in undesirable jobs. An equitable distribution of unemployment would probably raise the white unemployment rate by at least 1 percent. In this context, dualism can be considered as a way of minimizing the potential economic and social grievances resulting from unemployment and other forms of economic injustice. Given the tendency of the economy over the last eight years to function at levels where unemployment seldom falls below 5 percent, white workers are only protecting a narrow economic interest by excluding Negroes from many occupations. Because of a lack of political and social power, the Negro

[5] Joseph W. Garbarino, "Income Policy and Income Behavior," and Murray Edelman and R. W. Fleming, "Unemployment and Wage—Price Policies" in [Arthur Ross, ed., *Employment Policy and the Labor Market* (Berkeley: University of California, 1965)].

labor force has not been able to impose its own political constraint concerning the level of unemployment it will tolerate. One impact of the current civil rights movement may be to reduce the permissible rate of Negro unemployment. . . .

CONCLUSION

Segregation in the Northern labor market has been as efficient a mechanism for subjugating Negroes to second-class status as segregation in housing and education. In Chicago the process of allocating jobs to white workers is so effectively separated from the process of allocating jobs to Negro workers that year after year the differentials between white and Negro workers are maintained. At the same time, a large segment of the Negro labor force is relegated to the role of an urban peasantry destined to live off welfare payments and white paternalism. The Negro labor force, unlike those of other large ethnic groups, has not been allowed to assimilate into the metropolitan labor market. One hundred years after emancipation and forty-five years after urbanization, Negroes in Chicago are still systematically restricted in both the skills they may acquire and the extent to which they can utilize any given level of skills.

Racial dualism in the urban labor market is a structural phenomenon. While this does not necessarily mean that the social and economic order depends on segregation, it does tell us that our basic social and economic institutions have to be revamped in order to achieve equality. A dual structure based upon race is not merely a slight deviation from some acceptable norm as to how the labor market should function, but an essential feature of urban labor markets and American race relations.

Several implications immediately follow from this conclusion. (1) Programs and policies to eliminate segregation in the labor market have to be more extensive than those that now exist. Changes on the demand side —the removal of discriminatory barriers in hiring—can have only limited impact so long as conditions on the supply side remain stationary: inferior Negro public schools, housing segregation. (2) So long as current programing is continued under the same institutional assumptions—that the labor market is not divided racially—Negroes can make advancements only during periods of exceptional economic growth. Current programs are still applicable only in situations where the labor market is tight. And (3) the current pattern of racial disparities will perpetuate itself so long as only the market mechanism is relied upon as a corrective device and so long as supportive institutions that help shape the supply of labor continue their racist policies. Individual decision-making units in the labor market—the large firm or union—cannot by themselves produce changes in the institutional framework. At most, their policies can result in marginal adjustments. Concerted action and long-range planning by all important groups—employers, unions, placement agencies, and government—are necessary to produce the structural changes for the erosion of the dual structure. The labor market, if allowed to operate only through its own internal forces, does not generate sufficient economic or social pressure to eliminate racial disparities.

Recent events in the labor market can be evaluated against this background. So far the main institutional impact of the civil rights movement in Chicago has been in the area of employment, as both school and housing segregation have remained the same or even increased since Birmingham. On the demand side of the labor market, there has been a partial lowering of discriminatory barriers as firms seek to comply with new laws and federal executive orders. An even greater lowering of barriers has been brought about by the labor shortages created by the present five-year-long economic boom.

In most major firms absolute racial restrictions have been removed. The biggest changes have been in those firms which are U.S. government contractors and therefore subject to review under the President's Equal Employment Opportunity Program. A few Negroes are now moving into professional and managerial positions for which, regard-less of qualifications, they never would have been considered a few years ago. In some firms a fair number of female clerical workers are being hired.

However, these breakthroughs into new job classifications usually involve only a handful of Negro employees. They provide a symbolic token that the firm no longer discriminates absolutely. Most firms are pursuing only cautious programs of integration designed to be easily observable so as to satisfy government enforcement officers and civil rights groups. The current interest of many firms in race relations and the expensive rituals undertaken to indicate this interest still have not produced a major alteration in the employment structure. The openings in the better jobs are still minimal. The National Industrial Conference Board reports on a survey of forty companies: "Negroes, generally, still are being hired for low-paying, low-status jobs. The number of [Negroes] being employed in nontraditional Negro jobs is very small." The NICB further states: "There is a gap between policy and practice in the area of Negro employment. Few of the companies studied are doing as well as they want to do or so well as their top officers think they are doing."[6]

The current status of the Negro worker in the Chicago labor market may be characterized by the statement that although some discriminatory barriers on the demand side have been slightly lowered, most on the supply side still remain. Regarding the employment of semiskilled and unskilled workers by firms subject to compliance with the President's Equal Employment Opportunity Program, one close observer of discrimination in Chicago comments: "In the past, personnel men used to discriminate against nine out of ten Negro applicants; today they only discriminate against eight out of ten."

[6] "Chief Executives View Negro Employment," *The Conference Board Record* (May 1965), 32.

THE CHARACTERISTICS OF MARGINAL INDUSTRIES

Barry Bluestone

This excerpt describes the economic characteristics of jobs in the secondary labor market. It makes clear that the economic determinants of such low-wage jobs are deeply rooted, and that one cannot expect sudden changes in the basic structure of employment available to disadvantaged workers. Bluestone also presents another piece of the more basic argument that labor market segmentation is becoming increasingly distinct over time.

This reprinted portion is from the second half of an article called "Lower-Income Workers and Marginal Industries" from Louis Ferman *et al.*, eds., *Poverty in America.*

Bluestone is a research associate of the Institute of Labor and Industrial Relations at the University of Michigan.

A "character" sketch . . . applied to low-wage industries permits some insight into the dynamics of the low-wage sector of the economy. While it may not allow a perfect understanding of all low-wage jobs, it does unveil the economic and social forces conducive to the persistence of poverty employment within the confines of a materially affluent society.

Growth rate of average hourly earnings. Delehanty and Evans report that between 1958 and 1963, the gain in average hourly earnings in all manufacturing was 17 percent, while the gain in low-wage industries was limited to 13.6.[1] Over a longer period, 1953 to 1963, the median increase for low-wage two-digit industries was only 30 percent while the median in other manufacturing industry exceeded 45. The differential in wage growth rates is also reflected in the relative changes in wages in broader employment categories. Between 1947 and 1966, wages in non-durable goods and retail trade rose less rapidly than wages in all manufacturing, and overall, low-wage industries within

[1] George E. Delehanty and Robert Evans, Jr., "Low-Wage Employment: An Inventory and an Assessment," Northwestern University, mimeo, no date, p. 9.

manufacturing produced the smallest gains both relatively and absolutely.

Rather than closing, the earnings gap between low-wage industries and most high-wage industries appears to be growing. Relative to the average worker in society, the working poor wage-earner is more poor today than he was 20 years ago, and although some workers in low-wage industries have escaped absolute poverty in the sense that they have broken through the artificial $3,000 threshold, their income position, relatively speaking, has deteriorated. Small decreases in the percentage of low-wage employment among industries in recent years . . . reflect a minor reduction in absolute working poverty, but camouflage the fact that wage increases have not been spread throughout the industry. Rather, wage dispersion within the low-wage industries has been reduced, possibly due to upward pressure on lowest wages because of broader coverage of minimum wage laws.

Demand for labor in low-wage industry. All things equal, industries with increasing demand for labor are generally expected to have wages increasing at a faster pace than those where labor demand has slackened. Yet in this regard, empirical evidence on low-wage industry appears equivocal. While a number of low-wage industries have had steadily declining employment consistent with slow rather than rapid wage advance, other low-wage industries have had relatively high employment growth rates.

Lumber and wood products, textile mill products, leather and leather goods, laundries and cleaning services, and footwear are prime examples of the declining low-wage industry. On the other hand, apparel and related products, furniture and fixtures, and above all, retail trade, contradict the expectation as all of these have had healthy advances in employment without eliminating their poverty wage scales. A number of industries have had large decreases in employment yet have not fallen prey to low wages. Over the last two decades both mining and primary metal industries have had absolute decreases in non-supervisory production personnel yet have managed to keep wages at a high level. Indeed primary metal industries have increased wages at a rate in excess of the average for all manufacturing firms. Obviously all things have not been equal in the economy, and hence other factors must be called upon to explain the dimensions of low-wage industry.

Productivity of low-wage industries. When the productivity of a firm increases, presumably wages can be raised, profits can be increased, prices can be lowered, or a combination of the three can occur. In oligopolistic industries, productivity has been rising fairly steadily and the result, at least in part, has been expanding wages and profit margins, often at the same, or higher, growth rate as the productivity rate. When low-wage manufacturing industries are investigated, they are found, on the average, to possess productivity growth rates consistent with the gains in the rest of manufacturing. Using the ratio of the Federal Reserve Board's "Production Index" divided by total employment as a measure of productivity for the years 1958–1963, Delehanty and Evans found a 26 percent median increase in productivity for low-wage two-digit manufacturing classifications. For the remaining manufacturing sectors, the median increase was slightly *less,* 25 percent. Nevertheless, absolute productivity in the low-wage sectors was found to be well below that in non-low-wage industries. The value-added per production worker man/hour in the low-wage sectors was only $3.63 while in other manufacturing industry the median was more than double, $8.17.[2]

The low absolute productivity of labor in low-wage industry, no matter whether the cause is too little complementary capital or inefficient management, partly explains the

low level of wages in the poverty industries. But the productivity gains in low-wage industry are not reflected in the relative wage rate changes in low-wage industry. Rather than contributing to higher wages, productivity increases are either being absorbed into broader profit margins or otherwise into lower prices due to raging competition. Productivity, then, cannot alone explain the plight of the low-wage industry and its poverty-stricken workforce.

Profits. Periodically, it is suggested that poverty wages are the result of employee exploitation by profit-grubbing monopolistic firms. Indeed, firms maintaining influence in labor markets can artificially reduce wages below the return due to workers based on their productivity and thereby accrue higher money profits for the company. In some low-wage industries where the local labor market is at the mercy of a company town, no doubt exploitation of this kind is practiced. Yet in general, the evidence points to low-profit margins in the bulk of low-wage industry.

Using Stigler's study of capital and the return on capital in manufacturing, Delehanty and Evans computed the median rates of return (profit margins) over the years 1948 to 1957 for both all manufacturing and an isolated set of low-wage industries. The median for the former was 7.33 percent while for low-wage industry the median was limited to 5.75 percent, a considerably smaller profit margin.[3] More recent data from the Federal Trade and the Securities and Exchange Commissions gave comparable results, although they showed a declining relative and absolute gap in the profit margin between all manufacturing and the low-wage sector.[4] Some wage exploitation may be occurring in a few specific industries; nevertheless, the low-profit margins recorded here and reported in addition by Gus Tyler[5] of the International Ladies' Garment Workers Union lead us to believe that individual low-wage industries, by and large, have had little success in attempting wage exploitation. The working poor are being exploited by the economy as a whole rather than by the individual firms employing them.

[2] *Ibid.,* p. 11.

[3] *Ibid.,* p. 13.
[4] *Ibid.,* p. 14.
[5] Gus Tyler, "Marginal Industries, Low Wages, and High Risks," *Dissent,* Summer 1961, pp. 321–325.

Concentration and competition. The degree of market concentration in an industry or conversely market competition determines the ability of a firm to administer prices rather than be forced through economic pressure to submit to the ensuing set of market prices. When product market competition is fierce, because of a plethora of small firms competing where none can control the market, productivity increases tend to resolve into lower commodity prices rather than higher profit margins or higher wages. In contrast to mammoth oligopolistic industries which can set prices without fear of open price conflict, many relatively small firms which produce the same commodity cannot match the wages of the titans. Wage increases in manufacturing giants can be passed along at rates equal to productivity, while the competitive firm is often forced to lower prices rather than increase profits or wages. In some cases, the oligopolistic firm may be forced to raise wages even above productivity gains, paying for this by cutting into monopoly profits or by boosting the price of their products. The highly competitive firm is rarely in such a position.

Data from Kaysen and from Delehanty and Evans point to the much lower concentration ratios in the low-wage industries.[6, 7] For instance, the latter found that of the 1,132 five-digit product classes in all manufacturing, 23 percent were such that the four largest producers for each product made 60 percent or more of the total output. Prime examples are the industrial titans of automobile, steel, rubber, and aluminum. Among low-wage industry, however, only 9 percent of the product classes were produced in highly concentrated industries. Clearly the degree of competitiveness among the low-wage industries is greater than that for the rest of manufacturing, and the same generally holds, probably even to a greater extent, for retail trade and services, both low-wage sectors.

This analysis appears to account for the disparity between productivity and wage gains in the low-wage sector versus the better paying industries. While productivity in low-wage industries has kept pace with or in some cases has exceeded the rest of industry, wages and profits have not risen as quickly because of the raging price competition in the low-wage sector not present in the rest of the economy.

Nonetheless, a highly concentrated industry per se does not guarantee a higher wage scale, for there is nothing inherent in the size of a firm or in the absence of product market competition which accounts for better wages. Rather, oligopoly provides what might be called a "permissive economic environment" within which other forces can more easily work for higher wages.[8] Needless to say, such an economic climate is nonexistent for the frail, competitive, often low-wage, firm. A permissive economic environment entails capital-intensive production possibilities, the ability to set prices based on product demand conditions, high public visibility, low firm entry, and the opportunity for strong unionism.

Utilization of capital. Where each worker has a great deal of machinery at his command, output per man will be large and the wage bill correspondingly will be a small fraction of the total costs incurred by the producer. Such wages will have a tendency to be higher than where production is labor-intensive. Furthermore, resistence to wage increases will be less in the capital-intensive industry since wages make up a small part of operating costs.

Data on manufacturing production functions in the United States give adequate evidence to support the hypothesis that low-wage industries in general are less capital-intensive than more lucrative industries.[9] In four of six low-wage manufacturing industry classifications the extent of capital available was significantly related to the wage level.[10] In most cases, the correlation was also significant between the size of the firm and the amount of capital per worker. In both cases the same results certainly must extend to retail trade and services.

Part of the low-wage pattern found in labor-intensive firms is no doubt due to unexploited economies of scale and to the fact

[6] Carl Kaysen and Donald F. Turner, *Antitrust Policy: An Economic and Legal Analysis,* Harvard University Press, Cambridge, 1959. (See appendices.)
[7] Delehanty and Evans, *op. cit.,* pp. 19–20.

[8] Harold M. Levinson, "Unionism, Concentration, and Wage Changes: Toward a Unified Theory," *Determining Forces in Collective Wage Bargaining,* John Wiley and Sons, New York, 1967.
[9] George H. Hildebrand and Ta-Chung Liu, *Manufacturing Production Functions in the United States, 1957.* (As used in Delehanty and Evans.)
[10] Delehanty and Evans, p. 23.

that small wage increases, let alone large, add considerably to total operating costs of small firms which are weak in capital. Hence, the lack of capital in the low-wage firm accounts for some of the growing gap in relative incomes between the average worker and the working poor.

Product demand. Although there is little data on the demand for different products, it is plausible to posit that the demand for many low-wage industry commodities is quite elastic due to product substitutes and foreign competition. Only recently is foreign competition in the heavy goods industry beginning to dent domestic sales and prices in the high-wage sector. In textiles, miscellaneous manufacturing, watches and clocks and apparel, foreign competition has been fierce and in some cases has not completely destroyed a comparatively inefficient domestic industry only because of restrictive tariffs.

To the extent that a product has inelastic demand, wages can be raised at the expense of higher prices, as in the automobile industry. But where demand is highly elastic, a small increase in price reduces the demand precipitously. When cigar prices rise, smokers switch to pipes and cigarettes; when domestic textile prices rise, fashions turn to imported fabrics. Consequently, the low-wage firm has little recourse to a price increase as a means of boosting wages or profit margins for that matter. If the firm faces an elastic demand, it runs itself out of the market when it raises prices too high. The choice for workers in this industry becomes not low wages or high wages, but low wages or no wages. In the bituminous coal industry for example, the choice was against paying low wages to a multitude of coal-miners. Instead, the industry was mechanized; prices remained competitive but a great part of the workforce was eliminated. Many were thrown out of lifelong work, but those who survived the cut received an adequate wage for their continuing toil.

Public visibility. When General Motors Corporation announces net profits in excess of 20 percent per year, employs over 400,000 workers, and controls prices in a $20 billion-plus industry, the nation cannot help but take notice. The same holds for other major industries in the country. But the near invisible low-wage sector of the economy escapes the constant public scrutiny to which the industrial giants are subjected. A large firm can hardly escape paying relatively high wages even if there is little internal pressure from its workforce. The small "invisible" firm, on the other hand, often avoids the sharp eye of the government inspector and the acute sensitivities of an aroused public opinion. Consequently, low wages and poor working conditions have a much better chance of survival in the industries of the working poor. Similarly, laws are so drawn as to exclude many workers in the low-wage sector. As late as 1963, for instance, maximum wage laws excluded from coverage over one and one-half million restaurant workers, 489,000 hotel and motel employees, over a half million laundry workers, 700,000 hospital workers, over three million retail clerks, and, in addition, millions of farmers and thousands of loggers and agricultural processing workers.[11] Ironically, the minimum wage law covers *all* auto, steel, rubber, and aluminum workers where the average wage is over twice the minimum and literally no one earns below one and a half times the legal minimum wage.

Unionization. Although low-wage industry is not as highly unionized as high-wage manufacturing, it is not totally unorganized. Unions exist in many low-wage industries, but they are beset by a number of nearly insurmountable hurdles brought on by the characteristics of most low-wage industry. The same barriers account for the sectors of low-wage industry devoid of unionization.

There is nothing inherent in the nature of oligopolistic industrial giants which explains, not their ability, but their actual granting of higher wages. If we are to fully understand the causes of high wages and, consequently, those of low wages and working-poor jobs, it is necessary to include the all-important dimension of unionization.

A number of studies over the past few years have shown that greater rates of wage increases have been strongly associated with (1) a relatively high degree of oligopoly, (2) high profit rates, and (3) strong unions.[12] Yet these forces do not act independently, but rather bear systematic rela-

[11] AFL-CIO, "The Low-Paid Worker," *American Federationist*, August, 1964.
[12] See Arthur Ross and William Goldner, "Forces Affecting Interindustry Wage Structure," *Quarterly Journal of Economics*, Vol. 64, No. 2, May 1950, pp. 254–305; William G. Bowen, *Wage Behavior in the Postwar Period*, Princeton, 1960; Harold M. Levinson, *op. cit.*

tion to each other. High product market concentration and high profits provide the footing for a "permissive economic environment" in which strong unions can reap economic and social rewards for their members. Where an industry is inhabited by a few massive price-setting, highly mechanized, non-competitive, publicly visible, and highly profitable firms, entry of new firms is highly improbable and, indeed, quite rare. The needed initial resources are too vast to be accumulated by a newcomer. Consequently, unions, once they have become established, are relatively secure and free from the competition forced on them by an unorganized sector in the industry. Free to press for higher wages without fear of eliminating jobs by pricing their firm's product above unorganized competition, the union can demand their share of productivity and productivity gains, which in a capital-intensive industry are usually relatively high. With the industry held up to the inspection of both government and the public, the industry is doubly careful to refrain from "inappropriate" activities vis-à-vis their employees and their union. The high profits of the titans of industry present a choice target for union wage demands when bargaining sessions open.

In some high-wage industries, the product market nevertheless fails to be characterized by oligopolistic, highly profitable firms. High wages in these industries can usually be explained by the ability of the market to self-regulate entry or for unions to tightly control firm entry themselves. This is usually due to the "spatial" characteristics of the industry. The coal industry located in Appalachia is controlled in this way by the United Mine Workers. The Teamsters Union, which operates in a highly competitive industry, nevertheless reaps high wages for its members since it is able to control entry through over-the-road spatial agreements.

Consequently, we can conclude that most industries which are capital intensive, highly profitable, and free from raging competition have the *ability* to raise wages with relatively less pain and effort than other industry. Furthermore, it is precisely this economic environment which provides the most suitable conditions for strong unions. They can tackle the ability of their industries to pay high wages and turn it, through collective bargaining and the threat of collective action,

into real wage advances for their members. In other industries where unions can control entry and organize the whole market, high wages are also possible, although sometimes, as in the bituminous coal case, at the expense of eliminating many jobs.

In the low-wage sector, we have found nearly the opposite conditions. And, indeed, to a great extent, the low-wage industries represent the end result of a "repressive economic environment." Absolute productivity is well below that of all industry; less capital is utilized in production; profit rates are smaller, and most importantly, competition flourishes. The ability of many low-wage industries to pay adequate wages without drastically cutting employment is seriously open to question. Furthermore, the repressive environment decidedly stymies union organization and the pressure of unions for higher wages. Where an industry is so established that entry is free and open to new, unorganized firms, we can expect weak unions and most probably low wages. Where industries are marked by easy entry, fierce national and international competition, highly elastic product demand, low profits, and low productivity, we can almost be assured of two things: if a union exists at all, it is bound to be weak and ineffective, and there will surely be large numbers of working poor. Such is the case in textiles, apparel and related products, cigar manufacturing, fertilizer manufacture, and so forth. Many of the same characteristics are found in agriculture and the retail and service trades.

The same characteristics do not always apply to all industries which pay low wages and employ America's working poor. Some fail to pay higher wages because of foreign competition, watches and clocks for instance. Some, such as nursing care and retail trade, fail primarily because of low advances in productivity. Others fail for the most part due to one or more of these factors plus elastic demand for the product, e.g. cigar manufacturing.[13] Most fail, however, because of the competitiveness of their product markets.

[13] Note that no working poor are in the cigarette industry although over one-half of all cigar workers are paid low wages. This is mostly due to the fact that cigarette manufacture is capital-intensive, oligopolistic, highly profitable, strongly unionized, and faces an inelastic market for its product. In the cigar industry the conditions are reversed.

It is interesting to note that precisely where the market approaches its theoretical best—in the firms furthest from monopoly and closest to laissez faire—the market cannot supply jobs adequate enough to feed a man's family satisfactorily. In part, this arises because of the fact that the marginal industry exists in an economy alongside of oligopolies. As Gus Tyler has put it most eloquently,[14]

Just as small industry must lose out to oligopoly in the struggle for the market, so too, must the worker in the competitive, mobile, low-profit trades lose his standing relative to the worker in the mechanized, immobile, high-profit industries.

The 25 percent profit return on original investment not uncommon in steel and autos as contrasted with the 1 percent profit in garments does not derive from an inherent virtue of metal over fabrics,

[14] Tyler, *op. cit.*, pp. 323–324.

but from the monopoly character of the former and the competitive character of the latter. The workers in the latter industries suffer although many of them possess skills as great or even greater than those required in the basic industries.

The inadequate incomes of most of the working poor are not of their own making. If we are to blame them for anything it must be for not having the good fortune to complete an education topped off by a college degree. Rather we must blame the economic system which in too many instances provides less than an adequate job for those of adequate talents. In dealing with the working poor it is not enough to deal with the problems of individuals—too little schooling, not enough training, inadequate housing and filthy neighborhoods, no hope, and no potential power. We must also find solutions to an economic system which continues to propel a poverty-wage sector right into the decade of the '70s.

THE ECONOMICS OF RACISM

Michael Reich

This short essay summarizes some of the differences in orthodox and radical analyses of the economics of racism. Reich suggests some statistical tests of the two models and summarizes some important empirical evidence supporting the radical view. He concludes that racism serves a critical economic function by weakening the strength of the working class and promoting competition and class divisions among them.

Written originally for this book of readings, the essay draws on the author's work in progress for his doctoral dissertation in economics at Harvard University, "Racism and the White Income Distribution." Reich is a teaching fellow in economics at Harvard University.

In the late 1950's and early 1960's it seemed to many Americans that the elimination of racism in the United States was finally being achieved, and without requiring

SOURCE: *Michael Reich, an essay written for this book. The author wishes to acknowledge the help of Samuel Bowles, who encouraged him to work on this problem and has provided critical guidance at every stage.*

a radical restructuring of the society. The civil rights movement was growing in strength, desegregation orders were being issued, and hundreds of thousands of blacks were moving to Northern cities where discrimination was supposedly less severe than in the South. Government reports seemed to validate the optimism: for example, by 1969 the gap between blacks and whites in median years of schooling for males aged 25 to 29 years old was only one fourth the gap that had existed in 1960.[1]

But by 1970 the optimism of earlier decades had vanished. Despite new civil rights laws, elaborate White House conferences, special ghetto manpower programs, the War on Poverty, and stepped-up tokenist hiring, racism and the economic exploitation of blacks has not lessened. During the past twenty-five years the absolute male black-white income gap has more than doubled, while there has been virtually no permanent improvement in the relative economic position of blacks in America. Median black incomes have been fluctuating at a level between 47 percent and 62 percent of median white incomes, the ratio rising during economic expansions and falling to previous low levels during recessions.[2] Segregation in schools and neighborhoods has been steadily increasing in almost all cities, and the atmosphere of distrust between blacks and whites has intensified. Racism, instead of disappearing, seems to be on the increase.

Racism has been as persistent in the United States in the twentieth century as it was in previous centuries. The industrialization of the economy led to the transformation of the black worker's economic role from one of agricultural sharecropper and household servant to one of urban industrial operative and service worker, but it did not result in substantial relative improvement for blacks.

Quantitative comparisons using Census data of occupational distributions by race show that the occupational status of black males is virtually the same today as it was in 1910 (the earliest year for which racial data are available).[3]

This paper presents a radical analysis of racism and its historical persistence in America, focusing on the effects of racism on whites. The paper contrasts the conventional approach of neoclassical economic analysis —with its optimistic conclusions concerning the possibility of eliminating racism—with a radical approach—which argues that racism is deeply rooted in the current economic institutions of America, and is likely to survive as long as they do. A statistical model and empirical evidence are presented which support the radical approach and cast doubt on the conventional approach. The specific mechanisms by which racism operates among whites are also discussed briefly.

THE PERVASIVENESS OF RACISM

When conventional economists attempt to analyze racism, they usually begin by trying to separate various forms of racial discrimination. For example, they define "pure wage discrimination" as the racial difference in wages paid to equivalent workers, i.e., those with similar years and quality of schooling, skill training, previous employment experience and seniority, age, health, job attitudes, and a host of other factors. They presume that they can analyze the sources of "pure wage discrimination" without simultaneously analyzing the extent to which discrimination also affects the factors they hold constant.

But such a technique distorts reality. The various forms of discrimination are not separable in real life. Employers' hiring and promotion practices, resource allocation in city schools, the structure of transportation systems, residential segregation and housing quality, availability of decent health care, behavior of policemen and judges, foremen's

[1] "The Social and Economic Status of Negroes in the United States, 1969," Bureau of Labor Statistics Report No. 375 (October, 1967), p. 50.
[2] The data refer to male incomes, and are published annually by the U.S. Census Bureau in its P-60 Series, "Income of Families and Persons . . . ." Using data for the years 1948 to 1964, Rasmussen found that, after controlling for the effects of the business cycle, the average increase in the racial ratio of median incomes was only .3 percent per year, or 5 percent over the 16 years. See David Rasmussen, "A Note on the Relative Income of Nonwhite Men, 1948–64," *Quarterly Journal of Economics*, February, 1970. Thurow, using a slightly different technique, estimated that no relative increase in black incomes would occur after unemployment was reduced to 3 percent. See L. Thurow, *Poverty and Discrimination* (Washington, D.C.: Brookings Institution, 1969), pp. 58–61. And Batchelder found that stability in the ratio over time despite migration of blacks from the South to the North; within regions in the North the ratio declined. Alan Batchelder, "Decline in the Relative Income of Negro Men," *Quarterly Journal of Economics* (November, 1964).

[3] Since income data by race are not available before 1940, a relative index must be based on racial occupational data. Hiestand has computed such an index: he finds at most a 5 percent increase in blacks' status between 1910 and 1960; most of this improvement occurred during the labor shortages of the 1940's. See D. Hiestand, *Economic Growth and Employment Opportunities for Minorities* (New York: Columbia University Press, 1964), p. 53.

prejudices, images of blacks presented in the media and the schools, price gouging in ghetto stores—these and the other forms of social and economic discrimination interact strongly with each other in determining the occupational status and annual income, and welfare, of black people. The processes are not simply additive, but are mutually reinforcing. Often, a decrease in one narrow form of discrimination is accompanied by an increase in another form. Since all aspects of racism interact, an analysis of racism should incorporate all of its aspects in a unified manner.

No single quantitative index could adequately measure racism in all its social, cultural, psychological, and economic dimensions. But, while racism is far more than a narrow economic phenomenon, it does have very definite economic consequences: blacks have far lower incomes than whites. The ratio of median black to median white incomes thus provides a rough, but useful, quantitative index of the economic consequences of racism for blacks as it reflects the operation of racism in the schools, in residential location, in health care—as well as in the labor market itself. We shall use this index statistically to analyze the causes of racism's persistence in the United States. While this approach overemphasizes the economic aspects of racism, it is nevertheless an improvement over the narrower approach taken by conventional economists.

COMPETING EXPLANATIONS OF RACISM

How is the historical persistence of racism in the United States to be explained? The most prominent analysis of discrimination among economists was formulated in 1957 by Gary Becker in his book *The Economics of Discrimination*.[4] Racism, according to Becker, is fundamentally a problem of tastes and attitudes. Whites are defined to have a "taste for discrimination" if they are willing to forfeit income in order to be associated with other whites instead of blacks. Since white employers and employees prefer not to associate with blacks, they require a monetary compensation for the psychic cost of such association. In Becker's principal model white employers have a taste for discrimination; marginal productivity analysis is invoked to

[4] University of Chicago Press.

show that white employers hire fewer black workers than efficiency criteria would dictate —as a result, white employers lose (in monetary terms) while white workers gain from discrimination against blacks.

Becker does not try to explain the source of white tastes for discrimination. For him, these attitudes are determined outside of the economic system. (Racism could presumably be ended simply by changing these attitudes, perhaps by appeal to whites on moral grounds.) According to Becker's analysis, employers would find the ending of racism to be in their economic self-interest, but white workers would not. The persistence of racism is thus implicitly laid at the door of white workers. Becker suggests that long-run market forces will lead to the end of discrimination anyway—less discriminatory employers, with no "psychic costs" to enter in their accounts, will be able to operate at lower costs by hiring equivalent black workers at lower wages, thus driving the more discriminatory employers out of business.[5]

The radical approach to racism argued in this paper is entirely different. Racism is viewed as rooted in the economic system and not in "exogenously determined" attitudes. Historically, the American Empire was founded on the racist extermination of American Indians, was financed in large part by profits from slavery, and was extended by a string of interventions, beginning with the Mexican War of the 1840's, which have been at least partly justified by white supremacist ideology.

Today, transferring the locus of whites' perceptions of the source of many of their problems from capitalism and toward blacks, racism continues to serve the needs of the capitalist system. Although an individual employer might gain by refusing to discriminate and agreeing to hire blacks at above the going black wage rate, it is not true that the capitalist class as a whole would profit if racism were eliminated and labor were more efficiently allocated without

[5] Some economists writing on discrimination reject Becker's "tastes" approach, but accept the marginal productivity method of analysis. See, for example, L. Thurow, *op. cit.* The main substantive difference in their conclusions is that for Thurow, the entire white "community" gains from racism; therefore, racism will be a little harder to uproot. See also A. Krueger, "The Economics of Discrimination," *Journal of Political Economy*, October, 1963.

regard to skin color. I will show below that the divisiveness of racism weakens workers' strength when bargaining with employers; the economic consequences of racism are not only lower incomes for blacks, but also higher incomes for the capitalist class coupled with lower incomes for white workers. Although capitalists may not have conspired consciously to create racism, and although capitalists may not be its principal perpetuators, nevertheless racism does support the continued well-being of the American capitalist system.

Capitalist society in turn encourages the persistence of racism. Whatever the origins of racism, it is likely to take root firmly in a society which breeds an individualistic and competitive ethos, status fears among marginal groups, and the need for visible scapegoats on which to blame the alienating quality of life in America—such a society is unlikely magnanimously to eliminate racism even though historically racism may not have been created by capitalism.

Racism cannot be eliminated just by moral suasion; nor will it gradually disappear because of market forces. Racism has become institutionalized and will persist under capitalism. Its elimination will require more than a change of attitudes; a change in institutions is necessary.

We have, then, two alternative approaches to the analysis of racism. The first suggests that capitalists lose and white workers gain from racism. The second predicts the opposite—that capitalists gain while workers lose. The first says that racist "tastes for discrimination" are formed independently of the economic system; the second argues that racism is symbiotic with capitalistic economic institutions.

The two approaches reflect the theoretical paradigms of society from which each was developed. Becker follows the paradigm of neoclassical economics in taking "tastes" as exogenously determined and fixed, and then letting the market mechanism determine outcomes. The radical approach follows the Marxian paradigm in arguing that racial attitudes and racist institutions must be seen as part of a larger social system, in placing emphasis on conflict between classes and the use of power to determine the outcomes of such conflicts. The test as to which explanation of racism is superior is, in some ways, an illustrative test of the relative ex-

planatory power of these competing social paradigms.

The very persistence of racism in the United States lends support to the radical approach. So do repeated instances of employers using blacks as strikebreakers, as in the massive steel strike of 1919, and employer-instigated exacerbation of racial antagonisms during that strike and many others.[6] However, the particular virulence of racism among many blue- and white-collar workers and their families seems to refute the radical approach and support Becker.

THE EMPIRICAL EVIDENCE

Which of the two models better explains reality? We have already mentioned that the radical approach predicts that capitalists gain and workers lose from racism, while the conventional Beckerian approach predicts precisely the opposite. In the latter approach racism has an equalizing effect on the white income distribution, while in the former racism has an unequalizing effect. The statistical relationship between the extent of racism and the degree of inequality among whites provides a simple, yet clear test of the two approaches. This section describes that test and its results.

First we shall need a measure of racism. The index we use, for reasons already mentioned, is the ratio of black median family income to white median family income (B/W). A low numerical value for this ratio indicates a high degree of racism. We have calculated values of this racism index, using data from the 1960 Census, for each of the largest 48 standard metropolitan statistical areas (SMSA's). It turns out there is a great deal of variation from SMSA to SMSA in the B/W index of racism, even within the North; Southern SMSA's generally demonstrated a greater degree of racism. The statistical technique we shall use exploits this variation.

We shall also need measures of inequality among whites. Two convenient measures are

[6] See, for example, David Brody, *Steelworkers in America: The Nonunion Era* (Cambridge: Harvard University Press, 1960); Herbert Gutman, "The Negro and the United Mineworkers," in J. Jacobson, ed., *The Negro and the American Labor Movement* (New York: Anchor, 1968); S. Spero and A. Harris, *The Black Worker* (New York: Atheneum, 1968), *passim.*

(1) S_1, the percentage share of all white income which is received by the top 1 percent of white families, and (2) G_w, the Gini coefficient of white incomes, a measure that captures inequality within as well as between social classes.[7]

Both of these inequality measures vary considerably among the SMSA's; there is also a substantial amount of variation in these variables within the subsample of Northern SMSA's. Therefore, it is interesting to examine whether the pattern of variation of the inequality and racism variables can be explained by causal hypotheses. This is our first statistical test.

A systematic relationship across SMSA's between racism and white inequality does exist and is highly significant: the correlation coefficient is $-.47$.[8] The negative sign of the correlation coefficient indicates that where racism is greater, income inequality *among whites* is also greater. This result is consistent with the radical model and is inconsistent with the predictions of Becker's model.

This evidence, however, should not be accepted too quickly. The correlations reported may not reflect actual causality, since other independent forces may be simultaneously influencing both variables in the same way. As is the case with many other statistical analyses, the model must be expanded to control for such other factors. We know from previous inter-SMSA income distribution studies that the most important additional factors that should be introduced into our model are (1) the industrial and occupational structure of the SMSA's; (2) the region in which the SMSA's are located; (3) the average income of the SMSA's; and (4) the proportion of the SMSA population which is black. These factors were introduced into the model by the technique of multiple regression analysis. Separate equations were estimated with G_w and S_1 as measures of white inequality.

In all the equations the statistical results were strikingly uniform: racism was a significantly unequalizing force on the white income distribution, even when other factors were held constant. A 1 percent increase in the ratio of black to white median incomes (i.e., a 1 percent decrease in racism) was associated with a .2 percent decrease in white inequality, as measured by the Gini coefficient. The corresponding effect on S_1 was two-and-a-half times as large, indicating that most of the inequality among whites generated by racism was associated with increased income for the richest 1 percent of white families. Further statistical investigation revealed that increases in racism had an insignificant effect on the share received by the poorest whites, and resulted in a small decrease in the income share of whites in the middle-income brackets.[9]

THE MECHANISMS OF THE RADICAL MODEL

Within the radical model, we can specify a number of mechanisms which further explain the statistical finding that racism increases inequality among whites. We shall consider two mechanisms here: (1) total wages of white labor are reduced by racial antagonisms, in part because union growth and labor militancy are inhibited, and (2) the supply of public services, especially in education, available to low- and middle-income whites is reduced as a result of racial antagonisms.

Wages of white labor are lessened by racism because the fear of a cheaper and underemployed black labor supply in the area is invoked by employers when labor presents its wage demands. Racial antagonisms on the shop floor deflect attention from labor grievances related to working conditions, permitting employers to cut costs. Racial divisions among labor prevent the development of united worker organizations both within the workplace and in the labor movement as a whole. As a result, union strength and union militancy will be less, the

[7] The Gini coefficient varies between 0 and 1, with 0 indicating perfect equality, and 1 indicating perfect inequality. For a more complete exposition, see H. Miller, *Income Distribution in the United States* (Washington, D.C.: Government Printing Office, 1966). Data for the computation of G_w and S_1 for 48 SMSA's were taken from the 1960 Census. A full description of the computational techniques used is available in my dissertation.

[8] The correlation coefficient reported in the text is between G_w and B/W. The equivalent correlation between S_1 and B/W is $r = -.55$. A similar calculation by S. Bowles, across states instead of SMSA's, resulted in an $r = -.58$.

[9] A more rigorous presentation of these variables and the statistical results is available in my dissertation.

greater the extent of racism. A historical example of this process is the already mentioned use of racial and ethnic divisions to destroy the solidarity of the 1919 steel strikers. By contrast, during the 1890's, black-white class solidarity greatly aided mineworkers in building militant unions among workers in Alabama, West Virginia, Illinois, and other coalfield areas.[10]

The above argument and examples contradict the common belief that an exclusionary racial policy will strengthen rather than weaken the bargaining power of unions. But racial exclusion increases bargaining power only when entry into an occupation or industry can be effectively limited. Industrial-type unions are much less able to restrict entry than craft unions or organizations such as the American Medical Association. This is not to deny that much of organized labor is egregiously racist.[11] But it is important to distinguish actual discrimination practice from the objective economic self-interest of union members.

The second mechanism we shall consider concerns the allocation of expenditures for public services. The most important of these services is education. Racial antagonisms dilute both the desire and the ability of poor white parents to improve educational opportunities for their children. Antagonism between blacks and poor whites drives wedges between the two groups and reduces their ability to join in a united political movement pressing for improved and more equal education. Moreover, many poor whites recognize that however inferior their own schools, black schools are even worse. This provides some degree of satisfaction and identification with the status quo, reducing the desire of poor whites to press politically for better schools in their neighborhoods. Ghettos tend to be located near poor white neighborhoods more often than near rich white neighborhoods; racism thus reduces the potential tax base of school districts containing poor whites. Also, pressure by teachers' groups to improve all poor schools is reduced by racial antagonisms between predominately white teaching staffs and black children and parents.[12]

The statistical validity of the above mechanisms can be tested in a causal model. The effect of racism on unionism is tested by estimating an equation in which the percentage of the SMSA labor force which is unionized is the dependent variable, with racism and the structural variables (such as the SMSA industrial structure) as the independent variables. The schooling mechanism is tested by estimating a similar equation in which the dependent variable is inequality in years of schooling completed among white males aged 25 to 29 years old.[13]

Once again, the results of this statistical test strongly confirm the hypotheses of the radical model. The racism variable is statistically significant in all the equations and has the predicted sign: a greater degree of racism results in lower unionization rates and greater amounts of schooling inequality among whites. This empirical evidence again suggests that racism is in the economic interests of capitalists and other rich whites and against the economic interests of poor whites and white workers.

However, a full assessment of the importance of racism for capitalism would probably conclude that the primary significance of racism is not strictly economic. The simple economics of racism does not explain why many workers seem to be so vehemently racist, when racism is not in their economic self-interest. In extra-economic ways, racism helps to legitimize inequality, alienation, and powerlessness—legitimization which is necessary for the stability of the capitalist system as a whole. For example, many whites believe that welfare payments to blacks are a far more important factor in their high taxes than is military spending. Through racism, poor whites come to believe that their poverty is caused by blacks who are willing to take away their jobs, and at lower wages, thus concealing the fact that a substantial amount of income inequality is inevitable in a capitalist society.

Racism also provides some psychological

[10] See footnote 6.

[11] See Herbert Hill, "The Racial Practices of Organized Labor," in J. Jacobson, ed., *The Negro and the American Labor Movement* (N.Y.: Anchor paperback, 1968).

[12] In a similar fashion, racial antagonisms reduce

the political pressure on governmental agencies to provide other public services which would have a pro-poor distributional impact. The two principal items in this category are public health services and welfare payments in the Aid to Families with Dependent Children program.

[13] These dependent variables do not perfectly represent the phenomena described, but serve as reasonable proxy variables for these purposes.

benefits to poor and working-class whites. For example, the opportunity to participate in another's oppression may compensate for one's own misery. The parallel here is to the subjugation of women in the family: after a day of alienating labor, the tired husband can compensate by oppressing his wife. Furthermore, not being at the bottom of the heap is some solace for an unsatisfying life; this argument was successfully used by the Southern oligarchy against poor whites allied with blacks in the inter-racial Populist movement of the late nineteenth century.

In general, blacks as a group provide a convenient and visible scapegoat for problems that actually derive from the institutions of capitalism. As long as building a real alternative to capitalism does not seem feasible to most whites, we can expect that identifiable and vulnerable scapegoats will always prove functional to the status quo. These extra-economic factors thus neatly dovetail with the economic aspects of racism discussed in the main body of this paper in their mutual service to the perpetuation of capitalism.

THE ECONOMIC EXPLOITATION OF WOMEN

Marilyn Power Goldberg

The function of economic exploitation of women bears important similarities to the function of racism, and we should understand the former in order to appreciate the simultaneous importance of both. In each case, secondary classes of workers are created by the system of social and economic institutions, permitting the payment of low wages and the preservation of poor working conditions. This is an excerpt from a somewhat longer article of the same title, which appeared originally in *Liberation Magazine*.

Mrs. Goldberg is a graduate student in economics at the University of California at Berkeley and a member of Women's Liberation.

There are many ways in which capitalism endeavors to keep the pressures on it from becoming too great. One of the most important is by creating divisions in the work force, in order to keep wages low and otherwise limit the power of labor. It does this by creating a labor hierarchy, through differences in working conditions and through perpetuating reinforcing ideology, so that skilled workers will feel superior to unskilled, white to black, and male to female. At the same time capitalism repeatedly tells all workers that they have never before had it so good, that they are better off than workers (blacks, women) have ever been before. The division of the labor force is of further importance to capitalism because it allows cer-

tain groups, namely minorities and women, to be super-exploited, used as a marginal work force in order to smooth over cycles in the economy, and to perform vital but menial and poorly paid jobs. Ideology is very important in perpetuating these super-exploited groups, as it affects not only society's assumptions about them, but also their expectations about themselves.

Capitalism did not invent the nuclear family, or the concept that the role of women is to mind the home and the children. These institutions go back thousands of years, to the origins of private property, when man the hunter began to acquire land and desired heirs to pass it on to. But capitalism actively promotes the isolated family unit and the woman's role in it, through such propaganda devices as the glorification of motherhood, in order to facilitate its economic exploitation of both men and women.

SOURCE: *Marilyn Power Goldberg, "The Economic Exploitation of Women,"* Liberation Magazine, October, 1969.

SOCIALIZATION TO BE SECONDARY

Women are taught from the time they are children to play a serving role, to be docile and submissive, get what they want by being coy instead of aggressive. They are socialized to expect that they will spend their lives as housewives and mothers—for toys they are given the tools of their trade: dolls, tea sets, frilly dresses, and so on. They are never encouraged to think in terms of a career, unless it be one which is an extension of the serving, subordinate role in the family, such as nursing or being a secretary. As they grow they learn that it is unfeminine and therefore abhorrent to be self-assertive or to compete with men. Thus most women mature with the understanding that their primary role is that of housewive and mother and that, while they may by chance work, their contribution will be merely supplemental and temporary; they will not have a career. This is true despite the fact that most women who work are essential to support themselves and their families: 70 percent of women who worked in March 1964 supported themselves or others, or had husbands who earned less than $5,000 in 1963.[1] In a survey of women who graduated from college in 1957, while most were working or planned to work at some point in their lives, only 18 percent planned to have a career.[2] Another survey taken in 1964 found much the same result, although of Negro women college graduates, 40 percent planned a career, and many women who do work feel guilt pangs about being outside the home (although most of them face their traditional household tasks unaided at the end of the work day).[3] In a study of working wives in the Detroit area in 1956, nine out of ten often felt that a job makes personal relations in the home more difficult, hurts the husband's pride, or disrupts the home.[4]

These attitudes which women have learned about themselves and their work make them a convenient, cheap marginal labor force for capitalism. Because they con-

sider their economic contribution supplementary even when it is necessary to maintain a decent standard of living for their families, they are more willing than men to accept low pay and poor working conditions. Because they have been socialized to be docile and accept subordinate positions, they are far less likely than men to organize or create trouble for the employer. As they feel responsible to continue their role as housewives and mothers while working (and there are no facilities to relieve them of this burden), they are forced to accept a very low economic position and, even if skilled, to be exploited as a cheap labor force. They are bound to search for work near their homes, and very often for only part of the day or the year. Thus, they are in a poor bargaining position vis-à-vis their employers. This situation is further exacerbated by the tendency of many women to work until their children are born, drop out of the work force for ten, fifteen, even twenty years, then return to work after their children are grown. Thus they never acquire seniority or qualify for retirement and other benefits—employers, who are reluctant to promote women to prestigious or high-paying jobs, have an excuse not to do so. Besides these considerations of the detrimental effects the traditional roles of women have on their economic position, there is also plain discrimination on the part of employers, who are reluctant to hire women to positions of importance or where they will have authority over male workers; and who, given the opportunity, prefer to promote men, and to lay off women. Many labor unions also discriminate, and not only show no interest in organizing women, but frequently negotiate preferential treatment or pay for male workers.

PART-TIME WORKERS—A MARGINAL WORK FORCE

Women constitute a significant proportion of the supply of part-time workers. While 66 percent of all men in the labor force worked full-time, full-year in 1965, only 39 percent of the 33.8 million women who worked, or 13.1 million, did so. Of the rest, 10 million worked full-time less than a full year, and 10.6 million worked part-time for all or part of the year.[5] By 1967, 42.1 per-

[1] Women's Bureau, U.S. Department of Labor, *Fact Sheet on the Relative Position of Women and Men Workers in the Economy.*
[2] Valerie Oppenheimer, "The Sex-Labeling of Jobs," *Industrial Relations* (May, 1968), p. 231.
[3] *Ibid.*
[4] Harold Wilensky, "Women's Work," *Industrial Relations* (May, 1968), p. 234.

[5] Eli Ginzberg, "Paycheck and Apron-Revolution

	1967	1966	1965	1964
Total who worked during year	100.0	100.0	100.0	100.0
Full-time (35 hrs. or more)	70.6	70.1	70.2	69.4
50–52 weeks/yr.	42.1	40.1	39.8	38.5
27–49 weeks	13.0	14.0	14.8	15.4
1–26 weeks	15.5	16.0	15.6	15.5
Part-time	19.4	29.9	29.8	30.6
50–52 weeks	9.9	9.9	9.0	9.3
27–49 weeks	6.2	6.2	6.0	6.4
1–26 weeks	13.3	13.8	14.7	14.9

SOURCE: "Work Experience of the Population," *Monthly Labor Review,* June 1969.

cent of women who worked, worked full-time, full-year, an increase probably due in large part to the drafting of men to fight the Vietnam War.

Thus, women form a marginal work force, important for several reasons. First, as indicated above, part-time or temporary workers never achieve seniority or become eligible for fringe benefits. Thus an employer might well find it more economical and convenient to hire two such workers to perform basic or menial chores, rather than invest in one full-time, full-year worker. Temporary workers can be taken on or let go according to fluctuations in business, taking the brunt of cycles and uncertainties which otherwise might spread to the rest of the economy. They are the last to be hired and the first to be fired. Business offices in particular feel this need, as they have no product which can be stockpiled in case of waning demand. If they have over-hired, their employees simply go idle. This has been institutionalized in the flourishing temporary worker agencies—the Kelly Girl and so on—allowing an employer to hire extra help by the week or the month. Women form a significant portion of this temporary office work force. Ninety-seven percent of all stenographers and typists are women, and one-third of all women workers were in clerical work—the most in any job category.[6] The importance of temporary workers as a marginal work force is indicated by the rapid growth in this job category. In the years 1950–1965, the average annual increase of

part-time jobs for women was 300,000, or just below the average increase in full-time male workers.[7] Women workers' role concept facilitates their acceptance of part-time or temporary work. Thus, of the 17.6 million women who worked less than full-time throughout the year, while 22 percent did so because they were going to school and 26 percent either could not find full-time work or were kept from working by illness, disability, or other reasons, a full 52 percent chose to work in order to take care of their homes.[8]

UNEMPLOYMENT

One of the important aspects of temporary workers, as mentioned above, is precisely their "temporary-ness." That is, they can be taken on in time of need, and let go when the need is finished. Women are ideally suited to this purpose, both because they consider their income of supplementary, and therefore secondary, importance to the family and are therefore less likely to put up a fight; and because they tend not to enter the unemployment roles but rather to disappear back into their homes. They are not "unemployed," they are housewives. Further, labor unions tend to be male supremacist, and are unlikely to fight the laying off of women workers. The unemployment rate for women is still higher than for men—5.3 percent in 1965, as compared with 3.2 percent for men. If the number of women who return to their homes could be included, the figure would undoubtedly be much higher.

in Woman Power," (sic), *Industrial Relations* (May, 1968), p. 194.
[6] Gertrude Bancroft McNally, "Patterns of Female Labor Force Activity," *Industrial Relations* (May, 1968), p. 195.

[7] *Ibid.,* p. 197.
[8] *Ibid.,* p. 194.

Women have a higher unemployment rate for several reasons. First, their tendency to divide their career between work and home means they have a higher turnover in labor force participation. Thus, since many of them are occasional and seasonal workers, they are more exposed to the risks of unemployment. Second, the lack of maternity leave means that pregnancy results in loss of job. Third, in industry they tend to have less seniority than men, and custom and sentiment favor laying off women in preference to men, since women's work is considered secondary and even an aberration, taking employment away from men (once again, women bear the brunt of economic fluctuations). Fourth, since women have a more narrow range of job opportunities, stemming from a reluctance to hire them in many occupations, and their frequent concomitant lack of training in these fields, they do not have as many potential employment opportunities. And finally, there is an element of discrimination which means that many employers will not hire a woman for a job she is qualified for, especially if there are also male applicants for the position. For nonwhite women the problem is even more serious; they tend to have an unemployment rate twice that of white women at 7.8 percent in 1968, as compared with 3.9 percent for white women.[9]

WORK CYCLE OF WOMEN

The tendency of women to drop in and out of the labor force in their life cycle further leaves them open to economic exploitations. Two-thirds of women in the age group 18 to 25 worked at some time in 1965. However, in the age group 25 to 34, this figure dropped to one-third.[10] This drop is sufficient to give employers an excuse to pay their young women employees less, and not to promote them to positions of importance, since there is a danger that the women will work for a short time and then quit to marry or have children. This danger is increased by the fact that their husbands' careers are not yet settled, and the women's work being secondary, if he wants to leave the area, she must quit. When women return to the labor force after their children have grown, they have not worked for a long time, so that employers discount their previous experience and whatever skills they might have had are considerably rusty. Currently, 58 percent of women aged 45–54 work, more than any other group except aged 18–25.[11]

JOB DISCRIMINATION— SEX-TYPING

Whether working full-time or part-time, women tend to be employed in the less remunerative occupations, frequently in work which is an extension of their role in the family—that is, secondary, serving work; traditional housewives' tasks of cooking, cleaning, etc.; tasks requiring patience, waiting; work requiring an attractive appearance; and work dealing with children. They are rarely placed in positions requiring individual initiative or decision-making, and almost never in a position of supervising or giving orders to men. A survey shows that 74 percent of employers in New Haven and 53 percent of employers in Charlotte preferred men for administrative and executive positions.[12] It was felt that men should deal with other men, such as most clients, other management people, suppliers, and so on, and that it was not appropriate for a women to do so. Also, male supervisors were felt to command more respect, even from women workers. Men, after all, are accustomed to give orders to women, not receive them, in the home as well as on the job; and women are used to taking orders from men, and, looking at other women as rivals and competitors, would resent taking orders from them.

The sex-typing of jobs available to women is evident from the great concentration of women in certain occupations. Ninety-seven percent of all stenographers, typists, and private household workers are women, as are two-thirds of all health service workers, teachers (except college), waitresses and clerks, and other clerical workers.[13] Many of these jobs remain female-dominated at least in part because they combine a need for a fairly high level of training and education with very low pay (stenography, nursing, teaching).

9 Women's Bureau, U.S. Department of Labor, *Report of the Task Force on Labor Standards,* 1968.
10 Gertrude Bancroft McNally, p. 197.

11 *Ibid.,* p. 194.
12 Valerie Oppenheimer, p. 199.
13 Gertrude Bancroft McNally, p. 195.

	men	women	w as % of m	men	women	w as % of m
White	$6,497	$3,859	59.4	$1,419	$863	60.8
Non-White	4,285	2,674	52.4	639	327	51.2

SOURCE: U.S. Department of Labor, Women's Bureau, *Fact Sheet on the Relative Position of Women and Men Workers in the Economy.*

DIFFERENCE IN INCOME

The economic exploitation of women is indicated by their low median income in comparison with men. In 1965, women received a median of $2,098, or 40 percent of the male median of $5,194.[14] This inequality can be explained in part by the tendency discussed above for women to be relegated to part-time and/or part-year work, but even women who work full-time, full-year make only around three-fifths of the male median for the same work load. This relative earning position, moreover, has not improved in the last twenty-five years, except for non-white women. White men have the highest median income, then non-white men, then white women, and finally non-white women. The following table shows the median income for full-time, full-year male and female workers.

Calculating from this table, white women had an income which was 90.1 percent of that of non-white men, and non-white women had 41.0 percent of white men. It may be noted that white women and non-white men

[14] *Ibid.*

have exchanged relative economic positions since 1939.

In the category of full-time, full-year jobs, the discrepancy between the median incomes of men and women exists not only in general, but also within every occupational field. For example, in 1965, for sales workers, the median income for women was $3,000, for men $7,000; for managers and officials, $4,500 for women and $8,600 for men; and for professionals, $5,500 for women and $8,200 for men.[15] From these figures, we can see that the lower pay for women is not simply due to their being employed in the less remunerative occupations, although this is an important factor; they are also paid less than men for doing the same or similar work. Indeed, among full-time, full-year workers, the median income of women as a proportion of the median income of men has fallen from 1939 to 1964 in every major industrial group in which the number of women employed is significant.[16]

[15] *Ibid.*, p. 196.
[16] See *Fact Sheet on the Relative Position of Women and Men Workers in the Economy.*

PUTTING-ON THE POVERTY PROGRAM

David Wellman

Wellman's classic description of a program for "disadvantaged" youth illustrates the futility of one of the principal liberal policies intended to solve ghetto employment problems. Programs cannot simply "motivate" young ghetto workers to accept and stay with jobs unless the basic structure of employment opportunities available to them is changed. As the chapter introduction

SOURCE: *David Wellman, "Putting-On the Poverty Program," originally from* Steps, *reprinted with permission from Radical Education Project.*

also argued, the perceptions of the job market described in this selection are much too accurate for them to change simply because others want them to change. The selection has been excerpted from a longer piece of the same title which first appeared in an underground magazine at the University of California at Berkeley called *Steps.* The article was later reprinted by the Radical Education Project, and a different version of the same piece once appeared in *Trans-Action* magazine.

Wellman has been a graduate student in sociology at the University of California, works at the Institute for Race Relations at Berkeley, and has written often for movement publications.

"I guess these kids just don't want jobs. They're unwilling to try and help themselves. The clothes they wear are loud; they won't talk decent English; they're boisterous; and they constantly fool around. They refuse to take this program seriously."

"But isn't there a job shortage in Oakland?" I asked. "Does it really matter how they act?"

"There's plenty of jobs. They're just not interested."

It was the summer of 1966. The man with whom I was speaking was a counsellor for the Youth Opportunities Center in West Oakland. At the time, he was working on a federally sponsored program known as TIDE. I was observing the program for some graduate research that I was conducting. The purpose of TIDE was to help lower class youth become employable on the job market. The program ran for four weeks. I observed two four-week sessions. Youth from the ages of 16 to 22 were selected by local poverty program workers in the Bay Area. To make the program attractive for unemployed ghetto youth, the government paid participants five dollars a day. Two groups were involved: twenty-five young men and twenty-five young women. These groups met separately, only coming together periodically on common projects. I worked exclusively with the male group.

The young men who participated in the program had a distinctive style. They were "cool." Their hair was characteristically "processed" in one form or another. All sported a kind of sun glasses which they called "pimp's glasses." (These are very lightly tinted glasses, with small frames, which look like "granny glasses.") Their clothes, while usually inexpensive, were "loud" and ingeniously altered to express style and individuality. They spoke in a "hip" vernacular. Their vocabulary was small, yet very expressive. These young men are part of a "cool world" in the ghetto. They represent a distinctively black, working-class culture.

To most liberals these men are "culturally deprived" or "social drop-outs." Most of them had flunked out of or been kicked out of school. Few had any intention of getting a high school degree. They had long and serious arrest and prison records. They seemed uninterested in "making it" in terms of majority social values and norms. They were skeptical, critical, and hostile toward both the TIDE program [and] white society in general.

The TIDE workers were liberals: sincere, well-meaning people. Those things which, for the young men, defined their own special culture were, for the TIDE workers, symptoms of cultural deprivation. They assumed that if the young men would only act a little less "cool" and learn to smooth over some of their unfortunate encounters with white authorities, they too could become full-fledged working members of society and find their place in the sun. The men were told that the aim of the program was to help them get jobs. TIDE would not train them for jobs. Instead it would train them to *apply* for jobs. They were going to learn how to take tests, how to make a good impression during a job interview, how to speak well, and how to fill out an application form properly. To accomplish these things, they would play games like dominoes to ease the pain associated with numbers and arithmetic; they would conduct mock interviews, take mock tests, meet with management representatives, and go on tours of places where employment was a good possibility for them. They were told to consider the TIDE program as a "job." That is, they were to be at the YOC office on time, dressed as if they were at a job, and be docked if they were late or made trouble. If they took the program seriously and did well, they were told, they stood a pretty good chance of getting a job at the end of four weeks. The unexpressed aim of TIDE then, was to prepare Negro youth for white society. Public government would serve as an employment agency for white, private enterprise.

It was obvious from the outset that the program was aimed at changing the youth by making them more acceptable to employers. Their grammar and pronunciation were constantly corrected. They were subtly told that their appearance would have to be altered for them to get a job. "Don't you think you could shine your shoes?" "Haven't you got trousers that are pressed better?" "It's not a good idea to wear tee-shirts and jeans to a job interview." Promptness, a virtue few of them possessed, was lauded. The penalty for tardiness was being put on a "clean-up committee" or being docked.

For the liberal white TIDE workers the program became a four-week exercise in futility. They seemed to feel that they weren't asking very much of the men. All they really asked was that they learn to make a good impression on white society. This "simply" entailed dressing a little better, increasing one's vocabulary, learning the art of taking tests, and broadly speaking, accepting the "rules of the game." This was "all" they demanded. And yet the men were uncooperative. They fooled around, often refused to take the program seriously, and insisted upon having a "good time." The only conclusion TIDE workers could arrive at was "they just don't want jobs."

What belies this proposition is the seriousness with which most of the men took *actual and distinct job possibilities*. For example, when told there was a job at such-and-such a factory and that a particular test was required, the men studied hard and earnestly applied for the job. The TIDE program *itself*, however, seemed to be viewed as only distantly related to getting a job. The men wanted jobs, but indicated that they felt their inability to take tests and fill out forms was not the problem. They talked about the shortage of jobs available to people without skills. They would pump the YOC people daily about job openings. Their desire for work was obviously not the problem.

Yet, one could hardly deny that the young men fooled around and refused to meet the program on its own terms. If ambition was not the problem, how then do we understand the fact that the men rarely took TIDE seriously?

To one way of thinking, TIDE really didn't demand much of the men. It simply asked that they change certain outward appearances. From the perspective of the men, however, the program seemed to demand a great deal. It asked that they change their manner of speech and dress. It asked that they ignore their lack of skills and society's lack of jobs. It asked that they act as if their arrest records were of consequence in obtaining a job. It asked, most importantly, that they pretend *they*, and not society, bore the responsibility for unemployment. TIDE didn't demand much of the men: only that they become white.

What took place during the four-week program, then, was a daily struggle between white, middle-class ideals of conduct and behavior, and the mores and folkways of the black community. The men were handling TIDE in the same manner that the black community has *always* treated white invasions and threats to its self-respect. They were using subtle forms of subversion and deception.

Confronted by a hostile society and lacking the social tools necessary for material well-being, members of the Negro community have devised ingenious mechanisms for coping with this hostility and simultaneously maintaining their self-respect and human dignity. Historians and sociologists alike have pointed to subtle forms of slave subversion, the content and ritual of Negro spirituals, and recently to the meaning of the Blues as means by which the black man in America has struggled to preserve his integrity as a human being. Many of these devices have persisted until today. They are currently to be found within the structure and culture of the black community. Some of the devices are new. They reflect new forms of struggle with current problems.

"Putting someone on" ("putting the 'hype' on someone," or "running a 'game' on a cat") seems to be an important device used by Negroes to maintain their personal integrity. "Putting someone on" is used as much in relations with black people as it is in relations with members of the white community. In both instances it allows one to maintain personal integrity in the face of a hostile or threatening situation. To "put someone on" is to publicly lead him to believe that one is "going along with" what he has to offer or say, while at the same time privately rejecting the offer, and subtly subverting it. "Putting someone on" may or may not be malicious, but this is not a defining characteristic. "Putting someone on" fails if the other person catches on: he is no longer "put-on." This allows the individual who is "putting someone on" to take pride in the feeling that he has "put something over on" the other person, often at his expense. It thereby allows each party to feel that it has been "successful." "Putting someone on" is to be contrasted with "putting someone down." This is an active and public process involving both defiance and confrontation.

TIDE was evidently interpreted by the men as a threat to their self-respect, as being defeating, useless, and humiliating. They responded to it in much the same way as they would to people inside and outside the ghetto who seemed to threaten their concept of dignity. Sometimes TIDE was "put on." Sometimes it was "put down." It was only taken seriously when it met the needs of the men. And then, only on *their* terms—without a loss of human dignity.

PUTTING-ON THE YOC

There was almost no open defiance or hostility toward those in charge of TIDE. It seemed as if the men were going along with the program. Two things, however, first led me to believe that if the men "accepted" the program, they did so only on their *own* terms. They all appeared to have a "tuning out" mechanism. They just didn't "hear" certain things. For example, one young man was a constant joker and spoke incessantly. It mattered little to him whether or not someone else was speaking or if the group was supposed to be working on something. When he was told to "knock it off" (which was always) he simply never "heard" the command. On the other hand, when he was involved with the program and interested, he could hear just fine and responded to speakers quite adequately. "Tuning out" was, moreover, often a collective phenomenon. For instance, there was a radio in the room where the men worked. They would play it during lunch and coffee breaks. When the instructor would enter and tell them that work was to begin, they all seemed to be on a wave length frequency that differed from their instructor's. He would tell them that time was up, but they would continue listening and dancing to the music as if there were no one else in the room. However, without so much as acknowledging the instructor and without a word to each other or to him, when *they* were finished listening the radio went off and the session began.

This "tuning out" mechanism was frequently in operation. Conversations began and ended without any response to instructors. Men would embark on "projects" of their own during a class: looking out the window and talking to people on the street; fighting with each other; or reading comic books. During each of these "projects" they seemed "deaf" to the teacher. It is important to note that this "deafness" was *systematic*. When they were interested or wanted to participate in the program, the men were no longer "deaf." They "tuned out" and "turned on" when *they* saw fit and at no other time. In this respect, there was little authority or control that instructors could exert over the young men: authority was undercut by deafness. The men were "going along with" the program—in a way. They weren't challenging it. But they were undermining its purpose: putting it on.

The second technique which I found the men using as a means of selectively accepting the program was "playing stupid." When they wanted to they could be incredibly "stupid." A major part of the program, for instance, was devoted to teaching them how to fill out employment applications properly. They were given lengthy lectures on the importance of neatness and lettering on these forms. They were expected to fill out such forms at least two or three times a week. After having filled them out a number of times, some of the men suddenly didn't know their mother's name, the school they last attended or their telephone numbers.

This "forgetfulness" or "stupidity" was sometimes duplicated during mock job interviews, which were conducted almost daily. Five or more of the men would serve as "employers" and interview their fellow trainees for an imaginary job. The "interviewers" usually took their job seriously. But after it became apparent that the interview was a game, many of the interviewees developed into hopelessly incapable job applicants. They didn't have social security numbers, they could not remember their last job, they didn't know what school they had gone to, and they didn't know if they really wanted the "job." To the absolute frustration of the interviewers and instructors alike, the "prospective workers" simply behaved like incompetents. Interestingly enough, when the instructor told them one morning that this time the interview was "for real" and that those who did well would actually be sent out on a job interview with a "real" firm, the "stupid" and "incompetent" transformed literally overnight into model job applicants.

The responses to learning how to take tests for jobs and how to pass a driver's test were similar to the responses to mock interviews and filling out practice applications. The YOC used many of the tests that various government agencies gave to prospective workers. These included preference tests, intelligence tests, and aptitude tests. The men were required to take these tests almost daily. Some of the tests were boring and easy to catch on to. For example, the examiner would read off a number and those being tested would have to circle that number on an answer sheet. The first few times they took these tests most of the men worked hard to master them. After they had gotten the knack of it, however, and found themselves still without jobs and taking the same tests, their response changed radically. Some of them no longer "knew" how to do the test. Others found it necessary to "cheat" by looking over someone else's shoulder. Still others flunked tests they had passed the day before. Yet when they were informed of job possibilities that existed at the Naval Ship Yard or with the Post Office, they insisted on giving and taking the test themselves. In one instance, some of them read up on which tests were relevant for a particular job and then practiced that test for several hours by themselves. Their "stupidity" was a put-on. It was a way of ridiculing the tests and subverting the ritual of humiliating "practice" without openly challenging the program or its workers.

These two mechanisms for dealing with the TIDE program were used differently and at different times by many TIDE participants. Some men "tuned out" and "played stupid" more consistently than others. These men were usually less interested than others

in being acceptable to white society. Overall, however, there was little variation in behavior. "Stupidity" occurred when jobs were unavailable.

"Tuning out" and "playing stupid" were only two of the many ways in which the TIDE program was regularly "put-on." TIDE was supposed to be viewed as a "job" by those participating in it. As anyone who has been employed recently knows, any good job includes as part of the normal routine a number of legitimate "breaks" for coffee, lunch, and so on. The young men "employed" by TIDE were rather well acquainted with this ritual, and were very insistent that it be included as part of their job too. Since they were given a voice in deciding the content of the program, "breaks" were made a must for their daily routine. And no matter what the activity, or who was addressing them, "breaks" were religiously adhered to by the men. The program started at 9:30 a.m. They decided their first break would be for coffee at 10:30. This break was to last until 11:00. And while "work" was absolutely not allowed to proceed a minute past 10:30, it was usually 11:15 or so before they actually got back to business, just before their lunch break. Lunch began exactly at 12:00. Theoretically, work resumed at 1:00. This usually meant 1:15, since they had to listen to "one more" song on the radio before work could begin. The next break did not come until 2:30 p.m. The afternoon break was to last until 3:00. However, since they were finished at 3:30, and because it took another 10 minutes to get them back to work, the men could often talk their way out of the remaining business scheduled between 3:00 and 3:30. Considering they were being paid five dollars a day for five hours of work, they didn't have a bad "hustle." Of the five hours considered as "work," almost half were regularly devoted to "breaks."

"Games" were another important part of the TIDE program subverted by the "put-on." Early in the program the instructor told the men he thought it might be helpful for them to master math and language by playing games—dominoes, scrabble, and various card games. The men considered this a fine idea. But what their instructor had intended for a pastime during the breaks, involving at most an hour a day, the men rapidly turned into a major part of their instruction. They set aside 45 minutes in the morning and 45 minutes in the afternoon for games. But since they participated in these games during their breaks as well, "games" soon became a stumbling block to getting sessions back in order after "breaks." The instructor would say: "Okay, let's get back to work." To which the men would sometimes reply: "But we're already working on our math—we're playing dominoes and you said that would help us with our math." While usually said in half-seriousness, it was a difficult concept for the instructor to answer and overcome. According to *his* definition, they *were* working on their "math." With his authority undercut in this way, he had no alternative but to allow them to continue for a few minutes more. When he again called for order, the men would demand to be allowed to "finish" their game. Since finishing a game was a vaguely defined notion at best, they would usually get their way. More and more time, then, was whittled away from the substantive aspects of the program.

It finally got to a point where the instructor decided that "games" would only be a formal part of the program on certain days. The idea of using games to master certain useful techniques had been used by the men to undercut and subvert the over-all program and the instructor knew it—though could *not* admit it. He therefore had to curtail the abuse. The games "put-on" had been found out, and so had failed. The men could no longer use games as a "put-on." But games were trimmed from the program only at the expense of constant struggle between the men and their instructor. Games became a constant and unresolved issue. On the days when games were not formally part of the program, the men would continue to play them during breaks. In this way, games would usually extend into the formal sessions anyway. And on days when they *were* part of the program, games encroached upon the rest of the session as before.

To familiarize the men with the kinds of jobs potentially available to them when they had finished the TIDE program, their instructors took them on excursions to various work situations. The instructor presented them with different opportunities for such trips, and they were to decide which they would take. The criteria the men used for choosing trips are significant. They were most interested in excursions involving an entire

day. It hardly seemed to matter what *sort* of company they visited, so long as it took all day. They would only agree to half-day trips if there were no other alternative, or if there were some possibility that the company would give away "free samples." So, for example, even though it was pointed out to them that the Coca-Cola Company was not hiring, they wanted to go there. They knew they could get free cokes. They also wanted to go to many candy and cookie factories for much the same reason. In contrast, they turned down a trip to a local steel mill which they knew was hiring. The fact that it was hiring had become irrelevant for them. TIDE was not designed to get them an interview. Its purpose was to show them what sorts of jobs might be available. Given the circumstances, they reasoned, why not see what was enjoyable as well as available.

It was obvious that the men used trips like these to get away from the dull, daily routine in the YOC office. The trip to a steel mill, though previously rejected in favor of more enjoyable possibilities, was soon considered a good idea after all when the other alternatives fell through. If they didn't go to the steel mill, they would have to work in the office.

Their behavior on the trips themselves provides still another indication of the way the men used these excursions for their own ends. They were not very interested in the company conducting the tour. They seemed more interested in the bus ride out there, the possibility of a free lunch, or just fooling around. This apparently "frivolous" interest might seem a product of the kind of tours they chose: tours of bottling plants, of Fort Ord, and of cookie factories. Interestingly enough, however, their behavior altered only slightly when they visited more promising job possibilities, such as the Alameda Naval Air Station, the Oakland Naval Supply Station, and various container factories.

The trip to the Naval Air Station, for example, was an all-day trip. But the men spent most of their time putting "the make" on a cute young WAVE who was their guide for the day. She had a very difficult time keeping her "cool." They were quite adept at the game of provoking her, and played it the entire day.

To some extent, this behavior can be accounted for by the fact that the tour did not focus on potential job situations. Instead, it focused on the "interesting sights" of the base. Nevertheless, when they toured possible job situations, such as the warehouses and loading docks, their behavior scarcely changed. They were much more interested in visiting the air control tower, the aircraft carriers, and the mess hall than they were in seeing what work they might eventually do. Apparently the tour was viewed as an outing, or a "good time," and not as a job seeking situation. TIDE had told them it would not get jobs for them. It would show them how to apply for jobs. Since they were not there to apply for a job, they wanted at least to enjoy themselves. When the tour got boring or they got tired, they even refused to see the sights. They insisted on sleeping in the buses or listening to their transistor radios on the lawn. One thing the tour did produce, however, was a great deal of discussion about the war in Vietnam. Almost none of the men were interested in serving in the armed forces. Some of them would yell at passing sailors through the bus windows: "Vietnam, Baby!" or "Have a good time in Vietnam, man!"

The trip to the Oakland Naval Supply Station was similarly received. It was less interesting, however, and there was no pretty young lady guide to take them through the base. Although there were more potential jobs at this location, again the spirit of an outing prevailed.

The men cleverly manipulated this tour to meet their own needs and interests. While they were being shown the assembly line that packaged material, where they might possibly work, they drifted instead into the more interesting control room (replete with computers and television cameras) where they hardly had the qualifications to work. When they were taken on a tour of the warehouses, where again they might possibly work, they fell to the sides and spoke with friends who were already working there. The relationship between touring a possible work situation and actually being offered a job there was far too oblique to be of interest. They transformed the experience, therefore, into one which more adequately satisfied their interests and enthusiasms.

It might seem that what I have described so far indicates that these men "went along with" the program, but were in fact reluctant to get a job. I would, on the contrary, regard their behavior as a "putting-on" of the YOC.

Each of the above examples shows the men accepting the program, *on their own terms,* and inverting it to meet their own needs, *while at the same time* leading those in charge to think that the explicit aims of the program were being carried out. In this respect, each example is a classic "put-on." And when the men were not "putting-on" the YOC, they were "putting-down" the people and assumptions associated with it.

PUTTING-DOWN THE YOC

"Putting something down" is almost the reverse of "putting someone on." It is a more active and public process. It involves, among other things, confrontation and defiance. When someone is "put-down" he knows it. The success of a "put-down" depends on his knowing it, whereas a "put-on" is only successful when its victim is unaware of what is happening. There were many aspects of the TIDE program which were actively "put-down" by the young men involved.

Among the most glaring "put-downs" were those aimed at the kinds of jobs for which the men were learning to apply. These jobs usually involved unskilled labor: post office work, warehouse and longshore jobs, truck driving, and assembly-line work. Some work was also to be had in the service industry, while some was outright menial labor: chauffers, janitors, bus boys, and so on. The reaction of most of the men to this limited prospect was best expressed by a question asked of the instructor by one young man:

"How about some tests for IBM?" he inquired with a straight face.

The room was in an uproar. They thought that was a great question. Many of them were hysterical with laughter. They seemed to feel they had really put this cat down hard. His response was typically bureaucratic, yet very disarming.

"Say, that's a good suggestion. Why don't you put it in the suggestion box?"

They didn't seem able to cope with that retort and so things got somewhat back to normal.

However, when employers came to the TIDE sessions to show the men how an interview should be conducted, they were treated in similar fashion. These employers usually represented companies which hired men for unskilled labor. They came to illustrate good interview technique. They did *not* come to interview men for real jobs. Their visits were sort of helpful-hints-for-successful-interviews sessions. One of the more socially mobile men was usually chosen to play the role of job applicant. The entire interview situation was played through. Some employers even went so far as to have the "applicant" go outside and knock on the door to begin the interview. The men thought this was both odd and funny, commenting to the employer:

"Man, you've already seen the cat. How come you making him walk out and *then* walk back in?"

The employer responded with a look of incredulity: "But that's how you get a job. You have to sell yourself from the moment you walk in that door."

The men seemed unimpressed and continued to crack jokes among themselves about the scene. The interview continued. The employer would put on a real act, beginning the interview with all the usual small talk he'd normally use to draw people out and put them at ease.

"I see from your application that you played football in high school."

"Yeah."

"Did you like it?"

"Yeah."

"Football really makes men and teaches you teamwork."

At about this point the men would get impatient.

"Man, the cat's here to get a job, not talk about football!"

"When are you going to tell him about the job?"

A wise-cracker chimed in: "Maybe he's interviewing him for a job with the Oakland Raiders."

The point of all this was usually well taken by the employer, and he would begin to ask questions more germane to the particular job. He would ask about the "applicant's" job experience, his draft status, school record, interests, skills and so on. The young man being interviewed usually took the questions seriously and answered frankly. But after awhile, the rest of the group would tire of playing this game and begin to ask (unrecognized, from the floor) about the specifics of a "real" job.

"Say man, how much does this job pay?"

"What kind of experience do you need?"

"What if you got a record?"

"How many days off do you get?"

The employer would politely remind them that this wasn't a "real" interview. But this would only satisfy the young men for a short while, and they would soon resume their questions. It didn't take long to rattle the interviewer completely. Sometimes the instructor would intervene and tell the men that the gentleman was there to help them, and would request that they treat him more gently. Again, this would stifle revolt for only a short while. Then, in a mood of outright defiance, they might begin playing dominoes while the interview went on. If this didn't evoke an irritated response, they might begin to play the game rather enthusiastically by loudly slapping down the dominoes each time they scored a point. In one instance, several of the men began slapping the tables rhythmically with dominoes, during the interview. That got the response they were looking for.

"Look!" said the employer, who had completely lost control of the situation. "If you're not interested in learning how to sell yourself why don't you just leave the room so that others who are interested can benefit from this?"

"Oh no!" was the response of the ringleaders, "We work here. If you don't dig us, then *you* leave!"

It wasn't too much later that he did.

Sometimes during these interviews the very nature of the work being considered was "put down." During an "interview" for a truck driving job, some of the men began to ask the employer about salesman jobs. Others asked him about executive staff positions. They weren't very interested in talking about a job driving a truck. They continually interrupted the interview with "irrelevant" questions about the role of an executive. They wanted to know how much executives were paid and what they did to get their jobs. At one point the employer himself was asked point-blank how much he was paid, what his experience was, and what he did. To some extent they had turned the tables and were enjoying the opportunity to interview the interviewer. He finally told them, in fact:

"I'm here to *do* the interviewing, not to *be* interviewed."

In spite of this they managed to return to interviewing him. And when they weren't doing that, they were asking him about the qualifications necessary for other, more skilled jobs. In most such situations it became quite clear that they were not interested in the kinds of jobs most employers had to offer—not interested enough, that is, to participate seriously in a mock interview for an imaginary job.

The young TIDE participants were remarkably unimpressed, moreover, by the status of an employer. Regardless of his rank, the men treated their visitors as they would their peers. Sometimes visiting employers were treated more harshly and with genuine, open defiance. On one tour of a factory the men were escorted by the vice-president in charge of hiring. To some people this might have been considered an honor, and the man would have been treated with an extra ounce of deference. To the TIDE participants, however, he was just another guide. And after informing the men of the large number of unskilled positions available, he was asked about hiring some of them, on the spot. He responded by saying that this was just a tour and that he was in no position to hire anyone immediately. Some of the men were noticeably irritated at this answer. One looked at him and said:

"Then you're just wasting our time, aren't you?"

Although shaken, the executive persisted, telling the men about technical operations at the plant. Throughout his talk he referred to his audience as "boys."

"Now, when you boys come to apply for a job you will need proof of a high school education."

"If you boys want to work here you will need to join the union."

This constant reference to "boys" was obviously bothering the men. Each time the word would crop up, they squirmed in their seats, snickered, or whispered angrily to each other. The vice-president seemed unaware of the hostility he aroused. But finally, one of the bolder men spoke up firmly.

"We are young mens!, not boys."

The speaker blushed nervously and apologized. He made a brave attempt to avoid repeating the phrase. Habit, however, was victorious and the word slipped in again and again. Each time he said "you boys" he was corrected, aloud, and with increasing hostility. For a while it seemed as though the young men were more interested in catching him saying "you boys" than in anything else he said. . . .

Throughout the entire TIDE program

the young men had been "putting-down" people and projects. The men used the context of a government training program as a protective device which enabled them to "put down" institutions and individuals otherwise impervious to attack. TIDE provided insulation for them. And it offered an opportunity for meeting with people otherwise unavailable to them. In addition, the men rapidly developed a high degree of group consciousness upon which they could fall back for protection and inspiration. Armed in this manner, they then went out to "get" or "put down" normally inaccessible institutions. When consulted about whom they wanted to come and speak to them (which the men seemed to interpret as "come be put down by them"), they called for the police, a city councilman, state assemblymen, businessmen, and officials of the poverty program. Almost all these people were "put down" in one way or another when they appeared at the YOC. The TIDE people were anxious to have these visitors. TIDE workers thought it was a good idea for the young men to meet with community leaders and officials, in order to show them that these leaders were interested in their problems and would help if the men would show a little initiative. The men "showed initiative" by inviting important people to speak with them: to be "put down" by them. They "put on" the YOC in order to "put down" this array of visitors. The "put-downs," then, were also a "put-on" of the YOC. By using the program as a cover for airing their grievances, the men were, in effect, altering TIDE to meet their needs.

As the program was conceived by the government, TIDE did not meet the needs of the young men. Indeed, it wasn't meant to. The Great Society was trying to run a game on black youth. It wanted them to cease being what they were. It wanted to lead them into white middle-class America. It tried to trick them by leading them to believe that America was interested in getting them jobs.

But there aren't many jobs in America for young men who have arrest records, who lack skills, and who are black. There aren't jobs for black youth who refuse to accept white America's definition of self-respect and integrity. The young men knew that. TIDE knew it too. The very jobs over which TIDE had some control (that is, government jobs) are rarely filled by people with the backgrounds of ghetto youth. But TIDE didn't train the youth to work. It attempted to train them to pretend that there was no problem.

The men saw through it. They diagnosed it as a sham. They rejected its invitation into white America.

When a "put-on" is detected, it fails.

TIDE was more than a "put-on" of black youth. It was also an attempt to persuade the youth to "put on" potential employers. By training men to speak well, dress well, fill out application forms properly, and to take tests easily, TIDE evidently sought to "fool" employers into hiring these young men. But this was never made explicit to the men. Why, then, didn't TIDE workers just come right out and say it: "Look men. What we're suggesting is that you put on your employers; make them believe you're someone you're not."

The suggestion is absurd. The reasons for its absurdity are revealing.

It wouldn't work. This "new" approach would really not be new. It would only assert more openly that black culture is not acceptable to white society. It would still be asking the men to pretend they were someone else. It would still imply that there is something wrong with who they are. Finally, it would assume that there is work for those who want it. The young men knew there wasn't.

It could never happen. To suggest that the young men had to "put on" employers in order to win jobs implies that the employers have some responsibility for unemployment and racial exclusion. But the TIDE program, indeed much of the Great Society, assumes that the door to happiness—to America—is open if people will seek to enter on middle-class terms. "Teaching" the TIDE participants to "put on" the interviewer runs counter to the assumptions which are held dear by the poverty program and the nation. It would be impossible for government

representatives even to entertain such a step.

Our hypothetical proposition would also threaten the morale of the TIDE workers. I'm sure that most of them were well-intentioned, good, liberal people. They are also human beings. And as human beings they must strive for personal integrity in their work situation. Their job is not an enviable one. Facing fantastic barriers, they must try to get work for people. Their success is limited. But for them to recognize that society bears most of the responsibility for inequality would be to render their work worthless. To ask them to admit that their work is a "put-on" is to threaten their concept of self-worth. The institutional framework of the TIDE worker, like that of most welfare workers, therefore calls forth an orientation which holds the client, and not society, responsible for his situation.

The TIDE worker, then, would never consider asking the men to "put on" employers. Faced with defeat and frustration, as they were, they responded predictably: "they just don't want jobs." Ironically enough, the institutional requirements of northern liberalism have called forth a response very similar to the familiar line of southern racism. Wasn't it the "old fashioned" southern bigot who used to say: "Negroes don't have jobs because they are lazy and shiftless"? There is a difference to be sure. The southerner felt that black people are inherently shiftless and lazy. Thus, they are destined to be without jobs of consequence. Most modern liberals seem to view black people as temporarily hindered by psychological and cultural impediments. Inequities in the employment and opportunity structure of America, they seem to suggest, are minor in comparison with the deficiencies of black people themselves. What black people need, according to the liberals, is cultural enrichment and the ability to "sell themselves" to white society. In the end, northern liberals and southern racists agree: the problem is mainly with Negroes.

PRIVATE INDUSTRY AND THE DISADVANTAGED

Jules Cohn

The following selection represents part of a larger study of the "urban affairs" programs of 247 large corporations, programs instituted largely in response to the appeals of government and business leaders after the report of the National Advisory Commission on Civil Disorders in 1968. This chapter discusses the scope and impact of job development and training programs for "disadvantaged" workers. It belies conventional liberal notions that such programs can succeed primarily through moral suasion and subtle psychological sensitivity to the problems of lower-skilled workers. It suggests, instead, that the structure of corporate institutions and the structure of the larger economy determine the extent and success of such programs. When the corporations want to fill empty or new jobs, they can apparently train anyone they choose. If they don't want to, they won't.

The selection is Chapter Four of Cohn's book, *The Conscience of the Corporations: Business and Urban Affairs,* published in 1970. The book is not intended as a radical critique of corporate programs, but this selection illustrates some important pieces of the radical argument about employment problems and is the most recent available study of very recent corporate efforts.

Cohn is a political scientist who worked at the McKinsey Corporation, a management consulting firm, while preparing his study. He is continuing his research with another company, the Economic and Manpower Corporation in New York.

Responding to imperatives in the Kerner Report, and to appeals from Federal, state, and local officials, many of the country's largest corporations, in the wake of the urban riots of 1967, agreed to undertake recruitment and training programs for the disadvantaged.[1] Donations to charities, the traditional public service strategies of big business, would be supplemented (or replaced, in some companies) by a new approach: the direct and affirmative action of hiring people formerly considered unemployable.

By the spring of 1970 the National Alliance of Businessmen (NAB) reported that its member companies had already employed over 400,000 of the disadvantaged, or four-fifths of the total population of the "hard core" of the urban poor identified in the Kerner Report.[2] NAB's figures have been questioned by many, and there is considerable debate about the number of eligible candidates who have been hired and trained.[3]

further handicapped by psychological and sociological factors, has given way to a new term, the "disadvantaged." Labor Department criteria define the hard core or disadvantaged as "poor persons who do not have suitable employment and who are either: (1) school dropouts; (2) under 23 years of age; (3) 45 years of age or over; (4) handicapped; or (5) subject to special obstacles to employment." (The latter "obstacles" include those caused by racial discrimination.)

[3] NAB figures, which cover recruitment and training carried out through the publicly subsidized JOBS program, administered in cooperation with the Department of Labor, are derived from estimates provided on a voluntary basis by participating companies. Because of the difficulty in verifying data on the number of hires, terminations and retentions over measured periods, NAB's totals have to be treated as very broad estimates. Even if its figures are close to correct, in the absence of statistical information about the characteristics of each new employee, it is impossible to determine the extent to which the disadvantaged rather than the merely unemployed benefited from special programs. Nor is there reliable information about the extent and scope of training programs. But, as others have pointed out, even if some of the reported hirings are unfounded, "nothing is lost except the cred-

SOURCE: *Jules Cohn, "Private Industry and the Disadvantaged,"* The Conscience of the Corporations: Business and Urban Affairs, *Johns Hopkins Press, 1970.*

[1] See *The Report of the National Advisory Commission on Civil Disorders* (N.Y.: Bantam, 1968).
[2] The stigmatizing term "hard core," referring to poor people who lack vocational skills and are

Corporate efforts are alternatively evaluated as triumphant, disastrous, or merely promising, depending on the evaluator's perspectives, ideology, and data sources. Harsh or beneficent judgments are continually being made by mayors, governors, legislators, the bureaucrats who report to them, and, of course, by businessmen and their public relations representatives.

On only one point is there general agreement: The problems that arise in hiring and training the disadvantaged are tough ones, and the objectives of corporate programs, as presently defined, are not easily realized. Though it is difficult to determine how many of the disadvantaged have actually been served by industry's programs—a quantitative measure—it is possible to analyze and assess the qualitative aspects of corporate programs. In my nationwide study of 247 companies, data were gathered about enrollees in these programs and their experiences. The kinds of training provided, costs entailed, problems encountered and short-term successes of nearly 100 programs were studied. This chapter reports on programs under way in a group of representative major corporations, and identifies factors influencing their success or failure. The nature of the training challenge, the advantages and disadvantages of respective program types, from the standpoint of the needs of trainees but also the requirements of managers and supervisors, are discussed. Comparative costs of subsidized and unsubsidized programs are also identified. Finally, some issues arising out of the new mythology and technology of vocational training and counseling are discussed.

DEGREE OF PARTICIPATION VARIES BY INDUSTRY

Of the 247 major companies I studied, nearly one third reported programs for the disadvantaged, and said they had hired a total of 8,000 from this special group, providing training for two fifths of the total. But the majority of companies who hired the disadvantaged did so without offering special training.

Participation in programs varied by in-

ibility of NAB." Sar Levitan, Garth Mangum, and Robert Taggart III, *Economic Opportunity in the Ghetto.* Baltimore: The Johns Hopkins Press, 1970, p. 30.

dustry. In my sample (but also in all corporate efforts for the disadvantaged), the greatest percentage of participants is found in aerospace companies, financial institutions (including banks, savings and loan companies, and insurance) and manufacturers of electronic and computer equipment. Companies reporting meager or no efforts predominate in merchandising, metal manufacturing, petroleum, farm and industrial machinery, and chemicals . . . . Labor-intensive industries and those dependent on government favors and/or goodwill are· at the head of the class.

"Don't compare us with aerospace or insurance," said the president of a new conglomerate, admitting that his company's efforts were slim. "The insurance companies have more cash than we do, and aerospace has to go out of its way to be a good citizen in order to keep the government money flowing." Another observer insisted that, "it wasn't until after the Detroit riots that the automakers got busy. If their factories were in East Cupcake, they wouldn't be so energetic."

Some companies say they are unable to participate because they lack proper equipment, or training staff, or sufficient space. Others claim that their production schedules cannot be adapted to the needs of the disadvantaged, or that their supervisors are unable to cope with the special training requirements of new programs. Or they protest that their manpower needs are specialized, and that they rarely have openings for unskilled workers.

Many companies reported that they were making their urban affairs contributions through donations programs, assignment of staff to community projects, or economic development loans for minority-group businessmen. "We decided to settle on spending more money to support other people's endeavors, rather than take on the headaches ourselves," said one executive. For his company, as well as for dozens of others, cash outlays are seen as more affordable than the stresses and strains expected from programs for the disadvantaged. New kinds of people in the company, new ways of training them, new attitudes in hearing grievances, and new rules of behavior for employees are among the side effects feared by those who decline to participate.

It cannot be denied that hiring and training the disadvantaged simply makes more sense for certain industries than others. The need for unskilled workers has, understandably, proved to be the best incentive. Some respondents said they would have invested in special training programs even if the riots had never occurred and the Kerner Report had never been written. "We were willing to try anyone and anything," said the personnel director of a large utility in Chicago. "Our older sources of manpower were drying up. Prejudice wasn't functional in this company any more. So no one had to force us to give this new category of job candidates a try."

The spotlight that was focused on unemployed nonwhites in urban centers has caught the attention of recruiters in companies hardpressed for candidates to fill lower level jobs. For these companies, hiring programs for the disadvantaged were set up not as social service but as an attempt to maintain and protect normal operations. Thus telephone companies in Newark, Chicago, New York, Cleveland, San Francisco were among the first employers of the disadvantaged, as they desperately sought to fill operator jobs in inner city stations spurned by others in the labor market.

Companies undertaking programs for the disadvantaged face many challenges. The uninterrupted flow of literature from promoters and advocates of industry participation emphasizes the special needs of the new employees. They eventually come to learn, too, about the need to train managers and supervisors, and the economic requirements of the new programs. There are dollar costs to meet, for profitability must be protected, and financially sound cost structures and production quotas maintained. There are also institutional costs to anticipate.

A PLETHORA OF TRAINING

The kinds of programs created by industry, as well as the expectations of industry leaders, have been influenced by some assumptions about training needs in programs for the disadvantaged. These assumptions are embodied in the Federally subsidized JOBS program, but also in programs conducted by business without government support. Because of the particular view of the nonwhite disadvantaged worker that they express, and their view of training requirements, they affect the costs, the shape, the

conduct of programs, but also whether or not a company will be willing to undertake training at all.

The major dogma, propounded over and over again in the rhetoric recited by proponents of programs for the disadvantaged, and in the "human interest" stories prepared by journalists for the business press, is that the disadvantaged are profoundly different from the rest of us. They come from a different culture, have a different view of the world, different work habits, expectations, and values. Because they are so different, jobs alone are not enough to solve the problem they present to us, according to the assumptions that influence program development. And conventional job training, the kind traditionally carried out in industrial settings, is not enough either. New approaches to training are said to be essential for program success.

Industry's efforts for the disadvantaged have placed primary emphasis on training as an essential concomitant of employment. Companies participating in JOBS, or influenced by it, have been encouraged to bombard disadvantaged employees, their coworkers and supervisors, with a plethora of training: For [the] newly hired employee, there must be specially designed vocational training to teach him requisite job skills. But to cope with his "cultural differences," he will need "attitudinal training" or psychological counseling. Co-workers and supervisors are said to need "orientation" to prepare them for the challenges presented by the disadvantaged, and sometimes psychological counseling as well.

Most of the assumptions about training needs embodied in programs for the disadvantaged are unsubstantiated by research data or practical experience. They are derived instead from the notions of government policy makers and academicians about the characteristics of the nonwhite (Spanish-speaking and black) disadvantaged unemployed. Whether or not they are valid, they have to a considerable extent deflected interest from employment as an end in itself to the conviction that employment is meaningless without training. And they have encouraged the development of a training technology within the private sector, as personnel departments have been reorganized and sometimes expanded to include those who specialize in meeting the challenges said to be presented by the disadvantaged. They have contributed to the costs of employing the disadvantaged by prescribing additional budgetary items. And while they have created jobs and demand for trainers, counselors, psychologists, lecturers and assorted visiting consultants, they have probably discouraged many corporate managers from recruiting the disadvantaged.

The remainder of this chapter reviews and assesses the typology of corporate programs for the disadvantaged. Training is emphasized in varying degrees in each of the programs to be reviewed. The extent to which training is necessary, or is a deflection from the goal of providing employment is a question in need of further research. Probably most important as a research question is what kind of training is needed? What kinds of training do more harm than good? What are some of the unanticipated consequences of psychological counseling for the disadvantaged, of the attempt to "adjust" them to the corporate world? And what are some of the consequences of the well-intended but potentially explosive "orientation" programs for supervisors and co-workers? Answers to some of these questions will be suggested in the program analyses and descriptions that follow.

A TYPOLOGY OF CORPORATE PROGRAMS

There are four basic models of corporate programs for training the disadvantaged: (1) on-the-job; (2) in a vestibule setting; (3) in a subsidiary intended to be "spun off" to community groups; or (4) in a company-owned subsidiary. . . .

On-the-Job Programs

On-the-job training is the most commonly selected approach in the companies I studied: 80 percent of all new hires, in the 39 companies offering training along with jobs, are enrolled in programs of this type. The economics suggest the reason. The on-the-job approach does not require costly separate facilities or special training staffs. On the surface at least, companies can undertake training without changing ongoing production procedures.

This approach offers little opportunity for auxiliary training or basic skills education. For the most part, the burden of providing for the needs of the new workers falls on line personnel. The problems faced by line managers forced to train, coach, and guide new employees as they learn to adjust to the production environment, are among the most serious in the on-the-job approach. A fundamental aspect of any vocational training program is that the trainer as well as the trainee be motivated, the latter to apply the knowledge that he is acquiring, and the former to want to pass on what he knows and encourage the worker to stay on the job. When the trainer sees his new charges as burdens, added to his normal work load by a management that appears to be indifferent to his day-to-day problems, he is not likely to feel very cooperative. The trainee can easily become his scapegoat, the target of a displaced grudge against management. Managers who commit themselves to on-the-job programs must give thought to providing incentives for supervisors. A foreman will not do an adequate job simply because he heard a rousing speech by the company president. Nor is it enough to lecture him about the social value of working with the poor.[4] Understandably, he will expect to be paid for the extra work (and frequently longer hours) entailed. The corporate spokesman who pledges his company to participation in programs for the disadvantaged, however noble his intentions, must be sensitive to the problems of his foremen. Otherwise, he will do more harm (to relations among whites and nonwhites in his company, to his foremen and supervisors, to the feelings of the disadvantaged, who will feel the wrath of their supervisors) than good. A few companies have come to see that material incentives are needed to assuage irritation among the latter and to encourage their cooperation. Though extra compensation or lightened work loads are rarely provided, revised or relaxed production deadlines have been tried in some companies to relax pressures on supervisors and co-workers.

In addition to the training challenge itself, and problems with foremen and super-

[4] See Frank Riessman, "Jobs Are Not Enough for the Hard Core." Address before the American Society for Training and Development. Mimeographed, available from New Careers Center, New York University, New York, N.Y. 10003.

visors discussed above, high turnover rates are also a major concern in companies with on-the-job programs. Vestibules and subsidiaries, described below, had markedly lower attrition than on-the-job programs. Retention rates in the latter averaged 30 percent in companies I studied; in the former, rates were 43 percent. And there is an interesting difference in the way people drop out. On-the-job trainees often "just never come back Monday morning," with foremen left to speculate about what happened. On the other hand, dropouts from vestibule or subsidiary programs are said to seldom simply disappear, according to my respondents. Usually they announce that they will be leaving, or give cue of their intentions. (Sickness, family problems, acceptance of another job or the desire to seek another job are the commonest explanations of voluntary resignations offered in all programs.) One can hypothesize that enrollees in on-the-job programs less readily develop identification with the company, the supervisor, or the work unit, than those in other types of programs, and that they therefore tend to resign by fading away, deciding that explanations are not necessary. In the more personal or supportive training environment provided by the vestibule and subsidiary, the enrollee perhaps feels more of an incentive to explain his actions, and to believe that the company and its representatives care about him.

Even though formal vocational training is provided by fewer than half of the companies in my study, belief in its importance is growing. Very high turnover rates among the new hires, particularly in the first weeks on the job, have brought home the message: Adequate training may cost less than high attrition resulting from indifferent or no training.

On-the-job training can range from an hour to several days of coaching, sometimes by specially trained supervisors. Only occasionally are psychological counseling services and remedial education programs available, with psychologists and teachers on call during work and lunch hours. One of the large automobile manufacturers hired a team of psychologists, who claimed special knowledge of the problems of the disadvantaged. Members of the team were authorized to serve as peripatetic advisers, wandering along the assembly line, available to foremen, co-workers, and disadvantaged new hires on request. A manufacturer of pharmaceuticals hired a remedial reading teacher to hold classes during lunch breaks. In both companies first priority was given to training the new employee to do his job. Auxiliary services were assigned the second priority.

A few companies that offer on-the-job training make efforts to help members of the regular work force prepare for the new employees. Lecture and seminar programs of varying lengths and intensity are offered. Because they are generally prepared by an urban affairs staff and seldom by social scientists or, at the other but equally attractive extreme, by disadvantaged people themselves, the quality and results of these programs are not impressive. By means of filmstrips, lectures, or seminars, a company's regular troops, or stratified selections of them, are indoctrinated with messages presumably meant to inspire cooperation with the new programs but are just as likely to provoke anxieties about the new-comers and antagonism toward them. Most of the material presented develops the idea that disadvantaged employees are profoundly different from the rest of us, and that their behavior will at first, at least, seem strange and exotic. The differences are emphasized, and explained on the basis of culture (they come from a different one) or class. Orientation classes provide an unnecessarily dramatic overture to the arrival in some companies of the disadvantaged. The training department in a division of one of the telephone companies issued a packet of materials labeled "urban orientation," containing "problem-solving" exercises for supervisors of the disadvantaged:

Incident #2

A traffic operator, who reports to you, has just requested 3 days off to have an abortion. Outline below what action you would take.

Incident #3

One of your employees reported to work this morning obviously affected by alcohol consumed before coming to work. He has been boisterous all morning, and during lunch period insulted a fellow employee who has reported the incident to you. Outline below the action you would take.

Incident #4

You have learned that an installer who reports to you is carrying his small tools home with him and, on his own time, working on installation jobs he started earlier. Outline below the action you would take.

Incident #5

You have recently added a disadvantaged person to your work team. There has been no open problem but you have heard there is a great deal of smoldering discontent among many of the other members of the work team. Acceptance of the new man is important, because, if he is to make the maximum contribution to the team, he must work closely with other members of the work force. Outline what action you would take.

Incident #6

One of your newly hired employees' mode of dress is causing you real problems. He is doing satisfactory work but is having difficulty in relating to his fellow workers and the customers. The employee insists on wearing a beard and loud, weird-looking clothing. His manner of dress has caused several customers to request that he not be sent back to residence on any future service calls. Indications are that this man could make a good employee if he would shave and dress in an acceptable manner. Outline what action you would take.

The above illustrations of corporate "urban orientation" materials are alarmist and sensational, tending as much to provoke prejudice as to lessen it. But the telephone company trainers to whom I spoke insisted that the exercises were valuable, and that they prepared supervisors for what could actually happen. Readers interested in more examples of the dogma and stereotyping contained in orientation material are referred to publications of the American Management Association, and the National Industrial Conference Board. They will find much material dedicated to the proposition that the behavior of the hard-core or disadvantaged worker will shock the sensibilities of co-workers and supervisors, who are, of course,

well-adjusted, well-mannered, and properly motivated.

The automobile makers, who probably took on a larger share of the disadvantaged than any other industry in the period immediately following publication of the Kerner Report, at first provided no special training for the new employees.[5] They assigned most of their operations and assembly jobs, sometimes after a few hours of orientation. But as turnover rates began to climb, they realized that intensive effort was needed. General Electric also intensified its training approach after a period of trial and error. When managers noted unusually high turnover rates, they set up a specially designed program of orientation and counseling for the new employees.

Vestibule Training

Conducted in an isolated facility by a special training staff, this approach provides a kind of halfway house to help the disadvantaged adjust to "the world of work" by learning the habits and discipline expected during a workday, and also learning the basic features of the jobs they will do.

The aim of the vestibule approach is to ease the attitudinal and morale problems of the newly hired disadvantaged worker by providing him with an opportunity to practice his job before assuming the responsibilities that would be necessary in an actual production environment. He can acquire vocational skills under the tutelage of foremen who are expected and paid to be sympathetic and patient on personal as well as work problems. In the vestibule, the foreman is concerned with the trainee and not with production. Despite the attractiveness of the vestibule as a training environment, only 18 of the 247 companies I studied had settled on this approach. Most of those who decided against the vestibule strategy were put off by the extra costs involved in obtaining and equipping the separate facility, and

---

[5] Levitan, Mangum, and Taggart have suggested that the automobile companies were probably motivated to hire large numbers of the disadvantaged as much by a tightening labor market as by a "blossoming" of their social consciousness. For in the peak production periods of 1967–1968, when demand for output was high, but the available labor supply low, they had nowhere else to go for unskilled help. Levitan, Mangum, Taggart, *op. cit.*, p. 31.

in paying a separate training staff. Companies with vestibule programs point out that in the long run costs balance out—for they insist that attrition and turnover rates are significantly lower than in on-the-job programs.

The vestibule approach has several other attractions. By assuring that disadvantaged workers will take their places in normal operations only after acquiring basic skills and work habits, it minimizes the extent to which their arrival in the plant or office will provoke hostilities from on-the-line workers resentful of their effect on ongoing production processes. Because the special attention and dispensation required by disadvantaged workers can arouse antagonism on the part of other workers, isolating trainees during the period in which they need help most can help guard against conflict.

The vestibule can protect trainees from seasonal layoffs that hit other parts of a company, by making it possible to classify them as employees of a special division, and exempting them from seniority rules. But the claim is not always substantiated by experience. Thus, the trainees in Chrysler's vestibule operations were laid off, along with other employees, when the company had to terminate its programs, in March 1970, in the face of a slumping economy. (Chrysler's JOBS contract of $13.8 million to hire and train 4,450 production workers in seven plants was cancelled.)[6]

Vestibule programs still in operation include an interesting one created by Lockheed in Sunnyvale, California. To the delight of those who argue that corporate urban affairs efforts can be income producing, the aerospace giant seemed to have forged a successful business enterprise out of the challenge to train the disadvantaged.[7] It created a facility to prepare disadvantaged workers for referral to jobs in 41 companies belonging to a specially formed consortium in the Bay Area. The aerospace company thus was able to put its training expertise to good use. On the East Coast, Western Electric estab-

lished programs in Newark, New Jersey, and Baltimore, Maryland.

Community-Owned Subsidiaries

In order to assist economic development efforts in slum communities, several companies set up subsidiaries intended to be spun off for eventual ownership by neighborhood groups. These subsidiaries provide jobs and training for the disadvantaged in a community setting. Because they are frequently managed and supervised by non-whites, they also provide management training opportunities. Only a handful of companies in my study chose this strategy for providing jobs and training, but it will be discussed here in some detail because of its potential significance in the drive to develop black (and brown) managers and entrepreneurs, and its popularity not only with community groups but with exponents of theories of "black capitalism."

Setting up a subsidiary intended for spinning off to a community group requires an economic commitment greater than on-the-job or vestibule training programs. It also saddles the parent company with a long-term moral responsibility. The subsidiary has to be capitalized and supported until it can manage on its own. The parent corporation must be a dependable purchaser or salesman of its products, through its own divisions, or its network of other contacts. Some community-owned companies have been given government contracts to help them get started, but most still depend on their parent companies which must also, as a rule, help with management problems, by providing advice on financial, production, marketing, and distribution practices.

Commitment to a subsidiary intended for community ownership involves the corporation in neighborhood relations on a greater scale than other kinds of training programs. Community groups become monitors of the enterprise, and make demands and requests that corporate leaders sometimes view as intrusive or unnecessary. As a constituency they are quite different from absentee stockholders. For one thing, they aren't absent, they are right there, sometimes demanding a review of employment and operating procedures, and other corporate policies. The subsidiary will one day be theirs, and they want to follow its progress, evaluating the

[6] Reported in *The Wall Street Journal,* March 3, 1970.
[7] Lockheed's experience with programs for the disadvantaged is described in James D. Hodgson and Marshall H. Brenner, "Successful Experience," *Harvard Business Review,* September–October 1968, pp. 148–156. Also see "The New Business of Business," by Jules Cohn, *Urban Affairs Quarterly,* Fall, 1970.

implementation of the parent's commitment. Companies that set up subsidiaries meant for spinning off include:

Aerojet-General, which established the Watts Manufacturing Company in Los Angeles in 1966, funded by a $500,000 Labor Department job training grant, a $2.5 million Defense Department contract, and two government set-asides at $1.5 million. Watts Manufacturing makes postal equipment, canvas and metal products, packaging materials, and housewares. It employs about 200 people.

EG&G, which established a metal fabrication plant in the Roxbury section of Boston. Fifty percent of the company's stock was to be offered to employees and community residents within 5 years. Sixty employees.

Fairchild Hiller, which created FAIRMICCO, a metal, wood, and electrical fabricating plant in Washington, D. C. One hundred employees. Fairchild and Model Inner City Community Organization (MICCO), partners in the operation, are to hold eventually only 10 percent of the stock; most of the rest is for employees. FAIRMICCO was funded by Labor Department training grants and by assistance from the Economic Development Administration.

Xerox, which, with other companies in Rochester, New York, established Fighton, a small manufacturing company. Fighton, owned by community stockholders, had a major contract with Xerox.

General Electric, which helped set up Progress Aerospace Enterprises, an electronic components manufacturing company in Philadelphia, managed by black engineers (from GE), with a guarantee of business from GE.

Mattel, which assisted Shindana Toys, a minority-owned business in Los Angeles. Shindana received management assistance from Mattel, as well as an initial credit line of $150,000.

Few subsidiaries intended for community ownership have fared well. In the main, their problems have been economic. EG&G's facility failed before it could be spun off to the community. There was considerable turmoil and strain, attributed to problems in management and financing. It closed, in April 1970, at an estimated loss to the parent company of $500,000. Bernard J. O'Keefe, president of EG&G, blamed other businesses in the area, as well as the Federal government, for failing to provide markets for the small company's products. "Everyone was

hopped up over this thing 2 years ago," he said. "Company presidents would say, 'sure, we'll buy from you.' This would be passed down through vice presidents to the purchasing agent, whose job is to buy it at the lowest price. He'd give $500 to $1,000 worth of business, which is worse than nothing at all. I guess I know what blacks mean when they talk about tokenism."[8]

According to O'Keefe, EG&G underestimated the time and money needed to make a success of the project, and had difficulty, too, in finding the right managers. "This kind of venture attracts the people who are 'socially committed' and doing the job on their own time, but not the people who are concerned about costs or meeting budgets."[9]

Watts Manufacturing Company, created by Aerojet-General, also had problems but found someone to rescue it. The subsidiary was purchased from Aerojet in April 1970 by the Chase Manhattan Capital Corporation, a Small Business Investment Company (SBIC), for $1.1 million. Terms of the purchase provided that shares of the subsidiary would be placed in an escrow fund for eventual purchase by employees (most of whom are black) over a 7-year period. (Watts Manufacturing would thus continue to be eligible for contracts under the Federal minority business procurement program.) The terms of the purchase provided that Chase would retain its equity as employees buy stock, but the SBIC would retain a 20 percent interest in the company. "It's a pretty fair business deal that should make money for everyone," said Louis L. Allen, CMCC president.[10]

Company-Owned Subsidiaries

Wholly owned subsidiaries for training the disadvantaged were set up by North American Rockwell (NARTRANS in Los Angeles), Control Data (in North Minneapolis), AVCO Manufacturing (in the Roxbury section of Boston), and about three dozen other companies. In many ways these subsidiaries are similar to those intended to be spun off: They are generally managed by

8 *Business Week,* January 31, 1970.
9 Quoted in *Fortune,* May, 1970, p. 74.
10 Quoted in *Business Week,* May 9, 1970, p. 26. For Allen's own report on earlier activities of Chase Manhattan's SBIC see Louis L. Allen, "Making Capitalism Work in the Ghettos," *Harvard Business Review,* May–June, 1969.

nonwhites, are designed on a small scale (50–200 employees), and obtain their production equipment from the parent company's surplus stock. But they are not meant for spinning-off to the community, and are operated without participation by local groups.

Companies selecting this approach are attracted by the fact that by providing programs in separate facilities they can escape the need to alter ongoing production operations in existing locations. The special needs or problems of the trainees are kept away from the rest of the company. Only after careful screening, preceded by a period of training and actual work experience, are participants in these programs transferred into normal operations. Like the vestibule and the subsidiary planned for eventual spin-off, this approach has enabled companies to set lower wage scales for the disadvantaged without meeting objections from union negotiators, who—at least to date—have been willing to exempt *separated* operations from union scales.

But both types of subsidiary introduce costs and complications avoidable in on-the-job training and vestibules. Once created, the new shop or factory has a life of its own, and an audience. It is harder to close down than a pilot training project in an existing plant, using existing facilities. Its problems and achievements are more visible than those in programs that are part of normal operations. Constant vigilance, including attention to its products and their marketing, as well as to the progress of training efforts, is needed in order to ward off the many problems that can beset a subsidiary.

Of the 247 companies in my study, only 11 set up subsidiaries. And the number of employees and trainees participating in them is small. A total of only about 1,000 disadvantaged workers are reported involved in the programs I studied. Upgrading had been achieved, according to my data, for 125 employees, but few of these were transferred to jobs in parent companies.

TRAINING: COSTS AND OTHER ISSUES

Whatever the total number of jobs provided by industry's programs for the disadvantaged, there is ample evidence to show that the country's major companies can be induced to undertake recruiting and training efforts. The key questions for businessmen (and for government policy makers) are: What are the training requirements? How much will training cost? How can these costs be met?

Costs

When special training efforts are involved, employing the hard-to-employ involves higher costs than employing other job candidates. Auxiliary services—psychological counseling, remedial education, and social work—are sometimes provided, as well as expenditures for medical care, reimbursement for transportation, child care, etc. Accordingly, even companies that already have large training technologies incur extra costs when they hire the disadvantaged. In companies where training for entry-level jobs was never an allowable cost, budgets have to be increased by a new item. Moreover, companies sometimes pay for training of trainers and for orientation and training of supervisors.

There are wide variations in cost estimates, depending on the type of company, its location, and the kind of training undertaken. Federal grants made under the JOBS program averaged $2,800 in 1968 and $3,000 in 1969 per trainee. But by the spring of 1970, this amount would be cut back to $1,800. Companies supporting their own programs without government help report costs as high as $4,000. Lowest costs are reported in the insurance and banking industries, where estimates are placed at $2,200 per trainee, compared to about $1,000 for other entry-level employees. Companies in the aerospace industry quote costs as high as $3,000 for each disadvantaged trainee, compared with $1,500 for other new hires. Costs of higher turnover and absenteeism contribute to company estimates.

Has any company not lost money on its programs? To date, no one has reported that hiring the disadvantaged has brought direct economic benefits, but companies include in their calculations of the return realized by their efforts such factors as enhancement of their reputation with consumers, government, and potential critics. And a few with growing needs for unskilled labor are able to appreciate the value of the new manpower sources discovered by their programs.

For companies in the banking, insurance, and utilities industries, the improvement of training capabilities for the disadvantaged has led to improvements in training programs for other employees. And a limited number of companies are now producing goods and services formerly purchased on the open market but now turned out by the new employees during training periods. Though some companies have been accused of exploiting the JOBS program by claiming costs in excess of expenses incurred, it must be noted that other companies, including many large and prominent ones, have declined the opportunity to receive government benefits, and are paying for their programs themselves.

There are many reasons why a company might prefer to avoid participating in government-administered programs. The determination to pay its own bills rather than draw on public funds is only one. Participants in the JOBS program are required to hire only those applicants who have been classified by government interviewers as meeting the criteria that define the disadvantaged. Many companies prefer to do their own screening, apply their own definitions, and avoid entanglement with public bureaucracy.

In his case study of IBM's new plant for disadvantaged workers in the Bedford-Stuyvesant section of Brooklyn, Edward C. Banfield reported that the plant manager and his assistants decided to postpone the hiring of workers with serious problems until a "productive" work force had been created and tested. "He was aware that the Management Review Committee expected him to dig deep into the hard core, as Eastman Kodak, for example, was doing. He would dig eventually, but not right away." Thus, for the time being anyway, IBM would turn away the unmotivated, alcoholics, addicts, etc.[11] Some critics offered another explanation, and accused IBM of "creaming" the top of the labor supply in the neighborhood, to avoid the truly disadvantaged.[12] Whatever the reason, the intrusion of government bureaucrats is considered by some companies to be more burdensome than paying the costs of hiring and training disadvantaged workers. Participation has also been inhibited by fears that payroll records, personnel folders, and training practices will be reviewed. In my study, a little more than half of the companies operating programs for the disadvantaged were doing so with the help of government funds.

Training: A False Issue

In the business press and at workshops and seminars conducted by urban affairs consultants, poverty politicians, ideological academicians, industrial and even clinical psychologists, the notion that the disadvantaged cannot be reached by normal techniques of manpower management has been popularized. A new technology of training is necessary, it is argued, and sizable investments are required to pay counsellors, teachers, sensitivity trainers. The government's own JOBS program legitimates (and stimulates) substantial training expenditures by providing subsidies for them, and for services to trainees to supplement vocational guidance. Many companies that boast of their training capabilities (IBM, AT&T, some of the aerospace companies) increased their training budgets even more than usual when they decided to recruit the disadvantaged.

But perhaps the training task is not as onerous or costly as the literature and the sales talks of the consultants suggest. Jobs alone have motivated many members of the hard core, and vocational training alone without psychological support services has succeeded, too. The companies I studied developed different techniques of training, and proceeded at varying speeds, and no one asserted that the key factor for success was the provision of auxiliary services. "We had the requisite training skills right here," said one company president, "only we didn't know it at first."

It would appear from the data that it is not as difficult to motivate and train the disadvantaged as many people think. With retention rates at the 30–40 percent level, industry's programs prove that the performance of the hard core of the poor in entry-level jobs is not markedly inferior to that of other new hires. Many corporate leaders and their line department heads, including per-

[11] Edward C. Banfield, "An Act of Corporate Citizenship," in Peter B. Doeringer, ed., *Programs To Employ the Disadvantaged*. Englewood Cliffs, N.J.: Prentice-Hall, 1969, p. 39.
[12] See John A. Hamilton, "The Business of Business Is Still Business," *The New York Times*, February 10, 1969, p. 38.

sonnel directors, feel that they were led to expect greater problems with the new programs than they actually encountered.

THE FUTURE OF CORPORATE PROGRAMS

The key challenge in corporate programs for the disadvantaged is how to pay for them, not how to conduct them. Costs need to be kept at levels reasonable enough to attract industry participation. Impassioned appeals for community service and alarming news reports from inner city neighborhoods will not be enough to sustain corporate interest in any program over the long term.

By stressing the importance of training and auxiliary services, rather than jobs alone, Federal manpower policy has served to increase businessmen's expectations about the costs of programs, and to influence the kinds of programs they create. The basic issue posed by the emphasis on training must, therefore, be resolved if realistic cost projections are to be made. Some suggest that the Federal government ought to subsidize jobs rather than training. Senator Gaylord Nelson, Chairman of the Subcommittee on Employment, Manpower and Poverty of the Labor and Public Welfare Committee, has proposed that the Department of Labor earmark a portion of its budget allotment designated for manpower training to develop job programs instead, especially among the young. Other techniques that would shift government's emphasis onto jobs alone are needed.

It is possible that the basic problem of the disadvantaged is discrimination, and intensified government efforts to enforce antidiscrimination legislation are indicated. Stronger enforcement would perhaps encourage more companies to participate in hiring programs, particularly if extraneous training costs could be pared down.

The business recession in the spring of 1970 proved that cutbacks and slowdowns in industry are particularly hard on corporate programs for the disadvantaged. Many companies terminated their programs, or refused appeals to begin new ones, blaming the recession for their demurrals. In addition to layoffs of nearly 7,000 hard-core workers at Chrysler, and the cancellation of the company's $13.8 million contract with the Labor Department, the recession has already affected enrollees dismissed from jobs at General Motors, and in the steel industry.

Community group spokesmen and other urban crisis-watchers interviewed in May 1970 expressed concern that the recession and the layoffs it engendered would be the cause of summer riots. *The New York Times* quoted Douglas Fraser, National Director of the United Automobile Workers unit at Chrysler Corporation, as saying, "I just wonder whether we haven't done more harm than good with this program. We built up hopes and then we pull the rug out from under them."[13]

If the recession continues, and more programs are terminated, attempts to train and upgrade the disadvantaged will be defeated not by their problems, or the lack of skills on the part of their trainers, but by the leveling off of the economy, and by cost structures, subsidy policies, and problem definitions that made it impossible for programs to outlast a business slump.[14]

[13] *The New York Times,* April 11, 1970.
[14] It is noteworthy that the National Alliance of Businessmen in early 1970 announced a new strategy to attract participation in the JOBS program by companies thought to be immune to recession. NAB would attempt to find jobs for the disadvantaged in service industries (schools, hospitals, small businesses not directly dependent on manufacturing). Other companies enjoying "employment stability," such as the telephone companies, banks and food processors, would be encouraged to participate.

THE POLITICAL ECONOMY OF BLACK CAPITALISM

Barry Bluestone

This essay provides a critical perspective on the potential importance of ghetto economic development or "black capitalism." Bluestone argues that fundamental structural changes in the economy would have to occur before "black capitalism" could make much difference in the lives of ghetto workers.

The essay appeared in a different form in the *Review of Radical Political Economics* and has been substantially revised by the author for this volume.

Bluestone is a research associate of the Institute for Labor and Industrial Relations at the University of Michigan.

Back in 1960 four black students sat down at a white-owned Greensboro, North Carolina, lunch counter and asked to be served. Later, freedom rides, sit-ins, peaceful marches, and finally urban rebellion became vehicles for black expression *against* racism and *for* a fair share of American abundance. In most cases, the corporate sector responded with indifference, if not open hostility, to these anguished cries for social and economic justice. It was only when the smoke from ghetto uprisings could be, seen in their suburbs that corporate management began to realize that the economic, political, and social problems in the tense ghetto could potentially explode into their problems as well.

In the absence of a response from private enterprise, the federal government reacted to the clamor for justice by offering a portfolio of inadequately funded reforms. Beginning in 1962, Congress aimed its anti-poverty strategy in the direction of injecting job skills into the poor in an effort to transform the unemployed and unskilled into useful inputs for the expanding business sector. Later a spectrum of "Great Society" programs was introduced. Typically these programs were designed to outfit "misfits" with the qualities necessary to compete effectively in the evolving labor market.

For most of the ghetto poor, however, the so-called "war on poverty" was a badly fought, inadequately armed skirmish. The ghetto survived the "war," rooted to the inner-city soil very much as it was before the

days of the New Frontier. Some small segment of American minorities may have been aided by federal anti-poverty schemes, but the logic of the economist cannot be denied: the marginal benefits from the poverty programs aimed at refurbishing people rather than the refurbishing of economic and social institutions were purchased at high cost.

Out of the rubble of incinerated ghettos has grown a fresh perspective on the liberation of black America: "black economic self-determination." It entails black ownership, operation, and control of business enterprise. Militant black leaders have called it controlling the black economy. Mr. Nixon has called it "getting a piece of the action." Under the rubric of "black capitalism"—a term coined by the mass media—a previously disinterested or hostile corporate establishment has shown enthusiastic support for the strategy. But it is an illusion that black militants and white corporation executives share the same political-economic perspective, for the "black economic self-determination" of the militants and the "black capitalism" of the business establishment have little in common. The former scheme may portend a viable inner-city political movement accompanied by new jobs within an internally controlled inner-city economic base, while "black capitalism" may lead to a few more jobs for the black community, but inevitably at the expense of greater inner-city subservience to the white economic structure.

THE GHETTO ECONOMY

According to recent estimates, blacks constitute over 11 percent of the population, yet own or operate less than 1 percent of the

SOURCE: *Barry Bluestone, "Black Capitalism: The Path to Black Liberation,"* Review of Radical Political Economics, *I, May, 1969. Reprinted here as "The Political Economy of Black Capitalism."*

nation's five million private businesses.[1] Fewer than 3½ percent of the non-white labor force are managers, officials, or proprietors, while 14.2 percent of white employment is found in such occupations. While one of every forty whites is a proprietor of some sort, only one in a thousand blacks is so situated. The distribution of business enterprise is, indeed, even more dismal than these statistics imply, for an overwhelming proportion of black-owned business is extremely small-scale and marginal, lying at the periphery of the American economic structure. It comes as no surprise that the black customer, even in his own neighborhood, inevitably faces a white man when he buys his furniture, his clothing, or his vegetables.

This condition has become increasingly intolerable within the black community. In Watts, in Detroit, in Newark, and in numerous other black communities, the targets of Molotov cocktails were white-owned storefronts, neon-lit symbols of a "honky"-dominated culture and of an entrenched lily-white economy. The condition is made more intolerable by the fact that the inner-city poor pay more for what they buy in the ghetto and receive poorer quality than the suburban rich.[2] Ghetto blacks suffer from living in a "company town" with a "company store" and rarely accumulate enough to escape. With the routes to the outside world blocked by segregated housing and low income, black leadership has turned inward to its own community to find the means of escape.

Blacks are becoming more determined to expropriate the company store and develop it to fill the needs of the community, not the pocketbooks and bank accounts of absentee landlords and shopowners. The initial demand calls for blacks to take over or buy out ghetto shops, manage them, and reap the profit that might accrue from such enterprise. More far-reaching, however, is the expressed desire to expand the ghetto's economic base. For it is clear that while the expropriation of retail shops, laundries, and small-scale customer service industries will place black faces behind the shop counters, the misery of low

incomes and constant subservience can never be overcome by small-scale superficial means. Development of a production center as well as a distribution sector is necessary to generate a viable economy.

Such a development, however, necessarily requires capital and expertise, two commodities which are not native to the inner city and which must be imported from White America. For this reason, many black communities are turning to the federal government and large-scale private enterprise for aid. The response from Washington and especially from the elite of the corporate sector has been more than mildly enthusiastic.

THE NEED FOR ECONOMIC DEVELOPMENT

The real problem in the inner cities of America is not white faces behind drugstore counters, a phenomenon little more than skin deep.[3] Rather the root problem is the total lack of income generating production in the ghetto, the ubiquitous hallmark of a poor community. For all practical purposes the inner city is an underdeveloped region, suffering from decades of colonial rule which implicitly, if not systematically, deprived ghetto inhabitants of the physical and human capital fundamental to economic and social development. Denied the educational resources and the physical infrastructure necessary to develop technical skills and provide an efficient means of production, and at the same time denied access to the corporate sector through discriminatory practices in housing, in the schools, on the job, and in the capital market, the ghetto has been forced to rely on its one remaining resource: cheap labor. This it exports at a going rate of $1.60 an hour and sometimes less. During periods of extremely tight labor markets, all but 10 percent of the supply is exploited; during periods of recession, as much as 40 percent is left to seed. The ghetto is forced to survive on poverty wages, welfare payments, and anything it can beg, borrow, or steal.

Such an economy, lacking its own means of production and distribution, acts as a sieve. Income injected into the ghetto economy quickly dissipates into outlying suburbs

[1] Sar Levitan, "Community Self-Determination and Entrepreneurship: Their Promises and Limitations," *Poverty and Human Resource Abstracts*, Vol. 4, No. 1, January–February 1969, p. 18.

[2] David Caplovitz, *The Poor Pay More*, The Free Press of Glencoe, New York, 1963.

[3] This is not to deny the psychological and cultural advantages which accrue to the black community from gaining control over its own environment.

and outside investment. In economic terms, the inner city has a very small multiplier, approaching the value of one. Instead of remaining in the ghetto, passing from grocer to baker to candlestick-maker in return for services or goods supplied, the income dollar brought into the black community in the morning, through a small payroll or welfare check, gets spent that afternoon in a white-own ghetto store, and leaves in the evening for the suburbs and beyond. Such an income cycle considerably reduces the real income of the community and, what is worse, prevents the accumulation of any meaningful savings which could be turned to investment. The lack of black-owned enterprise thus accounts in part for the continuing leakage of capital from the ghetto.

Indeed, the cycle described here need not necessarily result in a depleted region. If the multiplier of an area fails to rise much above one, but the region is productive, exporting valuable goods and services to the outside world, affluence is assured. This is the case of the white suburb. Inner-city productive capacity, however, lies undeveloped, exporting services lightly valued by a market controlled by monopoly capital.

To reverse this condition would require the development of black-owned distribution centers in the way of wholesale and retail outlets as well as services, and more importantly, the development of a black-owned and operated production sector, capable of developing and manufacturing goods for sale both for inner-city use and for export. In this manner, injections of income into the inner city are greatly expanded and the income multiplier enhanced. While under present circumstances, a great part of the gain from welfare checks accrues to the white middle class, a developed inner city with a production and distribution matrix would be in a position to take full advantage of income injections. Leakage would be reduced to a minimum and could be spent where the comparative advantage of buying imports was greatest. Under an ideal system of inner-city economic development, the black community would no longer be forced to pay more for less.

THE MANY GUISES OF "BLACK CAPITALISM"

In response to the call for black economic development, scores of "black capitalism"

schemes have been unveiled, each with its own particular ideology and structure. Strategies range from large established corporations entering the ghetto to set up centrally controlled subsidiaries which capitalize on surplus labor and low wages, to perspectives which foresee community ownership and control of large-scale production and distribution centers, a form of "black socialism."

The simplest case is the traditional one. With a small amount of acquired capital, either saved or borrowed, private black entrepreneurs buy out individual white stores and manage them according to time-honored custom. Drugstores, grocery markets, and clothing outlets remain marginal, reaping small profit, adding only slight employment opportunity and little income to the community. The only critical difference is the black face behind the counter and the fact that the small trials and tribulations of capitalist ownership now accrue to a black rather than a white soul. To be sure, direct external control is minimal under this plan (although the competitive marketplace continues to set the boundaries of success). But to see in this strategy a means of economic development is overly optimistic, for almost by definition, the traditional scheme fails to aggregate enough capital for investment in profitable large-scale enterprise.

A significant alternative to "corner store" capitalism is posed by direct white corporate intervention in the ghetto economy. A case in point is that of Aerojet-General, a prime defense contractor, entering the ghetto of Los Angeles. In 1966, following the Watts riot, Aerojet-General developed the Watts Manufacturing Company and placed a Negro business leader in the president's chair.[4] Aerojet's philanthropy created several hundred new jobs in a riot-torn city, providing some marginal improvement in a post-marginal condition. However, it has done little to realign the relationship of the black community to the white power structure. The control of the Watts subsidiary does not emanate from the ghetto; rather the "black" company remain subservient to Aerojet and it is to the father firm that WMC, Inc. pays deference, and in the long run, possibly profits. Other firms including AVCO, Raytheon, Lockheed,

[4] William E. Zisch, "The Private Sector's Role in the Urban Crisis," Industrial Relations Center, California Institute of Technology, Pasadena, California, 1968.

and Ling-Tempco-Vought have attempted similar projects utilizing government subsidies.

An alternative to direct corporate intervention in the ghetto is the development of indigenous black corporations. The most famous and successful of these efforts remains the Opportunities Industrialization Center program pioneered by the Rev. Leon H. Sullivan in Philadelphia.[5] Sullivan envisions in his plan a bright future for the Negro entrepreneur.[6]

I see the African American becoming a part of American capitalism—in fact, joining the free enterprise system worldwide.

For all the years that my brothers and sisters—and my poor ancestors—have been a part of America, we have been outside the door of free enterprise, outside the door of capitalism. What I want to see is my black brothers walking through the door of free enterprise, not as "black capitalists" but as black men who can join the whole free-enterprise system and share its benefits.

The Reverend adds,[7]

I think of myself and what I'm doing as "black power" itself—it is black, it is capitalism, it is American. I will never be satisfied until every black adult in America owns a piece of this country individually or mutually, even if it is no more than two square feet of earth or a share of stock.

Beginning with a quarter of a million dollars raised from his church, Sullivan invested in a million-dollar apartment complex. Later "Progress Plaza," the largest black-owned shopping center in the world, was established with sixteen privately owned shops. Not content, Sullivan's acquired financial acumen directed him into the aerospace industry where he created Progress Aerospace Enterprises with management borrowed from the General Electric Corporation and a G.E. subcontract for $2.5 million of component production for the U.S. moon

mission. In addition, the OIC's Zion Investment Corporation has established the Progress Garment Manufacturing Company in Philadelphia which employs seventy-five workers. With this beginning, Sullivan believes he is on the way to creating "black power."

Management responsibility for Sullivan's Investment Corporation rests in a board of directors selected by its 3,500 shareholders. The waiting list for stock ownership is in excess of 2,000 families. But Philadelphia has over a half million blacks and so Rev. Sullivan's private enterprise scheme has fallen well short of serving even 3 percent of Philadelphia's ghetto population including children. Whether capitalism can work for the black working class as well as the bourgeoisie remains a moot point. How much of the black community can escape poverty and powerlessness, even with the aid of white corporate support, cannot be exactly determined.

In addition, there is some doubt as to whether the OIC will be able to remain independent from the white power structure. It has been assured the scarce resources of capital and technical expertise from the white community, but only after establishing an Advisory Board of twenty-five "influential" business leaders. George Champion, chairman of the board of Chase Manhattan Bank, heads up this board.

A fourth strategy is now being developed by a small group of black businessmen, economists, and accountants in Detroit.[8] With an inventory showing less than 35 percent of the ghetto economic base owned by blacks, and a $50,000 gift from Henry Ford II, the Inner City Business Improvement Forum (ICBIF) set out to build a black infrastructure within the inner city to stem the outward flow of black-earned dollars. Over the past three years, ICBIF's leadership has evolved a "community concept of comprehensive inner-city development" which stresses the need to develop retail outlets controlled by the black community, and the absolute necessity of establishing a production sector and black banking system to accumulate internally generated investment funds. Shying away from the paternalistic New Detroit Committee, founded by promi-

[5] *U.S. News and World Report,* " 'Black Capitalism' at Work: What's Happening in Philadelphia—An Exclusive Interview," February 17, 1969, p. 63.
[6] *Ibid.*
[7] *Ibid.*

[8] Information on the Inner City Business Improvement Forum (ICBIF) was obtained from interviews with the organization's past executive secretary, Walter McMurtry.

nent city businessmen even before the 1967 ghetto conflagration cooled, ICBIF has turned increasingly to the government for seed capital.

In 1968 a supermarket was established on Detroit's East Side to serve a large part of the surrounding black community. ICBIF provided 10 percent of the funds, while a leading city bank and the Small Business Administration picked up the first and second mortgages to supply the rest of the initial capital outlay. One-dollar shares are now being sold in the community to assure that profit from the supermarket goes to the community consumer rather than suburban interests. The board of directors for this supermarket and similar ventures created by ICBIF is chosen by the "block" clubs in the serviced areas. This, along with a strict limit on an individual's stockholdings, ensures democratic control of each enterprise.

In addition to the supermarket, ICBIF has now established a metal stamping plant, a plastics plant, and an iron foundry which is community controlled. Through such activities the black community in Detroit is beginning to gain some margin of control over the estimated $750 million which annually pass over inner-city store counters. Free of external manipulation, black community control is gained over an independent economic structure which can interact with the white-controlled economy from a position of comparative advantage rather than subservience. But whether even this scale of independent black enterprise is sufficient for economic viability, free of white support, is questionable.

There is yet another form of "black economic development," a form which is avowedly political and only secondarily economic in nature. The economic development strategy, in essence, is no more than an organizational tool for building an indigenous inner-city political base. By investing small amounts of capital, either generated internally or "hustled" from guilt-ridden whites, a nascent community-controlled black economic sector is launched, providing some new employment opportunities, but more importantly, a rallying point for community action. Profits from the enterprise are plowed back into the organization both for further business expansion and for political action. In this manner, the community organization becomes self-sufficient and free from external control. As the economic substructure expands, the political organization matures, benefiting from a well-financed base. Educational and cultural activities can be added to the political thrust of such a movement, thus creating an integrated program of community action.

It should be patently clear that each of the strategies outlined above can be evaluated according to two potentially conflicting criteria: first, the speed with which the plan leads to economic development as measured by rising employment, incomes, and capital outlays; and second, whether the scheme possesses a structure and dynamic conducive to economic and political liberation as measured by economic self-sufficiency and political influence. The conflict between the pace of development and self-determination arises from the scarcity of capital and expertise in the ghetto. For the inner-city community to develop economically over a short period of time, much capital and talent must be imported from the white community. Inevitably, large-scale importation leads to surrendering some control over the direction of development.

Thus while one scheme leads rapidly to investment in the ghetto by white business, it almost assuredly fails to promise radical change in the structure of power relations between white and black. On the other hand, development carried out solely by the black community may contribute some political freedom, but at the cost of continued economic stagnation. A conscious decision must then be made by the black community as to which road it chooses to travel, and indeed, how much "liberty" should be surrendered to hasten the development process. For the black community, it will seldom be permissible to have one's cake and eat it too.

THE CORPORATE INVASION OF THE INNER CITY

When the black community decides which development route to travel, the decision will not be made in a vacuum. Already the corporate establishment has offered its services to the inner city. The Watts Manufacturing Company of Aerojet is only one of many forms of aid being extended to the ghetto as black leaders turn their attention to economic development. Some companies have offered technical assistance, while others have contributed investment funds directly to black capitalist projects, and still others have created the means for long-term development loans.

Why has the corporate establishment leaped enthusiastically to the aid of black capitalist development when in the recent past it was a bastion of reaction against the war on poverty and legislation aimed at eliminating racial discrimination? It is good practice in answering this question to look at who stands to make the profit and who the loss.

Corporate management increasingly understands that growing unrest in the inner city threatens a smooth-running society. As Detroit burned, the auto plants were forced to shut down production; when production resumed, militant black groups like the League of Revolutionary Workers gained new strength within the plants. Demands for greater control over jobs and the economic environment were heard not only on 12th Street, but on the assembly lines at the Rouge Plant as well. Because of such developments, corporate managers have awakened to the fact that while what's good for America might not always be good for General Motors, what's bad for the American ghetto is increasingly bad for the company. Viewed from this perspective, an explosive inner city is a menace to the corporate establishment and the interests it defends.

To those responsible for maintaining efficient production on the assembly lines of the corporate sector, black capitalism has become one possible alternative to black chaos. If black capitalism works, the hope is that the black community will turn inward toward constructing a new set of economic conditions within the inner city rather than turning outward with attempts at reconstructing the conditions of power within the white business community. Black capitalism seems to offer some relief from the chaos, if not from its causes.

Increasingly, management also realizes that its own autonomy can be better preserved and long-run profits augmented by reducing the role of the federal government in developing the ghetto. By forging an alliance between black capitalists and themselves and foreclosing a nascent government-black producer coalition, corporate managers and owners can look forward to lower input costs (in terms of intermediate goods used

by large-scale industry in final goods production) and can spare themselves future competition both for government contracts and in the manufacture of some products. Furthermore, a smaller federal role in poverty programs and a larger corporate role in developing all black subsidiaries in the inner city could lead to a reduced emphasis on legislation aimed at discriminatory policies within the corporate sector. Legislation which now prohibits the federal government from contracting with firms which fail to live up to fair practice codes might be enforced less stringently. The public relations boost derived from lending a helping hand to the poor as well as the tax saving from discontinued Great Society programs are also viewed as boons to big business.

The corporate elite's positive attitude toward black ghetto enterprise is bolstered by the fact that white corporate profit will not be endangered by the introduction of the black capitalism strategy envisioned by the corporate establishment. The reason is simple. This strategy foresees the black community providing only two goods: (1) retail services to fill the community's needs for vegetables, meats, drugstore products, television repair, and other services, and (2) small-scale manufacture of intermediate goods for the industrial sector to use in the production of automobiles, washing machines, and computers. In the first case, the corporate sector is left unharmed by black capitalism for the corporate sector sells very little at the retail level. In the second, ghetto manufacturing firms will actually contribute to the corporate sector's profits, not deplete them, by providing cheaper intermediate goods for the major industries to use in final goods production. Excess profits of the largest industrial giants can be invested in the inner city (without fear of retaliation from the government anti-trust division) to establish subsidiaries which provide them with cheap parts and labor hired at less than union scale.

Side-stepping unions in the already organized intermediate goods industries is a difficult, if not risky, enterprise for the corporate leadership. Since the 1950's, such attempts by large corporations have been rare. Now, however, the opportunity for circumventing union power (with the blessing of government and the aid of the black community) has emerged. The small plant can pay half the going wage of unionized vendor operations, and yet still pay wages above the level normally offered low-skilled workers in the ghetto. In this way both the ghetto and the corporation benefit. Such a symbiotic relationship between the corporate elite and the community poor at the expense of the unionized working class has the potential for being the most exotic in a long line of techniques developed by industry for curbing union strength.

Other strategies for utilizing black capitalism to produce higher white corporate profit show equal ingenuity. For example, during the short-lived period of five-year/ 50,000 mile automobile warranties, auto industry executives developed a scheme whereby pre-delivery automobile diagnostic centers would be established in the ghetto, using black labor and white corporate capital and expertise. Such black-owned centers, manned by trained black auto mechanics, would test new cars at company expense before delivery to their prospective buyers. In this way fewer repairs would be required at cost to the auto industry and customer satisfaction would be reinforced. However, before the diagnostic centers were financed, the shorter car warranty was reinstated by the industry. Now the auto industry is no longer responsible for repairing much of its built-in obsolescence, and consequently the industry's savings from pre-delivery diagnosis and adjustment are reduced. The upshot is that the auto executives' enthusiasm for the centers waned considerably and the project now lies on the scrap heap.

Last, but not least, mention must be made of the profits which can be gleaned from government subsidy programs designed to induce big business participation in inner-city development. With such subsidies or tax incentives as specified in legislation like the Community Self-Determination Bill, for example, little effort is required on behalf of the corporate structure to create a "ghetto-industrial" complex including cost-plus contracts, loss write-offs, and tax-free subsidies. The corporate establishment is more than happy to help the black community—especially if it receives a little help itself.

"BLACK CAPITALISM" RECONSIDERED

Business brought into the ghetto by the white corporate establishment may very well add something to the inner-city environment. Some new jobs will be created, the average wage in the core city may rise a bit, and a few enterprising blacks will no doubt succeed in escaping the ghetto altogether. For some, a new sense of pride may develop. But what is equally true is that no black capitalism scheme which relies on the white establishment for sustenance will lead to a form of inner-city economic development which can result in black sociopolitical liberation. It is not in the interest of big business to develop a viable black economic sector, competitive in the new growth industries. Under white-dominated black capitalism, the best the black community can do is vie with the blue-collar unionized sector for a share of the intermediate goods market.

But if corporate intervention in the ghetto will not create a viable economy, can independent private black capitalism, unaided, but also unencumbered by the mixed blessing of corporate involvement, lead the black community to freedom? The answer is probably no. Independent private black enterprise cannot serve as the catalyst for economic development and political power.

It is a sad fact that private small-scale enterprises pay poverty wages, reap little profit, and consequently contribute little to economic development per se. While black retail capitalism will boost the inner-city multiplier by some small amount, the additional income generated will fail to raise a significant number of blacks from poverty. Consider, for instance, the average hourly wage rates paid in retail trade across the nation in the mid-1960's:[9]

Limited price variety stores	$1.31
Eating and drinking places	1.14
Drug and proprietary stores	1.56
Gasoline service stations	1.52
Apparel and accessory stores	1.70
Retail food stores	1.91

These were average rates; the inner-city wage levels helped to keep them this low. In addition, statistics on low-wage industry profits indicate that there is little room to raise these wage rates much beyond such low levels.[10]

[9] Barry Bluestone, "Lower-Income Workers and Marginal Industries," in Ferman, Kornbluh, and Haber, *Poverty in America*, 2d ed., University of Michigan Press, Ann Arbor, 1968.
[10] George Delehanty and Robert Evans, Jr., "Low-Wage Employment: An Inventory and an Assessment," Northwestern University, mimeo, no date.

This is due to the high degree of business competition in the retail field, which subjects the small firm to a profit and wage squeeze. Add to this the additional costs which small-scale business in the inner city must bear because of higher insurance costs, uninsured losses due to crime, and the higher cost of inner-city transportation, and the picture of low wages and low profits comes sharply into focus. While the sight of black faces behind ghetto drugstore counters may be psychologically comforting, it is not economically productive.

A small private production sector will also fail to add much viability to the ghetto economy. It is highly unlikely that individuals from the black community will have the ability to raise sufficient capital, independent of white business and government, to initiate enterprise in the growth sectors of the economy: electronics, computers, automation equipment, etc. To be successful in these industries requires enough capital to keep pace with rapid technological change. In addition, the efficient size of manufacturing firms is usually beyond the capacity of private capital resources owned by individuals in the ghetto. And even if capital could be raised by private black entrepreneurs to develop one or two competitive manufacturing firms in the inner city, the marginal benefit to a ghetto the size of that in Detroit, Chicago, New York, Los Angeles, or even Cleveland would be insignificant in producing a catalyst for full-scale economic development.

Inevitably, the end product of black entrepreneur capitalism is not the creation of an inner-city economic infrastructure, but the development of a larger black bourgeoisie which, given rising incomes, will emigrate from the ghetto taking along a large part of the wage bill and all of the profit. The tendency toward greater class stratification in the black community is thereby reinforced, with continued low wages and welfare incomes in the inner city and a richer, only slightly more numerous, black middle class on the outside. Again income will flow outward, leaving the bulk of ghetto residents no better off, save for a few more low-wage jobs and a few more black faces behind drugstore counters. Profits are reaped by an enlarged black middle class, while the losses continue to be borne by the poor.

AN ALTERNATIVE . . .

Even if blessed with normal profits, privately owned black enterprise will fail to aggregate enough capital for the creation of a viable inner-city economy. Because of the large capital input needed to initiate a community-wide enterprise, the tendency under private black ownership will be to buy up over time scattered small-scale enterprises rather than accumulate the capital necessary for large-scale high profit investment. In this way independent private black capitalism is doomed to corner store capitalism; inefficient, noncompetitive in the national economy, low-wage, and low-profit. There will be little in the way of savings for reinvestment and development.

Community-owned enterprise is the alternative to white-dominated ghetto development and small-scale private black capitalism. Inner-city residents can pool both the capital they own and that which can be coerced from the government on a "no-strings" basis, and under democratic rule, invest in cooperative industry on a relatively large scale. Supermarkets, department stores, banks, and intermediate-size factories can then be the first order of business—not corner drugstores. Creating business centers that are relatively crime-proof compared to sidewalk shops, taking full advantage of scale economies, and aggregating profits will ensure lower costs and larger reinvestment potential. As the black community owns the industry cooperatively, the wages and dividends from such enterprise will remain within the inner city. Those who choose to leave the ghetto would not be allowed to extract more capital from the community than the small amount they originally contributed (with some interest) and employment in the community enterprise will be conditional on community residence. Escape from the ghetto remains open, but not at the expense of the majority of the ghetto community. In order to maximize reinvestment so as to build as viable and diversified an inner-city economy as possible, capital and wage income leakages must be kept to a minimum. Community ownership and control ensures that the escape from poverty is open to the entire black community, not merely the fortunate few. Both on efficiency and equity grounds, black cooperative enterprise is preferable to private black capitalism.

. . . AND A REALISTIC PERSPECTIVE

Despite grandiose plans and even federal support, the black community must be cautioned against placing too much faith in any form of black economic development, even black cooperativism or black ghetto socialism. No scheme can automatically lead to economic and political freedom. To be sure, hundreds and possibly even thousands of jobs will be created and many businesses may ultimately become black controlled. But in the final analysis, the market determines which business survives and which fails. And unlike the textbook model, the American market, manipulated largely by the already existing corporate structure, allows few new small independent enterprises to reach the stratum of big business. The inner city, starved for capital and expertise—even with federal aid—begins far back in the field of potential money-winners. Mythologizing the possibility of the black community creating through its own industry the route to equal affluence with whites will be in vain. As a *goal*, black economic development may only lead to frustration. Yet as a *means*, black economic self-determination through community ownership of capital may provide the path to black liberation.

The act of striving toward an inner-city economy yields a powerful tool for organizing the black community into a coherent political force capable of extracting concessions on jobs, housing, income, and dignity from the government and from the corporate establishment. While black socialism alone may not be capable of rooting out poverty, it may root out powerlessness and thus gain for the black community the indirect means to freedom from poverty and the manifestations of racism. In the striving for economic independence, not only is dependence on the white power structure for jobs and welfare reduced, but the economic incentive to coalesce within the black community increases as well. Jobs and income are created within the community and it is from such a base that political and social power are born.

Black community enterprise will have a considerable impact on the whole economy and society, not because it can successfully compete directly with white enterprise, but because income generated from community enterprise can be used to develop a well-financed political organization, capable of confronting City Hall or Washington with a united front. If in the past, the black movement has been stifled by a lack of financial support, especially once it diverged from the strict integrationist political line, the community movement will now have a self-financed base. For while a large part of the "profit" from black community enterprise can be reinvested in expanded business projects, a part can also be earmarked specifically for political activity.

Taken in this context, black community enterprise not only places black faces behind drugstore counters, and allows a moderate scale production sector, but more importantly, it facilitates the creation of an indigenously financed, strictly independent, political force within the ghetto. Unlike black capitalism which fails to create either an economic infrastructure capable of pulling the black community out of poverty or a meaningful community-controlled power base, and unlike corporate intervention in the ghetto which adds longevity to white economic and political dominance over the black community, black cooperative enterprise in an inner-city "socialist" economy promises a new hope for political and social liberation. What this requires is an ICBIF-type program, but one which is geared more directly to the political needs of the black community. Emphasis must be placed on developing political structures based on community-owned enterprise.

Black enterprise must not be judged on whether it succeeds in the accountant's ledger, but whether it succeeds ultimately in the struggle to redistribute a just share of political and social power toward the black community.

CUBA'S WORKERS, WORKERS' CUBA

Maurice Zeitlin

The following selection describes the lives of workers and the organization of work in Cuba. The radical analysis of ghetto employment problems argues that those problems derive from the structure of basic capitalist institutions. The argument implies that a different set of social institutions and priorities would create an entirely different set of working conditions. This article illustrates that basic point. In Cuba, as Che Guevara wrote, "The ultimate and most important revolutionary aspiration is to see man freed from alienation." The implications of that priority pervade Zeitlin's description of work in Cuba.

The selection represents roughly half of a special supplement Zeitlin prepared for the recent Harper Torchbook edition of his book, *Revolutionary Politics and the Cuban Working Class*. In the rest of the supplement, Zeitlin describes recent aggregate social and economic trends in Cuba, accenting both the successes and failures the regime has experienced since his book first appeared in the early 1960's.

Zeitlin teaches sociology at the University of Wisconsin, and recently edited a book of readings called *American Society, Inc.*

Miguel Mendoza, carpenter, 57 years old, [lives with] his wife and seven children in a former storefront room no larger than ten feet square, on Zapata Street No. 24 across from the Colón cemetery in Havana. It has no inside running water, though there is a faucet nearby. One electric light hangs in the room's center. To him, these quarters, to which he moved a few weeks before I met him, were far better than those he had in the past. His wife, looking much older than her 43 years, agreed. The table, the bunk beds, a few chairs, some shelves with a few pots and dishes were, she told me, their first possessions. "We are all revolutionaries, ready to fight and die if necessary," she said. "Before the revolution, we had nothing, Miguel spent his time in the street; now our children are in school. He has secure work; for us there is no scarcity. . . ."

Sra. Mendoza's comment underlines the vast change in the lives of the poor and of the working class as a whole which even the most modest improvements in living conditions has meant; to most workers, who lived lives of great privation before the revolution, to whom unemployment and underemploy-

SOURCE: *Maurice Zeitlin, "Cuba's Workers, Workers' Cuba, 1969" from* Revolutionary Politics and the Cuban Working Class, 1970. *Reprinted by permission of the author and Harper & Row, Publishers, Inc.*

ment were a constant threat, the present does not appear austere at all. This was summed up well (in the typically eloquent and radical departure from conversational language Cubans use when speaking about their revolution) by a chunky, heavy-fisted, but soft-spoken miner at the Matahambre copper mine at the westernmost tip of the island:

"The life under the capitalist system was a life condemned to death below the earth—and your children also; that's what they were good for. They were lucky if they made sixth grade; that was really special. Only the strongest could work. Those without good physiques could not. The revolution came and now your children are completing basic secondary education, and you, if you want to improve yourself, attend classes at the *Facultad Obrera-Campesina* [Worker-Peasant Faculty].

"You went down in the mine in the morning before the dawn and saw no daylight; it was dark when you emerged from the pit. You took a piece of bread and maybe some meat with you into the mine, if you were among the more fortunate ones; and by the time you ate it, it was grimy and decomposed; but you had to eat it.

"So the revolution comes and it is concluded that the miners must not eat below any more, that they must come to the surface to eat. And you get milk, bread, an egg and meat, *gratis.* . . ."

"Look, I don't mean this in any way personally," another miner told me, "but listen, American. There used to be a *barrio* here they are called the *barrio americano,* where only Americans lived, the administrators, technicians, and so forth; and on the door of their social club was a sign, 'Only for members.' Now that's a social club for all of us. We are all members now. Everyone.

"A polyclinic has been constructed—there was no hospital here before, just one room. Now we have one with forty-four beds, built in 1964 or 1965—I'm not sure. There were no chances for you and your kids. Now there is work for everyone; there are eight six-hour shifts—the shifts used to be eight hours— and all the miners are studying, as are their children; and there are workers' sons from the shop who are now studying even to be engineers.

"The only thing the capitalist enterprise left us was the hole in the ground and in our stomachs. There were three hundred for every job."

The austerity program of the Cuban government has not noticeably dampened the workers' morale, because they see it as part of a common effort to develop their country, from which they have already benefited considerably; the rationing, the endless lines, the shortages seem, paradoxically, to have intensified the revolution's élan and heightened social solidarity. Most important, the egalitarian ethos of the revolution has been accentuated by its egalitarian practice.

"Everyone is on the *libreta*" (ration card), a black brewery worker in Manacas told me. "Everyone has his quota, according to his family's needs, no more or less. This, at least, is what I can see for myself. René [the administrator] stands in line like the rest of us. His wife and mine buy at the same store. No one has privileges now. What there is is for everyone."

Wages and salaries reflect the same pattern of social equality. It continues to be the practice in Cuba, contrary to that in the Soviet Union until quite recently, to maintain a narrow gap between the income of production workers and clerical, administrative, and technical personnel. In fact, it may be more correct to say that there simply is no gap, because there is, as yet, no systematic relationship between occupation and income in

Cuba. There is a mix between what the workers call the *sueldo histórico,* or the wage they had been receiving in 1961 when wages were frozen, and the new wage and salary scales which have been established in industry, services and in the predominantly publicly-owned agricultural sector. Plants where productivity was high and the workers had strong trade unions before the revolution, earned wages far higher than workers in similar jobs elsewhere that required equivalent skills and training; often unskilled workers in the organized plants earned more than skilled workers where unions were weak or nonexistent. This irrationality in the wage system hit skilled workers the hardest and intensified their sense of exploitation. The establishment of a standardized wage system was, therefore, an imperative necessity, not merely from the standpoint of rational planning but for equity and social justice, and one strongly supported by the workers, so far as I could tell, even in the "privileged" industries.

In my lengthy talks with workers, privately, informally, and in small groups, I probed for resentment, but found none. I expected the workers whose wages were frozen at their "historic" level to resent this; and I especially expected resentment from workers newly transferred into these plants who are earning far less on the newly established scales than veteran workers still on the "historic" ones. Instead, their responses to my questions were quite the opposite, and phrased in terms of justice and equity for the *other* workers. "It would not be proper to take what the privileged workers won from the capitalist enterprises away from them; they fought for themselves, as they had to," a black streetcar conductor now working at the paper mill in Cárdenas told me. Another man, at the cement plant in Mariel, said, "Every worker's goal was to get his son a job here. Fathers, sons, brothers, nephews helped each other get into the plant. We had a very strong union here. You went up the scale strictly by seniority. There was no such thing as self-improvement. You had no opportunity to study. Some guys in the extraction of ore earned seven hundred dollars a month with overtime. Most of them have renounced their overtime pay, though some haven't; it would have meant a great sacrifice. I myself have. New fellows coming into the plant know that they'll earn the same as workers elsewhere with the same skill and danger involved in their work. That's what counts. The fact is that the wage means very little now—"

"Because," I interrupted, "there's nothing to buy."

"Of course, to be truthful, because there is not much to buy. But mainly because so much is free, and my wife is working also. Everyone has work now, so that a family that had only one earner before now probably has a son, maybe even the wife, working. My wife leaves our kids at the *círculo infantil*—she knows they are well cared for, and it costs us nothing."

A worker at the cement plant in Mariel said:

"This is not conceivable by someone outside the revolutionary process [a favorite Cuban phrase now], I suppose. My consciousness has risen. The revolution was not Communist or even socialist, and neither was I. Something moved us all—what, was not clear—but we struggled. Some of us read and talked about things being different someday. Now we have free work clothes, work shoes, education for ourselves and our children, free health and medical attention, free X-rays, and drugs, vacations with pay; and if someone is not able to work because of illness or accident, he gets his full pay, because we are an outstanding plant with the Banner of the Heroes of Moncada. We don't have to worry about the future. Before, that was our biggest preoccupation—what would happen to your kids if you got sick or lost your job? That's over. By 1970, we won't pay any rent, and we hardly pay anything now, anyway—ten percent of our wage. We get free breakfasts in the plant; we'll be getting free lunches soon; and it only costs fifty cents anyway. Transportation is a nickel. If I want to make a phone call, I go to the corner and it costs me nothing. Little by little, we aren't even thinking in terms of individual earnings any more."

Under the newly established scales, the administrator of the plant earns no more than the most skilled worker, and may earn less. Especially skilled technicians may receive higher salaries than administrators, but these are also within a narrow range of variation. At the textile plant in Ariguanabo, for instance, which is Cuba's most important cotton textile mill, equipped with modern machinery and employing 2,700 workers, the administrator earns $250 monthly. A section technical chief earns $400 monthly. Skilled workers earn $1.75 an hour, which amounts to about $300 a month (figuring an eight-hour day, five days a week), while the lowest-paid *peón* or unskilled worker earns 55¢ an hour, or about $95 a month. At the Venezuela sugar central, which employs 1,700 workers and is the largest central in Cuba, the administrator earns $300 monthly, his assistant $250; the least skilled worker 50¢ hourly, or about $87 monthly; and a skilled worker $1 hourly, or about $173 monthly. These figures are typical of those in the other plants I visited and apparently is the pattern throughout industry.

Outside of industry, the new wage and salary scales have a similar pattern; the salaries of government officials range from $200 or $250 for typical functionaries to a high of $700 a month for Cabinet Ministers. There are certain limited perquisites of office. Many government functionaries have drivers and cars assigned to them for use on government business, mostly four-cylinder compact Volgas or Alfa Romeos, though an occasional Chevy or Ford still serves the Revolutionary Government. Functionaries, especially those dealing directly with foreign visitors, also have expense accounts which allow them to indulge more often than other Cubans in meals at the few remaining plush restaurants frequented still by the wealthy who have not chosen to leave. Public property and accessible to all, such restaurants are a luxury few Cubans can yet afford.

In general, however, from what I could observe, Cubans in the highest positions in government and industry live simply, and the gap between their life styles and those of ordinary workers is no greater, and perhaps less, than that indicated by differential income levels. Expropriated country homes and private yachting clubs, rather than becoming the opulent quarters of a new elite of government bureaucrats and party officials, as has occurred in other Communist countries as diverse as Yugoslavia and the Soviet Union, are now restaurants, resorts, schools, and museums open to everyone. The mansions along Quinta Avenida (Fifth Avenue[!]) in Marianao house scholarship students from worker and peasant families, or are being used as government office buildings. . . .

The egalitarian social reality of Cuba is

most evident precisely where one would expect to find it least evident, inside the factories, mines, and mills, in the social relations between production workers and administrative, technical, and clerical personnel. Informal social relations are direct, and there do not seem to be distinctions of status involving particular and subtle patterns of deference and obeisance to persons in authority. The social barriers (which functionalist sociologists rationalize as inherent in industrialism) between manual and nonmanual workers have disappeared from such modern industrial plants as the cement factory, paper mill, and copper mine I visited. The absence of these barriers is manifested in surface things such as the disappearance of jackets and ties from office personnel and the universal use of *compañero* (we have no word precisely equivalent; a mixture of fellow, mate, companion, and comrade), rather than *señor*.

The comments of a statistician at the paper mill in Cárdenas, in the midst of a spontaneous discussion between several workers and a visiting American sociologist outside the factory diner, point this up:

"Look, I am an office worker. Does that mean anything now? No, I am a worker like other workers. Before, we thought we were something special. We came in our starched shirts and ties, our fine clothes, sat in our air-conditioned offices, and looked down on the millworkers. They could not even pass through our doors without special permission. Now all that has changed.

"I am a worker like other workers. The administrator is a worker among workers. You want to see him, you see him. You do not have to stand and mumble and hope that you will sometime see someone who will take your complaint to the front office. You enter, like a worker who knows he is the owner here, and you ask to see the administrator. Naturally, he has meetings and a great deal of work. He cannot always just stop and speak to you anytime you wish. This is just. But you know that there is a correct reason why he can't see you, and you understand. Usually, this does not happen. You just ask to see him and do, or anyone else whom you might want to see. There are no privileges."

There has been a conscious de-emphasis on the hierarchical authority structure typical of industrial plants elsewhere. There is an attempt to encourage flexible cooperation between co-workers who have different but interdependent tasks, stressing that production is a common effort in the collective interest, and the responsibility of everyone. At the Venezuela sugar central, for instance, a black worker wearing a grease-stained beret, whom I had interviewed seven years earlier, said that "the system of work has changed completely, because we work for ourselves now. The workers, together, resolve the problems of production, in accordance with our knowledge. We have given up overtime pay. The quality of our work is much improved. We guarantee that equipment is maintained in good condition, that repairs are done when necessary, and that production continues. No one has to watch us any more. The administrator has good relations with the workers. He is concerned with the workers' interests and in easing our work. The fact is that we work like hell, throwing ourselves into it [*metiendo la manga y el cola*]."

The quality of relations at this workplace is indicated, I think, by the fact that as I sat in a corner of the mechanics shop talking privately to an old shoemaker now working at the central, other workers kept wandering over to listen or to make their own comments until I stopped asking them to leave simply because it was impolite to do so. After a few moments, the entire shop of 25 workers or more was involved in a spontaneous discussion of my questions, some joining the crowd, others leaving to return to their work. There was not the slightest indication, that I could sense, that the workers felt that it was anything but their right to rest and talk to their visitor. . . .

The workers' sense of ease around administrative and supervisory personnel (typically referred to as *responables*), as well as clerical and technical employees, and the radical narrowing of the social distance between them, is undoubtedly a general consequence, on the one hand, of the recent . . . destruction of the old class structure, in which the workers were considered social inferiors and manual work demeaning, and, on the other, of the Revolutionary Government's philosophical and practical emphasis on social equality. However, it is also the direct result of specific practices in the workplace which sustain the egalitarian and nonauthoritarian quality of these relationships.

The authority of those toward the top of the formal structure of the plant is limited and hedged in a number of ways. That "fundamental managerial prerogative" which even the most powerful industrial unions in America have not altered in any essential way—the authority to dismiss workers—does not reside in the hands of the plant officials. Workers cannot even be discharged for cause —negligence, frequent tardiness or absence from work; "back-talk" cannot be penalized by firing or even by fining the offending worker. The typical sanction applied is to transfer the worker—at the same pay—to other, less desirable work in the plant, or ultimately to transfer him out of the plant altogether.[1] "This is a blow," as a young engineer at the cement plant in Mariel put it, "because most workers—at least here—are friends and relatives of each other. They've known each other and worked together a long time. The only thing you can do is talk to him [the worker involved], try to explain to him what he lacks in his work, talk and keep talking. And don't think that those who make mistakes at work aren't often understanding workers, who do a lot of volunteer overtime and so forth, or that they aren't revolutionaries. They are ready to die for the revolution tomorrow but can't do a day's work today. Like this fellow Jorge, who is really a swell guy. He works watching the cement tank, making sure it stays clean and keeps level, and so on, and he's let the thing overflow three times this year already. Either he's 'studying'—reading on the job—or talking to a *compañero,* who is also not working when he should be. So I've talked to him, and Miguel [the administrator] has talked to him —and, well, he says he'll change, and we can only hope so. . . ."

A brewery worker who had been sanctioned and transferred to another department explained to me:

"The administration understands the workers, and I can say this since I've had my own troubles with them. The administrator is respectful [*cariñoso*] of the workers. So is the Chief of Personnel. Everything is said without insult, if you have to be talked to. I had an argument with some guys here. So I got in a fight. The Personnel Chief broke it up and I was pretty mad and said some rough words; I lacked respect and was penalized. I was transferred to another department. I did wrong. They were right."

The decision to request the Ministry to transfer a worker for cause cannot be made by the administrator alone. It requires the combined agreement of the local union leaders, the Communist Party "nucleus" in the plant, and the administrative staff, and the request must then be approved by the Ministry; it is not granted without review. The Party nucleus is made up mostly of production workers, and all of them have been chosen (in a combination of elitist and democratic practice described below) by the workers themselves; the union leaders are elected by the workers and work in the plant also; it is therefore a rare offense which receives even this sanction. Moreover, even in the event that the union leaders agree with the Party leadership and administration, the worker can appeal to the *Consejo de Trabajo,* or Work Council, elected by and composed of the workers in the plant. It is charged with hearing, investigating, reviewing, and deciding on the grievances of individual workers. These Councils grew out of the original *Comisiones de Reclamaciones,* or Grievance Commissions, established when Che was Minister of Industries. Unlike those three-man Commissions, however, which included representatives of the factory administration, the Ministry of Labor, and the workers in the factory, the Work Council is composed entirely of five elected workers representing the workers in the plant. These *Consejos* are apparently regarded by the workers as genuinely representative councils which adjudicate individual grievances fairly and efficiently.

As to the trade unions, however, from what I could observe, and from the vague and infrequent references to them by the workers I interviewed, they seem to have "withered away." The workers do not have an *independent organization* which takes the initiative in the plant, industry, or country as a whole, to assure, let alone demand, improved working conditions or higher wages; no organization exists, as an autonomous force, to protect and advance the immediate interests of the workers, as they see them, independent of the prevailing line of the Communist Party or policies of the Revolutionary Government. The distinction in practice between the role played by the Ministry of Labor and that of the CTC-R, the Workers

---

[1] Labor Law No. 1126 in force since January 1, 1965, permits more severe sanctions, including wage deductions and dismissal. In practice, however, under Labor Minister Captain Jorge Risquet, such sanctions are rarely imposed.

Federation—if it is clear in formal terms—is not clear to ordinary workers. Nor, indeed, does this distinction seem clear to some of the government officials and national leaders I spoke with.

One reason for the unions' failure to play a sufficiently independent role as workers' advocate is that many union officials (such men, for instance, as Conrado Bequer, former head of the Sugar Workers Union, or Jesús Soto, former Organizational Secretary of the CTC-R), who were independent trade unionists before the revolution, have taken positions in the government which demand entirely different roles of them, as administrators, planners, and political leaders. The newer union officials had limited experience, if any, as trade union leaders before the revolution, and their conceptions have been shaped largely in terms of the developmental objectives of the revolution. This is true on the local as well as the national level. While I discovered several ex-trade union officials in the plants I visited, they were not now involved in the leadership of the union. Many, even on the plant level, had been part of the *Mujalista*-run labor bureaucracy and had been thrown out of their positions early in the revolution. They had never been genuine workers' representatives, in any case. Others had simply taken on new tasks as the revolution developed.

At the Matahambre copper mine, in a conversation I had with several workers, one of them recalled their past union leaders this way:

"My boy, look, what we had in the mine before, put simply, as we miners say in our vulgar way, was a bunch of *marrecones* and sons of whores. The union officials were worse than useless to us; they wore revolvers on their hips and kept *us* in line, not the company. You ask why we tolerated such [poor working] conditions here and this is the answer. Most of them have already gone to the United States. Those that really tried to fight the company got their heads cracked; the good ones couldn't survive."

The unions exist on the local and plant level and have a variety of functions, the central one of which is the protection of the workers' interests in the plant. The unions function essentially, however, less as workers' independent organizations than as committees delegated by the workers to represent them on a day-to-day level concerning working conditions, as well as to provide for the distribution of scarce resources to the workers on a fair basis. One important function of the unions, for instance, is to investigate the living conditions of its members, establish priorities in accordance with the relative comfort or dilapidation of their dwellings, and decide on the allocation of housing as it becomes available. (Other, rather more idiosyncratic services are rendered by the unions also. At the cement plant in Mariel, for instance, I was informed by one worker that "the union bought a cow from our dues, and we keep it in a field nearby and take turns caring for it—which really is little work. We milk it and have plenty of milk for ourselves [despite the rationing]." On the plant level, the unions are active in proposing and initiating changes in the conditions of work which alleviate stress and make work less demanding. At the Ariguanabo textile plant, for instance, the union was responsible for proposing and establishing an arrangement to allow the workers to smoke during working hours. Since smoking is so hazardous there, especially in the cotton mill, this change was an important one to the workers.

"Look," a 64-year-old worker who began work there in 1937 (six years after it opened) remarked, "we work more freely. The workers are trusted. In the old days if they caught you smoking, that was it. You got thrown out. Now we have a place to take a break, to rest, to light a cigarette and talk when we feel the need. Someone else tends your machine when you take a break, and you do the same for him. There is a certain companionship at work now."

Since such changes may also be initiated by the workers through general assemblies of the entire work force, or in given departments, called not only by the union itself but also by the administration, the Party nucleus, or the Workers Council, the specific social function of the union as *the* organization of the workers devoted to protecting and advancing their interests has tended to disappear. In a revolutionary context in which the identity of interests between the workers and the administration is stressed continually (a sign on the desk of Agustín Hernández, the administrator of the Venezuela sugar central, reads: "The prestige and authority of the administrator will be directly related to the real links he has with the mass of workers in his unit"), and the workers themselves believe in it, the distinction between the Party, Workers Council, general assembly, and the union as means of furthering their interests has become vague in their minds. Nor, they say, do they feel the need for an independent organization. They have (what to an observer from the U.S. seems to be) a naïve faith in the harmony of interests between themselves, the administration of the plant, and the Revolutionary Government. The differences that do arise can be resolved, the workers insist, by free discussion and without conflict.

This may be true at the moment, and I think from my own observations that it is, and probably will be as long as sufficiently rapid economic growth seems assured by present policies. However, the problems of development are difficult and intractable, especially in the perilous international conditions in which the revolutionaries must resolve them. Tendencies toward the bureaucratization of decision-making in industry are strong under ordinary conditions. Pressed by Cuba's need for accelerated growth, such tendencies could be increased; administrators, anxious to fulfill and overfulfill quotas, and to respond to the political demands made on them by the Revolutionary Government, might be tempted to concentrate more and more decisions in their own hands and to utilize increasingly tougher methods to discipline the workers. This, of course, is contrary to the present premise and practice of the revolutionary leadership. Like its emphasis on flexible cooperation in the plant between coworkers, the leadership's egalitarian emphasis, and its refusal to countenance special privileges, is also a conscious decision. Again, however, the possibility exists that under the social pressures of what Che called "the weeds that shoot up so easily in the fertilized soil of state subsidization," of vested interests that may emerge (risen careerists, bureaucrats, and political opportunists), and of some members of the old privileged strata incorporated into positions of authority in the economic administration, government, or Party, the thrust toward social equality clearly evident at present could be subtly, even unconsciously, deflected.

To prevent such "bureaucratic deformation" of the revolution, as Lenin termed it, whether in industry or government, Lenin argued (*against* Trotsky) that the workers had to have the freedom to organize to protect both their immediate interests on the job and their relative share of the national income, and that their spokesmen had to have the freedom to represent those interests, while at the same time defending the revolutionary regime. (In practice, Lenin and his comrades were to curtail rights that they upheld in principle.) The Cuban leaders recognize this principle, and assert, at least privately, that they are not satisfied with the present situation in the unions. I was told by Carlos Rafael Rodríguez, for instance, that he feels that the unions have been inadequately concerned with the defense of the day-to-day interests of the workers and overconcerned with spurring the workers to meet production targets. In his book-lined office in the headquarters of the Communist Party's Central Committee in Havana, he said that "what was originally Che's antibureaucratic thesis [to keep the political leadership functions of the Party and the specific union functions separate] became an antidemocratic thesis. The unions are transmission belts of the Party directives to the workers but have insufficiently represented the workers to the Party or the Revolutionary Government. They cannot merely be instruments of the Party without losing their purpose. Administrators, after all, can also be *hijos de putas* [sons of whores], and if they are, the workers have to be able to throw them out—and, for that matter, do the same with any bureaucrats. . . ."

The workers I spoke to throughout the country in long, often very probing conversations felt confident that they could "throw out" any *hijo de puta* they felt was maltreating them. While the concrete changes in working conditions scarcely seem to be profound alterations of the workers' role in the productive process, the cumulative impact of such changes has given the workers a sense of well-being and freedom at work, rather than estrangement from it. The cynicism which is the characteristic informal philosophy of manual workers elsewhere, and expresses their resentment and sense of exploitation, apparently has disappeared among Cuban workers. The conditions under which they work *have* changed radically. Even where, as among formerly "privileged workers," their standard of living outside the plant has not improved materially, or may even have lowered, the health and safety conditions in the plant have improved considerably, and the pace and intensity of the work have lessened, bringing them a better life on the job. Most workers, therefore, seem to identify strongly with the revolutionary leadership and to be really willing to work extra hours without overtime pay, and to do voluntary work in the plant or in agricultural production, planting coffee or citrus-fruit trees or cutting sugar cane. As one worker put it to me, "Everyone wants to be able to tell his grandchildren that he was in the harvest of the 'ten million.' "

However, one consequence of their present economic security (or the abolition of what Max Weber called "the whip of hunger") and of their sense of freedom in the plant is that while productivity measured by what each worker produces per day (because he works longer hours) and per unit wage cost has risen considerably, according to government figures, productivity per man-hour apparently has not. "Absenteeism" also continues to be a problem throughout industry. Captain Jorge Risquet, the Minister of Labor, claims that "a vanguard with Communist consciousness [*conciencia*] at work has been developing, but at the same time there is still a rear guard whose conduct reflects the ideology of the capitalist past. . . . As the number of centers winning the Heroes of Moncada Banners rises, and as volunteer work, the 'advanced workers' movement [of outstanding workers honored by their fellows], develops, and more and more workers renounce overtime pay, all of which are expressions of the growth of Communist consciousness, there has also been an accentuation and spread of absenteeism, negligence, and inadequate use of the workday. . . ."

Risquet attributes the residue of "capitalist ideology" among the workers, interestingly enough, not to those who were workers before the revolution, or are the sons of workers, but to those who were previously self-employed petit bourgeois, "lumpen," or vagrants, who must now work in industry. In part, it is probably true that such new workers have not yet adapted to the discipline of industrial work, and that this is a contributing factor to the absenteeism and lowered productivity. It is also certain that the administration of production is still in the hands of inadequately skilled and trained individuals in many places throughout the country, as workers have risen from the ranks rapidly to assume administrative and technical responsibilities. And while the effect of the embargo imposed by the U.S. and the changeover to Soviet technology is no longer a major problem, this still continues to pose serious obstacles to productive efficiency, requiring often crude and improvised methods to be used.

There is an unavoidable dialectic here between the growth of consciousness and the abolition of alienation—of which the revolutionary leaders are quite aware. The workers have lessened the pace and intensity of their work—where possible—because that in itself is an important gain of the revolution. Consciously or unconsciously, they seem to have decided that the benefits of increased production should not come at the expense of their improved life on the job. Until now, the Revolutionary Government has responded to this dialectic by attempting to deepen consciousness. The emphasis has been on persuasion, exhortation, education, rather than on the imposition of punitive sanctions. "Even though they are *legally in force*," as Risquet puts it, "fines, suspensions, etc., are typical capitalist sanctions . . . which are equally obsolete and harmful, and we have refrained from imposing them and will continue to do so. . . . If we think that sanctions are the only way or the best way to combat these antisocial manifestations, we are wrong. Sanctions must be the last resort. Education and re-education through collective criticism and the help of other workers are the basic weapons in this struggle. . . ."

The workers meet regularly to discuss production goals. The goals of their factory, mine, or mill in the National Plan are submitted to them at the year's beginning. The goals for the plant as a whole and for particular departments are discussed, section by section, and, in most plants, in a general assembly of the entire work force. Once approved or modified by the workers—usually to increase the targets—the plan returns to the relevant Ministry (there are now five industrial Ministries in place of the former unified Ministry of Industries) for further study, and then is sent back to the plant for the workers' final approval. The workers I spoke with evidently considered themselves deeply involved in this process and claimed that the assemblies, run jointly by the administration, union, and Party leadership, were genuine exchanges of ideas and that the plan was often substantially changed by their suggestions.

The revolutionaries have thus far rejected punitive sanctions; and they have rejected what they consider to be "capitalist" or material and individual incentives—which is the path the Soviet Union took and has accentuated further recently by introducing criteria of profitability at the level of the enterprise to govern production. Fidel has spoken out strongly against what he considers to be capitalist tendencies in the Soviet Union and Eastern European socialist countries, and his heretical call to "build communism simultaneously with building socialism" is the doctrinal principle guiding the revolutionary leadership. It is the quest to build what Che called "the new man," rejecting "Communist economics without Communist morality."

"The capitalist society," to quote Risquet again, "is based on the power of money; it is guided by the principle that a man is worth as much as he owns. A thief lucky enough to amass a fortune becomes an illustrious man and he might even get to be president of the republic. Our society is based on merit. And the most precious things a man can amass are his record and the awareness that he has fulfilled his duty and the tasks of his generation, his homeland, and his revolution."

This conception of socialist morality is at the heart of the Cuban revolution's uniqueness among Communist states, because it is combined with an egalitarian practice and a rejection of individual and material incentives in favor of collective and moral ones. Talking to Cuban workers throughout the country, it becomes quickly apparent that these are not merely revolutionary slogans, but commitments deeply felt by many. In their descriptions of what it means to be a Communist, and what is required to merit membership in the Party, the workers emphasized moral qualities. As the cook at the paper mill put it, "You cannot join the Party unless the workers who know you best and work with you think that you are deserving. You must be of good morality. You must be an advanced worker, you must have the respect of your fellows in everything and be an example of discipline and sacrifice."

Most important, while it is hard to know in even the lengthy interviews I had how much is cliché and how much consciousness, many of the workers themselves emphasize that they are engaged in the construction of a new society, shorn of the exploitation of man by man and based on the premise of producing for the common good rather than individual profit. It is evident that they have talked about these questions, and thought about them. This came out clearly in my discussion with several miners. The mine's administrator, Captain Jesús Parra, a young mulatto wearing a sleeveless undershirt, grimy and sweaty with Matahambre's red earth, had just stated that "the reason for our being is for the benefit of the workers" when a miner broke in to give an example in the new Law No. 270. It gives the workers in a plant that wins the Banner of the Heroes of Moncada retirement and disability benefits equal to 100 percent of their wages. Otherwise workers retire at 70 percent of their pay, up to $250 a month. I suggested that this sounded like a "material stimulus" rather than a moral one—which brought a startled look to the worker's face. Captain Parra grinned. "Do you *really* consider that a 'material incentive'?" he asked. "I do not think so. We understand that other socialist countries have fallen into capitalist habits and forms. But we have learned from this. We have applied collective, not individual, measures. Only a small minority of the workers do not merit the collective benefits which go through them to their families. Workers cannot have their wages reduced as a sanction. They cannot be fired. They know they have work. It is a moral principle of the revolution that we cannot *punish* the families of those who avoid their responsibilities. But shall we also *reward* those few equally?"

"Didn't Fidel say something about building Communism simultaneously with socialism?" I asked.

The previous miner, rather tough, responded:

"I don't understand. It seems to me to be simple justice. Those who do not sacrifice, who sit on their shit, do not merit such rewards. Only those who sacrifice do. And it is us, not some distant government or Jesús [the administrator], who decides who merits and who does not. We know, after all, who works. We decide, department by department, who has done his share and who hasn't. And it isn't as if they don't have a chance to change their situation. We talk to them. We try to explain to them that the old ways are no good any more. That the bosses are gone. That we work for ourselves now and that they are cheating on *us*. And they *do* change. How many of the twelve hundred miners here do you think did not benefit from Law No. 270? A handful, a few, not more than a dozen. Is there something wrong with this? How can this create privileges? It is the majority who gain."

At this point, professor that I am, I gave a brief lecture about developments in the Soviet Union and its use of Stakhanovism. "The principle of individual and material rewards," I said, "became the basis of their development, rationalized by the slogan 'From each according to his ability, to each according to his work'; texts from Lenin and Stalin were cited to justify and allow the growth of ever-wider gaps in status and material welfare between ordinary and privileged workers, the heroes of socialist labor, and especially between the workers and technicians, scientists, administrators, and even party bureaucrats. Was it not based on the same principle of individual merit and sacrifice that the ideals of socialism were distorted in such a way?"

Everyone was listening very carefully. Jesús Parra broke the silence. "This will not happen here. We, as I have already said, are conscious of errors elsewhere in the socialist world. Our emphasis, as the *compañero* says, is on collective benefits, not individual ones, benefits which cannot be bought and sold, which cannot enter the marketplace, and which cannot be hoarded and accumulated, but which can only better the lives of all the workers in their work, and in their lives as a whole. The changes in the conditions of work in this mine, and in every workplace in this country, directly benefit all workers. The free education, medical care, nominal rents, the work clothes and shoes and hot meals provided *gratis*—these are earned by all the workers and received by all the workers. Such is the way we choose to go."

Contrary to Captain Parra and the miners, however, the 100 percent retirement benefits are clearly material incentives rather than moral ones, and have—at least so far—benefited only a small fraction of the workers in the country, somewhere around 6 percent, according to government sources. While this is, from what I could tell, a rare departure from the central emphasis on moral suasion and collective benefits, this tension between contrasting paths of development under socialism is critical for the future course of the revolution. The revolutionaries have not chosen to adopt the existing models of Soviet development, or succumbed to the pressures of those who urge them to do so. I can guess from discussions with "highly placed" sources, though, that there continue to be serious differences within the leadership on this question; and that there are those who argue that absenteeism and inadequate productivity are reflections of the lack of individual incentives, on the one hand, and of insufficient "discipline," on the other; if they win, Cuba will be taking the road already trod by the Communists elsewhere.

There are signs that "labor brigades" organized along military lines, as well as the actual utilization of "conscript labor," are already quite important in agricultural work, especially in sugar-cane harvesting. Of course, that the Army is engaged in "productive work" is not in itself reason to believe that "paramilitary forms of labor organization" are increasing. It is difficult to sort out the tendencies and countertendencies in any revolution, especially the Cuban, since its leadership continues to be independent, pragmatic, and experimental, bound in reality by little of the "Marxist-Leninist" dogma espoused by Communists elsewhere. The Fidelistas' independent leadership of the struggle for power, despite the old Communists' derogation of it as "bourgeois romantic" and "adventurist," and their success at putting through a socialist revolution 90 miles from the United States, when the Communists were urging a more moderate course and slower pace, have taught the Fidelistas to question the revolutionary judgment of the Communists, as well as to accentuate their own independent and pragmatic politics. Yet the counterpressures are great. It would be easier in the short run to abandon their dreams of an egalitarian and nonauthoritarian socialism and adopt Soviet political economic models. Neither Soviet nor "Western" economists think the revolutionaries can successfully utilize moral suasion and collective rewards to motivate and maintain the commitment of the Cuban people to development. . . .

. . . [T]he revolution's social base among the workers and peasants is secure. There is no serious internal opposition to the revolution; there is no threat from within. The revolution has been a profoundly liberating experience for the Cuban people; they are conscious of themselves as historical actors, and have learned to believe in themselves, to take the implausible for granted and the unprecedented as certain—as "no one," they will tell you, "who has not lived within the revolutionary process can understand."

"The most transcendental changes are within us," they say, "the ones that you cannot see, that are visible only to ourselves. No one who knows the Cuban past as only we can, of whoredom and corruption, of the infinite capacity to deceive oneself and others, to sell oneself to the highest bidder in all things, to lack faith in anything but the vulgar and to accept the obscene as natural —no one who lived this past as we did can doubt the great changes in our beings.

"What was Cuba?—an insignificant whorehouse for the West, a country known only for its sugar and the delights of the flesh, a country of 'simple blacks and *tropicales*,' and now we are trying to create 'the new man.'"

Such talking of creating the "new man," while it has its element of Spanish overstatement, self-flattery, and romanticism, is real. To create that "new man" will require not merely new economic but also new political forms. It will require the consciousness and the will of the revolutionaries; indeed, it will require an effort even more "decisive" for the revolution's future than the present one to produce ten million tons of sugar. Without it, they will not create that form of socialism which Che dreamt of. "The socialist society that we want," he said, "is absolutely democratic; it is based on the needs and the aspirations of the people, and the people have a major role in all decisive points."

The revolutionary leaders have consciously rejected the Soviet model of "how to construct Communism." Cuba is "the black sheep of the family," as Fidel put it, "because it does not follow the beaten path even if that path leads nowhere!" But that Soviet path included not only material incentives and vast inequalities, but also the use of force to repress dissent and the establishment of a monopoly of political power in the hands of the Communist Party. Social inequality and authoritarian controls reinforce and strengthen one another. If the revolutionaries in Cuba reject the one, they must reject the other. "Our task," Che told me in 1961, "is to enlarge democracy within the revolution as much as possible. As you have well said, we are pragmatic. . . . We feel that the government's chief function is to assure channels

for the expression of the popular will. What forms this will take, we cannot say yet. This will depend on the political system to be elaborated."

Elaborating this political system is now on the order of the day. The revolutionaries have avoided this task so far in part because of their fear of prematurely institutionalizing forms which will freeze their relations with the people, and prevent that spontaneity and improvisation and the sense of common effort and participation which has characterized their activity so far. The revolutionaries have acted to a great extent, as I wrote several years ago, as if unconsciously guided by a paraphrase of the German socialist Rosa Luxemburg's famous revolutionary axiom: "Mistakes committed by a genuine revolutionary government are much more fruitful and worthwhile historically than the infallibility of the very best central committee." Most important, they have no models which they simply can adopt wholesale. Political forms in the Communist countries, especially in the Soviet bloc, have led, in Che's words, "into dogmatic extremes, into cold scholasticism, into isolation from the masses"; they do not want to "create salaried workers docile to official thinking nor 'fellows' who live under the wing of the budget, exercising 'freedom' in quotation marks."

"We are," Che wrote, "seeking something new that will allow a perfect identification between the government and the community as a whole, adapted to the conditions of the building of socialism peculiar to our country, and avoiding as much as possible the commonplaces of bourgeois democracy transplanted to the society in formation (such as legislative houses, for example). There have been some experiments intended to gradually create the institutionalization of the revolution, but without too much hurry. The major thing holding us back has been the fear that any formal mechanism might separate us from the masses and the individual, making us lose sight of the ultimate and most important revolutionary aspiration: to see man freed from alienation."

Anyone who thinks the answers to the revolutionaries' dilemma are easy has not thought seriously about the questions. The establishment of socialist democracy will require the same pragmatism, experimentalism, and boldness, and the "same strong feelings of love for the people" (Che) and revolutionary optimism that have brought them this far, and have allowed them to transform the prerevolutionary social structure more profoundly and rapidly than has any other "socialist" revolution anywhere. Some questions that they must deal with, while yet involved in a struggle for development, are: How can they guarantee a free press when there is no private ownership of enterprises? What sort of representative system—and what kind of judiciary—is compatible with public ownership of the means of production and central planning? How are the technical requirements of expertise and authority in a planned economy to be reconciled with popular elec-

tion of government officials? What forms will prevent bureaucratic control of the new society? And how can they do all this while defending the revolution?

Whatever the answers the revolutionaries give to these questions in practice, it is unquestionable that they must choose soon between that "beaten path that leads nowhere" and one far more difficult for not having been trodden before, toward the establishment of socialist democratic political forms commensurate with the revolution's egalitarian and liberating content. "Then," in the vision that Che bequeathed the revolutionaries, "they will come to sing the song of the new man with the authentic voice of the people."

EMPLOYMENT BIBLIOGRAPHY

I. IMPRESSIONS OF EMPLOYMENT PROBLEMS

Elliot Liebow, *Tally's Corner*, Little, Brown, 1967, Chapter II.
Claude Brown, *Manchild in the Promised Land*, Macmillan, 1965.
Harvey Swados, "The Myth of the Happy Worker," in Swados, *A Radical's America*, 1961.
Paul Jacobs, "Bringing Up the Rear," in A. M. Ross and Herbert Hill, eds., *Employment, Race and Poverty*, 1967, Harcourt, Brace.

II. DEFINITIONS OF EMPLOYMENT PROBLEMS

Manpower Report of the President, April, 1968, pp. 13–80. All the different dimensions of problems, including "subemployment."
Seymour Wolfbein, *Employment and Unemployment in the United States*, 1964, Science Research Associates, pp. 1–40. Definitions of the labor force and of unemployment.

III. MAGNITUDES OF EMPLOYMENT PROBLEMS AND THEIR TRENDS

Report of the National Advisory Commission on Civil Disorders, 1968, Bantam, pp. 236–265. Useful summary of ghetto problems.
Manpower Report of the President, 1970, pp. 119–138. Recent figures on relations of employment and poverty.
Victoria Bonnell and Michael Reich, "Workers and the American Economy," pamphlet available from New England Free Press (391 Tremont St., Boston). Excellent collection of data on workers' conditions.
Tom Kahn, "The Economics of Inequality," in Louis Ferman *et al.*, eds., *Negroes and Jobs: A Book of Readings*, 1968, University of Michigan Press, pp. 15–28. Summary data on extent of black employment problems.
Marion Hayes, "A Century of Change: Negroes in the U.S. Economy," *ibid.*, pp. 53–64. Good collection of historical data.
Dale Hiestand, *Economic Growth and Employment Opportunities for Minorities*, 1964, Columbia. Some more historical figures, perhaps the most interesting.
Arthur M. Ross, "The Negro in the American Economy," in Ross and Hill, eds., *Employment, Race and Poverty, op. cit.*, pp. 3–48. Assessment of trends toward equality of employment opportunity, with pessimistic conclusions.

Robert A. Gordon, *The Goal of Full Employment*, 1967, Wiley, pp. 1–16, 117–192. Analytic discussion of changes in status of disadvantaged groups.

Harold M. Baron and Bennett Hymer, "The Negro Worker in the Chicago Labor Market," in Julius Jacobson, ed., *The Negro and the American Labor Movement*, 1968, Anchor paperback, Part I, pp. 232–254. Interesting figures on problems in one city.

IV. THEORIES OF PERSONAL INCOME DISTRIBUTION

A. Marginal Productivity Perspectives

Gary Becker, *Human Capital and the Personal Income Distribution*, University of Michigan, 1967. Principal statement of human capital view.

Jacob Mincer, "The Distribution of Labor Incomes: A Survey with Special Reference to the Human Capital Approach," *Journal of Economic Literature*, March, 1970, pp. 1–26. Interesting but difficult discussion, arguing the special importance of the human capital approach.

Melvin Reder, "A Partial Survey of the Theory of Income Size Distribution," in Lee Soltow, ed., *Six Papers on the Size Distribution of Income and Wealth*, 1969, National Bureau of Economic Research, pp. 205–254. Difficult, differing slightly with human capital emphasis.

James E. Meade, *Equality, Efficiency and the Ownership of Property*, 1964, Oxford University Press. Emphasizes the likelihood of increasing inequality in an economy governed by marginal productivity distributions.

B. Class Perspectives

Karl Polanyi, "The Self-Regulating Market and the Fictitious Commodities: Land, Labor and Money," in George Dalton, ed., *Primitive, Archaic and Modern Economies*, 1968, Doubleday, Anchor.

Karl Marx, "The Labor Theory of Value and the Theory of Exploitation," in Robert Venable, ed., *Marx on Economics*, pp. 29–105.

Karl Marx, *Capital*, Vol. I, Chapter 25, sections 1–4 (pp. 671–711, Modern Library edition). More on the labor theory of value.

Joan Robinson, *Essay on Marxian Economics*, 2d ed., 1967, St. Martin's Press. Some comparisons of conventional and Marxian explanations of the distribution of income.

V. ANALYSES OF EMPLOYMENT PROBLEMS

A. People or Jobs?

Lester Thurow, *Poverty and Discrimination*, 1969, Brookings, Chapters V–VI, pp. 66–110. Excellent summary of interpretation that employment problems derive from too low productivities, from little "human capital."

Gary Becker, "Investment in On-the-Job Training," in Mark Blaug, *The Economics of Education*, 1968, Penguin, pp. 183–207. Interprets success in acquiring skills on the job as a function of individual productivities.

Michael Piore, "On-the-Job Training in a Dual Labor Market," in Arnold Weber, ed., *Public-Private Manpower Policy*, 1969, I.R.R.A. In addition to the selection in his volume, a statement of the dual labor market theory and its implications for training possibilities.

Baron and Hymer, "The Negro Worker in the Chicago Labor Market," *op. cit.*, Part II, pp. 254–285. On the dynamics of the dual labor market.

Peter Doeringer and Michael Piore, *The Internal Labor Market*, 1971, D. C. Heath. Importance of institutionally structured labor markets, inside firms.

Barry Bluestone, "Lower-Income Workers and Marginal Industries," in Louis Ferman *et al.*, *Poverty in America*, 1968 revised edition, University of Michigan Press, pp. 273–302. Arguing the importance of changing industries rather than people.

Peter Blau and Otis Dudley Duncan, *The American Occupational Structure*, 1967, Wiley, skim pp. 1–206, read pp. 207–242. Differences in access to occupational mobility among whites and blacks in particular.

Thomas Vietorisz and Bennett Harrison, *The Economic Development of Harlem*, 1970, Praeger. The structure of problems in one ghetto, illustrating the characteristics of the secondary market.

B. Discrimination

By Race

Lester Thurow, *Poverty and Discrimination, op. cit.,* Chapter VII, pp. 112–138. Compares various theories.

Gary Becker, *Economics of Discrimination*, 1957, Chicago Press, pp. 1–24, skim pp. 25–81, read pp. 82–132. A marginal productivity theory of racial discrimination.

Paul Baran and Paul Sweezy, *Monopoly Capital*, 1966, Monthly Review Press, pp. 249–280. Neo-Marxist analysis of "Monopoly Capitalism and Race Relations."

Harry J. Gilman, "Economic Discrimination and Unemployment," *American Economic Review*, December, 1965, pp. 1077–1096. Attempt to measure empirically the effects of discrimination on unemployment rates.

Sterling Spero and Abram Harris, *The Black Worker*, 1968, Atheneum. Written originally in 1930, a historical discussion of early patterns of discrimination.

By Sex

Peggy Morton, "A Woman's Work Is Never Done," *Leviathan*, May, 1970. All the ways women face discrimination.

Margaret Benston, "The Political Economy of Women's Liberation," *Monthly Review*, September, 1969. Economic functions of discrimination by sex.

M. and J. Roundtree, "More on the Political Economy of Women's Liberation," *Monthly Review*, January, 1970.

C. Economic Growth and Automation

Technology and the American Economy, Report of the National Commission on Technology, Automation, and Economic Progress, 1966, U.S. Government Printing Office. Generally optimistic conclusions.

Charles C. Killingsworth, *Jobs and Income for Negroes*, 1968, National Manpower Policy Task Force. Intelligent discussion of effects of both growth and changing labor market demands.

Lester Thurow, *Poverty and Discrimination, op. cit.,* Chapter IV, pp. 46–65. Interesting analysis of effects of growth.

Georges Friedmann, *Industrial Society: The Emergence of the Human Problems of Automation,* 1955, Free Press. A sociological study of the impact of automation on conditions of work.

Jack Stieber, ed., *Employment Problems of Automation and Advanced Technology: An International Perspective,* 1966, St. Martin's. Comparative.

D. Labor Unions

Ray Marshall, "Racial Practices of Unions," in Ferman *et al.*, eds., *Negroes and Jobs, op. cit.,* pp. 277–297. Good summary of figures and facts.

Herbert Hill, "The Racial Practices of Organized Labor," in Arthur M. Ross and Hill, eds., *Employment, Race and Poverty, op. cit.,* pp. 365–402. Useful discussion by labor secretary of NAACP.

John E. Hutchinson, "The AFL-CIO and the Negro," in Ross and Hill, eds., *ibid.,* pp. 403–433. Tactful analysis of problems in major labor affiliation.

Julius Jacobsen, ed., *The Negro and the American Labor Movement, op. cit., passim,* especially pieces by Karson and Radosh, pp. 155–187, and by Rosen, pp. 188–208.

Ray Marshall, *The Negro and Organized Labor,* 1965, Wiley.

E. Operations of the Labor Market

Melvin Lurie and Elton Rayack, "Racial Differences in Migration and Job Search," in Ferman *et al.,* eds., *Negroes and Jobs, op. cit.,* pp. 358–381. The difficulties some blacks have in finding work.

Joseph C. Ullman and David P. Taylor, "The Information System in Changing Labor Markets," *Proceedings* of the 18th Annual Meeting of the Industrial Relations Research Association, December, 1965, pp. 276–289. Summary of the results of the Chicago labor market study, and role of information in job outcomes.

H. L. Sheppard and H. Belitsky, *The Job Hunt,* 1966, Johns Hopkins Press, *passim.* Study of job-finding behavior of unemployed men in Erie, Pa.

John F. Kain, "Housing Segregation, Negro Employment and Metropolitan Decentralization," *Quarterly Journal of Economics,* May, 1968. Rigorous statistical test of hypothesis that housing segregation reduces job opportunities for ghetto workers by increasing their distance from jobs.

Joseph Mooney, "Housing Segregation, Negro Employment and Metropolitan Decentralization," *Quarterly Journal of Economics,* May, 1969. Another view of Kain's results with different tests and slightly different conclusions.

F. Sociological Factors

Harold L. Sheppard and H. E. Shriner, "Family Structure and Employment Problems," in Ferman *et al.,* eds., *Negroes and Jobs, op. cit.,* pp. 174–186. Useful summary.

Kenneth B. Clark, "Sex, Status and Underemployment of the Negro Male," in Ross and Hill, eds., *op. cit.,* pp. 138–148.

Hylan Lewis, "Culture, Class and Family Life Among Low-Income Urban Negroes," *ibid.,* pp. 149–173.

VI. POLICY PERSPECTIVES

A. General

Report of the National Advisory Commission on Civil Disorders, 1968, Bantam, pp. 413–424. Useful summary of standard liberal policy approaches.

James Sundquist, "Jobs, Training and Welfare for the Underclass," in Kermit Gordon, ed., *Agenda for the Nation,* 1968, Brookings, pp. 49–76. Very good summary of the public issues.

Sar Levitan and Garth L. Mangum, *Federal Training and Work Programs in the Sixties,* 1969, National Manpower Policy Task Force. Useful summary of policies.

B. Legal Approaches

Richard Nathan, *Jobs and Civil Rights,* 1968, Brookings. Summary discussion of legal approaches to equalizing employment opportunities.

William Landes, "The Effect of Fair-Employment Laws," *Journal of Political Economy,* July–August, 1968. Rigorous statistical attempt to measure their effects.

C. Public and Private Training

Sar Levitan and Garth L. Mangum, *Making Sense of Federal Manpower Policy,* 1967, National Manpower Policy Task Force. Summary of intentions of government training assistance.

R. J. Solie, "Employment Effects of Re-training the Unemployed," *Industrial and Labor Relations Review*, January, 1968. One of the several important quantitative studies of effects of training on some workers.

Peter B. Doeringer, ed., *Programs to Employ the Disadvantaged*, 1969, Prentice-Hall. A collection of case studies of private training programs, with excellent summary and introduction by editor.

Peter B. Doeringer and Michael Piore, *The Internal Labor Market*, 1971, D. C. Heath, Chapters VII–VIII. Interesting discussion of the problems posed for manpower policy by the structure of internal labor markets.

Jules B. Cohn, *The Conscience of the Corporations: Business and Urban Affairs*, 1970, Johns Hopkins, *passim*. Results of study of training programs (and other "urban" programs) in 247 large corporations, with skeptical conclusions.

D. Economic Development and Black Capitalism

Gerson Green and Geoffrey Faux, "The Social Utility of Black Enterprise," in W. F. Haddad and G. Douglas Pugh, eds., *Black Economic Development*, 1969, American Assembly, pp. 21–37. Clear statement of the case for black capitalism.

John Kain and Joseph Persky, "Alternatives to the Gilded Ghetto," *The Public Interest*, Winter, 1969, pp. 74–88. Argument against investing in ghettos, and for the importance of dissolving the ghettos through decentralization.

"Community Development Corporations," *Yale Law Journal*, 1971. A comprehensive study of the need and vehicles for economic development.

Richard Cloward and Frances Fox Piven, "Corporate Imperialism for the Poor," *The Nation*, October 16, 1967. Warnings about corporate interest in ghetto development.

Anthony Downs, "Alternative Futures for the Ghetto," *Dædalus*, Fall, 1968, pp. 1331–1378.

E. Government Guaranteed Employment

Garth L. Mangum, "Government as Employer of Last Resort," in Sar Levitan *et al.*, eds., *Toward Freedom from Want*, 1968, Industrial Relations Research Association. Good summary of need and problems.

3 Education

Editor's Introduction

We Americans have suffered such losses of humane communality that we cannot allow ourselves to see the waste of life that stares us in the face.
Our very sense of crisis is often nothing more than a refined technique of avoidance. Thus we have a "problem of the schools," and talk to each other solemnly about improved facilities, better methods of instruction, more supervision, ignoring all the while the painful truth that what children need most is for the lives of their elders to make sense.
We are our children's problem. . . .

—George Dennison[1]

By 1970 most Americans seemed relatively familiar with the failures of urban schools. What we knew then from statistics and glimpses of shattered lives, we once only guessed. I suppose that our suspicions first crystallized in the mid-1950's, when middle-class America gasped at the movie *Blackboard Jungle.* Sputnik temporarily shocked us into worrying about all schools, but the publication at the end of the decade of James Bryant Conant's *Slums and Suburbs* forced us to focus still more clearly on the inadequacies of slum schools.[2] The sense of uneasiness had grown throughout the fifties, and Conant's book perfectly reflected the development of our concerns. We were thinking about education in a narrow, purely programmatic framework. Critics measured the schools' failures by their dropout rates. They hoped to improve school performance by fiddling with teacher/pupil ratios and classroom size.[3]

During the 1960's, however, the critics' specificity eroded. Nearly everything that happened in education during the decade combined to convince us that smaller classes and better counseling did not constitute sufficient solutions to the failures of schools. On the one hand, a steady succession of writing about ghetto schools by sensitive observers like Clark, Kozol, Kohl, Herndon, and Featherstone presented blistering evidence of the generality of failure in those schools—of the futility of planning with numbers, of the oppressiveness not only of the educational bureaucracy but of the larger ghetto society itself.[4] And on the other hand, the rebellion against the educational system among white middle-class youth, launched somewhat decorously at Berkeley in 1964, had penetrated deeply into the high schools and junior high schools by 1970.[5] Privileged students in the best schools, guaranteed of graduate degrees and occupational security, were rejecting the system which promised them success. The country was being forced to recognize that something else was wrong with its schools besides the low achievement scores of black students in ghetto schools. Some of the most sophisticated schools were performing brilliantly in meeting traditional objectives, but they were failing miserably in satisfying the demands of a new generation of students for social relevance and human priorities.

In this chapter on education, I have concentrated on the failures of ghetto schools because they have had a much more important effect on the ways in which the public responded to the "urban crisis." As this introduction and the readings should make clear, however, a radical

[1] From an article in "Annual Education Review," *The New York Times,* January 12, 1970, p. 52.
[2] *Slums and Suburbs* (N.Y.: McGraw-Hill, 1961).
[3] One of the first school systems to act on those specific programmatic perspectives was the New York City school system, which instituted its More Effective Schools program in ghetto schools, attempting to improve the quality of education by smaller class sizes and more teacher time available for counseling.
[4] See the bibliography at the end of this chapter for references to most of these authors' works.
[5] By 1970 books were being published about high school "revolutionaries" just as the campus rebellions had been a pet subject for publishers several years before.

analysis of current educational problems in our central cities helps illuminate the dissatisfactions of white students in suburban schools as well. In the general radical perspective, the very different dimensions of failure in ghetto schools and suburban schools reflect the same basic features of educational institutions in American society.

In this introduction to the readings, there are four sections. First, I have discussed the several ways in which we define and measure the failures of central-city schools. Second, I have briefly outlined the conservative and liberal perspectives on those problems. Third, I have discussed at greater length the structure of the radical analysis of those problems. Finally, I have summarized the purpose and contents of the readings.

DIMENSIONS OF FAILURE IN GHETTO SCHOOLS

We now recognize four different levels on which ghetto schools in central cities have been failing.

First, students in ghetto schools do not continue as far in school as students in most other schools; we have faulted ghetto schools for failing to stimulate them. (Some critics have obviously blamed the students for their lack of motivation.) This was the first level of failure we began to measure. Conant popularized the use of "dropout" rates as an index of this problem, comparing the varying percentages of students who graduate from different high schools.[6] Although it is still true that fewer students graduate from high school in predominantly black central-city systems than in white suburban systems, this difference in the number of years of schooling completed by blacks and whites has been narrowing rapidly in recent years.[7] Now, it begins to appear that "truancy rates" constitute a better measure of the *quantity* of schooling that different students receive. It seems to have become more and more routine for students to graduate rather automatically from central-city schools, as long as they appear occasionally in class. Although larger numbers of students are nominally completing high school, they are tending to spend fewer and fewer days in school each year. The truancy rates in New York City ghetto high schools, for instance, had reached nearly 50 percent per day by early 1970.[8]

Second, among students receiving a constant *quantity* of schooling—among those graduating from high school, for instance—black students in ghetto schools seem to learn "less" in school. Traditionally, we have used standardized achievement test scores to measure the *quality* of schooling at different levels, even though achievement test scores represent somewhat imperfect measures of quality. Using achievement test scores from over 600,000 American students, the federally sponsored survey, *Equality of Educational Opportunity* (widely known as the "Coleman Report" after its principal author), reported that black students had lower achievement scores than white students at every grade level, that only a portion of this difference could be explained by the poorer socioeconomic backgrounds of black students, and that the gaps in achievement scores tended to grow larger at higher educational levels. The report concluded from these separate results that white students received much higher quality education while in school than did black students.[9]

Third, we count these first two failures doubly. We have come to hope that schools in ghetto areas would *compensate* for the impoverished family and social background of many ghetto students, making up for their disadvantages in readiness to learn when they begin school. By the standards of the Coleman Report this goal would require that ghetto schools narrow the educational gap between blacks and whites as they proceed through school. In fact, as noted above, the gap between achievement scores of blacks and whites widens.

Fourth, ghetto schools suffer failures of commission as well as omission. Plainly and simply, the schools seem to destroy many students who pass through their doors. With their authoritarianism, their arbitrary bureaucratic practices, their preoccupation with order and compliance, the schools seem to create confusion, alienation, and rebellion where little existed before. In

[6] Conant, *op. cit., passim.*
[7] U.S. Bureau of the Census, *The Social and Economic Status of Negroes in the United States, 1969* (Washington: 1969), p. 50.
[8] See several stories in *The New York Times* during January, 1970.
[9] James S. Coleman *et al., Equality of Educational Opportunity* (Washington: U.S. Government Printing Office, 1966), p. 21.

different ways with different stories, several recent books have described the tragic oppression of many students in ghetto schools.[10] Jonathan Kozol meant it—ghetto schools bring "death at an early age."

CONSERVATIVE AND LIBERAL VIEWS

Conservative and liberal views of the educational problems described above begin with similar *analyses* of those problems; I would argue that their views on the sources of the problems begin with exactly comparable assumptions about the role of education in society and the ways in which it has failed for some.[11] The two views seem to differ primarily in their *prescriptions* for social solution of those problems. In this section, I have concentrated on describing the basic assumptions shared by the two perspectives about the present and potential role of education in American society. I have followed that discussion with a brief description of their differing programmatic views.

Conventional liberal and conservative analyses of educational failures in this country begin from a set of four related assumptions about education in an advanced society like the United States. The assumptions derive from the perspectives' common views of the functioning of the economic marketplace.

First, the analyses assume that the principal utility of educational achievement derives from education's influence on economic productivity.[12] Economists call it "returns to education," or, more mechanistically, "returns to investments in human capital."[13] They presume that more education will increase the level of an individual's general skills, thus increasing his "marginal productivity," and will consequently increase the amount of money he can expect to earn in his lifetime. Since additional years of education are clearly associated with higher individual earnings on the average in the United States, economists argue that increased education for those who are poor can play a significant role in lifting them out of poverty.[14] And because "adult education, training and retraining are difficult, slow and costly processes . . ." as James Tobin acknowledges, "our main hope must be in the education of our children."[15]

Second, the analyses assume that cognitive achievement tests accurately reflect the skill dimension through which education effects increased productivity. Those with more education are more productive, they presume, especially because they have learned how to read and reason more skillfully. This assumption has been mirrored in the Coleman Report, which used achievement test scores as the best available measure of educational outcomes. The assumption has acquired even more importance in a new strain of economic analysis—the analysis of educational production functions. From this new perspective, economists are trying to understand how to allocate resources in education most efficiently. Toward that end, they are studying how much various inputs contribute to outputs in education: do teachers with master's degrees contribute much more than teachers with bachelor's degrees to one unit of output; do extra library facilities add substantially to the reading scores of students; or does the educational level of a child's parents fundamentally determine the child's educational success? In all such cases, analysts have used standardized achievement test scores as the appropriate measure of educational output, and have studied the statistical determinants of variations in test scores among schools and among individual students.[16]

[10] See the books by Kohl, Holt, Kozol, and Herndon listed in the first section of the bibliography at the end of the chapter.

[11] There is one important difference, I suppose, in that conservatives tend to emphasize individual failures while liberals tend to concentrate on environmental causes of individual failures, but this difference concerns the concept of "blame" and does not affect the basic structure of their assumptions.

[12] For a useful general source, see Mark Blaug, ed., *The Economics of Education* (London: Penguin, 1968).

[13] See Gary Becker, *Human Capital* (N.Y.: NBER, 1964).

[14] For evidence for the country as a whole, see Herman Miller, *Rich Man, Poor Man* (N.Y.: Crowell, 1964).

[15] Tobin, "Raising the Incomes of the Poor," in Kermit Gordon, ed., *Agenda for the Nation* (Washington: Brookings, 1968), p. 91.

[16] Samuel Bowles provides a useful summary of this strain of analysis and its limitations in "Towards an Educational Production Function," in W. Lee Hansen, ed., *Education, Income and Human Capital* (N.Y.: NBER, 1970).

Third, the analyses assume that the role of education in a democratic society has been and can be that of guaranteeing equality of economic opportunity. As John H. Fischer has written,[17]

The dependence of democracy on popular education has been a continuing theme in our history. But it was not until the end of World War II that the country began seriously to consider the full implications of that relationship, and later still that it officially acknowledged the corollary proposition that to limit a man's education is to limit his freedom.

Education had been the route through which other disadvantaged groups had achieved social mobility, many observed, so it could also provide equality of opportunity for presently disadvantaged groups. If the rest of society somehow conspired to produce inequalities in the social and economic structure, then schools would counter those pressures by keeping open the yellow brick road.

Fourth, the analyses have also assumed that education has played an essential role in increasing opportunities for social and economic mobility over time. This involves a set of three related assumptions: first, that the income distribution has become more equal over time; second, that the amount of inter-generational mobility within that distribution has increased; and third, that increasing inter-generational mobility in the acquisition of education has played an important causal role in effecting the first two phenomena.[18]

Together, these four principal assumptions about education produce a single coherent perspective on educational objectives: that to improve the productivity of the low-skilled and the poor—in order to equalize their economic opportunities—we must improve their education; that to improve their education in that sense, we must raise their level of cognitive achievement by improving their abilities to read and reason; that the schools can effect this increasing equality of opportunity because they have played that role historically; and that, in general, it is becoming easier for the schools to fulfill this equalizing function because our society is continuing to become more educationally mobile (and simultaneously more meritocratic) over time.

Beginning with these shared objectives, liberals and conservatives diverge in their policy recommendations. Conservatives argue that most educational problems derive from the monopolistic control the government exercises over the public school system; most parents have no choice over their children's schools. Conservatives suggest a competitive private market for education, in which all families would have a freedom of choice among wide varieties of private schools for their children. (This exactly manifests their general faith in the efficiency and optimality of the competitive market system, discussed in Chapter One.) Schools providing superior education would be in heavy demand, flourishing and expanding. Those providing inferior education would be forced to improve or would eventually go out of business. The general quality of education in the market would therefore improve. And since some families would be too poor to be able to afford private schools, conservatives urge government subsidies to poor families for the education of their children, guaranteeing all parents some choice about schools.[19]

Liberals, as Chapter One noted, have more faith in the government and slightly less faith in the private market system. They tend to assume that private individuals in the market could not combine effectively to establish decent schools, and that government intervention would be necessary to foster cooperation. They therefore urge wide varieties of government initiatives in education, all designed to effect an equality of educational opportunity among children by providing schools of equal quality. In recent years, they have suggested many potential solutions: compensatory education in ghetto schools, with more teachers and smaller classes; community control of ghetto schools, to promote relevant education in ghetto communities; widespread busing of ghetto children to suburban schools, to allow wider exposure of poor children to their middle-class peers; and educational "parks," in which mammoth area-wide schooling complexes

[17] "Race and Reconciliation: The Role of the Schools," *Dædalus,* Vol. II of *The Negro American,* Winter, 1966, p. 24.
[18] For a brief discussion of the inter-relations among the hypothesized trends, see Peter Blau and Otis Dudley Duncan, *The American Occupational Structure* (N.Y.: Wiley, 1968), pp. 112–113.
[19] Milton Friedman elaborates this position in the chapter on "Government and Education," in *Capitalism and Freedom* (Chicago: University of Chicago Press, 1962).

would provide the same education (and therefore the same opportunities) to everyone under the same roof.[20]

THE RADICAL VIEW

A radical analysis of education argues that the role of education in capitalist societies is determined by the structure of basic "system-defining" capitalist institutions. As Chapter One noted, these basic institutions help preserve class divisions in society and help stabilize patterns of production and distribution. Within that context, education tends to serve two primary functions in capitalist societies: first, to instill in individuals both the ideology and the set of individual personality traits upon which the capitalist mode of production depends; and second, to help preserve or create economic and social class divisions.[21]

According to this analysis, the current "failures" of ghetto schools reflect education's success at its appointed roles; in this view, the schools are not failing at but are in fact fulfilling their objectives. I have chosen to outline this argument in three stages. First, I have amplified the radical analysis of the function of education in the United States by summarizing the kinds of evidence radicals cite to refute basic liberal and conservative assumptions about education. Second, with that evidence in hand, I have briefly outlined the argument that current problems in ghetto schools derive from the functions of education in capitalist societies. And third, given that argument, I have discussed the kinds of circumstances in which ghetto education could "improve" and argued that those circumstances are precluded unless basic capitalist institutions change enough to permit radical changes in the functions of schools.

As the previous section suggested, the liberal and conservative analysis of education built from four principal assumptions. In summarizing the radical critique of those assumptions, I have first quoted the assumption from the previous section and then summarized the arguments and evidence against it.

1. ". . . to improve the productivity of the low-skilled and the poor—in order to equalize their economic opportunities—we must improve their education;"

This assumption implies that anyone can increase his income by increasing his education, or, in other words, that variations in income correspond to variations in educational attainment for everyone in the economy. The radical analysis counters that the pattern of class stratification in the United States constrains the potential of education for increasing individuals' income. For blacks, for instance, the strength of class barriers in the labor market is so great that the income of blacks does not vary significantly with their educational levels. To the extent that this is true, then one cannot assume that increasing educational attainment among blacks will necessarily increase their incomes. It has not in the past.

Statistical evidence seems to support this argument. In the United States, blacks do not appear significantly to increase their earning power unless they graduate from college; between the ninth and fifteenth grades of school, income does not vary significantly with educational attainment. In addition, there is some evidence that returns to education vary by class as well as race.[22] Because blacks and some lower-class whites seem to realize this, their incentives about education inevitably differ drastically from those of many whites.[23]

2. ". . . to improve their education in that sense, we must raise their level of cognitive achievement by improving their abilities to read and reason;"

Radicals argue that education does not increase individuals' productivity by improving their cognitive abilities. Rather, it produces a set of personality traits compatible with capitalist modes of production. It screens potential workers through a sieve, sorting them according to their

<hr>

[20] For one collection of basically liberal prescriptions, see U.S. Civil Rights Commission, *Racial Isolation in the Schools* (Washington: U.S. Government Printing Office, 1967).

[21] For some of the general argument, see the piece by Edwards and MacEwan in Chapter One above. One of the best recent radical arguments about education is Ivan Illich, "Why We Must Abolish Schooling," *New York Review of Books,* July 2, 1970.

[22] On both of these points, see the evidence in the Supplement among the readings in this chapter.

[23] This of course should not imply that these groups should not continue in school. It simply means that they may not continue in school if schooling is justified solely on economic grounds.

capacities to work persistently, to respond to incentives like wages, to conform to work require-ments, and to defer gratification. Gintis summarizes much of this argument in his selection below. Ivar Berg has presented extensive evidence on this point, showing that education bears little relationship in the United States to determinants of productivity on the job except through its effects on personality.[24] Edgar Friedenberg has also sketched the mechanisms through which education induces those highly productive characteristics.[25] Elsewhere, Gintis summarizes varieties of evidence that educational attainment varies principally with those kinds of per-sonality characteristics.[26] The implication is clear—if we want to improve the economic oppor-tunity of our disadvantaged citizens, we should teach them to acquiesce, conform, and defer. We cannot expect that an improvement in their reading abilities will have any effect on their economic status.[27]

3. ". . . the schools can effect this increasing equality of opportunity because they have played that role historically;"

Radicals argue that schools have not functioned to improve equality of opportunity, but rather that they have functioned to preserve class stratifications. "Curriculum has always been used to assign social rank," as Ivan Illich puts it.[28] There are many pieces of evidence that the entire structure of social and economic institutions in the United States reinforces this educa-tional role. First, it has been shown that the socioeconomic class of parents bears a consistently positive relationship to the quality of schools available for their children; children from higher classes are afforded higher class rank through the distributive process of schooling.[29] This effect has been documented for a single city,[30] for a state at the elementary and secondary level,[31] and for a state at the college and university level.[32] Excerpts in this chapter from the studies by Sexton and Hansen and Weisbrod illustrate this kind of evidence. Second, it has been effectively demonstrated that both cognitive achievement and "productive" personality traits vary directly with the quality of school resources; the better the resources, the more productive the schooling for its students.[33] Finally, we have plentiful evidence that the effects of government finance of education tend to reinforce this class inequality of resources among localities, primarily through the practices and priorities of state legislatures.[34] None of this evidence should be regarded as the unfortunate residue of a more hierarchical past, for it corresponds to evidence about the role of publicly supported institutions in other areas. The schools, like other public institutions, tend disproportionately to benefit the more advantaged classes.

4. ". . . in general, it is becoming easier for the schools to fulfill this equalizing function because our society is continuing to become more educationally mobile (and simultaneously more meritocratic) over time."

Radicals argue that educational mobility has not been increasing over time in this country. Rather, they argue that the schools have become increasingly important in the distribution of class status over time, and that they have therefore tended to militate increasingly against social mobility. Illich makes the argument through an analogy with the historical role of religion:[35]

School has become the world religion of a modernized proletariat, and makes futile promises

[24] In his book, *Education and Jobs: The Great Training Robbery* (N.Y.: Praeger, 1969), and in an article summarizing some of the book's findings, "Rich Man's Qualifications for Poor Man's Jobs," *Trans-action*, March, 1969.
[25] In his classic study, *Coming of Age in America* (N.Y.: Vintage Books, 1967).
[26] In Chapter Six of his doctoral dissertation, "Alienation and Power: Toward a Radical Welfare Eco-nomics," Harvard University, 1969.
[27] Illich has some particularly interesting comments on this problem in "Why We Must Abolish Schooling," *op. cit.*
[28] *Ibid.*, p. 12.
[29] For a good summary of the evidence, see James Guthrie *et al., Inequality and Schools* (Washington: The Urban Coalition, 1969), Chapter Two.
[30] In Patricia Cayo Sexton, *Education and Income* (N.Y.: Viking, 1964); and in Martin Katzman, "Dis-tribution and Production in a Big City School System," *Yale Economic Essays*, Spring, 1968.
[31] See Guthrie *et al., op. cit.*
[32] W. Lee Hansen and Burton Weisbrod, *Benefits, Costs and Finance of Public Higher Education* (Chicago: Markham, 1969).
[33] For various pieces of the evidence, see Bowles, *op. cit.*, Guthrie *et al., op. cit.*, and Gintis, *op. cit.*
[34] Summarized in Guthrie *et al., op. cit.*, Chapter Four.
[35] "Why We Must Abolish Schooling," *op. cit.*, p. 11.

of salvation to the poor of the technological age. The nation-state has adopted it, drafting all citizens into a graded curriculum leading to sequential diplomas not unlike the initiation rituals and hieratic promotions of former times. The modern state has assumed the duty to enforce the judgment of its educators through well-meant truant officers and job requirements, much as did the Spanish kings who enforced the judgments of their theologians through the conquistadors and inquisition.

As other chapters have shown, social mobility has not been increasing in this country.[36] The Supplement among the readings in this chapter summarizes some evidence that inter-generational educational mobility has not been increasing either. There seems little reason to assume, given that evidence, that the schools' potential for equalizing economic opportunity is increasing.

Given these pieces of the radical argument, the radical explanation for ghetto educational problems flows quite directly. Educational institutions in the ghetto help reinforce the lower-class status of ghetto blacks. Schools in the ghetto help channel ghetto blacks to lower-class occupations and to prepare them psychologically to accept lower-class status. It seems clear by now that many young blacks understand these facts about their schools, learning from their elders' experience in the world that their schools offer them nothing worth acquiring. They understand that they have little control over their own fates, because race so thoroughly determines individual outcomes in society regardless of individual characteristics.[37] And for valid historical reasons, they are much less likely to accept their indoctrinations toward lower-class status than have previously disadvantaged groups. As Chapter Two also suggested, previously disadvantaged groups in this country have moved through a period of migration—first European immigrants and then black migrants from the South. Their acts of migration grew out of and preserved a sense of hopefulness about improving their lives. This helped induce them to develop the patience, perseverance, and deferred gratification which both the economy and the schools seem to reward. Now, many blacks are growing up in the ghetto, at the bottom of society with no hope of improving their status or that of their children. They are fully aware of the class structure in society and the role of the schools and work patterns in preserving that class structure. Their circumstances do not induce them to be patient with the schools. Indeed, they are likely to become particularly impatient. And with their impatience in school, they are likely neither to develop skills nor to acquire the personality characteristics through which education can bring them rewards in the larger society. The response of the schools is to try even harder to fulfill their roles, by becoming more authoritarian and demanding of those personality characteristics.

There appear to be only three ways this constellation of circumstances could change enough for ghetto schools to improve and for blacks to "apply" themselves more traditionally to their educational advancement.

First, if the class structure of the economy changed enough so that blacks could realize equal returns with whites for additional years of education or additional educational achievements, then they might apply themselves more consistently. Both their schools and their educations would probably improve as a result. Second, the economy could begin to reward different sets of characteristics, demanding creativity in its workers rather than conformity, or originality rather than docility. The schools would inevitably change, tending to emphasize those characteristics. They would loosen their structures and relax their expectations. Students would probably respond to this newer freedom by developing their creativity and originality. Third, the schools could seek an independence of the more basic institutions. They could try to ignore the demands of the economy for certain kinds of personalities and could establish for themselves independent sets of objectives. They could try, in George Dennison's terms, to respect and respond to the "present lives of children."[38]

None of these three possibilities seems to me at all likely. The first would require a restructuring of all our social institutions, for—as the chapter on employment argued more extensively —racism pervades our society and serves almost indispensable functions in the stabilization of

[36] See the Supplement among the readings in the chapter on poverty.
[37] Analyses of the Coleman Report have shown that those black students who have a relatively greater sense of control over their own destinies perform better in school, other factors held constant. See Bowles, *op. cit.*
[38] In *The Lives of Children* (N.Y.: Random House, 1969).

the capitalist system. We cannot easily replace those functions with some other stabilizing phenomenon adequately enough to ensure equal opportunities in the economy for members of minority groups. The second would require a fundamental change in both the process and objectives of economic production in this country. Conforming, deferring, persevering workers seem absolutely necessary to the preservation of profits for owners of capital. Independent, creative workers would not fit well with the ways in which production is managed. The third would require of the schools an independence of society that they have never achieved.[39] Were the schools to achieve this independence—through the pursuit of different objectives—the economy would have to find different mechanisms for the development of suitable personality structures among its workers. It seems impossible to anticipate both the shape of those mechanisms and their impact on the schools.[40]

In short, ghetto schools will continue to "fail" in liberal terms (but succeed in the "system's" terms) unless basic economic institutions stop placing demands on educational institutions, or unless some other institutions arise to satisfy those demands.

THE READINGS

The first three selections provide some basic Impressions, Definitions, and Magnitudes of ghetto education problems. Janet Sideman's short piece describes the experience of one intelligent, expressive, and energetic black student in a ghetto school. His story highlights both the ways in which schools try to channel those students and the ways in which students react to the schools. The brief selection from the Coleman Report and the special supplement to the readings provide evidence about different dimensions of inequality in American schools, relating the failures of ghetto schools to the general pattern of educational inequalities in education.

The second group of readings expands some (but not all) of the radical analysis. First, Bennett Harrison's essay provides some graphic evidence that education does not improve the economic opportunities of ghetto blacks; his analysis supplements many other pieces of evidence (based on national data) by examining patterns of returns to education within specific ghetto populations. Next, the pieces by James Coleman and Samuel Bowles provide some perspective on the nature of disagreement between liberals and radicals in their analyses of educational problems. In his article, Coleman interprets the evidence of the Coleman Report and argues for integration as a primary means of achieving equality of educational opportunity. His discussion assumes that educational and economic opportunity can be equalized regardless of the structure of basic economic institutions. Bowles, on the other hand, replies that the quality of schools does make a difference to educational outcomes on the margin but that the schools are effectively powerless to counter basic social and economic forces establishing class inequality among different groups. The next two selections provide some evidence on the ways in which schools support and promote class inequalities. The selections from Patricia Cayo Sexton's book offer evidence about a large city public high school system. The short article by Hansen and Weisbrod outlines some evidence for a liberal State higher education system. The final selection by Gintis synthesizes much of the radical view—presenting the basic argument that education serves the demands of the economic system by instilling productive personality characteristics and by inducing students to accept class divisions in the economy. Together, the pieces thoroughly amplify the two basic pieces of the radical analysis of education—that schools

[39] For especially interesting arguments on this issue, see Florence Howe and Paul Lauter, "The Schools Are Rigged for Failure," *New York Review of Books,* June 20, 1970.
[40] At this point, one can finally relate these arguments to white upper-middle class students' rejection of the schools. Like ghetto students, white upper-middle class students are not relying on the schools to help them move up in society—not because they are stuck at the bottom but because they are effectively stuck at the top. Many of them have no use for the kinds of personality structures both the schools and society reward, because they are not seeking to improve their economic status *and* because they recognize the alienation incumbent to those sets of characteristics. So they reject the mechanisms through which the schools develop those personality traits. And because that function so thoroughly defines education's role in this country, they conclude ultimately by rejecting the entire set of educational institutions. See Herbert Gintis, "New Working Class and Revolutionary Youth," *Review of Radical Political Economics,* Summer, 1970.

serve the basic social institutions by preparing productive workers and by promoting class divisions among them.

A final piece of reading illustrates how different schools might be if they were able to function independently of the economic system. The excerpt from George Dennison's brilliant book, *The Lives of Children*, suggests a very distant vision of human and humane education in which schools concentrate on developing the potential of their students as human beings rather than their productive potential in an alienating economic system.

DEATH OF A DROPOUT

Janet Sideman

This story provides a tragic glimpse of the reality of ghetto schools. It illustrates both the responses of those schools to problem students and the classic dimensions of student rebellion against the schools and their economic functions.

The selection originally appeared in *The New Republic*.

In early May [1967], newspapers reported that Clarence Brooker, age 19, Negro, was accidentally killed by a policeman in the Northeast section of Washington, D.C. A policeman was patrolling his regular beat, when he saw a group of boys milling about the street. Complaints from shopkeepers had already been received about them. The policeman stopped in front of the group and one of the boys, Clarence Brooker, dropped a bag of cookies onto the sidewalk. The bag broke, the crushed cookies were strewn over the street, the policeman attempted to arrest Brooker for disorderly conduct. There was a struggle and a chase, two shots were fired, and the boy was finally apprehended. It is unclear where he died, but the policeman was surprised that Clarence Brooker was dead at all. No one had realized that he had a bullet in his back, since there was no external bleeding. An investigation was demanded and the case is now before a grand jury. Among other items of interest mentioned in the reporting was that Clarence Brooker, besides having a police record, was also a high school dropout—one of many. (The dropout rate in the District's senior high schools last year was 12.3 percent.)

About two years ago I taught eleventh grade English in a Northeast Washington high school that had a special program for dropouts. Clarence Brooker was one of my students. The program had an all Negro enrollment. Most of the students lived in the Northeast ghetto section.

On the opening day of school I was informed that, although books had been ordered, they had not yet arrived, and I should

SOURCE: *Janet Sideman, "Death of a Dropout," from the June 3, 1967, issue of* The New Republic. *Reprinted by permission of* The New Republic. *Copyright © 1967, Harrison-Blaine of New Jersey, Inc.*

not count on them arriving at all. When I met the class, I asked them to write about something they enjoyed doing or that interested them. I mentioned that we would have no books for a while, but if I knew what they liked, I could base class work on this. They kept asking when the books would come. I said I didn't know, but you didn't have to carry a book to school in order to learn.

The students began writing, and after about 15 minutes, some began handing their papers in. The girls returned to their desks and sat, staring into space. The boys were more restless, and some got up and left the room. Browsing through the papers, I remarked that no one had crossed anything out or erased. You expect changes in written work. All the compositions were about half a page and in beautiful "penmanship." The letters were even, perfectly formed and slanted from left to right. The right-hand margins were as straight as a ruler. The compositions could be "classified" (using the professional jargon) as those that "demonstrated skills had not been learned" and those that were "literate." Here is an example of the former:

"Well I like everyone in the class. I have no pick. I am new here but that don't mean that I take of myself. The reason I here is because I drop out of school but I well like it here. The thing that interest me most is getting of school and having my diploma so I can say that I lest finish school without having to shy."

The other group wrote pieces something like this:

My name is .... My address is ....
I like school a little. My favorite subjects are English and Math. My favorite sports are softball and football. I would like to finish school and become a clerk-typist. I came here because I know how hard it is to get a good

job without a high school diploma. And I wouldn't want to be referred to as a dropout. I don't think it's going to be hard to finish school because I'm beginning to like going here."

Clarence Brooker was one of the first to finish, and after he brought the paper to my desk, he wandered from the room, returned, and roamed up and down the aisles, looking to see what the others were writing.

He had wide shoulders and was very muscular, which made him seem taller than he was. The photo of him in the newspapers gave the impression that he looked dull and impassive, but he had a very expressive face. His handwriting was clear, almost feminine because he paid such attention to details. The Os and As were perfect circles, the loops of the Ys and Gs were of equal length. His name was written in the upper right-hand corner, the date beneath it of equal length. "English XI" was in the left-hand corner, "Composition" in the middle.

"My interest is girls, booze and money, but the reason I came back is because I want my diploma. My diploma will help me very much in the future.

"My plan in the near future is to join the Air Force, and in order to join, I have to have my diploma.

"After I finish my service career, my other three interests will go into effect."

So from the English teacher's viewpoint Clarence was way ahead of the game—he was literate. That is, he conjugated verbs properly, he knew when to begin a new paragraph, he even had a good "clincher sentence," and the textbook tells us this is one of the most difficult problems in writing a composition. He had followed the assignment, he told me what interested him. He even had a bit of originality left in him. One of the better students in the class. So why had he dropped out? Because school had no relation to his life.

Dropouts are like nonchurchgoers; both might feel guilty or worried, but they soon discover their everyday lives are not altered by nonattendance. They can sleep late. There are no immediate consequences, and the future? Well, that is a long way off. Who knows if it was the air force that brought Clarence Brooker back? Anyway he carried an additional burden. He had more energy than was good for him and he didn't know what to do with it. That's the last thing you want from the congregation. They're only required to know when to rise, when to kneel, and to wait patiently while the organist finds the right page.

A few days later I requested another piece of writing. I began the sermon by asking the class to try to put their feelings into words. If they were interested in something, they should try to examine why. My words were stilted, but 30 wary faces do not make you very relaxed. "You have a language as a means of guiding and controlling your lives, so you can express ideas and understand situations. Do you think you would be able to have thoughts without a language?" I concluded. The girls dutifully began writing their names and the date at the top of the blue-lined paper. Clarence Brooker and some boys around him started laughing and yawning. What was the trouble? Clarence answered for them. They were bored. They knew what interested them, but I would never let them write about it. Yes I would, what was it?

"Sex," Clarence answered.

"You can write about it, but since I want you to put feelings into words, you might think I was trying to pry into your private lives, and that is not what I intended. Maybe you would feel freer with something less personal." He insisted that was what they really wanted to write about, and I agreed. Could they use a dictionary? Of course, that's what it was there for. Clarence had a perpetual grin on his face and after some writing would mutter something to those around him. The dictionary was passed from desk to desk. Snickers went around the room, pounding on desks, glances to see who would begin first.

"The point of this is to use words not noise."

I was uneasy, maybe I had overstimulated them. Teachers are always warned about this. The boys had been discipline problems before, the girls were pregnant or already mothers. It is important that limitations be set. Clarence was one of the first to finish, and waved his paper in the air as he brought it up. The bell rang while he was grabbing a pen away from one of the boys who had not yet finished. But nothing was produced that was stimulating, let alone overstimulating. The majority of the papers were definitions from the dictionary, with some moralizing attached.

"Sex is a division into male and female, relating to reproductive organs. Sex should mainly be active among adults who are married, but it doesn't always happen that way."

Here is the one Clarence Brooker wrote:

"Sex is, or shall I say, can be a form of both pleasure and relaxation. To me, sex is a *need* that has to be fulfilled by a member of the opposite sex. Some people use sex as a plaything, but sex should be regarded as being essential to life.

"Birth control pills should be abolished and so should abortions. Women getting rid of children should be sentenced to jail because it's a form of murder."

Grammatically correct, and the most original within the framework of the class, but not radically different. One newspaper article reported that Clarence committed rape and other sexual offenses, but his composition gives no hint of that. It is quite respectable today to consider sex a *need,* and many people agree with Clarence's view of birth control.

The next day the students wanted to hear the compositions and I read a few. They were very disappointed. I asked them if they could explain why, since they obviously had strong feelings about things, they could not express them in writing. The listlessness had begun, the wandering in and out, the slamming of the door, tapping feet. Their explanation was that they shouldn't be doing any writing or discussing at all.

"We want to get down to work." What was the definition of work in 11th grade English? Spelling, grammar, nouns, tests. And when are we going to get books?

I went to the central English department to see if I could get a book used by other D.C. schools. There happened to be one lying around, with Eleventh Grade English on it in capital letters.

"With this type of student, your classwork must have intensive structure," I was told. "Since it is lacking in the homes, the schools must provide it."

A lesson from the book was mimeographed. The sheets were passed out, heads were bent, *Adverbs* written in the center of the lined paper, numbers one to 20 to the right of the red vertical margin line. Correct the following sentences. (1) The parts of this camp stove fit together very simple. . . .

It was very peaceful. All the pens were moving in unison, a studious classroom scene.

Then Clarence Brooker was finished. If we had had books, I could have told him to begin the next lesson. He left the room, returned, wandered about. I told him I would correct his paper with him. Wasn't I going to grade it? I wrote an A in red ink. Wasn't I going to enter it in the record book? It was entered. Most of the students had done well. What was interesting was that students who could barely construct a sentence in a composition were able to recognize the incorrect use of an adverb in an isolated sentence. A student told me he was unable to pass the written part of the Civil Service Exam, would I give him additional work in grammar? I showed him one of his tests, where he was able to "correct the following verb forms," and substitute "I am" for "I is." Yet he always said "I is" and always wrote it in compositions. I never was able to convince him that the solution was not in additional exercises.

If the students could have defined what education meant to them, they would not have used words like understanding, ideas, or thought, for only words that could be attached to "things" had any meaning to them. They must have work. Work comes from a book and can be numbered and titled. A grade can be set down on paper and you can amass a collection of these papers to prove that you have been to school.

But what do you do with someone like Clarence Brooker, who is smart, who has this energy? He wanted work, but he wouldn't wait patiently when he finished, and he refused any other alternative. The class had been in session two weeks, and I decided to keep on mimeographing lessons for a while. I wasn't getting to know the class too well because Clarence was occupying most of my time. The wandering had developed into explosive noises. He wrote on other students' papers, he mimicked them. I spoke to him many times. Yes, he really wanted his diploma, he really did want to join the air force. He was very nice, his eyes responded to what I was saying. From a distance you would have thought we were having a conversation. You do very well in your work, maybe it's time for you to begin something new. Yes ma'am. Bring a book, any book, to class. Yes ma'am. He never did. Bring a book from the school library. Yes ma'am. He never went, he just wandered around the halls.

I asked another teacher if he had any "behavior problems."

"I never let them start," he answered. "From the first day, if there's any trouble, out they go. That's the only way to treat these kids. If you don't show them who's boss, they'll walk right over you. Besides, it's not fair to the rest of the class."

The school social worker said, "These children need authority because they don't get it on the outside. If the teacher doesn't show he is in control, it becomes very frightening for them."

I asked the principal if Clarence could be transferred to another class with a male teacher.

"We can't do it. He has to have eleventh grade English to graduate. Just drop him if he disrupts the class."

His classmates didn't have much sympathy with Clarence either. A girl spoke to me about him after class. "I know I shouldn't tell you how to run things, but you shouldn't let that boy in the class. We can't get any work done."

"But don't you think it's important that we try and see if we can't work something out with students like that?"

"I don't know about that. All I know is he's keeping me from learning."

So I hadn't followed the rules. I hadn't asserted my authority as teacher. If I could not make Clarence sit still, he had to be dropped. I had done neither, therefore he was walking all over me, which was to be expected.

"You really want to join the air force?"

"Yes."

"And you need a high school diploma to do that?"

"Yes."

"Then as a favor to me, I want you to think about something. Will you explain to yourself how you can want something badly, and yet, at the same time, do something that you know will give you the very opposite of what you want?"

"I'll try to stick it out," he answered. I had not got through at all. He didn't appear for the next few days, then came in late, left, then banged on the door glass until I started to go toward him. It dragged on for a few more days, then he was dropped. The policeman stationed in the building was instructed not to let him enter. I looked up his record to see what his other classes were and discovered that his other teachers had dropped him weeks before.

When I discussed this with other teachers and friends, I was advised not to take it personally. I didn't, and that's what made it so disquieting. I would have felt better if Clarence had been personally hostile, for that would have meant he had formed some opinion, passed some judgment.

Perhaps it is useless to investigate who was to blame for putting Clarence Brooker and hundreds of other dropouts on the street. The Negro child's education must be structured, it must be consistent. So he is taught to identify abstractions with visual things on the assumption that abstractions are too much for him to handle. He then becomes dependent on material symbols and equipment, and then in the cruelest inconsistency of all, is provided with schools. that have substandard equipment, and little or no material to satisfy this dependency. His private life is full of tension and conflict, so he is given work where tension and conflict are eliminated and he never learns to cope with them.

He faces inequality, therefore he is taught conformity, which is mistaken for equality. He never conceives of a class as a miniature community, where people of different character and ability have to live together. And he never experiences equality, since he must have authority, which by its very definition means that someone is above him.

Well, one May evening Clarence Brooker, who was too smart for his own good and couldn't stick it out, dropped a bag of cookies in front of a policeman and was shot. Did he know why he dropped it? The policeman symbolized authority? But this authority wasn't going to be walked over, he carried a gun to prove it. If he were not a dropout, would Clarence be alive today? Who can say? He got an A on his adverbs. He knew that the parts of this camp stove fit together very simply.

SEGREGATION AND ACHIEVEMENT IN THE PUBLIC SCHOOLS

James S. Coleman and Others

In 1966, the federal government published the results of a mammoth survey of students and schools in the United States, *Equality of Educational Opportunity*. The survey was intended to measure the extent of educational inequality in this country, and its results have become standard sources for analysis of achievement in the schools. This very brief excerpt from the report sketches one dimension of inequality in American schools—the large gaps in achievement scores between predominantly white and black schools. The Editor's Supplement following this excerpt summarizes evidence of other dimensions of inequality.

The leading author of the report, James S. Coleman, teaches sociology at Johns Hopkins and has recently advised President Nixon on educational policy.

SEGREGATION IN THE PUBLIC SCHOOLS

The great majority of American children attend schools that are largely segregated —that is, where almost all of their fellow students are of the same racial background as they are. Among minority groups, Negroes are by far the most segregated. Taking all groups, however, white children are most segregated. Almost 80 percent of all white pupils in 1st grade and 12th grade attend schools that are from 90 to 100 percent white. And 97 percent at grade 1, and 99 percent at grade 12, attend schools that are 50 percent or more white.

For Negro pupils, segregation is more nearly complete in the South (as it is for whites also), but it is extensive also in all the other regions where the Negro population is concentrated: the urban North, Midwest, and West.

More than 65 percent of all Negro pupils in the first grade attend schools that are between 90 and 100 percent Negro. And 87 percent at grade 1, and 66 percent at grade 12, attend schools that are 50 percent or more Negro. In the South most students attend schools that are 100 percent white or Negro.

The same pattern of segregation holds, though not quite so strongly, for the teachers

SOURCE: *James S. Coleman* et al., *"Segregation and Achievement in the Public Schools"* from Equality of Educational Opportunity (*Washington: U.S. Government Printing Office, 1966*).

of Negro and white students. For the Nation as a whole, the average Negro elementary pupil attends a school in which 65 percent of the teachers are Negro; the average white elementary pupil attends a school in which 97 percent of the teachers are white. White teachers are more predominant at the secondary level, where the corresponding figures are 59 and 97 percent. The racial matching of teachers is most pronounced in the South, where by tradition it has been complete. On a nationwide basis, in cases where the races of pupils and teachers are not matched, the trend is all in one direction: white teachers teach Negro children but Negro teachers seldom teach white children; just as, in the schools, integration consists primarily of a minority of Negro pupils in predominantly white schools but almost never of a few whites in largely Negro schools.

In its desegregation decision of 1954, the Supreme Court held that separate schools for Negro and white children are inherently unequal. This survey finds that, when measured by that yardstick, American public education remains largely unequal in most regions of the country, including all those where Negroes form any significant proportion of the population. . . .

ACHIEVEMENT IN THE PUBLIC SCHOOLS

The schools bear many responsibilities. Among the most important is the teaching of certain intellectual skills such as reading, writing, calculating, and problem solving. One way of assessing the educational opportunity offered by the schools is to measure how well they perform this task. Standard achievement tests are available to measure these skills, and several such tests were administered in this survey to pupils at grades 1, 3, 6, 9, and 12.

These tests do not measure intelligence, nor attitudes, nor qualities of character. Furthermore, they a.e not, nor are they intended to be, "culture free." Quite the reverse: they are culture bound. What they measure are the skills which are among the most important in our society for getting a good job and moving up to a better one, and for full participation in an increasingly technical world. Consequently, a pupil's test results at the end of public school provide a good measure of the range of opportunities open to him as he finishes school—a wide range of choice of jobs or colleges if these skills are very high; a very narrow range that includes only the most menial jobs if these skills are very low.

Table 1 gives an overall illustration of the test results for the various groups by tabulating nationwide median scores (the score which divides the group in half) for 1st-grade and 12th-grade pupils on the tests used in those grades. For example, half of the white 12th-grade pupils had scores above 52 on the nonverbal test and half had scores below 52. (Scores on each test at each grade level were standardized so that the average over the national sample equaled 50 and the standard deviation equaled 10. This means that for all pupils in the Nation, about 16 percent would score below 40 and about 16 percent above 60).

With some exceptions—notably Oriental Americans—the average minority pupil scores distinctly lower on these tests at every level than the average white pupil. The minority pupils' scores are as much as one standard deviation below the majority pupils' scores in the 1st grade. At the 12th grade, results of tests in the same verbal and nonverbal skills show that, in every case, the minority scores are farther below the majority than are the 1st-graders. For some groups, the relative decline is negligible; for others, it is large.

Furthermore, a constant difference in standard deviations over the various grades represents an increasing difference in grade level gap. For example, Negroes in the metropolitan Northeast are about 1.1 standard deviations below whites in the same region at grades 6, 9, and 12. But at grade 6 this represents 1.6 years behind; at grade 9, 2.4 years; and at grade 12, 3.3 years. Thus, by this measure, the deficiency in achievement is progressively greater for the minority pupils at progressively higher grade levels.

For most minority groups, then, and most particularly the Negro, schools provide little opportunity for them to overcome this initial deficiency; in fact they fall farther behind the white majority in the development of several skills which are critical to making a living and participating fully in modern society. Whatever may be the combination of nonschool factors—poverty, community attitudes,

TABLE 1

NATIONWIDE MEDIAN TEST SCORES FOR 1ST- AND 12TH-GRADE PUPILS, FALL 1965

| Test | Racial or ethnic group | | | | | |
	Puerto Ricans	Indian Americans	Mexican-Americans	Oriental Americans	Negro	Majority
1st grade:						
Nonverbal	45.8	53.0	50.1	56.6	43.4	54.1
Verbal	44.9	47.8	46.5	51.6	45.4	53.2
12th grade:						
Nonverbal	43.3	47.1	45.0	51.6	40.9	52.0
Verbal	43.1	43.7	43.8	49.6	40.9	52.1
Reading	42.6	44.3	44.2	48.8	42.2	51.9
Mathematics	43.7	45.9	45.5	51.3	41.8	51.8
General information	41.7	44.7	43.3	49.0	40.6	52.2
Average of the 5 tests	43.1	45.1	44.4	50.1	41.1	52.0

low educational level of parents—which put minority children at a disadvantage in verbal and nonverbal skills when they enter the first grade, the fact is the schools have not overcome it.

Some points should be borne in mind in reading the table. First, the differences shown should not obscure the fact that some minority children perform better than many white children. A difference of one standard deviation in median scores means that about 84 percent of the children in the lower group are below the median of the majority students—but 50 percent of the white children are themselves below that median as well.

A second point of qualification concerns regional differences. By grade 12, both white and Negro students in the South score below their counterparts—white and Negro—in the North. In addition, Southern Negroes score farther below Southern whites than Northern

Negroes score below Northern whites. The consequences of this pattern can be illustrated by the fact that the 12th-grade Negro in the nonmetropolitan South is 0.8 standard deviation below—or, in terms of years, 1.9 years behind—the Negro in the metropolitan Northeast, though at grade 1 there is no such regional difference.

Finally, the test scores at grade 12 obviously do not take account of those pupils who have left school before reaching the senior year. In the metropolitan North and West, 20 percent of the Negroes of ages 16 and 17 are not enrolled in school—a higher dropout percentage than in either the metropolitan or nonmetropolitan South. If it is the case that some or many of the Northern dropouts performed poorly when they were in school, the Negro achievement in the North may be artificially elevated because some of those who achieved more poorly have left school.

CLASS, RACE, AND EDUCATION

Editor's Supplement

The preceding selection from the Coleman Report highlights one aspect of educational inequality in this country, the disparity in achievement scores among schools with different racial compositions in different geographic areas. This brief supplement will summarize some scattered pieces of evidence on other elements of educational inequality. Four dimensions of inequality seem especially important: years of schooling, quality of schooling, returns to schooling, and inter-generational equality.

YEARS OF SCHOOLING

The level attained in school varies widely in this country by class and race, although racial inequalities have diminished substantially in very recent years.

In general, although the absolute level of educational attainment has increased considerably in the last century in the United States, the distribution of attainment has not become more equal. Roughly 20 percent of those born between 1890–1894 graduated from high school, 40 percent of those born between 1910–1914, and 60 percent of those born between 1930–1934.[1] Despite this rapid increase in numbers of high school graduates, however, inequalities in educational achievement have not diminished. One measures educational inequalities in the same way one measures income inequalities. In the U.S. income distribution, it has been true since World War II that the poorest 20 percent of families have received roughly 5 percent of total income received by individuals.[2] With education, one can measure the shares of different groups in total years of schooling attained by the population. If the distribution of educational attainment had become noticeably more equal over time, the most poorly educated group would

---

[1] Christopher Jencks and David Riesman, *The Academic Revolution* (Garden City: Doubleday, 1968), p. 77.
[2] See the Supplement in the chapter on poverty in this book.

have increased its share of total years of schooling. In fact, the distribution has hardly changed at all in recent years. The most poorly educated third of the male population born between 1910–1914 received 20 percent of total years of schooling, while the most poorly educated third born between 1930–1934 received 22 percent.[3]

Years of schooling vary substantially by socioeconomic class. In data collected from Project Talent, a nationwide survey of high school seniors in 1960, the proportion going to college varied directly according to the socioeconomic status of parents—whether or not the study controlled for variations in aptitude scores. Table 1 provides one set of illustrative results from that survey. Within a single city, years of schooling achieved also tend to vary with socioeconomic class, as Patricia Cayo Sexton found in her study of "Big City."[4]

TABLE 1
PROBABILITY OF COLLEGE ENTRY FOR A MALE WHO HAS REACHED GRADE 11*

| | | Socioeconomic Quartiles | | | |
		Low 1	2	3	High 4
Ability Quartiles	Low 1	.06	.12	.13	.26
	2	.13	.15	.29	.36
	3	.25	.34	.45	.65
	High 4	.48	.70	.73	.87

NOTE: The socioeconomic index is a composite measure including family income, father's occupation and education, mother's education, etc. The ability scale is a composite of tests measuring general academic aptitude.

* Based on a large random sample of U.S. high school students as reported in John C. Flannagan and William W. Cooley, *Project TALENT, One-Year Follow-Up Studies*, Cooperative Research Project Number 2333, School of Education, University of Pittsburgh, 1966.

Blacks leave school at lower levels than whites, although the gap between blacks and whites has closed rapidly in recent years. In 1960, for instance, 36 percent of nonwhite males between 25 and 29 years old had completed at least four years of high school, while 63 percent of their white peers had reached the same level. By 1969, fully 60 percent of black males in that age range had graduated from high school, while 78 percent of white males of the same age had completed at least twelve years.[5] The median educational level of blacks between 25 and 29 had climbed to 12.1 years by 1969; the median level for whites of the same age was 12.6 years.[6]

QUALITY OF SCHOOLING

The most prevalent measure of educational quality relies on comparisons of achievement test scores among students at a given grade level.[7] The preceding selection from the Coleman Report provides evidence on variations in achievement level by race. Further evidence from the report suggests that class differences are at least as strong. Measuring class by the Coleman Report's data on the presence of consumer durables in the home, a standardization of the Coleman data by class shows that average sixth-grade achievement scores among upper-class white students

[3] Jencks and Riesman, *op. cit.*
[4] Sexton, *Education and Income* (N.Y.: Viking, 1964), especially the chapter on senior high schools. See the selection from the book in this chapter.
[5] U.S. Bureau of the Census, "The Social and Economic Status of Negroes in the United States, 1969," Current Population Reports, Series P-23, No. 29, p. 51.
[6] *Ibid.*, p. 50.
[7] Considerable evidence indicates that variations in such achievement scores do not reflect simple differences among students in socioeconomic background, that the quality of schools has some kind of independent effect. For a general summary of the evidence, see James Guthrie *et al., Inequality and Schools* (Washington: The Urban Coalition, 1969).

were 43 percent higher than those for lower-class white students; that upper-class blacks scored 29 percent higher than lower-class blacks; and that lower-class whites scored only 19 percent above lower-class blacks.[8]

RETURNS TO SCHOOLING

Another quite different measure of educational quality relies on estimated monetary returns to years of schooling. Whatever the relationship between an additional year of schooling and additional income—whether it can be adduced to increased productivity or to the effects of a "screening process"—monetary returns to additional years of education represent one kind of reward available in society to those who continue in school. If the rewards are unequal, then those who receive fewer rewards have much less economic incentive to continue their education.

Evidence has accumulated that the monetary returns to education vary substantially between blacks and whites. Many analysts have found either of two principal results in different studies: first, that additional years of schooling are associated with statistically significant increases in monetary returns for whites but are not associated with returns for blacks (at least for certain schooling increments, especially grades nine through eleven); or second, that the returns associated with increased schooling are much larger for whites than blacks.[9] Randall Weiss found, for example, that an extra year of schooling (between grades one and twelve) was associated with $457.78 extra annual income among white males between 36 and 45 and with only $123.67 extra annual income among black males in the same group (controlling for age, marital status, and veteran status). Among blacks in other age groups, Weiss found no statistically significant association between income and education, even for the youngest group of blacks (between 26 and 35).[10]

One very small piece of evidence suggests that the returns to education also vary by class. In an unpublished study, John Conlisk found that a worker's earnings increase in direct relationship with the income of his parents, controlling for years of schooling attained by the worker.[11] And in their book, *The American Occupational Structure*, Peter Blau and Otis Dudley Duncan found that the socioeconomic status of male workers (an occupational index closely though not uniquely associated with income) increased as the father's socioeconomic status increased, controlling both for the worker's education and his father's education.[12]

INTER-GENERATIONAL EQUALITY

We tend to assume that the American educational system, if at one moment its resources and returns may not be equally distributed, at least helps promote increasing inter-generational equality. This implies that the children of the least-educated will have an increasingly good chance of moving up in the educational distribution over time, that they are increasingly less certain to become the least-educated of their own generation.

Some evidence has become available on this measure of equality, and it seems to belie our conventional assumptions. It does not appear that the American educational system has been promoting inter-generational equality. Jencks and Riesman report, for instance, that the percentage of the best-educated sixth in the male population who were born into that sixth (by virtue of their fathers' educations) had *increased* slightly between someone of like description born in 1897–1906 and one born in 1927–1936.[13] And William Spady finds much the same gen-

[8] Based on data from the federally sponsored Coleman Report (see the previous selection), standardized in an unpublished paper by Larry Seidman, 1968.
[9] For varieties of this evidence, see Giora Hanoch, "An Economic Analysis of Earnings and Schooling," *Journal for Human Resources*, Summer, 1967; Stephan Michelson, "Incomes of Racial Minorities," unpublished manuscript, 1968; and the selection in this chapter by Harrison.
[10] Randall Weiss, "The Effect of Education on the Earnings of Blacks and Whites," *Review of Economics and Statistics*, May, 1970, p. 154.
[11] "A Bit of Evidence on the Income-Education-Ability Interrelation," mimeo, 1968.
[12] Blau and Duncan, *The American Occupational Structure* (N.Y.: The Free Press, 1967).
[13] Jencks and Riesman, *op. cit.*, p. 101.

eral result.[14] In relative terms, Spady shows that the educational gaps between children with fathers of varying educational attainment have remained fairly constant over a period of forty years.

[14] William G. Spady, "Educational Mobility and Access: Growth and Paradoxes," *American Journal of Sociology*, November, 1967.

EDUCATION AND UNDEREMPLOYMENT IN THE URBAN GHETTO

Bennett Harrison

One of the important strands of the radical analysis of education is that the economic utility of education is constrained by the class structure of the economy. In the United States, radicals have observed, some groups are not able to improve their economic opportunities almost regardless of their education. Most of these observations have been based on an analysis of national data. Harrison summarizes some evidence based on local ghetto samples, a more relevant population base. His conclusions are striking confirmation of the general argument.

The paper, written originally for this volume, draws on the author's dissertation for a Ph.D. in economics, "Education, Training and the Urban Ghetto," University of Pennsylvania, 1971.* Harrison is now an assistant professor of economics at the University of Maryland.

SOURCE: *Bennett Harrison, "Education and Underemployment in the Urban Ghetto," written for this book.*

* All figures in this paper represent calculations from unpublished microdata files, including the Office of Economic Opportunity's 1966 and 1967 *Surveys of Economic Opportunity* (hereafter SEO) and the U.S. Department of Labor's 1966 *Urban Employment Survey* (hereafter UES). This is the most recent microdata available for use by independent researchers. When the 1968–70 Urban Employment Surveys become available, it will be interesting to test whether the conclusions based upon the 1966 data need to be revised. I suspect that this will not be the case.

I would like to acknowledge receipt of dissertation fellowships from the Office of Economic Research, Economic Development Administration, U.S. Department of Commerce; and from the Manpower Administration, U.S. Department of Labor. Additional support was provided by the Bureau of Business and Economic Research of the University of Maryland, and by the University's Computer Science Center. Constructive criticism of earlier drafts and materials was contributed by Benjamin Cohen, Susan Holland, Lawrence Klein, William Milligan, Mancur Olson, and Thomas Vietorisz.

There are at least seven million men and women in America who are labor force participants and yet who are poor. In the congested ghetto areas of our central cities, even the *most* stable families—those with both parents present and with the male head working full time—are unable to earn more than about $100 a week in the marketplace.[1] Individual ghetto male family heads earn considerably less than $100—when they work.[2]

Pending completion of my thesis, these findings are to be regarded as *distinctly preliminary*.
[1] On the labor force participation of low-income persons, see Harold L. Sheppard, *The Nature of the Job Problem and the Role of New Public Service Employment* (Kalamazoo, Mich.: W. E. Upjohn Institute, January, 1969). According to my calculations from the 1966 UES data files, median weekly family earnings in ten urban ghettos were highest in male-headed households in Central Harlem; a 95 percent confidence interval for this $103/week median is $85–$120.
[2] In Harlem, male household heads earned an individual median weekly wage of $84 during the UES survey week in November, 1966. The median for all Harlem workers was only $73. In

TABLE 1
PROPORTION OF GHETTO RESIDENTS HAVING COMPLETED
AT LEAST A HIGH SCHOOL EDUCATION BY 1966

N = 37,330

Ghetto and City	Aged 20			Aged 20–24		
	Black %	White %	Spanish-Speaking %	Black %	White %	Spanish-Speaking %
Roxbury (Boston)	45.4	42.8	19.8	57.1	61.2	13.6
Central Harlem (N.Y.C.)	45.2	46.0	26.6	69.2	76.5	44.9
East Harlem (N.Y.C.)	38.0	38.3	18.1	47.1	67.0	33.3
Bedford-Stuyvesant (N.Y.C.)	47.3	46.4	25.4	64.5	44.4	37.9
North Philadelphia	33.8	48.2	14.1	53.5	64.7	13.2
North Side (St. Louis)	29.7	27.0	44.4	52.9	57.1	50.0
Slums of San Antonio	43.4	47.8	17.7	80.6	53.3	39.0
Mission-Fillmore (S.F.)	52.5	54.3	37.5	71.7	79.7	57.9
Salt River Bed (Phoenix)	23.6	28.4	15.9	49.1	53.7	24.5
Slums of New Orleans	23.1	35.2	34.5	49.2	63.6	—

SOURCE: Author's computations from the unpublished 1966 Urban Employment Survey data files.

But ghetto residents are able to find work far less often than those living outside the slums.[3] Still others are involuntarily part-time employed—looking for full-time work but unable to find it.

The poverty areas of our central cities, and the more compact "hard-core" ghetto communities within them, contain families of many races and ethnic origins: blacks, Puerto Ricans, chicanos, Indians, and substantial numbers of whites. There is new evidence that ghetto workers—and blacks in particular —are investing in themselves through the mechanism of public education. In fact, blacks in the urban slums have achieved levels of schooling comparable to those of whites in the same neighborhoods, as shown

the North Philadelphia ghetto, employed workers earned on the average only $65/week. In the slums of New Orleans, their average rate of pay was only $58/week. Occupation by occupation, these median wage rates averaged only 40 to 60 percent of the corresponding 1966 annual average wage rates in the corresponding metropolitan area, as reported in *Employment and Earnings Statistics for States and Areas, 1939–66*.
[3] In the ten UES ghetto areas, the unemployment rate ranged from a low of 6.3 percent in the Bedford-Stuyvesant section of New York City to a high of 12.5 percent in the North Side ghetto of St. Louis. During the same period, the unemployment rates for New York and St. Louis as a whole were only 3.7 and 4.4 percent respectively.

by some of the figures in Table 1. Moreover, ghetto blacks seem to have achieved about the national nonwhite average for years of school completed.[4]

In spite of these achievements, nonwhites in the ghetto (of whom the large majority are black) continue to lag behind even ghetto whites in terms of earnings, unemployment rates, and job status. In general, for all races, the jobs to which ghetto workers have access are of poor quality and pay wages which are substandard by a number of widely accepted benchmarks.

[4] A third of the nonwhite workers living in the poverty areas of the nation's twelve largest cities in March, 1966, had completed at least twelve years of school, according to my calculations from the 1966 SEO tapes. About 38 percent of the blacks living in the ten UES areas (identified in Table 1) had attained at least that level of schooling by November, 1966. For the nation as a whole in 1966, only about 28 percent of the nonwhites aged 25 or more were high school graduates; see National Industrial Conference Board, *Economic Almanac* (N.Y.: Macmillan, 1967), p. 11. While no 1966 national statistics on the educational attainment of younger blacks have been published, Table 1 shows that—at least in the ghetto—younger blacks do better than the racial average; they *are* staying in school longer. Nationally, the rate of high school completion for black adults aged 20 and over is therefore probably somewhat greater than 28 percent. Note the similarity of the national and ghetto estimates.

EDUCATION AND THE ELIMINATION OF POVERTY

Neoclassical theories of unemployment and poverty are oriented almost entirely toward the "supply side."[5] Recent research efforts (including my own) indicate, however, that investments in the human capital of minority workers have *not* significantly contributed to eliminating poverty.[6] This suggests a need for revision of the current orthodoxy which asserts that poverty is a function of inadequate education and training. My own contribution to this critical literature has focused on the residents of eighteen central-city ghettos across the country.

Formal education is widely thought to be the principal instrument by which past generations of ghetto dwellers climbed out of the urban slums and into the American middle class.[7] Apparently, many take it for granted that the formula will work again—is working now—for the newest inhabitants of the urban ghettos. Public education, it is frequently argued, may in the last analysis be the most effective antipoverty instrument of all.[8] Under reasonable assumptions about the mix of academic, technical, and institutional ("sheepskin") prerequisites for skilled or at least semiskilled employment, we should expect to find that ghetto workers, like others, realize a meaningful return to the decision to remain in school. Certainly this has been the usual conclusion of studies on national samples,[9] and on suburbanites of both races in at least one American city.[10]

In a recently published study of the Harlem economy, a colleague and I found little evidence to support the conventional wisdom.[11] In models controlling for race, age, family size, relationship to household head, presence or absence of spouse, and sex, we estimated a marginal return to high school completion of only 17 cents above the expected hourly wage rate of a high school

[5] The originators of the antipoverty program decided that "poverty was to be eliminated by raising everyone's marginal product to the level where [they] would be able to earn an acceptable income. Education and training programs were to be the principal means for raising marginal products. . . . Increasing workers' human capital could eliminate poverty." Lester Thurow, "Raising Incomes Through Manpower Training Programs," in Anthony Pascal, ed., *Contributions to the Analysis of Urban Problems* (Santa Monica: The RAND Corporation, August, 1968), p. 3868.

[6] See, for example, the following: Ivar Berg, *Education and Jobs: The Great Training Robbery* (N.Y.: Frederick A. Praeger, 1970); Stephan Michelson, "Incomes of Racial Minorities" (Washington, D.C.: The Brookings Institution, 1968), unpublished manuscript; and Randall D. Weiss, "The Effect of Education on the Earnings of Blacks and Whites," *Review of Economics and Statistics*, May, 1970.

[7] See, for example, U.S. Commission on Civil Rights, *A Time to Listen . . . A Time to Act* (Washington, D.C.: U.S. Government Printing Office, 1967); Philip Hauser, "Demographic Factors in the Integration of the Negro," *Dædalus*, Fall, 1965, pp. 867–870; and Everett Hughes, "Anomalies and Projections," *ibid.*, p. 1134.

[8] In studying the "vicious circle of the 'Three E's', Education, Employment, and Environment" (sic), participants in a recent New Jersey conference on urban problems concluded: "After much research and study of the problem, it is now plain that the real place to begin to break through is in the area of education, because without correcting this problem first, the other two will . . . defy effective solution at all." David N. Alloway and Francesco Cordasco, *The Agony of the Cities* (Upper Montclair, N.J.: Montclair State College, 1969), p. 23. Philip Hauser firmly believes that "the Negro's major handicap in his efforts to advance in America . . . is undoubtedly to be found in his limited education and skills," Hauser, *op. cit.*, pp. 867–868.

[9] Studies which attribute an important income effect to education include Lowell Gallaway, "The Negro and Poverty," *Journal of Business*, January, 1967, pp. 27–35; W. Lee Hansen, "Total and Private Rates of Return on Investment in Schooling," *Journal of Political Economy*, April, 1963, pp. 128–140; H. S. Houthakker, "Education and Income," *Review of Economics and Statistics*, February, 1959, pp. 24–28; Elizabeth Waldman, "Educational Attainment of Workers," *Monthly Labor Review*, February, 1969, pp. 14–22; and Herman P. Miller, "Annual and Lifetime Income in Relation to Education," *American Economic Review*, December, 1960, pp. 962–986. A significant inverse relationship between education and unemployment is reported in Harry J. Gilman, "Economic Discrimination and Unemployment," *American Economic Review*, December, 1965, pp. 1077–1096; and Jeffrey K. Hadden and Edgar F. Borgatta, *American Cities: Their Social Characteristics* (Chicago: Rand McNally, 1965), pp. 138–140.

[10] Werner Z. Hirsch and Elbert W. Segelhorst, "Incremental Income Benefits of Public Education," *Review of Economics and Statistics*, November, 1965, pp. 392–399. This is a study of a St. Louis suburb.

[11] Thomas Vietorisz and Bennett Harrison, *The Economic Development of Harlem* (N.Y.: Frederick A. Praeger, 1970), pp. 19–30. The ghetto development project out of which this study emerged is described in Bennett Harrison, "A Pilot Project in Economic Development Planning for American Urban Slums," *International Development Review*, March, 1968, pp. 23–31.

dropout in Harlem. Moreover, when we stratified both unemployment and labor force participation rates by age, sex, and years of school completed, the resulting tables displayed a surprising absence of the expected inverse relationship between education and unemployment or the expected direct relationship between education and labor force participation. In fact, many of the cells showed precisely the *opposite* effects. From this, we hazarded a (most tentative) explanation, about which—after completing the thesis research on seventeen additional ghetto areas—I now feel considerably more confident. Perhaps education increases the expectations and standards of ghetto workers which, when unmet by discriminating or otherwise exploitative employers, leads to frustration. This in turn may reduce the job attachment of the worker. If presently employed, he or she may display greater absenteeism, more frequent recalcitrance when given orders by foremen, less patience with the more experienced and sometimes racist co-workers, and so forth. If the ghetto worker is *not* presently employed, then—although he is indeed searching for work—the change in his standards or expectations means that he will not accept just *any* job offered to him. If the offered positions do not meet his new standards, then he will reject the job and search further. In this way, he may remain unemployed for a relatively long period of time.

From my own independent thesis research, and from the recent work of other scholars (see footnote 6), it now seems clear that nonwhite workers in the urban slums have not been able to translate their additional schooling into more than token increases in earnings or reductions in the chances of being unemployed. Indeed, in a substantial number of cases I was unable to find statistically significant evidence of *any* income or employment effect at all, in models which controlled for age, race, sex, industry in which the worker is employed, city in which the worker lives, and participation by the worker in any of five different training programs.[12]

[12] The models employed in this study make no attempt to control for possible variations in educational returns attributable to differences in the *quality* of education. In this, I am following the precedent set by Gary Becker, in *The Economics of Discrimination* (Chicago: University of Chicago Press, 1957) who assumed that whites and

Central-City Poverty Areas in Twelve SMSA's

White workers in these geographically extensive low-income areas[13] earn on the average well over twice as much per extra year of schooling as nonwhites. The nonwhite payoff varies very much more than the white payoff—from city to city, from one industry to another, across the sexes, and by age. For nonwhite Houston women working in personal services, increased education actually *reduces* expected weekly earnings. And the older the woman, the greater the deficit. In one model, designed to isolate the effects of passage of important institutional milestones, the weekly wage of white high school graduates in the twelve sets of poverty areas is nearly $25 higher than that of whites who never entered high school. For nonwhites, the difference is only $8.83 (see Figure 1). High school, therefore, has *three times* as high a marginal payoff for ghetto whites as for ghetto nonwhites.[14] On the assumptions of a forty-year working life, a rectangular lifetime earnings distribution,[15] and a 6 per-

Negroes of equivalent age and sex were equally productive at the margin. It may be argued that the exclusion of quality controls in no way vitiates the results described in the text. Following Weiss (*op. cit.*), I shall assume that the "quality of schooling, grades, individual ability and motivation, and *parents'* income, education, and occupation [are] probably . . . correlated positively with years of school [such that] estimates of the increase in earnings associated with an additional year of school will [in the absence of controls for the above factors] be biased upward." In other words, my estimates of the marginal returns to education are, if anything, *overstated.*
[13] From the 61,517 persons aged 14 or more who are described in the March, 1966, SEO, I selected for analysis those 11,454 persons living in the nation's twelve largest SMSA's: Baltimore, Chicago, Cleveland, Detroit, Houston, Los Angeles, New York, Philadelphia, Pittsburgh, St. Louis, San Francisco, and Washington, D.C. These are the only areas that are individually identifiable on the current edition of the SEO tapes. For technical documentation on the definition of "poverty area" as employed in the SEO, see J. R. Wetzel and Susan B. Holland, "Poverty Areas of Our Major Cities," *Monthly Labor Review,* October, 1966, pp. 1105–1110.
[14] This is, of course, the mean size of the "payoff gap." At the .05 level, the difference *may* be anywhere from one to sixteen times, since 95 percent confidence intervals about the regression coefficients are $16–$32 for whites and $2–$14 for nonwhites.
[15] This is, of course, a most unrealistic assumption. But it is also an inexpensive one, and it

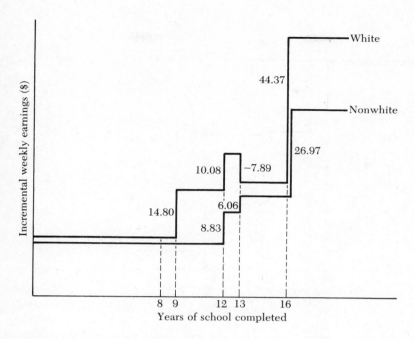

FIGURE 1
INCREMENTAL WEEKLY EARNINGS ATTRIBUTABLE TO EDUCATION
CENTRAL-CITY POVERTY AREAS IN TWELVE SMSA'S: MARCH, 1966

cent rate of time preference, the present value of the lifetime return to completion of high school is nearly $19,000 for whites but only $6,000 for nonwhites. Clearly, education has a very high opportunity cost for nonwhites living in the urban ghetto. There are any number of (largely illegal) activities out "on the street" that are capable of returning at least $6,000 in a *single* year.[16]

For whites, the risk of unemployment falls with years of school completed. Over the interval 9 to 12 years inclusive, the expectation of joblessness falls by 3.5 percent (see Figure 2). The average payoff per year of school completed over the entire range tested (0–18 years) is a 0.6 percent reduction (as indi-

cated by a less-than-satisfactory simple linear model). Among all twelve cities, fifteen industries, sex, and age, this payoff varies (for whites) by no more than 0.4 percent. For nonwhites, on the other hand, the average effect of education on unemployment, as well as the effect over the 9 to 12 interval, is zero! A *white* college graduate from the slums can expect to be involuntarily out of work nearly three weeks less per year than a white high school dropout who also lives in one of the urban ghettos in the sample. But the nonwhite college graduate faces exactly the same risk of unemployment as the high school dropout. There is, however, more intercity and interindustry variation around the nonwhite average "slope." Interaction models indicate that this slope attains a maximum payoff of −1.8 percent for twenty-year-old St. Louis women employed in personal services. Obviously, the demand for unskilled nonwhite workers varies substantially from one city to another, far more so than is the case for white workers from the ghetto. I interpret this to be yet another indirect manifestation of the presence of racial discrimination.

Additional researches into the structure of

facilitates computation. Actually, we need only require that blacks and whites in the ghetto have reasonably *similar* lifetime earnings distributions —whatever their specific shape. On different assumptions, the present values will of course be different.

[16] The preceding discussion is based upon comparative returns during a single survey *week*. Since nonwhites experience substantially higher annual unemployment rates than whites, the *annual* earnings "gap" is undoubtedly larger than that reported in the text.

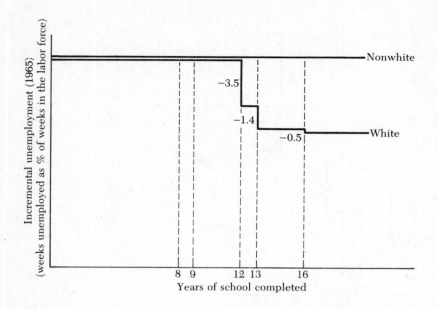

FIGURE 2
INCREMENTAL UNEMPLOYMENT RATES ATTRIBUTABLE TO EDUCATION
CENTRAL-CITY POVERTY AREAS IN TWELVE SMSA'S: MARCH, 1966

occupational status[17] lead to the conclusion that education facilitates the entry of both white *and* nonwhite ghetto workers into new occupations, and (at least for whites) leads to greater interoccupational mobility. Moreover, by national standards, these variations represent a "move up" into higher status positions. But this finding only confirms that the effects of racial discrimination pervade even these poorest neighborhoods in the urban economy, for, even though they share many similar problems associated with their common environment, ghetto residents diverge significantly by race insofar as their labor force status is concerned. Education may help members of both races to move into what are considered nationally to be more prestigious positions. But, once there, the *nonwhites* find themselves underemployed again: receiving earnings that are hardly above the levels enjoyed in the previous position, and facing the same expectations of

underemployment as before. For ghetto whites, on the other hand, the occupational mobility facilitated by education *is* translated into substantially higher earnings and significantly lower risks of joblessness. The contrast is dramatic.

Ten Racial Ghettos in Eight SMSA's

The earnings variable used with this sample[18] is hourly, rather than weekly, earnings, and the unemployment variable refers to the survey week rather than—as with the earlier sample—the previous year. In the ten urban ghettos studied, education has only a limited impact upon hourly earnings, and practically no effect at all upon the conditional probability of unemployment in any given week. Because of the relatively greater homogeneity of the population within each of these geographically rather compact areas, the regression results were not very sensitive to race.[19]

[17] These status calculations employ an ordinal prestige scale for detailed occupational categories, developed by the National Opinion Research Center and Professor Otis Dudley Duncan. See Duncan, "A Socioeconomic Index for All Occupations," in Albert J. Reiss Jr., ed., *Occupations and Social Status* (Glencoe, N.Y.: The Free Press, 1961).

[18] The UES areas in this sample are identified in Table 1. Usable records on 37,330 individuals aged 14 and over were available.
[19] Nearly 85 percent of the sample is nonwhite, i.e., Puerto Rican, Mexican-American, Indian, Asian, Negro, and other nonwhites. Maps of these UES and of the earlier SEO sample areas are contained in the thesis, and are available on request from the author.

A number of different earnings models yielded estimated returns of from 3 to 9 cents per hour for each additional year of schooling and—over the interval 9 to 12 years inclusive—an average return of 15 cents. Workers with at least some college received, on the average, only 20 cents more per hour than high school graduates who went directly to work and did not go to college. One model was designed to test for the existence of an upper limit to hourly wages and salaries in the ghetto, irrespective of education, i.e., the upper asymptote $e\alpha$ in the function $w = e\alpha - \beta E^{-1}$. Such limits were indeed found, ranging from a low of $1.56 per hour in San Antonio's chicano *barrios* to a high of $2.04 per hour in the Bedford-Stuyvesant ghetto of New York City. *No* amount of education would lead us to expect a Bedford-Stuyvesant worker of having an hourly wage of more than $2.04. That is the meaning of such a finding. All ten asymptotes were statistically significant.

When the UES data are pooled, increased schooling appears to reduce the probability of unemployment very slightly in the ghettos of New York, Philadelphia, St. Louis, and San Antonio. For the ten individual ghetto models, however, this effect was discovered only for the Salt River Bed section of Phoenix. The discrepancy appears to lie in the fact that, while each individual UES ghetto is relatively homogeneous with respect to race, the pooled sample contains many different minority groups. My pooled regression model did not attempt to capture this source of variation; had it done so, the results would undoubtedly have been far more consistent. In other words, for any given urban ghetto area, unemployment is *not* (with the single exception of the Phoenix slums) affected by increased schooling. In fact, the *individual* San Antonio model indicates that increased schooling actually *raises* the probability of unemployment, a finding whose implications we discussed earlier.

MINORITY ECONOMIC OPPORTUNITY OUTSIDE THE GHETTO

It has been suggested that a sample of ghetto residents is inherently biased, since those for whom education *has* paid off will presumably have moved out, leaving us with a sample skewed toward the "failures." A very recent (and decidedly unofficial) finding of the Bureau of Labor Statistics' Urban Employment Survey Group provides us with some remarkable direct evidence that the ghetto samples are probably *not* biased—at least not because of selective outmigration. Of 7,200 ghetto families in six cities who were to be reinterviewed by the BLS over a twelve-month period in 1968–69 (a period of exceptionally high mobility nationally), only 900 had moved from one residence to another. And of these 900 families, only 60 had moved *out* of the ghetto; all of the rest were either intraghetto moves (750) or involuntary relocations, for example, to jail or into the armed forces (90). In other words, the rate of outmigration from the urban ghetto, only two years after the date of the surveys we are analyzing, was less than 1 percent.

This same question about selective outmigration motivated the extension of my researches to urban workers living *outside* the ghettos, (*a*) in nonpoverty central-city neighborhoods, and (*b*) in suburban communities.[20] The results of these studies seem to validate the earlier findings. More important, they cast considerable doubt on the accuracy of some of our most cherished assumptions about the intrametropolitan spatial distribution of poverty and discrimination.

In terms of average economic opportunity, Figures 3 through 5 show that—for weekly earnings, annual unemployment, and occupational status among males—the white levels improve monotonically with "distance" from the core, while nonwhite opportunity increases somewhat with the "move" from the ghetto to the nonpoverty central city, but falls again with the further "move" out to the suburban ring. (When 95 percent confidence intervals are constructed around these means or medians, comparisons remain just as dramatic as in these figures.) For whites, employment opportunity definitely rises (or at least does not fall) as we move from the innermost to the outermost sample areas. For nonwhites, however, the three descriptors of employment opportunity show relatively little sensitivity to intrametropolitan residential location. Nonwhite earnings are significantly higher outside the ghetto than inside, but, once "outside," there is no significant difference between the median levels associated

[20] The source of these data is, again, the 1966 SEO.

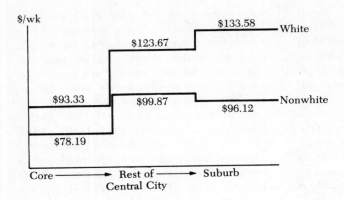

FIGURE 3
MEDIAN MALE EARNINGS—
BY INTRAMETROPOLITAN
LOCATION

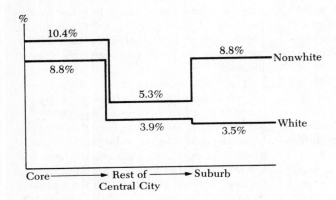

FIGURE 4
MEAN MALE UNEMPLOYMENT
RATES—BY INTRAMETROPOLI-
TAN LOCATION

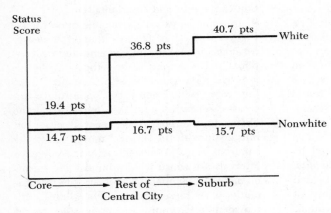

FIGURE 5
MEDIAN MALE OCCUPATIONAL
STATUS—BY INTRAMETROPOLI-
TAN LOCATION

with central-city as against suburban residence. Nonwhite unemployment rates in the
ghetto and in the suburbs are not statistically
different from one another, and may be only
slightly lower in the nonpoverty central city.
Finally, the indicator of occupational status
for nonwhite men is *totally* insensitive to
residential location.

Nor are the marginal returns to nonwhite
education significantly greater in the suburbs
than in the ghetto. In Table 2, the only sta-

tistically significant difference for nonwhites
is between the returns to college completion
for central-city residents who live (*a*) inside
and (*b*) outside the ghetto. To summarize the
more extensive thesis results for whites and
nonwhites, education is associated with increased mobility into what are nationally
considered to be higher status occupations.
For whites, this promise is realized; as education increases, whites move into new occupations where they receive higher earnings and

TABLE 2
PARTIAL REGRESSION RESULTS FROM MULTIVARIATE MODELS
BY RACE AND LOCATION OF RESIDENCE: MARCH, 1966

	Whites			Nonwhites		
Region	Incremental Return to H.S.	Incremental Return to College	Cumulative Effect*	Incremental Return to H.S.	Incremental Return to College	Cumulative Effect*
Central-City Poverty Areas	$24.88	$36.48	$61.36	$8.83	$33.03	$41.86
Rest of Central City	9.16	51.62	76.30	0†	53.50	53.50
Suburban Ring	32.80	65.32	98.12	0‡	38.87	38.87

* Sum of all individual "steps" in the step-function regression models.
† 79% of the observations in this cell displayed maximal schooling of ≤ 12 years.
‡ 85% of the observations in this cell displayed maximal schooling of ≤ 12 years.

SOURCE: Author's calculations from the 1966 Survey of Economic Opportunity.

face lower expectations of unemployment. Moreover, these marginal improvements in white employment status are greater in the nonpoverty areas of the central city than in the poverty areas, and greater still in the suburbs. For nonwhites, however, the promise is *not* realized; as their education increases, nonwhites move into new occupations, but their earnings are hardly affected at all by anything short of a college degree, and there is no effect whatever on their chances of finding themselves without a job over the course of the year. Moreover, the cumulative effects do not differ from one sample region to another; e.g., there is no significant difference (at the 95 percent level) among the entries in the last column of Table 2.

Thus, it appears that urban nonwhites are severely constrained in their search for decent employment, irregardless of where in the metropolis they reside. There is no evidence to support the widespread belief that, through education, unskilled or semiskilled nonwhite workers presently living in the ghetto can be "suburbanized": relocated to the metropolitan ring, where their economic opportunities are assumed to be substantially greater. This belief is reflected in a widely quoted policy recommendation made by Professor John F. Kain. Government programs, says Kain, "should emphasize the strengthening of the Negro's ability to break out of the ghetto [by] education and job training and the expansion of suburban housing op-

portunities."[21] But my findings suggest that there is probably little to be gained from policies designed to rearrange the intrametropolitan spatial configuration of minority residences. In *no* part of the American city does the labor market "work" adequately for nonwhites. In particular, there is no evidence to support the assertion that nonwhite economic opportunity in the suburbs is greater than in the ghetto. Taken together with the increasing resistance of middle-class white Americans to all forms of social protest and particularly to integration—a resistance which implies that the social costs of enforced integration would be extremely high—one cannot react to these materials with anything other than the deepest pessimism about the potential effectiveness of policies for "suburbanizing" nonwhites who presently live in the urban ghetto. The costs of such policies would probably be very great, and the expected benefits now seem to be very small, at least in terms of short-run employment opportunity.

CONCLUSION

Do these findings suggest that public investment in ghetto schools should be cut back? I believe not, "Equal education should be a goal in itself, not diminished for its

[21] John F. Kain, "The Big Cities' Big Problem," *Challenge*, September/October, 1966, reprinted in Louis A. Ferman *et al.*, eds., *Negroes and Jobs* (Ann Arbor: University of Michigan, 1968).

failure to produce income for nonwhites."[22] And in any case, the problem is not that education cannot work for blacks and other minorities in American cities. The problem is that the educational system is not being permitted to function in its normal capacity. My findings, it seems to me, call rather convincingly for a change in emphasis away from concentration on the alleged defects of the ghetto poor themselves toward the in-

[22] Michelson, *op. cit.*, pp. 8–28.

vestigation of defects in the market system which constrains the poor from realizing their potential. Only through a direct transformation and augmentation of the demand for their labor can the economic situation of ghetto dwellers be improved. Attempts to change the worker himself—whether to remedy his personal "defects" or to move him to a "better" environment—have not worked up until now, and there is no evidence to support the belief that they will work in the future.

EQUAL SCHOOLS OR EQUAL STUDENTS?

James S. Coleman

The federal report called *Equality of Educational Opportunity*, from which a preceding selection presented excerpts, had an important impact on educational policy discussions in the late 1960's. Widely known as the "Coleman Report" after its leading author, the report seemed to imply that integration of the schools was a necessary requirement for achieving educational equality among the races. Coleman himself provides one central view of the report's implications. Opinions like his formed an important component of liberal analyses of educational problems. In the selection following this, Samuel Bowles provides a more radical response to the same problems and evidence.

Coleman teaches sociology at Johns Hopkins and has recently advised President Nixon on educational policy.

The Civil Rights Act of 1964 contains a section numbered 402, which went largely unnoticed at the time. This section instructs the Commissioner of Education to carry out a survey . . . "concerning the lack of availability of equal educational opportunities" by reason of race, religion or national origin, and to report to Congress and the President within two years. The Congressional intent in this section is somewhat unclear. But if, as is probable, the survey was initially intended as a means of finding areas of continued intentional discrimination, the intent later became less punitive-oriented and more future-oriented: i.e., to provide a basis for public policy, at the local, state, and national levels,

SOURCE: *James S. Coleman, "Equal Schools or Equal Students?" The Public Interest, No. 4, Summer, 1966. Copyright © 1966 by National Affairs, Inc.*

which might overcome inequalities of educational opportunity.

In the two years that have intervened (but mostly in the second), a remarkably vast and comprehensive survey was conducted, focussing principally on the inequalities of educational opportunity experienced by five racial and ethnic minorities: Negroes, Puerto Ricans, Mexican Americans, American Indians, and Oriental Americans. In the central and largest portion of the survey, nearly 600,000 children at grades 1, 3, 6, 9, and 12, in 4000 schools in all 50 states and the District of Columbia, were tested and questioned; 60,000 teachers in these schools were questioned and self-tested; and principals of these schools were also questioned about their schools. The tests and questionnaires (administered in the fall of 1965 by Educational Testing Service) raised a considerable controversy in public school circles and among some parents, with concern ranging from Federal encroachment on the local education system to the spectre of invasion of privacy. Nevertheless, with a participation rate of about 70% of all the schools sampled, the survey was conducted; and on July 1, 1966, Commissioner Howe presented a summary report of this survey. On July 31, the total report, *Equality of Educational Opportunity*, 737 pages, was made available. . . .*

The summary of the report has appeared to many who have read it to be curiously "flat," lacking in emphases and policy implications. Much of the same flatness can be found in the larger report. The seeming flatness probably derives from three sources: the research analyst's uneasiness in moving from description to implications; the government agency's uneasiness with survey findings that may have political repercussions; and, perhaps more important than either of these, the fact that the survey results do not lend themselves to the provision of simple answers. Nevertheless, the report is not so uncontroversial as it appears. And some of its findings, though cautiously presented, have sharp implications.

Perhaps the greatest virtue of this survey —though it has many faults—is that it did not take a simple or politically expedient view of educational opportunity. To have done so would have meant to measure (a) the objective characteristics of schools—number of books in the library, age of buildings, educational level of teachers, accreditation of the schools, and so on; and (b) the actual extent of racial segregation in the schools. The survey did look into these matters (and found less inequity in school facilities and resources, more in the extent of segregation, than is commonly supposed); but its principal focus of attention was not on what resources go into education, but on what product comes out. It did this in a relatively uncomplicated way, which is probably adequate for the task at hand: by tests which measured those areas of achievement most necessary for further progress in school, in higher education, and in successful competition in the labor market —that is, verbal and reading skills, and analytical and mathematical skills. Such a criterion does not allow statements about

absolute levels of inequality or equality of education provided by the schools, because obviously there are more influences than the school's on a child's level of achievement in school, and there are more effects of schools than in these areas of achievement. What it does do is to broaden the question beyond the school to all those educational influences that have their results in the level of verbal and mathematical skill a young person is equipped with when he or she enters the adult world. In effect, it takes the perspective of this young adult, and says that what matters to him is, not how "equal" his school is, but rather whether he is equipped at the end of school to compete on an equal basis with others, whatever his social origins. From the perspective of society, it assumes that what is important is not to "equalize the schools" in some formal sense, but to insure that children from all groups come into adult society so equipped as to insure their full participation in this society.

Another way of putting this is to say that the schools are successful only insofar as they reduce the dependence of a child's opportunities upon his social origins. We can think of a set of conditional probabilities: the probability of being prepared for a given occupation or for a given college at the end of high school, conditional upon the child's social origins. The effectiveness of the schools consists, in part, of making the conditional probabilities less conditional—that is, less dependent upon social origins. Thus, equality of educational opportunity implies, not merely "equal" schools, but equally effective schools, whose influences will overcome the differences in starting point of children from different social groups.

This approach to educational opportunity, using as it does achievement on standardized tests, treads on sensitive ground. Differences in average achievement between racial groups can lend themselves to racist arguments of genetic differences in intelligence; even apart from this, they can lead to invidious comparisons between groups which show different average levels of achievement. But it is precisely the avoidance of such sensitive areas that can perpetuate the educational deficiencies with which some minorities are equipped at the end of schooling.

What, then, does the survey find with regard to effects of schooling on test achievement? Children were tested at the beginning

---

* [Ed.: See the selection from the Coleman Report above for part of the summary from the report.]

of grades 1, 3, 6, 9, and 12. Achievement of the average American Indian, Mexican American, Puerto Rican, and Negro (in this descending order) was much lower than the average white or Oriental American, at all grade levels. The amount of difference ranges from about half a standard deviation to one standard deviation at early grade levels. At the 12th grade, it increases to beyond one standard deviation. (One standard deviation difference means that about 85% of the minority group children score below the average of the whites, while if the groups were equal only about 50% would score below this average.) The grade levels of difference range up to 5 years of deficiency (in math achievement) or 4 years (in reading skills) at the 12th grade. In short, the differences are large to begin with, and they are even larger at higher grades.

Two points, then, are clear: (1) *these minority children have a serious educational deficiency at the start of school, which is obviously not a result of school;* and (2) *they have an even more serious deficiency at the end of school, which is obviously in part a result of school.*

Thus, by the criterion stated earlier—that the effectiveness of schools in creating equality of educational opportunity lies in making the conditional probabilities of success less conditional—the schools appear to fail. At the end of school, the conditional probabilities of high achievement are even *more* conditional upon racial or ethnic background than they are at the beginning of school.

There are a number of results from the survey which give further evidence on this matter. First, within each racial group, the strong relation of family economic and educational background to achievement does not diminish over the period of school, and may even increase over the elementary years. Second, most of the variation in student achievement lies within the same school, very little of it is between schools. The implication of these last two results is clear: family background differences account for much more variation in achievement than do school differences.

Even the school-to-school variation in achievement, though relatively small, is itself almost wholly due to the *social* environment provided by the school: the educational backgrounds and aspirations of other students in the school, and the educational backgrounds

and attainments of the teachers in the school. *Per pupil expenditure, books in the library, and a host of other facilities and curricular measures show virtually no relation to achievement if the "social" environment of the school—the educational backgrounds of other students and teachers—is held constant.*

The importance of this last result lies, of course, in the fact that schools, as currently organized, are quite culturally homogeneous as well as quite racially segregated: teachers tend to come from the same cultural groups (and especially from the same race) as their students, and the student bodies are themselves relatively homogeneous. Given this homogeneity, the principal agents of effectiveness in the schools—teachers and other students—act to maintain or reinforce the initial differences imposed by social origins.

One element illustrates well the way in which the current organization of schools maintains the differences over generations: a Negro prospective teacher leaves a Negro teacher's college with a much lower level of academic competence (as measured by the National Teacher's Examination) than does his white counterpart leaving his largely white college; then he teaches Negro children (in school with other Negro children, ordinarily from educationally deficient backgrounds), who learn at a lower level, in part because of his lesser competence; some of these students, in turn, go into teacher training institutions to become poorly trained teachers of the next generation.

Altogether, *the sources of inequality of educational opportunity appear to lie first in the home itself and the cultural influences immediately surrounding the home; then they lie in the schools' ineffectiveness to free achievement from the impact of the home, and in the schools' cultural homogeneity which perpetuates the social influences of the home and its environs.*

Given these results, what do they suggest as to avenues to equality of educational opportunity? Several elements seem clear:

a) For those children whose family and neighborhood are educationally disadvantaged, it is important to replace this family environment as much as possible with an educational environment—by starting school at an earlier age, and by having a school which begins very early in the day and ends very late.

b) It is important to reduce the social and

racial homogeneity of the school environment, so that those agents of education that do show some effectiveness—teachers and other students—are not mere replicas of the student himself. In the present organization of schools, it is the neighborhood school that most insures such homogeneity.

c) The educational program of the school should be made more effective than it is at present. The weakness of this program is apparent in its inability to overcome initial differences. It is hard to believe that we are so inept in educating our young that we can do no more than leave young adults in the same relative competitive positions we found them in as children.

Several points are obvious: It is not a solution simply to pour money into improvement of the physical plants, books, teaching aids, of schools attended by educationally disadvantaged children. For other reasons, it will not suffice merely to bus children or otherwise achieve pro forma integration. (One incidental effect of this would be to increase the segregation within schools, through an increase in tracking.)

The only kinds of policies that appear in any way viable are those which do not seek to improve the education of Negroes and other educationally disadvantaged at the expense of those who are educationally advantaged. This implies new kinds of educational institutions, with a vast increase in expenditures for education—not merely for the disadvantaged, but for all children. The solutions might be in the form of educational parks, or in the form of private schools paid by tuition grants (with Federal regulations to insure racial heterogeneity), public (or publicly subsidized) boarding schools (like the North Carolina Advancement School), or still other innovations. This approach also implies reorganization of the curriculum within schools. One of the major reasons for "tracking" is the narrowness of our teaching methods—they can tolerate only a narrow range of skill in the same classroom. Methods which greatly widen the range are necessary to make possible racial and cultural integration within a school—and thus to make possible the informal learning that other students of higher educational levels can provide. Such curricular innovations are possible—but, again, only through the investment of vastly greater sums in education than currently occurs.

It should be recognized, of course, that the goal described here—of equality of educational opportunity through the schools—is far more ambitious than has ever been posed in our society before. The schools were once seen as a supplement to the family in bringing a child into his place in adult society, and they still function largely as such a supplement, merely perpetuating the inequalities of birth. Yet the conditions imposed by technological change, and by our post-industrial society, quite apart from any ideals of equal opportunity, require a far more primary role for the school, if society's children are to be equipped for adulthood.

One final result of the survey gives an indication of still another—and perhaps the most important—element necessary for equality of educational opportunity for Negroes. One attitude of students was measured at grades 9 and 12—an attitude which indicated the degree to which the student felt in control of his own fate. For example, one question was: "Agree or disagree: good luck is more important than hard work for success." Another was: "Agree or disagree: every time I try to get ahead someone or something stops me." Negroes much less often than whites had such a sense of control of their fate—a difference which corresponds directly to reality, and which corresponds even more markedly to the Negro's historical position in American society. However, despite the very large achievement differences between whites and Negroes at the 9th and 12th grades, *those Negroes who gave responses indicating a sense of control of their own fate achieved higher on the tests than those whites who gave the opposite responses. This attitude was more highly related to achievement than any other factor in the student's background or school.*

This result suggests that internal changes in the Negro, changes in his conception of himself in relation to his environment, may have more effect on Negro achievement than any other single factor. The determination to overcome relevant obstacles, and the belief that he will overcome them—attitudes that have appeared in an organized way among Negroes only in recent years in some civil rights groups—may be the most crucial elements in achieving equality of opportunity —not because of changes they will create in the white community, but principally because of the changes they create in the Negro himself.

TOWARDS EQUALITY OF EDUCATIONAL OPPORTUNITY?

Samuel Bowles

Bowles responds in this selection to orthodox interpretations of ghetto educational problems and particularly to the kinds of analyses of the Coleman Report illustrated by the preceding selection. Bowles's discussion illustrates several important facets of the radical analysis of education, particularly his argument that educational inequalities reflect inequalities in the larger setting of social and economic institutions.

The article is based on a talk Bowles gave at a conference on the Coleman Report. The discussion was later revised and printed in a special issue of the *Harvard Educational Review.*

Bowles is an assistant professor of economics at Harvard and has written numerous articles on the economics of education.

I have been billed in some quarters as a critic of the Equality of Educational Opportunity survey, and the Coleman Report.[1] For many years to come, however, all of us, both critics and supporters (and even those hardy few who simply want to find out how our educational system works) will repeatedly return to the Coleman data. This is our great debt to Professor Coleman and his co-workers.

I will concentrate here on the problem of achieving equality of educational opportunity. Because the evidence contained in the Coleman Report is central to this question, I will focus on a number of the important aspects of the Report and the underlying survey. I suspect that much of the interest in the Coleman Report has been aroused by concern for gaining a greater measure of equality of opportunity for Negroes. For this reason, I will emphasize the achievement of equality of educational opportunity between races. However, let me urge you not to lose sight of the gross inequalities of educational opportunity among social classes, i.e., between rich whites and poor whites, and between rich Negroes and poor Negroes.[2]

I intend to show:

(1) that while the Coleman Report understates the effectiveness of devoting more resources to the education of Negro children, equality in the resources devoted to the education of children of different racial groups will not achieve equality of educational opportunity;

(2) that equality of educational opportunity implies major changes in society at large and, in fact, cannot be achieved by the efforts of the educational system alone; and

(3) that the achievement of equality of educational opportunity will require changes in the distribution of political power between races and among social classes.

EQUALITY OF EDUCATIONAL OPPORTUNITY THROUGH EQUAL SCHOOLS?

My first point is that the achievement of equality of educational opportunity requires inequalities in the amounts of resources devoted to the education of black children and white children, and of rich children and poor children.

There is nothing new about compensatory education; programs designed to give Negro children a higher level of school resources than whites have been in existence for years. Some of these programs have been investi-

SOURCE: *Samuel Bowles, "Towards Equality of Educational Opportunity?" Harvard Educational Review, 38, Winter, 1968, 89–99. Copyright © 1968 by the President and Fellows of Harvard College.*

[1] James S. Coleman *et al., Equality of Educational Opportunity* (Washington: U.S. Government Printing Office, 1966).
[2] Cf. William Spady, "Educational Mobility and Access in the U.S.: Growth and Paradoxes," *American Sociological Review*, XXXII (November,

1967), and *Project Talent, One Year Follow-up Studies* (Pittsburgh, Pa.: School of Education, University of Pittsburgh, 1966), p. 96ff. Also *U.S. Census of Population 1960, PC (2) 5A, School Enrollments,* Table 5.

gated, and a number of studies have reported their ineffectiveness. A recent evaluation of the More Effective Schools Program in New York, for example, showed that the very large increase in per-pupil expenditures was associated with a comparatively minor increase in grade level achievement on most tests.[3] Moreover, the findings in the Coleman Report itself have been taken by some as an indication that the level of school resources devoted to the education of children of any race has very little effect on the level of achievement. Professor Coleman has written that the evidence in the Report revealed that "the physical and economic resources going into a school had very little relation to the achievement coming out of it," and that "variations in teacher salaries (and a number of other resource measures) had little relation to student achievement when the family backgrounds of the students were roughly equated."[4]

These findings have raised difficult questions for the nation's educators, for if increases in per-pupil expenditures, higher teacher salaries, and a number of other conventional remedies for low scholastic achievement in fact have virtually no effect on achievement, what grounds are there to press for the allocation of increased funds to education? And, if the conventional remedies don't work, what new educational policies are required?

I believe that the evidence does not support the hypothesis that school resources are ineffective in increasing achievement levels. I intend to show that the inference that per-pupil expenditure, teacher salaries, and other measures of school resources have very little relationship to student achievement is open to serious question and that, in fact, the evidence of the Equality of Educational Opportunity survey itself suggests that student achievement is sensitive to the level of resources devoted to the school. At the close of this section I will suggest that while the effect of additional school resources on Negro student achievement could be substantial, a sizeable racial deficiency in achievement scores would remain even if we were to equate the presently measured characteristics of the quality of schooling of white and of nonwhite children. Let me make

it entirely clear that in suggesting the importance of school resources as a determinant of educational achievement in the schools, I do not intend to denigrate the importance of peer-group influence and the social backgrounds and attitudes of students.

We cannot hope to measure the effects of school resources on achievement without developing adequate measures of the school resources themselves. Yet the measurement of school resources in the survey appears to me to be highly inadequate.[5] Consider first the treatment of instructional expenditure per pupil. This measure would appear to be a rough index of the amount of instructional resources devoted to each student. However, the measure used in the analysis in the Report was not a school-by-school per-pupil expenditure, but rather an average of instructional expenditures per student within an entire school district. School-to-school differences within a district (even differences between secondary and elementary schools) were simply ignored. Even those inputs which were measured on a school-by-school basis are subject to some of the same measurement errors because the use of these measures necessarily ignores differences in the amount of resources devoted to children in different tracks within the same school.

A further problem arises because students who attend schools characterized by high levels of educational inputs, more often than not, come from higher social-class backgrounds and have attitudes conducive to educational achievement. The authors of the Report were obviously faced with the difficult statistical task of disentangling the effects of achievement associated with these overlapping characteristics of students. The method of statistical analysis adopted in the Report, however, is incapable of distinguishing among the overlapping effects of family background, attitudes, and school resources.

The inference that school resources are relatively ineffective in increasing achievement levels is based on the finding that when the social background of the students is controlled first, the level of school resources adds very little predictive power to the analysis.

[3] (New York: Center for Urban Education, 1967).
[4] James S. Coleman, "Towards Open Schools," *The Public Interest*, No. 9 (Fall, 1967), 20–27.

[5] For a more complete discussion of the data collected for the Report and the statistical methods used, see Samuel Bowles and Henry M. Levin, "The Determinants of Scholastic Achievement— An Appraisal of Some Recent Evidence," *Journal of Human Resources*, II (Winter, 1968).

Recent reanalysis of the data shows that controlling the level of school resources first, produces radically different results. For example, the amount of variance in achievement scores of twelfth-grade Negro students explained by the variable "teachers' verbal ability" more than doubles if this variable is brought into the analysis first, rather than after the social background variables.

Both approaches, however, give misleading results. Let me try to explain why this is so. Assume that we want to predict the weight of children on the basis of knowledge of both their age and their height. Because heights and ages of children are closely associated, we can predict a child's weight if we know only his age nearly as well as when we know both his height and his age. If we ran the analysis the other way around, i.e., first controlled for height and then investigated the additional predictive power associated with the variable age, the results would of course be reversed. We would find very little additional predictive power associated with age.

A similar statistical difficulty arises in the Coleman analysis because the level of resources devoted to a child's education and the child's own social background are not independent. When we control for the social class of the student, we implicitly control also for some part of the variation in school resources. The additional predictive power associated with the explicit addition of school resources to the analysis thus represents a downward-biased estimate of the real relationship between school resources and achievement. There is no rigorous statistical or compelling theoretical reason for controlling first for social background. In particular, it is not relevant that much of the effect of family background is felt first, prior to a child's entry into school, for the Coleman analysis is cross-sectional and does not take into account in any way the time sequence of the explanatory variables. By choosing to control first for social-background factors, the authors of the Report inadvertently biased its analysis against finding school resources to be an important determinant of scholastic achievement.

Fortunately for us, we do not have merely to speculate about the importance or direction of these biases, for the data which form the basis of the relevant portion of the Report have kindly been made available to me for reanalysis; and they reveal that school resources have a statistically significant relation to scholastic achievement, particularly for Negro children. Let me explain the apparent contradiction. When we talk about the effectiveness of a school input or a social background factor on scholastic achievement, we may talk either about the closeness of the association between the variable and achievement or about the magnitude of a change in achievement associated with a change in the variable. For purposes of educational policy-making, we clearly want to use the second approach; that is, we want to know how much change in achievement is associated with change in, say, class size, teacher quality, or student attitudes. Although the material was not published in the Report, the authors did in fact estimate what I believe to be the relevant quantities: namely, how large an effect on achievement do changes in school resources and other variables have?

Their decision not to publish this material was unfortunate, because the closeness of association measures which they did publish not only fail to shed much direct light on the educational policy issues at hand, but they are also subject to a number of statistical shortcomings such as those previously mentioned. The unpublished estimates avoid the most serious of these shortcomings.

Preliminary analysis of the computer runs which form the basis of the section of the Report on the effects of school resources indicate that the achievement levels of Negro students are particularly sensitive to the quality of the teaching staffs assigned to them.[6] The survey employed a number of measures of teacher quality; not surprisingly, the one most closely associated with student verbal achievement appears to be the teacher's score on a verbal facility test.

While these results must be subjected to further scrutiny, the implication is that, contrary to the Coleman conclusion, significant gains in Negro students' achievement levels can be made by directing additional resources to their education. Research currently in process[7] indicates that the cost of major changes in the quality of the teachers of Ne-

[6] I am currently using the Coleman data and other sources to generate new estimates of the relationship between school inputs and achievement.
[7] This research, using the Equality of Educational Opportunity Survey data, is being carried on at the Brookings Institution under the direction of Henry Levin.

gro students would not be prohibitive; in fact, the cost would be far below the per-pupil expenditure increases involved in many of the existing compensatory education programs. I do not minimize the practical difficulties involved in making improvements in the quality of the teachers of Negro students, nor do I intend here to endorse any particular form of compensatory education. There are no simple answers to these questions. What I seek to emphasize is that the evidence of the Coleman study itself, far from documenting the ineffectiveness of increased school resources, indicates that teacher quality is a major determinant of scholastic achievement among Negro students and that feasible changes in the level of quality of the teachers of Negro students would bring about significant changes in the achievement levels of these students.

Let me make my position clear: the type of compensatory educational program I am talking about does not involve simply spending more money on Negro than on white students, although more money will be necessary. We must go beyond the measure of money resources and concentrate on those school inputs which appear to have the greatest effect, i.e., on the basis of present data, teacher quality. Of course, in developing programs of compensatory education, we must not exclude consideration of other programs, such as the social-class or racial integration of the school, which may also have significant effects on achievement. Moreover, our present knowledge of the relationship between school inputs and achievement is still too rudimentary to justify much confidence in policies designed directly from the quantitative estimates of the effects on achievement of any particular school inputs. Many of the proposed solutions to our current educational problems imply increases in school resource levels considerably beyond our present range of observations, and therefore beyond the applicable range of our present statistical estimates.

More generally, the intelligent formulation of educational policies requires not only a more adequate theory of the learning process under various school and community conditions, but a far more complete description of the school, including such aspects as the atmosphere of the classroom and more exhaustive measurement of teacher attitudes. Detailed longitudinal case studies hold out some possibility of capturing the dynamic process of the development of cognitive skills, at least in the particular cases to which they apply.

After this lengthy statistical excursion, let me return to my first main point. The same evidence mentioned earlier suggests that were we merely to raise the quality of the teaching resources devoted to the education of Negroes to the level of that currently devoted to whites, we would significantly improve Negro achievement. Nevertheless, we would reduce the gap in Negro and white verbal achievement at grade 12 by only a little more than a quarter.[8] This estimate may be on the low side, since I have been able to estimate the impact of equating only a limited number of imperfectly measured teachers' characteristics. For example, we probably do not equalize the educational levels of teachers when we equate the degree levels that the teachers of Negro students have to those of teachers of whites, since the teachers of Negroes are more likely to be Negroes who have suffered serious deficiencies in their own education.[9] Even with more nearly ideal measures of teacher quality, however, a substantial gap would certainly remain. Equal school inputs will not produce equal school outputs.

EQUALITY OF ECONOMIC OPPORTUNITY THROUGH EDUCATION?

Let me move on now to my second point, which is that the burden of achieving equality of educational opportunity should not, and cannot, be borne by the educational system alone. The achievement of some degree of equality of opportunity depends in part upon what we do in the educational system but also, to a very large degree, upon what we do elsewhere in the economy, in the polity, and in the society as a whole.

First, given the importance of student attitudes and social-class background in the learning process, it may well be that no

[8] This result is based on the regression equations underlying Table 3.25.2 in Coleman *et al., op. cit.,* and evidence in the Report on differences between the means of the teacher quality variables for whites and Negroes. Naturally these calculations are subject to some error, although probably not enough to alter the substantive point being made here.
[9] Cf. Coleman *et al., op. cit.,* Ch. 4.

feasible program of compensatory education could overcome the educational disabilities imposed upon Negro children by racial discrimination and, in addition, upon poor Negro children by their lower-class origins. Closing the achievement gap may require changing student attitudes towards schooling and towards themselves; this can hardly be accomplished except through, or at least in conjunction with, an all-out social assault on racism and on the poverty and the powerlessness of the poor.

But closing the educational gap is not enough. Let me follow Professor Coleman in suggesting that equality of educational opportunity has to do with the effects of education rather than the inputs into education.[10] I will broaden the concept of the effects of education to include some of the crucial determinants of the distribution of economic well-being in our society, namely, the effects of education on jobs and the effects of education on income.

Education is obviously only one of the many influences on earnings and its effects differ considerably between racial groups. Differences in years of schooling appear to explain less than a third of the variance of earnings among individuals after account has been taken of race, region, sex, and age.[11] On the basis of U.S. Census returns, we find that Negroes gain considerably less from an additional year of education than do whites.[12] Discrimination in the labor market, as measured by the ratio of expected lifetime earnings of whites with a given level of schooling to the expected lifetime earnings of Negroes with a similar level of schooling, rises with increasing years of education through the completion of college. For example, the estimated lifetime earnings of nonwhite males with eight grades of education is 64 percent of that for whites with a similar level of schooling; the analogous fraction for those

with 12 years of schooling is 60 percent.[13] This means that with each additional year of education, short of postgraduate study, Negroes benefit less, both absolutely and relatively, than whites in terms of increased income. This situation obtains in the North as well as the South. Indeed, one competent piece of research using U.S. Census data suggests that for Negroes in the North, the economic gains associated with additional years of education beyond the eighth grade are comparatively minor, and that at a number of points in the educational career of a Negro youth, staying in school for an additional year results in an actual reduction in the present value of expected lifetime earnings.[14]

In part, these depressing results arise from the fact that the labor market rewards additional education in white children with a much lower probability of unemployment. This is not nearly as true in the case of Negroes. Let me give you two examples. For Negroes and whites with the lowest level of education, only one to four years of schooling, the rates of unemployment among males twenty-five years of age and above were roughly equivalent. For high shool graduates, the Negro unemployment rate was fully two times as large as the white unemployment rate.[15] Moreover, in 1964 the unemployment rates for male high school drop-outs under twenty-four years of age was 25 percent higher for nonwhites than for whites. By comparison, for high school graduates, the

[10] This position is advanced by Professor Coleman in his article in [the same issue of the *Harvard Educational Review,* Winter, 1968].

[11] G. Hanoch, "Personal Savings and Investment in Schooling" (Unpublished doctoral dissertation, University of Chicago, 1965), 42–47. (Mimeographed.)

[12] See *U.S. Census of Population 1960,* PC (2)7B, *Occupation by Earnings and Education,* Table 1. See also Stephan Michelson, "Equating Racial Incomes: On the Efficacy of Employment and Education Policies" (Washington: The Brookings Institution, 1967). (Mimeographed.)

[13] Based on 1960 Census returns for workers aged eighteen to sixty-four; H. Miller, *Income Distribution in the United States.* U.S. Census Monograph, 1966, p. 165.

[14] G. Hanoch, *op. cit.,* p. 90 ff. The present value of lifetime earnings is the sum of expected earnings over an individual's working life with future earnings discounted at some interest rate. Present values were computed with a variety of discount rates, ranging from 2 to 20 percent. A recent study of 2500 draft rejects aged 17 to 25 indicated low returns to schooling of the poor generally. Among that group an additional year of schooling contributes only an additional $37 to expected annual earnings. See W. Lee Hansen, B. Weisbrod and W. Scanlon, "Determinants of Earnings: Does Schooling Really Count?" (Unpublished preliminary paper.)

[15] *U.S. Census of Population 1960,* PC (2) 5B, *Educational Attainments.* These figures refer to 1960. Similar figures are reported in the *Monthly Labor Review* (March, 1966), "Educational Attainment of Workers in March 1965" for 1962, 1964, and 1965.

nonwhite unemployment rate was more than twice that of whites.[16]

Of course these differences in the gains from education reflect, among other things, differences in the quality of education received by the different races. It is extremely difficult to measure the economic impact of this quality difference, but the available evidence suggests that the economic gains from additional education would differ substantially for Negroes and whites even if the two racial groups had equal achievement scores. For example, the Coleman Report indicates that the mean Negro verbal-achievement score in the metropolitan Northeast is roughly one standard deviation behind the whites at grades 1, 3, 6, 9, and 12; a constant fraction of the whites score above the Negro mean achievement level at all grade levels.[17] Yet the fraction of whites earning more than the Negro mean by years of schooling shows a general rise from grade to grade. For example, among males with eight years of schooling, 66 percent of the whites earn above the Negro mean. Among high school graduates, the figure is 74 percent.[18] Thus, while Negro achievement levels are by this measure no farther behind the whites' at the higher than at the lower grades, Negro income levels fall increasingly far below the income of whites with each additional year of schooling. Or to use a slightly different measure, we know that by grade 12, Negro achievement levels are approximately three years behind the whites. Yet mean earnings of nonwhite twelfth-grade graduates fall far short of the earnings of whites with eight years of schooling.[19] The earnings gap considerably exceeds the learning gap.[20]

Let me state two conclusions. First, the achievement of equality of educational opportunity, if this concept is measured only by equivalent achievement scores, would take us only a small part of the way towards the achievement of equality of opportunity in the society at large, but it will take us some of the way.

Secondly, if we choose to define equality of educational opportunity in terms of the economic results of education, then in addition to equalizing achievement in school, we must tackle the problem of racial discrimination in the job market directly.

EQUALITY OF EDUCATIONAL OPPORTUNITY: WHO WANTS IT?

This brings me to my third and last point, namely, that the achievement of equality of educational opportunity in our society will probably require major changes in the distribution of political power. Decision-making in the educational system is a sensitive barometer of the power relations within a society. The selection processes, the promotion probabilities, and the formulation of educational policy reflect who really counts and who really governs.

Professor Coleman and his co-authors have made it painfully clear to us that, left to the benevolence of those who presently count, our system of education does not achieve equality of educational opportunity. There is ample evidence that we have not arrived at equality of educational opportunity; there is very little evidence that we are moving closer to its achievement.[21] Let me suggest that this situation has not come about by accident.

Raising Negro achievement levels confers definite benefits on those directly involved, and on many not so directly involved. But if we view the individual gains from education in relative rather than absolute terms, equality of educational opportunity is a two-way street. Some stand to benefit by it and others stand to lose. The competition for places in good colleges and the competition for good jobs must cause many white parents to regard the narrowing of racial discrepancies in educational opportunity with mixed feelings, or worse.

Those who stand to gain are the objects

[16] "Employment of High School Graduates and Drop-outs in 1964," Table A (U.S. Department of Labor, Bureau of Labor Statistics, Special Labor Force Report, No. 54, June, 1965).

[17] Coleman et al., op. cit., p. 273.

[18] The figures refer to workers aged twenty-five to sixty-four in the North and West (U.S. Census 1960, PC [2] 7B). If only workers in the age category twenty-five to thirty-four are considered, or if Southern workers are included, the same general picture emerges.

[19] The figures refer to male workers twenty-five to sixty-four years old in the North and West (U.S. Census 1960, PC [2] 7B).

[20] In a recent study of white-nonwhite income differentials, Stephan Michelson concludes that equating both the quantity and quality of schooling between races would reduce the racial income disparity by less than half. Cf. S. Michelson, op. cit.

[21] Cf., for example, W. Spady, op. cit.

of my attention here. Yet we must recognize that the achievement of equality of educational opportunity involves very real conflicts of interest. More specifically, it will involve favoring the interests of the poor and the powerless to the detriment of the interests of those better endowed with wealth and influence. Are we ready to take this road? Is Congress? Is City Hall?

If I am correct in suspecting that in most cases the answer is no, then we are faced with a choice. We can, of course, continue to make recommendations directed towards particular causes of low achievement among Negro children, ignoring the underlying dynamics of the system which produces these results. Or we may broaden our attack and attempt to increase the degree of participation in educational decision-making and to transfer power to groups presently excluded from influence.

Many of our policy decisions in education can have little effect on the distribution of political power. But I believe that many options open to us could have the effect of mobilizing poor communities, particularly of mobilizing Negro communities to exert their interests more effectively in the making of educational policy. For example, greater parental involvement in school decisions could have the effect of developing political and organizational skills in the ghetto, and building a political base which may allow the Negro community to make felt its claims for a larger share of educational and other social resources. The immediate effects of such programs on the scholastic achievement of children in school are of course unknown. But if the above analysis is correct, the immediate effects on scholastic achievement must be considered along with the long-run effects on the distribution of political power, on the attitudes of parents and students, and on the degree of racial discrimination in employment.

Let us continue to ask *what* school policies should be adopted. But let us also ask *who* should decide, and *how*. We must, of course, attempt to right the particular wrongs which we observe today; but we must attempt as well to understand why our system of decision-making in education has worked so consistently to the disadvantage of Negroes and the poor. Let us first understand it and then let us change it.

EDUCATION AND INCOME: SENIOR HIGH SCHOOLS

Patricia Cayo Sexton

This and the following selection provide two important glimpses at some evidence of a basic radical contention about education in the United States—that the educational system helps reinforce class inequalities. The excerpt is taken from the chapter on senior high schools in Mrs. Sexton's book, *Education and Income*, a study of the public schools in a large American city (which she identifies only as "Big City").

Mrs. Sexton teaches sociology at the City University of New York and has written several other books on urban education.

High schools in Big City are much like elementary schools in their social class characteristics. The differences among schools,

SOURCE: *From* Education and Income: Inequalities in our Public Schools *by Patricia Cayo Sexton. Copyright © 1961 by Patricia Cayo Sexton. All rights reserved. Reprinted by permission of The Viking Press, Inc.*

however, are sometimes less clearly defined than in the smaller and more homogeneous elementary schools. High schools are large institutions drawing students from a wide geographic area, some from very low and some from very high income pockets. Because of this, differences among high schools tend to be rather muted in some cases.

Nevertheless, social class is very apparent at the high-school level in a number of significant ways. Social class distinctions are also present *within* each high school, much more than within each elementary school, though it was not our purpose to explore these distinctions, interesting as they may be.

In some ways high schools reveal the operation of the social class system better than elementary schools do. In Big City all elementary-school children, regardless of origins or aspirations, study much the same subjects and proceed through the same curriculum. It is only at the high-school level that they begin to go their separate ways. In the high schools students are very methodically sorted out into various categories—like mail in a post office—depending on the school's appraisal of their destination in life.

In elementary schools students are often separated into "ability" groups, usually of a rather temporary nature. At the high-school level this "ability" grouping system usually becomes greatly exaggerated and more permanent and inflexible in character.

Some high schools in Big City sort students into "ability" groups (on the basis of IQ tests) which are so rigidly segregated that students in one group have little or no contact with students in other groups. Some schools, avoiding his kind of semi-caste system, sort their students into subtler types of "ability" groups.

In addition to "ability" separations, all high schools in Big City sort students into three basic curriculums, chiefly on the basis of presumed "ability"; these curriculums are: college preparatory, vocational (and commercial), and general (the catch-all category). Placement in these curriculums may determine the student's entire future life. If a student is placed, for example, in a general or vocational curriculum (at ages ranging from twelve to fourteen), he will have great difficulty qualifying for college entry or remaining in college should he be admitted. His chances, therefore, of moving into professional or highly skilled jobs will be similarly limited.

In principle, of course, and on paper, the child and the parent have the final say about curriculum selection. In actual practice, however, the school often makes the decision. Students who are not thought qualified for college prep are persuaded to take other courses, or they are simply not ad-mitted. Students regarded as qualified for college prep are persuaded to enter. The school's guiding hand is often firm and directive. The lower-income parent, knowing little about school affairs or vocational preparation, is usually willing to follow the school's lead.

Another basic element in this sorting process is the high-school drop-out. About 50 percent of all students in the city drop out of school before completing the twelfth grade. Without a high-school diploma, these students are virtually frozen into the occupational and status positions of their parents and their social class. As we shall see, the heaviest concentration of drop-outs is in the lowest-income groups.

Still another aspects of the sorting and selecting process is the social system of the high school and the student's increasing awareness of his status and social position in relation to other students. Albert Hieronymus says that "in elementary grades there appears to be little grouping along class lines, while in high school 70 to 75 percent of students' 'best friends' come from their own social class." The high-school student's sudden awareness of his position, and his acceptance or rejection of it, seem to have a marked influence on his attitudes and on his school activities.

There are only seventeen high schools in Big City, excluding schools which are wholly or largely vocational. The family income levels in these seventeen schools, according to revised Census data, are [shown on p. 202].

Because there are so few schools, major income group divisions have been made at every one thousand dollars of income instead of every two thousand, as in the elementary schools. As a result there are five major income groups . . . .*

CURRICULUM ENROLLMENT

Not all school systems separate students into different curriculums in high school. A school system adjacent to Big City, which has a reputation for being one of the best in the country, does not make curriculum separations at all, but simply guides students into various subjects according to their interests.

* [Ed.: In the sections that follow, the author refers to these income groups as group I, group II, etc.; group I is the lowest-income group while group V is the highest-income group.]

SCHOOL	INCOME IN SCHOOL AREA
1	$5043
2	5315
3	5452
4	5643
5	5700
6	6260
7	6600
8	6893
9	7220
10	7324
11	7486
12	7685
13	8000
14	8114
15	8430
16	8724
17	9503

This system is typical of many throughout the country.

Big City, however, makes these curriculum separations. All high schools in the city offer three distinct courses of study, or curriculums: college preparatory, general, and business-and-vocational. The business-and-vocational curriculum is designed for those students who plan to work in offices or in the trades, skilled or semi-skilled. The general curriculum is designed for those who do not seem to fit anywhere else. Most of the students who enroll in this curriculum will eventually become unskilled workers.

Since students are usually only fourteen when they enter high school (fifteen if they enter from junior high school), the decision to enter a fixed curriculum, with its occupational limitations, seems very premature. What is more, the decision seems unnecessary. A student who wants to prepare for college can take suitable courses without being put in a special curriculum and segregated from students in other curriculums. In fact, all students could be processed through high school on the assumption that they might some day want to go to college. At fourteen most students know little about college or about the occupational possibilities open to them. They are too young to make an informed and free choice of curriculums; as a consequence the choice is very heavily influenced, if not actually made in most cases, by teachers and counselors and, in upper-income groups especially, by parents.

Considering the accelerated tempo of technological change and the resulting changes in the nature of work assignments, it may be doubted that schools can successfully train students for particular work assignments. Certainly employers would prefer potential employees who are literate rather than partially trained in an already outmoded "vocational" skill. Consequently, it would seem wiser to concentrate on "general" education at all levels.

By the school's own standards, curriculum choices are very often misguided. Professor Samuel A. Stouffer says: "A nation-wide survey shows that among seniors in the top 30 percent of ability, a third of the boys and nearly half of the girls were not, at the time of the survey, in college preparatory courses." Curriculum assignments are often made on the basis of social class factors; again, Stouffer says: "It is known, for example, that even very able boys from working-class homes who fail to make really good grades in the seventh and eighth grades are seldom advised to take a college preparatory course. This is not equally true of boys from white-collar homes."

Indications of the influence of social class on curriculum assignments are shown in Table 1.

Almost half the students in group I are enrolled in the free-floating general curriculum. This is five times the enrollment in group V.

Only 19 percent of students in group I are enrolled in college preparatory; in group V, 79 percent are enrolled.

Enrollments in all three curriculums follow a regular income pattern in the major income groups. The only exception is the unusually heavy enrollment of group II in the business and vocational curriculum.

In interpreting college-preparatory enrollments it should be kept in mind that many of the group V students enrolled in non-college curriculums are probably lower-income students who "happen" to attend this highest-income high school, and that well over half the students in lower-income groups drop out of school before graduation. Thus it cannot be said that 19 percent of *all* group I students take college-preparatory courses. Counting drop-outs, and considering the cur-

TABLE 1
CURRICULUM ENROLLMENTS—
PERCENTAGE OF STUDENTS IN
EACH SCHOOL

Income Group	College Preparatory	Business and Vocational	General
1 $5000—	15%	30%	55%
2	19	41	40
3	16	27	57
4	18	27	55
5	25	40	34
6 $6000—	25	40	35
7	15	60	25
8	34	39	27
9 $7000—	33	35	32
10	54	23	24
11	37	33	30
12	35	34	31
13 $8000—	50	25	25
14	59	17	24
15	53	22	25
16	64	19	17
17 $9000—	79	11	10
I ($5000—)	19	33	48
II ($6000—)	25	46	29
III ($7000—)	40	31	29
IV ($8000—)	57	21	23
V ($9000—)	79	11	10

I remember when I was a freshman mother wanted me to take home economics, but I didn't want to. I knew I couldn't rate. You could take typing and shorthand and still rate, but if you took a straight commercial course, you couldn't rate. You see, you're rated by the teachers according to the course you take. They rate you in the first six weeks. The teachers type you in a small school and you're made in classes before you get there. College prep. kids get good grades and the others take what's left. The teachers get together and talk, and if you are not in college prep. you haven't got a chance.

From long experience with the situation, we suspect that approximately the same prestige attaches to the college-preparatory curriculum in Big City; those who are "in" are usually enrolled in college prep, and those who are "out" are usually in general or vocational curriculums.

Through the use of separate curriculums and other devices, including segregated groupings of various sorts, the schools establish a class system which is more rigid in its way than the class system in the outside world, since all students have curriculum and "ability" labels which segregate them from other students in a clearly defined rank order. In this school social system, the college-preparatory curriculum is the upper class, the vocational curriculum the middle, and the general curriculum the lowest class. Within this class structure there is apparently little movement either up or down. Once assigned to a curriculum and status level in the high school, students seldom change to other curriculums and class categories.

This curriculum-class system is neither necessary nor inevitable, since, as has been noted, numbers of high-ranking school systems do not make these distinctions at all. It is observed in *Who Shall Be Educated?* that "one of the more significant social experiments of our time is being carried on in a number of city high schools in the Middle West and West." In these schools "all students are in a single curriculum, with many individual electives, but without hard and fast divisions into college-preparatory, commercial, vocational, etc." The consequence of this system is that there are "no divisions on the basis of which claims to social status can be made. All kinds of students are in the same English, mathematics and history

riculums the drop-outs would have been enrolled in, the percentage would be much lower than this.

What effect does enrollment in one or another of these curriculums have on a student's chances for social and academic success? One senior high-school girl quoted in Hollingshead's Elmtown study claimed that enrollment in the college-preparatory curriculum was the key to success in high school.

If you take a college preparatory course, you're better than those who take a general course. Those who take a general course are neither here nor there. If you take a commercial course, you don't rate. It's a funny thing, those who take college preparatory set themselves up as better than the other kids. Those that take the college preparatory course run the place.

courses, regardless of their college-going intentions."

The system is not equally popular with all elements in the community, however. "The schools in these cities are criticized by many upper-middle-class people because they do not have 'high standards' and do not 'prepare well for college.' Yet a comprehensive and careful study of the college records of students from several of these schools shows that in college they do as well as or better than do the graduates from traditional college-preparatory curricula and traditional high schools with a college-preparatory emphasis."

"It is probable," the authors conclude, "that the criticisms coming from upper-middle-class people come in part from uneasiness over the threatened disintegration of social-status lines in the high school with the disappearance of clearly marked differences among curricula."

Naturally these "upper-middle-class criticisms" cannot be regarded as legitimate objections to the single-curriculum system. On the contrary they seem to argue in favor of it, for in a democratic society we cannot justify giving artificial support to the status claims of upper-class groups. As an instrument of democracy, the schools should work to reduce class barriers rather than to reinforce them. The single curriculum therefore seems fairer, just as efficient, and much more in keeping with democratic goals than the class-curriculum system now used in Big City and elsewhere. Yet no audible criticisms have been made in Big City of the system, and some people are prepared to go even farther than curriculum divisions. The citizens' committee recommended in its final report that all high-school diplomas awarded to students in the city should "include a notation of the school from which the student has graduated and the curriculum completed." Thus students are to bear class labels not only in school but presumably for the rest of their lives.

"ABILITY" GROUPS

The schools employ various means of segregating students. In addition to curriculum divisions, "ability" grouping is another commonly used segregation device.

This device is used to some extent at the elementary-school level, where students are often grouped somewhat informally according to teacher-rated "ability" in subjects such as reading and arithmetic; in some schools there is a growing tendency to separate students into different homeroom groups on this basis.

At the high-school level, "ability" groupings often become highly formalized and systematized. It is very difficult to get exact information about these groups. No records are kept in Big City concerning their use, and administrators seem reluctant to discuss them—either because they do not know much about them or because they regard the subject as too sensitive. According to the best reports, however, all high schools in Big City use "ability" groupings, some more than others.

One high school in the city (school number 10) uses a system that results in almost complete segregation of the various "ability" groups. When a student enters this high school he is assigned to a home room on the basis of his rated "ability" (IQ, marks, etc.). He stays with this home room throughout most of his school career. He attends classes almost exclusively with the other members of his home-room group, and it is only when he begins taking elective subjects that he has any real contact with other students in the school. In effect, he is almost completely isolated socially and intellectually from students in other "ability" groups.

This is about as complete and rigid a system of segregation as can be found in Big City schools. In view of the close relationship between "ability" ratings and social class position, these separations result in a system of social class segregation as well as a presumed system of "ability" grouping. (We hasten to add that, in this case, these groupings do not result in racial segregation, since there are very few non-whites in this school.)

Segregation in other schools in the city is not so complete, apparently, as it is in school 10. All schools in groups IV and V however use rather rigid systems, while none of the schools in groups I, II, and III (except school 10) are reported to put heavy emphasis on "ability" segregation. It appears, then, that this type of segregation, like curriculum segregation, is most popular with upper-income groups, perhaps because of their desire to prevent contact with lower-income students in the same school. At any rate almost all the demand for segregation of this kind has come traditionally from upper-income groups.

Because no information was available, it was not possible to examine the social class composition of "ability" groups in Big City schools. Judging by the "ability" ratings used in the schools, it seems inevitable that lower-income children would be assigned to lower-ranking groups and upper-income children to higher-ranking groups. This distribution has been observed in other school systems. Lloyd Warner, for example, found that each grade in Old City schools was divided into three sections, A, B, and C, according to rated "ability." Over a three-year period an analysis of the social class positions of 103 girls revealed that, of the 10 "upper-class" girls, eight were in section A (the highest ability group), one in B, and one in C. Of the 53 "lower-class" girls, only 6 were in section A, 28 in section B, and 19 in section C.

Factors other than "ability" entered into the group assignments, as one of the teachers in Old City observed.

Of course, we do some shifting around. There are some borderliners who were shifted up to make the sections more nearly even. But the socialites who aren't keeping up their standard in the A section were never taken into B or C section and they never will. They don't belong there socially. Of course, there are some girls in A section who don't belong there socially, but almost every one of the socialites is in A.

Sections are supposed to be made up just on the basis of records in school but it isn't and everybody knows it isn't. I know right in my own A section I have children who ought to be in B section, but they are little socialites and so they stay in A.

And so it is that family background and all the symbols of social class inevitably count for something when honors are being awarded by the schools and when status assignments are being made. They may not always count as much as they do in Old City, but it appears that they always count.

Warner describes the effect (or perhaps the intention) of educational segregation: "The school, besides purveying knowledge to the children, keeps or helps to keep the children in groups according to social class.

Thus, children learn to like being with people of their own class or higher and to dislike being with people of lower classes."

Despite the undesirable consequences of segregation, the citizens' committee in Big City recommended that "ability" groups be continued and extended. It was also recommended that the schools "identify the more able students as early as possible and make provision for advanced work." These recommendations were made even though, in a report to the citizens' committee, this statement of doubt was made about the value of "ability" groupings: "Under the impact of current criticism of education, additional impetus is being given to homogeneous grouping. The sad fact remains, however, that there is little definitive research to indicate that gifted children learn more in homogeneous groups . . . than they would learn in well-taught, undivided groups."

The tendency to segregate students at increasingly early ages seems especially dangerous. Very young children are easily molded to form. If they are put in "slow" groups, they will *be* slow, since this is expected of them, and each semester they will fall further behind the "fast" groups which are moving ahead at an accelerated pace.

We do not wish to minimize the problems teachers sometimes have in adjusting course work to a single group of students operating at different achievement levels. Under present classroom conditions, this is undeniably a deeply troublesome problem for teachers and students alike. But segregation, we would suggest, is not the answer. Perhaps a new solution can be found which will permit all students to move ahead at their own individual pace, with help and encouragement for those who have trouble and fall behind.

Lacking such a solution, which would provide for individual rather than group progress, perhaps a more flexible system of "ability" groupings can be settled on, where need is obvious and where consequences cannot be damaging.

A more flexible system would group children on a temporary basis in *each* subject. Thus a child might be in one group in reading, a second group in arithmetic, and still a third group in writing. The weakness of such systems is, however, that the child who is at one level in one subject tends to be at the same level in most other subjects. As a result, the system proves to be more rigid than it might appear. Also, it often becomes much more permanent than originally intended, as students tend to remain in assigned groups.

In addition, such systems can impose extra burdens on teachers, who must then contend with perhaps three distinct "classes" or sub-groups within a class, each of which requires separate texts, tests, and lesson plans.

Some schools have tried to solve the problem of heterogeneous class groupings by using remedial teachers instead of "ability" groups. In this system the student having trouble with his lesson is given individual remedial aid during each class period by teachers specially assigned to this job. He is not put into a "slow group" where he may get little or no extra attention. Instead, his individual learning needs are attended to so that he may keep up with the rest of his group.

Interestingly, as will be noted elsewhere, Soviet schools do not use ability groupings. They tend to focus instead on a totally dif-ferent solution. In the Soviet school the child who finishes his work quickly is given the responsibility of helping the child who is having trouble with his lesson. By this means one child is given experience in leader-ship, service to others, and the familiarity with subject matter that only a teacher ac-quires, while the other is given the needed help with his lessons. Also, older students in the school are often given responsibility for helping younger students who require extra help and attention.*

Students themselves can obviously be a valuable source of assistance to the class-room teacher. They are in fact a great un-tapped source of remedial aid for children with learning problems, and perhaps even with emotional problems. It would seem that special efforts should be made to tap these rich resources.

* [Ed.: See the recent book by Urie Bronfen-brenner, *Two Worlds of Children, U.S. and U.S.S.R.* (N.Y.: Russell Sage, 1970).]

THE EQUALITY FICTION: CALIFORNIA HIGHER EDUCATION

W. Lee Hansen and Burton A. Weisbrod

The State of California is supposed to have the most liberal, accessible public system of higher education in the country. If education helps promote equality and social mobility anywhere in the United States, one ought to find evidence of that impact in the California college system. Even there, however, the educational system helps perpetuate class divisions; the state subsidizes the best education for the wealthiest families, reinforcing the initial advantages of children from those homes. This selection summarizes the results of a book by the authors; the summary appeared in *The New Republic*.

The authors teach economics at the University of Wisconsin and are associated with the University's Institute for Research on Poverty.

The claim that the American system of higher education contributes to equality of educational opportunity is largely fiction. This year well over $11 billion of tax funds

SOURCE: *"The Equality Fiction: Bottom Dogs Subsidize Top Dogs"* by W. Lee Hansen and Burton A. Weisbrod from the September 13, 1969, issue of The New Republic. *Reprinted by permis-sion of* The New Republic. *Copyright © 1969, Harrison-Blaine of New Jersey, Inc.*

spent on higher education will seriously vio-late the egalitarianism principle. Seemingly, public colleges and universities are open to all, but the truth falls far short of this. In practice, a perverse redistribution of higher education subsidies from low-income to high-income families takes place. Those with the most need for higher education are getting the least in terms of public benefits.

Studies of public higher education have

recently been completed for the states of California, Florida, and Wisconsin. Because our study of California is the most comprehensive we shall focus on it.

The following material is drawn from our book, *Benefits, Costs, and Finance of Public Higher Education,* Markham Publishing Company, Chicago, [1969].

California possesses a vast and in many respects a model system of public higher education. Tuition is zero. College campuses abound, with at least a junior college in every sizeable community. And it has the largest percentage of any state's high school graduates going on to college. Undergraduate students all receive large public subsidies, although the amounts differ greatly with the type of school attended. A student fortunate enough to attend the University of California in the mid-1960s received an average subsidy of about $5,000, but a California State College student only $3,000, and a junior college student about $1,000. Of course, some got even larger subsidies: a student completing four years at the university received a total subsidy of over $7,000. By "subsidy" we mean the difference between tuition—which in California is zero—and the sum of average instructional costs (professors' salaries, operating expenses, etc.) and capital costs (the value of services provided by building, equipment, and land).

Many youngsters, however, receive no subsidies at all, because they do not go to college (or, at least, not to a public college in their own state), and many others receive little, because they are in college only briefly.

The highest subsidies go to students at the University of California (UC). But UC accepts only the upper eighth of all high school graduates, and these are largely children from well-to-do family backgrounds. Students from families with incomes above $25,000 are four times as likely to be eligible as are those from families with incomes below $4,000. Moreover, among eligible students, twice as large a percentage from high-income families actually attend the UC as do those from low-income families. The selectivity process restricts the availability of large subsidies to all but high-income families. The end result is that California's three higher education systems—the University, the State Colleges (SC), and the Junior Colleges (JC)—educate three different general classes of students and, in turn, provide three different levels of subsidies. (The same is true for many other states—including Florida, Wisconsin, Michigan, and Illinois, to name a few—that have a multiple-tiered higher education system.) The UC has the highest-income students—their family incomes average more than $12,000—and provides the largest subsidies—$5,000 per student. Meanwhile, the JCs attract the lowest-income students—with $8,800 average family income—and provide the lowest subsidies—about $1,000. The SC students are in between, with family incomes of $10,000 and subsidies of $3,800. Thus, the average subsidy received by students at the UC is 30 percent greater than that received by SC students, and is 400 percent greater than the JC subsidy—in spite of the fact that "need," as reflected by family income, runs in the opposite direction.

The upshot: even in California, with its extensive higher education system, over 40 percent of families with college-age children receive *no public subsidy at all,* while a most fortunate ten percent receive subsidies over $5,000.

Consideration of the taxes people pay does not alter these striking redistributional effects. There is no satisfactory way to isolate the taxes that go for education, and so we can only compare *total* state and local taxes (for all public services) with the subsidies provided by public higher education. However, higher education consumes roughly 10 percent of state and local tax revenue in California, whose state-local tax system is essentially proportional to income over most of the income range.

The inescapable conclusion is that the structure and financing of public higher education in California heightens rather than narrows inequalities in economic opportunities. The situation is no different in other states. State tax systems are either proportional (to income) or regressive (i.e., high-income taxpayers pay a smaller percentage of their income in taxes than low-income persons).

Nationally, a larger percentage of low- than of high-income youngsters drop out of high school and so are not eligible to receive any higher-education subsidies. Those low-income students who are eligible to go to higher educational institutions most often wind up at institutions where the education subsidy is lowest. And they are more likely to drop out before graduation. For these and other well-known reasons, the cards are stacked against low-income youngsters. Yet because tax revenues are used to support higher education, the anomalous result is lower-income families not only do not receive significant amounts of public higher-education subsidies but actually pay a larger fraction of their income in taxes to support higher education than do more affluent families. At a time when pressures are mounting to reduce disparities between privileged and disadvantaged, it is clear that something has gone awry. The mythology of equal educational opportunity for all is just that: mythology.

It is clear that the present structure and financing of public higher education needs to be reformed. One important possibility is to revamp the tax structure, making state and local taxes more progressive. This would increase taxes most for higher-income families and wipe out some but not all of the redistributive effects. But it wouldn't discriminate between families with and without children in college, or between those in public and in private colleges.

Another approach is to set tuition much closer to the full instructional and capital costs of college, and then to provide financial aid to students who cannot afford the full cost. This is essentially what private schools now do through their financial aid programs. Judging from the recent actions of state legislatures in raising tuition and fees, there is some sentiment for moving in this direction even at public colleges. Unless, however, every increase in tuition for those who can afford it is accompanied by an increase of loan and scholarship funds for those who cannot afford it, the goal of greater equality of opportunity will continue to be only a distant vision. Unhappily, while tuition rates at public colleges are rising rapidly, student-aid funds are lagging and federal student-loan and scholarship funds are actually drying up.

More important than either of these reforms, public subsidies should be available to *all* young people, not just college students. Those for whom the best way to increase earning power is through apprenticeships, on-the-job training or night school deserve an equal chance in their struggle for productive and satisfying lives.

REPRESSIVE SCHOOLING AS PRODUCTIVE SCHOOLING

Herbert Gintis

The following selection provides an important statement of one of the basic radical contentions about education—that it prepares workers for their roles in the production process by repressing them as human beings.

The selection comes from a much longer article by Gintis, "New Working Class and Revolutionary Youth," which has appeared in *Socialist Revolution* and in the *Review of Radical Political Economics*. In that article, Gintis argues that recent revolutionary attitudes about education among youth constitute a basic and fundamental challenge to the capitalist system because of the intrinsic and functional importance of educational institutions in supporting that system.

Gintis is a lecturer in the Graduate School of Education at Harvard University and an associate of the Center for Educational Policy Research.

The function of education in any society is the socialization of new individuals in ac-

SOURCE: Herbert Gintis, "Repressive Schooling as Productive Schooling," in "New Working Class and Revolutionary Youth," from Socialist Revolution, May–June, 1970.

cordance with predominant social and cultural patterns: on the one hand, schooling represents a major force in the institutionalization of dominant *value, norm, and belief systems* necessary to the integration of individuals in society; on the other, schooling provides the individual *competencies* necessary for the adequate performance of social roles. Thus educational systems are fundamental to the *stability* and *functioning* of any society.[1]

A description of the characteristics of education *in a society devoted to economic rationality* begins by noting its exclusion from ties to family and community: new citizens are developed in isolation from the *general* pattern of social activity, and the educational process shrinks to a *separate* and *jurisdictionally distinct* sphere, the sphere of *educational institutions*. This shrinkage follows from the more fundamental removal of economic functions from family and community for two reasons. First, the rationalization of production places ever-increasing demands on the individual because these productive relations are not part of the "normal social relations" of the family and the community and hence cannot be developed through the gradual integration of the child into family and society. Second, the fact that technologies develop over time in response to the criterion of maximal efficiency means the requisites for adequate job performance—the very competencies which must be developed in the child—must change fairly abruptly from generation to generation. An educational system imbedded in the fabric of family and community cannot respond to the rapidly changing demands imposed by the economic system.

This independent status provides the educational system with the *flexibility* to execute functions basic to the operation of capitalism. Among these are (*a*) the preservation of social statuses along class lines; (*b*) the transmission and preservation of cultural norms, attitudes and values to the degree that they are compatible with an increasingly materially-oriented economy, (*c*) the training of a technocratic stratum capable of developing new technologies favorable to capitalist development; and (*d*) the generation of an educated work force, with competence for adequate role performance in complex, alienated work environments. I shall focus on the last of these functions, one central to the question of educated labor as a class,

and the role of (potentially) revolutionary youth.

The problem of instilling in the individual a set of *competencies* for adequate job performance reduces to the need for a *structure of individual motivation* compatible with capitalist organization and a set of *individual capacities* including both *technical capability* for handling the cognitive tasks of the object world of production, and the *personality traits* necessary for the execution of these bureaucratic tasks. These requirements limit the manner in which an educational system can aid the "human development" of the individual in two basic ways. First, many personality types are simply *incompatible* with prerequisites of individual motivation and capacity for adequate job performance. Thus a truly spiritual individual, or an individual who values aesthetic, physical, or interpersonal activities may be psychologically incapable of working in an alienating work environment. In this sense, basic *competence* for job performance is incompatible with non-capitalist values. Second, the development of economic motivations and capacities may be so exacting in terms of the time and energy required for their development, as to severely limit the time and energy that may be devoted to the development of individual capacities of *direct* importance to the individual, as opposed to capacities important through his increased "economic productivity." As capitalist technologies become ever more highly developed, it is likely that time and energy demands required for competence be correspondingly increased, so that the general dimensions of individual personality development compatible with fulfillment of economic roles be severely limited. *In this situation, the educational system tends to become functionally reduced to its role in generating labor for the economy, and the development of the individual becomes more or less fully tailored to the needs of "economic rationality."* This *excision* of educational institutions from the social fabric, and their resulting *reduction* to the fulfillment of economic functions, to the exclusion of its function in the human development of individual personality represents, I claim, the setting within which revolutionary youth must be analyzed.

Further, the problem of *motivation* toward adequate job performance on the part of workers begins with a *social context* of labor

---

[1] Cf. Talcott Parsons, "The School Class as Social System: Some of Its Functions in American Society," *Harvard Educational Review*, 1959; and Alex Inkeles, "The Socialization of Competence," *Harvard Educational Review*, June, 1966.

characterized by the worker's *alienation from the work process* and his *alienation from his product*. Alienation from work activities results from the worker's entrance into no social relations with fellow workers, through which the organization of production could be determined, and through which the resulting pattern of work activities could develop over time in response to the introduction of new technologies. As a result of this form of alienation, personal and interpersonal benefits of work play no part in the determination of actual modes of production and the diffusion of new modes of production.[2]

That the worker is alienated from his work activities is a simple fact of capitalist organization independent of the way in which the worker *perceives* his relation to his job. Thus it is conceivable that the worker, despite this alienation, be fully socialized to accept the activities involved, and indeed to accept them *willingly;* the pattern of work activities, while failing to fulfill even minimal conditions for fully human activities, might correspond closely to the manifest needs and desires of "properly socialized" workers. Nevertheless, for most workers, their work activities represent *the least preferred activities* they habitually undertake; given the choice, and if there were no adverse effects on income, most workers would choose not to work at all. In this sense *workers are not motivated to work by the nature of their work activities.*

If workers are not naturally motivated by the process of production itself, they might yet be motivated by the *goal* of production —by the attributes of the product itself, and the social benefit deriving from productive activity. The reflection of the social value of production in the individual motivation of the worker seems to require that he *identify in some fundamental way with the social unit.* Yet under capitalism the worker is alienated from his product in the sense that he enters into no social relations as a community-member, in terms of which production goals are defined—what is to be produced, for what use, and for whom. Hence we may conclude (what is empirically obvious, in fact) that *workers are not motivated*

to produce by either intrinsic or social value of production.

The alienation of the worker from his work process and product—a natural result of his lack of control over the relevant decisions—requires the motivation to efficient and harmonious performance, in a situation where he is at best indifferent to both the *process* and *goals* of production. In this situation, motivation must be responsive to incentives in the form of *indirect and external reward*: money or social power. To respond predictably, persistently, and efficiently to such external reward requires an extensive process of socialization, and the educational system has historically risen, in the course of the industrial revolution, in response to this need, and as the prime source of this training. The authority relations and structure of incentives in schools *mirrors* the work environment in just this respect: learning is not supposed to take place, nor does it, through the student's intrinsic interest in the *process* of learning, nor in his intrinsic interest in the *goal* of this process—the possession of knowledge. The student must learn to operate efficiently in an educational environment, unmotivated by either the process or the product of his activities—in short, in an *alienated educational environment*. The *reward* for adequate behavior is in all cases *external,* in the form of grades, threat of failure, or more subtle interpersonal sanctions. The first and final goal of educational systems is that of inducing the student to *internalize the value of rewards* external to the learning process itself, and to operate efficiently and with high motivation in the alienated school environment.[3]

The psychological manifestations of "motivation according to external reward" are not obvious; one might generalize that such individuals undervalue *process and activity* as opposed to *outcome, status,* and *individual material reward* to *subjective value,* and *being* to *becoming.* Yet in general the psychological syndrome of alienated labor does not conform to well-known psychological categories. It cannot be confused with "deferred gratification," with "degree of ego-control," or any other common psychological construct. Indeed, it represents a unique and special syndrome, found perhaps in some people in any society, to some extent in all

[2] For a description of the powerlessness of union activity in controlling aspects of the work process, see André Gorz, *Strategy for Labor* (Boston: Beacon Press, 1965).

[3] Cf. Robert Dreeben, *On What Is Learned in School* (Reading, Mass.: Addison-Wesley, 1968).

individuals, but in a majority and to an overwhelming extent only in modern industrial society.

Motivation according to external reward must be considered the *central ingredient in the psychological manifestation of alienated labor.* That American labor is alienated in this sense is borne out by the entire history of industrial psychology: virtually all tests as to the relation between the worker's attitude toward his job and product and his efficiency and adequacy on the job, point to *no* relation.[4] In essence, American workers perform *independently* of their valuation of work process and product, and hence are alienated according to our use of the term.

The structure of motivation is not the only element in the socialization of competence of the individual through schooling. Equally important, perhaps, is the question of the *capacity for role performance* under conditions of modern capitalist technology. Here I shall emphasize that the most important capacities supplied by the educational system are not cognitive, skill- and knowledge-oriented capacities, but capacities embodied in *particular forms of personality organization.* In other words, while schooling significantly increases the earnings of workers, *one cannot account for the increases in terms of the cognitive development of the worker*—for workers of given educational attainment, possession of information on intelligence, on verbal or mathematical achievement, reasoning ability, etc., *have very low predictive value for eventual occupational success.*[5] Thus whatever capacities are in fact supplied through education must take the form of non-cognitive traits: schooling creates productive workers almost uniquely through the molding of personality, and for all but a small "technological stratum" consisting of scientists, engineers, physicians, and the like, not through the development of the *level* of cognitive activity (although, as I shall later discuss, schooling does repress non-cognitive development, hence leading to a predominance of cognitive *modes* of individual response desirable in bureaucratic organization), nor through the provisionment of concrete work skills—which can easily be acquired on the job.[6] Moreover, an analysis of modern technology shows that the traits characteristic of efficient job functioning are harmful to the development of the worker as a human being, and can be inculcated only in an educational environment characterized by rigid relations of authority between teacher and student, an environment devoid of love and positive, constructive personal interaction; in short, in a *repressive* educational environment.

The importance of individual orientation to authority derives from the predominantly *bureaucratic structure of "modern" productive enterprise.* This structure is characterized as a functionally specific and highly circumscribed organization of individual roles, institutionally ordered and subject to a hierarchy of control. The personality traits rewarded and penalized in the classroom seem admirably suited to the generation of workers who fit harmoniously in a system of hierarchical authority, and the concomitant personality changes induced through schooling represent a central element in the contribution of schooling to individual productivity.

If a proper *subordination* is required for adequate worker functioning in a bureaucratically organized form or office, a proper worker *discipline* is of no less importance. In the words of Weber,[7]

> *Organizational discipline in the factory is founded upon a completely rational basis. . . . The optimum profitability of the individual worker is calculated like that of any material means of production. On the basis of this calculation, the American system of "Scientific Management" enjoys the greatest triumphs in the rational conditioning and training of work performances. The final consequences are drawn from the mechanization and discipline of the plant, and the psychophysical apparatus of man is completely adjusted to the demands of the outer world, the tools, the machines—in short,*

[4] A. H. Brayfield and W. H. Crockett, "Employee Attitudes, and Employee Performance," *Psychological Bulletin,* Vol. 55, No. 2, 1955.

[5] See Herbert Gintis, "Production Functions in the Economics of Education and the Characteristics of Worker Productivity," in "Alienation and Power: Towards a Radical Welfare Economics," Ph.D. dissertation, Harvard University, unpublished, 1969.

[6] Indeed, nearly all the studies of the "returns to vocational education" have shown these programs to have no "economic value" to the worker.

[7] Max Weber, "The Meaning of Discipline," in Hans Gerth and C. Wright Mills, *On Max Weber: Essays in Sociology.*

to an individual "function." The ever-widening grasp of discipline irresistibly proceeds with the rationalization of the supply of economic and political demands.

More recently, we find a similar emphasis in Merton:[8]

> Bureaucratic structure exerts a constant pressure upon the official to be "methodical, prudent, disciplined." If the bureaucracy is to operate successfully, it must attain a high degree of reliability of behavior, and an unusual degree of conformity with prescribed patterns of actions. Hence the fundamental importance of discipline. . . . Discipline [requires] . . . strong sentiments which entail devotion to one's duties, a keen sense of the limitation of one's authority and competence and methodical performance of routine activities.

A third aspect of adequate functioning in bureaucratic roles involves the *modes of thought* typically applied by the worker. Roughly, the advancement in level of bureaucratic organization proceeds with the necessity of the worker's employing a greater preponderance of *cognitive* as opposed to *affective* modes of mental functioning:

> Bureaucratization . . . very strongly furthers the development of "rational matter-of-factness" . . . . When fully developed, bureaucracy also stands in a specific sense under the principle of sine ira ac studio. Its specific nature, which is welcomed by capitalism, develops the more perfectly the more the bureaucracy is "dehumanized," the more completely it succeeds in eliminating from official business love, hatred, and all purely personal, irrational, and emotional elements which escape calculation. This is the specific nature of bureaucracy and it is appraised as its special virtue.[9]

To what extent is this emphasis on cognitive, as opposed to affective, modes of personal organization developed in the classroom? According to Robert Dreeben, the very *structure* of the social relations in education is conducive to cognitive orientation:[10]

[8] R. K. Merton, "Bureaucratic Structure and Personality," *Social Forces*, 1940.
[9] Max Weber, "On Bureaucracy," in Gerth and Mills, *op. cit.*
[10] Robert Dreeben, *op. cit.*

> Although affectation is not proscribed in schools, it is expressed less intensely and under more limited circumstances. In the long run, matter-of-factness in the accomplishment of specific tasks governs the relationship between teachers and pupils, and teachers are customarily expected to be friendly but to avoid intense expressions of either verbal or physical affection . . . members of a classroom are expected to help and like one another because they are engaged in performing a multitude of individual and collective tasks, and not because they love one another.

The bureaucratization of work is a result of the capitalist control of the work process, as bureaucracy seems to be the sole organizational form compatible with capitalist hegemony. If bureaucracy in the factory is a "given" of productive organization, it follows that the development of increasingly cost-minimizing technologies will be limited to *those technologies compatible with bureaucratic organization.* Potentially "efficient" technologies which are destructive of bureaucratic organization will *not* be introduced, and the development of technology in these directions will be prevented. Thus it is not clear that bureaucracy is indeed itself "economically rational" as opposed to a necessary instrument for the *application* of economically rational criteria by capitalists, in the interests of profit maximization. As a result of this ambiguity, we cannot say whether the personality characteristics associated with adequate job-performance in a bureaucracy are required *directly* by efficiency criteria in production, or only *indirectly* as a concomitant of capitalist hegemony. In either case, *the educational system must act as a repressive force in the production of workers who fit harmoniously in an alienating and bureaucratic work environment,* and in either case education is productive only insofar as it is repressive. . . .

[Ed.: Gintis then relates recent student unrest—the emergence of "revolutionary youth"—to the economic and social functions of education. He concludes:]

Revolutionary youth is the first step in the radicalization of educated labor—in the transformation of educated labor from a simple emergent social class to a true agent of social change. That schools "fail" to produce "productive" workers does not mean that they do not produce workers at all; rather, it means that they produce workers who do not operate properly in alienated work environments. That is to say, they produce workers who *rebel against their alienation and lack of control in the process of production.* The dysfunctionality of education then lays the basis for the development of a *radical force in the factory and office.* Radical activity around issues of student power is *indirect* in this sense: that it acts to sow the seeds for genuine class struggle, but does not itself engage in this struggle.

The student's demand for "control over his life and the social relations of education" is at the same time *revolutionary* and *con-structive,* much as industrial unions were both revolutionary and constructive in an earlier stage of the development of capitalism —both sow the seeds for true class consciousness, both can take place within the existing institutional structure, both begin to outline basic aspects of a new society, and in both cases, their final contributions to social change depend on the *level* and *quality* of the political activity that guide their development. It is a basic radical precept that *consciousness and solidarity develop through struggle,* and the struggle for student power, in proper political form, contributes directly to the growth of consciousness, and indirectly creates the preconditions for the extension of struggle to other sectors of society.

THE LIVES OF CHILDREN

George Dennison

These excerpts from Dennison's book provide a glimpse of how education might be different in a world with different priorities. Dennison describes the way his First Street School operated and the vision it created of small schools dedicated to developing children as human beings.

Dennison now writes free-lance, publishing mainly fiction. The First Street School folded because it could no longer finance itself.

There is no need to add to the criticism of our public schools. The critique is extensive and can hardly be improved on. The processes of learning and teaching, too, have been exhaustively studied. One thinks of the books of Paul Goodman, John Holt, Greene and Ryan, Nat Hentoff, James Herndon, Jonathan Kozol, Herbert Kohl; and of such researches as those of Bruner and Piaget; and of Joseph Featherstone's important *Report.* * The question now is what to do. In the pages that follow, I would like to describe one unfamiliar approach to the

SOURCE: *Excerpts from* The Lives of Children, *by George Dennison. Copyright © 1969 by George Dennison. Reprinted by permission of Random House, Inc.*

* [Ed.: See the bibliography at the end of this chapter for complete references to most of these works.]

problems which by now have become familiar. And since "the crisis of the schools" consists in reality of a great many crises in the lives of children, I shall try to make the children of the First Street School the real subject of this book. There were twenty-three black, white, and Puerto Rican in almost equal proportions, all from low-income families in New York's Lower East Side. About half were on welfare. About half, too, had come to us from the public schools with severe learning and behavior problems.

Four things about the First Street School were unusual: first, its small size and low teacher/pupil ratio; second, the fact that this luxurious intimacy, which is ordinarily very expensive, cost about the same per child as the $850 annual operating costs of the public schools; third, our reversal of conventional structure, for where the public school conceives of itself merely as a place of instruction, and puts severe restraints on the relationships between persons, we conceived of ourselves as an environment for growth, and accepted the relationships between the children and ourselves as being the very heart of the school; and fourth, the kind of freedom experienced by teachers and pupils alike.

Freedom is an abstract and terribly elusive word. I hope that a context of examples will make its meaning clear. The question is not really one of authority, though it is usually argued in that form. When adults give up authority, the freedom of children is not necessarily increased. Freedom is not motion in a vacuum, but motion in a continuum. If we want to know what freedom is, we must discover what the continuum is. "The principle," Dewey remarks, "is not what justifies an activity, for the principle is but another name for the continuity of the activity." We might say something similar of freedom: it is another name for the fullness and final shape of activities. We experience the activities, not the freedom. The mother of a child in a public school told me that he kept complaining, "They never let me *finish* anything!" We might say of the child that he lacked important freedoms, but his own expression is closer to the experience: activities important to him remained unfulfilled. Our concern for freedom is our concern for fulfillment—of activities we deem important and of persons we know are unique. To give freedom means to stand out of the way of the formative powers possessed by others.

Before telling more of the school, I must say that I was a partisan of libertarian values even before working there. I had read of the schools of A. S. Neill and Leo Tolstoy. I had worked in the past with severely disturbed children, and had come to respect the integrity of the organic processes of growth, which given the proper environment are the one source of change in individual lives. And so I was biased from the start and cannot claim the indifference of a neutral observer. Events at school did, however, time and again, confirm the beliefs I already held—which, I suppose, leaves me still a partisan, though convinced twice over. Yet if I can prove nothing at all in a scientific sense, there is still a power of persuasion in the events themselves, and I can certainly hope that our experience will arouse an experimental interest in other parents and teachers.

But there is something else that I would like to convey, too, and this is simply a sense of the lives of those who were involved—the jumble of persons and real events which did in fact constitute our school. The closer one comes to the facts of life, the less exemplary they seem, but the more human and the richer. Something of our time in history and our place in the world belongs to Vicente screaming in the hallway, and José opening the blade of a ten-inch knife —even more than to Vicente's subsequent learning to cooperate and José to read. So, too, with other apparently small details: the fantasy life and savagery of the older boys, the serenity and rationality of the younger ones, teachers' moments of doubt and defeat. Learning, in its essentials, is not a·distinct and separate process. It is a function of growth. We took it quite seriously in this light, and found ourselves getting more and more involved in individual lives. It seems likely to me that the actual features of this involvement may prove useful to other people. At the same time, I would like to try to account for the fact that almost all of our children improved markedly, and some few spectacularly. We were obviously doing something right, and I would like to hazard a few guesses at what it might have been. All instruction was individual, and that was obviously a factor. The improvement I am speaking of, however, was not simply a matter of learning, but of radical changes in character. Where Vicente had been withdrawn and destructive, he became an eager participant in group activities and ceased destroying everything he touched. Both Eléna and Maxine had been thieves and were incredibly rebellious. After several months they could be trusted and had become imaginative and responsible contributors at school meetings. Such changes as these are not accomplished by instruction. They proceed from broad environmental causes. Here again, details which may seem irrelevant to the business of a school will give the reader an idea of what these causes may have been. A better way of saying this is that the business of a school is not, or should not be, mere instruction, but the life of the child.

This is especially important under such conditions as we experience today. Life in our country is chaotic and corrosive, and the time of childhood for many millions is difficult and harsh. It will not be an easy matter to bring our berserk technocracy under control, but we *can* control the environment of the schools. It is a relatively small environment and has always been structured by deliberation. If, as parents, we were to take as our concern not the instruction of our children, but the lives of our children, we would find that our schools could be used in a powerfully regenerative way. Against all that is shoddy and violent and treacherous and emotionally impoverished in American life, we might propose conventions which were rational and straightforward, rich both in feeling and thought, and which treated individuals with a respect we do little more at present than proclaim from our public rostrums. We might cease thinking of school as a place, and learn to believe that it is basically relationships: between children and adults, adults and adults, children and other children. The four walls and the principal's office would cease to loom so hugely as the essential ingredients.

It is worth mentioning here that, with two exceptions, the parents of the children at First Street were not libertarians. They thought that they believed in compulsion, and rewards and punishments, and formal discipline, and report cards, and homework, and elaborate school facilities. They looked rather askance at our noisy classrooms and informal relations. If they persisted in sending us their children, it was not because they agreed with our methods, but because they were desperate. As the months went by, however, and the children who had been truants now attended eagerly, and those who had been failing now began to learn, the parents drew their own conclusions. By the end of the first year there was a high morale among them, and great devotion to the school.

We had no administrators. We were small and didn't need them. The parents found that, after all, they approved of this. They themselves could judge the competence of the teachers, and so could their children—by the specific act of learning. The parents' past experience of administrators had been uniformly upsetting—and the proof, of course, was in the pudding: the children were happier and *were* learning. As for the children, they never missed them.

We did not give report cards. We knew each child, knew his capacities and his prob-

lems, and the vagaries of his growth. This knowledge could not be recorded on little cards. The parents found—again—that they approved of this. It diminished the blind anxieties of life, for grades had never meant much to them anyway except some dim sense of *problem,* or some dim reassurance that things were all right. When they wanted to know how their children were doing, they simply asked the teachers.

We didn't give tests, at least not of the competitive kind. It was important to be aware of what the children knew, but more important to be aware of *how* each child knew what he knew. We could learn nothing about Maxine by testing Eléna. And so there was no comparative testing at all. The children never missed those invidious comparisons, and the teachers were spared the absurdity of ranking dozens of personalities on one uniform scale.

Our housing was modest. The children came to school in play-torn clothes. Their families were poor. A torn dress, torn pants, frequent cleanings—there were expenses they could not afford. Yet how can children play without getting dirty? Our uncleanliness standard was just right. It looked awful and suited everyone.

We treated the children with consideration and justice. I don't mean that we never got angry and never yelled at them (nor they at us). I mean that we took seriously the pride of life that belongs to the young—even to the very young. We did not coerce them in violation of their proper independence. Parents and children both found that they approved very much of this.

Now I would like to describe the school, or more correctly, the children and teachers. I shall try to bring out in detail three important things:

1) That the proper concern of a primary school is not education in a narrow sense, and still less preparation for later life, but the present lives of the children—a point made repeatedly by John Dewey, and very poorly understood by many of his followers.

2) That when the conventional routines of a school are abolished (the military discipline, the schedules, the punishments and rewards, the standardization), what arises is neither a vacuum nor chaos, but rather a new order, based first on relationships between adults and children, and children and their peers, but based ultimately on such truths

of the human condition as these: that the mind does not function separately from the emotions, but thought partakes of feeling and feeling of thought; that there is no such thing as knowledge *per se,* knowledge in a vacuum, but rather all knowledge is possessed and must be expressed by individuals; that the human voices preserved in books belong to the real features of the world, and that children are so powerfully attracted to this world that the very motion of their curiosity comes through to us as a form of love; that an active moral life cannot be evolved except where people are free to express their feelings and act upon the insights of conscience.

3) That running a primary school—*provided it be small*—is an extremely simple thing. It goes without saying that the teachers must be competent (which does not necessarily mean passing courses in a teacher's college). Given this *sine qua non,* there is nothing mysterious. The present quagmire of public education is entirely the result of unworkable centralization and the lust for control that permeates every bureaucratic institution.

In saying this, I do not mean that the work in a free school is easy. On the contrary, teachers find it taxing. But they find it rewarding, too—quite unlike the endless round of frustrations experienced by those at work in the present system. . . .

I hope it is clear that I have not been proposing First Street as the model for a system of education. I do certainly propose it as a model for the indispensable first step. And since the first step is in fact the continuing foundation, I do propose the kinds of relationships we established at First Street, the kinds of freedom enjoyed by teachers and children and parents, the respect for experience, the absence of compulsion, the faith in the inherent sociability of children; I do propose all these as the environmental model for an entire system, for they belong intrinsically to the educational experience, and not just to the rationale of a school. As a school we were far too limited to provide a pattern for other schools (which will have problems of their own), and this, I am sure, has been so obvious that I hardly need mention it. A pattern has been suggested by others, however, and there were many times—our good days, our best trips through the city—when this pattern drifted before my eyes: all

through the city, but especially in the poorer neighborhoods, where the need is greatest, there are little one-, two-, and three-room schools for young children in storefronts and ground-floor apartments, several to a block. The teachers live in the neighborhood and the schools belong intimately to the life of the block. Adults, adolescents, and the young all have a role and a stake in the schools; all are joined in a natural continuum. The adolescents are part-time aides, tutors, leaders in games and expeditions. Some are salaried, others are volunteers. All know the young, for they are neighbors' children, and brothers and sisters. Parents come and go as they like. Some cook lunches, help on trips, supervise cleanup and special work details. Some are salaried, some are volunteers. They are not working with younger members of "the public," but with their own children's playmates. The children in the schools feel secure and cared for. They have formed dependable relationships with adults who are important to them, and whom they see in the streets. They have made friends and working alliances with other children on the block. They know whom they belong to, and who belongs to them. The gigantic public schools, in the meantime, have been transformed into centers of specialized activities. Some are devoted to the arts, others to physical sciences, others to social studies conducted as community action. The children gather at these centers at specified times to make use of laboratories and special equipment, and ·for games and athletic competition, and to produce plays and pageants, and to taste the excitement of the larger world that is spread out all around them. And it *is* excitement, for though they gather now in large numbers, they are not rendered anonymous, but still know whom they belong to, and who belongs to them. There is a lively rivalry between the block schools, and much opportunity for social exchange. Nor are these larger centers known any longer simply as schools. They have become community centers and belong absolutely to the people of the neighborhood. They are filled with adults at night, and with youths and children. There are social dancing and games, orchestra, films, jazz groups, facilities for crafts, open classes for adults, meeting rooms for political action. And there is no one present, not a soul, who believes that the buildings, or any of their functions, belong to the State. They belong to those who use them. The uses are so intimately a part of life that the idea of compulsion has come to seem grotesque. The educational bureaucracy has dwindled to almost nothing, and responsibility now rests where it should: on the shoulders of those who are closest to the children, and those who, for reasons of their own, care most.

The idea of block schools, storefront schools, mini-schools, has been put forward on a number of occasions by Paul Goodman and Elliott Shapiro. The existence of First Street itself owed a great deal to Goodman's influence. I would like to quote the words of both. They are available elsewhere, and perhaps need not be repeated here. But they are important, and will bear repeating.

Nat Hentoff gives us the words of Shapiro in *Our Children Are Dying* (an unfortunate title, I think, for a positive and valuable book):

Take this neighborhood. It's poor. Stores go out of business, leaving many vacant storefronts—some with back yards—that could be used as classrooms. From 110th to 145th Streets and between Seventh and Eighth Avenues, there are the equivalent of forty to fifty potential classrooms. Why not use them primarily for young children— with the back yards as school-yards, and with libraries interspersed here and there? The libraries would be for parents as well as children and could be open until eight or nine in the evening. We would be coming right into the heart of the community, creating the kind of reciprocal relationship between the community and the schools that you don't find anywhere in this city— or in the country. We'd be on constant display, and people would be welcome to come in and see what we're doing. And if they wanted to, they could help as parent aides. The plan would take care of classroom shortages and would represent real decentralization. It could be a stimulus toward the creation of a new society. I've proposed this idea to the Board, with the estimate that it would take $4,000 to transform each vacant store into a classroom. The Board's estimate was $10,000, but even $10,000 isn't that much when you consider that the average classroom in a regular school costs more than $60,000 to construct. . . . The storefront classrooms could increase the possibilities of integration.

As you spread out along the avenues, you would break through district lines and move into neighborhoods that would allow for different racial balances. (Shapiro points out, too, that the way to attract middleclass whites to ghetto schools is to make precisely these schools the very best.)

At the Borough President's hearings on decentralization in November of 1967, Paul Goodman put the case like this:

For ages six to eleven, I propose a system of tiny schools, radically decentralized. As one who for twenty years has urged democratic decentralization, I am of course interested in the Bundy Report, but here I am thinking of decentralization to the level of actual operation. By tiny school I mean twenty-eight children with four teachers (one grown-up to seven children), and each tiny school to be largely administered by its own staff and parents, with considerable say, also, for the children, as in Summerhill. The four teachers are:*

A teacher regularly licensed and salaried. Since the present average class size is twenty-eight, these are available.

A graduate from the senior class of a New York college, perhaps just embarking on graduate study. Salary: $2,000. There is no lack of candidates to do something interesting and useful in a free setting.

A literate housewife and mother, who can also prepare lunch. Salary: $4,000. No lack of candidates.

A literate, willing, and intelligent high school graduate. Salary: $2,000. No lack of candidates.

Such a staff can easily be racially and ethnically mixed. And it is also the case, as demonstrated by the First Street School, that in such a small setting, with individual attention paid to the children, it is easy to get racially and ethnically mixed classes; there is less middle-class withdrawal when the parents do not fear that their children will be swamped and retarded. (We have failed to achieve integration by trying to impose it from above, but it can be achieved from below, in schools entirely locally controlled, if

* [Ed.: This was the report, prepared by a committee chaired by McGeorge Bundy and appointed by New York's Mayor Lindsay in 1968, which recommended a particular plan for decentralization of New York City schools.]

we can show parents it is for their children's best future.)

For setting, the tiny school would occupy two, three, or four rooms in existing school buildings, church basements, settlement houses otherwise empty during school hours, rooms set aside in housing projects, storefronts. The setting is especially indifferent since a major part of activity occurs outside the school place. The setting should be able to be transformed into a clubhouse, decorated and equipped according to the group's own decision. There might be one school on every street, but it is also advisable to locate many in racial and ethnic border areas, to increase intermixture. For purposes of assembly, health services, and some games, ten tiny schools could use the present public school facilities.

The cost saving in such a setup is the almost total elimination of top-down administration and the kind of special services that are required precisely because of excessive size and rigidity. The chief uses of central administration would be licensing, funding, choosing sites, and some inspection. There would be no principals and assistants, secretaries and assistants. Curriculum, texts, equipment would be determined as needed—and despite the present putative economies of scale, they would be cheaper; much less would be pointless or wasted. Record keeping would be at a minimum. There is no need for truant officers when the teacher-and-seven can call at the absentee's home and inquire. There is little need for remedial personnel since the staff and parents are always in close contact, and the whole enterprise can be regarded as remedial. Organizational studies of large, top-down directed enterprises show that the total cost is invariably at least 300 percent above the cost of the immediate functions, in this case the interaction of teachers and children. I would put this 300 percent into increasing the number of adults and diversifying the possibilities of instruction. Further, in the conditions of New York real estate, there is great advantage in ceasing to build $4,000,000 school buildings, and rather fitting tiny schools into available niches.

Goodman describes the pedagogical advantages of such a system, with special reference to the teaching of reading. He then goes on to make a point which tends to outrage teachers and educators. It is one that I agree with, and have seen borne out in my own teaching experience.

I am assuming that for the first five school years, there is no merit in the standard curriculum. For a small child everything in the environment is educative, if he attends to it with guidance. Normal children can learn the first eight years' curriculum in four months anyway, at age twelve.

I would like to quote the rest of Goodman's address, for it sums up a great many things succinctly, many of which we experienced as life issues at First Street.

I see little merit, for teaching this age, in the usual teacher-training. Any literate and well-intentioned grown-up knows enough to teach a small child a lot. Teaching small children is a difficult art, but we do not know how to train the improvisational genius it requires, and the untrained seem to have it equally: compare one mother with another, or one big sister or brother with another. Since at this age one teaches the child, not the subject, the relevant art is psychotherapy, and the most useful course for a normal school is probably group therapy. The chief criterion for selection is the one I have mentioned: liking to be attentive to children. Given this setting, many young people would be introduced to teaching and would continue with it as a profession; whereas in the New York system the annual turnover approaches twenty percent, after years of wasted training.

As I have said, however, there are fatal political and administrative objections to this proposal. First, the public school administration does not intend to go largely out of business. Given its mentality, it must see any radical decentralization as impossible to administer and dangerous, for everything cannot be controlled. Some child is bound to break a leg and the insurance companies will not cover; some teen-ager is bound to be indiscreet and the Daily News will explode in headlines.

The United Federation of Teachers will find the proposal anathema because it devalues professional perquisites and floods the schools with the unlicensed. Being mainly broken to the public school harness, most experienced teachers consider free and inventive teaching to be impossible.

Most fatally, poor parents, who aspire for their children, tend to regard unrigidly structured education as downgrading, not taking the children seriously, and also as vaguely immoral. In the present black power temper of Harlem, the possible easy intermixing is itself not desired. (Incidentally, I am rather sympathetic to black separatism as a means of consolidating the power of black communities. But children, as Kant said, must be educated for the future better society which cannot be separated.)

In spite of these fatal objections, I recommend that instead of building the next new school building, we try out this scheme with 1,200 children.

Shapiro, too, mentions the suspicion with which the poor look upon free activities in school. Certain of the First Street parents, similarly, objected to the noise, the lack of punishment, and the apparent disorder of our classes. They thought we were horsing around. But they were in contact with other of the parents, who did not share their views; and of course they noticed the changes in their own children. Before the year was well out, they had reversed their opinions. This seems a more likely pattern than settled opposition. Shapiro mentions some relevant events. He had just become principal of Public School 119 in Harlem. The parents, for many years, had been apathetic.

The parents didn't trust us, and they had good reason not to. One of the problems with parents in this kind of neighborhood is supposed to be that they're nonverbal. But they often have good reasons for not saying much to school administrators. They're thinking, "Why don't the children have readers to take home, and why don't they have more other things, too?" But often the parents don't ask, because they sense the principal is loyal to the system and not to the children, and they figure, "What's the use? He's not going to do anything to change the system." So it's an act of intelligence on their part to refuse to enter into what would be a phony dialogue.

Here the parents were slow to accept that we were talking honestly about the deficiencies of the school. We told them what we were doing was impaired because we didn't have resources to do very much. That kind of admission was something new in their experience. We admitted, for example, that we didn't have enough books, and finally we got the parents to write to the Board and ask for more. Between their efforts and ours we did get more, and then we discovered that many of the same parents who had seemed inarticulate were very verbal and quite sophisticated. We began with only ten parents coming to meetings, but eventually we were getting seven hundred and fifty at important meetings. The other day the room was so full that I, one of the speakers, had to stand in the hall.

Let me say a word here of the effect of First Street on the pupils' parents. It is one of the most important things, and I haven't said much about it.

There was a great deal of contact between parents and teachers. It was continuous and purposeful, and gradually became more social and diverse. There were chats after school with the mothers who came for their children. But all parents had all teachers' phone numbers, and they called frequently to ask questions, give information, make complaints and suggestions. The parents got to know one another. The social exchange itself was inspiriting, but soon there was much more, for they had many needs in common and found that they could help one another. They swapped clothing, took care of one another's children, chipped in and hired an older child to escort the young ones to school. Some banded together and devised strategies for confronting the Department of Welfare (they have continued—now in stronger and more political forms). Some became interested in civil rights, and are now involved in black power and community actions. Many invited the kids to their homes. Many helped at school during special activities and on trips. Several took turns cooking lunches (fried chicken was one's specialty), and the girls took turns transporting these lunches, wrapped in foil, from home to school. (Our fried-chicken days were notable.) One father, a restaurateur, held open house for us once a week. The improvement in the kids had a strong effect on family life, not only because hope was revived, but because the kids were no longer sources of trouble and criticism. As the kids became happier, so did the parents. Not all changes took communal forms. Some were romantic. One mother blossomed suddenly into an off-Broadway actress. Two found new husbands. Was this an effect of the school? Who knows? A woman looks prettier when she isn't frantic with worry and depressed by the feeling of isolation. I claim it for the school. All these parental changes had further effects on the children. To some small extent, these new relations among their parents turned the neighborhood in the direction of community.

EDUCATION BIBLIOGRAPHY

I. IMPRESSIONS OF EDUCATIONAL PROBLEMS

Kenneth Clark, *Dark Ghetto*, 1965, Harper & Row, pp. 111–153.

Herbert Kohl, *36 Children*, 1967, New American Library.

Jonathan Kozol, *Death at an Early Age*, 1967, Houghton Mifflin.

Nat Hentoff, *Our Children Are Dying*, 1968, Viking Compass.

John Holt, *How Children Fail*, 1964, Pitman.

James Herndon, *The Way It Spozed to Be*, 1968, Simon and Schuster.

II. DEFINITIONS AND MAGNITUDES

U.S. Civil Rights Commission, *Racial Isolation in the Public Schools*, 1967, U.S. Government. Summary of extent and effects of schooling inequality.

James S. Coleman *et al.*, *Equality of Educational Opportunity*, 1967, U.S. Government. Results of comprehensive survey on educational inequality.

John C. Flanagan *et al.*, *The American High School Student*, 1964, Project Talent. Results of a large survey, covering thousands of students through time.

Kenneth B. Simon and Vance W. Grant, *Digest of Educational Statistics*, 1967, U.S. Government.

III. ANALYTIC PERSPECTIVES

A. Economic Returns to Years of Schooling

Theodore Schultz, "Investment in Human Capital," in Mark Blaug, ed., *The Economics of Education*, 1968, Penguin, pp. 13–33. Original statement of human capital perspective on returns to education.

Herman Miller, *Rich Man, Poor Man*, 1964, T.Y. Crowell, pp. 148–173. Summary of figures on "The Cash Value of Education."

Giora Hanoch, "Personal Earnings and Investment in Schooling," *The Journal of Human Resources*, Summer, 1967. Summary of economic returns for different groups of the population.

Gary Becker, *Human Capital*, 1964, National Bureau of Economic Research. Major generalization of economic interpretation.

Mark Blaug, ed., *The Economics of Education*, op. cit., pp. 45–261. A series of pieces discussing the technical problems with the human capital perspective on returns to education.

Peter Blau and Otis Dudley Duncan, *The American Occupational Structure*, 1967, Wiley, *passim*. An examination of the effect of education on occupational status, rather than monetary earnings.

B. Inequality of Economic Returns

Lester Thurow, *Poverty and Discrimination*, 1969, Brookings, pp. 66–95. Empirical evidence of inequality of returns by race.

Thomas Ribich, *Education and Poverty*, 1968, Brookings, *passim*. On the ineffectuality of education among poor people.

Randall Weiss, "The Effect of Education on the Earnings of Blacks and Whites," *The Review of Economics and Statistics*, May, 1970. Striking empirical evidence that education does not pay for blacks.

Stephan Michelson, "Incomes of Racial Minorities," 1968, Brookings (mimeographed). Comprehensive empirical study of unequal returns to education.

C.   What Is the Real Socioeconomic Function of Education?

Robert Dreeben, *On What Is Learned in School*, 1968, Addison-Wesley. General model of the role of education in screening students for their attitudes, inducing conformity in those who continue.

Ivar Berg, *Education and Jobs: The Great Training Robbery*, 1969, Praeger. Varieties of evidence that educational skills bear little relationship to productivity on the job, that education produces attitudes, not skills.

Edgar Friedenberg, *Coming of Age in America*, 1967, Vintage. Classic study of the mechanisms through which conforming attitudes are instilled by the educational system.

Paul Lauter and Florence Howe, *Conspiracy of the Young*, 1970, World. Essays on the role of education in American society.

Ivan Illich, "Why We Must Abolish Schooling," *New York Review of Books*, July 2, 1970. Strong statement on the function of schooling in maintaining class inequalities.

Alex Inkeles, "Social Structure and the Socialization of Competence," *Harvard Educational Review*, June, 1966. Interesting analysis of socialization functions of schools.

Talcott Parsons, "The School Class as a Social System: Some of Its Functions in American Society," *Harvard Educational Review*, Fall, 1959.

D.   The Determinants of Scholastic Achievement

James Guthrie *et al.*, *Schools and Inequality*, 1969, The Urban Coalition, Chapter IV. Summary of evidence on effect of schools on achievement.

Samuel S. Bowles, "Towards an Educational Production Function," in W. Lee Hansen, ed., *Income, Education, and Human Capital*, 1971, National Bureau of Economic Research. Theoretical and analytic problems involved in measuring effectiveness of different school inputs.

Martin Katzman, "Distribution and Production in a Big City Elementary School System," *Yale Economic Essays*, Spring, 1968. Analysis of the effect of resource allocation on school achievement within the Boston school system.

E.   Schooling Inequalities: Class or Race?

Harvard Educational Review, *Equal Educational Opportunity*, Winter, 1968. A series of articles debating the different causes and elements of inequality.

Patricia Cayo Sexton, *Education and Income*, 1964, Viking. Effect of socioeconomic class in producing educational inequalities.

W. Lee Hansen and Burton Weisbrod, *Benefits, Costs and Finance of Public Higher Education*, Markham, 1969. Study of the class inequalities in higher education systems, with particular striking evidence about California's ostensibly equalizing system.

Robert E. Herriot and Nancy Hoyt St. John, *Social Class and the Urban School*, 1966, Wiley.

Christopher Jencks and David Riesman, *The Academic Revolution*, 1968, Doubleday, pp. 61–90. Strong evidence on class inequality in American education.

F. Trends in Schooling Inequality

Jencks and Riesman, *The Academic Revolution, op. cit.*, pp. 90–154. Varieties of evidence that inequality has persisted through time in the United States.

Christopher Jencks, "Social Stratification and Mass Higher Education," *Harvard Educational Review,* Spring, 1968. Further discussion of the persistence of class inequality.

William Spady, "Educational Mobility and Access in the U.S.: Growth and Paradoxes," *American Journal of Sociology,* November, 1967. Evidence that educational mobility has not increased in this century in the United States.

IV. POLICY ISSUES

A. Integration versus Compensatory Education and Community Control

Joseph Alsop, "No More Nonsense About Ghetto Education," *The New Republic,* July 22, 1967. Argues the case for increased compensatory education in ghetto schools.

R. Schwartz, T. Pettigrew, and M. Smith, "Fake Panaceas for Ghetto Education: A Reply to Joseph Alsop," *The New Republic,* September 23, 1967. The case for integration.

Joseph Alsop, "Ghetto Schools," *The New Republic,* November 18, 1967. The end but not the resolution of the exchange.

Henry M. Levin, ed., *Community Control of Schools,* 1969, Brookings. Series of articles on the reasons for and the mechanisms for achieving community control.

U.S. Civil Rights Commission, *Racial Isolation in the Public Schools,* 1967, U.S. Government, *passim.* Strongest argument available on necessity of integration for improving school quality.

Harvard Educational Review, Equal Educational Opportunity, Winter, 1968. Several articles clarifying the issues in the debate between integration and community control.

B. Mini-Schools and Educational Vouchers

George Dennison, *The Lives of Children,* 1969, Random House. A strong argument for mini-schools, based on the description of his experience with his own small experimental school.

Christopher Jencks, "Is the Public School Obsolete?" *The Public Interest,* Winter, 1966. Presents arguments for relaxing public monopoly on school systems, for freeing possibility of everyone starting his own school, with public financial assistance.

Henry M. Levin, "The Failure of the Public Schools and the Free Market," *The Urban Review,* June, 1968. Some of the implications of funding schools versus funding parents for their children's education.

Center for the Study of Public Policy, *Education Vouchers,* 1970, Center for the Study of Public Policy (56 Boylston St., Cambridge, Mass.). Proposal for a demonstration project of educational vouchers, presenting issues and difficulties with such a scheme.

4 Poverty

Editor's Introduction

While income and wealth taxation may help a bit to dry up these well-springs of material inequalities, the real attack on them comes from civil rights groups, anti-poverty campaigns, anti-monopoly drives, etc., all working within the context of capitalism; from socialists who call for the nationalization of means of production; and from Maoists, hippies, and others who are rebelling against the capitalist mentality with its heavy emphasis on selfishness and material rewards. It might well be that this last movement poses the ultimate threat to material inequalities—the hippies rather than the Internal Revenue Service.

—John G. Gurley[1]

It may have been true in 1962 when Michael Harrington published *The Other America* that "the America of poverty is hidden today in a way that it never was before. Its millions are socially invisible to the rest of us."[2] But by 1970 the poor had been detected, inspected, and injected many times. A War on Poverty had been declared, many commissions had studied the problem, and the poor themselves had organized to demand a larger slice of the pie.

But with all the new attention on the poor, the problem of poverty had neither been solved nor adequately understood. Millions of Americans remained poor throughout the sixties, while the public seemed increasingly to confuse symptoms, causes, systems, and cultures of poverty. Even the experts failed to agree on analyses or solutions. Reporting on one seminar of leading poverty experts held in the late 1960's, for instance, Daniel P. Moynihan concluded, "There was no common understanding as to the nature of poverty or the process of deliberate social change."[3] In the face of programmatic failure and analytic confusion, despite all the promises and wars, as Michael Harrington wrote in 1970, "Society has failed to redeem the pledges of the sixties and has taken to celebrating paper triumphs over poverty."[4]

In this chapter I have tried to sort through some of the confusion and summarize different perspectives on the poverty problem. In the first section I have presented three definitions of poverty and some estimates of the magnitude of poverty according to each definition. In the second section I have briefly sketched the liberal and conservative views of poverty and potential solutions to the problem. In the third section I have outlined the radical analysis. The fourth section briefly introduces the purposes and contents of the readings.

DEFINITIONS AND MAGNITUDES

Any society effectively establishes its own definition of poverty—there is no eternally fixed standard applicable to all social circumstances. Within any specific society, one can isolate several ways of defining poverty. Each of those ways of defining poverty typically involves society's preferences about the shape of its income distribution.

An income distribution expresses the proportions of families in a society which earn varying levels of income during a specific period of time, like a year. In 1968 in the United States, for instance, 10.3 percent of American families earned less than $3,000, 12.1 percent earned $3,000 to $4,999, 14.5 percent earned $5,000 to $6,999, and so on.[5] An income distribution represents

---

[1] See the selection by Gurley among the readings below.
[2] (London: Penguin, 1962), p. 10.
[3] In Moynihan, ed., *On Understanding Poverty* (N.Y.: Basic Books, 1969), p. 19.
[4] "Betrayal of the Poor," *Atlantic Monthly*, January, 1970, p. 71.
[5] "Income in 1968 of Families and Persons in the United States," Bureau of the Census, *Current Population Reports*, Series P-60, No. 66, p. 1.

the outcome of a complicated market process: potential earners acquire skills, shop for jobs, learn more skills on the job, receive income from property, win lotteries, and so on. All of those activities are summarized by a family's final market income. Given the distribution of market incomes, a society then manifests its preferences about the final shape of the distribution. It can decide that some people should not earn as much money as the market permits, for instance, taking some of their market income and distributing it to those who have earned less. Or it can decide that every family should receive exactly the same income, achieving an exact equality in the final income distribution.

Society's implicit and explicit preferences about changes from the market distribution of income to the final distribution of income constitute its definitions of poverty. Three kinds of definitions seem especially important in the United States: an explicit definition of "absolute poverty," an explicit definition of "relative poverty," and an implicit definition suggested by social programs designed to eliminate poverty.

An "absolute" definition of poverty specifies a "minimum subsistence income"—an income level below which the society feels that families should not be forced to live. It might represent the smallest income necessary to prevent families from starving, or it might allow slightly more comfortable subsistence. The U.S. Government has formally accepted and codified an absolute definition of poverty, developed by the U.S. Social Security Administration. The definition relies on Department of Agriculture calculations of the cost of food for a "nutritionally adequate" family diet—the least expensive food items necessary to maintain a family in relatively decent health. It then multiplies that food cost by three, relying on studies during the 1950's which suggested that one third of low-income family budgets were spent on food. By 1970, the government considered that a family of four with less than $3,800 annual income lived in poverty. By that definition, roughly 22 million Americans, or 11 percent of the population, were poor in 1970.[6]

Although this absolute definition of poverty has been officially established by the government, it has been widely criticized by others.[7] Most critics attack it for establishing much too low a level of income as the absolute poverty line; they argue that many families earning more than this amount should also be considered poor.[8] According to Michael Harrington, for instance, at least 12 million more Americans should be considered poor by absolute standards.[9]

An editor's supplement on trends in poverty among the selections below summarizes trends in poverty measured by this absolute definition, and sketches some of the criticisms of that definition.

A "relative" definition of poverty compares the income of those at the bottom of the income

[6] The definition was developed by Mollie Orshansky of the Social Security Administration. It begins with an estimate of the cost of the "economy" food plan used by the Department of Agriculture, taking into account price variations by region (farm and non-farm), age of head-of-household (aged and non-aged) and number of children in a family. The "economy" food plan is meager, designed for "temporary or emergency use when funds are low." (Orshansky, "Counting the Poor . . . ," *Social Security Bulletin*, January, 1965, p. 12.) The varying costs for food are then multiplied by three to derive the final poverty levels for different family sizes (by region and age of head). The multiple was derived from a 1955 study of budgets, but a later study suggested that families now spent smaller shares of their income on food— a 1960–61 study implied a multiple of four rather than three, which would have produced a much higher poverty line and estimates of many more poor people. Interestingly, the choice of the multiple may have been based on politics. The Council of Economic Advisers originally proposed that anyone with less than $3,000 be considered poor, estimating in 1963 that 34 million persons were poor. "More refined estimates, if they were to be politically acceptable, had to be consistent with CEA's estimate of the size of the problem." (Martin Rein, "Problems in the Definition and Measurement of Poverty," in Louis Ferman *et al.*, eds., *Poverty in America* (University of Michigan Press, 1968), rev. ed., p. 125.) A multiple of three produced an aggregate estimate of poverty very close to the CEA estimate, so it seemed appropriate. For references on this definition and alternative definitions, see the bibliography at the end of the chapter. At the time of writing, the most recently published figure was for 1968, an aggregate, weighted national average of $3,531 for a family of four.

[7] For the best discussion of problems with the definition, see Martin Rein, "Problems in the Definition and Measurement of Poverty," *op. cit.*

[8] Many argue, for instance, that one should use a "lower-than-moderate" budget standard developed by the Bureau of Labor Statistics, which required roughly $6,000 for a family of four and was hardly generous. See U.S. Department of Labor, Bureau of Labor Statistics, "Three Standards of Living," BLS *Bulletin*, No. 1570-5 (1969).

[9] "Betrayal of the Poor," *op. cit.*, p. 72.

distribution with that of more affluent families. Given total output in society and average standards of living, a society can express some preferences about how equally total income should be distributed among its members. One society might wish for nearly perfect equality of income, while another might accept the degree of inequality already reflected in the final market distribution of income. The more equal the desired income distribution, the higher will be the income level established as the definition of "relative" poverty. A society in favor of considerable income equality might feel, for instance, that any family earning less than 80 percent of the social median family income should be considered relatively poor and should receive some income transferred from more affluent families. The President's Commission on Income Maintenance Programs has argued that relative definitions of poverty become increasingly important as societies become more affluent:[10]

As a society's general standard of living rises, increasingly expensive consumption patterns are forced on the poor, not in order to catch up, but in order to remain a part of that society. Moreover, as society's normal standard of living rises the poor will seek to emulate it— since they are part of society—and feel increasingly deprived if they cannot.

The United States has rarely considered relative definitions of poverty, and the government has never adopted an official definition of poverty in relative terms. As the next section will suggest, liberal and conservative perspectives informing public policy on poverty have always emphasized absolute rather than relative definitions. Nonetheless, many academicians have found a definition proposed by Victor Fuchs as a rather sensible minimal relative standard. By this relative definition, any family earning less than one half the national median family income would be considered poor. This does not involve very great equality, for it says that families earning as little as $4,500 a year would be included among the non-poor if the national median income were $8,000. Throughout the period since World War II, the percentage of Americans who were poor by this definition remained constant at roughly 20 percent.[11] Not surprisingly, there are now more Americans considered poor relative to our aggregate affluence than there are Americans considered poor by an absolute measure of the minimum they need to survive.[12]

A third definition of poverty involves interpretation of social efforts to help the poor. In the United States, historically, society has publicly supported only those families whose household head was *unable* to work. If a family head worked but earned very little money, the American public has traditionally been reluctant to consider his family worthy of support. Public assistance, as we have called it, was always intended as "a 'residual program' to aid those considered unable to enter the labor force."[13] In fact, during the 1960's, only one third of Americans considered poor by the official definition of absolute poverty actually received any kind of public assistance.[14] Lumping all government transfer programs together, including Social Security, unemployment compensation, and public assistance, Christopher Green estimated for the early 1960's that transfers filled less than half the total poverty gap (the difference between final market income and absolute poverty level) for those who were still poor in the final income distribution.[15]

According to this implicit social definition of poverty, therefore, Americans have defined poverty more by capacity to work than by market income. If a household head was able to work, the public has felt he should accept his market income as his final family income.

THE LIBERAL AND CONSERVATIVE VIEWS

Liberal and conservative perspectives on poverty follow precisely from the theories of the State and the normative predispositions of the two paradigms outlined in Chapter One.

[10] President's Commission on Income Maintenance Programs, *Poverty Amid Plenty* (Washington: U.S. Government Printing Office, 1969), p. 38.

[11] Fuchs, "Comment on Measuring the Low-Income Population," in Lee Soltow, ed., *Six Papers on the Size Distribution of Wealth and Income* (N.Y.: National Bureau of Economic Research, 1969), pp. 198–202; and President's Commission, *Poverty Amid Plenty, op. cit.*, p. 40.

[12] This, however, has been true only recently, since 1960.

[13] *Poverty Amid Plenty, op. cit.*, p. 46.

[14] See Robert Lampman, "Expanding the American System of Transfers to Do More for the Poor," *Wisconsin Law Review*, 2 (1969), pp. 548–549.

[15] Christopher Green, *Negative Taxes and the Poverty Problem* (Washington: Brookings, 1967), p. 33.

Both perspectives emphasize absolute definitions of poverty. Since they accept the market system as an essentially just system for the allocation of resources, they tend basically to accept the pattern of income distribution resulting from that system. Writers in both perspectives acknowledge, however, that some people are not able to work and that some others earn too little to maintain their families at a "minimum" standard. Conservatives tend to emphasize absolute definitions of poverty more singularly than liberals; some liberals urge a slight equalization of the market distribution, although they do not advocate modification of the market process by which initial incomes are determined.

Both perspectives therefore tend to urge a system of income redistribution which would establish a basic floor to incomes but would disrupt the market system of income determination as little as possible. Both liberal and conservative economists have objected to traditional public assistance programs in this country because they have not effectively established comprehensive or adequate income floors, and because they have tended to undercut the market system of wage incentives. On the former grounds, public assistance programs have historically included only portions of the poverty population, and have provided basic living allowances far below officially accepted absolute poverty standards.[16] On the latter grounds, economists have argued that public assistance programs traditionally provided a disincentive to work; for each dollar of employment earnings, the programs subtracted a dollar from public assistance allowances, imposing an effective 100 percent tax on work income.[17]

Based on those criticisms, liberals and conservatives have joined in suggesting various forms of a basic redistribution scheme—typically called "negative income taxation."[18] Most proposals have suggested a minimum income allowance and a tax rate on additional earnings of only one third to one half of extra work income.[19] In response to this stream of proposals, the Nixon Administration finally offered its Family Assistance Plan to Congress for approval in 1970. At the time of writing, the eventual Congressional outcome seems unclear. Most probably, a variation on the basic Nixon plan will be enacted by the middle of 1971 at the latest. The plan will probably provide roughly $2,000–$2,400 cash equivalent to a family of four with no income, and would take away 50 percent of any additional earned income. A family of four earning $2,400 from employment, for instance, would receive roughly $3,600 in final income, including government transfers.[20]

In the long run these proposals would not basically affect the shape of the distribution of income in the United States, since they would tend simply to establish a floor under final income. Liberals and conservatives have tended not to emphasize the issue of relative poverty because they assume society is not interested in that issue. If society decided that it wanted to equalize the distribution of income, both perspectives imply, then it would be able to pick whatever final distribution it wanted. As Walter Heller wrote in the excerpt included in Chapter One, the set of liberal theories of the state "points the way to achieving any combination of Government services, income redistribution and economic redistribution, and economic stability we set our sights on."

Both analyses assume further that the existence of progressive income tax statutes in the United States provides sufficient documentation of general American preference for government redistribution of income from the more affluent to the poor. Otto Eckstein says simply, "Adam Smith argued that taxes should be *proportional* to income. . . . Today, we have gone one step further. We favor *progressive* taxes. . . ."[21] Since society favors progressive taxation in general, the perspectives imply, it would be able to establish a *more* progressive system of taxation and transfer if it wanted. Those who favor such redistribution need simply mobilize a majority of public opinion.

[16] The low standards have been especially prevalent in the South. For criticisms on these grounds, see the selection by the President's Commission on Income Maintenance Programs below.

[17] See *ibid.*, below.

[18] See Green, *op. cit.*, or James Tobin, "Raising the Incomes of the Poor," in Kermit Gordon, ed., *Agenda for the Nation* (Washington: Brookings, 1968).

[19] For a summary of proposals, see Theodore Marmor, ed., *Poverty Policy: A Sourcebook of Cash-Transfer Proposals* (Los Angeles: Aldine, 1971).

[20] Based on latest newspaper reports, in midsummer 1970, of versions most likely to pass Congress.

[21] Eckstein, *Public Finance* (Englewood Cliffs, N.J.: Prentice-Hall, 1964), p. 56.

THE RADICAL VIEW

The radical perspective on the problem of poverty differs from the liberal and conservative views in two fundamental respects. First, radicals tend to emphasize relative rather than absolute definitions of poverty. Second, radicals argue that any kind of meaningful redistribution of income cannot possibly be achieved in the context of current capitalist institutions. Both of those premises derive directly from the general radical paradigm discussed in Chapter One.

Radicals argue, first of all, that man cannot be free until society separates man's activities as producer from his needs as consumer. He must be freed, as Max Weber put it, from the "whip of hunger." Although members of society should have widely varying opportunities to engage in different kinds of productive activities, radicals argue, they should receive fundamentally equal allocations of social resources. Thus the famous Marxist dictum, "From each according to his abilities, to each according to his needs." This set of normative predispositions obviously implies a primary concern with the relative shape of the distribution of income, in present societies, rather than with the definition of absolute levels of poverty.[22] The distribution of income and resources, radicals urge, should approach perfect equality (adjusted for need).

This kind of equality cannot possibly be achieved in capitalist societies based on the private ownership of property, according to the radical analysis, for two reasons.

First, the market distribution of income tends to become increasingly unequal in a market system based on private ownership of property. As James Meade has concluded from his extended analysis of the distributional implications of the market system, in most cases[23]

Efficiency pricing would require that an ever-increasing proportion of output accrued to property owners and the distributional dilemma would to this extent be intensified. . . . The question which we should ask is: What shall we all do when output per man-hour of work is extremely high but practically the whole of the output goes to a few property owners, while the mass of the workers are relatively . . . worse off than before?

Second, radicals argue that the State cannot and will not achieve a fundamental equalization of income in capitalist societies. This argument derives from the radical theory of the State, and was summarized by Paul Sweezy in his exposition of that view: "Let us summarize the principles underlying the use of the State as an economic instrument within the framework of capitalism. In the first place, the State comes into action in the economic sphere in order to solve problems which are posed by the development of capitalism. In the second place, where the interests of the capitalist class are concerned, there is a strong predisposition to use the State power freely. And, finally, the State may be used to make concessions to the working class provided that the consequences of not doing so are sufficiently dangerous to the stability and functioning of the system as a whole."

Radicals suggest that capitalists would oppose a meaningful redistribution and equalization of income for two reasons. First, it would totally undermine the wage-incentive system in a society where work is fundamentally alienating. If workers can receive a decent income from the State without working, and if their work in society is unsatisfying, why should they work? As John Gurley argues in his selection among the readings below, "If people were willing to work for non-material reasons—for the sheer love of it, to serve their country, to serve others, to serve God—material incomes . . . could be distributed equitably in the first place. . . ."

This State refusal to upset the only potent work incentives in a capitalist society like the United States has clearly surfaced in recent debates about the Nixon Administration proposal for income maintenance. Congress and the Administration have insisted that those able to work must work before they can receive adequate income from the government. In testimony before the Senate, the Secretary of Labor tried to reassure Congress: "If the person has no skills . . . he or she will have to take an unskilled job. . . . We are not remaking the American labor market in this bill and fully realize that people are going to have to do the work that is available in our economy. . . ."[24]

[22] See some of the discussions in the pieces by Edwards and MacEwan and by Sweezy in Chapter One above.
[23] Meade, *Equality, Efficiency and the Ownership of Property* (London: Unwin, 1965), p. 26.
[24] Quoted in *The New York Post*, August 5, 1970, p. 18.

Second, radicals also argue that the State would not and could not meaningfully redistribute income in a capitalist society because the State serves the interests of the capitalist class and because capitalists are interested primarily in maintaining or increasing their relative share of income. Radicals point to three kinds of evidence about the government impact on the distribution of income to support their argument that the State protects the capitalists' relative share.

1. Although our society nominally prefers progressive taxation, according to liberal views, radicals argue that the net effect of government taxes in this country is plainly not progressive. At best, the total impact of government taxes is proportional, as official government figures summarized by Gabriel Kolko in his selection below would suggest. At worst, as Gurley argues, a more accurate measurement of the impact of government taxes would demonstrate actually regressive patterns of impact.

2. In view of these figures on the impact of taxes, liberals often argue quite justly that one must look at the distribution of government expenditures among income classes (as well as the distributional burden of taxes) in order totally to assess the impact of the State. These analyses pose extremely intractable statistical problems, however, and one can question the assumptions involved in any set of such estimates. How does one allocate among income classes the $80 billion the government spends on national defense, for instance? Does everyone benefit equally from the expenditure, or do defense firms and their owners benefit most? Some estimates of the distributional impact of government expenditures have been made.[25] One summary of such estimates is presented in Table V of the Editor's Supplement on "Recent Evidence of Government Impact" among the readings in this chapter. According to that set of estimates, which the government itself supports, the net government impact in 1965 was progressive up to $4,000, proportional from $4,000 to $15,000, and progressive above $15,000. For varieties of reasons, these estimates surely overestimate the progressivity of government impact at the tails of the distribution, particularly because they rely on official measures of tax impact.[26] In any case, throughout the dominant middle range of the income distribution, they suggest proportionality at best.

3. Finally, and most important, radicals argue that such calculations fundamentally misstate the total impact of the State on the distribution of income. These estimates begin from a common starting point, for they both measure government impact on the final market distribution of income.[27] Neither set of statistical calisthenics asks a more important preliminary question: What impact has the government had on determining which citizens end up in which income classes in that final market distribution of income? Michelson states the point directly: "The process by which people receive money . . . is not independent of ordinary government action."[28] He cites one example of the importance of this impact on the *process* of income generation. The government spends money on schools, spending different amounts on different schools. Those who attend the schools learn different amounts, attain different levels of school depending largely on what they learn and how much it's worth, find jobs based substantially on how far they've gone in school, and then earn different amounts of money. Standard estimates of the differential impact of government expenditures on education look only at how much money the government spends on schools attended by the children of families with different incomes. But those estimates have nothing to do with the real effect of the government expenditure, and therefore with the real benefits it provides. Michelson summarizes the implications of estimating the impact of eventual benefits from education, rather than looking solely at the distribution of current government expenditures:[29]

If low-class children are taught that they will be high school graduates at best, then laborers, the finding that these people tend not to go to college surely cannot be written off as exogenously determined taste. Because the chances of going to college vary by income class, and future

[25] See principally, W. I. Gillespie, "The Effect of Public Expenditures on the Distribution of Income," in R. A. Musgrave, ed., *Essays in Fiscal Federalism* (Washington: Brookings, 1968), pp. 122–168.
[26] See the selection by Gurley below, for a summary of most of the mis-estimates.
[27] This discussion is drawn from Stephan Michelson, "The Economics of Real Income Distribution," *Review of Radical Political Economics,* Spring, 1970, pp. 75–86.
[28] *Ibid.,* p. 78.
[29] *Ibid.,* pp. 82–83. See readings in the chapter on education for evidence of some of his points.

income is strongly a function of college graduation (for whites), the high-income students are gaining more from their college-preparatory, elementary, and secondary schooling than are the low-income students from their presumably non-college directed schooling. . . . The result is a biased benefit in favor of the higher income classes within each race, and in favor of whites over nonwhites.

Now when these children from high-income families achieve their increment to lifetime income which . . . education has provided, they will be taxed at higher rates than the children of the poor, who now earn less. . . . All will see this money being spent rather equally by race and income in the . . . school system, and many will say . . . that government has effectuated a redistribution from [the rich] to the poor. Yet their present before-tax income position is itself a direct result of this equal expenditure, which produced a very unequal benefit in their favor when they were in school, and continues in their children's favor now. Thus the analysis taking pre-tax incomes as given leads to exactly the opposite conclusion from that of a correct analysis. And carrying this analysis over two generations shows, I believe, that this class bias in the benefits to education is large enough to dominate the apparent redistribution to the lower classes of the traditional analysis.

Many readings throughout the rest of this book suggest the extensive and important ways in which government expenditures help reinforce the class biases of private-sector institutions. These effects seem large enough, as Michelson argues, not only to undercut the importance of conventional benefit estimates but also thoroughly to support the radical contention about the role of the State. The implication of that contention for the problem of poverty seems clear: although the government may help establish a floor under incomes to help stabilize the system, it will hardly be very conscientious about trying to equalize the distribution of income. If the distribution of income seems unnecessarily unequal now, it will probably seem just as unequal many years from now.

THE READINGS

Because public discussion of the poverty problem has been so frequently confused, I have relied heavily on Editor's Supplements in this chapter. With those supplements, the selections are divided into three main clusters.

First, three selections provide Impressions, Definitions, and Magnitudes. First, Jimmy Breslin watches the moon landing with a poor family on welfare in New York, and perfectly evokes the extraordinary contrast between the family's poverty and the social affluence applied to the space program. Anthony Downs summarizes some basic figures on the distribution of absolute poverty among city residents, and the composition of the urban poor. The first Editor's Supplement summarizes a wide variety of evidence on trends in absolute poverty, relative poverty, and the distribution of wealth.

A second group of readings presents the basic issues involved in the kinds of public assistance available in the past and potentially available in the future. The first selection, from the report of the President's Commission on Income Maintenance Programs, provides a critique of traditional forms of public assistance in this country, emphasizing their selectivity and disincentives to work. A second selection, by Christopher Green, outlines the analytic characteristics of transfer-by-taxation proposals—or negative income taxes, as they are commonly called. His selection emphasizes the extent to which the proposals do not interfere with the process of income generation but serve only to establish a floor below which final incomes would not fall. The second Editor's Supplement summarizes the features of several specific income maintenance proposals, including the plan proposed by President Nixon to Congress; none of the proposals offers very ample minimum allowances for fear of disincentive effects.

A third group of selections provides some of the evidence with which radicals support their view of the State. Gabriel Kolko provides an interesting historical summary of the radical argument that the real impact of government taxes has not been progressive. The third Editor's Supplement provides several pieces of more recent statistical evidence supporting Kolko's basic argument on the impact of government taxes. Finally, John Gurley argues that those kinds of estimates of government impact fundamentally understate the extent to which the government tolerates market inequalities and the extent to which the government does not redistribute income as liberals tend to assume. Evidence on the real impact of government expenditures, of the sort that Michelson has urged we consider, has not been included here because the readings in other chapters serve effectively to illustrate some of that evidence.

MOONWALK ON SUTTER AVENUE

Jimmy Breslin

Breslin watches the moon landing with a family on welfare in Brownsville, a rapidly decaying slum in New York City. Better than any statistics, the selection illustrates the distribution of income in this country.

The article is reprinted in its entirety from *New York Magazine,* for which Breslin writes regularly. He formerly wrote a regular column for *The New York Post,* and recently wrote a best-selling novel, *The Gang that Couldn't Shoot Straight.* Breslin ran for New York City Council President on Norman Mailer's ticket in 1969.

It began raining in the early evening of Sunday, July 20, 1969. The kids crowded under the marquee of the Premier, the moviehouse on the corner of Sutter Avenue and Hinsdale Street in Brownsville, which is in Brooklyn. The marquee said the movie showing inside was *Las Sicodalics.* The smeared showcase windows had glossy photos of Puerto Rican girls in undergarments. When somebody pushed open one of the Premier's doors, a thick, sour smell came out of a lobby which must have been ornate in the thirties and forties. The smell from the lobby mixed with the smell of the wet garbage in the gutter in front of the Premier. None of the kids standing under the marquee noticed the smell.

Ralph DuBois, who is 15, twirled a long, varnished stick that had rows of finger-width notches carved into it. He stopped twirling it long enough to show you the knobbed head of the stick. He had burned an evil-looking face into the wood.

"That's Africa, like you see," Ralph said.

"Oh."

"It was hard to do," he said. He began twirling the stick. "I made it in school."

"What school are you in?"

"A 'special' school."

"What special school is that?"

"My *personal* 'special' school." They all laughed.

"What are you doing for the summer?" he was asked.

"Work," he said. He held the stick up to your face and spun it with a flourish. "Wanna know where I work at?"

"Where?"

"Nearest crap game."

"Where is the nearest crap game?" he was asked.

"Usually right around the corner. But it rainin' now, so we got to wait for dry sidewalk."

"Isn't the moon landing on television now?" he was asked.

"Guess so," he said.

Gregory Dyer, who is 12 and who was wearing a wine polo shirt and a pink beret, stepped forward. "They got peoples on the moon, I know that," he said.

"They do?"

"Yeah. They all look like me. The peoples on the moon all like me. So you through when you get to the moon. Y'unnerstan? On the moon, you gotta look like me. Black. Black on the moon, black on Mars, black on the stars."

"Why aren't you watching television to see if there are men on the moon?" he was asked.

"I can't, account of my mother, she watchin' Alfred Hitchcock."

When the rain let up a little, I went across the street to Borinquen's grocery store to buy a pen. The cramped area in front of the counter was crowded, so I stepped back and leaned against the meat counter and waited. Only one of the trays in the window of the meat counter had meat on it. The meat was a thin slab which once was red but now had gray in it. The sides were curling up. The tray next to it had green peppers and two cans of Ballantine beer. On the other trays, flies covered the dried meat blood on the wax paper.

Alongside the grocery store was the Cuchifritos, a stand that sold Spanish food. Next to the food stand was an empty corner lot, enclosed with a high chicken-wire fence. The kids had come over from the Premier movie house and were standing at the fence and throwing rocks into the lot. The lot was covered with mounds of garbage. Each time a kid threw a rock into the lot, a rat would come out of the garbage and make his way over to the wall and disappear through an opening into the Cuchifritos stand.

Ralph DuBois poked his carved stick through the wire fence and began rapping it on an empty beer can. A rat came out from under the beer can and in one motion headed toward the wire fence. DuBois was wearing sneakers and the tips of his feet were sticking through the wire fence. "Eeeyahhh!" he shouted. He jumped back from the fence.

The rat changed direction. It moved with this quick, but not fast, scurry to the wall of the Cuchifritos stand. Then it disappeared. All the kids picked up rocks and began throwing them into the lot, and everywhere there were these shapes moving through the garbage to the wall. Twenty to twenty-five rats showed themselves.

"More rats here than in the whole world," DuBois said.

"Big rats, little rats, baby mice," one of the kids said.

"You should see when the Cuchifritos closes and everybody goes home," DuBois said. "The rats run around inside the stand. Then they come out here on the sidewalk. They are all over the corner. You come home late and you come to the corner here and there are hundreds of rats on the sidewalk."

The corner traffic light was red and Spanish music came from two of the three cars waiting for it to change. In the third car, an old red convertible, the voice on the radio was saying, ". . . man's incredible initial conquest of the universe, a 240,000-mile flight through space—and now, the unbelievable, a lunar landing . . ."

Angelo Cora, who is 35, was leaning against the car parked at the curb. He wore a dark blue polo shirt, black pants and sandals. His arms were folded cross his chest. When I introduced myself to him, he unfolded his arms to shake hands. The streetlight caught these little streaks of scar tissue on the inside of his elbows. Needle marks.

He saw me looking at them, and he smiled.

"Two months home now," he said.

"Where were you?"

"Hospital for bein' an addict. But no more addict, man. I'm two months home now. I go to the Civic Center Clinic. It's at 44 Willoughby. They help all the addicts there. It's a good thing. This is the first time in my life I ever felt good."

"How long were you on it?"

He smiled again. "Fourteen years."

"How much of a habit?"

"Twenty, twenty-five dollar a day," he said.

"How did you get it?"

"Crack cribs. You know, go into apartments and steal. I got caught a few times. Between prison and hospitals, I was off the streets three years. Now, man, I'm two months home and I really don't need it. But, man, this whole neighborhood. It's addicts."

"Are these kids addicts?" I asked, pointing to the ones by the fence.

He shrugged.

"Any of you kids use narcotics?" I called out.

"Why, you got somethin' for me?" one of them said. They all laughed.

Angelo held out his hands. "You see, you can't say anything to them. Like you couldn't say anything to me, either. I never thought about gettin' caught. I was just contented. You go 'round contented. Everything is beautiful, man. The street here, the rats there, it don't mean nothin'. You get contented. You're out of it. It's very hard to tell somebody he shouldn't try. Because when he does, he likes it so much."

There was another red light and one of the car radios was saying, ". . . at this moment, Neil Armstrong is preparing to be the first man to walk on the moon . . ."

"Hey, didn't they do that yet?" Cora said.

"I guess they didn't," I said.

"We ought to go watch it on television someplace," he said. "It's a terrific thing. We beat the Russians to the moon. It makes me happy, man."

There was a bar on the opposite corner, but there was no television set inside. Cora said he knew a place where we could watch the men walk on the moon. The sister of a girl who had been his wife lived on Sheffield Street and Cora said she would let us come in. We got into a car and began driving there.

At night, the streets of Brownsville are like a well-bombed target. On each block there are half-demolished buildings. Their corroded insides of staircases and broken walls and sagging floors are outlined by the car headlights. Most of the streetlights are broken, and with no light coming from the houses, you drive on some blocks through complete darkness. On many of the streets, the rows of four- and five-story houses have been almost abandoned. Windows and doorways have tin sheets nailed over them. Here and there in a block, a lone light will show. One person, or one family, will be living with the rats in the building. The people in these lone apartments must keep somebody awake all night, because the kids from the neighborhood come into these buildings and set fires in the empty apartments. The firehouse serving the neighborhood, Ladder 103, is so busy that the company rarely comes back to the station after a call. It stays out on the streets, going from fire to fire, sometimes two and three in a single block.

It has been like this for a long time in Brownsville. A year and a half ago, I went to visit the nuns working at the Good Shepherd center on the corner of Hopkinson and Sutter. The stores on the corners were empty and the apartments over the stores were empty and the broken glass from the windows covered the sidewalks. And here, in the rain on this Sunday night, the corners were as they were, except now stripped cars sat there. One of the cars had crashed into the light pole. It sat on rusted haunches on the sidewalk. Several buildings down Hopkinson Avenue, the faint blue light of television showed from an apartment window. When you looked in the window, you could see a woman sitting on a kitchen chair in a bare room and watching the moon coverage on a small television set. There was a noise behind you at the curb. Something had moved in one of the trash cans sitting in the sprawl of spilled garbage.

Here and there in the ruins of Brownsville there are neatly painted wooden signs proclaiming that a housing project will be erected on the spot. Under the proclamation is the name of the politician, and of the various urban experts, in charge of the housing program. These signs have been standing in Brownsville for many, many months. Just as the same signs have been standing for the same months and months on Roosevelt Avenue in Chicago and Twelfth Avenue in Detroit and Joseph Avenue in Rochester. The story of a city in this nation in the 1960s is a sign with a politician's name on it, and only the name on the sign changes.

As we drove, the news announcer on the car radio was talking about the technical skill it took to get the lunar landing ship down onto the surface with its four legs evenly touching.

The place Angelo took us to was a frame house sitting in a lot that was filled with old cars. He went to a door with a torn screen and called in Spanish. A woman opened the door.

"I was asleep," she said. She had a sundress thrown over a nightgown. Her name was Clara Pagan. She was plump and her face looked 40. She is only 26.

A clock in the small, clean kitchen said it was 10:45. In a box-like bedroom off the kitchen two teenage nieces of Clara Pagan sat on a bed and watched a small portable television.

"Columbia, this is Houston . . ."

"They coming out now," one of the girls said.

"They haven't been out yet?" Angelo said. The girls shook their heads. "Wow, we're in time," Angelo said. He clapped his hands and sat on the bed.

Clara Pagan leaned in the doorway and watched.

"You tell your mailman?" Angelo said to her. She shrugged. "You better," he said. "I told you, the new rule says that if the mailman puts the check in your mailbox and somebody steals it, then they won't replace the check anymore."

On the television, there still was the "simulated" tag across the screen. Walter Cronkite talked in fatherly tones to the country, and every few seconds the metallic, mechanical voices of the spacemen—"Houston, this is Eagle . . ."—came through.

"I have to watch for the mailman because this is bad out here," Clara said. "They steal, they do everything. This gang of kids. The Devils. Very bad. Coloreds and Puerto Ricans. They steal and beat up people. You can't go out at night. They stab you. Last night they were running down the street all covered with somebody's blood."

"How much relief do you get?" she was asked.

"I get $115.95 every two weeks," she said. "It's supposed to be more, but now I don't know. They going to cut down."

"They used to give carfare to the people going to clinics," Angelo said. "Now they don't give that anymore. They cut out carfare for people on relief."

"How long have you been on relief?" she was asked.

"For a year. I have two children. The baby is only a year old. I worked all my life, but I cannot go and leave the baby. My husband leave me a year ago. He went home to Puerto Rico. So now I stay home." She made a face. "Relief is no good."

"Why isn't it good?" she was asked.

"They come and look. They always *axt* you about a husband. They come to house one time at 6:30 in the night. I was surprised. She didn't say anything to me. She just walked by me and she look in the draws and the closets. She look all over."

"She look for a man's clothes," Angelo said. "To see if she's living with a man."

"I don't like relief," Clara said.

On the television, the "simulated" line suddenly said "live from the surface of the moon." The picture was upside down. It was fixed. Now you could watch the simple,

staggering act of a man coming down a step-ladder and onto the surface of the moon.

Clara Pagan kept talking. "I was on relief when I was with my mother," she said. "She had TB. My father died. I was with my brothers and sisters. Relief, it was no good then. No good now."

Images skipped across the screen. The astronauts romped on the moon.

"Smell it?" Clara said.

"Smell what?"

"The dogs. The old lady downstairs keeps dogs in the cellar and she never cleans. The smell makes you sick. The rats and the roaches come."

". . . Eagle, this is Houston. Can we get you two together so we can see the two of you . . ."

"Look at this," Clara Pagan said. "They have them pose for pictures like children in the park."

"Look at it, you can't believe it," Angelo Cora said, holding out his arms. In the bright light of the room, you could see that he has needle scars all up and down the insides of his arms.

Clara Pagan walked over to the stove and lit a cigarette. She came back to the doorway with the cigarette in her mouth and she watched American men walk on the moon.

"Some day I'm going to get off relief," she said.

WHO ARE THE URBAN POOR?

Anthony Downs

Downs sketches the statistical dimensions of urban poverty—who are the poor in cities, how many are they, and what's happening to them. Downs's figures draw primarily on 1960 numbers, but more recent evidence suggests that the distributions and composition of the urban poor did not change much during the 1960's. Mainly, the urban poor became more dominated by blacks and by female-headed families.

This selection comes from a larger pamphlet with the same title. Downs is vice-president of the Real Estate Corporation in Chicago and an occasional teacher of economics. He has written widely, including *An Economic Theory of Democracy*.

SOURCE: *Anthony Downs, "Who Are the Urban Poor?" Committee for Economic Development, Supplementary Paper #26, October, 1968.*

In 1966, there were 29.7 million persons living in poverty in the entire United States —or 15.4 percent of the total population. Of these persons, 20.1 million (68 percent) were white, and 9.6 million (32 percent) were nonwhite.[1] Thus, there were twice as many poor whites as poor nonwhites. But the *incidence* of poverty (the probability of being poor) was 11.8 percent for all whites, as compared to 41.4 percent for all nonwhites.

The 224 metropolitan areas of the United States contained 125.3 million people in 1966, or 65 percent of the nation's total population. Slightly more than half of all metropolitan area residents (66.9 million) lived in suburbs; the remainder (58.4 million) lived in central cities. About 15.2 million poor persons lived in these metropolitan areas, or 51 percent of all U.S. poor. Thus, metropolitan areas as a whole contained a less-than-proportional share of poor persons. But within those areas, the proportion of poor in central cities was almost double that in the suburbs. Table 1 shows the proportions and number of poor persons in key geographic areas both inside and outside of metropolitan areas for 1966.[2]

Thus, central cities contain a higher proportion of poor persons than the nation as a whole, though a lower proportion than any non-metropolitan areas. In contrast, suburbs contain a substantially smaller proportion of poverty than any other part of the nation.

Within metropolitan areas, the number of poor persons and the incidence of poverty for whites and nonwhites are shown in Table 2.[3] These figures show that the incidence of poverty is higher in central cities than in suburbs for both whites and nonwhites. They also indicate that about 57 percent of the 9.4 million poor persons living in central cities are white, and about 43 percent are nonwhite. In contrast, about 84 percent of the 5.7 million poor suburbanites are white, and only 16 percent are nonwhite. Further, about 62 percent of all the 15.2 million poor persons in metropolitan areas live in central cities.

Another conclusion implicit in Table 2 is that racial segregation in the suburbs does not result solely—or even mainly—from economic-class discrimination. In 1966, the suburbs were 95 percent white. The 5 percent nonwhite fraction contained 21 percent of the metropolitan-area nonwhite population. But suburbs contained 47 percent of the poor white metropolitan-area population. Moreover, poor whites comprised about 7 percent of total suburban population—or more than *all* nonwhites (who comprised 5 percent), even though 72 percent of suburban nonwhites were *not* poor.

Data concerning recent trends in the number of poor persons in metropolitan areas are not available. However, it is reasonable to

[1] The data in this section are mostly from U. S. Department of Commerce, *The Extent of Poverty in the United States, 1959 to 1966,* Current Population Reports, Series P-60, No. 54, Washington, D.C., May 31, 1968. We will hereafter refer to this publication simply as *The Extent of Poverty.*
[2] Mollie Orchansky, "Counting the Poor: Before and After Federal Income-Support Programs," in *Old Age Income Assurance, Part II: The Aged Population and Retirement Income Programs,* a compendium of Papers submitted to the Subcommittee on Fiscal Policy, Joint Economic Committee, Washington, D.C., December 1967. We will hereafter refer to this article simply as "Counting the Poor."

[3] *Ibid.*

TABLE 1

Area	Percentage of Total Population in That Area in Poverty	Number of Poor Persons in That Area (in millions)*
United States	15.4%	29.7
Metropolitan Areas	12.1%	15.2
Central cities	16.2%	9.5
Suburbs	8.6%	5.7
Non-metropolitan Areas	21.4%	14.6
Rural nonfarm	23.1%	7.4
Farm	22.5%	2.4
Urban	18.7%	4.8

* Numerical sub-totals may not add to totals because of rounding.

TABLE 2

| | Poor Whites | | Poor Nonwhites | |
Area	Number (in millions)	As % of All Whites	Number (in millions)	As % of All Nonwhites
Metropolitan Areas	10.2	9.3%	5.0	32.1%
Central cities	5.4	11.7%	4.1	33.3%
Suburbs	4.8	7.5%	0.9	27.3%

assume that these trends are quite similar to those concerning the number of poor people in the nation as a whole.[4] In 1959, there were 38.9 million poor persons in the United States, based upon the definition of poverty explained previously. By 1966, this total had dropped by 9.2 million (or 23.6 percent) to 29.7 million—even after correcting for changes in the price level between those two dates. Since the U.S. population was rising during these seven years, this absolute drop caused an even larger fall (30.3 percent) in the *proportion* of all citizens who are poor —from 22.1 percent in 1959 to 15.4 percent in 1966. Thus, the record-level economic prosperity prevalent during this period, plus various public policies regarding poverty, markedly reduced over-all U.S. poverty—and presumably that in metropolitan areas, too.

However, this reduction in poverty was not experienced to an equal degree by all parts of the population. Poverty among whites dropped from 28.2 million in 1959 to 20.1 million in 1966, or 28.7 percent. But poverty among nonwhites fell from 10.7 million in 1959 to 9.6 million in 1966, or only 10.3 percent. In part, this disparity resulted from much faster population growth among nonwhites. But even the *proportion* of poor in total population declined faster among whites (from 18.0 percent to 11.8 percent, or by 34 percent) than among nonwhites (from 54.6 percent to 41.4 percent, or by 24 percent). Presumably, the same disparity prevailed in metropolitan areas. . . .*

The 15.2 million poor persons in all U.S. metropolitan areas in 1966 can be [distributed among families headed by five types of people.] Using the best available information, and supplementing it with some extrapolation and interpolation where necessary, we have developed estimates for 1966, which are shown in Table 3.[5] . . . The numerical and percentage breakdowns for the metropolitan area as a whole reveal the following significant conclusions:

1. *The largest group of poor persons in metropolitan areas consists of children under 18.* The 6.3 million such children constitute 41.7 percent of all poor persons in these areas. This is about the same as the proportion of all poor children among all poor persons for the United States as a whole.

2. *The second largest group of metropolitan-area poor consists of elderly persons (65 or over).* The 2.876 million persons in this group make up 18.9 percent of all such poor.

3. *The third largest group of metropolitan-area poor is comprised of adults in households headed by a man who is employed but earns a very low income.* The adults in these households total 2.393 million persons, or 15.7 percent of all metropolitan-area poor. If all the children under 18 are distributed to the five other groups (since the children

[4] The following data are from *The Extent of Poverty*.

* [Ed.: Since Downs compiled these data, some more recent figures directly provided much of the information he was inferring. In metropolitan areas, the absolute number of poor people declined from 18.3 million in 1959 to 13.2 million in 1967, and from 17 percent to 10 percent of the total metropolitan population. The number of poor persons living in central cities fell from 11.3 million to 8.3 million over those years, or from 20 percent to 14 percent of total central city residents. However, the number of poor blacks living in the central cities of the 24 largest metropolitan areas (those with more than one million residents) increased slightly between 1959 and 1967, from 2.0 million to 2.1 million; this was primarily a function of the large increases in black population within those cities. See U.S. Bureau of the Census, "Trends in Social and Economic Conditions in Metropolitan Areas," *Current Population Reports*, Series P-23, No. 27, February 7, 1969, pp. 51–67.]

[5] Estimates by the SYSTEMETRICS division of Real Estate Research Corporation based on data from *The Extent of Poverty* and "Counting the Poor."

TABLE 3

MILLIONS OF PERSONS IN POVERTY IN EACH TYPE OF
HOUSEHOLD IN ALL METROPOLITAN AREAS—1966

Type of Household	Adults	Children	Total	Percent of Total
Headed by females under 65	1.974	2.347	4.321	28.4%
Headed by unemployed males under 65	1.137	1.133	2.270	14.9%
Headed by disabled males under 65	0.479	0.477	0.956	6.4%
Headed by employed males under 65	2.393	2.384	4.777	31.4%
Headed by persons 65 or over	2.876	—	2.876	18.9%
All persons	8.859	6.341	15.200	100.0%

actually live in households headed by adults in those groups), then the total number of persons in male-headed households with employed heads is probably about 4.8 million (including children), or over 31 percent of all poor persons in metropolitan areas. Furthermore, some of the female-headed households in poverty also have employed heads with low incomes. Thus, *the poverty of about one-third of all poor persons in metropolitan areas stems from low earnings, rather than unemployment or inability to work caused by disability or old age.* Moreover, low wage jobs are responsible for at least twice as much poverty in metropolitan areas as is unemployment.

TRENDS IN POVERTY

Editor's Supplement

As the Introduction to this chapter of readings suggested, analysts have used varying measures and definitions of poverty. Many definitions of poverty have been proposed, each intended as a refinement of its predecessor.[1] Within each definition, analysts have employed slightly different statistical assumptions or statistical sources to produce real estimates of incidence. For political purposes, writers on poverty have typically chosen to emphasize those measures which best support their conclusions.

It would take volumes, in short, to assess adequately all the discussions of poverty trends in the United States. Rather, this supplement aspires, first, to present a bare skeleton of estimates, most of them rather widely accepted, suggesting some of the less disputed measures in trends in poverty; and, second, to offset some conventional conclusions about poverty which seem to me unjustifiably optimistic. The supplement concentrates on three means of measurement: absolute poverty, relative poverty, and relative wealth.

TRENDS IN ABSOLUTE POVERTY

As described in the Introduction to this chapter, measures of the incidence of absolute poverty count the number of people whose incomes fall below a strictly defined poverty threshold, a

[1] See the bibliography at the end of this chapter for references.

dollar measure of the income necessary for minimum subsistence. For the United States, most analysts now accept for most purposes the Social Security Administration's definition of poverty, which will have reached roughly $3,800 for a family of four in 1970.[2]

Using that definition of poverty, or a rough counterpart, most analysts tend to argue that the United States has experienced an enormous reduction in the incidence of poverty over the past fifty years and especially in the more recent post-World War II era. In the 1969 *Economic Report of the President*, the Council of Economic Advisers concluded, "With the general rise in family incomes in the postwar period, the incidence of poverty . . . has declined sharply."[3] Although the decline is indisputable, its extent and significance should be very carefully questioned.

First, the evidence about long-run trends in poverty is difficult to interpret. The Social Security Administration's definition of poverty has been applied only since 1959. For estimates of poverty trends before 1959, analysts have resorted to a wide variety of definitions and statistics. The most important differences in long-term estimates of poverty involve a single issue: Should estimates reflect our current definitions of poverty, themselves a function of currently available, institutionally determined commodity baskets, or should they incorporate historical standards of poverty, which are based on the quantity and kind of goods necessary for subsistence in earlier periods? The difference between the two definitions produces profoundly varying historical estimates of the poverty population. For instance, Oscar Ornati estimated that roughly 39 percent of the population in 1929 lived below a "subsistence" level defined by 1960 standards, while only 26 percent would have been considered poor by 1929 standards. I personally prefer estimates based on historical—rather than current—standards of poverty, principally because the variety, availability, and quality of goods necessary for minimum subsistence change radically over time. As the poverty population becomes more urban, for instance, the poor must pay for much more of their food, rather than growing it. And as society becomes more bureaucratic, telephones increasingly become a necessity for everyone, including the poor, in order adequately to negotiate bureaucratic channels.

Table 1 presents a set of historical estimates of absolute poverty which I find quite reasonable.[4] They depend on historically determined definitions of poverty, and include two separate definitions of poverty, a "subsistence" definition and an "adequacy" definition. In 1960, the "subsistence" standard for a family of four was $2,660, the "adequacy" standard $4,350. The Social Security Administration's definition for 1960 considered roughly $3,000 as the appropriate poverty standard; the two historical standards therefore envelop the SSA definition. Table 1 suggests four important conclusions about trends in absolute poverty defined by historically determined standards, conclusions about which I find relatively little disagreement in the literature:

1. Between 1929 and the end of World War II, the number of Americans living in absolute poverty declined absolutely, although the singular nature of the Depression and war years makes it difficult to pinpoint exactly when those declines occurred.

2. The percentage of families in poverty declined even more sharply during that period, since the population itself grew.

3. Between 1947 and 1960, the number of poor Americans remained roughly constant, barely dropping by the "subsistence" measure and increasing more substantially by the "adequacy" measure.

4. Since the population grew between 1947 and 1960, this relative constancy in numbers of poor reflected a slight decline in the percentage of Americans who were poor. By the "subsistence" standard, the incidence of poverty decreased from 15 percent to 11 percent; by the "adequacy" standard from 28 percent to 26 percent.[5]

[2] At the time of writing, the most recently published official threshold was the standard for 1968, a weighted national average of $3,531 for a family of four.
[3] *Economic Report of the President*, January, 1969 (Washington, D.C.: U.S. Government Printing Office, 1969), p. 153.
[4] For an intelligent summary of a variety of historical estimates and their problems, see Herman Miller, "Changes in the Number and Composition of the Poor," in Margaret S. Gordon, ed., *Poverty in America* (San Francisco: Chandler, 1965).
[5] This conclusion in particular differs from those based on the current definitions of poverty, which suggest a much more substantial decline in the incidence of poverty. Using the original measure of $3,000 (in

TABLE 1

TRENDS IN ABSOLUTE POVERTY, 1929–1960

| Year | Below "Minimum Subsistence" Level | | Below "Minimum Adequacy" Level | |
	Number of Persons (millions)	Percent of Households	Number of Persons (millions)	Percent of Households
1929	31.8	26	52.2	43
1935–36	33.9	27	57.3	46
1941	21.6	17	41.5	32
1944	12.1	10	19.2	15
1947	21.3	15	38.1	27
1950	20.1	14	41.8	28
1951	18.9	12	37.4	25
1952	17.8	12	33.2	22
1953	22.7	14	35.7	23
1954	23.0	14	42.7	27
1955	19.9	12	45.3	28
1956	18.1	11	42.4	26
1957	17.7	10	42.9	25
1958	22.7	13	49.0	28
1959	21.3	12	46.8	27
1960	19.9	11	46.1	26

NOTE: The marked discontinuity in numbers and percentages between 1941 and 1944 and between 1944 and 1947 is due to the combination of the following factors: the table deals with civilian population only; there was a significant change in income distribution during these years; and there was a large upgrading of budget standards between 1944 and 1947 while between 1941 and 1944 budget standards remained relatively unchanged.

SOURCE: Oscar Ornati, *Poverty Amid Affluence* (N.Y.: The Twentieth-Century Fund, 1966), p. 158.

After 1960, everyone seems to agree on a set of "official" statistics tracing trends in absolute poverty, but many differ substantially in interpreting those statistics. The statistics derive from an application of the SSA poverty definition to Census Bureau distributions of income among American families. Table 2 summarizes figures on the number of poor and the percentage of families in poverty based on these sources. They suggest a very great decline in absolute poverty, from 22.4 percent to 12.8 percent of the population between 1959 and 1968. Government officials have cited these figures with pride. Mollie Orshansky reports, "Eight successive years of plenty had raised incomes to the point where no more than two Americans were counted poor at the end of the period for every three so designated at the beginning."[6]

As noted in the Editor's Introduction, the SSA definition of absolute poverty, like any other, embodies many arbitrary assumptions. Criticisms of the *level* of the SSA definition were mentioned in the Introduction—for instance, that the definition understates the poverty threshold. More important for the purposes of this supplement, the use of the same definition to measure trends throughout the 1960's has also been severely criticized as sketching too rosy a picture of the decline in poverty during the 1960's.

Criticisms of the SSA definition for measuring changes in poverty over time focus primarily

constant dollars), for instance, the Council of Economic Advisers estimated a decline in the precentage of families who were poor from 32 percent in 1947 to 21 percent in 1960. As noted in the text, however, this application backwards of current standards of poverty ignores the substantially increased costs (in constant dollars) of maintaining minimum subsistence standards over time as a result of technology and migration; large flows of black migration from the rural South to the urban North came between 1947 and 1960, for instance, substantially increasing the constant dollar costs to those blacks of reaching a given standard of living. For CEA estimates, see *Economic Report of the President*, January, 1964, p. 57.

[6] Mollie Orshansky, "Progressing Against Poverty," U.S. Department of Health, Education, and Welfare, Social Security Administration, *Research and Statistics Note*, December 10, 1968, p. 1.

TABLE 2
TRENDS IN ABSOLUTE POVERTY, 1959–1968

Year	Number of Poor (in thousands)	Percentage of Population
1959	39,490	22.4
1960	39,851	22.2
1961	39,628	21.9
1962	38,625	21.0
1963	36,436	19.5
1964	36,055	19.0
1965	33,185	17.3
1966	28,510*	14.7*
1967	27,769*	14.2*
1968	25,389*	12.8*

* These numbers incorporate a slight revision in the definition.

SOURCE: U.S. Bureau of the Census, *Current Population Reports*, P-60, No. 68, December 31, 1968, pp. 21, 24.

on its use of a constant food-costs-to-total-income ratio of one to three.[7] This ratio was derived from a Department of Agriculture study made in 1955. By 1960–61, another study had found that the ratio should more properly be approximately one to four. Mollie Orshansky argued against using this study, and stuck to the one-to-three measure.[8] Whatever her arguments, the trends in relative price increases during the 1960's document the need to move toward the later study. Between 1959 and 1968, the price of food at home rose by only by 16.7 percent, while the cost of other commodities and services of special importance to the poor rose much more rapidly. The cost of medical care rose by 45.1 percent, for instance, while the cost of public transportation rose by 38.5 percent and the cost of general services by 34.9 percent. Even the cost of shelter increased by 24.2 percent.[9]

Most reasonably, then, one could suggest moving to a food/income ratio of one to four at least for 1968, if not for 1959. Using the same cost of food in 1968 prices and the one-to-four ratio, one computes a weighted 1968 poverty threshold of $4,548 for a family of four. Applying this definition to the 1968 income distribution, one would estimate that roughly 37.5 million Americans were poor in 1968—not 25.4 million as Table 2 suggests—or roughly 19 percent of the population. Referring back both to Tables 1 and 2, it seems clear that the decline in number of poor Americans would be very slight by these more appropriate standards. After making essentially the same calculations, Michael Harrington concluded, "The fact is that society . . . has taken to celebrating paper triumphs over poverty. . . . By using the erroneous assumptions of the Eisenhower fifties, the government abolished the poverty of 12 million Americans who were still poor."[10]

Table 3 provides official estimates of changes in the composition of the poor. Although these estimates are based on the same assumptions as those in Table 2, there is no reason to believe that the composition of a more accurately estimated poverty population would differ substantially from that suggested by these figures. The principal implications of Table 3 seem clear: increasing proportions of poor families during the 1960's were urban, black, and headed by females.

[7] See especially Michael Harrington, "The Betrayal of the Poor," *Atlantic*, January, 1970, pp. 71–72; and Martin Rein, "Problems in the Definition and Measurement of Poverty," in Louis Ferman *et al.*, eds., *Poverty in America*, rev. ed. (Ann Arbor: University of Michigan Press, 1968), pp. 123–125.
[8] Despite the fact, for instance, that the later study documented a decline in the food/income ratio of 5.6 percent during the 1950's. See Alan Haber, "Poverty Budgets: How Much Is Enough," *Poverty and Human Resources Abstracts*, I, No. 3, 1966, p. 6.
[9] U.S. Bureau of Labor Statistics, "Consumer Price Index, July, 1968."
[10] Harrington, *op. cit.*, pp. 71–72.

TABLE 3

SELECTED CHARACTERISTICS OF FAMILIES BELOW THE
POVERTY LEVEL IN 1968 AND 1959

(Numbers in thousands. Negro data from 1959 from the 1-in-1,000 sample of the 1960 Census)

| | 1968 | | | | 1959 | | | |
| | | | Percent Distribution | | | | Percent Distribution | |
Selected Characteristics	Number Below Poverty Level	Percent Below Poverty Level	Below Poverty Level	Above Poverty Level	Number Below Poverty Level	Percent Below Poverty Level	Below Poverty Level	Above Poverty Level
Sex and Race of Head								
Total	5,047	10.0	100.0	100.0	8,320	18.5	100.0	100.0
Male head	3,292	7.3	65.2	91.9	6,404	15.8	77.0	93.0
Female head	1,755	32.3	34.8	8.1	1,916	42.6	23.0	7.0
White	3,616	8.0	71.6	92.0	6,185	15.2	74.3	94.3
Male head	2,595	6.3	51.4	85.3	4,952	13.3	59.5	88.0
Female head	1,021	25.2	20.2	6.7	1,233	34.8	14.8	6.3
Negro and other races	1,431	28.2	28.4	8.0	2,135	50.4	25.7	5.7
Male head	697	18.9	13.8	6.6	1,452	44.2	17.5	5.0
Female head	734	52.9	14.5	1.4	683	72.0	8.2	0.7
Residence								
Total	5,047	10.0	100.0	100.0	8,320	18.5	100.0	100.0
Nonfarm	4,553	9.5	90.2	95.3	6,624	16.1	79.6	94.3
Farm	494	18.8	9.8	4.7	1,696	44.6	20.4	5.7
Age of Head								
Total	5,047	10.0	100.0	100.0	8,320	18.5	100.0	100.0
14 to 24 years	437	13.2	8.7	6.3	622	26.9	7.5	4.6
25 to 54 years	2,731	8.6	54.1	64.2	4,752	16.0	57.1	68.0
55 to 64 years	678	8.2	13.4	16.6	1,086	15.9	13.1	15.6
65 years and over	1,201	17.0	23.8	12.9	1,860	30.0	22.4	11.8
Size of Family								
Total	5,047	10.0	100.0	100.0	8,320	18.5	100.0	100.0
2 persons	1,831	10.5	36.3	34.2	2,850	19.6	34.2	31.7
3 and 4 persons	1,431	7.1	28.4	41.2	2,420	12.8	29.1	44.9
5 and 6 persons	991	10.2	19.6	19.3	1,793	20.2	21.6	19.3
7 persons or more	794	24.7	15.7	5.3	1,257	45.6	15.1	4.1
Employment Status of Head								
Total	5,047	10.0	100.0	100.0	8,320	18.5	100.0	100.0
Employed	2,410	6.0	47.7	83.1	4,536	12.8	54.5	84.3
Unemployed	146	19.3	2.9	1.3	559	33.1	6.7	3.0
In Armed Forces or not in labor force	2,491	26.0	49.4	15.6	3,225	40.8	38.8	12.7

SOURCE: U.S. Bureau of the Census, *Current Population Reports*, Series P-60, No. 68, December 31, 1969, p. 4.

TRENDS IN RELATIVE POVERTY

The most common measure of relative poverty calculates the percentage of total personal income earned by the poorest fifth among all families. Trends in this measure over time represent relatively unbiased estimates of the effect of changes in the income distribution on those at its bottom end.

With this measure, one finds fairly close agreement about historical trends in relative poverty. First, it appears that relative poverty declined slightly between 1929 and 1947, as Table 4

TABLE 4
PERCENTAGE DISTRIBUTION OF AGGREGATE MONEY INCOME
AMONG FAMILIES 1929–1968

Year	Lowest Fifth	Second Fifth	Third Fifth	Fourth Fifth	Highest Fifth	Top 5%
1929	— 12.5 —		13.8	19.3	54.4	30.0
1935–36	4.1	9.2	14.1	20.9	51.7	26.5
1947*	5.0	11.0	16.0	21.8	46.1	21.3
1947*	5.1	11.8	16.7	23.2	43.3	17.5
1948	5.0	12.1	17.2	23.2	42.5	17.1
1949	4.5	11.9	17.3	23.5	42.8	16.9
1950	4.5	11.9	17.4	23.6	42.7	17.3
1951	4.9	12.5	17.6	23.3	41.8	16.9
1952	4.9	12.2	17.1	23.5	42.2	17.7
1953	4.7	12.4	17.8	24.0	41.0	15.8
1954	4.5	12.0	17.6	24.0	41.9	16.4
1955	4.8	12.2	17.7	23.4	41.8	16.8
1956	4.9	12.4	17.9	23.6	41.1	16.4
1957	5.0	12.6	18.1	23.7	40.5	15.8
1958	5.1	12.4	17.8	23.7	41.0	15.8
1959	5.1	12.1	17.8	23.6	41.4	16.3
1960	4.9	12.0	17.7	23.4	42.1	16.9
1961	4.8	11.7	17.4	23.6	42.5	17.2
1962	5.1	12.0	17.3	23.8	41.7	16.3
1963	5.1	12.1	17.6	23.6	41.6	15.8
1964	5.2	12.0	17.6	24.0	41.1	15.4
1965	5.3	12.1	17.7	23.7	41.3	15.8
1966	5.5	12.3	17.7	23.7	40.7	14.8
1967	5.4	12.2	17.5	23.7	41.2	15.3
1968	5.7	12.4	17.7	23.7	40.6	14.0

* The first estimates for 1947 come from Source (a) below; the second come from (b).

SOURCES:
(a) 1929–1947: U.S. Census Bureau, *Historical Statistics of the United States: Colonial Times to 1957.*
(b) 1947–1964: U.S. Census Bureau, Technical Paper No. 17, *Trends in the Income of Families and Persons in the U.S.: 1947 to 1964.*
(c) 1965–1968: U.S. Census Bureau, *Current Population Reports,* Series P-60, No. 66, December 23, 1969.

shows. The share of the poorest 40 percent increased from 12.5 percent to 16.0 percent of total income. Between 1935–36 and 1947, the share of the poorest fifth barely increased, from 4.1 percent to 5.0 percent. Since World War II, however, relative poverty remained roughly constant in the United States; the share of the poorest fifth fell from 5.0 percent in 1947 to 4.1 percent in 1961, and then rose back to about 5.4 percent in 1967. (Its spurt to 5.7 percent in 1968 should be regarded with caution. One cannot tell yet whether that figure simply represents the effects of inflation.) Table 4 summarizes the shape of the income distribution and the extent of relative poverty between 1929 and 1968, presenting estimates for the shares of aggregate money income among quintiles of families and among the richest 5 percent of families. Table 4 clearly belies a central illusion about the American income distribution, the illusion that it has become much more equal over time as the country has grown more prosperous. Quite simply, it has not.

TRENDS IN RELATIVE WEALTH

The distribution of wealth in the United States has always been much less equal than the distribution of income. Trends in the distribution of wealth are difficult to estimate, since data on its distribution are hard to develop.

One principal source has been available for information about changes in the distribution of wealth. Table 5 summarizes the information developed by Robert Lampman in his pioneering

TABLE 5
SHARE OF PERSONAL SECTOR WEALTH HELD BY TOP
WEALTH-HOLDERS, SELECTED YEARS, 1922–1956

Year	Top 1 Percent of Adults	Top 0.5 Percent of Adults	Top 2 Percent of Adults
1922	31.6	29.8	33.0
1929	36.3	32.4	—
1933	28.3	25.2	—
1939	30.6	28.0	—
1945	23.3	20.9	—
1949	20.8	19.3	—
1953	24.2	22.7	28.5
1956	26.0	25.0	—

SOURCE: Robert J. Lampman, *The Share of Top Wealth-Holders in National Wealth* (New York: National Bureau of Economic Research, 1962), p. 24.

study, *The Share of Top Wealth-Holders in National Wealth*. Again drawn from Lampman's study, Table 6 distributes total wealth among kinds of assets for the years 1922 through 1953.

TABLE 6
CONCENTRATION OF OWNERSHIP OF WEALTH BY TYPE OF ASSET, 1922–1953

Type of Property	1922	1929	1939	1945	1949	1953
Real estate	18.0	17.3	13.7	11.1	10.5	12.5
U.S. Govt. bonds	45.0	100.0	91.0	32.5	35.8	31.8
State and local bonds	88.0	*	*	*	77.0	*
Other bonds	69.2	82.0	75.5	78.5	78.0	77.5
Corporate stock	61.5	65.6	69.0	61.7	64.9	76.0
Cash	—	—	—	17.0	18.9	24.5
Mortgages and notes	—	—	—	34.7	32.0	30.5
Cash, mortgages, and notes	31.0	34.0	31.5	19.3	20.5	25.8
Pension and retirement funds	8.0	8.0	6.0	5.9	5.5	5.5
Insurance	35.3	27.0	17.4	17.3	15.0	11.5
Miscellaneous property	23.2	29.0	19.0	21.4	15.0	15.5
Gross estate	32.3	37.7	32.7	25.8	22.4	25.3
Liabilities	23.8	29.0	26.5	27.0	19.0	20.0
Economic estate	33.9	38.8	33.8	25.7	22.8	27.4

* Sample leads to estimates in excess of 100 percent.

SOURCE: Robert Lampman, *op. cit.*, p. 209. Lampman urges that, because of potential sampling errors, each individual item in this table "be treated with caution," and that the entire table "be used in evaluating any single figure in it." *Loc. cit.*

Lampman's data suggest trends exactly comparable to those in the distribution of money income presented in Table 4. The distribution of wealth becomes slightly more equal from 1922 through the end of World War II, but then less equal from the end of World War II through 1956.

Have the trends Lampman isolated continued since 1956? Only one other source of information permits extrapolation, data developed from the *Survey of Financial Characteristics of*

Consumers for 1963.[11] These data confirm Lampman's figures, pointing to a continuing increase in the concentration of wealth. According to the survey, the wealthiest 0.34 percent of consumer units owned 22 percent of total wealth, and the wealthiest 1.2 percent of consumer units owned 35 percent of total wealth.[12] An interpolation of those figures, according to the shape of the curves calculated by Lampman, suggests that the wealthiest 1 percent owned at least 32 percent of total wealth, an increase of nearly 25 percent in their share between 1956 and 1963. Whether the distribution of wealth followed the pattern of the income distribution in the late 1960's and became slightly more equal again could not be determined at the time of writing. Since corporate profits after taxes had increased from 5.8 percent of gross national income in 1963 to 6.9 percent in 1969, it seems unlikely that the concentration of wealth diminished during the same period.[13]

[11] Dorothy S. Projector and Gertrude S. Weiss, *Survey of Financial Characteristics of Consumers* (Washington, D.C.: Federal Reserve Board, 1966).
[12] *Ibid.*, pp. 136, 151.
[13] U.S. Department of Commerce, *Survey of Current Business*, January, 1964, and January, 1970.

FEDERAL PUBLIC ASSISTANCE PROGRAMS

The President's Commission on Income Maintenance Programs

This brief survey summarizes most of the kinds of criticisms leveled at the recent system of public assistance in this country. Many agreed on the criticisms, leading to formulation of more general income maintenance proposals, and, indirectly, to the Nixon Administration's Family Assistance Plan.

The commission was appointed by President Johnson, although it issued its report under President Nixon. It was chaired by Ben Heineman. The report was called *Poverty Amid Plenty: The American Paradox.*

THE ORIGINS OF EXISTING PROGRAMS

The existing system of income maintenance programs originated in the Depression of the 1930's when millions were unemployed. As it has evolved over 35 years, it has been based on a three-pronged strategy of employment, social insurance, and Public Assistance. In our society the great majority of people obtain their income and social status through employment. The strategy thus assumed that monetary and fiscal policies would guarantee sufficient employment at

SOURCE: *The President's Commission on Income Maintenance Programs, 1969.*

adequate wages for most people, while education and training programs would assist others in developing their employment potential. If there were enough jobs, adequate education would assure young people a place in the labor force. In addition, a family or individual would need protection against changes in the unemployment rate and against the crippling losses of income when the breadwinner retires, dies, or becomes disabled. Finally, Public Assistance would be necessary as a "residual program" to aid those considered unable to enter the labor force.

This analysis gave birth to the Social Security System, which provided partial income replacement to workers and their families upon retirement or death. More recently it has provided income to disabled workers and health insurance for the aged. State Unemployment Insurance programs were encouraged by Federal legislation to keep those who were briefly unemployed from becoming paupers. The Public Assistance system was constructed as an optional State program, jointly financed by all levels of government, to provide aid for particular categories of the poor: the blind, the aged, the disabled, and dependent children and their guardians. Generally, able-bodied male workers were ineligible for assistance under any of these programs. Training and manpower programs have been developed to increase the earning power of employables—but only recently. Other transfer programs have been created for special groups deemed deserving and in need—such as veterans—and a variety of subsidized goods and services—such as housing, health, and food—have been made available to various income groups.

The strategy behind the income maintenance programs of the 1930's was aimed at the lack or loss of employment rather than directly at the problem of poverty. Today, however, the context of poverty and our view of it are vastly different from that era. We have learned to manage the economy so that catastrophic unemployment no longer is a significant threat. While the economic growth of recent decades has multiplied vastly the output of the economy, we have learned that a very substantial portion of poverty and unemployment is chronic, beyond the control of individuals or the influence of rising aggregate demand. The American economy holds the promise of continued economic growth, a growth in which all Americans *could* share, but in which some may not.

In the mid-1960's an effort was made to mount a war on poverty; the main emphasis was placed on programs to expand opportunities. Social service, training, counseling, and related programs grew rapidly. But on the income maintenance front we attempted to fight the war with old weapons. We sought to improve old programs by raising benefits, easing eligibility requirements, and extending coverage. Now every month on the average, 24 million Americans receive Social Security checks, 10 million are helped by Public Assistance, and 1.1 million draw Unemployment

Insurance benefits. But many of the poor remain untouched by any of these programs.

CRITIQUE OF CURRENT PROGRAMS

We have done much to help the poor in our midst. But we have not reassessed our theories or changed our program structure. We have not developed a National program which (1) provides economic security to all those in need, not just those in certain categories, (2) provides aid in an efficient, dignified, consistent fashion, and (3) preserves the incentives that have provided much of our unique growth as a Nation and as individuals. The present income maintenance system has not succeeded for several reasons.

Programs Focus on the Unemployable Poor

One of the major obstacles in the development of an adequate National income maintenance program has been the reluctance to supplement the incomes of employed and *potentially* employable persons. We have assumed that the labor market would provide such persons with sufficient income. But many persons are at least intermittently unemployed due to both cyclical and structural reasons. In 1968, a good year in terms of employment opportunities, monthly unemployment averaged 2.8 million persons. During the course of the year, a total of 11 million persons experienced some period of unemployment.

The major program dealing with the temporarily unemployed but employable person is Unemployment Insurance. However, in 1968 this insurance did not provide compensation for nearly two-thirds of total unemployment because of gaps in coverage and expiration of benefits. Not only are payments limited to a specified length of time, but Unemployment Insurance benefits levels are low. In most States they are below the poverty level for families with children.

The program of Aid to Families with Dependent Children is aimed primarily at families with absent or incapacitated fathers. An Unemployed Father component of this program (AFDC–UF) can provide benefits to households headed by unemployed able-bodied men, but the eligibility requirements are stringent. Only 25 States have chosen to implement this program since its enactment in 1961, and less than 100,000 families are benefiting from it.

In 1966 there were 2.6 million poor families headed by nonaged able-bodied men.[1] These men, and their 10 million dependents, were excluded from Federally-assisted Public Assistance, although a few received locally-financed General Assistance. That exclusion may have weeded out a few potential malingerers and saved a few dollars in the short run, but in the long run it has produced harmful social and economic effects.

The structure of existing welfare programs encourages the real or feigned breakup of poor families, since unemployed or poorly paid fathers generally must leave home if their families are to become eligible for AFDC benefits. AFDC benefits vary by family size and provide a predictable if low income, while wages are subject to the vagaries of a labor market characterized by diminishing need for low-skilled workers.

The employment potential of AFDC recipients—and hence the rationale for treating them separately from working men and women—is unclear. The employability of incapacitated AFDC fathers obviously is limited. The education and skill levels of many AFDC mothers severely limit their employment opportunities in the current job market, especially since the demand for low-skilled workers has been declining. Partially because of this, provisions were enacted recently which allow AFDC recipients to work and still retain part of their grants.

While many AFDC recipients could increase their total income from this provision, the employed poor and the employable poor are put at a further disadvantage vis-à-vis welfare recipients. These work incentives make increasingly frequent the inequitable situation in which a poor family headed by an employed worker may have significantly lower income than an AFDC family which the male head has deserted.

Thus, the lack of a program which aids working men and women not only creates economic disincentives and encourages family breakup; it also is socially divisive, because it is possible for the incomes of some aid recipients to exceed the incomes of low earners of the same family size. The understandable resentment that has developed against welfare programs sometimes has been interpreted to mean that all efforts to assist the poor are resented by the nonpoor and especially by the marginally nonpoor—who have somehow "made it on their own." But malevolence need not be the source of this resentment. Clearly, resentment can spring from a sense of unfairness because programs reverse positions and ranks in the income distribution for no justifiable reason.

The potential for reversing positions in the income distribution exists under the welfare system because we have largely clung to the notion that employment and receipt of welfare must be mutually exclusive. This view is untenable in a world where many employable persons have potential earnings below assistance payment standards. In developing programs to eliminate poverty, exclusion of the employable and the working poor from categories aided by the Government would be justifiable only if all who worked achieved adequate incomes. This is not the case.

Social Insurance Benefits Depend on Earnings

Social insurance programs protect workers and their families against the loss of earnings from some of the hazards of industrial life. Each social insurance plan is built around one of several carefully specified risks that have been identified as potential interruptions to earnings. Old Age, Survivors, and Disability Insurance, Unemployment Insurance, Workmen's Compensation, and other forms of social insurance generally pay benefits based on earning levels before employment is interrupted.

These programs have departed somewhat from strict insurance principles because they also provide benefits to some persons who have contributed little or nothing, and the ratio of benefits to contributions declines as the size of contributions increases. Despite this they do not provide adequate benefit levels for the very poor. They pay adequate benefits only to those with strong labor force attachments and relatively high earnings records. Because eligibility for social insurance is related to employment, it cannot reach effectively those who are poorest—

[1] U.S. Department of Health, Education, and Welfare, Office of the Assistant Secretary (Planning and Evaluation), *Poverty Status Tabulations, 1966.*

those who have fleeting or irregular labor force ties. Moreover, low wage earners will receive low social insurance benefits. The poor worker will become a poor beneficiary. And the system's coverage is still denied to the most poorly paid workers and to the poor who are not employed at all.

Programs Deal Differently with Categories of the Poor

Federal assistance and social insurance programs are designed to provide aid to selected categories of the poor. Programs are designed to cover only certain risks or to benefit only certain groups, such as persons who are old, blind, or disabled, veterans, and farmers.

One consequence of this categorical approach has been the exclusion from Public Assistance of many who are unquestionably in need of help. Part of this exclusion has been by design, as in the case of the employed or employable poor. Other exclusions result because it is impossible to design categories which can cover all cases of need, anticipate the wide variety of human circumstances, and change in response to new manifestations of need. So, we exclude many and arbitrarily include others.

Similarly, it has proven impossible to spell out and devise social insurance programs for all the possible risks to earnings. While old age, death, severe disability, and involuntary unemployment are fairly obvious risks, others —such as partial mental and physical disorders—are not so obvious or so easily covered. It is more difficult to design programs for those who cannot work due to psychological disorders than for those with physical disabilities, although they may be equally unemployable.

Public Assistance Programs Are State and Local Programs

Public Assistance was designed as a residual program for unemployable persons which would wither away in the face of effective employment and social insurance programs. Instead it has grown increasingly larger. Employment has not guaranteed economic security to workers. Social insurance does not cover all workers, or provide adequate benefits to those with inadequate earnings. Thus, the primary burden of providing basic economic security for many Americans has fallen on Public Assistance programs. These responsibilities go far beyond those originally intended for the programs.

Public Assistance provides Federal matching funds for State Public Assistance programs that operate within loose Federal guidelines. The programs exist at State option, and the decision to implement or ignore each of the various cash assistance and service programs is left to the States. The Federal Government can provide financial encouragement for participation, but it cannot compel States to offer these programs.

This local option arrangement has consistently thwarted efforts at National welfare reform. The Federal administering agencies simply have not been able to develop uniform practices and procedures in the 50 States. New administrative guidelines may be issued at the Federal level with comparatively little information on how they will be interpreted and instituted at lower levels of government. The multiplicity of governments involved has made effective policy coordination nearly impossible. The major power of the Department of Health, Education, and Welfare for affecting State programs is the power to withhold funds. But the burden of such action falls primarily on the poor rather than on the State, so such a step never has been taken. Hence, it is not surprising, given resource limitations at the State level, that several of the more significant welfare reforms in recent years have been the result of court decisions rather than National legislation or Federal administrative action.

Clearly, it is somewhat misleading to talk of Public Assistance as a single set of program components, since there are at least 50 State programs with considerable intra-State variations. This multiplicity of programs has several effects: program benefits are generally low; program coverage is restricted; administration is subject to local discretion; and programs differ markedly from State to State in benefit levels, program coverage, and administrative practices.

There are wide differences both in the treatment of needy individuals who fall into the same categories—because of variations in State benefit levels—and in the treatment of needy persons in different categories. Within the Aid to Families with Dependent Children Program, in January 1969 for example, average grants per recipient ranged from $10 per month in Mississippi to $65 in Massachusetts. For Old Age Assistance the range was from $36 per person monthly in Mississippi to $115 in New Hampshire.

Average grants reflect the variety of factors taken into account by States in determining payment levels and eligibility. Among these factors are amounts of income from other sources and family composition. The data below, however, show maximum payments for cases with no other income under the various programs.

Type of Case	Maximum Monthly Payment	
	Low State	High State
AFDC (4 persons)	$55	$332
AFDC (6 persons)	88	423
OAA (1 person)	50	182

These are the amounts that would be paid if the assistance unit had no other income. Six States set maximum AFDC payments for families of four persons at a level almost identical with those for single aged women under OAA. One State actually pays the family less. Differences in benefit levels by State far exceed cost-of-living variations. These programs thus act to accentuate rather than to reduce the sharp differences in living standards across this Nation.

The administration of Public Assistance stands in marked contrast to other public programs such as Social Security and the Federal personal income tax. In both of those, administrators have little discretion in dealing with individuals and follow objective rules and procedures. The determination of eligibility, need, and grant levels in Public Assistance on an individual case-by-case basis gives a great deal of discretion to officials at the lowest level. They have the power to interpret regulations broadly or narrowly, to give or withhold assistance. Moral fitness requirements not characteristic of more impersonally run programs often are imposed, and administration of the program may be harsh and stigmatizing. While such individual discretion is not misused always or perhaps even generally, the *potential* for abuse and the way in which this potential affects Assistance clients compels us to emphasize here the types of problems we have encountered in the system.

Some recipients of Public Assistance have not had sufficient access to information regarding the rules which govern them or the benefits to which they are entitled. In many areas, this information has been systematically kept from them as well as from the general public. Thus more stringent interpretations of regulations may be made in times of budgetary pressure. Various forms of coercion may be used to impose conditions on the recipient of aid. Recipients may be harassed by investigators and their private lives may be exposed to governmental scrutiny seldom found in an open society.

Programs Provide Benefits-in-kind

There are also governmental programs which supplement low incomes through direct provision of goods and services or subsidies to consumers. The major in-kind programs provide subsidized housing, health care, and food.

Federal housing programs reach low and middle-income families through a number of means, including public housing, mortgage insurance, rent supplements, and urban renewal. The limited funds allotted to these programs have restricted their scale. There are approximately 700,000 units of Public Housing, for example, while the number of families potentially eligible as tenants exceeds seven million. These housing programs require a basic financial capability if families are to repay loans—despite very low interest rates—or to pay rent—even subsidized, modest, below-market rents. Hence, many of the poorest families are excluded.

Two major programs assist families and individuals in paying for health care. The Medicare program, enacted in 1965, provides medical care benefits to those over age 65. Part A, under which virtually the entire aged population is enrolled, primarily covers hospitalization. Part B, under which approximately 90 percent of the aged are enrolled, costs enrollees $4 per month for coverage of physicians' fees. Because of deductibles, co-insurance formulas, limitations of benefits, and non-coverage of out-of-hospital drugs, Medicare pays only 40 percent of the health care costs of aged persons.

The Medicaid program assists States in furnishing medical care under State Public Assistance programs. Many of the poor are screened out of the program due to stringent income tests and a variety of State-imposed non-income eligibility requirements. Medicaid covers a minority of low-income persons, and generally does not provide fully for even this group.

Two major programs have been developed to subsidize food for low-income families: the Commodity Distribution program, which provides for direct distribution of certain commodities, and the Food Stamp program, which sells stamps at a discount to low-income families, with which they can purchase food at commercial grocery stores. Both programs give low-income households an opportunity to supplement their diet, but neither program is designed to assure a participating household of an adequate diet. Moreover, non-food needs go unmet. These needs often deter persons from buying stamps since outlays for stamps tie up scarce dollars and may leave families unable to meet other needs, such as rent. Commodity programs have been unpopular with recipients because the range of foodstuffs generally is limited and many of the commodities are not very palatable. Both the Commodity and Food Stamp programs are administered by local welfare departments and are governed by State Public Assistance eligibility requirements which exclude many of the poor. These exclusions, plus the reluctance or inability of many persons to buy the Food Stamps, have limited program beneficiaries to only one-fourth of the poor.

In-kind programs are a response to both the limitations of the market—which cannot always make available an adequate supply of housing and health services at low cost—and the inadequate incomes of the poor. Government efforts thus far have not compensated successfully for either of these factors. Programs have been funded at low levels, and responsibility for their implementation and operation often rests with the States. Hence, not all of the poor have been reached. Many of those who have participated have had their range of choice severely limited by earmarked benefits. In-kind programs aimed to supplement low incomes generally do so less well than direct cash payments. Programs which provide a money income supplement allow for greater consumer choice, and permit greater flexibility of family resources than governmental programs which attempt to set family priorities and allocate family resources. Moreover, we feel that the market system is more efficient at distributing goods and services than direct governmental distribution.

THE COMMON FEATURES OF TRANSFER-BY-TAXATION PLANS

Christopher Green

This selection includes all of Chapter Five of Green's book, *Negative Taxes and the Poverty Problem.* The selection outlines the variables from which one chooses in devising a scheme for generalized income maintenance. It clarifies the nature of that choice, illustrating the interrelationships among minimum allowance level, tax rate, and total program cost. Green is now a professor of economics at McGill University in Canada.

The different types of transfer-by-taxation plans which were discussed in the preceding

SOURCE: *Christopher Green*, Negative Taxes and the Poverty Problem. *Copyright © 1967, by The Brookings Institution, 1775 Massachusetts Avenue, N.W., Washington, D.C.*

chapter are basically similar. Furthermore, all transfer-by-taxation contains three basic variables: (1) a guaranteed minimum level of income that varies with family size or family composition or both; (2) a tax rate or rates applied against a tax base; and (3) a breakeven level of income where the tax liability equals the allowance guarantee. Any two of these variables determine the outcome of the third.

THE BASIC VARIABLES

The interrelationships of these three variables of transfer-by-taxation can be clarified by simple illustrations. If a family is guaranteed $3,000 and a tax rate of 50 percent is applied against the family's income (excluding the guaranteed allowance), the breakeven level of income will be $6,000 for the family. That is, at $6,000 the family's income tax liability of $3,000 (.50 times $6,000) equals the guaranteed allowance of $3,000. Suppose it were desirable to make the family's breakeven level of income $3,000 and to guarantee $1,500. The transfer-by-taxation tax rate would be 50 percent—or some combination of rates which averaged 50 percent on $3,000 of family income. Finally, a breakeven level of income of $3,000 and a 25 percent tax rate would mean an income guarantee of $750 (.25 times $3,000). Only if the guarantee is $750 is the net allowance[1] reduced to zero by a flat 25 percent tax rate when income reaches $3,000.[2]

Once it becomes clear that the essentials of transfer-by-taxation can be reduced to three basic variables, it is easy to understand why there is, in principle, no difference between the Rhys-Williams social dividend plan, the Lampman or Friedman negative rates taxation plans, and the Tobin plan which is a cross between the two types.[*] The only important difference between these plans lies in the magnitude of the guaranteed minimum income or allowance, the level of the tax rate, and the breakeven level of income.

All the social dividend schemes described in Chapter IV begin with the choice of a guaranteed minimum income (which varies with family size) and the choice of an income tax rate which will finance the plan. These choices determine the magnitude of the third variable, the breakeven level of income. In simple algebraic terms:

[1] The net allowance is equal to the guaranteed allowance less the tax on the family's income.
[2] Throughout this discussion, "income" refers to the family's income excluding the allowance.
[*] [Ed.: For details of these and other plans, see the Supplement following this selection.]

$$(1) \qquad Y_g/t_s = R$$

where

Y_g = guaranteed minimum income,
t_s = social dividend tax rate,
R = the breakeven level of income—or the level of income at which the net allowance is reduced to zero.

The righthand side of equation 1 may be thought of as the "outcome" of sociopolitical decisions involving the magnitudes on the lefthand side of the equation. This does not mean that in social dividend taxation the breakeven level of income, R, is not a matter of concern for policy makers. It simply means that social dividend taxation is characterized by an emphasis upon a guaranteed minimum income and a tax schedule which reduces the guarantee to zero at some point. This is true of the Tobin plan which differs from social dividend taxation in its more modest proportions and in its failure to specify how the cost is to be financed. It is also true of tax credit schemes which would convert the personal exemptions under present tax systems into a credit financed by a tax on income.

The emphasis in negative rates taxation is somewhat different. A breakeven level of income is first determined. In the case of Friedman's plan, the breakeven level of income is the value of exemptions and deductions allowed a family; for the plan by Lampman it is the family's poverty line. When the breakeven level of income is combined with a negative tax schedule, a guaranteed minimum income level is determined. The equation for negative rates taxation might be written as:

$$(2) \qquad Rt_n = Y_g,$$

where

t_n = the negative tax rate (or rates)

and R and Y_g are the same as in equation 1 above.

The negative rates taxation equation might also have been written as:

$$(3) \qquad Y_g/R = t_n.$$

The emphasis here is upon a breakeven level of income and a guaranteed minimum income. The outcome is the negative tax rate. It is difficult to say whether proponents of a negative rates plan, after having chosen a breakeven level of income, put more empha-

TABLE 1

ALLOWANCE FOR A FAMILY OF FOUR UNDER TWO TRANSFER-BY-TAXATION PLANS

Type of Plan	Family's Income Before Allowance				
	$ 0	$ 500	$1,000	$2,000	$3,000
Negative Rates Taxation:					
(1) Poverty income gap or unused EX-MSD*	$3,000	$2,500	$2,000	$1,000	$ 0
(2) Allowance based on 40% of poverty gap or unused EX-MSD	1,200	1,000	800	400	0
Social Dividend:					
(3) Basic allowance guarantee of $1,200 (equal to 40% of poverty line)	1,200	1,200	1,200	1,200	1,200
(4) Tax liability with 40% income tax rate	0	200	400	800	1,200
(5) Net allowance, (3)–(4)	1,200	1,000	800	400	0

* Both the Lampman poverty line and the value of exemptions and minimum standard deductions (EX-MSD) are $3,000 for a family of four.

sis on the negative tax rate or upon the guaranteed minimum income. The answer probably is "both equally."

The tax base, at first glance, would seem to differentiate negative rates taxation from social dividend taxation or the Tobin plan. In negative rates taxation, the tax base is the gap between some "standard"—such as the value of personal exemptions and minimum standard deductions (hereafter EX-MSD) allowed a family or the family's poverty line—and the family's income. In social dividend taxation and in the Tobin plan the tax base is the family's income before allowance. In fact, this difference is superficial. For example, it is easy to show that a negative rates plan which fills X percent of a family's poverty income gap is the same as a plan which guarantees a minimum income equal to X percent of the family's poverty line and taxes the family's income at an X percent rate. This is shown in Table 1. The first plan shows what happens under a typical negative rates taxation plan with a negative tax rate of 40 percent applied against the family's poverty income gap or the family's unused EX-MSD. The second resembles a social dividend plan in that it guarantees a family of four $1,200 (40 percent of $3,000) and taxes the family's income at a 40 percent rate. Lines 2 and 5 show that both plans, given the family's income, produce identical results.[3]

[3] The similarity between negative rates taxation

THE SIMILARITY OF TRANSFER-BY-TAXATION AND OTHER MINIMUM INCOME PLANS

It is interesting to consider whether any plan which guarantees a minimum income differs, in principle, from a transfer-by-taxation plan. That is, if a plan completely unrelated to the tax system is devised, will it not in substance be the same as a transfer-by-taxation plan? The answer would seem to be yes. If, as an example, some federal bureau were established with the duty of assuring all families a minimum income, it would necessarily have to implement a plan consisting of a "tax rate" and a breakeven level of income in addition to the guaranteed minimum. This is because the bureau would be forced to decide on a rate at which the guaranteed allowances are reduced as a family's income rises. Once this is determined, the rate (or rates) in conjunction with the guarantee will determine a breakeven level of income. In addition, the bureau would have to secure financing in some form, even though the means of financing might be completely unrelated to the plan itself.

Some writers, as noted in Chapter IV, have proposed raising the income of families with income deficiencies to some predetermined level.[4] This effectively means equating the

and social dividend taxation is further illustrated by comparing their allowance formulas. . . .

[4] See Edward E. Schwartz, "A Way to End the

TABLE 2
THE SCHWARTZ PLAN*

Earned Income	Tax on Income (percent)	Allowance	Total Income
$ 0– 999	60	$3,000–2,400	$3,000–3,399
1,000–1,999	70	2,399–1,700	3,399–3,699
2,000–2,999	80	1,699– 900	3,699–3,899
3,000–3,999	90	899– 0	3,899–3,999
4,000–4,499	100	0	4,000–4,499

* Guarantees a minimum income of $3,000 to all families.

SOURCE: Edward Schwartz, "A Way to End the Means Test," *Social Work*, Vol. 9 (July 1964), page 9.

minimum income guarantee and the break-even level of income. The outcome is a 100 percent tax rate on the negative taxable income of allowance recipients. Sometimes modifications are made in order to mitigate the potential disincentive to work produced by a 100 percent tax on earned income. One modification takes the form of an allowance premium equal to some percentage of the family's earned income.[5] If a family is guaranteed $3,000 and has earnings of $2,000, it might be allowed $1,000 (which would fill the gap) plus some percentage of its earned income. The difficulty with this modification is that it produces what tax experts call a "notch" problem. That is, it is possible for some families, whose before-allowance income made them worse off than some other families, to have a higher after-allowance income than that of previously better-off families. For example, suppose two four-member families have, respectively, $2,000 and $3,200 of income before an allowance is made.[6] Assume the guaranteed minimum income for a four-person family is $3,000. The $3,200 family does not qualify for any allowance because its before-tax income is above the guarantee. The $2,000 family qualifies for a $1,000 allowance plus a

premium of, say, 20 percent of its $2,000 earnings. Its after-tax and after-allowance income is $3,400.

This notch problem can be remedied by extending eligibility for receiving an allowance to families whose before-tax income is above the guaranteed minimum income level. Schwartz, one of the proponents of the fill-the-gap approach, has suggested such a remedy. Under his modified plan, outlined in Table 2, as earned income rises, the allowance falls until a breakeven point is reached at $4,000. This plan, aside from the progressivity in the tax schedule, is equivalent to a social dividend plan with a $3,000 guarantee and a 75 percent tax rate on income below the breakeven level of income.

In sum, simply filling the gap is equivalent to a negative rates plan with a 100 percent negative tax rate. If the disincentive effect of such a plan is to be avoided without producing a notch problem, the fill-the-gap plan resembles a social dividend plan. The same analysis may be applied to public assistance, social insurance, and family allowance programs designed to guarantee a minimum income.[7] Although this study is confined to transfer-by-taxation plans, such a limitation is not necessary except to the extent that it reduces the number of specific plans to be examined.

Means Test," *Social Work*, Vol. 9 (July 1964), pp. 3–12; Robert Theobald, ed., *Free Men and Free Markets* (New York: C. N. Potter, 1963), Appendix, pp. 192–197.
[5] This approach is taken by Theobald, *op. cit.*
[6] It is assumed for simplicity that the income of these families is composed solely of earnings.

[7] A recent guaranteed minimum income proposal appears in U. S. Department of Health, Education, and Welfare, Advisory Council on Public Welfare, *Having the Power, We Have the Duty* (June 1966).

ALTERNATIVE INCOME MAINTENANCE PROPOSALS

Editor's Supplement

The preceding selection outlined the common characteristics of income maintenance, or transfer-by-taxation schemes.[1] It suggested that three principal choices surround a decision about an appropriate program—the level of basic (zero-income) allowance, the tax rate on additional earned income, and the total cost of the program. A choice of specific values for any two of those parameters will determine the value for the third for any given income distribution.

Many different proposals have been made for income maintenance programs. I have summarized five different proposals here to illustrate the ways in which choices about the determinant variables differ from program to program. At the time of writing (July, 1970), it seems impossible to predict the exact form in which the Nixon Administration's Family Assistance Plan will be enacted by Congress (if it is indeed passed). I have summarized the version of the plan which the Administration submitted to Congress. I have also summarized proposals by Milton Friedman, an early suggestion by James Tobin, a proposal by the President's Commission on Income Maintenance Programs, and a later proposal by Tobin. The features of each program described include (a) the basic allowance for a family of four with zero income; (b) the tax rate on additional earned income; (c) the break-even point where the transfer from the government falls to zero; and (d) the estimated additional federal cost (beyond currently mandated public assistance costs) for the late 1960's. Each of the proposals described presumes that all families, headed by either male or female, would be eligible if family earned income fell below the break-even point. The Nixon proposal included a provision (extremely difficult to enforce) that those able to work must accept jobs in order to receive assistance. The Friedman proposal suggested suspending all other social services to the poor, on his (typically conservative) assumption that income maintenance would provide enough money for the individual to buy such services on the market; all other proposals would continue present social services to those who need them, simply effecting a separation between income maintenance and social service.

	ZERO-INCOME ALLOWANCE (family of four)	TAX RATE ON ADDITIONAL EARNED INCOME	BREAK-EVEN POINT (family of four)	ADDITIONAL FEDERAL COST
Nixon Family Assistance Plan[2]	$1,500	50%	$3,000	$2 billion
Friedman's Negative Income Tax Proposal[3]	$1,500	50%	$3,000	$2 billion
Tobin's Early Proposal[4]	$1,600	33⅓%	$4,800	$9 billion
President's Commission on Income Maintenance[5]	$2,400	50%	$4,800	$6 billion
Tobin's Later Proposal[6]	$3,200	50%	$6,400	$17 billion

[1] Another form of income maintenance was at times suggested in the 1960's but was eventually discarded —a scheme called children's allowances. This would provide a fixed allowance per child to all families, not just those of the poor. It was usually suggested to avoid political resistance from non-poor families to an increase in assistance to the poor. It eventually dropped from public discussion because it was a very inefficient way to provide assistance to the poor. For a discussion of the program and a brief for its adoption, see James Vadakin, *Children, Poverty and Family Allowances* (N.Y.: Basic Books, 1968).
[2] Based on *The New York Times*, various issues, 1970. Later, after the Nixon plan was submitted to Congress, it decided to include in the basic allowance a provision that everyone could receive the full statutory allowance of food stamps from the Department of Agriculture. For a family of four, this would typically provide about $800–$900 a year in extra monetary assistance. This made the Nixon proposal

very similar to the Income Maintenance Commission Proposal, the fourth in the table, but the commission was appointed by a Democratic President, so the Nixon plan retained the food stamp equivalent instead of converting it to cash; this way, it could differentiate its basic proposal from a "Democratic proposal."

3 Under Friedman's proposal, a family's total exemptions and standard deductions would be retained under present income tax rules. The difference between allowed exemptions and deductions ($3,000 for most families of four) and earned income would be computed, and the family would receive 50 percent of the difference. Thus, the program would be exactly the same as the Nixon plan (in its original version) for that family size. See Milton Friedman, *Capitalism and Freedom* (Chicago: University of Chicago Press, 1962).

4 From James Tobin, "Improving the Economic Status of the Negro," *Dædalus,* Fall, 1965, pp. 889–895.

5 See the commission's report, *Poverty Amid Plenty* (Washington: U.S. Government Printing Office, 1969), Appendix C.

6 See James Tobin, "Raising the Income of the Poor," in Kermit Gordon, ed., *Agenda for the Nation* (Washington: Brookings, 1968), pp. 105–114.

TAXATION AND INEQUALITY

Gabriel Kolko

This selection provides some of the historical evidence which radicals use to
argue that the government does not seek to redistribute income from the rich
to the poor. Kolko sketches the origins of heavily progressive taxation in the
New Deal, and shows that the progressivity of the tax system is primarily
an illusion. The wealthy are typically able to evade most of the heavy burden of
statutory tax rates for upper income brackets. Kolko's book, *Wealth and Power
in America,* from which this has been reprinted, was published in 1962.
More recent figures supporting Kolko's earlier data are summarized in the
Editor's Supplement following this selection.

Kolko teaches history at the State University of New York at Buffalo, and
has written several other books about twentieth-century America.

It is widely believed that, as Ernest van
den Haag and Ralph Ross put it, "the effect
of progressive income taxes in diminishing the
income of the upper brackets is too plain to
need rehearsing."[1] But the impact of Federal
income taxes on the actual distribution of
wealth has been minimal, if not negligible.
The desire to avoid the burden of high taxes
has given rise to new factors in the distribution of wealth, which have so complicated the
picture that a change in form has been mistaken by many for a basic change in content.
A careful study of the topic will hardly sustain this illusion.

Contrary to common belief, heavy taxation of upper-income groups did not begin
with the advent of the New Deal; it began
only with the approach of United States involvement in World War II. Higher income
taxation came as a response of the Roosevelt
Administration to world events and not as a
result of a conscious commitment to a social
policy of reducing inequalities in the distribution of wealth.

As a matter of historical record, the New
Deal was not seriously interested in taxation
as a means of income equalization—despite
its frequent assertions that it was. Roosevelt
actively supported the Revenue Act of 1934,
but his support for the somewhat stronger
1935 Act was equivocal and was finally ob-

tained only because he feared the growing
appeal of Huey Long's "Share-the-Wealth
Clubs" and attacks by progressives in Congress. Even so, in a number of important
areas, the provisions of the two Acts were
hardly designed to redistribute wealth effectively or reduce the capital accumulations of
the rich. The estate-tax rates, which the 1932
Act set at 2 percent for each bracket above
$70,000, were raised to 3 percent on amounts
above $70,000 and up to $4.5 million, after
which the rate dropped to 2 percent. The
corporate income tax was raised from 12 percent to 15 percent in 1936, to 19 percent in
1939; not until 1942 was it raised to 40
percent.[2]

Before 1941, the New Deal practice on
personal-income taxation was, despite its difference in verbiage, essentially a continuation of that of the Hoover Administration. In
1929 and 1940, when the national personal
income was almost the same, Federal receipts from personal income taxes were virtually identical—$1,323 billion in 1929 and
$1,393 billion in 1940. But in 1941, the Fed-
eral personal income tax, increased because
of the growing military budget, produced
revenue one-half more than in 1940, although
personal income increased only 14 percent.
In 1944, personal income was twice the 1940
level, but the tax yield was twelve times as
great.[3] While much of this increased burden

SOURCE: *Gabriel Kolko, "Taxation and Inequality,"
from* Wealth and Power in America, *rev. ed.,
Frederick A. Praeger, Inc.*

[1] Ralph Ross and Ernest van den Haag, *The
Fabric of Society: An Introduction to the Social
Sciences* (N.Y.: Harcourt, Brace, 1957), p. 398.

[2] Roy G. and Gladys C. Blakey, *The Federal Income Tax* (New York: Longmans, Green & Co.,
1940), pp. 366–73; and Louis Eisenstein, 'The
Rise and Decline of the Estate Tax,' *Federal Tax
Policy for Economic Growth*, p. 830 ff.

[3] Office of Business Economics, *National Income,*

fell on the upper-income groups—enough to stimulate their search for new ways to avoid the highest tax brackets—the major weight fell on income groups that had never before been subjected to the income tax.

Thus, the ironic fact is that the extension of the income tax to middle- and low-income classes was the only original aspect of the New Deal tax policy.

TAXATION: THEORY AND PRACTICE

The feature of the income-tax structure that purportedly has had a major impact is the extremely steep tax rates (up to 91 percent) on the very largest incomes. Actually, the resulting varied and ingenious methods of tax avoidance have substantially lessened the importance of these theoretically high rates.

Since 1941, members of the economic elite have attempted to receive their income in nontaxable forms or to postpone receiving it until retirement, when they will be in lower income brackets. There has been a strong downward shift in income-bracket levels, with an increasing proportion in the $25,000–$100,000 bracket, and in some years there has been an absolute drop in the number of returns reporting more than $100,000. More important, however, has been the trend away from the forms of income subject to high tax rates (salaries, wages, and certain types of property income) and toward tax-free interest, capital gains, and many other forms of income taxed at much lower rates or not at all. The proportionate importance of these forms of income to total income rises sharply in every income category over $10,000 a year.

Under Roosevelt, up to 1941, the actual, as opposed to the theoretical, tax rates on very high incomes were not very different from those under Herbert Hoover. Theoretically, the statutory tax is levied on straight income, none of which is derived from capital gains or other sources taxed at lower rates, from which no deductions are made, and no evasion attempted. In 1932, the highest possible tax rate on incomes of $1 million and up was 54 percent, but only 47 percent was actually collected. In 1938, the maximum theoretical tax rate had increased to 72 percent, but only 44 percent was collected. By

1954 (Washington, D.C.: Government Printing Office, 1954), p. 471.

1957, the highest possible tax rate was 91 percent, but only 52 percent was collected.[4] As J. Keith Butters, Harvard economist, has written in his major study of taxation and the rich, *Effects of Taxation—Investment by Individuals* (1953), "By far the most striking and significant feature . . . is the large excess of theoretical over actual tax rates on upper bracket individuals when these rates are computed for income inclusive of all net capital gains."[5]

The income of the richest tenth is reduced less than 10 percent by Federal income taxes. And, of course, the other tenths also show a net reduction in earnings after income taxes. Thus, it should come as no surprise that the distribution of income by tenths after Federal income taxes, shown in Table 2, is practically the same as the distribution before taxes [shown in] Table 1. . . . The slight changes in income-shares effected by the income tax have benefited income-tenths in the upper half almost as frequently as income-tenths in the lower half. These fundamental facts have been ignored by those who interpret the tax system on the basis of their arbitrary preconceptions rather than on the basis of its actual effects.

THE REVOLUTION IN TAXATION

Now we see that progressive taxation of incomes has not been applied to the economic elite sufficiently to change the distribution of income-shares, and that although the economic elite has been subject to heavier Federal income taxation since 1941, the same factor that stimulated a higher tax rate on the rich also produced, for the first time in American history, permanent and significant income taxation of low- and middle-income earners.

In 1939, only 4.0 million families or persons were subject to Federal income taxation; in 1940, 7.5 million; in 1941, 17.6 million; in 1944, 42.4 million; and in 1957, 46.9 million.[6] Similarly, the share of the national

[4] All calculations from data in Bureau of Internal Revenue, *Statistics of Income for 1939, Part I* (Washington: G.P.O., 1943), pp. 63–64, and *Statistics of Income—Individual Income Tax Returns for 1957* (Washington: G.P.O., 1959), p. 20.
[5] J. Keith Butters et al., *Effects of Taxation—Investment by Individuals* (Boston: Harvard Business School, 1953), p. 85.
[6] Daniel Creamer, *Personal Income During Business Cycles* (Princeton, N.J.: Princeton U Press,

TABLE 1
PERCENTAGE OF NATIONAL PERSONAL INCOME,
BEFORE TAXES, RECEIVED BY EACH INCOME-TENTH*

	Highest Tenth	2nd	3rd	4th	5th	6th	7th	8th	9th	Lowest Tenth
1947	33.5	14.8	11.7	9.9	8.5	7.1	5.8	4.4	3.1	1.2
1948	30.9	14.7	11.9	10.1	8.8	7.5	6.3	5.0	3.3	1.4
1949	29.8	15.5	12.5	10.6	9.1	7.7	6.2	4.7	3.1	0.8
1950	28.7	15.4	12.7	10.8	9.3	7.8	6.3	4.9	3.2	0.9
1951	30.9	15.0	12.3	10.6	8.9	7.6	6.3	4.7	2.9	0.8
1952	29.5	15.3	12.4	10.6	9.1	7.7	6.4	4.9	3.1	1.0
1953	31.4	14.8	11.9	10.3	8.9	7.6	6.2	4.7	3.0	1.2
1954	29.3	15.3	12.4	10.7	9.1	7.7	6.4	4.8	3.1	1.2
1955	29.7	15.7	12.7	10.8	9.1	7.7	6.1	4.5	2.7	1.0
1956	30.6	15.3	12.3	10.5	9.0	7.6	6.1	4.5	2.8	1.3
1957	29.4	15.5	12.7	10.8	9.2	7.7	6.1	4.5	2.9	1.3
1958	27.1	16.3	13.2	11.0	9.4	7.8	6.2	4.6	3.1	1.3
1959	28.9	15.8	12.7	10.7	9.2	7.8	6.3	4.6	2.9	1.1

* In terms of "spending units."

SOURCE: Previously unpublished data for 1947–58 are reproduced by permission of the Board of Governors of the Federal Reserve System, and data for 1959 by permission of the Survey Research Center.

TABLE 2
PERCENTAGE OF NATIONAL PERSONAL INCOME
RECEIVED BY EACH INCOME-TENTH AFTER FEDERAL INCOME TAXES

	Highest	2nd	3rd	4th	5th	6th	7th	8th	9th	Lowest
1947	31(−2)*	15	12	10	9	8(+1)	6	5(+1)	3	1
1949	28(−2)	15	13(+1)	11	9	8	7(+1)	5	3	1
1950	27(−2)	15	13	11	10(+1)	8	7(+1)	5	3	1
1951	28(−3)	15	13(+1)	11(+1)	9	8	7(+1)	5	3	1
1952	27(−3)	15	13(+1)	11	10(+1)	8	7(+1)	5	3	1
1953	28(−3)	15	12	11(+1)	9	8	7(+1)	5	4(+1)	1
1954	27(−2)	15	13	11	9	8	7(+1)	5	4(+1)	1
1955	27(−2)	16	13	11	10(+1)	8	6	5(+1)	3	1

* Numbers in parentheses indicate change in percentage points from before-tax income.

SOURCE: Bureau of the Census, *Statistical Abstract of the United States—1957* (Washington, D.C.: Government Printing Office, 1957), p. 309. These data, collected by the Survey Research Center, include capital gains but exclude income-in-kind.

personal income subject to Federal income taxes was 10 percent in 1939, 24 percent in 1941, and 43 percent in 1957.[7] The net effect, since there was a fairly stable distribu-

1956), p. 153; Bureau of Internal Revenue, *Statistics of Income—Individual Returns for 1957*, p. 23.
[7] Joseph A. Pechman, 'What Would a Comprehensive Individual Income Tax Yield?' *Tax Revision Compendium*, I. 258.

tion of income over that period, was to tax lower- and middle-income classes that had never been taxed before. This was done by reducing the minimum tax exemption and extending the tax scale. In 1957, 66 percent of all reported incomes were taxed at the base rate of 20 percent. For married couples, taxable income began at $3,500 in 1929, $2,500 in 1935 and 1936, $1,500 in 1941, $1,000 in 1944, and $1,200 from 1948 on.

Inflation sharply increased this trend by reducing the value of both incomes and exemptions, and its influence continues. The percentage of Federal revenue yielded by personal-income taxes increased from a scant 9 percent in 1916 to 18 percent in 1941, 41 percent in 1946, and 53 percent in 1960. At the same time, the percentage of Federal revenue yielded by corporate-profits taxes grew from 8 percent in 1916 to 26 percent in 1941, and 30 percent in 1946, and fell to 28 percent in 1960.[8]

In this process of incorporating more and more of the American population into the Federal income tax system, a moderate degree of progressive taxation has been maintained. The income tax is practically the only major tax that is not basically regressive. Nevertheless, the income tax paid by the average family in the lowest income-fifth—in 1957, amounting to 3.3 percent of their income—constitutes a greater hardship for those living on an emergency budget than does the tax burden of 13.7 percent paid in the same year by the average family in the richest income-fifth.[9]

The basic tax rate on taxable income (i.e., income after all deductions for dependents, charitable donations, medical expenses, etc.) begins at 20 percent. A major proportion of legitimate expenses is unclaimed annually, and most of this can, we know, be attributed to low- and middle-income families.[10] Fewer than 10 percent of those earning less than $2,000 take credit for deductible expenditures beyond their dependents and the flat 10 percent allowed on the short form.[11] This failure is due in large part to the complexity of filling out a "long form" for deductions. Deductions, it should be pointed out, must be quite high before they will save a family anything. For example, a family that can claim no deductions for interest, state taxes, donations, casualty losses, or the like must have medical expenses amounting to at least 13 percent of its total income before it will save anything.

Joint-filing provisions for husbands and wives, intended to lower their tax burden, were of no benefit in 70 percent of the joint returns filed in 1957, which were from low- and middle-income groups.[12] In the upper-income brackets, however, the joint return can be of enormous benefit. On an income of $35,000, it can realize a peak saving of 40 percent of the tax bill.[13]

THE COMBINED IMPACT OF ALL TAXES

Most recent commentators who have credited the Federal income tax with redistributing income have ignored the fact that it is only one of a number of taxes—and the only one that is in some measure progressive. Therefore, any discussion of distribution of income after taxes must consider the consequences of all taxes.

In general, local and state taxes are regressive. More than half—59 percent in 1958—of all state tax revenues come from sales taxes. About one-half of the expenditures of an average spending unit earning a cash income of less than $1,000 a year are subject to general sales or excise taxes, but only one-third of the expenditures of those earning $10,000-plus are so taxed.[14] In effect, corporations present the public with additional hidden taxes. The corporation income tax is, as the *Wall Street Journal* puts it, "treated by the corporations as merely another cost which they can pass on to their customers."[15] It has been variously estimated that one-third to one-half of this tax is shifted to the consumers. Furthermore, at least two-thirds of

[8] William Crum *et al.*, *Fiscal Planning for Total War* (New York: National Bureau of Economic Research, 1942), pp. 172, 174; *Economic Report of the President—1958*, p. 174; Tax Foundation, *Reexamining the Federal Corporation Income Tax* (New York: Tax Foundation, 1958), p. 22; *The Budget of the U.S. Government for the Fiscal Year Ending June 30, 1960* (Washington: G.P.O., 1959), p. M-12.
[9] Selma F. Goldsmith, 'Income Distribution by Size—1955–58', *Survey of Current Business*, April 1959, p. 16.
[10] C. Harry Kahn, 'Personal Expense Deductions', *37th Annual Report, National Bureau of Economic Research*, 1957, p. 49.
[11] Daniel M. Holland and C. Harry Kahn, 'Comparison of Personal Taxable Income', in U.S. Senate, Jt. Committee on the Economic Report, *Federal Tax Policy for Economic Growth and Stability*, 84th Cong., 1st Sess. (Washington: G.P.O., 1955), 331–32.

[12] Bureau of Internal Revenue, *Statistics of Income—1957*, p. 37; Lawrence H. Seltzer, 'The Individual Income Tax', *39th Annual Report, National Bureau of Economic Research, 1959*, p. 74.
[13] Holland & Kahn, *op. cit.*, p. 333.
[14] Tax Foundation, *Federal Excise Taxes* (New York: Tax Foundation, 1956), p. 47.
[15] *Wall Street Journal*, 5 May 1958, p. 1.

American corporations add all payroll-tax costs to their prices.[16]

The Tax Foundation has calculated actual taxes paid as a percentage of income for all income classes in 1958 (see Table 3). Its figures show that state and local taxes are regressive, and that all Federal taxes combined, although tending to be progressive, fall much more substantially on the low-income classes than is generally realized. Included in its calculations are all local, state, and Federal personal-income taxes; inheritance, estate, and gift taxes; corporate-profit taxes (it assumes that one-half of this is shifted to the public); excise and sales taxes; customs and property taxes. Excluded are the highly regressive social-insurance taxes, which take 7.3 percent of the total income of those earning $2,000 or less but only 1.5 percent in the $15,000-plus class.

These Tax Foundation data indicate that the combined American tax system is scarcely "progressive" and hardly in accord with the image of it nourished by most social scientists and students of contemporary America.[17] If, despite innumerable loopholes, the Federal income tax has introduced a moderately progressive but greatly misunderstood and overemphasized taxation, the Federal excise and customs—and most major local and state —taxes have seriously lessened its impact. The income tax paid by the lower-income classes is, for the most part, money that would otherwise go for essential personal and family needs; in this light, the tax burden is substantially heavier for the lower-income classes than for the higher-income classes.

WELFARE AND INCOME INEQUALITY

Theoretically, it would be possible for the revenues from regressive taxation to be directed to welfare expenditures for lower-income groups, and for the inequality of income distribution to be reduced thereby to a significant extent. This has actually been achieved, in the eyes of a number of proponents of the income-redistribution thesis. "Through a combination of patchwork revisions of the system—tax laws, minimum wage laws, subsidies and guarantees and regulations of various sorts, plus labor union pressures and new management attitudes— we had repealed the Iron Law of Wages," wrote Frederick Lewis Allen in *The Big Change*. "We had brought about a virtually automatic redistribution of income from the well-to-do to the less well-to-do."[18] The plausibility of this thesis has only been strengthened by the attacks of conservatives on the alleged "welfare state" created by the Roosevelt Administration.

However, this viewpoint is not sustained by a careful examination of the motives for the revisions in the tax structure: The reason

TABLE 3
PERCENTAGE OF 1958 TOTAL INCOME PAID IN FEDERAL, STATE, AND LOCAL TAXES,* BY INCOME CLASS

Income Class (in dollars)	Share of Taxes (in percent)		
	Federal	State and Local	Total†
0– 2,000	9.6	11.3	21.0
2,000– 4,000	11.0	9.4	20.4
4,000– 6,000	12.1	8.5	20.6
6,000– 8,000	13.9	7.7	21.6
8,000–10,000	13.4	7.2	20.6
10,000–15,000	15.1	6.5	21.6
15,000–plus	28.6	5.9	34.4
Average	16.1	7.5	23.7

* Social-insurance taxes are not included.
† Because of rounding, items do not always add up to totals.

SOURCE: Tax Foundation, *Allocation of the Tax Burden by Income Class* (New York: Tax Foundation, 1960), p. 17.

[16] Lewis H. Kimmel, *Taxes and Economic Incentives* (Washington: Brookings Institution, 1950), p. 182.

[17] Even this inadequate progression is an improvement over the distribution of the total Federal, state, and local tax burden in 1938–39. In that fiscal year, the total Federal tax burden as a percentage of the income of every income class was about equal in every income class up to $10,000 (roughly equal to $20,000 in 1958), when it began to rise steeply. State and local taxes, as a whole, were mildly regressive. See Temporary National Economic Committee, *Who Pays the Taxes?* (Washington: G.P.O., 1940) Monograph #3, p. 6.
[18] Frederick Lewis Allen, *The Big Change* (New York: Harper & Brothers, 1952), p. 286.

for high taxation, at least since 1933, has been not to redistribute income but to pay for extraordinary costs—primarily military from 1940 on—in the most expeditious way. We have not taxed the rich to give to the poor; we have taxed both the rich and the poor and, at least since 1940, contributed only a small fraction of the proceeds to the welfare of the poor.

Consider, for example, 1958. In that year, Federal revenue from personal-income, estate and gift, corporate-profit, and excise and customs taxes, excluding the self-financing social-insurance program, amounted to $69 billion.[19] The families and unattached individuals in the $0–$2,000 class contributed $1.066 billion, those in the $2,000–$4,000 class contributed $4.971 billion. But the Federal government spent only $4.509 billion on what by the most generous definition may be called "welfare." Included were all expenditures for public assistance, public health, education, and "other welfare," and half of the outlay for farm parity prices and income, and public housing. In 1949, Federal expenditures for welfare were $2.037 billion; in 1954, they were $2.451 billion, and in

[19] Tax Foundation, *Allocation of the Tax Burden by Income Class*, pp. 14–15; Bureau of the Census, *Statistical Abstract—1959*, p. 368.

1955, $4.062 billion. In each of these years, however, the total Federal tax payments of the spending units earning less than $4,000 were greater than these welfare expenditures. If all Federal welfare expenditures went to the $0–$4,000 class—which was certainly not the case—this class more than paid for them.

In brief, welfare spending has not changed the nature of income inequality, nor raised the standard of living of the lowest-income classes above what it would have reached if they had not been subjected to Federal taxation. It might be claimed that these classes must assume some responsibility for the nation's "larger obligations," but this is not an argument advanced by those who assert that we have redistributed income through taxation and welfare measures. . . .

The complexity of the effect of taxation should not be allowed to obscure the basic trends—the growing tax burden on the low- and middle-income classes, and the huge disparity between theoretical and actual tax rates for the wealthy. The conclusion is inescapable: Taxation has not mitigated the fundamentally unequal distribution of income. If anything it has perpetuated inequality by heavily taxing the low- and middle-income groups—those least able to bear its burden.

RECENT EVIDENCE OF GOVERNMENT IMPACT

Editor's Supplement

Since Kolko revised his book in 1962, more recent figures have become available on the net impact of government taxes and expenditures on the American income distribution. Although several changes both in the tax structure and in tax rates were implemented during the 1960's and the level of government expenditures increased enormously during the same period, none of Kolko's conclusions were affected significantly by subsequent developments. The following five tables, all taken from a useful summary article by Joseph Pechman, published in late 1969, summarize the most recent evidence available at the time of writing. Their implications seem clear. At the end of the 1960's, just as at the beginning, available evidence provides no support for the contention that one of government's functions in the United States has been to correct the market distribution of income by substantial redistribution from the rich to the poor.

Source for all five tables is Joseph Pechman, "The Rich, the Poor, and the Taxes They Pay," *The Public Interest*, No. 17, Fall, 1969, pp. 23, 24, 27, 28, and 33 respectively.

TABLE 1
BEFORE-TAX INCOME SHARES,
CENSUS DATA (PERCENT)

Year	Top 5 Percent of Families	Top 20 Percent of Families
1952	18	42
1957	16	40
1962	16	42
1967	15	41

SOURCE: Bureau of the Census. Income includes transfer payments (e.g., social security benefits, unemployment compensation, welfare payments, etc.), but excludes capital gains.

TABLE 2
BEFORE-TAX INCOME SHARES, TAX DATA (PERCENT)

Year	Top 1 Percent of Tax Units	Top 2 Percent of Tax Units	Top 5 Percent of Tax Units	Top 10 Percent of Tax Units	Top 15 Percent of Tax Units
1952	9	12	19	27	33
1963	8	12	19	28	35
1967	9	13	20	29	36

SOURCE: *Statistics of Income*. Income excludes transfer payments, but includes realized capital gains in full.

TABLE 3
EFFECTIVE FEDERAL TAX RATES ON TOTAL INCOME (PERCENT)

Year	Top 1 Percent of Tax Units	Next 1 Percent of Tax Units	Next 3 Percent of Tax Units	Next 5 Percent of Tax Units	Next 5 Percent of Tax Units
1952	33	20	16	14	12
1963	27	20	16	14	13
1967	26	18	15	13	12

SOURCE: *Statistics of Income*. Total income is the sum of adjusted gross income and excluded capital gains, dividends, and sick pay.

TABLE 4
SHARES OF TOTAL DISPOSABLE (i.e., AFTER-TAX) INCOME (PERCENT)

Year	Top 1 Percent of Tax Units	Top 2 Percent of Tax Units	Top 5 Percent of Tax Units	Top 10 Percent of Tax Units	Top 15 Percent of Tax Units
1952	7	10	16	24	30
1963	7	10	17	26	33
1967	7	11	17	26	34

SOURCE: *Statistics of Income*. Disposable income is total income less federal income tax paid.

TABLE 5
TAXES AND TRANSFERS AS PERCENT OF INCOME, 1965

| | Taxes | | | | |
Income Classes	Federal	State and Local	Total	Transfer Payments	Taxes Less Transfers
Under $2,000	19	25	44	126	−83*
$ 2,000– 4,000	16	11	27	11	16
4,000– 6,000	17	10	27	5	21
6,000– 8,000	17	9	26	3	23
8,000–10,000	18	9	27	2	25
10,000–15,000	19	9	27	2	25
15,000 and over	32	7	38	1	37
Total	22	9	31	14	24

* The minus sign indicates that the families and individuals in this class received more from federal, state, and local governments than they, as a group, paid to these governments in taxes.

SOURCE: *Economic Report of the President,* 1969. Income excludes transfer payments, but includes realized capital gains in full and undistributed corporate profits.

THE REAL IMPACT OF FEDERAL TAX POLICY

John G. Gurley

The following selection originally appeared as part of a review by Gurley of Joseph Pechman's *Federal Tax Policy* (1966). Gurley had high praise for the book, but he also felt that it represented some important faults of the orthodox economic perspective on the tax system, "the most important being the romantic and uncritical view of the society we live in."

Indeed, Pechman's summary statement in the book seemed uncritical:

Despite all its faults, the achievements of the tax legislative process have been impressive on balance. . . . The overall distribution of federal taxes continues to be substantially progressive despite the strong forces arrayed against progressive and equitable taxation. Imperfect as it is, the tax legislative process has produced a tax system that contributes to the nation's welfare. (Federal Tax Policy, p. 49.)

Gurley responded by writing his own summary of the tax system's impact and function, substantially more critical than Pechman's. (In the selection which follows, Gurley's general, mainly favorable comments on Pechman's book have been deleted; Gurley's assessment of the tax system has been retained.)

Since Pechman wrote his book, one should note, he seems to have changed his tone considerably. In a 1969 article in *The Public Interest,* from which the tables in the preceding supplement were taken, Pechman concludes:

It may be that, at some distant future date, the well-to-do and the rich will

SOURCE: *John G. Gurley, "Federal Tax Policy: A Review Article," reprinted as "The Real Impact* of Federal Tax Policy" *from* The National Tax Journal, XX, 3, September, 1967.

have enough income to satisfy not only their own needs, but also to help relieve the tax burdens of those who are less fortunate. In the meantime, the tax system will continue to disgrace the most affluent nation in the world. ("The Rich, the Poor, and the Taxes They Pay," *p. 43.*)

Gurley is a professor of economics at Stanford University.

THE RICH

In dealing with the individual income tax, one of Pechman's major points is that the nominal or potential tax rates are far above the rates actually paid by the various income groups. If we take total income to be adjusted gross income including all realized capital gains,[1] then potential average tax rates for the single taxpayer run from about 14 to 70 percent, if all of this income is fully subject to tax. Because, however, much of this income is not subject to tax for one reason or another, or receives favorable tax treatment, the actual average rates start from less than 1 percent on the lowest income group and rise to only 29 percent on those with incomes of $150,000 to $200,000, and then fall to 27 percent on the still richer.

At the lower income levels, the actual tax rate is much below the potential mainly because of personal exemptions and personal deductions. These factors continue to exert strength through the middle and upper-middle income ranges, but in addition the income splitting provision and the favorable treatment of realized capital gains become increasingly important. The capital gains provisions clearly dominate the picture at the highest income levels. These provisions permit the rich to pay only half the tax they would otherwise be liable for, and personal deductions lower their taxes still more—to a third of the potential levels.[2] So, in these terms, the individual income tax turns out to be only moderately progressive throughout most of the income classes and actually regressive on incomes above $200,000.

That is where Pechman leaves the story, but there is much more to it than that. Although only a part of the realized capital gains reported in any year is a realization of gains actually made in that year (the rest is a current realization of gains made in previous years), such reported gains on the average greatly understate the year's actual capital gains (realized and unrealized). For example, over the period 1955–65, the average annual capital gains on corporate stock, other business equities, and tangible assets (mainly land) were at least $60 billion.[3] Over the same period, realized capital gains reported by taxpayers were on the average only $10 billion per year.[4] Thus, a year's true capital gains were at least 6 times the reported-realized gains.

When these true capital gains are taken into account, the degree of progression of the individual income tax is reduced still further from where Pechman left it. This may be seen as follows. As incomes rise, net worth rises much faster: net worth is about $2\frac{1}{2}$ times income on the average in the lower income levels; it is 10–15 times income at the highest income levels. As net worth rises, the "price-sensitive assets"—corporate stock, other business equities, and

[1] Plus excludable sick pay and excludable dividends.

[2] This material was reported by Pechman at the 1964 annual meetings of the American Finance Association (and later by Richard Goode, *The Individual Income Tax*). The results are based on a special file of about 100,000 tax returns for 1962. However, one can come close to these results by using the information regularly published by the U. S. Treasury Department in *Individual Income Tax Returns;* the approximation of the excluded portion of capital gains at each income level is the important step.

[3] I have used various sources to obtain this and other estimates in this section. For net worths at various income levels, see "Survey of Financial Characteristics of Consumers," *Federal Reserve Bulletin*, March 1964. See also Robert Lampman, *The Share of Top Wealth-Holders in National Wealth* (NBER, 1962). For indications of capital gains on corporate equities, see *Flow-of-Funds, Assets and Liabilities, 1945–65*, Board of Governors of the Federal Reserve System, October 20, 1966, p. 25, along with the companion publication, *Flow of Funds, Annual 1946–65*, October 20, 1966, p. 28. I have also drawn from Raymond W. Goldsmith and Robert E. Lipsey, *Studies in the National Balance Sheet of the United States*, Vol. I (NBER, 1963), pp. 43–7, 170–75, 181–84, from George Katona and John B. Lansing, "The Wealth of the Wealthy," *Review of Economics and Statistics*, February 1964, and from *Individual Income Tax Returns*, U. S. Treasury Department, IRS, 1964, pp. 8–10, 113–18.

[4] This figure includes the excludable portion of realized capital gains.

land (excluding houses)—rise much faster, from about 5 percent of net worth at the lower end of the income scale to 60 percent and more at the upper. As price-sensitive assets rise, the rate of capital gain on them increases. Thus, compared to lower and middle income groups, the rich have huge net worths relative to their incomes, mostly in equities and land, on which they make extremely large capital gains, only a small part of which is realized. So, when true capital gains are substituted for realized capital gains in Pechman's income classes, the incomes at the lower end are raised very little and those at the upper end are raised enormously. Hence, the ratio of taxes paid to true total income rises much more slowly over the entire income range than Pechman shows. The average tax rate at the upper end, instead of being around 30 percent as Pechman calculates it, is probably around 20 percent. The fact is that the rich are not being soaked; instead, they are soaking up wealth very rapidly in ever-increasing amounts.

At the present time, there are around 200,000 families with an average income (including all capital gains) of more than $150,000, 80 percent of which consists of returns on property—capital gains, dividends, interest, rents, and business profits. The average net worth of these super rich is about $1 million, about ⅔ of it in corporate stock, other business equities, and land. These families comprise only ⅓ of 1 per cent of all families, but their net worth is 15 per cent of the total, and they own 30 percent of all corporate stock held by families, 25 percent of all other equity in business and professions, and a large share of the land. During most of the postwar period, capital gains on these assets have been huge; some of the gains have been taxed at relatively low rates, but most of them have not been taxed at all and probably never will be.

The individual income tax has hardly made a dent in the buildup of this massive concentration of wealth, despite the façade of progressive rates, principally because the super rich receive over half their incomes in capital gains and have the political power to prevent any serious taxation of these gains. While, as I have said, the individual income taxes paid annually by these privileged families average only 20 percent of their true incomes, their taxes are of course a much smaller percentage of their net worths— around 2–3 percent—which is about equal to the inflation-induced capital gains each year on their asset holdings, and which is less than the rates paid on net worth by many, less-affluent families. While in terms of income, the individual income tax becomes regressive only at very high income levels, in terms of wealth or net worth, it becomes regressive at relatively lower levels.

So when Pechman appears so pleased by the "attractive feature" of progression to individual income taxation (p. 50), I can only ascribe it to a temporary lapse into a dreamy, make-believe world. That it may be a temporary lapse is suggested 13 pages later where we find him saying:

Graduated expenditure taxes are often proposed as a method of avoiding or correcting the defects of the income tax base, particularly in the top brackets where the preferential treatment of capital gains, tax-exempt interest, depletion allowances, and other favorable provisions permit the accumulation of large fortunes with little or no payment of income tax (p. 63).

While in the real world, then, as Pechman recognizes, the individual income tax touches the super rich very lightly, this is doubly true for the estate and gift taxes. In fact, the latter for many years have been something of a joke among public finance experts, a joke which Pechman tells as follows:

Estate and gift taxes are levied only on a small proportion of privately owned property in the United States. About 3 percent of the estates of adult decedents and less than one-fourth of the wealth owned by the decedents in any one year are subject to estate or gift taxes. The relatively small size of the tax base is explained in part by the generous exemptions which exclude a large proportion of the wealth transfers, and also by defects in the taxes that permit substantial amounts of property to be transferred free of tax (p. 182).

The reason for this state of affairs is that the super-rich families who have seen to it that their capital gains are largely untouched are exactly the ones who have prevented any substantial taxation of their estates. The super rich have super power, and they have used it. Pechman's explanation is more romantic:

One can only guess why the estate and

*gift taxes have not been more successful.
A possible explanation is that equalization of
the distribution of wealth by taxation is
not yet accepted in the United States. In
some countries, economic classes tend to be
fairly stable with little crossing-over by
succeeding generations. In the American
economy, membership in economic classes
is fluid. The average family in the United
States still aspires to improved economic and
social status, and the estate and gift taxes
are erroneously regarded as especially
burdensome to the family which is beginning
to prosper through hard work and saving*
(p. 180).

It is true that the "equalization of the distribution of wealth by taxation is not yet
accepted," but it is surely only the wealthy
who do not accept it. The millions of poor
have not voted against such equalization for
any reason, and especially not in the belief
that they are part of a fluid upstream. The
poor know better than that because they are
the children of the poor. And neither is there
concerted opposition by middle-class families
to a more equal wealth distribution. Instead,
there is powerful opposition to any such
change in the status quo by the top 1 or 2
percent of families who own more than 35
percent of the wealth.

THE POOR

I have mentioned the poor. About 20 percent of our families have incomes (including
transfer payments) below $3,000, and over
40 percent of "unrelated individuals" have
incomes below $1,500. These 14 million eco-
nomic units have an aggregate net worth substantially less than that of the few super rich.
Indeed, over 40 percent of the poor have a
net worth less than $1,000 per family; only
7 percent of the poor own any stock at all,
and these holdings are very small; they have
few liquid assets. A fifth of the poor live in
trailers, parts of other families' dwellings, in
abandoned shelters, etc.[5]

Nevertheless, the poor pay taxes. They are
hardly affected by the estate and gift taxes,

[5] In this section, I have drawn from: *Poverty in
the United States,* Committee on Education and
Labor, Washington, D.C., 1964; Mollie Orchansky, "Counting the Poor: Another Look at the
Poverty Profile," *Social Security Bulletin,* January
1965; Michael Harrington, *The Other America;*
and Margaret S. Gordon (ed.), *Poverty in
America.*

but as a group they do pay individual income
taxes—on the average, about 3 percent of
their total incomes including transfer payments and capital gains. In addition, these
families have been subjected to two sets of
highly regressive taxes—the federal excises
(including custom duties) and the payroll
taxes—which in 1965 brought to the federal
government revenues equal to 75 percent of
those collected from the individual income
tax. According to estimates presented by
Pechman, the poor pay 5–6 percent of their
incomes (including transfers, etc.) in excise
taxes and 4–5 percent in payroll taxes (assuming forward shifting of the employer tax).
The super rich also pay these taxes, but such
levies are very tiny as a percentage of their
incomes. As Pechman points out, these taxes
are regressive, and recent increases in payroll taxes "have raised the tax burden on low
income wage earners substantially. . . . In
1966, the federal payroll tax will be the highest tax paid by at least 25 percent of the
nation's income recipients, and $350 million
will be paid by persons officially classified as
living below poverty levels" (pp. 166, 168).
He later adds: "Given the present importance of the payroll taxes and the increases
in tax rates already scheduled, the effects of
these taxes on the distribution of income can
no longer be disregarded" (p. 177).

While Pechman does not present estimates
of the incidence of state and local taxes, he
does claim that as a whole they are regressive (p. 202); and this is no doubt true above
a relatively low level of income, considering
that consumption and property taxes and
charges and fees comprise over 80 percent of
all revenue of state and local governments
(excluding that from the federal government). Pechman also presents some evidence
that corporations, in the face of a long-term
rise in the corporation income tax, have been
able to raise rates of return before tax sufficiently to maintain their after-tax returns,
probably by more efficient use of capital.
Still, it is likely that some or most of this tax
has been a burden on owners of capital.

These considerations do not permit any
definite statements about the overall relative
tax burdens on rich and poor. However, if
we confine ourselves to the federal individual
income, estate, excise, and payroll taxes, it
would seem, from the information presented
above, that the poor may spend around 12–
14 percent of their total incomes to pay these

taxes, while the comparable tax burden on the super rich is around 25 percent.[6] If we now try to take account of the regressive state and local taxes and the (probably) progressive corporation income tax, it is difficult to see how the richest 200,000 families could have a tax burden as much as twice that of the 14 million poor.[7] This is not much of a difference considering the vast gulf separating the two groups. Furthermore, since the super rich have wealth that, relative to their incomes, is several times higher than that possessed by the poor, it is almost certain that on a wealth basis the poor pay a higher tax rate than the rich. . . .

THE CORPORATIONS

There are today more than 1.2 million U.S. corporations, but the largest 600 of them ($\frac{1}{20}$ of 1 percent) own half of all corporate net assets and receive half of all corporate net income; each of the largest 600 has on the average net assets of at least $1 billion.[8] These gigantic corporations are controlled largely by the super rich who own most of the stock, and in controlling these 600 corporations they control most of what goes on in the business world.

In recent years, corporations as a whole have prospered greatly. Corporate profits after tax have risen by 80 percent in the last five years—twice the growth rate of GNP. One result is that manufacturing corporations' rate of return (after tax) on stockholders' equity is now at the highest level since the very early postwar years; in the last five years it has risen from 9 percent to 14 percent. And this has occurred in the face of rapidly rising capital consumption allowances and steeply rising interest costs, both of which are part of gross returns to property

but neither of which is included in the above rates of return.

Some of this bonanza to corporations since 1961 is attributable to the economy's higher growth rate and to its fuller utilization of resources. A large part, however, as Pechman clearly brings out, is owing to the very favorable tax treatment that corporations have recently received. Since 1954 corporations have increasingly taken advantage of liberalized provisions regarding capital consumption allowances—accelerated depreciation. In addition, in 1962, service lives of "facilities," as guidelines to depreciation, were reduced in manufacturing industries by about 15 percent, thereby allowing corporations to accelerate capital consumption even more. Further, in 1962, an investment tax credit of as much as 7 percent of qualified new investment was given to corporations. After 1964 the corporation income tax rate was lowered from 52 percent to 48 percent. (And, of course, firms engaged in extracting oil and gas and other minerals from the ground continue to receive a depletion allowance which is much more generous than depreciation allowances.) These measures have enabled corporations to reduce their stated profits by inflating capital consumption allowances, and to pay less taxes on these profits through the tax credit and lower tax rates.

As Pechman shows, the result is that federal corporation income taxes as a percentage of profits before tax plus capital consumption allowances fell from 33 percent in 1954 to about 26 percent in 1965 (p. 111). The reduction in taxes paid by corporations, at 1966 levels of profits and investment, as a result of these measures was around $6½ billion, which becomes $8 billion if the effect of depletion allowances is included.[9] Pechman calculates that the generous depreciation allowances and the investment tax credit have boosted the rate of return on 10-year assets from 10 percent to 12½ percent, which is a remarkable jump of 25 percent. In brief, corporations have cleaned up in the past several years.

These corporate windfalls, however, probably have stimulated business investment and so contributed to the higher growth rate which the economy has enjoyed since 1961. That is to say, to achieve investment levels

[6] Twenty percent on income tax, 4 percent on estate and gift taxes, and 1 per cent on excises and payroll taxes. The estimate on estate and gift taxes is based on information in Pechman, pp. 252, 271, 276.

[7] A recent study shows that families with incomes below $3,000 pay the same percentage of their incomes for all state and local taxes plus the federal corporate income tax as do families with incomes of $15,000 and over. See *Tax Burdens and Benefits of Government Expenditures by Income Class, 1961 and 1965,* Tax Foundation, Inc., 1967.

[8] See, for recent years, *Corporation Income Tax Returns,* U. S. Treasury Department, IRS.

[9] See Pechman, pp. 121–22, 124, for some of the figures. The totals are mine.

compatible with an acceptable output growth rate, it has been thought necessary to "slip" an extra several billion dollars a year to the handful of huge corporations that account for most of the business investment. This raises the general question of whether these and other extravagant payoffs (e.g., capital gains) to the wealthy are too costly a way to achieve our saving-investment goals. This is, of course, an old problem in economics—income distribution vs. growth—but it is especially pertinent to raise it now when many economists, including Pechman, seem so satisfied with the growth performance of the economy and so complacent about the costs of achieving it.

TAXES AND SOURCES OF INEQUALITY

At one point, Pechman notes that, while in a democracy such as ours incomes are (naturally?) distributed unequally, income taxes can largely take care of the problem. There are a few points to make about this attitude. First, as I showed above, while income (and wealth) taxation is progressive, when all capital gains are taken into account the redistribution achieved by such taxation is not impressive. Second, income and wealth taxation is increasingly likely to give rise to allocative inefficiencies as the gap between the pre-tax income distribution and the post-tax one that society wishes to achieve widens. While this gap is not tremendous in our society, it is large enough to insure that our tax-transfer system disturbs work, saving, investment, and other incentives—and, I think, more seriously than Pechman is willing to admit. Third, even if a tax-transfer system could smoothly produce equity out of inequity, many people might prefer another economic system that produced equity to begin with. Finally, while a tax-transfer system may strike, directly or indirectly, at some sources of material inequalities, it is mainly an ameliorative measure, a way of smoothing ruffled feathers without removing the causes of the difficulty.

Why is it that our income distribution, even when lifetime incomes are considered and even when differences in investment in human capital are taken into account, is so bad to begin with? Part of the answer is that, given the demands for various abilities and skills, some of these talents are exceptionally scarce and others most plentiful (at some uniform compensation); so the former receive fabulously high compensations, and the latter virtually nothing. Much of this gross maldistribution of abilities and skills is artificially imposed by privileged groups or by the mores and practices of society. It can be attacked in various ways—by widening educational opportunities, weakening monopolistic positions, reducing discriminatory practices, encouraging initiative by the underprivileged, etc.

The maldistribution of wealth, although partly a result of income inequalities, also contributes importantly to them. High incomes are often based on nothing more than the "talent" that certain people have in inheriting large fortunes. The maldistribution of such "talents" can be corrected by inheritance taxes that mean something, by progressive income taxes that over longer periods weaken abilities to accumulate assets, or by nationalization of land and other means of production.

A final source of income inequalities, though generally not recognized as such, is the pervasiveness of the "capitalist mentality" in our society: the fact that our economy runs mostly on self-interest and material incentives, so that tasks simply don't get done unless there are monetary payoffs for them. Since allocative efficiency demands such payoffs, and since there is such a maldistribution of abilities and skills, gross income inequalities are the result. If people were willing to work for non-material reasons—for the sheer love of it, to serve their country, to serve others, to serve God—material incomes (but not necessarily non-material ones!) could be distributed equitably in the first place, without much if any loss in allocative efficiency, and without the aid of an elaborate tax-transfer system.

While income and wealth taxation may help a bit to dry up these wellsprings of material inequalities, the real attack on them comes from civil rights groups, anti-poverty campaigns, anti-monopoly drives, etc., all working within the context of capitalism; from socialists who call for the nationalization of means of production; and from Maoists, hippies, and others who are rebelling against the capitalist mentality with its heavy emphasis on selfishness and material rewards.

It might well be that this last movement poses the ultimate threat to material inequalities—the hippies rather than the Internal Revenue Service.

POVERTY BIBLIOGRAPHY

I. IMPRESSIONS OF URBAN POVERTY

Herb Goro, *The Block,* 1970, Random House.

Richard Conot, *Rivers of Blood, Years of Darkness,* 1968, Morrow.

Richard Elman, *The Poorhouse State: The American Way of Life on Public Assistance,* 1968, Dell.

Herbert Krosney, *Beyond Welfare: Poverty in the Supercity,* 1966, Holt, Rinehart and Winston.

Edgar May, *The Wasted Americans: Cost of Our Welfare Dilemma,* 1964, Signet.

II. DEFINITONS OF POVERTY

A. Absolute Poverty

Alan B. Batchelder, *The Economics of Poverty,* 1966, Wiley paperback, pp. 3–9. Simple, general discussion of issues in definition.

Council of Economic Advisers, *Economic Report of the President,* January, 1964. Definition of poverty as less than $3,000 income.

Mollie Orshansky, "Counting the Poor: Another Look at the Poverty Profile," in Louis A. Ferman *et al.,* eds., *Poverty in America,* rev. ed., 1968, University of Michigan paperback, pp. 67–84. Now-official U.S. government definition in its original presentation.

Martin Rein, "Problems in the Definition and Measurement of Poverty," in Ferman *et al., op. cit.,* pp. 116–131. A criticism of the Orshansky definition.

Burton A. Weisbrod and W. Lee Hansen, "An Income-Net Worth Approach to Measuring Economic Welfare," *American Economic Review,* December, 1968, pp. 1315–1329. Includes an index on income from property in definition of poverty.

Harold Watts, "An Economic Definition of Poverty," in Daniel P. Moynihan, ed., *On Understanding Poverty,* 1969, Basic Books, pp. 316–329. Provides several measures of the "poverty gap."

Gerald Rosenthal, "Identifying the Poor: Economic Measures of Poverty," in Moynihan, ed., *op. cit.,* pp. 330–342. Summary discussion of issues.

B. Relative Poverty

President's Commission on Income Maintenance Programs, *Poverty Amid Plenty,* 1969, U.S. Government Printing Office, pp. 37–40. Summary discussion of need for relative poverty definition.

Victor Fuchs, "Redefining Poverty and Redistributing Income," *The Public Interest,* No. 8, Summer, 1967. Relative poverty definition proposed.

Victor Fuchs, "Comments on Measuring the Low-Income Population," in Lee Soltow, ed., *Six Papers on the Size Distribution of Wealth and Income,* 1969, National Bureau of Economic Research, pp. 198–202. Relative poverty as one half the national median income.

Henri Theil, *Economics and Information Theory,* 1966, Rand McNally, pp. 121–128. A survey of various measures of income inequality.

III. COMPOSITION AND TRENDS

A. American Poverty

Trends and Composition of Absolute Poverty

Alan B. Batchelder, *The Economics of Poverty, op. cit.*, pp. 11–44. General historical trends.

Mollie Orshansky, "The Shape of Poverty in 1966," *Social Security Bulletin*, March, 1968. Detailed composition by official definition.

U.S. Bureau of the Census, "Poverty in the United States, 1959–1968," *Current Population Reports*, Series P-60, No. 68, December 31, 1969. Detailed composition and trends.

Herman Miller, "Changes in the Number and Composition of the Poor," in Margaret S. Gordon, *Poverty in America*, 1965, Chandler Press paperback, pp. 81–101. General evaluation of historical statistics.

Oscar Ornati, *Poverty Amid Affluence*, 1966, Twentieth Century Fund, pp. 27–31. Original formulation of historical trends.

Trends in Relative Poverty

Herman Miller, *Rich Man, Poor Man*, 1964, Crowell, pp. 37–55. Useful discussion of figures on relative distribution, in popular style.

Herman Miller, *Income Distribution in the United States*, 1966, U.S. Government, Chapters 1–2. Technical companion to *supra*.

Edward C. Budd, "Postwar Changes in the Size Distribution of Income in the U.S.," *American Economic Review*, May, 1970. More recent, more varied measures than Miller.

Wealth Inequality

Robert J. Lampman, *The Share of Top Wealth-Holders in National Wealth*, 1962, National Bureau of Economic Research, Chapters 1, 4–7. Pioneering study of concentration of wealth.

Dorothy S. Projector and Gertrude S. Weiss, *Survey of Financial Characteristics of Consumers*, 1966, Federal Reserve Board. Slightly more recent.

B. Urban Poverty

Report of the National Advisory Commission on Civil Disorders, 1968, Bantam paperback ("Kerner Commission Report"), pp. 258–260. Summary calculations.

Anthony Downs, *Who Are the Urban Poor?*, 1968, Committee for Economic Development. Comprehensive study of available statistics.

Daniel P. Moynihan, "Poverty in Cities," in James Q. Wilson, *Metropolitan Enigma*, 1968, Harvard University Press, pp. 335–349. Interesting analytic discussion.

Dick Netzer, *Economics and Urban Problems*, 1970, Basic Books, pp. 13–20. Useful summaries of trends.

David M. Gordon, "Income and Welfare in New York City," *The Public Interest*, No. 16, Summer, 1969, pp. 64–88. Various measures for one city.

C. Black Poverty

St. Clair Drake, "The Social and Economic Status of the Negro in the United States," in Talcott Parsons and K. Clark, eds., *The Negro American*, 1966, Houghton Mifflin, pp. 3–46. Excellent summary of figures and trends.

Rashi Fein, "An Economic and Social Profile of the Negro American," in Parsons and Clark, *op. cit.*, pp. 102–133. A good supplement to Drake.

Herman Miller, "Poverty and the Negro," in Leo Fishman, ed., *Poverty Amid Affluence*, 1966, Yale University Press paperback, pp. 99–123. Another useful summary of trends by Miller.

D.   International Comparisons

Simon Kuznets, "Quantitative Aspects of Economic Growth of Nations: Distribution of Income by Size," *Economic Development and Cultural Change*, XI, 2, Part II, January, 1963, pp. 1–80. Difficult but best available summary of international comparisons of income size distributions.

Irving Kravis, "International Differences in the Distribution of Income," *The Review of Economics and Statistics*, November, 1960.

IV.   ANALYSES OF POVERTY

A.   Poverty Over Time and Economic Growth

General

Robert Lampman, "Population Change and Poverty Reduction," in Fishman, ed., *Poverty Amid Affluence*, pp. 18–42. What different growth rates might mean for the reduction of poverty.

Lowell Gallaway, "The Foundations of the 'War on Poverty'," *American Economic Review*, March, 1965, pp. 122–131. Statistical analysis of the relation of growth rates and poverty levels.

Henry Aaron and Gallaway, discussion of Gallaway, *ibid.*, *American Economic Review*, December, 1967, pp. 1229–1244.

W. H. Locke Anderson, "Trickling Down . . . ," *Quarterly Journal of Economics*, November, 1964, pp. 511–524. A similar kind of analysis.

T. Paul Schultz, "Secular Trends and Cyclical Behavior of Income Distribution in the United States: 1944–1965," in Soltow, ed., *Six Papers . . .* , pp. 75–100.

The Black Share of Growth

James Tobin, "On Improving the Economic Status of the Negro," in Parsons and Clark, eds., *The Negro American, op. cit.*, pp. 451–471.

Alan B. Batchelder, "Decline in the Relative Income of Negro Men," *Quarterly Journal of Economics*, November, 1964, pp. 525–548.

B.   Composition of Poverty

Lester Thurow, *Poverty and Discrimination*, 1969, Brookings, Chapter III, "The Causes of Poverty." Cross-sectional analysis among states.

Woo Sik Kee, "The Causes of Urban Poverty," *Journal of Human Resources*, Winter, 1968, pp. 93–99. Similar analysis for cities.

Alan B. Batchelder, "The Special Case of the Negro," *American Economic Review*, May, 1965. Descriptive analysis.

James Morgan *et al.*, *Income and Welfare in the United States*, 1962, McGraw-Hill. Read Chapter 1, skim pp. 15–186, read pp. 187–256. Very dry treatment of interesting data.

C.   Class or Race

Stefan Thernstrom, "Poverty in Historical Perspective," in Moynihan, ed., *On Understanding Poverty, op. cit.*, pp. 160–186. Wise discussion of two centuries.

Irving Kristol, "The Negro Is Like the Immigrant," *The New York Times Magazine*, September 11, 1966. Argues what title says.

Report of the National Advisory Commission on Civil Disorders, op. cit., "Comparing the Immigrant and the Negro Experience," pp. 278–282. Argues black experience not like immigrant experience.

Otis Dudley Duncan, "Inheritance of Poverty or Inheritance of Race," in Moynihan, ed., *On Understanding Poverty, op. cit.,* pp. 85–110. Concludes the latter.

V. THE ROLE OF THE STATE

A. In Theory

Conservative View

Milton Friedman, *Capitalism and Freedom,* 1962, University of Chicago Press, pp. 25–36.

Liberal Views

Walter Heller, "Reflections on Public Expenditure Theory," in E. S. Phelps, ed., *Private Wants and Public Needs,* 1962, Norton paperback, pp. 124–136.

Otto Eckstein, *Public Finance,* 1968, Prentice-Hall, pp. 1–19.

Richard Musgrave, *The Theory of Public Finance,* 1959, McGraw-Hill, pp. 3–27.

Marxist Views

Paul Sweezy, *The Theory of Capitalist Development,* 1968, Modern Reader paperback, pp. 239–253.

Rudolph Goldscheid, "A Sociological Approach to Problems of Public Finance," in Richard A. Musgrave and A. Peacock, eds., *Classics in the Theory of Public Finance,* 1958, Macmillan, pp. 202–213.

Mancur Olsen, *The Logic of Collective Action,* 1965, Harvard University Press, pp. 98–110. Contrasts liberal and Marxist positions.

V. I. Lenin, *The State and Revolution,* 1965, China Books, Chapter 1.

B. In Practice

Gabriel Kolko, *Wealth and Power in America,* 1965, Praeger, "Taxation and Inequality," pp. 30–45.

Joseph Pechman, "The Rich, the Poor and the Taxes They Pay," *The Public Interest,* No. 17, Fall, 1969.

John Gurley, "Federal Tax Policy: A Review," *National Tax Journal,* September, 1967, pp. 319–327. Criticizes conventional, "romantic" view of state.

W. I. Gillespie, "The Effect of Public Expenditures on the Distribution of Income," in Richard Musgrave, ed., *Essays in Fiscal Federalism,* 1968, Brookings, pp. 122–168. Basic statistical study.

James T. Bonnen, "The Absence of Knowledge of Distributional Impacts . . . ," in U.S. Congress, Joint Economic Committee, *Analysis and Evaluation of Public Expenditures,* Vol. I, 1969.

Stephan Michelson, "The Economics of Real Income Distribution," *Review of Radical Political Economics,* II, 1, Spring, 1970, pp. 75–86. Urges new methods of assessing real impact of government.

VI. PAST AND FUTURE PROGRAMS

A. Past Programs

Public Assistance

President's Commission on Income Maintenance Programs, *Poverty Amid Plenty, op. cit.,* pp. 45–55. Summary of failures.

Christopher Green, *Negative Taxes and the Welfare Problem,* 1967, Brookings paperback, pp. 34–41. Some useful analyses.

Daniel P. Moynihan, "The Crises in Welfare," *The Public Interest*, 1967.

Lora S. Collins, "Public Assistance Expenditures in the United States," in Otto Eckstein, ed., *Studies in the Economics of Income Maintenance*, 1968, Brookings, pp. 97–174. Statistical analysis.

Unemployment Compensation and Minimum Wages

Milton J. Nadworny, "Unemployment Insurance and Income Maintenance," in Sar Levitan *et al.*, eds., *Towards Freedom from Want*, 1968, Industrial Relations Research Association. Summary of issues.

J. J. Kaufman and T. G. Foran, "The Minimum Wage and Poverty," in Levitan *et al.*, *op. cit.* Summary of issues.

Anti-Poverty Programs

Sar Levitan, *The Great Society's Poor Law*, 1969, Johns Hopkins Press.

Peter Marris and Martin Rein, *Dilemmas of Social Reform*, 1967, Atherton Press.

James Sundquist, ed., *On Fighting Poverty*, 1969, Basic Books, *passim*.

B.   Impending and Future Programs

President's Commission on Income Maintenance Programs, *Poverty Amid Plenty*, *op. cit.* Good source of figures and recommendations.

Theodore Marmor, ed., *Poverty Policy: A Sourcebook of Cash-Transfer Proposals*, 1971, Aldine. A compendium of different plans.

George Hildebrand, *Poverty, Income-Maintenance and the Negative Income Tax*, 1967, N.Y. School of Industrial and Labor Relations at Cornell, esp. pp. 9–12 and 65–68. Another summary of plans.

James Tobin, "Raising the Incomes of the Poor," in Kermit Gordon, ed., *Agenda for the Nation*, 1968, Brookings, pp. 77–116. Balanced analysis.

Theodore Schultz, "Public Approaches to Minimize Poverty," in Fishman, ed., *Poverty Amid Affluence, op. cit.*, pp. 165–181.

Christopher Green, *Negative Taxes and the Poverty Problem*, 1967, Brookings, *passim*.

Nathan Glazer, "Beyond Income Maintenance—A Note on Welfare in New York City," *The Public Interest*, No. 16, Summer, 1969, pp. 102–120. Argues that income maintenance solves few problems.

Robert J. Lampman, "Transfer Approaches to Distribution Policy," *American Economic Review*, May, 1970.

5 Crime

Editor's Introduction

What is there to say? We've got a living to earn. There wouldn't be any prostitution if there weren't a demand for it.

—New York City prostitute[1]

The poor youth growing up in the slum has little incentive to emulate Abraham Lincoln when he sees the homage which society pays to the corrupt. Such a boy will probably never have the opportunity to embezzle funds from a bank or to promote a multimillion dollar stock fraud scheme. The criminal ways which we encourage him to choose will be those closest at hand—from vandalism to mugging to armed robbery. And, if he is very successful at these, perhaps he can work his way through the rackets to the high level where he, too, can open a Swiss bank account.

—Robert Morgenthau[2]

The American public has recently demonstrated a certain fickleness in its public fears about crime. During the mid-1960's, the country trembled through several summers of riot and rebellion in urban ghettos. A few years later, fears had focused more specifically on the threat of street crime—the muggings and robberies which emptied cities at night. As I write this in 1970, the public seems most preoccupied with campus disorder; one finds much less frequent mention of "crime in the streets."[3] A year from now, Americans may have returned to previous fears, or may have discovered new ones. It seems impossible to predict.

Whatever the vagaries of public concern about law and order, however, many of the late-60's fears about street and ghetto crime have become a permanent part of our responses to the urban crisis, fixed factors in the calculus of our political life. As Richard Harris has noted most clearly, the fear of ghetto and street crime ultimately dominated the tone of the 1968 presidential election.[4] Mayor John V. Lindsay of New York has himself described the extraordinary importance of electorate concerns about crime during his mayoral campaign of 1969.[5] Politicians have developed a kind of lexicography of code words to address public paranoia about urban crime. Fred P. Graham has described the development perfectly:[6]

Every nation has its equivalent of the mythical emperor who wore no clothes. In the fable, nobody could bring himself to believe what he saw until a child blurted out the truth, and then everyone had a laugh at the emperor's expense. In the United States the naked emperor was for years the high Negro crime rate; the boy who broke the spell was George Wallace, and nobody laughed. . . .

Governor Wallace did not shout that the emperor had no clothes; a politician with his segregationist credentials could make his point without calling a spade a spade. Instead, he preached incessantly about rising crime. Everyone knew that it was Negro crime that was being deplored. . . .

Soon, so many politicians had vowed that they weren't necessarily criticizing Negroes

[1] Quoted in *The New York Times*, May 29, 1970.
[2] Robert M. Morgenthau, "Equal Justice and the Problem of White Collar Crime," *The Conference Board Record*, VI, 8, August, 1969, p. 20.
[3] See, for instance, some comments in a survey of crime problems in six cities throughout the country, *The New York Times*, May 18, 1970.
[4] Richard Harris, *Justice* (N.Y.: Dutton, 1970).
[5] John V. Lindsay, *The City* (N.Y.: Norton, 1970).
[6] Fred P. Graham, "Black Crime: The Lawless Image," *Harper's*, September, 1970, p. 64.

when they demanded "law and order" that everybody understood that the term really was a racial slur of sorts.

Behind the political slogans, a debate of critical importance has been emerging in this country about the range of potential solutions to the problem of urban crime. While some have urged much more pervasive application of strict police power, others have worried about the possible erosion of civil liberties. As Graham summarizes the development, "A coincidence of events has heightened the traditional tensions between the forces of enforcement and of justice, and has greatly increased the likelihood of a constitutional crisis somewhere down the line."[7]

Those tensions reflect the ways in which liberal and conservative analyses have historically defined the problem of urban crime. The radical analysis of crime differs fundamentally from those two views, and one can best understand the dynamics of the debate between liberal and conservative solutions by exploring the radical view as well. In this introduction, I have summarized the dimensions of the problem, outlined the liberal and conservative views, and then presented the radical analysis. The section closes with a brief introduction to the contents and purposes of the reading selections.

DEFINITIONS AND MAGNITUDES

The problem of urban crime involves elements of both myth and reality. Factually, a great deal of serious crime occurs in large central cities, much of it committed by blacks. Subjectively, many Americans have blown the problem out of proportion, tending to view certain kinds of urban crime as the major threat to law and order in this country although those crimes account for small proportions of death, injury, and property loss.

The reading selections below from the Crime Commission Report and the Riot Commission Report provide excellent summaries of the Definitions and Magnitudes of the problem of urban crime. A few conclusions from those selections can serve adequately to highlight their implications.

First, they clearly indicate that many kinds of crime have increased rapidly in the United States, especially in central city ghettos. Seven crimes are grouped by the FBI as "Index Crimes" in their regular Crime Reports, and these seven crimes reflect the kinds of crimes stimulating fears about street and ghetto crime: willful homicide, forcible rape, aggravated assault, robbery, burglary, larceny (of $50 or more), and motor vehicle theft. These Index Crimes are committed twice as frequently in cities with more than one million people than on average throughout the country. Within those cities, they are committed most frequently in ghetto areas.[8]

Second, blacks tend to commit crimes *and* to be victims of crime much more frequently than whites. The most striking difference between white and black crime rates appears in the figures for numbers of youths (between 10 and 17) arrested for robbery per 100,000 citizens in that age group. Among whites, 27 youths per 100,000 were arrested for robbery in cities in 1967, while 550 black youths per 100,000 were arrested for the same crime.[9]

Third, some of the demographic conditions superficially responsible for high rates of urban crime will not soon disappear. Central city ghettos have been spreading continuously in many cities for years, and the numbers of black youths living in central city ghettos will apparently continue to rise.

Finally, these "urban crimes" account for rather small proportions of total personal harm and property loss in the United States. Four more frequent causes of "unnatural" death—car accidents, other accidents, suicide, and falls—were responsible for twelve times as many deaths as was willful homicide. The economic impact of illegal gambling, for instance, was twelve times greater than the economic impact of Index Crimes against property. And no one even counts the personal harm and property loss from industrial chimneys illegally spewing pollution.

The task of analyses of urban crime, therefore, includes explanation not only of its causes but also of public preoccupation with this particular kind of crime. Other kinds of crime and accidents seem statistically more serious than "urban crime," so why the public paranoia?

[7] *Ibid.*, p. 71.
[8] See the selections by the Crime Commission and the Civil Disorders Commission below.
[9] From Graham, *op. cit.*, p. 68.

Liberal and conservative analyses begin from a single common perspective on the problem of crime, but diverge rapidly in their discussions of its potential solution.

To each view, crime against person and property seems essentially to represent an individual aberration from basic social norms. As Chapter One noted, both perspectives view society as a circumstance of equilibrium and harmony satisfying the interests of all rational men. Those who disobey socially legislated rules by committing crimes against person or property can therefore be presumed to have acted irrationally. They can be regarded as maladjusted individuals, as social misfits.

In addition, both perspectives tend to assume that society views "urban crime" with special alarm because of the violence of the particular kinds of crime common in urban areas. Neither perspective would accept the radical contention, described below, that the relative concern of the legal and judicial system in this country actually reflects its bias against the lower classes, for neither perspective accepts the radical argument that the State favors one class over another.

To conservatives, criminals should be treated as criminals regardless of the social forces which may well have produced their criminality. They represent a threat to the safety of others and should be isolated until society can be sure of their good behavior. In policy terms, conservatives engage in two kinds of calculations. First, they discuss the potential deterrence of a variety of crime-prevention techniques. If only enough deterrent force could be mustered, they assume, crime could be stopped. Typically, they urge more police and more equipment to prevent crime. Second, they tend to favor preventive detention as a necessary means of protecting the social order from the threat of probable criminality. They make their argument, normally, on relatively pragmatic grounds. As Edward Banfield has formulated the equation, for instance:[10]

In any event, if abridging the freedom of persons who have not committed crimes is incompatible with the principles of free society, so, also, is the presence in such society of persons who, if their freedom is not abridged, would use it to inflict serious injuries on others. There is, therefore, a painful dilemma. If some people's freedom is not abridged by law-enforcement agencies, that of others will be abridged by law breakers. The question, therefore, is not whether abridging the freedom of those who may commit serious crimes is an evil—it is—but whether it is a lesser or a greater one than the alternative.

In contrast, liberals argue that civil liberties must in nearly all instances be protected, and that individuals cannot ultimately be blamed for many crimes caused by environmental factors. Some unfortunate imperfections in the social equilibrium, in effect, tend to push some individuals toward criminality. Three elements of this liberal response seem especially important. First, liberals insist that different kinds of crime must be distinguished from one another. They emphasize the diversity and complexity of crime in this society—urban crime, it seems, flows from one set of imperfections, organized crime from another, and corporate crime from a third. As the Crime Commission puts it, "No single formula, no single theory, no single generalization can explain the vast range of behavior called crime."[11]

Second, liberals argue that we cannot totally eliminate urban crime until we can eliminate its principal social causes—particularly racism and poverty. (They of course assume, as Chapter One noted, that we can solve those more fundamental problems.) To quote the Crime Commission again, "And so it is probable that crime will continue to increase . . . unless there are drastic changes in general social and economic conditions. . . ."[12]

Third, liberals also believe that crime can be partially reduced even if social and economic conditions do not improve, if we further rationalize our system of law enforcement and the administration of justice. We need more research, more analysis, more technology, more money, better administration and better personnel. Marvin Wolfgang concludes his analysis of the problem: "Urban crime might be reduced by significant proportions if more talent, time, and funds

---

[10] Banfield, *The Unheavenly City* (Boston: Little, Brown, 1970), p. 184.
[11] The President's Commission on Law Enforcement and the Administration of Justice, *The Challenge of Crime in a Free Society* (Washington: U.S. Government Printing Office, 1967), p. v.
[12] *Ibid.*, p. 5.

were put into public use to produce the kind of research findings necessary to make more rational informed decisions."[13]

Pulling all of those strands together, liberals argue that we must attack the problem of urban crime by improving our enforcement and judicial institutions at the same time that we move toward eliminating racism and poverty.

THE RADICAL VIEW

The radical analysis of urban crime derives directly from the general radical paradigm discussed in Chapter One. The radical perspective views crime as an inevitable consequence of the kinds of competitive and alienating institutions inherent in capitalist societies. It views urban crime in the United States as a specifically inevitable consequence of social and economic institutions in this country. In general, according to the analysis, many "crimes" are committed quite inevitably in a capitalist society; some are considered "illegal" and some are not.[14] Of those that are considered illegal, some are prosecuted and some are not. Of those criminals prosecuted, some receive severe punishment and some almost none. None of these eventualities is random, radicals argue. Each is consistent with the structure of basic institutions, for each in some way reinforces class divisions in society and the power of those in control of important institutions.

This view of crime in the United States consists of five principal hypotheses.

1. To the extent that the State serves the interest of the dominant classes in society, it can often perform its functions most effectively in "democratic" societies by permitting many laws to remain in its statutes while enforcing those laws selectively. For varieties of historical reasons, the selective enforcement of the law seems to arouse less fear for the erosion of democratic tradition than legally selective legislation. As long as statutes nominally outlaw racial inequality, for instance, inadequate enforcement of those laws seems to cause little furor. As a result, one should view the nature of laws which exist in such societies as less meaningful than the pattern of their enforcement. Laws may come to exist for eventually irrelevant historical reasons. Once they exist, the patterns of their enforcement tell us most about social attitudes toward crime.

2. Capitalist societies depend, as Chapter One argued, on basically competitive forms of social and economic interaction. Individuals cannot depend on society for economic security; they must fend for themselves, finding the best opportunities for providing for themselves and family. At any point in time, many of the best opportunities for economic survival open to different citizens will violate a historically determined set of statutes and laws. Although these activities are therefore technically illegal, they nonetheless constitute functionally similar responses to the organization of institutions in capitalist societies; they represent a means of survival in a society which does not guarantee survival to its citizens. Three kinds of crime in the United States provide the most important examples of this functional similarity: ghetto crime, organized crime, and corporate crime.

First, the prevalence of illegal activity in the ghetto, especially among younger black men, represents a perfectly rational response to their limited employment opportunities within the "legitimate" labor market—to the threat of unemployment, low wages in dead-end jobs, and pervasively alienating conditions in many jobs. The potential income in illegitimate activities is often higher (because of artificial barriers to competition), the work is typically less demeaning, and even the instability of income from some "illegal" activities like numbers running is less crippling than that in many "legitimate" jobs (from which ghetto workers can so easily be fired).[15] As Arthur Dunmeyer puts it in the selection on ghetto crime below: "In some cases this

---

[13] Wolfgang, "Urban Crime," in James Q. Wilson, ed., *Metropolitan Enigma* (Cambridge: Harvard University Press, 1968), p. 275.

[14] A "crime" in this sense obviously consists of an action which harms someone else in society, regardless of the law. Some "crimes" are not "illegal," like certain kinds of unsafe industrial production processes and certain kinds of unprotected consumer frauds. The argument also does not intend to imply that there is no crime in non-capitalist societies, like socialist societies. It suggests, rather, that the institutions of a capitalist society thoroughly inform the nature of crime in that society, and that crime in other kinds of society must be understood in different terms.

[15] For insights on all these factors, see Claude Brown, *Manchild in the Promised Land* (N.Y.: Macmillan, 1965); and *The Autobiography of Malcolm X* (N.Y.: Grove Press, 1964). One study has documented

is the way you get your drug dealers and prostitutes and your numbers runners. . . . They see that these things are the only way that they can compete in the society, to get some sort of status." The illegality of the activities does not obviate their economic necessity or their social attractiveness.

Second, as Donald Cressey illustrates in his selection in this chapter, what we call "organized crime" represents little more than the rational supply of illegal goods for which there is economic demand. These economic activities are illegal for varieties of historical reasons, but they are basically economic activities nonetheless. For those with access to the "organization," they offer better income and status than conventional jobs. The harm of the goods to society is certainly relative. In nearly every sense, for instance, the economics and functional importance of supply and demand for alcoholic beverages seems similar to the supply and demand for a drug like marijuana. The most important sociological differences between the two activities stem from the illegality of the latter and the consequences of its illegality.[16]

Third, corporate "crime" also represents a rational response to life in capitalist societies. Corporations exist to protect and increase the capital of their owners. If it becomes difficult to perform that function one way, corporate officials will quite inevitably try to do it another. When Westinghouse and General Electric agreed to fix their prices, for instance, they were choosing one of many alternatives for limiting the potential threat of competition to their price structures. Similarly, when Ford and General Motors proliferate new car model after new car model, each differing only slightly from its siblings, they are choosing to protect their price structures by what economists call "product differentiation." In both cases, the corporations are trying to diminish the vulnerability of their profits to the price-cutting that direct competition might involve. In one case, they use oligopolistic power quite directly. In the other, they rely on the power of advertising to generate demand for the differentiated products.[17] In the context of a perpetual race for profits and capital accumulation, each response seems reasonable; one happens historically to have been declared illegal.

3. Given this basic analytic similarity among several important kinds of crime, the pattern of social decisions about which crimes to prosecute and punish seems more meaningful. Apparently, our institutions prosecute and punish both crimes and criminals with principal reference to their class status in society. Corporations get away with illegal Swiss bank accounts while blacks in the ghetto face long sentences for marginal crimes. White suburban youths receive admonishment, as Ronald Goldfarb points out in his article below, while black ghetto youths serve several months before they are tried, waiting for jammed city courts to reach their cases. As Robert Morgenthau has written:[18]

We . . . find persons who publicly denounce crimes of violence while privately committing more "socially acceptable" white collar crimes. . . . There is, moreover, a national tendency to enforce the law against crimes of violence more vigorously than against the more sophisticated white collar crimes.

4. Public images of and responses to crime depend in large part, as Morgenthau notes, on the amount of violence involved. And yet, the amount of violence involved in these three fundamentally important kinds of crime in the United States seems to depend on the biased pattern of law enforcement. Many kinds of ghetto crime generate violence because the participants are severely prosecuted for their crimes and must try to protect themselves against arrest

the sources of crime among ghetto youths by comparing the attitudes toward the law and toward work of ghetto and middle-class youth. See Leonard Goodwin, "Work Orientations of the Underemployed Poor," *Journal of Human Resources,* Fall, 1969.

[16] This does not imply that such goods might not also be supplied illegally in socialist countries. It simply argues that (a) the goods are arbitrarily declared illegal in this society, (b) that the insecurity of existence in this kind of society leads people to find any means of supporting themselves, and (c) that criminal supply of illegal goods eventually becomes the best economic opportunity available to some Americans. One gathers, informally, that organized crime sometimes plays the same role in working-class Italian communities that ghetto crime plays in the ghetto.

[17] For a fascinating study of the economic costs involved in the continuous attempt by firms to differentiate their automobile products, see Franklin M. Fisher, Zvi Griliches, and Carl Kaysen, "The Costs of Automobile Model Changes since 1949," *Journal of Political Economy,* October, 1962.

[18] "Equal Justice . . . ," *op. cit.,* p. 18.

however they can. Other kinds of ghetto crime are tolerated by the police, like numbers running, and rarely involve violence. Similarly, organized crime has become violent, as Cressey notes below, principally because its participants are often prosecuted. As long as that remains true, the suppliers of illegal goods require secrecy, organization, and a bit of violence to protect their livelihood. Corporate crime, since it is tolerated by society, does not require violence to protect its continuation. Accountants at Lockheed did not need to force Defense Department agents at knife-point to ignore their distortions of cost figures in 1968 and 1969, for instance, because the defense officials were perfectly willing to go along.[19] This interaction between selective prosecution and violence leads to and reinforces a vicious circle of criminality for some.[20]

5. Finally, these vicious circles of enforcement, prosecution, and violence play an important role in helping legitimize class distinctions in the United States and in helping stabilize the American institutional structure. So many activities are technically illegal in this country that nearly all Americans commit crimes at some points in their lives; 91 percent of a national sample, according to the Crime Commission study, "admitted they had committed acts for which they might have received jail or prison sentences."[21] Only a small portion of that criminal nine tenths is ever arrested, prosecuted, or punished however.

The eventual institutional outcome of that pattern serves many useful functions. For instance, if an employer refuses a black a certain job because he is black, he can be called a racist. But if he turns down a black for that job because the black happens to have a criminal record, the employer can safely argue that he is merely protecting himself against a potential threat to his property. The fact that many blacks tend inevitably to have criminal records excludes them from many opportunities.[22] At another level, individuals are prosecuted for accidents because of negligent or drunken driving, but auto manufacturers are never prosecuted for the negligent construction of unsafe cars or their role in increasing the likelihood of death from air pollution. These patterns reinforce the apparent invulnerability of large institutions, confirming our conventional assumptions that individuals rather than institutions are always at fault.

Perhaps most important for its stability, society manages "legitimately" to keep thousands of men out of the job market or trapped in the secondary job market by perpetuating a set of institutions which serves functionally to feed large numbers of blacks into an oppressive prison system when young and discharge them as old or dead men. Were they in the job market, given economic institutions, they would probably be unemployed.[23] Were so many more blacks unemployed, blacks might pose an even more threatening challenge to the stability of the society. Instead, they are locked up or on the run most of their lives. And the importance of this phenomenon should not be underestimated. First, as Eldridge Cleaver and Malcolm X have both said many times, the same blacks keep reappearing in prisons throughout their lives. In Cleaver's words:[24]

I noticed that every time I went back to jail, the same guys who were in Juvenile Hall with me were also there again. They arrived there soon after I got there, or a little bit before I left. They always seemed to make the scene. In the California prison system, they carry you from Juvenile Hall to the old folks' colony, down in San Luis Obispo, and wait for you to die.

[19] See the article by Robert Sherrill in *Scanlan's Monthly*, August, 1970, for evidence on the Lockheed distortions.

[20] Perhaps the best example of this interaction is the cycle of drug addiction, robbery, and violent crime. Were heroin legal and free, addicts would not have to rob to support their very expensive habits. Given its illegality and the necessity of robbery to support their habits, many addicts are forced into increasingly desperate and often violent attempts both to rob and to avoid arrest. This pattern of attack and escape, always uncertain, feeds the factors leading to addiction, makes it more difficult for them to go "cold turkey," and intensifies the violence.

[21] See the selection from the Crime Commission Report below.

[22] On the importance of racism for employers, see the chapter on employment in this volume.

[23] For evidence that those with prison records have difficulty finding jobs, and therefore are most likely to return to prison, see Robert Evans, Jr., "The Labor Market and Parole Success," *Journal of Human Resources*, Spring, 1968.

[24] *The Post-Prison Writings and Speeches of Eldridge Cleaver*, ed. by Robert Scheer (N.Y.: A Ramparts book by Random House, 1969), pp. 154–155.

Then they bury you there. . . . I noticed these waves, these generations . . . graduating classes moving up from Juvenile Hall, all the way up.

Second, the numbers of blacks locked into that pattern of prison and recidivism are by no means insubstantial in relation to the numbers of blacks who are unemployed. A different set of institutions, which effectively ended the disproportionate prevalence of crime and conviction among blacks, would radically increase the number of blacks who were unemployed. In July, 1968, for instance, 317,000 black men were unemployed. At the same time, an estimated 140,000 blacks were serving time in penal institutions at federal, state, and local levels. If the percentage of black males in prison had been as low as the proportion of white men, there would have been only 25,000 blacks in jail. The phenomenon of ghetto crime, from society's perspective, keeps a lot of blacks out of trouble.[25]

In short, radicals argue that the problem of urban crime as we know and fear it should be regarded as a specific and inevitable feature of the American class and institutional structure. Like many of our crimes, it flows from a rational response to the competitiveness of our institutions. Unlike most other crimes, it is prosecuted heavily. The continued effect of this institutional pattern of prosecution and punishment exacts a heavy and deadening price from its victims; in that sense it plays a functional role in the context of larger social institutions by removing many from the labor force and by obviating the need to find decent work for those criminals. To eradicate urban crime, one would need both fundamentally to change the institutions which produce it and somehow to replace the functions it serves within those institutions. Since one of its principal functions is to help perpetuate the lower-class status of blacks without recourse to overt racism, eliminating the prevalence of crime among blacks would probably require more overt racism in order to preserve necessary class divisions.[26] More overt racism would necessarily accentuate the kinds of social forces which currently produce urban crime. If we eliminated urban crime, our institutions would tend to reproduce it. And it is in that sense that we must change the entire set of institutions in order to solve the problem.

To quote Eldridge Cleaver again:[27]

What we have in this country is a system organized against black people in such a way that many are forced to rebel and turn to forms of behavior that are called criminal in order to get the things they need to survive. Consider the basic contradiction here. You subject people to conditions that make rebellion inevitable and then you punish them for rebelling. . . .

Those who are now in prisons could be put through a process of real rehabilitation before their release. . . . By rehabilitation I mean they would be trained for jobs that would not be an insult to their dignity, that would give them some sense of security, that would allow them to achieve some brotherly connection with their fellow man. But for this kind of rehabilitation to happen on a large scale would entail the complete reorganization of society, not to mention the prison system. It would call for the teaching of a new set of ethics, based on the principle of cooperation, as opposed to the presently dominating principle of competition. It would require the transformation of the entire moral fabric of this country. . . .

The difference between liberal and conservative views of crime on the one hand and the radical view on the other has been clearly illustrated by a recent exchange in the legal literature. In a widely heralded article written in 1964, Herbert Packer, a leading American expert on criminal process, argued that most legal discussion of criminal procedure involves a conflict be-

---

[25] Based on official figures from the Bureau of Labor Statistics and the Bureau of the Census, disaggregated by race and age. These figures do not even include adjustment for the large numbers of black males who are never counted by official statistical surveys. In the 1960's, for instance, Census surveys failed to count roughly 20 percent of the total estimated black male population between 20 and 40 years old. Many of those missed by surveys, presumably, avoid the Census because they are on the run, working and hiding in the "illegitimate" labor market, afraid of anyone on an official mission. The numbers involved in this general cycle of prison and criminal activity, therefore, are probably much higher than the numbers of blacks in prison.

[26] In the same way, substantial elimination of housing segregation would probably require much more overt racism in American society. See the chapter on housing.

[27] *Post-Prison Writings . . . , op. cit.,* pp. 179, 182.

tween (or dialogue between) two different models of the criminal process.[28] Packer called one of these models the "Crime Control Model" and the other the "Due Process Model." The emphases embodied in each model closely resemble the difference in emphasis of the general conservative and liberal views of crime, respectively, as described in the preceding section. The Crime Control Model, according to Packer, "is based on the proposition that the repression of criminal conduct is by far the most important function to be performed by the criminal process." The Due Process Model, on the other hand, derives from "the concept of the primacy of the individual and the complementary concept of limitation on official power."[29]

In a reply to Packer's article, John Griffiths argued that Packer's two models represent qualitatively similar views of the relationship between the criminal and society, deriving from some common ideological assumptions about the law.[30] Griffiths calls this set of shared assumptions the "Battle Model of the Criminal Process." He argues that both the "conservative" and "liberal" views derive from a common vision of conflict and hostility between the aberrant individual on the one hand and the social order on the other. To illustrate the communality of the two models proposed by Packer, Griffiths suggests a third "model" which closely resembles the radical vision of how crime ought to be dealt with in society. Griffiths calls this the "Family Model of the Criminal Process." He suggests that society's treatment of criminals could be patterned after the treatment by families of those family members who betray the family trust. The Family Model begins from "an assumption of reconcilable—even mutually supportive—interests, a state of love."[31] In contrast to the Battle Model, the Family Model would propose that "we can make plain that while [the criminal] has transgressed, we do not therefore cut him off from us; our concern and dedication to his well-being continue. We have punished him and drawn him back in among us; we have not cast him out to fend for himself against our systematic enmity."[32]

The Battle Model, as Griffiths describes it, obviously reflects not only liberal and conservative views of crime but the reality of our social treatment of criminals. Griffiths' Family Model illustrates the fundamentally different priorities which would motivate institutional organization in a society where human needs were not sacrificed to the interests of a single dominant class, where institutions supported the growth and development of all individuals as humans.

THE READINGS

The first three selections provide some brief Impressions, Definitions, and Magnitudes. In a short excerpt, Bell Gale Chevigny describes the life of one "urban criminal." From his story, Arnold Kemp could clearly have been a successful businessman if he had grown up in white upper-middle class society. In the ghetto, however, the entire complex of institutions and attitudes he confronted led him into crime as a vocation. The two selections from government reports provide extremely useful summaries of the kinds of crime prominent in urban areas and the relative importance of that crime. As both selections clearly show, urban crime constitutes a small proportion of total crimes committed in this country.

The next four readings help elaborate the two most important points of the radical analysis. The first three illustrate the ways in which three primary forms of criminal activity constitute perfectly rational responses within our institutional structure. The testimony by Brown and Dunmeyer supports the argument that ghetto crime often offers the most plausible economic opportunity available to ghetto residents; Cressey's selection establishes the purely economic nature of "organized crime"; and Sutherland's selection describes the importance of corporate crime and the inevitable pattern of its evolution. Given the perfectly expectable existence of those activities, then, our institutions prosecute them with extraordinary selectivity. Ronald Goldfarb elaborates this basic argument quite briefly, suggesting several ways in which our judicial and enforcement institutions abound with class biases.

[28] Herbert Packer, "Two Models of the Criminal Process," *University of Pennsylvania Law Review,* 1964.
[29] Quoted in John Griffiths, "Ideology in Criminal Procedure, or a Third 'Model' of the Criminal Process," *Yale Law Journal,* January, 1970, p. 363.
[30] *Ibid.*
[31] *Ibid.,* p. 371.
[32] *Ibid.,* p. 412.

THE STORY OF ARNOLD KEMP

Bell Gale Chevigny

This selection sketches the life of one "urban criminal"—how he became one and what he thought about it. It comes from an article in *The Village Voice,* "After the Death of Jail, Rebirth like Raskolnikov," in which the author describes a number of ex-convicts whose experience in prison had changed their lives. Like Malcolm X, they had been "reborn" with a new sense of energy and purpose, moving from "semi-conscious" to fully conscious social protest. The article originally appeared in 1969.

In Arnold Kemp's history, I made my first acquaintance with this pattern [of rebirth]. In my class at Queens College, Kemp was more than a good student. In discussion he paid unusual attention, and he seemed to have a genuine love of explaining himself. He often bailed out the class when they were frankly behind in preparation, by summarizing the material and reading crucial passages aloud with a dramatic eloquence that spurred them on. At these times, his voice lost all traces of the stammer that afflicted him intermittently in conversation, and which sometimes reminded me oddly of Billy Budd, especially since something in his manner and the way Kemp carried his heavy-set body often suggested curbed force. As he wrote in one of his essays for class, the stammer had something to do with the turn his life had taken, since it led him at the age of nine into the white world of Mount Sinai Hospital for a speech therapy class and thence into the world of poetry, which he was asked to recite as an exercise. At the conclusion of the essay he wrote, "I was still a creature of my environment. The only difference was a ludicrous one: I now carried Stendhal or Faulkner next to my zip gun."

At the age of 15 Kemp dropped out of high school, became a pimp for two women, and began to make his way through Harlem's other rackets. At 17, with a fleeting intuition that the hustling life was a dead end, he tried to escape by joining the Air Force.

SOURCE: *Bell Gale Chevigny, "After the Death of Jail, Rebirth like Raskolnikov," from* The Village Voice. *Reprinted by permission of* The Village Voice. *Copyright © by The Village Voice, Inc.,* 1969.

Now in his early 30s, he looked back on his service. "I suppose I was hoping to find something to save me, but I didn't. I had a ball, I flew all over the world, I went to radio school and got three years' experience, and I was promoted to sergeant and got an honorable discharge. But when I applied for radio work at various airports in New York afterwards, I was turned down flat. I was back in the streets. Sometime in there I declared war on America."

As long as he operated in Harlem, Kemp was never arrested. "There's no way to rationalize my pre-prison life," he said now. "There's nothing I wouldn't have done if the price was right. Except that I was not petty. I didn't feed on my own. I played on vice, of course, but I never mugged old ladies. I never used force on the poor, black or white. What really interested me, actually, was making plans. I loved planning everything, figuring things out. People would come to me and I'd work something out for them and I wouldn't take anything for it."

Characteristically, then, when he made his big and fatal move, he planned it with his partner for three months, and arranged to avoid using force. The job was taking a $24,000 payroll from a supposedly impregnable new building of Bell Telephone in the Bronx. He was caught six weeks later through an informant. He laughs now at his belief that they could protect themselves by planning. "We deliberately fixed it so we couldn't harm anyone. We used toy pistols. We didn't plan to get caught, but we figured if we did, we'd be treated more leniently if we hadn't harmed anyone. But it was too much money." He says he heard the prosecutor say that if he had broken in on a storekeeper and beaten him up, it would have gone more easily for him. The telephone company sent down a battery of lawyers, he said, to make sure that the district attorney did not let him plead guilty to a reduced charge. Availed nothing by his honorable discharge and the fact that this was his first offense, he was sentenced to 10–12 years, and served seven before he was paroled.

"Jail did me some good," Kemp says, adding with his quiet irony, "I learned some things I had to, but I would have done that in two years as well as in seven." He sees three initial responses to prison life: to become depressed, sycophantic, or embittered. A fourth response—adopted by a minority—is to channel one's energy some other way. "I was in the first category for a few months and then in the fourth," says Kemp. "It didn't take me any time to decide I wasn't going back to commit crimes. Because it's stupid, it's a trap, it only makes it easier for them to neutralize you. It's hard to explain, because you can't say it's a question of right and wrong, but of being free or trapped."

He was first, briefly, at Attica Prison, where he said school was like a concentration camp, then at Wallkill, where although he was told by the director of education to forget about college education, he did get his Regents diploma. Like some inmates he also taught—elementary French, English grammar, typing, and even some business law. Unlike other men I talked with, he found some of the state-employed teachers not only competent, but anti-authoritarian and willing to supply an interested inmate with some of the literature forbidden by the authorities. "Most of the new black literature was forbidden—Brown, Baldwin, Fanon. So was anything revolutionary or political, anything about Cuba. These things circulated and were hidden in the pipes, in the kitchens,

anywhere. If you were caught with a book, 30 days were added to the time before you came up for parole."

Kemp feels that prison changed his values. "Before prison I was concerned with one thing only and that was money. I thought it was impossible to live without plenty of it. And yet even when I had the payroll, it was nothing. It was like confetti, I didn't use it. I'd go to the track or Miami. Or I'd fly four friends to Chicago for ringside seats, going first class for once. After being in the cage and deprived all that time it might have seemed hard not having money and going to school. But I found I didn't need things, and I used to need everything—silk suits, $50 shoes, everything. In fact, I was planning to go to school when I pulled the telephone company job. I was making enough money for it working in the Post Office, but I wanted to go to school in style."

With the acceptance of relative austerity came the birth of political awareness. Kemp makes one feel, as Malcolm's memoirs do, that ghetto crime is a semi-conscious and half-baked form of social protest. Attitudes in the street itself operate to keep that consciousness limited. The community protects the criminal, he believes, even him who exploits it, because he represents the defeat of the system. "At my trial there was a cheering section, respectable people offered me character references, and when I came out of prison I was a minor hero. Look at the way they *love* Adam Clayton Powell. They *love* him because he makes them experience vicariously what they can't do. But I think you have to change the system. I don't want a piece of the action. I want to be a part of the flood that washes away the whole system. This is what I try to tell the kids in Harlem who are like what I was—to fight with the Panthers or the Muslims or something more underground—but it's hard."

CRIME IN THE UNITED STATES

The President's Commission on Law Enforcement and the Administration of Justice

This brief selection from the Crime Commission Report outlines the magnitude of various kinds of crime in the United States. Pulling together varieties of official statistics on national crime, it makes clear that what we think of as "urban crime" constitutes only a small proportion of total crime. For the nation as a whole, many other causes of death and injury account for much more personal harm than the FBI Index Crimes against persons, and many other kinds of crime have much larger economic impact than Index Crimes against property.

THE AMOUNT OF CRIME

There are more than 2800 Federal crimes and a much larger number of State and local ones. Some involve serious bodily harm, some stealing, some public morals or public order, some governmental revenues, some the creation of hazardous conditions, some the regulation of the economy. Some are perpetrated ruthlessly and systematically; others are spontaneous derelictions. Gambling and prostitution are willingly undertaken by both buyer and seller; murder and rape are violently imposed upon their victims. Vandalism is predominantly a crime of the young; driving while intoxicated, a crime of the adult. Many crime rates vary significantly from place to place.

The crimes that concern Americans the most are those that affect their personal safety—at home, at work, or in the streets. The most frequent and serious of these crimes of violence against the person are willful homicide, forcible rape, aggravated assault, and robbery. National statistics regarding the number of these offenses known to the police either from citizen complaints or through independent police discovery are collected from local police officials by the Federal Bureau of Investigation and published annually as a part of its report, "Crime in the United States, Uniform Crime Reports." The FBI also collects "offenses known" statistics for three property crimes: Burglary, larceny of $50 and over and motor vehicle theft. These seven crimes are grouped

SOURCE: *The President's Commission on Law Enforcement and the Administration of Justice, 1967.*

together in the UCR to form an Index of serious crimes. Table 1 shows the totals for these offenses for 1965 [see p. 284].

The Risk of Harm

Including robbery, the crimes of violence make up approximately 13 percent of the Index. The Index reports the number of incidents known to the police, not the number of criminals who committed them or the number of injuries they caused.

The risk of sudden attack by a stranger is perhaps best measured by the frequency of robberies since, according to UCR and other studies, about 70 percent of all willful killings, nearly two-thirds of all aggravated assaults and a high percentage of forcible rapes are committed by family members, friends, or other persons previously known to their victims. Robbery usually does not involve this prior victim-offender relationship.

Robbery, for UCR purposes, is the taking of property from a person by use or threat of force with or without a weapon. Nationally, about one-half of all robberies are street robberies, and slightly more than one-half involve weapons. Attempted robberies are an unknown percentage of the robberies reported to the UCR. The likelihood of injury is also unknown, but a survey by the District of Columbia Crime Commission of 297 robberies in Washington showed that some injury was inflicted in 25 percent of them. The likelihood of injury was found higher for "yokings" or "muggings" (unarmed robberies from the rear) than for armed robberies. Injuries occurred in 10 of

TABLE 1*
ESTIMATED NUMBER AND PERCENTAGE OF INDEX OFFENSES, 1965

	Number	Percentage
Murder, non-negligent manslaughter	9,850	0.4
Forcible rape	22,467	0.8
Robbery	118,916	4.3
Aggravated assault	206,661	7.4
Burglary	1,173,201	42.2
Larceny, $50 and over	762,352	27.4
Motor vehicle theft	486,568	17.5
Total, crimes against person	357,894	12.9
Total, crimes against property	2,422,121	87.1
Grand Total	2,780,015	100.0

SOURCE: *Uniform Crime Reports*, 1965, p. 51.

* [Ed.: In the Crime Commission Report, this table is actually presented as a bar graph. I have presented it as a table, to save space, and have added the percentages.]

91 armed robberies as compared with 30 of 67 yokings.

Aggravated assault is assault with intent to kill or for the purpose of inflicting severe bodily injury, whether or not a dangerous weapon is used. It includes all cases of attempted homicide, but cases in which bodily injury is inflicted in the course of a robbery or a rape are included with those crimes rather than with aggravated assault. There are no national figures showing the percentage of aggravated assaults that involve injury, but a survey of 131 cases by the District of Columbia Crime Commission found injury in 84 percent of the cases; 35 percent of the victims required hospitalization. A 1960 UCR study showed that juvenile gangs committed less than 4 percent of all aggravated assaults.

Forcible rape includes only those rapes or attempted rapes in which force or threat of force is used. About one-third of the UCR total is attempted rape. In a District of Columbia Crime Commission survey of 151 cases, about 25 percent of all rape victims were attacked with dangerous weapons; the survey did not show what percentage received bodily harm in addition to the rape.

About 15 percent of all criminal homicides, both nationally and in the District of Columbia Crime Commission surveys, occurred in the course of committing other offenses. These offenses appear in the homicide total rather than in the total for the other offense. In the District of Columbia Crime Commission surveys, less than one-half of 1 percent of the robberies and about 1 percent of the forcible rapes ended in homicide.

Some personal danger is also involved in the property crimes. Burglary is the unlawful entering of a building to commit a felony or a theft, whether force is used or not. About half of all burglaries involve residences, but the statistics do not distinguish inhabited parts of houses from garages and similar outlying parts. About half of all residential burglaries are committed in daylight and about half at night. A UCR survey indicates that 32 percent of the entries into residences are made through unlocked doors or windows. When an unlawful entry results in a violent confrontation with the occupant, the offense is counted as a robbery rather than a burglary. Of course, even when no confrontation takes place there is often a risk of confrontation. Nationally such confrontations occur in only one-fortieth of all residential burglaries. They account for nearly one-tenth of all robberies.

In summary, these figures suggest that, on the average, the likelihood of a serious personal attack on any American in a given year is about 1 in 550; together with the studies available they also suggest that the risk of serious attack from spouses, family members, friends, or acquaintances is almost twice as great as it is from strangers on the street. Commission and other studies, moreover, indicate that the risks of personal harm are spread very unevenly. The actual risk for slum dwellers is considerably more; for most Americans it is considerably less.

Except in the case of willful homicide, where the figures describe the extent of injury as well as the number of incidents, there is no national data on the likelihood of injury from attack. More limited studies indicate that while some injury may occur in two-thirds of all attacks, the risk in a given year of injury serious enough to require any degree of hospitalization of any individual is about 1 in 3,000 on the average, and much less for most Americans. These studies also suggest that the injury inflicted by family members or acquaintances is likely to be more severe than that from strangers. As shown by Table 2, the risk of death from willful homicide is about 1 in 20,000.

Criminal behavior accounts for a high percentage of motor vehicle deaths and injuries. In 1965 there were an estimated 49,000 motor vehicle deaths. Negligent manslaughter, which is largely a motor vehicle offense, accounted for more than 7,000 of these. Studies in several States indicate that an even higher percentage involve criminal behavior. They show that driving while intoxicated is probably involved in more than one-half of all motor vehicle deaths. These same studies show that driving while intoxicated is involved in more than 13 percent of the 1,800,000 nonfatal motor vehicle injuries each year.

For various statistical and other reasons, a number of serious crimes against or involving risk to the person, such as arson, kidnapping, child molestation, and simple assault, are not included in the UCR Index. In a study of 1,300 cases of delinquency in

TABLE 2
DEATHS FROM OTHER THAN NATURAL CAUSES, 1965 (PER 100,000 INHABITANTS)

Motor vehicle accidents	25
Other accidents	12
Suicide	12
Falls	10
Willful homicide	5
Drowning	4
Fires	4

SOURCE: National Safety Council, "Accident Facts," 1965; Population Reference Bureau.

Philadelphia, offenses other than the seven Index crimes constituted 62 percent of all cases in which there was physical injury. Simple assault accounted for the largest percentage of these injuries. But its victims required medical attention in only one-fifth of the cases as opposed to three-fourths of the aggravated assaults, and hospitalization in 7 percent as opposed to 23 percent. Injury was more prevalent in conflicts between persons of the same age than in those in which the victim was older or younger than the attacker.

Property Crimes

The three property crimes of burglary, automobile theft, and larceny of $50 and over make up 87 percent of Index crimes. The Index is a reasonably reliable indicator of the total number of property crimes reported to the police, but not a particularly good indicator of the seriousness of monetary loss from all property crimes. Commission studies tend to indicate that such non-Index crimes as fraud and embezzlement are more significant in terms of dollar volume. Fraud can be a particularly pernicious offense. It is not only expensive in total but all too often preys on the weak.

Many larcenies included in the Index total are misdemeanors rather than felonies under the laws of their own States. Auto thefts that involve only unauthorized use also are misdemeanors in many States. Many stolen automobiles are abandoned after a few hours, and more than 85 percent are ultimately recovered, according to UCR studies. Studies in California indicate that about 20 percent of recovered cars are significantly damaged. . . .

ECONOMIC IMPACT OF INDIVIDUAL CRIMES

The information available about the economic cost of crime is most usefully presented not as an overall figure, but as a series of separate private and public costs. Knowing the economic impact of each separate crime aids in identifying important areas for public concern and guides officials in making judgments about priorities for expenditure. Breakdowns of money now being spent on different parts of the criminal justice system, and within each separate part, may afford insights into past errors.

For example, even excluding value judgments about rehabilitative methods, the fact that an adult probationer costs 38 cents a day and an adult offender in prison costs $5.24 a day suggests the need for reexamining current budget allocations in correctional practice.

Table 3 represents six different categories of economic impacts both private and public. Numerous crimes were omitted because of the lack of figures. Estimates of doubtful reliability were used in other cases so that a fuller picture might be presented. Estimates do not include any amounts for pain and suffering. Except for alcohol, which is based on the amount of tax revenue lost, estimates for illegal goods and services are based on the gross amount of income to the seller. (Gambling includes only the percentage retained by organized crime, not the total amount gambled.) The totals should be taken to indicate rough orders of magnitude rather than precise details.

The picture of crime as seen through cost information is considerably different from that shown by statistics portraying the num-

TABLE 3
ECONOMIC IMPACT OF CRIMES AND RELATED EXPENDITURES
(ESTIMATED IN MILLIONS OF DOLLARS)

General Class of Crime	Component	Component Amount	Class Total
1. Crimes Against Person (loss of earnings, etc.)	Homicide	750	
	Assault and Other	65	
			815
2. Crimes Against Property (transfers and losses)	Unreported Commercial Theft	1,400	
	Index Crimes (robbery, burglary, larceny $50+, auto theft)	600	
	Embezzlement	200	
	Fraud	1,350	
	Forgery and Other	82	
	Property Destroyed by Arson and Vandalism	300	
			3,932
3. Other Crimes	Driving Under Influence of Alcohol	1,816	
	Tax Fraud	100	
	Abortion	120	
			2,036
4. Illegal Goods & Services	Narcotics	350	
	Loan-sharking	350	
	Prostitution	225	
	Alcohol	150	
	Gambling	7,000	
			8,075
5. Public Law Enforcement, Criminal Justice	Police	2,792	
	Corrections	1,034	
	Prosecution and Defense	125	
	Courts	261	
			4,212
6. Private Costs Related to Crime	Prevention Services	1,350	
	Prevention Equipment	200	
	Insurance	300	
	Private Counsel, Bail, Witness Expenses	60	
			1,910

ber of offenses known to the police or the number of arrests:

—Organized crime takes about twice as much income from gambling and other illegal goods and services as criminals derive from all other kinds of criminal activity combined.

—Unreported commercial theft losses, including shoplifting and employee theft, are more than double those of all reported private and commercial thefts.

—Of the reported crimes, willful homicide, though comparatively low in volume, yields the most costly estimates among those listed on the UCR crime Index.

—A list of the seven crimes with the greatest economic impact includes only two, willful homicide and larceny of $50 and over (reported and unreported), of the offenses included in the crime Index.

—Only a small proportion of the money expended for criminal justice agencies is allocated to rehabilitative programs for criminals or for research.

Employee theft, embezzlement, and other forms of crime involving business, which appear in relatively small numbers in the police statistics, loom very large in dollar volume. Direct stealing of cash and merchandise, manipulation of accounts and stock records, and other forms of these crimes, along with shoplifting, appear to constitute a tax of one to two percent on the total sales of retail enterprises, and significant amounts in other parts of business and industry. In the grocery trade, for example, the theft estimates for shoplifting and employee theft almost equal the total amount of profit. Yet Commission and other studies indicate that these crimes are largely dealt with by business itself. Merchants report to the police fewer than one-quarter of the known offenses. Estimates for these crimes are particularly incomplete for nonretail industries.

Fraud is another offense whose impact is not well conveyed by police statistics. Just one conspiracy involving the collapse of a fraudulent salad oil empire in 1964 created losses of $125–$175 million. Fraud is especially vicious when it attacks, as it so often does, the poor or those who live on the margin of poverty. Expensive nostrums for incurable diseases, home-improvement frauds, frauds involving the sale or repair of cars, and other criminal schemes create losses which are not only sizable in gross but are also significant and possibly devastating for individual victims. Although a very frequent offense, fraud is seldom reported to the police. In consumer and business fraud, as in tax evasion, the line between criminal conduct and civil fraud is often unclear. And just as the amount of civil tax evasion is much greater than the amount of criminal tax fraud, the amount of civil fraud probably far exceeds that of criminal fraud.

Cost analysis also places the crimes that appear so frequently in police statistics—robbery, burglary, larceny, and auto theft—in somewhat different perspective. The number of reported offenses for these crimes accounts for less than one-sixth the estimated total dollar loss for all property crimes and would constitute an even lower percentage if there were any accurate way of estimating the very large sums involved in extortion, blackmail, and other property crimes.

This is not to say, however, that the large amounts of police time and effort spent in dealing with these crimes are not important. Robbery and burglary, particularly residential burglary, have importance beyond the number of dollars involved. The effectiveness of the police in securing the return of better than 85 percent of the $500 million worth of cars stolen annually appears to be high, and without the efforts of the police the costs of these crimes would doubtless be higher. As with all categories of crime, the total cost of property crimes cannot be measured because of the large volume of unreported crimes; however, Commission surveys suggest that the crimes that are unreported involve less money per offense than those that are reported.

The economic impact of crimes causing death is surprisingly high. For 1965 there were an estimated 9,850 homicide victims. Of the estimated 49,000 people who lost their lives in highway accidents, more than half were killed in accidents involving either negligent manslaughter or driving under the influence of alcohol. An estimated 290 women died from complications resulting from illegal abortions (nearly one-fourth of all maternal deaths). Measured by the loss of future earnings at the time of death, these losses totaled more than $1½ billion.

The economic impact of other crimes is particularly difficult to assess. Antitrust violations reduce competition and unduly raise prices; building code violations, pure food and drug law violations, and other crimes affecting the consumer have important economic consequences, but they cannot be easily described without further information. Losses due to fear of crime, such as reduced sales in high crime locations, are real but beyond measure.

Economic impact must also be measured in terms of ultimate costs to society. Criminal acts causing property destruction or injury to persons not only result in serious losses to the victims or their families but also the withdrawal of wealth or productive capacity from the economy as a whole. Theft on the other hand does not destroy wealth but merely transfers it involuntarily from the victim, or perhaps his insurance company, to the thief. The bettor purchasing illegal betting services from organized crime may easily absorb the loss of a 10-cent, or even 10-dollar, bet. But from the point of view of society, gambling leaves much less wealth available for legitimate business. Perhaps more important, it is the proceeds of this crime tariff that organized crime collects from those who purchase its illegal wares that form the major source of income that organized crime requires to achieve and exercise economic and political power.

CRIME IN URBAN AREAS

The National Advisory Commission on Civil Disorders

This second set of basic figures on crime provides a more specific picture of crime in urban areas and especially in urban ghettos. It emphasizes that crime rates within cities bear a fairly clear relationship to the poverty of urban neighborhoods, and that the victims of crime in poor neighborhoods are usually the neighborhood residents themselves, not random citizens living in other parts of the city.

Nothing is more fundamental to the quality of life in any area than the sense of personal security of its residents, and nothing affects this more than crime.

In general, crime rates in large cities are much higher than in other areas of our country. Within such cities, crime rates are higher in disadvantaged Negro areas than anywhere else.

The most widely used measure of crime is the number of "index crimes" (homicide, forcible rape, aggravated assault, robbery, burglary, grand larceny, and auto theft) in relation to population. In 1966, 1,754 such crimes were reported to police for every 100,000 Americans. In cities over 250,000, the rate was 3,153, and in cities over one million, it was 3,630—or more than double the national average. In suburban areas alone, including suburban cities, the rate was only 1,300, or just over one-third the rate in the largest cities.

Within larger cities, personal and property insecurity has consistently been highest in the older neighborhoods encircling the downtown business district. In most cities, crime rates for many decades have been higher in these inner areas than anywhere else, except in downtown areas themselves where they are inflated by the small number of residents.

High crime rates have persisted in these inner areas even though the ethnic character of their residents continually changed. Poor immigrants used these areas as "entry ports," then usually moved on to more desirable neighborhoods as soon as they acquired enough resources. Many "entry port" areas have now become racial ghettos.

The difference between crime rates in these disadvantaged neighborhoods and in other parts of the city is usually startling, as a comparison of crime rates in five police

SOURCE: *Report of the National Advisory Commission on Civil Disorders, 1968.*

districts in Chicago for 1965 illustrates. Taking one high-income, all-white district at the periphery of the city, two very low-income, virtually all-Negro districts near the city core, both including numerous public housing projects, and two predominantly white districts, one with mainly lower-middle-income families, the other containing a mixture of very high-income and relatively low-income households, the table shows crime rates against persons and against property in these five districts, plus the number of patrolmen assigned to them per 100,000 residents, as follows:

INCIDENCE OF INDEX CRIMES AND PATROLMEN ASSIGNMENTS
PER 100,000 RESIDENTS IN 5 CHICAGO POLICE DISTRICTS, 1965

Number	High-Income White District	Low-Middle-Income White District	Mixed High and Low-Income White District	Very Low-Income Negro District No. 1	Very Low-Income Negro District No. 2
Index crimes against persons	80	440	338	1,615	2,820
Index crimes against property	1,038	1,750	2,080	2,508	2,630
Patrolmen assigned	93	133	115	243	291

These data suggest the following conclusions:

—Variations in the crime rate against persons within the city are extremely large. One very low-income Negro district had 35 times as many serious crimes against persons per 100,000 residents as did the high-income white district.

—Variations in the crime rate against property are much smaller. The highest rate was only 2.5 times larger than the lowest.

—Both income and race appear to affect crime rates: the lower the income in an area, the higher the crime rate there. Yet low-income Negro areas have significantly higher crime rates than low-income white areas. This reflects the high degree of social disorganization in Negro areas described in the previous chapter, as well as the fact that poor Negroes, as a group, have lower incomes than poor whites, as a group.

—The presence of more police patrolmen per 100,000 residents does not necessarily offset high crime in certain parts of the city. Although the Chicago Police Department had assigned over three times as many patrolmen per 100,000 residents to the highest-crime area shown as to the lowest, crime rates in the highest-crime area for offenses against both persons and property combined were 4.9 times as high as in the lowest-crime area.

Because most middle-class Americans live in neighborhoods similar to the more crime-free district described above, they have little comprehension of the sense of insecurity that characterizes the ghetto resident. Moreover, official statistics normally greatly understate actual crime rates because the vast majority of crimes are not reported to the police. For example, a study conducted for the President's Crime Commission in three Washington, D.C., precincts showed that six times as many crimes were actually committed against persons and homes as were reported to the police. Other studies in Boston and Chicago indicated that about three times as many crimes were committed as were reported.

Two facts are crucial to understand the effects of high crime rates in racial ghettos: most of these crimes are committed by a small minority of the residents, and the principal victims are the residents themselves. Throughout the United States, the great majority of crimes committed by Negroes involve other Negroes as victims, just as most crimes committed by whites are against other whites. A special tabulation made by the Chicago Police Department for the President's Crime Commission indicated that over 85 percent of the crimes committed by Negroes between September 1965 and March 1966 involved Negro victims.

As a result, the majority of law-abiding citizens who live in disadvantaged Negro areas face much higher probabilities of being victimized than residents of most higher-income areas, including almost all suburbs. For nonwhites, the probability of suffering from any index crime except larceny is 78 percent higher than for whites. The probability of being raped is 3.7 times higher among nonwhite women and the probability of being robbed is 3.5 times higher for nonwhites in general.

The problems associated with high crime rates generate widespread hostility toward the police in these neighborhoods for reasons described elsewhere in this Report. Thus, crime not only creates an atmosphere of insecurity and fear throughout Negro neighborhoods but also causes continuing attrition of the relationship between Negro residents and police. This bears a direct relationship to civil disorder.

There are reasons to expect the crime situation in these areas to become worse in the future. First, crime rates throughout the United States have been rising rapidly in recent years. The rate of index crimes against persons rose 37 percent from 1960 to 1966, and the rate of index crimes against property rose 50 percent. In the first nine months of 1967, the number of index crimes was up 16 percent over the same period in 1966 whereas the United States population rose about one percent. In cities of 250,000 to one million, index crime rose by over 20 percent, whereas it increased four percent in cities of over one million.[1]

Second, the number of police available to combat crime is rising much more slowly than the amount of crime. In 1966, there were about 20 percent more police employees in the United States than in 1960, and per capita expenditures for police rose from $15.29 in 1960 to $20.99 in 1966, a gain of 37 percent. But over the six-year period, the number of reported index crimes had jumped 62 percent. In spite of significant improvements in police efficiency, it is clear that police will be unable to cope with their expanding workload unless there is a dramatic increase in the resources allocated by society to this task.

Third, in the next decade the number of young Negroes aged 14 to 24 will increase rapidly, particularly in central cities. This group is responsible for a disproportionately high share of crimes in all parts of the nation. In 1966, persons under 25 years of age comprised the following proportions of those arrested for various major crimes: murder—37 percent; forcible rape—60 percent; robbery—71 percent; burglary—81 percent; larceny—about 75 percent; and auto theft —over 80 percent. For all index crimes together, the arrest rate for Negroes is about four times higher than that for whites. Yet the number of young Negroes aged 14 to 24 in central cities will rise about 63 percent from 1966 to 1975, as compared to only 32 percent for the total Negro population of central cities.[2]

---

[1] The problem of interpreting and evaluating "rising" crime rates is complicated by the changing age distribution of the population, improvements in reporting methods, and the increasing willingness of victims to report crimes. Despite these complications, there is general agreement on the serious increase in the incidence of crime in the United States.

[2] Assuming those cities will experience the same proportion of total United States Negro population growth that they did from 1960 to 1966.

A WAY OF LIFE IN THE GHETTO

Claude Brown and Arthur Dunmeyer

In 1966 the "Ribicoff subcommittee" held a long series of hearings on urban problems, inviting both academic experts and many city residents. One of the most dramatic testimonies of the entire hearings involved Claude Brown, author of *Manchild in the Promised Land,* and Arthur Dunmeyer, a friend of Brown's from Harlem. Both of them had grown up poor and black in the center of a ghetto, and both had long records of crime and arrest as teenagers. Better than more detached analysis, their testimony underscored a basic fact of ghetto life—crime often offers more status, income, and dignity to many ghetto residents than "legitimate" employment. No matter how hard the ghettos are policed, this implies, the links to crime for many in the ghetto cannot really be broken until the nature of "legitimate" employment opportunities radically improves.

SENATOR RIBICOFF: What is the impact on the Negro from the rural South who comes up to the slums of New York? What happens to them physically, emotionally, mentally, morally? What do you find happens when they have to make their change? Your parents came and you were born here, or you were just a child in arms, and now you are older and you observe this. What happens to them then?

MR. BROWN: Once they get there and become disillusioned, they can see the streets aren't paved with gold, and there exist no great economic opportunities for them, they become pressured. Many of the fathers who brought the families can't take the pressure any more, the economic pressure. How can you support a family of five kids on $65 a week? So he just leaves. He just ups one day and leaves; maybe becoming an alcoholic. Maybe he just goes out one night and he is so depressed because he missed a day's pay. During the week—he was sick. He couldn't help it. And he wasn't in the union, and this depression leads to a sort of touchiness, I will say—to become more mundane, where in a bar a person can step on his foot and he or the person gets his throat cut.

SOURCE: *Claude Brown and Arthur Dunmeyer, "A Way of Life in the Ghetto,"* from The Federal Role in Urban Affairs, *Hearings Before the Subcommittee on Executive Reorganization of the Committee on Government Operations. U.S. Senate, 89th Congress, 2d Session, August 29–30, 1966.*

Somebody is dead. The other is in jail. He is going to the electric chair. It won't happen in New York today since they have abolished capital punishment. But this was one of the reactions.

Many of the physical reactions—they took out their frustrations on their kids—they beat the hell out of them. My father used to beat me nearly to death every day. Still they take it out on their wives. They beat their wives. It is just frustration that they feel. . . .

Or maybe the number runner on the corner digs Mama or something. She has got a couple of kids. He can give her $25 a week. All her husband can make is, say, $60 at most a week, and it isn't enough, and the $25 helps because she wants her kids to have the things that TV says that they should have.

You know, these are many of the reactions. And, then, there is the shooting. The guy comes home. He is trying. He comes home. He hears about his wife and he goes out one day, picks up a gun, he says "Oh, Lord, I have tried so hard. It is just not for me. It is my lot to always be a day late and a dollar short. But, this guy has been making it with my woman and he has got to die. This is an affront to my masculinity."

So he kills him. Then he is in jail. His family is on welfare or he is in the electric chair. These are emotional and physical reactions.

I will turn it over to you, Arthur.

MR. DUNMEYER: I would like to bring

this up also. In some cases this is the way you get your drug dealers and prostitutes and your numbers runners. You get people that come here and it is not that they are disillusioned. They see that these things are the only way that they can compete in the society, to get some sort of status. They realize that there aren't any real doors open to them, and so, to commit crime was the only thing to do, they can't go back. There is nothing to go back to. This is understood. This is why they came.

The only thing to do is to get something going to benefit yourself. It is a way to live, a way to have enough to keep your wife from going to bed with the butcher. It is a way to keep from killing the butcher. You kill him in small ways, by taking him off, by holding him up, by seeing that he don't hang out in the neighborhood after the store is closed. It is cheating. It is stealing. These things are just a way of life that come from this one particular thing.

This Negro comes to the promised land, as he says, and he finds that it isn't a promised land and he finds that there is nowhere else to go. There is nothing else to do. And he has the physical and the mental ability to do this particular thing. So he does it as a way of life.

Society has made this law to protect itself, not to protect this man in any way, just to protect itself so there is a law that he can't do this, and he doesn't recognize this law. Really, he doesn't recognize anything in society, because of this one particular thing. He sees there are no doors really open to him; and until these doors can be open to this man and this woman, there is going to be the same thing over and over again.

It is a matter of getting caught. Not a matter of taking or doing anything. It is a matter of getting caught and this is where it comes from.

MR. BROWN: I would like to add something more to this. In the Harlems throughout the Nation, it is like the crimes which society considers crimes, that the Negro who has migrated to the North has to resort to. My father he started—as it is related in the book—one of my most pronounced recollections is seeing my father cut a man's throat when I was at the age of 5. My father and I never got too close because there never was time. He beat the hell out of me quite often, and that was it. We couldn't talk. He had

too many problems, too many frustrations. And there were times when I would be bothering my sisters. I would hit them or something. They'd say, "I'm going to tell Daddy on you and he's going to cut your throat," and I say, "No, he ain't." But I never believed that he wasn't because I had seen him do it.

Anyway, my father started when he came, the only thing he knew was what his father had taught him as a trade, considered illegitimate by Internal Revenue Service, of course, but it was making corn liquor in the bathtub —White Light, King Corn, perhaps you heard of it in those terms. And so he did this and ran his parlor parties and his crap games.

When I was coming up I wanted things, too, as a child, that my parents couldn't give me because my father he wanted to be with his family, he wasn't going to jail and had to give up his way of life, and at this time he was making a little more money. Of course, by the age of 40 or 42 he was making, say, $75 a week, because he had been working on the job for about 15 years at that time and this was a big deal to him. But still, he couldn't afford to give me the things, buy the sport jackets and things that the kids were wearing at the time to go along with the fad of the community. Anyway, I took to selling drugs.

SENATOR RIBICOFF: How old were you when you started selling drugs?

MR. BROWN: I was selling drugs at 13.

SENATOR RIBICOFF: Thirteen?

MR. BROWN: Yes; heroin. Anyway, it is like, in the community, in the Negro ghettos throughout the country, these things that are considered criminal by society, the solid citizen, aren't considered criminal. It is like a war between them and us, the society which oppresses us, and us, the oppressed. When a guy goes to jail, it is OK. You are looked up to, if you are a successful hustler, you have a big Cadillac and you have always got $300 in your pocket, you are taking numbers, you are selling drugs, you are a stickup artist, you are anything, you are a prostitute, anything you may be doing, you are a con man, a hustler. Anybody you heard of, Jim Smith, the mayor, or somebody from Arkansas, this is the way you come up in Harlem. You learn these games at certain ages.

At 13 I learned how to cut drugs, how much quinine to put in cocaine. At the age of 15 I learned how to "Murphy" somebody. The "Murphy" is the flimflam. Anyway, had I been in the South, had I been in a better society, I would have been learning. I would have been in school and learning how to make it legitimately, but I wasn't. I was learning how to make it illegitimately, but these were the best possible ways to make it financially, to establish a decent place for yourself in America's greatest metropolis.

The TV's were saying, yes, get this, you know, have a car. Everybody should have a car. Even color TV, how are you going to get it? You can get it selling drugs. You can get it taking numbers. You know, you can get it playing the Murphy. You can get it if you ran around taking off people, sticking up people, this sort of thing. As long as you were making it, as long as you were a success, that is why in Harlem people respect the guy who is always clean.

You know, he has on a $200 silk suit every day, $55 alligator shoes and this sort of thing. He drives a big Cadillac, and, they know he is winning the war. He is a soldier, he is a real soldier. He is a general in the community. If he gets busted, well, he is just a prisoner of war. That is the way it is looked upon.

MR. DUNMEYER: Or you have a situation where you have got a white fellow from downtown. He is a gangster, and high in society. He can bring the dope in town. He imports it. He brings it uptown. He makes me feel important. I have the money that he has. I can dress the way he dresses. I can drive a car like he drives. I can take care of my family the way he takes care of his. And he is white. So if it is recognition by the white standards, then, I am getting recognition by the white. And this is very important, you are being looked up to in your community. It is just a way of life. So when you get struck, you take it until you get struck again. That is the way it is.

It is not a matter of a guy saying, "I want to go to jail. I am afraid of jail." Jail is on the street just like it is on the inside. The same as, like when you are in jail, they tell you, "Look, if you do something wrong you are going to be put in the hole." You are still in jail, in the hole or out of the hole. You are in jail in the street or behind bars. It is the same thing. . . .

ORGANIZED CRIME: DEMAND, SUPPLY, AND PROFIT

Donald R. Cressey

This selection summarizes the economics of organized crime, illustrating several more general points of the radical view of crime. Clearly, from Cressey's description, organized crime represents a relatively rational supply of "illegal" goods for which there is a demand; the organization and the violence grow out of the precautions necessitated by the goods' illegality. To eliminate the violence or even the criminal activity, one would have to legalize the goods or radically change the nature of employment incentives and satisfactions available in the "legitimate" labor market to participants in organized crime. Cressey's characterization of organized crime as a single monolithic organization, the Cosa Nostra, has since been criticized, but the critics have not disputed his analysis of the economic factors underlying these criminal activities or the reasons that they become organized. The critics have simply contended that we do not know enough to lump all such organizations together into one giant monopoly, as Cressey sometimes seems to do.

These excerpts come from Chapter Five of Cressey's book, *Theft of the Nation: The Structure and Operations of Organized Crime in America.*

SOURCE: Theft of the Nation: The Structure and Operations of Organized Crime in America *by Donald R. Cressey, pp. 72–78, 81–82, 90–99,* 100–101, 107–108. Copyright © 1969 by Donald R. Cressey. Reprinted by permission of Harper & Row, Publishers.

The underworld is what it is largely because Americans are too moral to tolerate human weakness, and because they are too great lovers of liberty to tolerate the tyranny which might make it possible to abolish what they prohibit.

—Walter Lippmann

The American confederation of criminals thrives because a large minority of citizens demands the illicit goods and services it has for sale. As Walter Lippmann observed at the end of the Prohibition era, the basic distinction between ordinary criminals and organized criminals in the United States turns on the fact that the ordinary criminal is wholly predatory, while the man participating in crime on a rational, systematic basis offers a return to the respectable members of society. If all burglars were miraculously abolished, they would be missed by only a few persons to whose income or employment they contribute directly—burglary insurance companies, manufacturers of locks and other security devices, police, prison personnel, and a few others. But if the confederation of men employed in illicit businesses were suddenly abolished, it would be sorely missed because it performs services for which there is a great public demand. The organized criminal, by definition, occupies a position in a social system, an "organization," which has been rationally designed to maximize profits by performing illegal services and providing legally forbidden products demanded by the members of the broader society in which he lives. Just as society has made a place for the confederation by demanding illicit gambling, alcohol and narcotics, usurious loans, and a cheap supply of labor, the confederation has made places, in an integrated set of positions, for the use of the skills of a wide variety of specialists who furnish these goods and services. Organized crime cannot become a social problem until a much broader segment of society perceives that the cost of the services provided is too high.

It is true, of course, that criminals who do not occupy positions in any large-scale organization also supply the same kinds of illicit goods and services supplied by the confederation. Perhaps a large proportion of the persons demanding illicit goods and services believes that they are being supplied by criminals who are unorganized and who, for that matter, are not very criminal. The existence of such a widely held belief would account for the fact that the public indignation which becomes manifest at the time of an exposure of the activities of members of the confederation—such as a Senate hearing, an Appalachian meeting, an execution of an informer—is sporadic and short-lived. A gray-haired old lady who accepts a few horse-racing bets from the patrons of her neighborhood grocery store is performing an illegal service for those patrons, just as is the factory worker who sells his own brand of whiskey to his friends at the plant. Law violators of this kind do not seem very dangerous and, if treated in isolation, such persons cannot be perceived as much of a threat to the social order. Accordingly, they tend to be protected in various ways by their society. The policeman is inclined to overlook the bookmaker's offenses or merely to insist that they not occur in his precinct, the judge is likely to invoke the mildest punishment the legislature has established, and the jailer is likely to differentiate such offenders from "real criminals."

We do not argue that such "mom and pop" kind of catering to the demands of the community is necessarily insidious, though by no means do we condone it. What is insidious is the fact that the providers cannot be individual entrepreneurs for long. "Gambling" cannot be perceived as a social problem until it is widely understood that bookmakers and lottery operators are organized to insure that *making* bets is gambling but *taking* bets is not. The nature of the bookmaking business is such, as we will show later, that bookmakers must join hands with others in the same business. Other illicit businesses have the same character. Nowadays, moreover, free enterprise does not exist in the field of illicit services and goods —any "mom and pop" kind of small illicit business soon takes in, voluntarily or involuntarily, a Cosa Nostra man as a partner.

By joining hands, the suppliers of illicit goods and services (1) cut costs, improve their markets, and pool capital; (2) gain monopolies on certain of the illicit services or on all of the illicit services provided in a specific geographic area, whether it be a neighborhood or a large city; (3) centralize the procedures for stimulating the agencies of law enforcement and administration of justice to overlook the illegal operations; and (4) accumulate vast wealth which can be used to attain even wider monopolies on illicit activities, and on legal businesses as well. In the long run, then, the "small operation" corrupts the traditional economic and political procedures designed to insure that citizens need not pay tribute to a criminal in order to conduct a legitimate business. The demand, and the profits, are too great to be left in the hands of "mom and pop" operators. As the Kefauver Committee reported about the demand for gambling services, "The creeping paralysis of law enforcement which results from a failure to enforce gambling laws contributes to a breakdown in connection with other fields of crime." Organization, not gambling or usury or narcotics distribution or labor racketeering or extortion or murder, is the phenomenon to worry about.

Despite the fact that most forms of gambling are illegal in most parts of the United States, a significant proportion of American citizens want to gamble. They spend about $5 billion annually betting legally at race tracks and an unknown amount gambling legally in Nevada. Estimates of the amount bet illegally each year range from $7 billion to $50 billion. While it is impossible to determine the calculations on which such estimates are made, there is a consensus among law-enforcement officials that illegal betting on horse races, lotteries, and sporting events totals at least $20 billion a year. Cosa Nostra members take about one-third of the gambling gross as their share, so if that gross is in fact $20 billion they acquire some $6 to $7 billion annually. In 1967, the United States spent about $30 billion on the Vietnam war. The total American budget for foreign aid is about $2 billion annually. The $6 or $7 billion going into the hands of organized criminals each year is not all profit. From this amount must be deducted the costs of doing business, such as wages, rent, bribery, and armaments. Neither can it be assumed that this amount is divided equally among the five thousand or so members of Cosa Nostra. But the profits are huge enough to make understandable the fact that any given member of Cosa Nostra is more likely to be a millionaire than not.

In most large American cities, the opportunity to gamble is provided by Cosa Nostra. Members of this organization do not themselves own and operate all the illegal betting and lottery enterprises, but those they do not own they control, or provide with essential services. The organization profits, thus, in three ways. It provides an enterprise for which there is a great demand and, accordingly, for which customers are willing to pay a high price. It secures, by direct intimidation and extortion, a portion of the profits of any competitors who attempt to meet part of the demand. And it provides, in exchange for a portion of profits, reinsurance ("lay-off") services, which any man taking bets needs if he is to avoid being a gambler. . . .

The usury business, usually called "loan-sharking" or "shylocking," consists simply of loaning money at rates higher than the legally prescribed limit, commonly 20 percent per week. No one knows how much revenue organized criminals earn each year from usury. Dollar for dollar, it is a better business than taking bets, but citizens gamble more dollars than they borrow from usurers. It is safe to say, as the President's Commission did, that the business is in "the multibillion-dollar range."

It is not necessary that usury be organized, in the way it is necessary that bet-taking be organized. Any criminal can play. But the criminal who would play must have three things not available to most criminals —customers, capital, and a method of collection. The members of the Cosa Nostra organization that provides illegal gambling for a community possess these three things. For that reason, a large proportion of all contemporary usurers are members of Cosa Nostra or are backed by them. One New York City usurer made a loan of a million dollars in the morning and another loan of a million dollars in the afternoon of the same day. Another man by means of usury increased his net worth from $500,000 in 1960 to $7,500,000 in 1964.

Usurers provide a service which is sorely needed, especially by gamblers and by others whose financial problems arise from a bit of shadiness. Many victims of usury operations are compulsive or eager gamblers who have borrowed from loan sharks in an attempt to recoup gambling losses. While they are not conspirators in the usury operation, they are compromised as conspirators in the gambling activity. As the former Director of the Chicago Police Intelligence Division has said,

The same degree of complicity usually applies to a businessman who wants to borrow money quickly, and for reasons best

known to himself doesn't want anyone to know about the loan. Oftentimes the mere making of such a loan violates ethical standards of his business or social affiliations. When such is the case, the co-conspirator factor indirectly applies and such businessmen rarely become complainants if they can manage to repay the loan.

Some years ago I did a study of embezzlers and found, among other things, that embezzlement is generally an attempt to solve an unsharable financial problem, a problem which the trusted person is ashamed of because it was created by some illegality, immorality, or "foolishness" which he is reluctant to admit to others. Because the trusted person's problem is unsharable, the sources of legitimate loans available to him are cut off. Some trusted persons solve their unsharable financial problems by embezzling. Perhaps others find the solution in the usurious loans available from loan sharks. But this embezzlement-preventing function of usury is not all gravy. In some embezzlement cases the unsharable financial problem is indebtedness to a loan shark. . . .

The interest rates are not constant. Usurers get whatever interest they can get. The commonest loan is the "six for five," which means that next Saturday you pay me six dollars for each five I hand you today. It comes to 20 percent per week. For $400, you pay $80 per week each week until such time as a lump payment of $480 is made. You leave an envelope containing $80 with a tavern owner each Saturday. The payments are due exactly at noon on Saturday, and if you come in at 12:15 at the end of the first week, you owe me another week's interest —on $480, not on $400.

Interest rates can be as low as one percent a week, and as high as 150 percent per week. The variation depends on four conditions— the relationship between the lender and borrower, the intended use of the money, the size of the loan, and the repayment potential. Some loan sharks service a neighborhood in the way a barber or shoe repairman services it. Their "six for five" interest rates on loans made to community residents do not fluctuate much. Even when their capital (often borrowed from a bigger loan shark) diminishes, they do not raise their rates. Loans are viewed as having a price rather than an interest rate, and the price tends to be steady,

just as the neighborhood barber's or shoemaker's prices tend to be steady. This type of loan shark often doubles as a bookmaker. Other loan sharks specialize in financing gamblers, at interest rates not lower than 5 percent a week—260 percent a year. Still a third type, occupying higher Cosa Nostra echelons, loans large sums, at rates of one or 2 percent per week, to other loan sharks and to rather affluent businessmen. Such a man is an especially important figure in the Cosa Nostra organization because he channels the syndicate's proceeds from bet-taking and narcotics into highly profitable circulation. He is known in police and Cosa Nostra circles as a "money mover." . . .

The interest on any loan of $10,000 is high enough to drive a prosperous businessman into bankruptcy. At 20 percent interest per week, such a loan costs $104,000 a year. After the borrower has been bled white, two sequential courses of action are taken. First, he is told to get more money. To stress the seriousness of this request, the usurer is likely to ask leading questions about the routes the borrower's children take to school, or about the shopping and social habits of his wife. These thinly veiled threats often send the borrower to father-in-law, uncle, and grandpa for all the money they possess. But if the borrower's desperate fund-raising campaign fails to produce more money, the usurer hires a goon to hang the borrower out a hotel window by his legs, to break his arms, to kick him in the stomach, or to take similar action. Collectors usually work on a commission basis, receiving half the amount of interest they collect. . . .

Someone estimates the cost of everything. The McClellan Committee estimated that the drug addicts in the United States spend about $350 million a year for heroin. The Committee estimated, further, that narcotics importers and wholesalers had a standard income of about 6 percent of this gross, something like the stockholders of a public-utilities corporation. This puts the profit of a few Cosa Nostra members, who are in the business of importing and wholesaling narcotics, at about $21 million annually.

Members of Cosa Nostra do not hustle a hundred dollars here and a hundred dollars there selling heroin to dope fiends. The profits in this retail operation are too low, and the risks are too great. Transactions with addicts are handled by independent "dealers" (the word "pusher" is rarely used on the street) who work like dogs to keep up their own habits or, consistently, their own cool style of living. Dealers make a dollar wherever they can find it. They usually have a few "holes" (women) whoring for them, and they might fence stolen property now and then. In fact, they might even steal the property before they fence it. Some own apartment houses or other income-producing property that doesn't take too much time away from their hustle. Such street-level narcotics dealers are indispensable to Cosa Nostra. Later we will show that they play roles which might be considered parts of the organization. However, the dealers rarely are members of Cosa Nostra.

Gambling money moves upward from the street through at least six levels of a personnel hierarchy. Narcotics move downward through the same hierarchy, except that they are not ordinarily handled by the street-level workers serving as bookmakers and lottery-ticket salesmen. Narcotics retailers do not work on the sharecropper plan utilized by bookmakers and lottery operators. Because the heroin business involves a commodity rather than a service, it operates like a legitimate importing-distributing-wholesaling-retailing business. Each member of the personnel hierarchy buys and then sells. The street-level dealer is an independent businessman who purchases at wholesale prices and sells at retail prices. He might or might not be required to buy from a specific wholesaler, at risk of his life. If the dealer, or anyone else in the heroin industry, doesn't have enough money to finance his purchases, he can always borrow from a usurer. Narcotics operators are good usury risks because drug addicts desperately need the product they have for sale.

At the top are importers of multi-kilo lots. At the next level are "kilo men," who handle nothing less than a kilogram of heroin at a time. A kilo man makes his purchase from an importer-supplier and receives delivery from a courier. He dilutes the heroin by adding three kilograms of milk sugar for each kilo of heroin. The product is then sold to "quarter-kilo men" and then to "ounce men" and then to "deck men," there being further adulteration at each stage in this process. Eventually, street dealers dispense it in five-grain packets called "bags" or "packs" or "balloons." The cost to the consumer is in excess of three hundred times the cost of the original kilo.

Use of the "kilo man" term varies from community to community. Sometimes it refers to all the men working at the three highest levels in the business organization— the importer, the man who buys from the importer, and the man to whom it is sold in bulk lots. This *third* man, rather than the second man, sells the drug to the "quarter-kilo men." In the San Francisco area, the "kilo man" terminology is rarely used, but the level of what is called "the big-time dealer" is about the same as that of "kilo men" in other cities. The "big-time dealer" buys heroin in pound lots, delivered by "runners" (couriers), who bring it from Los Angeles, at $3500 to $4000 per pound. The "big-time dealer" adds about 94 to 98 percent milk sugar to the heroin and sells it to a "piece man" at $250 an ounce. The "piece man" sells in ounce lots to a "spoon man," who cuts the ounces and sells to a "bag man," who in turn may divide the "spoons" into $10 "balloons" ($1/4$ to $1/2$ gram). Most street-level dealers handle "big bags," or "spoons," of about 2 grams and costing from $40 to $60, depending on the percentage of heroin. In the course of a year, a dealer may slide up and down the scale from "pieces" to "balloons," but Alan G. Sutter has shown that the prestige rests with the "piece man," and organizational positions for "piece men" persist, as do the other positions, even if they are vacated by specific dealers.

A major portion of the heroin used in the United States comes originally from Turkey. The heroin traffic is organized like an hourglass, with ten to fifteen Cosa Nostra members occupying the center section. The top section consists of hundreds of Turkish farmers, each of whom produces a small crop, and dozens of processors who refine the raw material first in Syria and Lebanon and then in southern France and Italy. The bottom section of the hourglass consists of the "piece men" or "quarter-kilo men" and all the street-level salesmen beneath them. The farmer in Turkey gets about $35 per pure kilogram of opium, and the addicts of New York pay about $225,000 for this much unadulterated heroin.

The bookmaker or lottery operator might

be required, at risk of his life, to split his gross with a Cosa Nostra clique. Members of Cosa Nostra, thus, rely on control of a large number of local bookmaking and lottery operations for their huge profits. However, the heroin business is not, on the retail level, organized like bookmaking is. Territory is not allocated, financial backing is not provided, and protection from arrest and imprisonment is not offered, let alone guaranteed. That is why dealing in heroin on the street is so much riskier than taking bets. Dealing is not riskier than bookmaking simply because the penalties for selling heroin are greater than the penalties for taking bets; the difference lies in the fact that the dealer has no organization behind him. A member of the Cosa Nostra "family" operating in a city might require that heroin dealers in his area buy from him or die, but once the dealer buys his drugs from the syndicate he is on his own. He does the best he can.

The importation and wholesale distribution of narcotics takes huge amounts of cash, like usury. Just anyone cannot get into the business. Even without the risks of imprisonment, the illegal business is risky enough. Fortunes are lost whenever a big shipment of narcotics is confiscated by customs agents or other law-enforcement officials. About 20 percent of the attempted flow is confiscated. Perhaps a shipment is hijacked now and then, as truckloads and shiploads of alcohol were hijacked during the period of Prohibition, but I have never heard of such an event occurring at the importation or wholesaling levels. The demand for heroin is great, and the fact that heroin is illegal makes it horribly expensive. For persons who are willing to risk imprisonment, who have enough capital to finance huge purchases, and who have enough additional capital to carry them through huge but temporary losses stemming from confiscations, the profits are enormous. Cosa Nostra members have these characteristics. Other persons also have them, of course, and for that reason Cosa Nostra has competitors in the narcotics importation and wholesaling business, especially on the West Coast.

Because American business and industry has been extensively unionized, industrialists and businessmen seek black-market labor. Cosa Nostra meets this demand, and frequently cheats the businessmen who make it. Fraud, extortion, and bribery are the basic crimes involved when Cosa Nostra members work as labor brokers. But these same crimes, plus income-tax evasion, are the foundations of all the organizations' activities. In order to differentiate Cosa Nostra's activities in the labor field from its activities elsewhere, law-enforcement personnel some years ago began using the term "labor racketeering" to refer to the former. Unfortunately, this term directs our attention away from the fact that all Cosa Nostra operations are, basically, racketeering. It is quite appropriate to speak of Cosa Nostra involvement in "usury racketeering," "business racketeering," and even, in the case of monopolizing illegal bet-taking businesses, "racketeering racketeering." All involve extortion of the kind used by Lord Clive, founder of the British Empire in India, who in his youth formed a gang of fellow delinquents to collect tribute from shopowners who did not wish to have their windows broken. All take organization.

Four fundamental operations are involved when Cosa Nostra members become labor brokers. Three of the operations, in their many variations, are provided as a service to greedy, crooked, or shady businessmen who have created the demand for a cheap supply of labor. In the fourth kind of operation, the Cosa Nostra member steals from his own union.

First, real unionization of some businesses is prevented by pretending, for a fee, that the shops are unionized. Nine men riding in two convertible-topped automobiles parked by the door of a sandwich shop. Two Cosa Nostra men walked into the shop. One handed the proprietor a business card and said, "You got to sign up with this union, right now." The proprietor, who had only four employees, replied, "I can't give you the answer right now." The second Cosa Nostra member was a bit persuasive: "Listen, you better sign, otherwise we know where you live." The man signed, but his employees never were really unionized. The employer paid their "initiation fee" and he regularly paid their "dues," all of which were simply pay-offs to the two men. He was never asked for a list of his employees, and the employees had no idea that they were union members. Since he paid his employees wages lower than the rates set by legitimate unions, the apparent extortion turned out to be a pretty jolly affair for all except the workers.

For a larger business, $5000 a year is a

cheap price for a nonunion "unionized" shop. One trucking firm is so well known to be controlled by Cosa Nostra that it is called a "mob's barn." The company is "unionized," but the workers do not get union wages. There is no "union trouble" in this company.

Second, in a variation of the first operation, employees are made members of fictitious "paper locals" which have been established in part to help greedy employers reduce labor costs. In the "sweetheart-contract" operation, a Cosa Nostra member for a fee writes a labor contract that cheats the workers out of wages and benefits they could legitimately obtain at the bargaining table. For example, most union contracts specify the names of the holidays to which the employees are entitled—New Year's, Christmas, Easter, Fourth of July, Rosh Hashanah, Passover, Washington's Birthday, Thanksgiving Day. But "sweetheart contracts" might restrict employees to only one or two holidays a year. In one such contract negotiated by the stupid Cosa Nostra president of a paper local, the only holiday granted to a work force made up exclusively of Catholic Puerto Ricans was Passover. A man who could neither read nor write was vice president of one fictitious Cosa Nostra local.

A company that manufactures chairs suddenly stopped manufacturing the cushions for the chairs. It began to purchase them, instead, from a newly formed company which was owned by a Cosa Nostra member. Shortly thereafter, a new union local was formed, and the son of the cushion company's owner became president of it. The union then "organized" both the chair company and the cushion company. About a dozen friends and relatives of the cushion-company owner were put on the payroll of the chair company.

In a beautiful double cross, two Cosa Nostra members acting as business agents for a real union local agreed to let a shopkeeper pay them fees for a highly favorable contract. But later they went back for more. They told the shopkeeper that they had never reported the fraudulent contract to the local, then handed him a new contract with a different local, and demanded another pay-off. The shopkeeper paid, but he reported the matter to the district attorney, who convicted the two men of extortion, despite the fact that the shopkeeper's hands were by no means clean. But the district attorney never

was able to find the second local, which simply disappeared. Its address was the same as that of a Cosa Nostra leader's office, but no union records could be found.

Fictitious locals are business properties. A low-level Cosa Nostra member engaged in gambling, usury, and narcotics financing simply purchased, for $30,000, a small-town union local from a Cosa Nostra boss. Later he sold a part interest in the local to a friend.

Third, employers are threatened with labor strife or mayhem if they do not pay under-the-table fees to the Cosa Nostra members heading union locals, "paper" or otherwise. This, of course, is the outright extortion called "labor racketeering." It need not be, however. One man paid a union to picket his competitor, believing that the competitor wouldn't be able to pay them off because he had already done so. He was wrong. The competitor paid the officers of the local a higher fee, and they picketed the originator of the plot.

It is not at all unusual for a Cosa Nostra union official to engage in a mild form of extortion by demanding that his relatives be put on the company payroll. In another thinly veiled form of extortion, some Cosa Nostra union "leaders" demand that the employing company hire them as "labor consultants." One company avoids paying some of its income taxes by overpaying one of its suppliers and then secretly taking the overpayment back. It uses the same scheme to bribe the president of a union local. Thus, it overpays a Cosa Nostra member for merchandise supplied by him. This man, in turn, passes the overpayment on to a second Cosa Nostra member, who is president of the local.

Cosa Nostra members have effectively used the National Labor Relations Board as part of their pressure for extortion. One man stated his "paper local's" terms to a shopkeeper, who refused them. The crook threatened to report him to the NLRB for unwillingness to negotiate, which is an unfair labor practice. As a variant, a Cosa Nostra union leader struck a company so that his brother, owner of a competing company, would get more business.

While some Cosa Nostra men get rich by threatening strikes or slowdowns if businessmen do not pay under-the-table fees, others make a nice living by offering their services in the settling of "labor disputes" of this kind. In April, 1968, *The New York Times* reported that a grand jury had indicted the vice president of Spartan Industries—of which the billion-dollar E. J. Korvette chain of discount stores is a wholly owned subsidiary—for perjuring himself in testimony about such an arrangement. The indictment said the vice president had made a move for labor peace by seeking the aid of three hoodlums, two of them reputed Cosa Nostra leaders. In return for the help of the three "labor consultants," companies formed by them were to be given contracts to provide Korvette's with basic services such as window washing and garbage collection. The vice president was to share in the profits of the companies. Specifically, the indictment charged that the vice president had committed perjury when he told a grand jury he had never asked a reputed lieutenant in a New York Cosa Nostra "family" to help him persuade an unidentified labor union official to "lay off" in his demands. The case has not yet come up for trial.

Fourth, funds are stolen or otherwise obtained illegally from union funds or from union pension and welfare systems. This varies from the simple fraud of putting one's wife on the payroll to overpaying a consultant for services rendered. Funds are commonly embezzled by sending large checks to lawyers for nonexistent services. One local borrowed money from its own welfare fund, then used the money to buy Cadillacs for each of its Cosa Nostra officials. Two union locals jointly "purchased" a Cosa Nostra member's summer home for $150,000 but never used it. One union official bought a great deal of jewelry at one store with embezzled union funds. He was reported to the police by an irate union member who happened to notice the purchase and said, "Something crooked must be going on as no one pays full retail prices for jewelry, especially union officers who have many contacts."

The industries which seem to be most susceptible to shakedowns and to connivance between employers and union officials are those employing unskilled or only semiskilled labor. Significantly, it is the unions serving such industries that are most likely to be controlled by Cosa Nostra members. Many of the New York companies engaged in housewrecking are nonunion, and even the companies having union contracts hire non-

union personnel on occasion. There is a saving of some $2.50 per hour per man, and this difference permits the dishonest company to underbid the honest companies, even when the dishonest company must pay an illegal fee to a corrupt union official. Cosa Nostra members seek control of the officers of union locals so they can get a share of the pay-offs. "Control" may be secured legitimately, by helping an officer win a union election. More frequently it is achieved illegitimately, by outright extortion from an honest or dishonest official.

The American demand for illicit goods and services produces huge Cosa Nostra profits, which are then invested in legitimate enterprises in politics. Robert F. Kennedy made the following statement while he was Attorney General of the United States: "What is at least disturbing—and for me insidious—is the increasing encroachment of the big businessmen of the rackets into legitimate business." Cosa Nostra members have been, and are, acquiring and operating legitimate enterprises, ranging from Las Vegas casinos to huge corporations, to butcher shops, to restaurants and bars. Moreover, some of them have deposited huge sums in Swiss banks, and they draw on these fruits of crime whenever they want to buy or corrupt another large piece of America. Carmine Lombardozzi, a New York Cosa Nostra leader, once obtained control of a Wall Street brokerage house, and used it fraudulently to sell stock to the public. . . .

There are four possible combinations of legitimate-illegitimate acquisition and legitimate-illegitimate operation of businesses, and Cosa Nostra members participate in all of them. Some businesses are legitimately purchased with the fruits of crime and operated legitimately. Others are legitimately purchased with the fruits of crime and operated illegitimately. A third possibility involves illegitimate acquisition and legitimate operation, while the fourth alternative is to acquire a business illegitimately and then to operate it illegitimately. No outsider knows which of these four types is dominant. There is a tendency to look at Las Vegas, where until recently the profits from illegal bet-taking and other crimes were secretly invested in certain legitimate casinos which were operated illegally (at least so far as income-tax payments are concerned), and then to assume that all businesses owned by Cosa Nostra members are operated illegally. It is quite possible, however, that most of the legitimate businesses owned by Cosa Nostra members are operated legitimately, at least most of the time. . . .

The principal operations of organized criminals are not independent of each other. Bet-taking, usury, narcotics distribution, labor fraud and extortion, corruption of government, and control of legitimate businesses all go together. Legitimate interests serve as an outlet for the vast amounts of money acquired illegitimately and also provide a tax cover. With the aid of lawyers and accountants, some of whom have done a tour of duty as employees of the Internal Revenue Service, members of Cosa Nostra now insure that it is extremely difficult to catch them in income-tax evasion. Ownership of legitimate enterprises creates an aura of respectability. Moreover, by investing in legitimate businesses the profits of illicit businesses, the member is able to make his money, which is the fruit of crime and therefore contraband, earn more money. When the contraband money is invested in legitimate businesses, it is almost impossible to trace it to its criminal source.

THE CRIME OF CORPORATIONS

Edwin H. Sutherland

This analysis of corporate crime thoroughly emphasizes a basic point of the radical analysis of crime. Crime in corporations—"white-collar crime," as it is often called—is frequent and pervasive. It often grows out of the normal competitive operations of business, but it is almost always treated differently than other kinds of crime. It must be considered "criminal" behavior, but is rarely punished in the way that lower-class crimes are punished. Sutherland concludes, therefore: "The assumption that an offender must have some such pathological distortion of the intellect or the emotions seems to me absurd, and if it is absurd regarding the crimes of businessmen, it is equally absurd regarding the crimes of persons in the lower economic class."
Sutherland pioneered the study of white-collar crime during the 1940's. This essay was one of the first he prepared on corporate crime. Although it appeared in the early 1950's and is thus descriptive of an earlier era, it is nonetheless the classic analysis of corporate crime. The behavior of corporations, from everything one reads, has hardly changed since Sutherland wrote.

About twenty years ago I began to study violations of law by businessmen and have continued the study intermittently to the present day. This study was begun for the purpose of improving the general explanations of criminal behavior. The theories of crime which were then current and which are still current emphasized social and personal pathologies as the causes of crime. The

SOURCE: *From* The Sutherland Papers *edited by Albert Cohen, Alfred Lindesmith, and Karl Schuessler. Copyright © 1956 by Indiana University Press. Reprinted by permission.*

social pathologies included, especially, poverty and the social conditions related to poverty, such as poor housing, lack of organized recreational facilities, the ignorance of parents, and family disorganization. The personal pathology emphasized in the earlier period was feeblemindedness; the early theory asserted that feeblemindedness is inherited and is the cause of both poverty and crime. At about the time I started the study of business crimes, the personal pathology which was used to explain crime was shifting from defective intelligence to defective emotions, as represented by such concepts as frustration, the inferiority complex, and the Oedipus complex.

These theories that crime is due to social and personal pathologies had considerable support from the fact that a very large proportion of the persons arrested, convicted, and committed to prisons belong to the lower economic class.

In contrast to those theories, my theory was that criminal behavior is learned just as any other behavior is learned and that personal and social pathologies play no essential part in the causation of crime. I believed that this thesis could be substantiated by a study of the violation of law by businessmen. Businessmen are generally not poor, are not feebleminded, do not lack organized recreational facilities, and do not suffer from the other social and personal pathologies. If it can be shown that businessmen, without these pathologies, commit many crimes, then such pathologies cannot be used as the explanation of the crimes of other classes. The criminologists who have stated the theories of crimes get their data from personal interviews with criminals in the criminal courts, jails, and prisons, or from criminal statistics based on the facts regarding such criminals. But when businessmen commit crimes, their cases go generally before courts under equity or civil jurisdictions or before quasi-judicial commissions, seldom before the criminal courts. Consequently, the criminologists do not come into contact with these businessmen and have not included their violations of law within general theories of criminal behavior.

I have used the term "white-collar criminal" to refer to a person in the upper socioeconomic class who violates the laws designed to regulate his occupation. The term "white collar" is used in the sense in which it was used by President Sloan of General Motors, who wrote a book entitled *The Autobiography of a White Collar Worker*. The term is used more generally to refer to the wage-earning class that wears good clothes at work, such as clerks in stores.

I wish to report specifically on a part of my study of white-collar crimes. I selected the seventy largest industrial and commercial corporations in the United States, not including public utilities and petroleum corporations. I have attempted to collect all the records of violations of law by each of these corporations, so far as these violations have been decided officially by courts and commissions. I have included the laws regarding restraint of trade; misrepresentation in advertising; infringement of patents, copyrights, and trademarks; rebates; unfair labor practices, as prohibited by the National Labor Relations Law; financial fraud; violations of war regulations; and a small miscellaneous group of other laws. The records include the life careers of the corporations, which average about forty-five years, and the subsidiaries as well as the main corporations. In this search, I have been limited by the available records found in a university library, and this is far from complete. I am sure that the number of crimes I shall report on is far smaller than the number actually decided by the courts and commissions against these corporations.

This tabulation of the crimes of the seventy largest corporations in the United States gives a total of 980 adverse decisions. Every one of the seventy corporations has a decision against it, and the average number of decisions is 14.0. Of these seventy corporations, 98 percent are recidivists; that is, they have two or more adverse decisions. Several states have enacted habitual criminal laws, which define an habitual criminal as a person who has been convicted four times of felonies. If we use this number and do not limit the convictions to felonies, 90 percent of the seventy largest corporations in the United States are habitual criminals. Sixty of the corporations have decisions against them for restraint of trade, fifty-four for infringements, forty-four for unfair labor practices, twenty-seven for misrepresentation in advertising, twenty-six for rebates, and forty-three for miscellaneous offenses.

These decisions have been concentrated in the period since 1932. Approximately 60 percent of them were made in the ten-year period subsequent to 1932, and only 40 percent in the forty-year period prior to 1932. One possible explanation of this concentration is that the large corporations are committing more crimes than they did previously. My own belief is that the prosecution of large corporations has been more vigorous during the later period and that the corporations have not appreciably increased in criminality.

Of the seventy large corporations, thirty were either illegal in their origin or began illegal activities immediately after their origin, and eight additional corporations should probably be added to this thirty. Thus, approximately half of the seventy corporations were either illegitimate in birth, or were infant and juvenile delinquents, as well as adult criminals.

All of the 980 adverse decisions were decisions that these corporations violated laws. Only 159 of these 980 decisions were made by criminal courts, whereas 425 were made by courts under civil or equity jurisdiction and 361 by commissions. The most important question regarding white-collar crime is whether it is really crime. That is a difficult and somewhat technical question, and I shall not attempt to deal with it here since I have published another paper on that question. The general conclusion stated in that paper is that the violations of law which were attested by decisions of equity and civil courts and by administrative commissions are, with very few exceptions, crimes.

The statistics which I have presented are rather dry and may not mean much to the average student who is not a specialist in this field, but the prevalence of white-collar crimes by large corporations can be illustrated more concretely. If you consider the life of a person, you find that from the cradle to the grave he has been using articles which were sold or distributed in violation of the law. The professional criminals use the word "hot" to refer to an article which has been recently stolen. For the purpose of simplicity of statement, I wish to use this word to refer to articles manufactured by corporations, but I shall expand the meaning to include any official record without restricting it to recent times and shall refer to a class of articles rather than articles manufactured by a particular concern. Using the word in this sense, we can say that a baby is assisted into this world with the aid of "hot" surgical instruments, rubbed with "hot" olive oil, wrapped in a "hot" blanket, weighed on "hot" scales. The father, hearing the good news, runs a "hot" flag up on his flag pole, goes to the golf course and knocks a "hot" golf ball around the course. The baby grows up surrounded by such articles and is finally laid to rest in a "hot" casket under a "hot" tombstone.

I now wish to describe in more detail violations of some of the specific laws and shall take first misrepresentation in advertising.

Although the Pure Food and Drug Law contains a provision prohibiting misrepresentation on the labels of foods and drugs, the administrators of that law have not published regular reports including the names of the corporations that have been found to be in violation of the law. I shall therefore restrict the discussion to the misrepresentations in advertisements which have been decided on by the Federal Trade Commission.

This is one of the less important white-collar crimes in comparison with the others. Decisions have been made in ninety-seven cases against twenty-six of seventy corporations. No decisions were made against forty-four of the seventy large corporations under this law. Of these forty-four corporations against which no decisions were made, twenty-seven may be classed as nonadvertising corporations. That is, they do not advertise for purposes of their sales, although they may advertise for general goodwill or for the goodwill of the newspapers and journals. They sell their products to expert buyers, who cannot be influenced by advertising. It would be a waste of money for U.S. Steel to distribute pamphlets among the expert buyers of its products, claiming that its products were made from the finest ores or with Bessemer steel imported from England or to show a picture of a movie star in a Pullman saying, "I always select railroads which use rails made by U.S. Steel, because they are better rails" or a picture of a baseball manager saying, "I feel that my players are safer if they ride the trains on rails made by U.S. Steel, because these rails are safer." If these large corporations which do not advertise for sales purposes are eliminated, approximately 60 percent of the large corporations which do advertise for sales purposes have decisions against them for misrepresentation in advertising.

These misrepresentations in advertising are not, in most cases, mere technical violations. The Federal Trade Commission each year makes a survey of several hundred thousand advertisements in periodicals and over the radios. From these they select about 50,000 which are questionable, and from these they pick out about 1,500 as patently false, making adverse decisions against about 1,000 of these each year. Also, in their selection, they tend to concentrate on certain products in one year and other products in other years. About 1941, they concentrated on false advertisements of vitamins and issued desist orders against about twenty-five firms on this one product. The advertisements of vitamins at that time claimed with practically no qualifications that vitamins would restore vigor, aid digestion, eliminate sterility, prevent miscarriage, increase sex vigor, decrease blood pressure, reduce neuritis, reduce insomnia, stop falling hair, cure hay fever and asthma, cure alcoholism, prevent tooth decay, eliminate pimples, make chickens lay more eggs, and keep the dog in good health.

Misrepresentations fall into three principal classes: First, some advertisements are designed to sell products which are physically dangerous, with the dangers denied, minimized, or unmentioned. Most of these advertisements are in the drug and cosmetic businesses. Only two of the seventy large corporations have decisions against them for advertisements of this nature.

Second, some advertisements exaggerate the values of the products, and this is equivalent to giving short weights. An extreme case of advertisements of this nature was a case decided against two hoodlums in Chicago about 1930. They sold a bottle of medicine at a price of $10 to a blind man with the claim that this would cure his blindness. When analyzed, the medicine was found to consist of two aspirins dissolved in Lake Michigan water. The hoodlums were convicted and sentenced to six months' imprisonment. The advertisements by large corporations are frequently of this class, except that they are not so extreme and are not followed by convictions in criminal courts and imprisonment. Garments advertised and sold as silk or wool are almost entirely cotton. Alligator shoes not made from alligator hides, walnut furniture not made from walnut lumber, turtle-oil facial cream not made from turtle-oil, Oriental rugs not made in the Orient, Hudson seal furs not made from the skins of seals are further instances of such misrepresentation. Caskets advertised as rustproof are not rustproof, garments as mothproof when they are not mothproof, garden hose as three-ply when it is only two-ply, and radios as "all-wave reception" that do not receive all waves. Electric pads are advertised with switches for high, medium, and low heat, when in fact they have only two degrees of heat. Storage eggs are sold as fresh eggs, old and reconditioned stoves as

new stoves, and worn and reconditioned hats as new hats. Facial creams sold as skin foods, corrective of wrinkles, do not feed the skin or correct wrinkles. Some corporations advertise that their tea is made from tender leaves, especially picked for these corporations, when in fact their tea is purchased from lots brought in by importers who sell the same tea to other firms. Cigarettes are advertised as having been made from the finest tobacco, for which the company pays 25 percent more, but other cigarettes are also made from the "finest tobacco" for which the manufacturers pay 25 percent more than they do for chewing tobacco.

The third class of misrepresentation overlaps the two preceding and is separated from them principally because certain advertisements do special injury to the competitors rather than to consumers. One mail-order company advertised its furnaces as containing features which no other furnaces contained, when in fact the furnaces of competitors contained the same features. Consumers Research Service, which claimed to make impartial and unbiased appraisals of automobiles, was found to be receiving payments from an automobile company for reporting that their cars were superior.

I wish to describe a few of the important cases of misrepresentation in advertising. A prominent automobile manufacturer originated the 6 percent installment purchase plan in 1935. This plan as advertised stated that the interest rate on unpaid balances on cars purchased on the installment plan was only 6 percent. The Federal Trade Commission, after an investigation, reported that the interest rate was actually in excess of 11 percent and that the exaggeration in the interest rate was nearly 100 percent. Before the commission had ordered the pioneer firm to desist from this misrepresentation, practically all the other large automobile companies adopted the same method of taking money under false pretenses. Again, in 1936, all the important automobile companies were ordered on two counts to desist from misrepresentation in advertising their cars. First, they quoted a price which did not include necessary parts and accessories, the price for the car as actually equipped being 10 percent higher than the advertised price. In addition, they added handling charges independent of transportation costs, which further increased the price required. Second, they advertised a picture of a car which was not the model actually named and priced. Again, in 1941, three of the four principal manufacturers of automobile tires were ordered to desist from misrepresentation in their advertisements of special sales prices on the Fourth of July and on Labor Day. These companies advertised prices which were reductions of 20 to 50 percent from the regular prices. When the Federal Trade Commission investigated, it found that the 20 percent reduction was actually only an 8 percent reduction and the 50 percent reduction only an 18 percent reduction. In addition, one tire company was found to have engaged in misrepresentation in two respects. First, it advertised that with its tires a car would stop 25 percent quicker. It did not say 25 percent quicker than what, but the implication was 25 percent quicker than with tires of other manufacturers; this was not true. Second, it made claims for the greater safety of its tires on the basis of the fact that these tires were used in the Indianapolis Speedway races, whereas in fact the Speedway tires had been especially constructed, so that there was no assurance that the company's tires for regular passenger cars were safer than other tires.

When the Federal Bureau of Investigation hunts kidnappers, it tries to find everyone who is in any way accessory to the kidnapping. The Federal Trade Commission, similarly, has attempted to some degree to bring into the picture those who are accessory to misrepresentation in advertising. They have, for instance, issued desist orders to many of the advertising agencies that prepare the advertising campaigns for the manufacturers. Though these desist orders have included many small and unimportant advertising agencies, they have included also the largest and most prominent agencies.

Also, practically all the newspapers and popular journals have participated in dissemination of false advertisements. These include publications which range from the Gannett publications at one extreme to the *Journal of the American Medical Association* at the other. Although the *Journal of the American Medical Association* claims that it does not carry advertisements which have not been checked and found to be true, it has for years carried advertisements of Philip Morris cigarettes. In earlier years, the Philip Morris Company had claimed that these cigarettes cured irritated throats and in later years

claimed that they produced less irritation in the throat than other cigarettes. As proof of their truth, these advertisements cited the opinions and experiments of physicians many, if not all, of whom had received payment for their statements. Competing tobacco companies employed other physicians, who performed experiments and gave testimony which conflicted with the testimony in the *Journal of the American Medical Association*. The Philip Morris Company made a grant of $10,000 to St. Louis University to test these propositions. The medical school insisted on complete freedom in its methods of testing and in making its report. The report was that no accurate method of testing throat irritation or of testing the effect of the substances in question had been devised and that conflicting claims of experimenters were all bunk. The Philip Morris Company gave no publicity to that report, but their advertisements continued to appear in the *Journal of the American Medical Association*.

I do not want to take the time to go into similar detail in regard to other types of violations of law, but I shall describe a few incidents involving violations of the National Labor Relations Law. This law was enacted first in 1933 and in more developed form in 1935. It stated that collective bargaining had proved to be a desirable policy and prohibited employers from interfering with the efforts of employees to organize unions for purposes of collective bargaining. A violation of this law was declared to be an unfair labor practice. Decisions have been made against forty-three of the seventy large corporations, or 60 percent, with a total of 149 decisions. Of these forty-three corporations, 72 percent are recidivists, or repeaters; thirty-nine used interference, restraint, and coercion; thirty-three discriminated against union members; thirty-four organized company unions; thirteen used labor spies; and five used violence. Violence has been confined largely to the steel and automobile industries. One steel corporation from 1933 to 1937 purchased 143 gas guns, while the police department of Chicago purchased in the same years only thirteen; the steel corporation also purchased 6,714 gas shells and grenades, while the Chicago police department purchased only 757. The corporations customarily argue that they purchase this military equipment merely to protect themselves against the violence of the unions.

Doubtless the equipment is used for protective purposes, but it is also used on some occasions for aggression. I wish to report one decision of the National Labor Relations Board concerning the Ford Motor Company. Henry Ford is reported to have said in 1937, "We'll never recognize the United Automobile Workers Union or any other union." The Ford Corporation organized a service department, under the supervision of Harry Bennett, an expugilist, and staffed it with 600 members equipped with guns and blackjacks. Frank Murphy, at the time Governor of Michigan and previously mayor of Detroit, said, regarding this service department, "Henry Ford employs some of the worst gangsters in our city."

In 1937 the United Automobile Workers Union was attempting to organize the employees in the River Rouge plant of the Ford Motor Company. A public announcement was made that the organizers would distribute literature at this plant at a specified time. Reporters and others gathered in advance. When a reporter asked a guard what they were going to do when the organizers arrived, the guard replied, "We are going to throw them to hell out of here." The organizers arrived, went with their literature up onto an overhead pass into one of the entrances. There they were informed that they were trespassing on private property. According to many witnesses they turned quietly and started away. As they were leaving, they were attacked by the service staff. They were beaten, knocked down, and kicked. Witnesses described this as a "terrific beating" and as "unbelievably brutal." The beating not only occurred on the overhead pass but was continued into the public highway. One man's back was broken and another's skull fractured. The cameras of reporters, who were taking pictures of the affray, were seized by the guards and the films destroyed. A reporter who was taking a picture from the highway was observed by a guard, who shouted, "Smash that camera!" The reporter jumped into the automobile of another reporter, and they were chased by the guards at a speed of 80 miles an hour through the streets of Detroit until they could secure refuge in a police station. According to prearranged plans, women organizers arrived later to distribute literature. As they alighted from the streetcar at the entrance to the plant, they were attacked by the guards and pushed back into the cars. One woman was knocked down and kicked. While these assaults were being committed, city policemen were present but did not interfere; the director of the service department was also present.

I wish next to give a few illustrations of embezzlement and violation of trust by officers of corporations. Seiberling organized the Goodyear Rubber Company and was its manager for many years. Because of financial difficulties in the corporation, he lost control of it in 1921. His successors found that Seiberling was short nearly $4,000,000 in his account with the company; that is, he had embezzled that amount from the company. The suits which were brought resulted in a settlement by which Seiberling agreed to reimburse the company. He not only did this but also secured credit from Ohio financiers and started the Seiberling Rubber Company, which has been quite successful.

President Sloan, Mr. Raskob, and other officers of General Motors developed a plan to pay bonuses to the officers and directors of General Motors. Under this plan, President Sloan secured a total payment from the corporation of $20,000,000 between 1923 and 1928. When suits were started in later years, these excessive payments prior to 1930 were not included in the suits because of the statute of limitations. The court held, however, that these officers had appropriated by fraudulent methods of calculating their bonuses approximately $4,000,000 and ordered them to repay this amount to the corporation.

George Washington Hill and other officers of the American Tobacco Company were criticized and sued for appropriating corporate funds for their enormous salaries and bonuses. One of these suits was to be tried before Judge Manton in the federal court in New York City. Shortly before the trial, Judge Manton suggested to the attorney for the American Tobacco Company that he needed to borrow $250,000. The attorney mentioned this to the assistant to the president of the American Tobacco Company, who mentioned it to Lord and Thomas, the advertising firm for the company, and Lord and Thomas lent Judge Manton the $250,000. Judge Manton decided the case in favor of the American Tobacco Company. Probably his decision was correct, but he was convicted of receiving a bribe, the attorney for the company was disbarred from practice in federal courts, and the assistant to the president, who made the arrangements, was promoted immediately after the decision to the position of vice president, where he was entitled to a bonus. In another suit, the American Tobacco Company paid from its own treasury $260,000 to the complainant, $320,000 to its law firm, and made other payments to bring the total for fixing this case to approximately a million dollars. A court later ordered the officers, against whom the suit was brought, to reimburse the corporation for these payments.

Finally, I wish to discuss the violation of the antitrust laws. Restraint of trade was prohibited by the Sherman Antitrust Act of 1890 and by several subsequent laws, as well as by the laws of most of the states. Decisions that such laws were violated have been made against sixty of the seventy large corporations in 307 cases. Three motion-picture corporations stand at the top of the list for restraint of trade with twenty-two, twenty-one, and twenty-one decisions, respectively. Thus, 86 percent of the seventy corporations have decisions against them for restraint of trade, and 73 percent of the corporations with such decisions are recidivists. Although no decisions have been made against the other ten corporations, other evidence indicates that probably every one of them has, in fact, violated these laws. These decisions tend to corroborate the statement made by Walter Lippmann: "Competition has survived only where men have been unable to abolish it." Not law but expediency and practicability have determined the limits of restraint of trade. Big Business does not like competition, and it makes careful arrangements to reduce it and even eliminate it. In certain industries, the negotiations among large corporations to avoid competition are very similar to international diplomacy, except that they are more successful.

For competition these businessmen have substituted private collectivism. They meet together and determine what the prices shall be and how much shall be produced; they also regulate other aspects of the economic process. This is best illustrated by the trade associations, although it is not limited to them. These trade associations not only fix prices and limit production, but also they have set up systems of courts with penalties for violation of their regulations. Their system of justice applies both to their own members, in which case they have a semblance of democracy, and also to nonmembers, in which case they resemble dictatorship and racketeering. Among ninety-two trade associations investigated in 1935 to 1939, twenty-eight had facilities for investigating or snooping on their members, eleven had provisions for fining those who violated regulations, and eighteen had provisions for boycotting the offenders.

Although businessmen often complain that the antitrust law is so vague that they cannot determine whether they are violating the law or not, a very large proportion of the decisions against these seventy corporations are for making agreements to have uniform prices; that is, not to compete as to prices. This practice is clearly in violation of the antitrust law, and no one at all acquainted with its provisions and with the decisions made under it could have the least doubt that such behavior is illegal. Also, many of the agreements limit production. Businessmen have insisted for at least seventy-five years on limiting production in order to keep prices from falling. Though many people have regarded as ridiculous the agricultural policy of killing little pigs, it is in principle the policy which industrial corporations have been using for many generations, long before it was ever applied in agriculture.

What significance do these violations of the antitrust law have? The economic system, as described by the classical economists, was a system of free competition and *laissez faire*, or free enterprise, as we call it today. Free competition was the regulator of the economic system. The laws of supply and demand, operating under free competition, determined prices, profits, the flow of capital, the distribution of labor, and other economic phenomena. When profits in an industry were high, other businessmen rushed into that industry in the hope of securing similar profits. This resulted in an increase in the supply of commodities, which produced a reduction in prices, and this in turn reduced profits. Thus, the excessive profits were eliminated, the prices were reduced, and the public had a larger supply of the commodity. Through this regulation by free competition, according to the classical economists, Divine Providence produced the greatest welfare of the entire society. Free competition was, to be sure, a harsh regulator. Cut-throat practices were general, and in the achievement of the welfare of the total society weaker establishments were often ruined.

Because free competition regulated the economic system, governmental regulation was unnecessary. The economic system of the classical economists developed primarily because business revolted against the governmental regulations of the feudal period, which were not adapted to the changing conditions of the eighteenth century. Government kept out of business after this system was established, except as it enforced contracts, protected the public against larceny and fraud, and enforced the principles of free competition by the common-law prohibition of restraint of trade.

During the last century this economic and political system has changed. The changes have resulted principally from the efforts of businessmen. If the word "subversive" refers to efforts to make fundamental changes in a social system, the business leaders are the most subversive influence in the United States. These business leaders have acted as individuals or in small groups, seeking preferential advantages for themselves. The primary loyalty of the businessman has been to profits, and he has willingly sacrificed the general and abstract principles of free competition and free enterprise in circumstances that promised a pecuniary advantage. Moreover, he has been in a position of power and has been able to secure these preferential advantages. Although businessmen had no intention of modifying the economic and political system, they have produced this result. The restriction of the principle of free competition has been demonstrated by the practically universal policy of restraint of trade among large corporations.

The restriction of free enterprise has also come principally from businessmen. Free enterprise means, of course, freedom from governmental regulation and governmental interference. Although businessmen have been vociferous as to the virtues of free enterprise and have, in general, insisted that government keep its hands out of and off business, businessmen above all others have put pressure on the government to interfere in business. They have not done this *en masse*, but as individuals or as small groups endeavoring to secure advantages for themselves. These efforts of businessmen to expand the governmental regulations of busi-

ness are numerous and have a wide range. One of the best illustrations is the early and continued pressure of business concerns to secure tariffs to protect them from foreign competition. Many statutes have been enacted as the result of pressure from particular business interests to protect one industry against competition from another, as illustrated by the tax on oleomargarine. Another illustration is the fair trade laws of the federal and state governments, which prohibit retail dealers from cutting prices on trademarked articles. The federal fair trade law was enacted in 1937. The bill was presented by Senator Tydings, as a rider to a District of Columbia appropriations bill, where it could not be discussed on its merits. The bill was prepared by the law partner of the Senator, and this law partner was the attorney for the National Association of Retail Druggists. The bill was supported by many national associations of manufacturers and dealers, who were opposed to the competitive principle and to free enterprise. The bill was opposed by the Department of Justice and the Federal Trade Commission, which have been attempting to preserve the principle of free competition and free enterprise.

In fact, the interests of businessmen have changed, to a considerable extent, from efficiency in production to efficiency in public manipulation, including manipulation of the government for the attainment of preferential advantages. This attention to governmental favors has tended to produce two results: First, it has tended to pauperize business in the sense in which charity tends to pauperize poor people; second, it has tended to corrupt government. But the most significant result of the violations of the antitrust laws by large business concerns is that these have made our system of free competition and free enterprise unworkable. We no longer have competition as a regulator of economic processes; we have not substituted efficient governmental regulation. We cannot go back to competition. We must go forward to some new system—perhaps communism, perhaps cooperativism, perhaps much more complete governmental regulation than we now have. I don't know what lies ahead of us and am not particularly concerned, but I do know that what was a fairly efficient system has been destroyed by the illegal behavior of big business.

Furthermore, the businessmen have practically destroyed our system of patents by the same procedures. The system of patents was authorized in our Constitution to promote the development of science and the arts. The patent system has become one of the principal methods of promoting monopoly. Not one patent in a hundred pays even the costs of registration. Patents are important for business establishments primarily because they can be used to eliminate or regulate competitors. This is illustrated by the variation in the extent to which corporations apply for patents and bring suits for infringement of patents. In industries such as steel, very few patents are secured and very few patent-infringement suits initiated, because establishments in this country are protected from competition by the heavy capital investment. On the other hand, in industries such as the chemical industry and the manufacture of electrical equipment, new competitors can start with a very small investment. The large companies protect themselves against competition by taking out patents on every possible modification of procedure, bringing suits on every possible pretext, and granting licenses to use patents only with a highly regimented and bureaucratic control. The patent is important principally because it is a weapon for fighting competitors. This can be seen in the practice of some of the small concerns, where widespread monopoly is not threatened. The Miniature Golf Corporation secured a patent on its vacant-lot recreation and filed scores of suits against anyone who used this method without a paid license from them. The Good Humor Corporation engaged in patent litigation for more than a decade with the Popsicle Company and other manufacturers of ice-cream bars to determine which firm had invented this contribution to science and the arts. Similarly, the Maidenform Brassiere Company and the Snug-Fit Foundations, Inc., were before the courts for many years regarding their patented designs, each charging the other with infringement.

The general conclusion from this study of the seventy large corporations is that the ideal businessman and the large corporation *are* very much like the professional thief:

First, their violations of law are frequent and continued. As stated previously, 97 percent of the large corporations are recidivists.

Second, illegal behavior by the corporations is much more prevalent than the prose-cutions indicate. In other words, only a fraction of the violations of law by a particular corporation result in prosecution, and only a fraction of the corporations which violate the law are prosecuted. In general, a few corporations are prosecuted for behavior which is industry-wide.

Third, the businessman who violates laws regulating business does not lose status among his business associates. I have mentioned President Sloan of General Motors and Seiberling (previously of the Goodyear Rubber Company), and many others could be mentioned who have appropriated the funds of their own corporations fraudulently and who have not lost status in their own corporations or in the eyes of other businessmen. Leonor F. Loree, chairman of the Kansas City Southern, knowing that his company was about to purchase stock of another railway, went into the market privately and secretly purchased shares of this stock in advance of his corporation, and then, when the price of the stock increased, sold it at the higher price, making a profit of $150,000. This profit, of course, was made at the expense of the corporation of which he was chairman, and he could make the profit because as an officer he knew the plans of the corporation. The courts, however, determined that this profit was fraudulent and ordered Mr. Loree to reimburse the corporation for the violation of his trust. Shortly after this decision became generally known, Mr. Loree was elected president of the New York Chamber of Commerce, perhaps in admiration of his cleverness.

Fourth, businessmen feel and express contempt for legislators, bureaucrats, courts, "snoopers," and other governmental officials and for the law, as such. In this respect, also, they are akin to the professional thieves, who feel and express contempt for police, prosecutors, and judges. Both professional thieves and corporations feel contempt for government because government interferes with their behavior.

Businessmen, being like professional thieves in these four respects, are participants in organized crime. Their violations of law are not identical and haphazard, but they have definite policies of restraint of trade, of unfair labor practices, of fraud and misrepresentation.

Businessmen differ from professional thieves principally in their greater interest in status and respectability. They think of themselves as honest men, not as criminals, whereas professional thieves, when they speak honestly, admit they are thieves. The businessman does regard himself as a lawbreaker, but he thinks the laws are wrong or at least that they should not restrict him, although they may well restrict others. He does not think of himself as a criminal, because he does not conform to the popular stereotype of the criminal. This popular stereotype is always taken from the lower socioeconomic class.

I have attempted to demonstrate that businessmen violate the law with great frequency, using what may be called the methods of organized crime. I have attempted in another place to demonstrate that these violations of law are really crimes. If these conclusions are correct, it is very clear that the criminal behavior of businessmen cannot be explained by poverty, in the usual sense, or by bad housing or lack of recreational facilities or feeblemindedness or emotional instability. Business leaders are capable, emotionally balanced, and in no sense pathological. We have no reason to think that General Motors has an inferiority complex or that the Aluminum Company of America has a frustration-aggression complex or that U.S. Steel has an Oedipus complex or that the Armour Company has a death wish or that the DuPonts desire to return to the womb. The assumption that an offender must have some such pathological distortion of the intellect or the emotions seems to me absurd, and if it is absurd regarding the crimes of businessmen, it is equally absurd regarding the crimes of persons in the lower economic class.

PRISON: THE NATIONAL POORHOUSE

Ronald Goldfarb

This brief selection summarizes some of the very important respects in which the administration of justice in this country demonstrates a bias in favor of the rich and against the poor. As with many of the other problems discussed in this book, the class bias seems thoroughly rooted in the entire institutional structure; it does not seem accidental or inadvertent.

Goldfarb is a Washington lawyer who has written widely on the problems of the system of prosecution and justice in the United States and its need for reform.

I recently read a fairy tale entitled, "Those Who Do Not Steal"* to my young daughter. It is about a poor man who was caught stealing an old piece of pipe and was thrown into prison. He asked to see the king to offer him a rare treasure, a pit that would grow into a tree that bore golden pears. The king asked the thief why he did not plant it himself. He replied that if the tree was to bear golden fruit it had to be planted by a person who had never stolen or cheated. As a little boy, the king had stolen something from his mother; he could not qualify. The chancellor said he could not because he was prepared to accept bribes. The same offer was made to the commander of the royal army who had reasons why he could not accept it; nor could the supreme judge or the warden of the prison. And so the story ends with the king letting the thief go free. To a remarkable extent, we have still in America a dual system of criminal punishment, one public, the other private, each operating very differently from the other. Our prisons are, in effect, a public welfare system of corrections for the poor.

SOURCE: Ronald Goldfarb, "Prison: The National Poorhouse," The New Republic, November, 1969. Reprinted by permission of The New Republic. Copyright © 1969 Harrison-Blaine of New Jersey, Inc.

* From The Fairy Tale Tree.

Those who can afford it have a private and informal corrections system of sorts. Perhaps the most succinct summary comes from Noah Pope, a little known resident-client of the Maryland House of Corrections in Jessup: "The jail is for the poor, the street is for the rich." An analysis by the D.C. Crime Commission concluded that offenders in the nation's capital are "predominantly Negro, male, poorly educated, youthful, products of broken homes and large families, unskilled and erratically employed." Which is to say, poor. Does this mean simply that the poor commit more crimes and perforce end up incarcerated more frequently?

It seems a common insight, if not a provable one, that all transgress but not all —in fact, very few—end up labeled and treated as criminal. Former Supreme Court Justice Tom Clark said that only 50 percent of all crime is reported. That figure was put at 90 percent at recent congressional hearings. One study of 6000 offenses admitted by youths in one area found that only 1.5 percent were "brought to public attention by arrest or juvenile court hearing." And of reported crime, only a very small fraction of the offenders are tried, convicted and go to prison. A survey of 1700 adults without criminal records brought out that 99 percent of those questioned had committed offenses for which they could have ended up in prison. The breakdown of these admitted but not punished offenses is interesting: "Businessmen and lawyers were highest in perjury, falsification, fraud and tax evasion; teachers and social workers in malicious mischief; writers and artists in indecency, criminal libel and gambling; military and government employees in simple larceny; mechanics and technicians in disorderly conduct; farmers in illegal possession of weapons; laborers in grand larceny, burglary and robbery; students in auto misdemeanors."

When upper- or middle-class people or their children get in trouble—drunk in public; paternity charges; fights; mischief in the school, neighborhood, country club, resort, downtown; even homicide—ordinarily, private action is quickly taken. The person's problem is analyzed sympathetically, the best treatment sought. Restitution, medical or psychiatric assistance, special educational steps, legal advice are enlisted from the family and community. Alcoholics who comprise about half our jail population are rarely

well-to-do; those children with sad faces in our juvenile institutions are not from homes in the affluent suburbs; most of the men and women caught, tried, convicted and sent to prison are poor.

A Berkeley criminologist and author, Professor Richard Korn, criticizing the hypocrisy of a system in which the rich get help and the poor get jail, has urged in a recent report to the Joint Commission on Correctional Manpower and Training that innovative and sympathetic community treatment of offenders should not be viewed as radical or even new. They are no more than what is provided "by the well-to-do on behalf of their deviant members": restitution, medical treatment, special schooling, training, and other sensible alternatives to imprisonment. He went on to say:

"A wholly private and unofficial system of correctional treatment has long been available to the violent scions of the socially fortunate. In every middle-class community there are psychiatrists specializing in the treatment of the errant youth of the well-heeled, frequently with the full approval of the police and judicial authorities. Should private outpatient treatment prove inadequate, there is a nationwide network of relatively exclusive residential facilities outside the home community. Every Sunday The New York Times publishes two pages of detailed advertisements by private boarding schools catering to the needs of 'exceptional youth' who are 'unreachable' by means of 'conventional educational methods.' It would be wrong-headed and disingenuous to cite these facts as instances of dishonest official connivance with wealth or privilege. If anything, they reflect an honest recognition that the private, unofficial treatment of offenders is vastly superior to most available public programs. Keeping children out of reformatories is a widely approved and worthy objective, irrespective of whether the children are rich or poor. The scandal lies in the fact that such alternatives are denied to the poor, through nothing more deliberate than the incidental fact of their inferior economic position."

Delinquency rates of college students in Ft. Worth, Texas, have been compared with the rates for others who got in trouble. While both groups committed similar crimes, the college group "enjoyed relative impunity." The investigators concluded that: "Whether a man becomes a confirmed criminal may well depend less on what he does to society than on what society does to him. Pranks that cause a college student some uncomfortable moments in the Dean's office may send an East Side youth to the reformatory. Unlawful possession of a revolver may result in a warning to a suburban home owner, a prison sentence to a tenement dweller. Taking a sum of money as 'honest graft' in business or public life is vastly different from taking the same amount from a cash register. . . . It is perhaps less important to show that good citizens are not always good than that these same citizens can commit crimes and still become eminent scientists, intelligent parents, leading teachers, artists and social workers, or prominent business executives."

Poor juvenile offenders not only pay more often and more heavily for their misconduct, they end up more frequently in terrible public institutions which their wealthier counterparts ordinarily are able to avoid.

The 1967 President's Crime Commission reported that 90 percent of the youth in America have done something for which they could be committed by a juvenile court. Yet, only five percent of the children in institutions for juvenile delinquency (that would be 20,000 of the 400,000 children in detention at the time of the last national crime commission survey) come from families in "comfortable circumstances."

A 1966 study in Contra Costa County, California, for the President's Committee on Juvenile Delinquency and Youth Development tells the story: 48.2 percent of juveniles arrested in California were released by the police after some informal handling and without charges being preferred. But in the upper-middle-class suburban community of Lafayette in Contra Costa County, 80 percent of them were released after arrest. Of the total juveniles arrested in California, 46.5 percent were referred to a juvenile court; in Lafayette, 17.9 percent. Of those who eventually were institutionalized, the California average was 5.3 percent; in Lafayette . . . , 1.3 percent. "These data," said the report, "clearly indicate that the . . . adjustments without benefit of the formal agencies of juvenile justice for middle class suburban youth at the law enforcement level is considerably above the national and state averages."

Typical juvenile crimes like vandalism,

truancy, illicit sexual relations are often repaired privately by upper- and middle-income families; but not among the poor. Poor children sometimes are put in institutions for their own good, regardless of the seriousness of their offense (for lack of a good home, for example), while children from prosperous backgrounds are usually released—also for their own good—even though they may have committed serious offenses. This differential treatment might be rationalized if public institutions accomplished for their wards what affluent families negotiate privately for theirs. But they don't. Most of these places are Dickensian; rising rates of young repeaters show that they do not work.

The poor defendant's dilemma is hard to document, but not to illustrate. A 1967 government review of federal criminal statistics showed that adult defendants with assigned counsel had their cases dismissed less often and were acquitted less frequently than comparable defendants who retained their own counsel.

Most crimes are misdemeanors. Poor misdemeanants do not have lawyers and, without counsel, go to jail more frequently and for longer terms. This corroborates what we know about the pretrial stage of the criminal justice process. Poor defendants who go to jail before trial subsequently get convicted and sentenced to prison more frequently than those able to afford bail and are released before trial.

Obviously, only the poor go to jail and have criminal records for failing to pay alimony, support, restitution or fines. Similarly, few wealthy people steal or commit crimes out of economic desperation. The point is: in the classes of offenses committed by rich and poor *equally*, it is rarely the rich who end up behind bars.

Take two cases in Maryland. In one, a 15-year-old black boy from a poor section of Baltimore, who had never been in trouble before, went with a gang to rob a store. In the course of the theft a resisting storekeeper was shot and killed by one of the youths who, without the subject's knowledge, had a gun. The boy was tried in the adult criminal court, convicted, sentenced to life imprisonment at the Maryland House of Corrections. He is not eligible for parole until he has served 15 years.

While serving that sentence (he is now 29), he might have read news accounts of the trial of a 24-year-old gentleman tobacco farmer from rural Charles County. This son of a prominent businessman and former state official was tried for assault, resisting arrest, and manslaughter arising out of a drunken episode at a fashionable society ball. After taunting a 51-year-old hotel barmaid (mother of 11) with racist insults, he struck her with a steel-topped cane because she was slow delivering him a drink. She collapsed and died. The judge sentenced him to six months in a county jail, allowing him to remain free for a while, however, so that he could oversee the harvesting of his crops.

What is of central importance is not the theoretical concern that our legal system in part discriminates between economic classes; but rather the question whether present discrimination in the use of our correctional programs and resources is wise and economical, as well as fair. Treating higher class offenders one way for their and our good, while treating poor offenders another way to their and our loss is by every standard wasteful as well as unjust. Noah Pope, Richard Korn and our law-and-order-minded President and Chief Justice all seem to agree that our public welfare corrections system, a billion dollar a year disaster, needs to be revised. The revision need not be so very radical. The lesson lies in what the more affluent do for their own.

CRIME BIBLIOGRAPHY

I. IMPRESSIONS, DEFINITIONS, AND MAGNITUDES

Eliot Asinof, *People vs. Butcher,* 1970, Viking. Description of one man's tragic encounter with police, jails, and courts.

Fred P. Graham, "Black Crime: The Lawless Image," *Harper's,* September, 1970. Useful discussion of the myth and reality of black crime.

Marvin Wolfgang, "Urban Crime," in James Q. Wilson, ed., *The Metropolitan Enigma,* 1968, Harvard. Summary of extent and definitions.

President's Commission on Law Enforcement and the Administration of Justice, *The Challenge of Crime in a Free Society,* 1967, U.S. Government, pp. 17–54. Extent and definitions of crime.

II. ANALYTIC PERSPECTIVES

A. General Analysis

President's Commission on Law Enforcement and the Administration of Justice, *The Challenge of Crime . . . , op. cit., passim.* For a commission report, surprisingly acute analysis of varieties of crime and their relationship to the system of enforcement.

James Q. Wilson, "Crime in the Streets," *The Public Interest,* No. 5, Fall, 1966. General sorting of issues.

Gordon Tullock, "An Economic Approach to Crime," *Social Science Quarterly,* June, 1969. A simple illustration of the orthodox economist's rational model of criminal behavior, a less technical version than Becker's article listed below.

Gary Becker, "Crime and Punishment: An Economic Approach," *Journal of Political Economy,* April, 1968. Generalized, technical analysis of incentives and deterrence in crime.

David M. Gordon, "Class and the Economics of Crime," in James Weaver, ed., *Current Economic Problems,* forthcoming. An attempt to compare radical and orthodox economic analyses of crime.

B. Ghetto and Youth Crime

Malcolm X, *Autobiography,* 1964, Grove, *passim.* Classic perspective of ghetto relation to crime.

Soledad Brother: The Prison Letters of George Jackson, 1970, Random House. The criminal and prison experiences of one ghetto black.

Belton M. Fleisher, *The Economics of Delinquency,* 1966, Quadrangle. The importance of income in determining crime rates.

Leonard Goodwin, "Work Orientations of the Underemployed Poor," *Journal of Human Resources,* Fall, 1969. Relation of their attitudes about work and about crime, compared with middle-class members.

Robert Evans, Jr., "The Labor Market and Parole Success," *Journal of Human Resources,* Spring, 1968. The importance of employability in determining recidivism rates.

C.   Organized Crime

Donald R. Cressey, *Theft of the Nation: The Structure and Operations of Organized Crime in America,* 1969, Harper & Row. Superb analysis of structure and role of organized crime.

Peter Mass, *The Valachi Papers,* 1968, Putnam. Insight into the workings of organized crime through eyes of one leader.

D.   Corporate and White-Collar Crime

Robert M. Morgenthau, "Equal Justice and the Problem of White Collar Crime," *The Conference Board Record,* August, 1969.

Gilbert Geis, ed., *White-Collar Crime,* 1968, Atherton Press. Large collection of articles on all varieties of white-collar and corporate crime, accenting sociological approach.

E.   Enforcement

James Q. Wilson, *Varieties of Police Behavior,* 1969, Basic Books. Interesting survey of the determinants of police response to crime.

J. H. Skolnick, *Justice Without Trial,* 1966, Wiley. On the importance of enforcement through pretrial settlement.

William Westley, *Violence and Police,* 1970, M.I.T. Classic early 1950's study of police attitudes finally published.

Paul Chevigny, *Police Power,* 1969, Pantheon. Account of a civil liberties lawyer's cases against police abuse of power.

6 Health

Editor's Introduction

At 97th Street and First Avenue, at Metropolitan Hospital, a woman and her sick child wait eight hours to see a doctor in the emergency room. On Wall Street, at the stock market, brokers rush for shares of American Medical Enterprises, Inc., a chain of profit-making nursing homes. In Brooklyn, a man returns from a long hospitalization to find that Blue Cross left him with a bill too big to manage on a cab driver's salary. In Santa Monica, a major aerospace firm outbids the competition and acquires yet another small company making computers for hospital use.

The American medical care system has never been too healthy for people who are sick. But for those who have a loose dollar to invest—whose main interest in health is "healthy" earnings, there couldn't be a better place to turn. Health, in America, has become a big, profitable business, and everybody's getting in on it—from the people who make perfume to the people who make napalm. The "health industry" used to mean just doctors and drug companies. Now it's doctors, drugs, hospital supplies, electronic equipment, computers, health insurance, construction, real estate, and profit-making chains of hospitals and nursing homes.

—Health Policy Advisory Council[1]

Throughout 1970, New York City hospitals were invaded by community groups from poor neighborhoods. The activists typically seized a floor or two, escorted some doctors out of the hospital, attracted scores of reporters, issued some demands for improved medical care in their communities, and vacated after a day or two of occupation. Increasingly, it seems, many among the poor have focused on health services in their complaints about the quality of American life. Their demands have usually been general, for they feel that the quality of health care available to them is inadequate in almost every area of medical service. Often, members of the hospital staffs have agreed.

With its enormous wealth, its advanced and sophisticated medical technologies, the glitter of its scientific achievements in other areas, the United States ought to be able to provide adequate medical care for everyone. Liberals and conservatives tend to argue that it falls short of that goal for simple, remediable reasons. Radicals suggest that it fails to provide adequate medical care because its social and economic institutions sacrifice human needs to the corporate quest for profits. This chapter outlines the nature of that disagreement. In the introduction, I have first described the problems, then sketched the respective analyses of the different perspectives, and finally introduced the readings.

DEFINITIONS AND MAGNITUDES

Health problems are easy to define. An individual is healthy when he isn't sick. A society is aggregately healthy when few of its citizens are sick. Typically, a wide variety of indices are deployed to measure the "health" of a society. Infant mortality rates are frequently measured, total mortality rates are often compared, and relative mortality rates within certain segments of the population are also charted. Finally, the prevalence of preventable or curable diseases is also studied.

[1] Health Policy Advisory Council, *Health-PAC Bulletin,* November 1969, p. 1.

By almost any standard, the United States performs very poorly in taking care of its citizens' health. Among the twenty North Atlantic countries belonging to OECD, for instance, the United States ranks eighth in infant mortality rates, tenth in total mortality rates, and twentieth in mortality rates among males between 45 and 54 years old.[2]

Worse still, some Americans suffer especially severe health problems—blacks and the poor in particular. Whites at birth can expect to live more than six years longer than blacks. And poor families suffer from chronic diseases which affect their employment or employability roughly four times as frequently as the non-poor.[3]

All of these disadvantages seem to converge in central-city ghettos, where poverty, racial discrimination, and urban density apparently combine to effect especially serious health problems. The selections below by Joyce Lashof and by the Commission on Civil Disorders summarize varieties of evidence of both health problems and inadequate medical care in ghetto areas. Other pieces of evidence document the same conditions. One study compared health indices in poor and non-poor areas of Chicago, for instance:[4]

It was found that the poverty area had a 60 percent higher infant mortality; 200 percent higher incidence of premature births; . . . 200 percent more new cases of tuberculosis; 550 percent more new cases of venereal disease; and 100 percent higher death rate from carcinoma of the cervix.

Another study found that infant mortality rates among blacks in the city of San Francisco were three times greater than white infant mortality rates.[5]

Less conventionally, one can measure the quality of medical care in other, less statistical ways. One can explore the kind of services provided, for instance—whether services are provided readily, cheerfully, and immediately, or whether they are proffered reluctantly, inefficiently, hostilely, and sluggishly. Or one can inspect the conditions under which treatment is provided— whether they involve concern for a patient's general welfare or suggest contempt for the patient. By these counts too, according to many different kinds of reports, medical care seems extremely inadequate for a large number of Americans, especially those in central-city ghettos.[6]

In general, one can distinguish two principal sources of especially severe health problems in urban poverty areas. First, there is much less prevention of disease in ghetto communities. Poor ghetto residents visit doctors less frequently for regular checkups than other citizens, follow less nutritional diets, wear less adequately protective clothing, and often have trouble finding and/or traveling to medical facilities.[7] Also, many ghetto residents suffer some diseases unique to their environments. For example, at least 400,000 poor children had lead poisoning in the United States in 1969, most of them in older ghetto communities in the Northeast; they contract the poisoning from eating chipped, lead-base paint in deteriorating housing.[8] Also, there were 14,000 cases of rat-bite in the United States in 1965, most of these in ghetto communities where rats feast on garbage and hide in rotten buildings.[9]

Second, when ghetto residents do become ill, they receive much less adequate medical service. They must wait longer for attention, must often use inferior hospital facilities, and must often solicit service from inexperienced or incompetent medical personnel.[10]

LIBERAL AND CONSERVATIVE VIEWS

To most liberal and conservative analysts, the solutions to these health problems seem especially simple, and in most cases the two perspectives agree.

[2] See additional figures in the selection by Fred Anderson in this chapter.
[3] For these and other figures, see the Lashof and Civil Disorders Commission selections below.
[4] Mark H. Lepper *et al.*, "Approaches to Meeting Health Needs of Large Poverty Populations," *American Journal of Public Health and the Nation's Health,* July, 1967, p. 1154.
[5] *City Health Officers News,* Vol. 8, No. 3, January, 1968, p. 3.
[6] See the selection by Fred Cook below for one illustration of these conditions.
[7] See Lawrence Bergner and Alonzo Yerby, "Low Income and Barriers to Use of Health Services," *New England Journal of Medicine,* March 7, 1968, pp. 541–546.
[8] An article in *Look* magazine, October 21, 1969, estimated 400,000. The president of the Citizens' Committee to End Lead Poisoning (CELP) estimated 500,000 (in a personal interview).
[9] *Report of the National Advisory Commission on Civil Disorders* (N.Y.: Bantam Books, 1968), p. 273.
[10] See evidence on this in the selection by Lashof below.

First, they argue that the poor suffer especially severe problems because they are poor. Subsidize their health costs, and much of the problem will be solved.[11]

Second, they admit that the health care sector has not been organized with perfect efficiency, and that some bottlenecks in the industry should be eased. They have been forced especially to reach this conclusion in very recent years; as Medicare and Medicaid have subsidized some of the costs of health care for the aged and the poor, medical costs have been soaring. From a strictly economic point of view, this implies an excess of demand over supply, or, more dynamically, that demand has increased much more rapidly than supply. This seems especially true of the supply of physicians' services, which has not increased fast enough in recent years.[12] As a result, liberals and conservatives argue, vast government subsidies should be applied to expand the supply of medical services—particularly to increase the capacities of medical schools and to construct more hospitals. When supply can catch up to demand, they assume, the market will function well.

Finally, many suggest that problems among the poor derive from their additional informational and locational disadvantages. The poor typically know less about health care than the non-poor, and know less about how to use medical facilities. In addition, older central cities often have older and less adequate medical facilities.[13] For these sources of the problem, there are also simple solutions. More facilities should be built in local communities. In particular, preventively oriented neighborhood health facilities should be constructed to reach out into poor communities, supplying information, discovering special health needs among the poor, and providing regular checkups.[14]

Notably, liberal and conservative analyses do not move beyond these prescriptions to suggest more fundamental reorganizations of the health care sector. They support the basic orientation of American medicine toward fee for service as the best way of remunerating doctors (as opposed to establishing standard salaries for doctors);[15] they do not advocate universal comprehensive *public* health insurance, tending rather to advocate public subsidy for the poor and private insurance for the non-poor; and they support the increasing orientation of American medicine toward huge medical complexes, built on research and technology, concerned more with the provision of facilities to doctors than the provision of service to patients.[16] In general, as with other problems in this book, they think that the market can work if a few inefficiencies can be overcome.

THE RADICAL VIEW

The radical analysis of health problems suggests that the entire structure of social and economic institutions in this country tends to preclude the adequate provision of health care to many Americans. Increasingly, the provision of health care has been tied to the priorities of profit-making institutions. As this has occurred, the institutions dominating the health care sector have become less and less concerned with the very human needs of patients.[17]

Traditionally, critics of medical care in this country have focused their complaints on the American Medical Association and the orientation of physician payment toward fees for service.[18] But since World War II, and especially in the last decade, the character of the health sector has changed radically. Now, the provision of medical care is growing more and more inter-

[11] For one of the best studies on the relationship between income and demand for health, see Richard Auster *et al.*, "The Production of Health: An Exploratory Study," *Journal of Human Resources,* Fall, 1969. See also H. and A. Somers, *Medicare and the Hospitals* (Washington: Brookings, 1967).
[12] See Rashi Fein, *The Doctor Shortage* (Washington: Brookings, 1967); Martin Feldstein, "The Rising Price of Physicians' Services," *Review of Economics and Statistics,* May 1970; and Herman and Anne Somers, *Doctors, Patients and Health Insurance* (Washington: Brookings, 1961).
[13] See both the Lashof and Civil Disorders Commission selections below.
[14] The Office of Economic Opportunity funded several of these experimental centers in the mid-1960's. See Lashof and Langer below.
[15] On the fee-for-service system, see Anderson below.
[16] For a nearly definitive discussion of this trend, see *The American Health System: Power, Profits, and Politics,* a Health-PAC book prepared by Barbara and John Ehrenreich (N.Y.: Random House, 1970).
[17] Much of this discussion is based on *ibid.*
[18] Especially for their blatant opposition to simple reforms like Medicare.

twined with the structure of big business in this country. Large enterprises like Blue Cross/Blue Shield provide health insurance. Large drug companies provide increasing proportions of medical supplies. And huge, frequently profit-making, hospital complexes become more and more tied to the price structures of huge medical suppliers.[19] These developments have several implications.

First, public subsidy of health care costs for the poor will have increasingly little effect. As monopoly powers gain more and more control over the price mechanisms within the health sector, they will be able to match increases in demand with price increases, preventing an increase in the supply of service.[20]

Second, as private health insurance plans like Blue Cross/Blue Shield consolidate their control of that particular market, it becomes increasingly difficult to advocate universal public insurance plans. And the difference between private and public insurance seems clear. With private, profit-making insurance plans, patients always face the possibility that the companies will raise their prices, refuse to cover certain costs, or refuse to insure certain high-risk categories of patients. Automobile insurance companies have fought frantically against proposals for a "no-fault" car insurance system; private health insurance companies would probably do the same.[21]

Third, as the provision of health care becomes increasingly dominated by large organizations, it becomes less likely that preventive programs sensitively geared to the subtle differences among residential communities can be developed. The problem of lead poisoning among small children in ghettos was ignored for years, for instance, mainly because middle-class doctors and large hospital organizations were not able to imagine that the problem could be serious. Public action against lead poisoning has been taken only after community groups have forced the medical establishment to pay attention.

Finally, and most important, it becomes less likely that the needs of patients will be considered as the health sector becomes more dominated by large corporations. The Ehrenreichs, in their article on the "medical-industrial complex," intend the analogy with the "military-industrial complex" quite directly. In both cases, corporations have been searching for safe, large, stable, effectively guaranteed outlets for their capital. Decisions about research, construction, supply and allocation within the health sector will increasingly be tied to profitability criteria.

And as the "medical-industrial complex" emerges, it becomes less and less possible over time to effect the kind of radical institutional transformation of the health sector which we seem to require. Formerly, one could somehow have envisioned public pressure pushing the government toward assumption of important planning, administrative and financial responsibilities in health —not completely socialized medicine perhaps, but an extension of public power comparable to the government's role in England and Scandinavia. Now with the new and apparently permanent involvement of major corporations in health, it is becoming increasingly improbable that the United States can redirect its health priorities without at the same time changing the ways in which American industry is organized and the ways in which monopoly capitalism works. To quote the Ehrenreichs,[22] to try fundamentally to change the health care system in this country will be increasingly

. . . to challenge some of the underlying tenets of the American free enterprise system. If physicians were to become community employees, if the drug companies were to be nationalized, then why not expropriate the oil and coal industries, or the automobile industry? There is an even more direct antipathy to nationalizing the health industry: a host of industries, including the aerospace industry, the electronic industry, the chemical industry, and the insurance industry, all have a direct stake in the profitability of the medical care system.

[19] See *The American Health System, op. cit.*
[20] This was clearly the result with the increase in funds available for Medicare and Medicaid. On some of the consequences, read the *Health-PAC Bulletin*, September, 1969.
[21] For a discussion on the profit structure of companies like Blue Cross, see the selection by the Ehrenreichs below.
[22] From *The American Health System: Power, Profits, and Politics*, a Health-PAC book prepared by Barbara and John Ehrenreich (N.Y.: Random House, 1970), prepublication manuscript.

THE READINGS

The first three readings provide Impressions, Definitions, and Magnitudes: Fred Cook the Impressions, and Joyce Lashof and the Civil Disorders Commission the Definitions and Magnitudes.

The next two readings provide superb amplification of this very brief summary of the radical analysis. Fred Anderson sketches the nature of problems in the American health sector, elaborating the insufficiency of liberal and conservative suggestions that we simply make the system more efficient. Barbara and John Ehrenreich document the most important recent trend in medical care, the emergence of the "medical-industrial complex." They argue that so many industries have now rushed into the health care sector that their power and presence will substantially determine the future directions of health care in this country.

A final reading provides an illustration of the extent to which health problems, like all the other problems in this book, are fundamentally dominated by the balance of power among various interest groups. Elinor Langer describes the establishment of a small neighborhood health center in Denver, and illustrates all the ways in which medical care—to be effective—must be provided by caring human beings sensitive to the human needs of their patients. She also describes the strong resistance to this tiny but effective reform. And, notably, her focus on resistance was apt. Her article appeared in 1966. Since then, the poverty program—which funded the medical center—has been stripped of most of its powers, lost most of its program money, and the hopes for centers like the one she describes seem to be growing dimmer every day.

THE DOOMED OF WATTS

Fred J. Cook

This excerpt from Cook's book, *The Plot Against the Patient,* illustrates the many ways in which residents of poor urban neighborhoods encounter health problems. They suffer not only because they are poor and eat relatively less nutritional food, for instance, but because the public health facilities provided for their neighborhoods are woefully inadequate.

He was born in Watts in August 1964, the youngest of five children and a welfare case. Dr. Sol White, a county health commissioner and a pediatrician, saw him for the first time four months after birth. Already the boy (let's call him C.J.) was a tiny bundle of suffering. He had bronchitis, eczema, cow's milk allergy, an umbilical hernia and a right anal hernia. The last required immediate surgery.

But C.J. was born in Watts.

Watts is the ghetto of southeast Los Angeles that was literally torn apart in the summer of 1965 in the nation's worst race riot. It is a sprawling warren with the population of a fair-sized city—344,000 residents, 50 percent of them fifteen years old or younger. Thirty-three percent of the 18–45 year group are unemployed. In the hard-core area of Watts, there is no hospital of any kind. Around the periphery are eight proprietary hospitals, only two of which are accredited. There is no emergency service available to the 344,000 residents of Watts except in unaccredited hospitals or in hospitals miles beyond its borders. There is no place in Watts for a four-month-old boy like C.J. to go for a hernia operation. The only alternative is Los Angeles' huge County General Hospital.

County General is a two-hour ride and six bus changes away from Watts, and it is chronically overwhelmed trying to treat and succor the human flotsam that daily flows through its doors. What hope is there for a four-month-old baby needing a hernia operation? Dr. White sighed and telephoned County General, trying to set up an appointment for C.J.

"I had to make the appointment for the next surgical date," Dr. White explained long afterwards. "If I had sent the mother and child to the hospital right away, they would have had to get there at seven in the morning in order to be seen around 10 A.M. in the regular clinic. Then they would have been referred to the evening clinic, and they wouldn't have been through until four or five in the afternoon—and then they would be put on a waiting list."

The waiting list at County. General at times seems infinite. When Dr. White saw C.J. again on December 29, 1964, no appointment had yet been made for surgery —C.J. was still on the waiting list. A few weeks later, in January, 1965, examining C.J. again, Dr. White found that, in addition to all his earlier ailments, he had a scalp infection and had developed a heart murmur. He sent the mother and baby to a pediatric cardiologist 20 miles away.

On January 28, 1966, a full year later, Dr. White saw C.J. again. The boy's heart murmur was still present. He also had tonsilitis, an ear infection and mild but persistent bronchitis. He had had incomplete immunization shots. He still had the hernias; he still had not had the needed operation. County General had been so swamped with cases, it had been working through such a backlog, that C.J.'s case had been postponed and postponed until the mother, Dr. White indicated, had eventually just given up.

Perhaps today, with greatly expanded federal medical programs—not just Medicare but the treatment of youthful indigents like C.J. under the California program that takes advantage of the Title XIX amendment to the Kerr-Mills Act—it might be easier for C.J. to get his much needed operation. He would at least be able to get a specialist who could assure him some continuity of care. But there is still no hospital in Watts. He would still have to go to County General, with its still long waiting list. It was, as one observer described it, "a helluva situation."

This nation has two kinds of medicine. One kind for those with insurance and money; one kind for those with nothing. It is not true that those with nothing get nothing. But they do sometimes get very close to nothing.

This, needless to say, is not the view of the medical establishment. Organized medicine has long trumpeted that Americans get "the best medical care in the world" and that "anyone can get care." Even in the aftermath of the bloody riots in Watts, one heard the same old refrains. One of the most prominent hospital authorities in Southern California acted as if Watts was just a lower class Beverly Hills, without hospitals of its own from choice. Why, he said, residents of the area could go to County General or Harbor General, and then there were those eight proprietaries scattered around the periphery of Watts.

"Every region is well served, if you travel," he said.

Fortunately, the report on the Watts riots prepared by the commission headed by John A. McCone, millionaire businessman and former director of the Central Intelligence Agency, tells a different and more candid story. The McCone commission wrote:

"Statistics indicate that health conditions of the residents of south central Los Angeles are relatively poor, and facilities to provide medical care are insufficient. Infant mortality, for example, is about one and one-half times greater than the city-wide average. Life expectancies are considerably shorter. A far lower percentage of the children are immunized against diphtheria, whooping cough, tetanus, smallpox and poliomyelitis than in the rest of the county.

"As established by the comprehensive reports of consultants to the Commission, the number of doctors in the southeastern part of Los Angeles is grossly inadequate as compared with other parts of the city. It is reported that there are 106 physicians for some 252,000 people, whereas the county ratio is three times higher. The hospitals readily accessible to the citizens in southeastern Los Angeles are also grossly inadequate in quality and in numbers of beds. Of the eight proprietary hospitals, which have a total capacity of 454 beds, only two meet minimum standards of professional quality. The two large public hospitals, County General and Harbor General, are both distant and difficult to reach. The Commission recognizes that the motivation of patients to take advantage of the medical facilities is an important factor in health conditions, but it appears that the facilities in the area are not even sufficient to care for those who now seek medical attention."

Statistics make this general description even more grim. A poverty report prepared by the Institute of Industrial Relations at UCLA for the Los Angeles County Commission on Human Relations found that in 1960, the Watts area contained only 17 percent of the city's population, but in category after category it harbored nearly 50 percent of the city's ills. It had 48.5 percent of amoebic infections, 42 percent of food poisoning, 44.8 percent of whooping cough, 39 percent of epilepsy, 42.8 percent of rheumatic fever, 44.6 percent of dysentery, 46 percent of venereal diseases, 36 percent of meningitis and 65 percent of reported tuberculin reactors. The death rate in Watts was 22.3 percent higher than for the remainder of the city.

It was clear that in health, as in all else, Watts existed in a vacuum of deprivation and suffering. There were only three specialists—two pediatricians and one radiologist—in the entire greater Watts area inhabited by 344,000 persons. And the first of these, Dr. Sol White, had come to the area only in 1959.

With no hospital of its own, Watts had no emergency service worthy of the name. The nearest approved emergency facility was in St. Francis Hospital in Lynwood, miles beyond its borders. The proprietary hospitals scattered around the periphery of Watts maintained walk-in clinics, but had no organized outpatient or emergency service. They had at the most a doctor or a nurse, who might be summoned and who *might* arrive sometime to give a patient in dire need some cursory attention. If the patient had insurance (less than one-fourth of the population of Watts did), he would, of course, be hospitalized if he needed it, and sometimes even if he didn't. But if he lacked resources of any kind, the most normal circumstance in Watts, he would usually be told to travel on to County General.

Three of the unaccredited hospitals in the Watts area had contracts with the city to provide some kind of emergency care, but Dr. White and others who had observed the situation at close hand were contemptuous of the quality of that care.

"If you can breathe and you're conscious, they send you on," Dr. White said in one interview. "Sometimes they don't even take X-rays or sew up an open wound."

The kind of things that happen in proprietary hospitals, where profit too frequently overrides humanity, is illustrated by some Los Angeles cases. In June, 1964, a four-year-old girl was scalded in the bathtub in her home. The accident happened on a Monday, and the parents did nothing until Thursday when they decided they had better take the child to a hospital. They found one private hospital's doors closed. Two other proprietaries refused aid, the family later said, because it was "too early in the morning." The child was finally taken to County General, where she died.

In another case, a seventy-two-year-old woman suffering from internal hemorrhaging was rushed to a hospital holding a city service contract. The hospital, learning she was on Social Security, which meant that it would receive only the small city contract fee, insisted her family take her on to County General. The family, not familiar with the city streets, got lost on the way, wandered around, finally arrived at County General, fortunately with the woman still alive.

On the other hand, Dr. White cites the case of a family that was well-fortified with hospitalization insurance. The parents took their five children to one of the proprietary hospitals, and they were all promptly slapped into hospital beds and kept there for days on end. What was the strange malady that had felled all five children at the same time? According to Dr. White: ringworm.

Such incidents brought the entire medical profession into disrepute in the disadvantaged and disgruntled world of Watts.

"We are not reaching the people," Dr. White conceded. "There is no image. I'm referred to as the 'eight to four.'" . . .

Built in 1932, County General is poorly planned, by modern standards. Its laboratories and X-ray departments are usually hopelessly inadequate to meet the burdens they must handle. It has a 3,000 bed capacity, and is chronically overcrowded. It is afflicted, like most hospitals in its circumstances, with an acute and growing shortage of nurses and other personnel. In an atmosphere of perpetual crisis, where the medical staff seems about to be buried under an avalanche of patients, County General treats the afflicted, administers to the maimed and saves lives.

The figures dealing with its operations are phenomenal. In mid-1965 County General had 6,351 employees and nearly 3,000 doctors, including volunteers. The attending medical staff, all private practice specialists, comprised one-fifth of the entire doctor population of Los Angeles, and these doctors donated on an average of two mornings a week without pay to County General patients. In 1964, the hospital cared for 121,071 bed patients, who stayed an average of eight days each. It performed 14,254 surgeries, saw 15,739 babies born. Outpatient visits totaled an incredible 892,800, and the emergency wards handled 205,529 cases—an average of one every three minutes around the clock, seven days a week. It all cost Los Angeles County $38,777,775.

The sheer pressure of numbers puts at times an almost insupportable burden upon the hospital staff. The staff handles 90 percent more patients per employee than the average of the four largest teaching hospitals in the United States, and Local 434 of the Los Angeles County Employees Union (AFL-CIO) has long contended that such figures spell out an understaffing crisis. In 1959, the union created a brief public flurry when it dramatized its case with an illustrative horror anecdote. The incident took place in Olive View Sanitarium, part of County General, when, according to a union spokesman, "a woman nursing attendant overseeing 50 male patients was recently attacked and almost killed in a darkened room."

The outcry engendered by the deed was purely temporary; the headlines died and nothing changed. Alfred Charlton, general manager of Local 434, insisted in early 1966 that the crisis in understaffing was as bad as ever, despite his union's years-long battle. He blamed budget limitations on hospital expenditures and deaf ears. The argument his union most often hears, Charlton said, is shocking from a humane view: it must face the fact, it is told, that its members are serving indigent patients who can't expect to receive top quality care.

There is an urgent need, Charlton insists, to double hospital staffs, a goal that might seem a bit of overblown union press-agentry, except for the acknowledged fact that in County General the staff handles 90 percent more persons per employee than the average in top-graded hospitals that are probably themselves somewhat shorthanded. Under existing circumstances, there is simply no leeway in County General or other county hospitals if someone becomes ill, has an accident or for some other reason misses a day of work. Then one attendant may have to do the work of four instead of two. Charlton says, one employee may be left to take care of 52 persons, all of whom need to be tended and turned over every couple of hours. When the crush reaches such propor-

tions, care inevitably is inadequate, and accidents happen.

Charlton cited the case of a 105-pound woman attendant who tried by herself to lift a heavy patient. The patient twisted in her arms, and in struggling to prevent a fall, the attendant strained herself and suffered a heart attack. There was some dispute about whether this was an industrial accident, but the woman attendant was finally awarded $18,000 in compensation and medical care for the rest of her life. Charlton has a thick dossier of similar cases. In 1962, he declared, the insurance premium for county hospital employees cost over $3 million; by 1964, it had doubled. When the Board of Supervisors became alarmed about this staggering cost factor, Charlton suggested that it might be cheaper to hire the number of hospital employees actually needed. "But that fell on deaf ears," he recalled.

MEDICAL CARE IN THE URBAN CENTER

Joyce C. Lashof

This short piece sketches the dimensions of various sources of health problems in central cities, and particularly the inadequacy of facilities available to the poor for health care. Dr. Lashof is the director of the community medicine section of Presbyterian-St. Luke's Hospital in Chicago.

The private practice of medicine in our inner cities has been declining steadily in recent years. Physicians in increasing numbers have left the inner city for the suburbs, and the community areas served by the urban hospitals have changed. A study of four community areas in Chicago showed a decline of 40 to 60% in the number of physicians practicing in these areas in 1966 as compared with 1953. One of these communities of 26,300 persons had only 4 doctors practicing in its area in 1965.[1] The

number of physicians in the Chicago area as a whole has increased at only half the rate that the population has grown.[2] Such a study illustrates the changing pattern of *medical care* in urban areas.

The distribution of physicians is clearly related to the socioeconomic and racial changes in urban centers. The migration into urban areas of both the Appalachian white and southern Negro and the flight of the prior urban white population have led to steady enlargement of poverty areas in the

SOURCE: *Joyce C. Lashof, "Medical Care in the Urban Center,"* Annals of Internal Medicine, 68:2, pp. 242–244.

[1] Rees, P. H.: Numbers and movement of physi-

cians in southeast Chicago 1953–1965. Working Paper no. 1. 13. Chicago Regional Hospital Study, July 1967.
[2] Rees, P. H.: The movement and distribution of physicians. Working Paper no. 1. 12. Chicago Regional Hospital Study, June 1967.

inner city. A large discrepancy in available medical manpower now exists between the poverty and nonpoverty areas, both quantitatively and qualitatively. In Chicago in 1965 there were 1.26 physicians per thousand population in nonpoverty areas of the city but only 0.62 per thousand in poverty areas. The ratio of board-certified specialists per thousand was 0.53 for the nonpoverty areas and only 0.18 for the poverty areas.[3] Studies carried out by the Hospital Planning Council of Chicago indicate that whereas suburban hospitals draw the majority of their patients from the immediate surrounding community many of the urban hospitals draw from a much larger service area with a minority of patients coming from the area in which the hospital is located.[4] Much of the patient distribution is related to the economic and racial changes that have occurred in the area. The difference in hospitals used by the poverty and nonpoverty groups is striking. Thirty percent of all admissions from the poverty communities in Chicago in 1965 were to Cook County Hospital. Among patients in one community 15 miles distant from the County Hospital 47% of hospital admissions occurred at County Hospital. This concentration is in sharp contrast to the diffusion of care provided to residents of the nonpoverty areas among whom no one hospital accounted for over 4% of all admissions.[5]

One cannot look at medical practice in the urban setting without also considering the rising cost of medical care. In 1950 medical care expenditures totaled $12.9 billion but rose to $43 billion in 1966, of which $10.9 billion came from public funds.[6] These rising costs have served to widen the gap between the medical care available to the affluent and to the poor. They also have made it increasingly difficult to define medical indigency. At the same time there has been

a decay of the tax base in the city, while the demands for health and social services have increased.

The large poverty areas in our inner city have produced health problems that we have not solved. Infant mortality, which has generally been accepted as a sensitive indicator of health conditions, has steadily risen in Chicago from 1958 to 1965. The average yearly infant mortality rate for the years 1958 to 1961 was 22.7 per 1,000 for whites and 37.9 per 1,000 for nonwhites. By 1965 the rate had risen to 28.8 per 1,000 for whites and 48.1 per 1,000 for nonwhites. Comparing morbidity and mortality statistics between the city and the state as a whole, Somers found that Trenton's tuberculosis and venereal disease rates were three to five times as high as those of New Jersey as a whole.[7] In addition, death rates from virtually all major causes—cancer, heart disease, accidents, etc.—in Trenton were higher than state and national rates. Dr. George James has calculated that 15,000 deaths in New York in 1964 could be attributed to poverty.[8]

Efforts to meet the problems posed by these changes have been made over the past two decades. Hospital outpatient departments have expanded, emergency room services have increased, board of health clinics have multiplied, and welfare medical care programs have developed. Unfortunately, these efforts have taken the form of piecemeal, uncoordinated, stopgap measures designed to meet the most obvious needs of the moment. This has resulted in a complex range of facilities and disease-oriented clinics. When we now look at what is available in our cities we find prenatal clinics, well-child clinics, family-planning clinics, tuberculosis clinics, mental health clinics, disease-detection programs, school health programs, and so forth, none of which are quantitatively adequate. In public health nursing alone, in some cities one can find board of health nurses, visiting nurse association nurses, teacher nurses, and tuberculosis control nurses. Funding may also come from different agencies of local, state, and federal government as well as from private voluntary agencies and foundations.

[3] Preliminary report on patterns of medical and health care in poverty areas of Chicago and proposed health programs for the medically indigent. *Chicago Board of Health Medical Care Report,* 1966, p. 16.
[4] Chicago Hospital Planning Council: Hospital discharge study 1965. IBM print-out sheets.
[5] Preliminary report on patterns of medical and health care in poverty areas of Chicago and proposed health programs for the medically indigent. *Chicago Board of Health Medical Care Report,* 1966, pp. 19–22.
[6] Blue Cross Reports. *Hosp. Cost Trends* 5: May–June, 1967.

[7] Somers, A. R.: An American city and its health problems: a case study in comprehensive health planning. *Med. Care* 5: 129, 1967.
[8] James, G.: Poverty and public health—new outlooks. I. Poverty as an obstacle to health progress in our cities. *Amer. J. Public Health* 55: 1757, 1965.

The dual system of medical care is most obvious when one compares the patterns of obtaining medical care followed by the indigent with those of the more affluent sector of our population. The basis of medical practice is a personal physician who takes responsibility for the total care of the patient, including preventive and curative services, coordination of speciality care, and arrangement for hospitalization when indicated. This concept, however, has not been part of our medical care system for the poorer segment of our society. Approximately 40% of people interviewed in four poverty communities of Chicago indicated that they had no family physician.[9] This segment depends on the numerous facilities listed above for their care. No one person takes the responsibility for coordinating care and evaluating total health needs. Thus, a population with the least sophistication is left on its own to determine the appropriate time and place to seek care. The physician seeing those patients usually takes care of acute needs but does little in health counseling or preventive services. If hospitalization is necessary the physician can merely refer a patient to a hospital, but it is not his decision as to whether the patient is admitted. It is estimated that not more than 40% of the physicians in Chicago who take care of welfare patients have hospital staff appointments. If the referring physician feels consultation is necessary or specialized workup is indicated he may give the patient a list of places where this may be obtained. Here, again, it becomes the responsibility of the patient to work his way through the maze and to have himself accepted for treatment. We have encountered families who had been attending five different hospitals and agencies, both public and private, in an effort to have their families' health needs met. Dr. Yerby[10] summarized the health care of the disadvantaged as being "piecemeal, often inadequate, underfinanced, poorly organized and provided without compassion or concern for the dignity of the individual."

Although it is probably true that there has never been enough medical care for any group, medical technology before World War II was such that the difference in care given by the voluntary sector and the public sector was not as great as it is at present. In the last two decades the deficits in the dual system have become obvious in that the voluntary sector has had the resources to exploit the scientific breakthrough while the "charity" system has been overwhelmed.

In an attempt to deal with the financial aspects of the problem, Congress enacted both Titles XVIII and XIX of the Social Security Act in 1965. Indecision in social policy is clearly reflected by the diametrically opposed approaches of these two laws. Title XVIII is based on the social insurance principle with all persons over 65 years of age eligible on the basis of having in the past paid taxes. Title XIX, on the other hand, provides a mechanism by which the states may provide health services for persons whom they define as unable to meet their medical bills on the basis of a means test. The accomplishments and problems presented by these laws are beyond the scope of this discussion, but clearly the effects of Titles XVIII and XIX are far-reaching, and a decision as to which approach will become dominant is not far off. The implications and the effect on social policy are clearly analyzed by Eveline Burns.[11]

In an effort to deal with the fragmentation of care, to improve accessibility of care, and to experiment with new models for delivery of health services, the Office of Economic Opportunity has nurtured and given financial support to the development of the neighborhood health center. The first such centers were developed by Tufts Medical School in Boston, and the Department of Health and Hospitals in Denver. Centers are now also open in New York (under the auspices of Morissania-Montefiore Hospitals), Chicago (under the auspices of Presbyterian-St. Luke's and Mt. Sinai Hospitals), and in Los Angeles (sponsored by the University of Southern California). An additional 36 centers have been funded in 26 cities. These centers are designed to bring a core of physicians, public health nurses, social workers, and community health aides together with other ancillary services into an organized group to attack the health problems of defined communities. The experiences of these

[9] Preliminary report of medical and health care in poverty areas of Chicago and proposed health programs for medically indigent. *Chicago Board of Health Medical Care Report*, 1966, p. 41.
[10] Yerby, A. S.: The disadvantaged and health care. *Amer. J. Public Health* 56: 5, 1966.

[11] Burns, E. M.: Social policy and the health services: the choices ahead. *Amer. J. Public Health* 57: 199, 1967.

centers should help define the health problems of the urban centers and, hopefully, offer one solution. Other experimental models are badly needed.

At the White House Conference on Health, Marion Folsom stated, "Health is a basic human right. Comprehensive, continuous and personal care should be available to all."[12] To reach this goal in our urban centers is a challenge to the medical profession.

[12] Proceedings of the White House Conference on Health, Nov. 3 and 4, 1965, Washington, D.C., p. 7.

HEALTH IN THE GHETTO

The National Advisory Commission on Civil Disorders

This excerpt from the "Riot Commission Report" supplements the preceding selection, providing additional information about the extent and sources of health problems in central city ghettos. It emphasizes that health problems and utilization of medical facilities vary both by income and by race in urban areas.

The residents of the racial ghetto are significantly less healthy than most other Americans. They suffer from higher mortality rates, higher incidence of major diseases, and lower availability and utilization of medical services. They also experience higher admission rates to mental hospitals.

These conditions result from a number of factors.

POVERTY

From the standpoint of health, poverty means deficient diets, lack of medical care, inadequate shelter and clothing, and often lack of awareness of potential health needs. As a result, about 30 percent of all families with incomes less than $2,000 per year suffer from chronic health conditions that adversely affect their employment—as compared with less than 8 percent of the families with incomes of $7,000 or more.

Poor families have the greatest need for financial assistance in meeting medical expenses. Only about 34 percent of families with incomes of less than $2,000 per year use health insurance benefits, as compared

SOURCE: *Report of the National Advisory Commission on Civil Disorders*, 1968.

to nearly 90 percent of those with incomes of $7,000 or more.[1]

These factors are aggravated for Negroes when compared to whites for the simple reason that the proportion of persons in the United States who are poor is 3.5 times as high among Negroes (41 percent in 1966) as among whites (12 percent in 1966).

MATERNAL MORTALITY

Maternal mortality rates for nonwhite mothers are four times as high as those for white mothers. There has been a sharp decline in such rates since 1940, when 774 nonwhite and 320 white mothers died for each 100,000 live births. In 1965, only 84 nonwhite and 21 white mothers died per

[1] Public programs of various kinds have been providing significant financial assistance for medical care in recent years. In 1964, over $1.1 billion was paid out by various governments for such aid. About 55 percent came from federal government agencies, 33 percent from states, and 12 percent from local governments. The biggest contributions were made by the Old Age Assistance program and the Medical Assistance for the Aged program. The enactment of Medicare in 1965 has significantly added to this flow of public assistance for medical aid. However, it is too early to evaluate the results upon health conditions among the poor.

100,000 live births—but the *relative* gap between nonwhites and whites actually increased.

INFANT MORTALITY

Infant mortality rates among nonwhite babies are 58 percent higher than among whites for those under one month old, and almost three times as high among those from one month to one year old. This is true in spite of a large drop in infant mortality rates in both groups since 1940.

NUMBER OF INFANTS WHO DIED PER 1,000 LIVE BIRTHS

Year	Less Than One Month Old		One Month to One Year Old	
	White	Nonwhite	White	Nonwhite
1940	27.2	39.7	16.0	34.1
1950	19.4	27.5	7.4	17.0
1960	17.2	26.9	5.7	16.4
1965	16.1	25.4	5.4	14.9

LIFE EXPECTANCY

To some extent because of infant mortality rates, life expectancy at birth was 6.9 years longer for whites (71.0 years) than for nonwhites (64.1 years) in 1965. Even in the prime working ages, life expectancy is significantly lower among nonwhites than among whites. In 1965, white persons 25 years old could expect to live an average of 48.6 more years; whereas nonwhites 25 years old could expect to live another 43.3 years, or 11 percent less. Similar but smaller discrepancies existed at all ages from 25 through 55, and these discrepancies actually became wider between 1960 and 1965.

LOWER UTILIZATION OF HEALTH SERVICES

A fact that also contributes to poorer health conditions in the ghetto is that Negroes with incomes similar to those of whites spend less on medical services and visit medical specialists less often.

PERCENT OF FAMILY EXPENDITURES SPENT FOR MEDICAL CARE 1960–61

Income Group	White	Nonwhite	Ratio White:Nonwhite
Under $3,000	9	5	1.8:1
$3,000 to $7,499	7	5	1.4:1
$7,500 & over	6	4	1.5:1

Since the lowest income group contains a much larger proportion of nonwhite families than white families, the overall discrepancy in medical care spending between these two groups is very significant, as shown by the following table:

HEALTH EXPENSES PER PERSON PER YEAR FOR THE PERIOD FROM JULY TO DECEMBER 1962

Income Racial Group	Total Medical	Expenses			
		Hospital	Doctor	Dental	Medicine
Under $2,000 per Family per Year:					
White	$130	$33	$41	$11	$32
Nonwhite	63	15	23	5	16
$10,000 and More per Family per Year:					
White	$179	$34	$61	$37	$31
Nonwhite	133	34	50	19	23

These data indicate that nonwhite families in the lower income group spent less than half as much per person on medical services as white families with similar incomes. This discrepancy sharply declines but is still significant in the higher income group, where total nonwhite medical expenditures per person equal, on the average, 74.3 percent of white expenditures.

Negroes spend less on medical care for several reasons. Negro households generally are larger, requiring larger nonmedical expenses for each household, and leaving less money for meeting medical expenses. Thus lower expenditures per person would result even if expenditures per household were the same. Negroes also often pay more for certain other basic necessities such as food and consumer durables, as is discussed in other sections of this Report. In addition, fewer doctors, dentists, and medical facilities are conveniently available to Negroes—especially to poor families—than to most whites. This is a result both of geographic concentration of doctors in higher income areas in large cities and of discrimination against Negroes by doctors and hospitals. A survey in Cleveland indicated that there were 0.45 physicians per 1,000 people in poor neighborhoods, compared to 1.13 per 1,000 in non-poverty areas. The result is fewer visits to physicians and dentists.

PERCENT OF POPULATION MAKING ONE OR MORE VISITS TO INDICATED TYPE OF MEDICAL SPECIALIST FROM JULY 1963 TO JUNE 1964

Type of Medical Specialist	Family Incomes of $2,000 to $3,999		Family Incomes of $7,000 to $9,999	
	White	Nonwhite	White	Nonwhite
Physician	64	56	70	64
Dentist	31	20	52	33

Although widespread use of health insurance has led many hospitals to adopt nondiscriminatory policies, some private hospitals still refuse to admit Negro patients or to accept doctors with Negro patients. And many individual doctors still discriminate against Negro patients. As a result, Negroes are more likely to be treated in hospital clinics than whites, and they are less likely to receive personalized service. This conclusion is confirmed by the following data:

PERCENT OF ALL VISITS TO PHYSICIANS FROM JULY 1963 TO JUNE 1964 MADE IN INDICATED WAYS

Type of Visit to Physician	Family Incomes of $2,000 to $3,999		Family Incomes of $7,000 to $9,999	
	White	Nonwhite	White	Nonwhite
In physician's office	68	56	73	66
Hospital clinic	17	35	7	16
Other (mainly telephone)	15	9	20	18
Total	100	100	100	100

THE GROWING PAINS OF MEDICAL CARE

Fred Anderson

This superb general analysis outlines the nature of health problems in the United States. It suggests that those problems derive from the ways in which health care is organized in this society, arguing that a basic reorganization will be necessary before the quality of health care improves. The selection after this one provides the second half of the radical argument—that increasing corporate dominance of health makes such reorganization within the current structure of institutions more and more difficult.

This selection comes from a three-part series by the same title in *The New Republic* in early 1970. It represents most of the first two parts of the series; the third part discussed alternative mechanisms for improving the financing of health care.

Anderson was a graduate student in political science before joining the staff of the National Academy of Engineering.

[Late in 1969] President Nixon, Secretary Finch and the Assistant Secretary for Health and Scientific Affairs, Dr. Roger Egeberg, gathered at the White House to tell the nation that it is about to face a complete breakdown in the delivery of health services. Many think the breakdown has already occurred. Long waits for an appointment with a physician, poor service, and astronomical medical bills have gradually become the rule, rather than the exception. The public does not understand how this state of affairs came about, nor why physicians, hospitals and insurers have not done something about it. Particularly irritating is the federal government's failure, though it paid 29.6 percent of the $53.1 billion spent on health in 1968. Long hours in the "waiting room," hurried and impersonal attention, difficulty in obtaining night and weekend care, reduction of services because staff is not available, high drug and treatment costs, loopholes in insurance coverage, and the like, tell only part of the story. The rest is told by statistics which smash any remaining confidence that we lead the world in health care. Fifteen other countries have longer average life expectancies. (Ten-year-old females have a longer life expectancy in twelve other coun-

tries, while the American male child of ten years is bested in 31 countries.) Infant mortality is less in 14 other nations. Five countries have better maternal mortality rates. Twelve have better records for ulcers, diabetes, cirrhosis of the liver, hypertension without heart involvement. Twenty have less heart disease.

Whatever life expectancy a white American has, subtract seven years from the life of his nonwhite counterpart. Infant mortality rates are two times as great for nonwhites as for whites. Infant mortality rates for Negro children in Mississippi or a Northern city are comparable to Ecuador's; nationwide, to Costa Rica's. Nonwhite maternal mortality is four times as great as the white rate. (The disparity in maternal death rates has grown from twofold to fourfold since the end of World War II.) In the city slums there is three times as much heart disease, five times as much mental disease, four times as much high blood pressure, and four times as many deaths before age thirty-five than there are nationwide.

The National Advisory Commission on Health Manpower (1967) reviewed 15 representative studies of the quality of health care services in the United States. Here are the findings in three of the studies: (1) a survey of medical laboratories sponsored by the National Center for Communicable Diseases (U.S. Public Health Service) found that 25 percent of reported laboratory results

SOURCE: *Fred Anderson, "The Growing Pains of Medical Care I, II, III," The New Republic, January 17, 24, and 31, 1970. Reprinted by permission of* The New Republic. *Copyright © 1970, Harrison-Blaine of New Jersey, Inc.*

on known samples were erroneous; (2) an evaluation of all major female pelvic surgery performed during a six-month period in a community hospital revealed that 70 percent of the operations which resulted in castration or sterilization were unjustified in the opinion of expert consultants; (3) the medical records of a random sample of 430 patients admitted to 98 different hospitals in New York City during May 1962 were reviewed by expert clinicians. In their opinion only 57 percent of all patients, and only 31 percent of the general medical cases, received "optimal" care.

Organized medicine attributes deterioration in health care to our failure to produce enough physicians for the growing demands for services. That's correct, to a point. Over the decade 1955–1965 "physician-directed services" rose 81 percent and hospital services 65 percent, although the increased output of physicians (22 percent) barely exceeded population growth (17 percent). In fact, the increase in physicians who went into patient care (12 percent) was *less* than population growth. Thus the availability of direct, personal treatment by a physician has diminished at a time when demand for medical care is going up rapidly. Demand has been so great that the expected undersupply of physicians should have occurred years ago. What happened? Physicians learned to delegate many tasks to other medical professionals, a practice which should be encouraged. Between 1955 and 1965, professional nurses increased by 44 percent, nonprofessional nurses 63 percent, X-ray technologists 56 percent, and clinical laboratory personnel 70 percent. Nevertheless, in the opinion of the National Advisory Commission on Health Manpower, the existing organization of medical care will soon require more physicians than the medical schools are capable of producing. "If additional personnel are employed in the present manner and within present patterns and 'systems' of care," said the Commission, "they will not avert, or even perhaps alleviate, the crisis." That seems to say that no number of additional physicians will be sufficient unless medical care is reorganized. But the Commission did not say how reorganization should be carried out.

What is so unsatisfactory about the organization of our present medical care system?

It consists by and large of physicians in practice alone, or in small groups, on a fee-for-service basis. The model is the independent business entrepreneur, and a strong sense of nineteenth-century individualism still guides professional conduct. (About 60 percent of physicians in direct care of patients are solo practitioners, even though less than two percent of current graduates go into general practice. Of physicians in office practice, about 72 percent still work on a fee-for-service basis.) The "nonsystem" of separate practitioners and few hospitals which grew up in the last century has somehow managed to underpin the vast array of interlocking referrals, specialties, clinics, hospital services and financial arrangements which exists today. That foundation is crumbling.

We cannot allow the further duplication of services, equipment and personnel, not only because of the high cost of redundancy, but because fee-for-service medicine is medically one-sided. It is adequate for episodic care for patients with a specific complaint. But such care, though good, is delivered in sporadic bursts. It is not the personalized, lifelong program of prevention, diagnosis, treatment and rehabilitation that it should be. Patients very rarely receive preventive screening or treatment. How could a fee-for-service bill be written for "diagnosing" and publicizing a dangerous playground? Who would be billed? The city? Parents? Fixing up several broken arms is a medical "service," with a going rate per arm. Getting embroiled with nonmedical "playground" issues is not, even though the expense of an ounce of prevention may be less than that for a pound of cure.

It is not quite fair to lay all the ills of the health care system at the feet of the practitioners who favor the fee-for-service system. The American Medical Association, as chief defender of fee-for-service, is almost a caricature of an Establishment, an easy target. But medicine has two Establishments, both of which contribute to our troubles. The second Establishment, hostile to the first, is based in urban hospitals. It is research and technology oriented, often salaried, and provides the world's best surgery and treatment for complex illnesses. The result is that though this is the best country in the world in which to have a serious illness, it is one of the worst countries in the world in which to have a non-serious illness. That part of medicine which most people encounter most often is mediocre. At the same time, we have outstanding open heart surgery, plastic surgery, surgical organ transplantation, and diagnostic skills. It is this paradox which makes it possible for a patient to read in the waiting room literature of America's latest triumph of medical technology, while failing to receive quick, effective and inexpensive treatment for a sore throat.

The strength of the new hospital-based Establishment is in its domination of the medical schools. Dr. Charles E. Lewis of Harvard's Center for Community Medicine and Medical Care believes that the inertia of medical schools and their affiliated teaching hospitals is the health care delivery system's chief problem. The schools and their hospitals turn out excellent clinicians, scientifically imaginative researchers, who appear more concerned with a patient's interesting electrolytes than with his humdrum good health. A department chairman, selected perhaps because he discovered subtle mechanisms of kidney function, makes the school's reputation (and much of its money) by his work and by the grants which he gets for research. No one can tell the collection of department chairmen who run a medical school, or their granting agencies, that the funds which they collect should go to teach students how to care for whole patients in the environment in which patients live.

The fee-for-service system has not adapted well to third-party payments, whether from insurance companies or from government. The public finds this awkward welter of insurance plans and complex federal programs confusing and vexing.

Picking one's way through the medical maze requires, in the words of Dr. Sidney Lee of Harvard Medical School, "the flexibility of a worm, the dexterity of a locksmith, and the hairsplitting ability of a Philadelphia lawyer." For instance, new employees at the Lawrence Radiation Laboratories in California are handed a chart which folds out like a roadmap into a description of eight programs and benefits for 21 selected services. In the 168 separate boxes of fine print are detailed the conditions of coverage and exclusions of each of the eight plans. Making sense of health insurance is a problem for all of us, even if we are not given "helpful"

charts. With approximately 1800 separate plans in existence to choose from, what are we to do?

Perhaps it would be worth working through the maze *if* private insurance provided complete coverage. It does not. *All* third-party payments, including federal programs and philanthropy as well as private insurance, accounted for only *half* of personal health care expenditures by 1966. The private health insurers make quite a fuss over how extensive their coverages are. They point out that about three-fourths of the population has some kind of hospitalization or surgical coverage and that the number is growing. But the important point is not that the number of persons covered is going up; it is that the insured are not getting much for their money. The insured three-fourths of the population has about one-third of its medical bills paid through insurance. Large categories of medical expenses, such as drugs, dental care, and nonhospital "ambulatory" office visits, are excluded from most policies. These exclusions are critical at a time when consumers spend about 20 percent of their health dollars on drugs, about 10 percent on dental care, and, according to a recent MIT study, another 25 percent to 50 percent for ambulatory care.

Government, principally through Medicare and Medicaid, has ventured into paying some of the medical bills of those least able to pay—the elderly and the poor. Medicare includes two related programs for insuring persons over 65 against the costs of hospitalization, physicians' services and related health care. There is no means test. Part A, Hospital Insurance Benefits, covers practically all persons over age 65. It draws its money from a special hospital insurance trust fund, in the case of social security beneficiaries, and general revenues, in the case of those not currently covered by Social Security. Part B, medical insurance for some (but nothing like all) physicians' fees and related costs, is financed by voluntary individual monthly payments, although the federal government also contributes from general revenues. Medicare functions quite smoothly, though hospitals complain of the paperwork and restrictions, and patients complain that in some hospitals they are discriminated against as Medicare patients. Lastly, and contrary to general belief, Medicare covers only about 35 percent of the total health bill of persons over 65.

Medicaid is more complicated. The primary recipients here are, in the bureaucratic phrase, the indigent "categorically needy": the aged, the blind, the disabled, and families with dependent children. Each participating state must submit a plan, and the categorically needy must be included. States are permitted, but not required, to include persons who are self-supporting, but have no reserves to meet medical expenses. These are (again, their phrase) the "medically needy." States may also extend Medicaid to those whose only qualification is poverty. But the federal government will pay only the administrative costs of providing them with medical care. State Medicaid plans must offer five basic services: inpatient hospital care, outpatient hospital care, other lab and X-ray services, nursing home services, and physicians' services. States may elect to provide five additional services for a comprehensive program.

We constantly hear that Medicaid was ill-conceived, that it slipped by Congress while its attention was on Medicare. It certainly was not ill-conceived. Medicaid is a ten-year plan designed to gently badger the states into providing comprehensive medical coverage for all medically and economically deprived persons by 1975. Inflation aside, one reason why Medicaid now gobbles up the dollars is because it is growing, exactly according to the plan set out in the original legislation. After four years of varying degrees of state acceptance, the plan does, however, seem to be a shambles: Medicaid currently serves limited categories of the poor and sick, through benefits of Byzantine complexity, which vary astonishingly from state to state (under Medicaid, New York averages $57 per inhabitant for medical assistance; New Hampshire, $5). The states abuse Medicaid, about a dozen of the states have rejected it altogether, and it is underadministered in Washington.

Skyrocketing costs under Medicaid have led to a well-publicized campaign to economize through administrative reforms. The Administration may actually believe that such tinkering with Medicaid, including November's frantic efforts of yet another Task Force, are the kind of "revolutionary change" which the President said he wanted when he drew attention to the crisis in health care. It would appear so, since the Administration's July report, billed as a major inter-agency study requiring five months to complete, spent most of its shot on administrative reforms. For instance, the government pins great hopes on the strict limits it recently set on fees of physicians participating in Medicaid. But physicians, angered by this effrontery, are likely to respond either by dropping out of Medicaid entirely, or raising their fees to the new legal maximum, causing costs to escalate further.

This sort of reform is worthless. All large institutional funds such as Medicaid, whether public or private in origin, are uncontrollably inflationary in the present *entrepreneurial fee-for-service system*. There is no effective way to police this vast undertaking. Through their right to determine "reasonable" fees, and behind the screen of the simple physician-patient contract for services, hospitals and practitioners are tempted to take what large third-party funds will allow. Proof is not hard to find. Medical costs were already increasing at twice the rate of increase in the Consumer Price Index when Medicaid and Medicare went into effect. But in that year physicians' fees shot up at almost three times the rate of general prices, while hospital charges, incredibly, increased. at five times the rate of general prices! Small wonder that the Senate Finance Committee felt obligated to inquire into possible fraudulent behavior among the 10,000 physicians who in 1968 "earned" $25,000 or more apiece from Medicaid and Medicare.

Federal bureaucratic inefficiency is not particularly to blame, as a recent experience of a private insurer shows. Blue Cross of Kansas, a comparatively simple, modestly financed scheme, recently made $250,000 available to its subscribers for walk-in care at the physician's office. Ten percent of the physicians participating used 50 percent of the fund, and $50,000 was paid out by Blue Cross for simple hypodermic injections alone. Four physicians gave most of the injections, collecting remarkably "reasonable" fees. Patients did not need the injections any more than they did before Blue Cross acted, nor did they request injections. Nevertheless, their physicians prescribed them, and patients, because they were not paying or because they had no idea what an injection should cost, did not object to the artificially high prices charged back to Blue Cross. . . .

COMPLETE REORGANIZATION

When the President told the nation [in 1969] that its health services were about to break down, he based his conclusion on a major, five-month interagency study. Considering the gravity of the news and the President's call for "revolutionary change," it's astonishing that the study hardly mentioned the one way that we might avoid a crisis—reorganization of the nation's entire health care system. Nothing else could rescue a system where physicians' fees are increasing at twice the rate of general prices, hospital costs are increasing at three times the rate of general prices, and scarce physicians provide fewer services, limited to episodic illnesses, for patients—patients, that is, who are not overlooked entirely because of race or class.

Reorganization, if effective, must include three components: group practice, comprehensive preventive care, and prepayment.

Group practice is not a new idea. Physicians learned quite some time ago to cut duplication of office expenses by going into business together. Decreasing overhead increases profits. Comprehensive preventive care, on the other hand, is a new idea. It reduces the present overemphasis on episodic, crisis medicine by requiring that physicians provide for prevention of illness, as well as for its cure, on a family and community basis. Prepayment is also a relatively new idea; it helps pass the savings of group practice on to patients: By paying in advance for total care, patients eliminate the itemized doctor's bill which lists a highly inflatable array of fees for each separate service.

These three concepts, when put together, would foster urban and rural group practices, with a variety of health professionals rendering comprehensive medical services, including family and community-centered preventive care, for a prepaid annual fee per group or person. Hospitals would be integrated with the group practices in a regional plan and would be expected to provide types of specialized or intensive care now unavailable to most people.

Solo practitioners, who may number as many as 175,000, have their own fully equipped offices and pay for them by passing the costs on to their patients. But when it is properly set up, a group practice cuts overhead by finding an optimal size for sharing underused resources, such as receptionists, record maintenance, instruments and buildings. Group practice has other benefits. It relieves the medical graduate of the burden of establishing an office and building up a practice. It facilitates collaborative treatment among physicians who know each other well. It makes possible regular hours, time off for vacation, "sabbaticals" for continuing and updating the physician's medical education, and other benefits of a collegial practice. These advantages probably account for the 26,000 physicians who by 1965 had chosen to go into groups, although very few of the 5450 practices had prepayment plans and almost none passed savings along to consumers.

The second component of reorganization, preventive medicine, poses a philosophical challenge to current medical thought about health care. Today, we must wait until we are ill (preferably *very* ill) before modern medicine can bring its sophisticated techniques into play. Hospitals, medical researchers, and, to a surprising extent, private practitioners prefer it this way: illness is impersonal, isolatable, scientific. People, thought of in terms of what's needed to *prevent* illness, are not nearly as tractable. Experimentation now taking place in the urban ghetto in a special kind of group practice may reverse this unfortunate trend.

Not only are these experimental urban neighborhood practices efficient (Dr. Harold Wise, Director of the Office of Economic Opportunity's South Bronx project, says that in his clinic 25 physicians do what normally would require 60); they are a new approach to health services as well. The urban clinics are staffed with a variety of professionals, including the usual complement of pediatricians, internists, and other specialists. But community health nurses, social workers, nutritionists and psychologists are added, in order to give preventive—as well as episodic—care to families. The neighborhood practitioners are critical of the fragmented care which hospitals provide in outpatient departments or emergency wards at night, or in clinics organized around organ systems and diseases—ear, nose and throat clinics, cancer clinics, burn clinics, chest clinics, medical clinics. The patient is critical, too. He sees this array as frustrating, senseless. Need we be told that diseased organs are found in people, people in families, and families in communities, and that overemphasizing the pathology of tissues may underemphasize simple good health? Good health may require intervention in the social, as well as medical, aspects of a patient's problem. As small as the clinics' impact is, they seem to be gaining: several medical schools have started pilot projects; OEO has 40 clinics in operation; Senator Percy and 22 colleagues have introduced legislation for a $295 million program similar to OEO's; and young health professionals, many through the Student Health Organization, intend to make the clinics work.

Oddly, the communities have not always accepted community medicine with uncloyed gratitude, from which an important fact can be learned. Community leaders want control of the health programs and a larger say in what services they will deliver. Thus, Harvard University, which claims the first university-sponsored prepaid group practice plan, has had to contend with community suspicion that Harvard will provide services only so long as the community is content to do no more than provide plenty of illnesses. Tufts University, also in Boston, found that the community's Columbia Point Health Association had ideas about community health which went well beyond the "programmed" level. These "people difficulties" show that medicine is not nearly in close enough touch with its consumers, even in the inner city where medicine has tried very hard. It leads one to wonder what middle-class patients might learn and say if they, too, had a voice in health care. Preventive family medicine, through dietetics, early screening, and broader consultation, could have a great effect on middle-class maladies: ulcers, diabetes, obesity, dental caries, cirrhosis of the liver, hypertension, heart disease, cancer, neurosis. It does not take a physician to realize that each of these can be prevented or detected quite early, and that families and communities contribute to cause and cure.

The last component in reorganization, prepayment, shifts attention once again to economy. Having agreed to a set lump sum to cover comprehensive care, physicians increase their income through internal savings below their predetermined annual income, not by gradually raising fees, here and there, for the uncountable number of separate services now available. Physicians in a prepayment plan must also give their time to patients whose health needs are greatest. This is a healthy contrast to the present situation, where all too often money determines what patients get. If Warbucks chooses to pay the prevailing rate, he can buy two hours of a Menninger's time for little Annie's sniffles. A prepayment group practice, in theory, must be more economical and apportion its talent and time on a health-oriented basis if it is to make money.

The Group Health Association of America estimates that almost eight million people are served, in part or in whole, by group health prepayment practices. About 25 of these are community plans, the largest of which are the Kaiser Foundation Health Plan (Western states), the Health Insurance Plan of Greater New York, the Community Health Association of Detroit, the Group Health Association of Washington, D.C. and the Group Health Cooperative of Puget Sound. Together, they care for up to four million people. The Longshoremen, the Hotel Union (New York), the Teamsters, the Mineworkers and other labor groups support a variety of plans with checkered coverages for another 3.5 to 4 million people. The collective experience of these plans has revealed some interesting facts: our outmoded system typically requires four hospital beds for every 1000 of population served; in the plans, half as many beds are enough, because office visits and outpatient care are more intelligently used, and because there is no built-in incentive to overutilize hospitals in order for the patient "to get his money back" from insurance plans (which usually provide generous benefits for hospitalization but almost nothing for outpatient care). The plans also keep drug costs down. For example, drugs for subscribers to the Seattle plan cost 50 percent less than the national average. The plans, then, are making dramatic savings in just those areas of health finance which are the most expensive, and usually they do it with substantial improvement in the quality of care rendered.

The Kaiser Foundation Health Plan, which now serves almost two million subscribers, has been particularly successful. Kaiser has saved its California subscribers 20 to 30 percent of the costs which Californians must meet if they are not in Kaiser's program. Further, under the terms of Medicare,

Medicaid, and private insurance plans, many services are not reimbursable unless delivered in hospitals, causing a tremendous overuse of hospitals and consequently lower uninsured expenditures for early detection and preventive care. By reversing the incentives Kaiser has cut hospitalization 30 percent and costs even more, and without higher outpatient costs.

But group practices *alone* will not get us better medicine at lower cost. Especially when organized by physicians themselves, they rarely pass savings on to patients. Community and labor plans like the ones above are exceptional, in spite of their successes in some parts of the country. Nor will adding the prepayment device to group practice cut into medical consumers' huge bills unless a way can be found to keep down the initial lump sum payments. The purchasers of medical care need to be able to find effective representation for themselves and to challenge abuses when there is an increase in annual prepayments. What is needed in fact is countervailing "patient power."

Although prepayment cannot do the whole job, it does lay a foundation for effective patient representation. National norms for what a medical consumer should pay for comprehensive care are already evolving, since a prepaid group practice is a manageable unit for quality review. (The plans mentioned have begun to develop a figure, leaving age differences aside, of around $130 a person a year.) With the evolution of standards costs for comprehensive services for individuals in various age groups, one is able to inquire why any particular group practice cannot hold its rates down to the norm. And given patients, services and profits, it is possible to develop a set of facts with which a group, an insurer, a consumer's representative or a government agency can criticize the quality of care rendered. For instance, the cost of *my* minor respiratory disorder is almost impossible to estimate. But the cost of 2000 of them can be estimated, and that information used for more rational health pricing, or, if need be, as a weapon in the consumer's battle for better care and reduced costs. Furthermore, united consumers can afford physicians, and economists, who are hired to protect *their* interests.

As matters now stand, no one really knows how to challenge physicians' fee scales.

(There is much talk and some effort directed to "quality control and review" under the federal programs, but review depends upon statistical analysis, and the needed data cannot be produced under the present organization of health care.) To make things easier, relevant statutes can be amended or passed to require annual reports to subscribers, where statutes do not already require this disclosure as part of corporation or partnership law. There is no good reason why the financing of health (the second largest of all our private industries, second only to education) should not be openly reported. Participants can negotiate collectively for coverage and for items of preventive care from which the community or group as such can benefit. Prepayment can make available additional kinds of health benefits which are unmanageable in a fee-for-service system. The large institutional funds may even do it for them. For instance, state Medicaid agencies have already bargained with the Clackamas County, Oregon, Physicians' Association and with 290 physicians in California's San Joaquin Valley to pay fixed per capita premiums for total care for Medicaid recipients. A private insurer, if it had to, could do the same.

The success of groups like Kaiser in cutting consumers' costs by 20 to 30 percent is encouraging. Similar savings nationwide could save $7.5 billion in hospital bills by 1975. But without being overly cynical one may ask why physicians, who are in short supply, would want to respond to the pressures of patients, who are in large supply, even if annual set rates are charged. There is no final guarantee that physicians would not keep the annual rates as high as they possibly can. But if they attempt to do so they will meet informed opposition where virtually none had existed before. They will have to push prices up under the scrutiny of consumers' representatives who know facts formerly unavailable—facts showing how much increase is due to real costs, normal inflation, waste, or higher incomes for physicians.

Either physicians will see the wisdom of economies in the financing of health care and in reorganization, or they will risk their prestige to demand even larger incomes and the continuation of wasteful practices which make life easier for the physician and harder for everyone else. Even if blinded sometimes by the preeminence which they enjoy in American society, physicians know that they are wide open to every kind of regulation and control once they lose the prestige that has made them so effective in Congress.

Many of them believe that group practice and prepayment, combined as described here, or in another way, are a means of preserving the private practice of medicine.

THE MEDICAL-INDUSTRIAL COMPLEX

Barbara and John Ehrenreich

This long selection clearly documents the emergence of a new "medical-industrial complex" in this country. The implications of that emergence are clear. If we desire a basic reorganization of our health care system—as the preceding selection argued we should—then we shall have to contend with an increasing domination of that system by large corporations in pursuit of profit.

The selection appeared originally as Chapter Seven of *The American Health System: Power, Profits, and Politics*, a Health-PAC book prepared by Barbara and John Ehrenreich. The Health Policy Advisory Center (Health-PAC) is a collective of radicals in New York City who do research and organizing on health care issues. Barbara and John Ehrenreich are members of the group.

Ever since Florence Nightingale, medical care has had an aura of selflessness and self-imposed poverty. The great modern hospital center, for instance, projects itself as a "non-profit" institution where "the few toil ceaselessly that the many might live." But behind the facade of the helpless sick and dedicated healers lies the 1960's greatest gold rush, a booming "health industry" churning out more than $2.5 billion a year by 1969 in after-tax profits.

In 1969 the nation spent over $62 billion on medical care, up more than 11 percent over [1968] and twice the 1960 level. $6 billion of this flowed into the hands of the drug companies; almost $10 billion went to the companies that sell doctors and hospitals everything from bed linen to electrocardiographs; $35 billion was spent on "proprietary" (profit-making) hospitals and nursing homes. The nation purchased $6 billion

worth of commercial health insurance and construction companies built about $2 billion worth of hospitals. Additional billions were raked in by private physicians. The health industry is big business, profitable business, and booming business. Stockbroker Goodbody and Company clued in its customers earlier this year: "Steady growth of the health industry . . . is as certain as anything can be"—as certain as death and taxes, in any event.

The great boom of the 1960's in the health industries is largely the product of government subsidization of the market. For years the government has directly or indirectly fed dollars into the gaping pockets of the dealers in human disease. In addition to direct payments for health care, for educating health manpower, and for hospital construction, it has granted tax deductions to individuals for their medical expenses, making their health dollars cheaper. It has expanded the purchasing power of "non-profit" hospitals by granting them tax exemptions, and, until recently, by not applying minimum wage or labor relations laws to them. It has directly supported basic biological and chemical re-

SOURCE: *Barbara and John Ehrenreich, "The Medical-Industrial Complex," from* The American Medical System: Power, Profits, and Politics, *by Health-PAC. Copyright © 1970 by Health Policy Advisory Committee, Inc. Reprinted by permission of Random House, Inc.*

search to the tune of billions of dollars as well as sponsoring the dramatic advances in electronics. These technologies underlie many of the most profitable sectors of the health industry. And in 1966, the biggest government subsidy of all—Medicare and Medicaid —got going. By 1969 federal, state and local governments directly picked up more than a third of the tab for the nation's health needs, and all signals were go for a steadily increasing government-guaranteed market. One likely mechanism: government subsidized national health insurance, to underwrite the entire medical care market.

Only a small part of the new money being spent on health has gone to improve health care. For instance, community hospitals spent 16 percent more money in 1968 than they did in 1967. But they provided only 3.3 percent more days of inpatient care and 3.7 percent more outpatient visits. (Nobody noticed any 13 percent increase in the quality of care.) A large fraction of the new money for the health care delivery system has, for all social purposes, simply vanished —as inflated costs for drugs, supplies and equipment, and as profits for doctors and hospitals.

In this section we take a look at the money for health which has surged through the delivery system of doctors, hospitals and drug stores to fuel an unprecedented boom in the health "industry"—the private companies which supply, equip, finance, build for and (sometimes) manage the health delivery system. Here, the dollar-for-dollar return as health benefits is, first, shockingly low, and second, perhaps not even that "healthy." From the outset, the aim of the health industry is not to promote the general well-being (in the long run, that would be self-defeating), but to exploit existing profitable markets and create new ones. The emphasis, then, is not on products and services which would improve basic health care for the great mass of consumers, but on what are essentially luxury items: computerized equipment for intensive cardiac care units, hyperbaric chambers, hospitals which specialize in elective surgery for the rich, expensive combination drugs, etc. Under the pressure of the industry's barrage of packaged technology, the health care delivery system is increasingly distorted towards high-cost, low-utilization, inpatient services.

Most of the money which flows through the delivery system to the health industry's drug and hospital supply and equipment companies never returns to the delivery system in any medically useful form, or in any form at all. First, a good 5 to 10 percent is raked off directly as profits, and these by and large vanish into the larger economy, going to stockholders and going to finance the companies' expansions into other enterprises. More and more of the health industry firms are conglomerates, whose holdings in drugs or hospital supplies help finance their acquisitions in cosmetics, catering or pet food.

Profits are only part of the story. There is no way of auditing the health industry companies to determine how much of their "costs" actually represents medically wasted, privately managed, surplus income. Prices are high, the health companies claim, not on account of profits, but because of the enormous cost of research, skilled manpower, meeting exacting standards, etc. But how much of the industry's research goes into a needless and dangerously confusing proliferation of marginally different products—like drugs which differ only in flavor, electronic equipment which differs only in console design, etc.? How much goes to plan the planned obsolescence in expensive hospital hardware? How much of the costs go for the design of appealing packaging? How much for million-dollar advertising and promotion campaigns? Money spent on these causes is not simply wasted. The needless proliferation of dazzlingly advertised and packaged products is a health hazard. It prevents the buyer, whether he is a doctor, a hospital administrator, or a patient, from making informed choices among products and mystifies him to the point where he will accept unquestioningly the industry's definition of what he needs and what he must pay for it.

DRUGS

The drug industry likes to think of itself as a sort of public service—dispensing life and comfort and at the same time upholding the American, free-enterprise way. *Forbes* magazine, which likes to think of itself as the "capitalist tool," much more honestly describes the drug industry as "one of the biggest crap games in U.S. industry." Any way you cut it, the drug industry is big and on the way to being bigger:

—$6 billion worth of drugs (prescription

and nonprescription) were sold in 1969, $6.5 billion will be sold in 1970, and so on, increasing at about 9 percent a year.

—There are 700 drug firms. Control is concentrated in the top fifteen, who sell more than half of all drugs.

—200,000 people are employed by drug companies all over the world. 100,000 of these are Americans and 20,000 of them are the "detail men" who push prescription pills to private doctors.

—The American drug industry is worldwide. Foreign sales are growing faster than domestic, as drug companies expand their foreign subsidiaries. The two leading drug imperialists are Pfizer, with 48 percent of its business abroad, and Merck, with 37 percent industry-wide; more than one quarter of sales are abroad.

—The industry spends one and a half billion dollars a year on advertising, twenty-five cents out of every sales dollar and more than three times as much as its spends on its much-heralded research and development effort.

What makes drugs the "biggest crap game," however, is profits. For the last ten years, the drug industry has held either first, second or third place among all U.S. industries in terms of profitability, outdistancing such obvious moneymakers as the cosmetics, aerospace, recreation and entertainment industries.

But the drug industry has seen better days. Earlier leaps in profits grew out of major breakthroughs: antibiotics in the late '40s, tranquilizers in the late '50s and early '60s and birth control pills in the early and mid-'60s. Nothing big has come along since "the pill" and even it is something of a disappointment. Efforts to push the pill beyond the 20 percent of eligible women who now use it have been checked by growing mutters about annoying and often lethal side effects. "We're in a trough right now," says a top Merck man, and some companies are beginning to wonder whether it's worth gambling on another wave of wonder drugs.

According to the industry's own probably inflated estimates, a really new drug takes about 10 years and $7 million worth of research. Hence more and more "new" drugs are not new at all. Over half released in the last 10 years are what are called "me, too" drugs: minor chemical modifications of old drugs, combinations of old drugs, old drugs

released in chewable form, time capsule form, half-dose form, in handy dispensers, and so on in endless, meaningless elaboration. Meanwhile some of the old best-sellers are threatened with patent expirations and anti-trust suits. Parke Davis has become too dependent on chloromycetin, and began to slip in profitability when the antibiotic's patent expired a couple of years ago. Similarly, Pfizer has lost an anti-trust suit which will loosen its grip on tetracycline. Overall drug industry profits slipped below 10 percent of sales in 1968 for the first time in years. (That's still way ahead of most industries.)

Then, as if the drug companies didn't have enough problems of their own, the federal government has shown increasing signs of being serious about regulating drug costs and quality. The Kefauver investigations into drug prices and the resulting federal drug law amendments had drug companies, by their own admission, "running scared" in the early sixties. The stiffer scrutiny of new drugs required by the 1962 law caused a sharp drop in the rate at which new products were introduced, and pushed many companies to expand abroad, in countries where drug-testing laws are more permissive.

But the most potentially far-reaching affront to the drug companies' independence was Medicare. Drug companies knew from the start that a healthy chunk of Medicare funds would find its way to their pockets. What they feared was that there might be some strings attached. The Pharmaceutical Manufacturers Association, in their right-wing public relations throwaway "Medicine at Work," editorialized in early 1965:

> What is the logic in socializing medical care (via Medicare) when health insurance programs can function so effectively and are expanding every day, in fact already covering most of our citizens? . . . If private initiative disappears there may never be enough time to repair the damage that will ensue . . . .

But a few months later the Pharmaceutical Manufacturers Association, at their national convention, spent a whole day in seminars on Medicare. When they emerged, *The New York Times* reported with cautious optimism that "some companies have accepted the fact that Medicare is here and with it has come a new opportunity for the industry."

Even though they reluctantly accepted

Medicare (and of course Medicare money for their pills), the drug companies saw the handwriting on the wall. Like the AMA, the drug industry knows that government subsidy can lead to government scrutiny. Drug costs are a big bill to swallow, and have already become the subject of repeated Congressional inquiry. If the government role in financing medical care expands beyond Medicare and the ruins of Medicaid, the government might begin to insist on generic drugs (as opposed to much more expensive but chemically identical brand-name drugs), price-setting, or other forms of profit-regulation.

When the neighborhood pusher feels the heat coming down on him, he begins to turn to new, but related, rackets. So with the drug companies, menaced by real or imagined regulation, the answer has been to diversify into anything which their technology and marketing skills prepare them for. As if by free association, drug companies have been turning to cosmetics, chemicals, hospital supplies and electronic equipment for hospitals. American Cyanamid (which owns Lederle Labs) now owns Breck (shampoo). Pfizer has bought Coty, Barbasol, Pacquin and Desitin (baby powders and oils). Richardson-Merrill acquired Clearasil; Smith, Kline and French has Sea and Ski; Syntex, Upjohn and Merck are all reaching into chemicals. Upjohn, Searle and Smith, Kline and French are all into medical electronics, with Searle, for instance, betting on Medidata, which makes computers for futuristic mechanized mass screening devices. Parke Davis, Abbott and Cutter Labs are getting into the booming hospital supplies industry.

All this diversification by the once-staid drug manufacturers does not represent a flight from drugs. Prescription drugs remain the most profitable line of the diversified companies, and the drug habit, once established, is hard to break. In fact, the most interesting trend in the drug industry is not diversification of the old guard, but the influx of new industries, all potential drug addicts. Chemical companies are leading the way. Dow Chemicals, of Saran Wrap and napalm fame, began buying up small drug companies in 1960, and is now a major contender in the measles vaccine market. Other chemical newcomers are 3M (formerly Minnesota Mining and Manufacturing, the conglomerate which makes, among other things,

Scotch Tape), Rohm and Haas, Union Carbide, Malinckrodt and DuPont. Cosmetic and soap companies, such as Bristol Meyers, Colgate Palmolive, and Helene Curtis are not far behind in the rush for the drug markets. Revlon now owns U.S. Vitamin and Pharmaceuticals; Cheeseborough, Pond has acquired Pertussin. One other industry which is being invaded by the drug firms has begun a counter-offensive, the medical supplies industry. Baxter, Becton-Dickinson and Johnson and Johnson have all bought into the drug industry.

You don't have to be a member of the chemical/drug/cosmetics axis to get in on the drug action. For instance, American Home Products, Inc., maker of Boyardee foods, Guldens mustard and Gay-pet products for animals also serves up nonprescription drugs such as Preparation H, Quiet World (a tranquilizer) and Sudden Action (breath freshener), and has become a big shot in the ethical drug world, owning Wyeth Labs as well as several smaller drug companies. Then there's Squibb-Beechnut which makes gum, babyfoods, candy, coffee, pastry, airlines' meals and operates drive-ins and snack bars, in addition to prescription drugs. Anybody who makes anything which can be swallowed, inhaled, absorbed or applied would like to make drugs . . . and vice versa.

HOSPITAL SUPPLIES AND EQUIPMENT

The story of the growth of the hospital supplies industry is the story of the explosive growth of the hospital as the central institution in the delivery of health care in America. In 1950 the nation spent $3.8 billion on hospital care. By 1965, the figure had risen to $13.8 billion, and in 1969, three years after Medicare and Medicaid, hospital expenditures were running at a $20 billion a year clip. About $7.5 billion of this went for goods and services. Much of it's mundane—food, bed linen, and dust mops, but billions went for more specifically medical equipment, from scalpels, syringes and catheters to X-ray equipment, electronic blood cell counters, and artificial kidneys. In addition to the hospital market, physicians, dentists, nursing homes, and medical research labs spend huge sums, measured in the billions of dollars, on similiar supplies.

The risks in the hospital supply industry

appear to be as low as the profits are high. Medicaid may have its ups and downs, but Medicare, at least, is here to stay. And only a gambler with a compulsion for losing would bet against the likelihood of continued growth in hospital expenditures and increased subsidy of the market by the government. The hospital supply companies have gotten the message. "The start of IPCO's new financial year on July 1, 1966," said the annual report of one of the major distributors and manufacturers of hospital goods, "also marked the beginning of the Federal Medicare program and supplementary state health programs [Medicaid]. The enormous increase in demand for institutional care . . . will, we believe, create a growing demand for the type of products IPCO distributes and manufactures." Like the man said, in the last dozen years IPCO's earnings have increased at a compound annual rate of 22 percent. In the same vein, an executive of the paper manufacturer of Kimberly-Clark, which has applied its technology to disposable bed linen and uniforms for hospitals, said, "The type of care usually provided under Medicare is the type that creates new opportunities for disposables." In 1951, $14 million worth of disposable products (including needles, syringes, and such standbys as paper plates) were sold. By 1965, the last pre-Medicare year, the market hit $100 million, and 1970 sales are expected to reach $300 million.

The stock market has been hot on the track. The month Medicare went into operation, stockbrokers Burnham and Co. prepared an analysis of the industry for their customers. One year later, the Value Line Investment Survey spoke of one hospital supply company as "operating in a sector of the economy that is virtually recession-proof." (The company, American Hospital Supply, has seen its earnings grow at 16 percent per year for the last decade. In the first half of 1969, earnings were up 19 percent over the corresponding period of 1968.) And despite the Medicaid flip-flops United Business Service listed eight hospital supply companies on its fall 1969 list of 200 top-growth stocks.

The traditional hospital supply companies —C. R. Bard, Becton-Dickinson, Baxter Labs, Sherwood Medical, Johnson and Johnson, IPCO, and American Hospital Supply— have been the big winners in the Medicare sweepstakes, with earnings up 15 percent to 25 percent a year over the last few years.

But the soaring profits and wide-open market are attracting new contenders, as well. Through acquisitions of existing hospital supply companies or through applying the technology of other markets to medical supplies, many of the big guns of American industry are out for a piece of the pie. 3M Company is getting in through its mastery of cellophane—it makes peel-open packages of sterile surgical supplies as well as surgical tapes and drapes and masks. Soapmaker Procter and Gamble goes for germicidal soaps and cleansers, rubbermaker B. F. Goodrich for anti-bacterial mattresses, and chemical company W. R. Grace for carbon dioxide absorbants for anesthesiology. Other big non-medical companies buying in are, for instance, American Cyanamid and the Brunswick Corporation (a conglomerate). Companies with past experience in medical technology are especially active, with such big drug companies as Smith, Kline and French, Searle, Parke Davis, Abbott, and Warner Lambert going into everything from blood bank equipment to cardiac pacemakers.

Supplies aren't the only thing booming in the hospital products industry. Medical electronics is moving out of the realm of science fiction and into the *Wall Street Journal*. A convergence of several factors has created a market currently running at about $350 million a year and expected to reach $1–$1.5 billion a year by the mid-1970's. For one thing, hospitals are buried under an increasing patient load. The volume of every service, from laundry to lab tests, from medical record-keeping to financial record-keeping, from diagnosis to intra-hospital communications, is growing at a staggering rate. At the same time, the cost of the labor to perform these functions is rising sharply, under the impact of the hospital workers' unionization movement, newly applicable minimum wage legislation, and an acute shortage of skilled medical manpower. The need of hospitals for cost-cutting technology has created a good sales pitch for the industry.

At the same time, years of government expenditures on defense and on medical research are flowering into a wealth of new technology to apply to hospitals. The new technology is expensive—out of reach of the solo practitioner—but the large hospital has both the volume to effectively use it and the financial resources to afford it. And the costs can be passed along to the government in the form of Medicare and Medicaid depreciation allowances. "Medicare is the computer manufacturer's friend," exults one trade journal.

Finally, some sectors of the electronics industry, at least, are under pressure to find new markets. The aerospace industry, for one, is in a trough, with NASA expenditures on the decline since 1965, Vietnam production past its 1968 peak, and a lag in new orders from the commercial airlines. Health —another government subsidized market— looks like a good pasture to head for.

One big chunk of the hospital electronic market is in computers. There are three types: general computers for business use (billing, accounting, payrolls, etc.); small machines built into other apparatuses (such as patient monitors); and computers for medical information and practice (diagnosis, medical record-keeping, and "total hospital information systems"). This last type of computer has not grown as rapidly as expected, due in part to the inherent irrationality of many hospital operations. (Installation of a major computer must be preceded by a thorough systems analysis of the hospital and rationalization of its procedures—often by experts supplied by the computer company.)

Most of the major computer companies are out for a share in the hospital market. They are joined by such outsiders as United Aircraft, Lockheed, Motorola, Xerox, and American Optical. Industry spokesmen estimate that upwards of a billion dollars' worth of computers will have been installed in hospitals by 1975.

The general medical electronics industry is growing even more rapidly. Practically everybody who knows an oscilloscope from a stethoscope is out for this one—Litton Industries, GE, International Rectifier, TRW, RCA, Varian and Siemens, among the big ones. Perhaps the most intriguing product is produced by Fairchild Space and Defense Systems Division of Fairchild Camera and Instrument. It's a "foreign body locator" patterned after mine detectors, for locating pieces of shrapnel bullets, or the safety pin baby has swallowed. As with the parent electronics industry, a plethora of smaller companies like those lining Route 128 around Boston are appearing on the fringes. Hospital journals feature ads for such companies as Astro Associates, Spacelabs, Inc., Laser Sys-

tems and Electronics, Inc., and Medidata Services, Inc.

Like drugs in an earlier era, medical electronics has the potential to revolutionize medical practice. At one level, new vistas in diagnosis and treatment are opened up by the electron microscope, fiber optics, high energy radiation sources, computer analysis of electrocardiograms, and the like. At a second level, the potentials of computer diagnosis may lead to new roles for the doctor and other health workers. Finally, the need for systems analysis to accompany the fully effective use of computers may have fallout in the form of partial rationalizations of hospital operations. There is no guarantee, of course, that any of these changes will work to the favor of the patient. Like the drug companies' "me too" drugs, innovations may rebound mainly to the favor of the manufacturers.

HEALTH INSURANCE

The growth of private health insurance is superficially one of the great success stories of American business. In 1940 only 12 million Americans had the most common form of medical insurance, coverage for hospital expenses. By 1967, no less than 175 million, or 83 percent of the civilian population, were covered by private hospital insurance. 100 million of these were covered by commercial, profit-making insurance companies, the rest by Blue Cross, Blue Shield, and independent plans. Many of these subscribers were insured for other kinds of medical expenses than hospitalization, as well. The private companies collected premiums totaling $5.86 billion and paid out $4.84 billion in benefits, administrative and selling expenses comprising much of the remainder.

Demand for health services has risen sharply since the forties, just as the cost of those services skyrocketed beyond the reach of the average consumer. Some sort of insurance against the financial catastrophe of getting sick has become a necessity. Meanwhile, the courts were recognizing fringe benefits as a legitimate area for collective bargaining, and mass purchasers of health insurance in the form of union and employer health and welfare plans emerged. For these reasons, the health insurance industry grew explosively in the late 1940's and early 1950's. By now more than a thousand companies, mainly life insurance companies, write health insurance. But the business is still dominated by a few giants: eight companies do almost two thirds of the business.

The companies get a huge gross income from their health insurance business, but the profit picture is a bit muddy. Insurance companies earn money in two ways: directly, from premiums paid by consumers, and indirectly, from the investment of premiums in corporate and government securities. On a direct sales of health insurance to individuals, the companies generally make an underwriting profit. But on group policies (e.g., policies covering all the employees of a certain firm), the industry claims to lose money overall—about a quarter of a billion dollars in 1967. And the investment income which the companies attribute to their health insurance business is, according to their claim, barely adequate to cover the underwriting loss.

Don't believe that the industry is writing health insurance for charity, though. Industry-wide, the companies take an apparent underwriting loss, but most of the bigger companies report substantial profits. The losses probably reflect the trouble smaller companies have had in predicting expenses in the face of escalating medical prices. Industry giants, such as Equitable, Prudential, Metropolitan, have all showed net underwriting gains over the last five years. And the two big companies that did not, Aetna and Connecticut General, had one bad year that outweighed substantial gains in the other years.

The real profits in health insurance may be very different. Insurance companies are good jugglers. Almost all companies link sales of health insurance to sales of life insurance, sometimes refusing to sell the one without the other. Thus the problems of allocating profits and costs between individual life, group life, individual health, group health and various other kinds of policies are enough to turn even an honest accountant's hair grey.

Finally, the insurance companies see health insurance, in the words of one insurance executive, as "not so much a separate product but rather another of the client's needs." In many cases, health insurance is thrown in at a low price as a sweetener or "loss leader" for a highly profitable package including life insurance, disability, and even

casualty insurance. The industry trade journals are full of such success stories as "Health Insurance—the Door Opener," and "Company Growth through Health Insurance."

For all these reasons, it is hard to say anything quantitative about the profits in the business. But health insurance is clearly an important component of the overall business of the life insurance companies. Health premiums alone account for 15–45 percent of the total gross income (including investments and all sorts of premiums) of the major companies. The entire life insurance industry had an after-tax income in 1967 of $9.1 billion, and had assets of $180 billion. The availability of such huge funds for investment makes control of the top companies a major source of corporate wealth and power. The health insurance business thus represents a significant piece of a very large pie indeed.

Despite its great size, the health insurance industry is about as functional as a dinosaur. Most Americans do have some kind of basic hospitalization insurance, but relatively few are covered for other medical expenses (40 percent for home or office physician visits, 9 percent for nursing home care, 2 percent for dental expenses). Moreover, the insurance companies, along with their non-profit buddy, Blue Cross, are caught in a cost squeeze: as prices for medical services rise, either the cost of insurance must go up or the expenses covered must be limited. Since commercial insurance companies set their premiums according to the medical experience of the individual group they are insuring, it is the elderly and other relatively high-risk groups who are squeezed out first.

The first consequence of the failures of commercial insurance came in 1965 when the companies were forced to relinquish older customers to Medicare. The companies' screams in response to Medicare had something of a theatrical quality. After all, the companies were ridding themselves of their least profitable customers. In fact, the year following Medicare saw a drop in company premiums but a much larger drop in benefit payments to consumers. But, as one company official said, "Most of us feel the loss of the over-65 market is not the important thing, but rather what Medicare will do to the business in 10 or 15 years." They feared that "Medicare has brought the country a giant step closer to socialized medicine" which could "all but eliminate the need for health insurance as it is sold today." According to *The New York Times,* the companies, "generally inspired more by the wish to discourage government expansion of Medicare than by the desire for the business that would be generated," cooperated with the government in setting up the program. About fifteen companies now serve as intermediaries in the administration of the program.

By 1968 it was again becoming evident that the health insurance companies were not able to provide adequate protection for many Americans. Under the influence of problems affecting other aspects of the insurance industry and under pressure from consumer groups, the companies' attitudes toward the government were shifting. Some industry figures openly hoped that the government would serve as guarantor of the companies' market rather than as a competitor. One plan for national health insurance, for instance, would have used government funds to subsidize the purchase of private health insurance by employers and employees. According to the president of Aetna: "A program of universal health insurance offers one way to spread the cost of medical care [between employer, employee and government]. It could be structured to retain the advantages of competition and the profit incentive. . . . I have full confidence in our ability to work successfully in partnership with government."

NURSING HOMES AND HOSPITALS

The age-old way of profiting from illness is by selling health services themselves. Doctors have always done it; so have what are called "proprietary" (profit-making) hospitals and nursing homes. During all the fuss about glamorous health hardware and electronics industries, old-fashioned health service profiteering hasn't been going out of style. If anything, nursing homes and hospital chains have become, at least to the adventurous investor, the hottest things going in the entire health industry, if not the entire stock market. Brokers and investment advisors liken the current boom in nursing homes and hospital chains to the boom in bowling alleys a few years ago or to that in computer software and fried chicken drive-ins today. In 1969 the nursing home industry, almost all of which is proprietary,

grossed $2.8 billion, up 21 percent over 1968 and up 529 percent from 1960. Proprietary hospitals trailed with $720 million in total "sales."

Only four years ago, the nursing home and hospital business was still a cottage industry. A family added a wing to their home and called it a nursing home. A doctor or group of doctors bought and ran their own hospital for their own patients. Four years ago, only five nursing homes and one hospital company were "publicly owned," i.e., sold stock on the open market. Now there are 50 publicly owned nursing home companies and six hospital companies. For both hospital and nursing home chains profits are running at about 5 percent of "sales," after taxes.

What put the profit into the traditionally "charitable" nursing home and hospital business? Medicare, more than anything else, is underwriting the boom. The expansion of Blue Cross and commercial insurance coverage has helped, of course, to create hosts of paying customers for the health service business. Clever management is another factor. Nursing home and hospital companies are able to cut costs through economies of scale, such as bulk purchasing for an entire chain of facilities, centralized administration, etc. But the voluntary (private, nonprofit) health sector also did much to set the stage for the entrance of the energetic profit-makers. Local voluntary hospital establishments, working with Blue Cross and the regional health planning agency, have done much to keep down the number of hospital and nursing home beds—creating a shortage which the profit-makers are eagerly filling.

Nursing homes are the ideal way to cash in on Medicare and Medicaid. Every oldster is at least partially covered and every oldster is a potential customer. Some of the largest publicly owned nursing home companies are: Extendicare, Four Seasons Nursing Centers of America, Medicenters of America (a franchise system owned by Holiday Inns), and American Automated Vending Corp. All are expanding: for instance, Four Seasons projects 100 additional homes per year. Some buy existing homes; others build their own. Some operate their own homes; others are selling franchises.

If hotels are profitable, nursing homes ought to be profitable. But hospitals would seem to be another matter. Costs are wild;

manpower is scarce and frequently irascible; funds are unreliable. To make a profit out of hospitals, you would have to forget all the old voluntary-sector inhibitions about hospitals as "a sacred trust" and a public service. This is exactly what the new hospital companies are doing: They select well-to-do neighborhoods and turn away any non-paying patients who might find their way in. They avoid outpatient and emergency services insofar as possible. They encourage short-term patients in order to gain a high turnover rate (the first few days in the hospital pay the most). They avoid expensive and difficult technology, by concentrating on simple illnesses and elective surgery, and by contracting out for services such as pathology and radiology.

Wherever they spring up, profit-making hospitals offer stiff competition for the local voluntaries. First they sell stock to local doctors, guaranteeing themselves a large medical staff and plenty of private patients. And of course the doctor/stockholders have a special interest in keeping the hospital running efficiently and profitably. Once in operation, the profit-maker skims off the cream of the local patient crop from nearby voluntaries—the not-too-sick, able-to-pay patients. Having cut costs in all the ways listed above, the profit-maker is then able to lure nurses away from local voluntaries by offering higher salaries.

What's most insulting is for a profit-maker to parasitize off a local voluntary—setting up shop near a voluntary which can handle patient-rejects and unprofitable services like obstetrics and outpatient care. This happened recently in Fort Meyers, Florida, where the Hospital Corporation of America (HCA) decided to locate a new 150-bed profit-maker near the already-underutilized voluntary Lee Memorial Hospital. When Lee Memorial protested against being left with the dregs of the patient supply, HCA president responded, "As proprietary hospitals we pay taxes. These taxes help support the tax-supported hospitals [voluntaries] which are in business to care for the nonpaying patient and were established for that purpose." Lee Memorial never intended to be that charitable, and is ganging up with the local power structure to drive out Nashville-based HCA. A recent *Fort Meyers News Press* editorial was entitled, "No Fast-Buck Hospital Needed Here."

If the hospital boom continues, it is likely to run into more and more organized opposition from voluntaries. Much of the opposition will be, on the surface at least, on moral grounds, although it is not clear why profits made by hospitals are any less "moral" than profits made by drug and hospital supply companies. The voluntary hospital leaders in many localities may be especially resentful because the men who head up hospital companies are not, by and large, the kind of men who would ever be chosen as trustees and directors of voluntaries. American Medicorp, which does business primarily in the South and Midwest, was founded by a couple of young Jewish lawyers from the North. The chairman and founder of HCA is an ex-retail druggist who made his first fortune in the Kentucky Fried Chicken chain of drive-ins. To fight the profit-making intruders, voluntaries may have to swallow their traditional antipathy to government "interference," and lobby for tougher laws regulating licensing and operation of hospitals.

In case government regulation is in the cards, many profit-making hospital companies are already one step ahead of the game—busily diversifying into hospital-related businesses. Beverly Enterprises, which owns 18 hospitals and nursing homes, is forming Career Development Corp., to train health personnel at a profit. Metrocare Enterprises, owner of nine acute-care hospitals, has purchased a construction firm and plans to build complete medical centers. Other companies are developing firms to provide ancillary services to hospitals. For instance, American Medical Enterprises, Inc. owns Cario-Pulmonary Services of America, Inc. (inhalation therapy); American Medicorp, Inc. has purchased Metropolitan Diagnostic Labs, Inc.

Coming from the other direction, a number of outside companies are diversifying into the profitable nursing home and hospital field. American Hospital Supply Corp. owns American Health Facilities, Inc., which constructs and furnishes nursing homes. Computer Research, Inc., runs Mental Retardation Centers, Inc.; and Cenco Instruments, Inc. has joined a nursing home consortium in Milwaukee.

The health industry has come a long way from the days of the one-horse patent medicine peddler with his line of liver pills and elixirs. Replacing him are the mammoth internationalist drug companies, whose corporate medicine chests are increasingly likely to include hospital supplies, computers and cosmetics along with a growing profusion of pills. Health insurance, which can trace its origins to pre-trade union workers' welfare funds, is now a key element of the nation's vast insurance industry. The hospital supply industry has outgrown its Band-Aid days and is branching into catheters, computers and artificial organs. Proprietaries, which used to be the dark horse of the delivery system, are forging multi-state chains and moving into more and more investors' portfolios. Two other components of the modern health industry bear watching: the hospital construction industry and the health policy consulting business. The "health consultant" of fifty years ago was likely to be the neighborhood barber; today such consultants include defense-oriented think tanks like Rand, the Institute for Defense Analysis and Research Analysis Corporation.

The health industry has changed rapidly in the last five or ten years, that is, in the short period that the federal government has begun to play an important role in regulating and subsidizing health services and products. Changes in the future may be just as rapid and unpredictable, but two trends seem to be almost built-in: First, the health industry will move increasingly into the mainstream of American industry. Corporate giants like Dow, DuPont, TRW, Lockheed are busily staking out their claims on the profit-rich health turf. Drug companies, once the heavy-weights of the health business, will be challenged by these newcomers. Second, the health industry will be pulling itself together into a more and more integrated monolith. The drug, hospital supply and hospital equipment industries have already begun to blur into a single "health products" industry. Profit-making hospital chains are creating vertical chains including construction and supplies and equipment. Insurance companies, so far aloof from the promiscuous merging in health products, may be about to take the plunge into hospital operation, following the lead of nonprofit innovators like Kaiser and HIP.

These developments in the health industry may have more impact on health services delivery than anything that happens in the next decade of medical research. What is emerging is an increasingly unified, significant sector of the U.S. economy with a major direct stake in the organization and finances of health services. In the past, drug companies dominated the health industry and they picked up their policy line from between the drug ads in the AMA publications: up with solo, fee-for-service practice, down with government intervention of any sort. There's more to the health industry today than drugs, and many of the booming newcomers have market perspectives which reach far beyond the traditional, doctor-centered delivery system. And diversification into Medicare-subsidized, hospital-oriented products has seriously compromised the purity of the policy line of the drug companies.

It was Medicare that transformed the old bogeyman of government "interference" into a Santa Claus for the health industry. The drug industry and even the commercial insurance industry have found that they can live more than comfortably with Medicare and Medicaid. And of course it was Medicare that sent the hospital supply, equipment and proprietary chain industries spiraling giddily into a boom. Within a few years the health industry may begin to outweigh organized consumer groups as the most powerful force lobbying for increased government subsidy for health services. The industry's interest, however, will be in subsidy with a minimum of regulation, as outlined, for instance, in some of the current proposals for a national health insurance. With national health insurance, the health industry could settle down to the kind of guaranteed security which the defense and aerospace industries enjoyed during the heyday of cold war spending.

When it comes to the health services delivery system, the health industry is again likely to line up with the medical "liberals" as opposed to the AMA-rear-guard. Although only the proprietaries (hospitals and nursing homes) actually deliver services themselves, all segments of the health industry have an interest in increasing the productivity and efficiency of the delivery system. Insurance companies, which foot part of the bill, want to see health services become cheaper, or at least to see people utilize more of the cheaper services (e.g., clinic visits, as opposed to hospital stays). Drug and supply and equipment dealers have an interest in increasing the total volume of health services delivered, since, for almost every provider/consumer encounter, a prescription is written, equipment is used, or a disposable is disposed of. This interest is not compatible with a fixation on solo physician practice—the least productive means for delivering health services. In fact, as far as the industry is concerned, there is no reason why the dispenser of drugs or the user of supplies and equipment should be a physician at all. The health industry may eventually join the ultra-liberal faction of the medical world in advocating group practice and extensive use of paraprofessionals (if not machines) in direct patient contacts.

The hospital equipment industry has an even more immediate interest in the development of more centralized, institutionalized health services delivery systems. The market for heavy hardware such as computers, patient-monitoring devices, multi-phasic screening equipment, etc., is necessarily health facilities which serve a large number of patients—rather than private offices. Furthermore, in order to absorb such equipment, health facilities must be moderately rational in their internal operations. (There's no point in getting a computer unless some of the hospital's operations are at least rational enough to program into it.) Looking beyond the individual facility, computer and electronics companies even have an interest in rationality at the regional level, i.e., in the development of multi-facility, regionally integrated health systems. The multi-hospital medical empire is the ideal market for computers to book admissions, for super-specialty hardware, and for TV systems to link outposts with centralized technical staff.

The danger in increasingly centralized, institutionalized health delivery networks is, of course, that they will eventually get wise to the health products industry. Bulk buyers of pills, supplies and equipment could begin to exert significant leverage over prices and quality even before government regulation becomes a serious threat. However, if government subsidy of the health services delivery system is generous enough, hospitals will probably go on as they are now—hardly bothering to ask the price of pills and supplies. So long as the government is standing by to pick up the tab, the health industry's interest is in a delivery system which is boundlessly productive and mindlessly extravagant: organ transplants should be prescribed as frequently as tranquilizers are today; normal people should periodically have their blood cleaned out with an artificial kidney machine; "search and destroy" operations should become part of normal diagnostic work-ups; and so on.

To say that the health industry has an interest in a certain kind of delivery system is one thing; whether it can do anything about it is another question. So far the answer is yes—the health industry is developing increasingly effective ways of influencing public and private policy in health services delivery. At the most obvious level, the very existence of equipment which can be used only in hospitals, of insurance which can be used only in hospitals, of insurance which can be used only for hospital care, etc., gives hospitals an edge over non-institutional delivery modes. At the level of government policy, the health industry can always join oil as an industry-wide lobby, testify in Congressional hearings, etc. Already, health industry people are beginning to show up regularly on important governmental panels and commissions. For instance, the McNerney Taskforce on Medicaid and National Health insurance includes the Director of Prudential Life Insurance Company. New York's 1966 Piel Commission, which was the launching pad for New York City's new Health and Hospitals Corporation (a public authority set up to run the municipal hospitals) included the chairman of the board of the Systems Development Corporation, a leading consulting firm in health.

There are more direct and intimate ways in which the health industry influences and interacts with the delivery system. Trustees and upper-level staff of medical schools and hospitals are always welcome on the boards and top staffs of health industry firms. Many hospital and medical school professionals moonlight as consultants to the health industry, thus acting as human bonds between the two worlds. Consulting in the other direction, industry to nonprofit delivery institutions, is more important in terms of volume and potential policy impact. For instance, Technomics Corporation, a consulting firm with links to the defense hardware industry, did much of the staff work for the Piel Commission.* Another consultant, MacKinsey

* [Ed.: The Piel Commission recommended the formation of a nonprofit public corporation to assume administrative responsibility for New York City's public hospitals. The plan was implemented in 1970.]

Corp., is under contract to get the New York City Hospital Corporation off the ground. Interestingly enough, such consultants' recommendations invariably feature heavy use of computers and other expensive hardware. . . . And as hospitals install more and more sophisticated "systems," executives with backgrounds in health industry firms are increasingly moving into jobs in hospital administration.

No one seems to be too alarmed about the growing rapport between the health industry and the health services delivery system. Far from it, it's become fashionable to look to the profit-motivated health industrial forces to lead the way out of the health services crisis. According to this view, what's been wrong with health services all along is that they've been isolated from the business world, cut off from "hard-headed management thinking," and of course, without the profit motive, "unstimulated to really produce." But there is no reason yet to trust that the "rationalizations" that the health industry brings to health services will look like rationalizations to the consumer. Judging from America's experience with the drug industry—the consumer can expect no mercy from the new Medical-Industrial Complex.

MEDICINE FOR THE POOR: A NEW DEAL IN DENVER

Elinor Langer

The author offers a simple description of how health problems in a central city ghetto might be attacked in a system with different priorities. She makes clear that the success of a health system depends not so much on its technology as on the balance of political power among groups seeking to influence institutions. This piece was written in 1966, when the poverty program had just begun. The later history of OEO provides ample illustration of the message of this article. As poverty programs seemed increasingly successful in organizing the poor as a political force, federal funds were pulled away from those programs until OEO now—in mid-1970—remains a mere shadow of its earlier intentions.

The author lives in New York and writes free-lance. When she wrote this article, she worked on the staff of *Science*.

One outpost of the War on Poverty that is drawing increased attention from health professionals these days is an unassuming former bakery in the heart of Denver's Negro–Spanish-American ghetto known as the Neighborhood Health Center. The Neighborhood Health Center is not the only product of the interest in medicine that is being shown by the Office of Economic Opportunity (OEO). Roughly analogous cen-

SOURCE: Elinor Langer, "Medicine for the Poor: A New Deal in Denver," Science, Vol. 153, pp. 508–512, July, 1966. Copyright © 1966 by the American Association for the Advancement of Science.

ters are operating in Boston and New York City, and the OEO has now agreed to fund five more—one in Watts, two in Chicago, one in the Bronx, and one in Bolivar County, Mississippi. So far, the amount of money spent and pledged amounts to less than $10 million, and the number of people eligible for the new services is only about 150,000. But, if the numbers are small, the aspirations of those behind the OEO projects are not. They believe not only that they may rescue medical care for the poor from the "poor law" and charity traditions that have characterized it, but that in doing so they may develop a model that will influence the direction of the rest of American medicine as well.

OEO has gone into the health business for two reasons. The first was a recognition of the reinforcing relationship between ill health and poverty—the realization, in the words of one of OEO's physician-grantees, that "the poor get sicker and the sick get poorer." Inevitably, the agency's involvement in health has in it a measure of political calculation as well. OEO's programs have brought it into conflict with a wide range of political and social interest groups around the country, and as the uproar has increased —and the Vietnam war has been used to justify congressional budget-pruning—the OEO has looked about for activities that fulfill its mandate of liberating the poor without disrupting the Johnson consensus. It was assumed that medical centers would be like Project Headstart—the system of preschools that the OEO is funding throughout the country—and that, just as no one could be against finding places for small children to play learning games, no one could be against finding places where impoverished families already draining municipal welfare and charity resources could go to find medical treatment more convenient and congenial. That calculation was probably wrong. As long as the OEO health centers were viewed as extensions of traditional social welfare institutions for the poor, they drew nothing from existing professional organizations and institutions but a rather benign indifference. Now they are seemingly flourishing, reaching out in new ways, and opposition—chiefly from organized medicine—is clearly on the rise.

At the same time, the neighborhood health centers are finding themselves involved in a very different kind of war. To a certain extent, the doctors who have started them are reformers—even radicals—within their profession. They are fighting decades-old battles—for comprehensive, family-centered, preventive medical care; for group practice; for the development of new kinds of health manpower that cuts across lines made fast by the domination of professional associations and certification and licensing boards. But they are doing all this through the War on Poverty and—at least in Denver —have found themselves confronting radicals with a very different set of priorities, militant leaders (particularly Spanish-American) seeking to use the centers not only to improve the health of their people but to advance their political power as well.

The health center pie has a great many other fingers in it, too. There are a variety of municipal apparatchniks defending established political and bureaucratic jurisdictions, and a number of interested citizens representing local banks, charities, newspapers, real estate interests, and so forth—the group referred to in every city as the "establishment" or "power structure"—that all have an interest in preserving the status quo. In Denver the bureaucracy and the establishment were slow to grasp the significance of the health center experiment. The obstacles they created were low-grade, the product more of inertia than of opposition. But as the center develops and expands—its sponsors have just applied to OEO for money to fund a second center—the vacuum around the health center is beginning to be filled in, and not all the voices are supportive. At this stage, however, the role of old municipal alliances in the effort to create new health institutions is not yet clear.

Denver's Neighborhood Health Center is in a northeastern part of the city known as the Curtis Park–Arapahoe area (after two housing projects located there). The area includes nearly 40,000 people, at least half of whom are classified as living in poverty. Nearly 31 percent of the families have incomes under $3000 a year. Thirty-four percent of those over 25 have completed less than 8 years of education, and 75 percent have less than 4 years of high school. Forty-six percent of the houses are judged substandard or deteriorating. In 1959 the infant mortality rate in the area was 65.1 per thousand; for Denver as a whole it was 58.5. The death rate for Curtis Park–Arapahoe was 16.8; for the city as a whole it was 9.5. About 40 percent of the residents are Negro; about 30 percent are of Spanish or Mexican origin (they are known in the record books as "Spanish surname"); the rest are white. Virtually no physicians maintain offices in the area.

Before the opening of the Neighborhood Health Center last March, Denver's poor were generally treated at Denver General Hospital or at one of a few charity clinics in the city. Denver General is probably neither much better nor much worse than most municipal hospitals. It has suffered during the past few years from the disaffiliation of its medical departments from those of the Colorado Medical Center, a unit of the state university also located in Denver. The disaffiliation, still a rankling issue, was the product of what some people refer to as a "town-gown" fight and others as a successful campaign by the right-wing elements in the local medical society. A gradual reaffiliation is now taking place, but, while the academic tie-in may improve the content of the medical services, it is unlikely to affect the style in which they are delivered.

For many of Denver's poor, Denver General is inaccessible, separated from their homes by a 60-cent bus fare on a line that is out of service on evenings and weekends. Long waits at depot-like waiting stations take patients away from their other obligations for large chunks of the day. Its clinics are specialized, and there is no one to guide the timid (or the non-English–speaking) through the basement rooms in which they are dispersed. There is little likelihood that a patient will see the same physician twice. There is a complicated fee schedule which demands intensive probings into personal resources to determine the scale of payment for the individual patients, and a kind of assumption that most of the poor must be chiselers. While leading members of Denver's medical society admit deficiencies in the city's provision for treating dental and psychiatric disorders, they claim that the quality of medicine practiced at Denver General is first-rate and that "the people get here somehow when they really need to." The poor refer to it as the "butcher shop," avoid it unless they are painfully ill, and are perhaps as concerned with the personal indignities they encounter (which they are surely capable of judging) as with the quality of the suturing (which they are not).

NEW STYLE SERVICE

The Neighborhood Health Center, although it is managed by the city's Department of Health and Hospitals (which also runs Denver General), has managed to avoid almost all these difficulties. Three Volkswagen microbuses, driven by neighborhood residents, pick up and drive home patients who are too ill or too poor to take the bus. An indoor nursery and an outdoor playground, also manned by neighborhood assistants, provide supervised care for well children while their parents or sisters are seeing the doctors. The waiting period is down to proportions more like those experienced by middle-class patients in the offices of private doctors. Every attempt is made to avoid discussing income with patients: efforts are made to check them out with the city's welfare agencies (or with Denver General), but no fee schedule has been adopted and so far all services have been offered free. Efforts are made to insure that not only individuals but whole families have their major point of contact with a single physician. Individual health records are summarized on a family record chart, reminding the alert doctor to ask a mother why she failed to bring her child back for his second shot.

The center's staff of about 130 includes 58 "neighborhood aides"—poor people living in the area served by the center and trained either there or at an earlier training program run by Denver University. These people run the switchboard, the reception area, and the transportation service and are also assigned as assistants to the various medical, dental, and other service departments. At least nine of them speak both English and Spanish and function as translators when the need arises. The center's nonmedical departments include nutrition, health education, social services, and environmental health, and are meant to function as a team, with referrals flowing two ways between the medical and nonmedical areas. There is also a research department that is attempting to develop data about utilization, social attitudes, and so forth. Specialized clinics are being established, but the center emphasizes "family medicine," and most serious and surgical cases are referred to hospitals. The center uses the part-time services of about 30 Denver physicians, drawn both from private general and specialty practice and from local medical institutions, and has a handful of doctors practicing there full-time. It is open virtually around the clock, with appointments scheduled until 10 p.m. on weekdays, and it has become a kind of hub for other community services from meetings of Alcoholics Anonymous to the offering of free legal aid by the Denver Bar Association. The whole enterprise is suffused with a kind of neighborly spirit that can best be described as "easiness." People waiting to see the doctors at Denver General look like "masses"; at the health center they look like individuals.

There is absolutely no doubt that the message of the health center is getting through to the neighborhood. By 3 July, the close of the 17th week of operation, the center had seen nearly 7000 individual patients—about 33 percent of the eligible residents. Even more surprising than the rate at which new patients are coming in is the discovery that 21 percent of the patients are individuals who have never been seen at Denver General. That figure should be interpreted with some caution: population calculations are based on the 1960 census, the population in question is fairly mobile, and it is therefore impossible to discover what proportion of that 21 percent represents newcomers. But it is clear that the health center is flooded, receiving over 1000 patients a week—more than twice its anticipated caseload.

RHETORIC OR REALITY?

Evaluation of the medical treatment that the patients are so enthusiastically receiving is a more difficult matter. Only medically trained evaluators could perhaps arrive at a definitive assessment of how the center's rhetoric—"comprehensive, family-centered care"—squares with the reality. The heavy caseload and the shakedown period have both taken their toll. Samuel Johnson, the young director of public health and preventive medicine of Denver's Department of Health and Hospitals, and the moving force behind the Neighborhood Health Center, readily admits to certain doubts. Johnson, 39, received his medical training at the University of Colorado and a Master of Public Health degree from Harvard in 1960. He is a former professor of preventive medicine at Colorado and still maintains a part-time position there. Johnson wonders whether his doctors are referring to each other as much as they might, and how thorough their examinations are. "What gets on the charts seems too much like what goes on them at large clinics," he commented in an interview with *Science*. "We were aiming for something more. I'm not worried about errors of commission but of omission. We want to do a total job." Nonetheless, Johnson believes that the quality of care is "above average" and

certainly equal to that available at Denver General. This view is corroborated by John Sbarbaro, a young physician assigned to the Denver Health Department while on temporary duty with the Public Health Service, and now acting as the center's chief medical officer. "We're sure the care here is average," Sbarbaro told *Science*, "but we want to make it better than average." There is already a weekly analytic "case conference" for the staff and visiting specialists; Johnson hopes to establish an outside visiting committee to review random patient charts as well.

Johnson and Sbarbaro, as well as the OEO in Washington, take particular pride in the fact that the health center was mobilized around rather typical resources such as exist in nearly every American city. Unlike the Boston project, for example, which is run by Tufts University Medical School and gives Tufts appointments to its staff physicians, the Denver project has drawn only on the local medical community. Now, the fee-for-service mystique is very strong among doctors in this country, and most doctors—particularly those representing organized medicine—are prone to conclude that if the center's salaried doctors relinquish private practice it must be because the services they offer are so bad they are unable to collect the fees. (The center's part-time doctors are paid $7.50 an hour; the full-time physicians average $5.93.) Accordingly, the center has been the butt of numerous charges, mostly made off the record, that its physicians are either incompetents who could not stand the competition or are senile citizens taking it on as a pension while awaiting the pasture. In fact, the center's doctors seem to have rather different motivations. Some are frankly idealists, eager to participate in a novel social experiment. Others are physicians disenchanted with the extensive "management" activities that private practice requires. "There are two things I like about practicing medicine here," commented one center physician. "One is that I can order tests, medicines, referrals, and so forth without worrying about my patient's pocketbook. The other is that I don't have to do any bookkeeping any more. Here I can do what I really want to do. See patients and practice medicine."

The center's medical society critics often seem to be comparing it to some unreal conception of what the alternatives are for the patients involved. One prominent member of the Denver Medical Society interviewed by *Science* complained that the center was inadequate because a mother's prenatal care would not come from the same obstetrician who would deliver her baby in Denver General. In a sense he is right: the division in obstetrical (and other) services certainly reinforces the "depersonalization" in medical care that the center hopes to combat. But the past record suggests that, if it were not for the Neighborhood Health Center, the mother would probably not bother with prenatal care at all.

If all is cheery in the waiting rooms, it has been somewhat less cheery behind the scenes. The problems of the Neighborhood Health Center began early when the original proposal became bogged down in the offices of Sargent Shriver, director of the OEO. Shriver's objections to the proposal were never made thoroughly clear either to his staff in Washington or to the applicants in Denver, but they appear to have included a feeling that the plan had to be as nearly perfect as possible—both because of the OEO's vulnerability in the Republican-dominated landscape of Colorado and because of the attention-getting potential of the plan as an experiment in medical organization. Working on the other side was a desire to give the poverty program some foothold in Denver, where most of the city's other proposals had already been vetoed as inadequate. Accordingly, the OEO dispatched two medical consultants to the scene. The proposal was then revised—to include, among other things, a greater concentration of resources in a single area than initially envisaged—and, after a time, Shriver reversed himself.

Since then, the health center has functioned without any substantial supervision from either the national office of the OEO or the regional office in Kansas City, neither of which is well equipped to provide the close guidance that the health center's sponsors might have liked. The center was also left pretty much alone by its parent agency, the Department of Health and Hospitals. And it has also functioned largely independently of the metropolitan agency that handles OEO projects, formerly known as Denver's War on Poverty, Inc., recently renamed Denver Opportunity (D.O.).

DENVER'S POVERTY PROBLEMS

Nearly all the urban antipoverty agencies in the country have had their difficulties, and Denver is a first-class example. For a variety of reasons—including control by the "establishment," insufficient representation of the poor, weak leadership that is constantly changing (the entire staff has just resigned), and massive disorganization—D.O. has been in exceptionally bad shape. It has managed to sponsor only a few projects, mostly small and mostly innocuous. To all intents and purposes, the Neighborhood Health Center is the only thing Denver has to show for its War on Poverty. And, accordingly, the health center became the focus of community politics and community tensions that in other cities have been spread out among a variety of programs.

The chief factor affecting the political relations of the Neighborhood Health Center with its clientele is the rising militancy of the area's Spanish Americans. In Denver, as in much of the Southwest, Spanish Americans are at the bottom of the heap, considerably below the Negro population in status and opportunity. Negro leadership, reflecting the upward mobility of its community, tends to be relatively moderate. The Spanish-American community, until recently in a state of almost total social disorganization—and lacking in access to the instruments of political power—is increasingly radical and increasingly in a hurry. When the local war on poverty began, it offered Spanish Americans one of their first opportunities to develop and use political power. The opening was the OEO's rhetorical commitment to "maximum feasible participation of the poor," and, because the city-wide poverty agency was virtually immobile, what the poor wanted to participate in was the Neighborhood Health Center. Their vehicle was an advisory board composed of neighborhood residents.

Among the issues raised by Spanish Americans on the advisory board are some with real relevance to the question of whether a medically innovative institution can be fused with a politically radical one. A case in point is a dispute over selection of neighborhood aides. These jobs are crucial to the success of the center both as an operating agency and as an experiment. The neighborhood aides give the center its distinctive character; they make it emotionally accessible to the area's residents; they help reduce the psychological gulf—a product of both class and function—that impedes communication between doctors and patients. As an experiment in "socialization" of the poor, the program seems already on the threshold of success. The jobs are a first step up the social ladder. Offering real responsibilities, not just make-work, they open up possibilities of better jobs in other places: a number of health center trainees are already beginning to move on to jobs with local industries or the municipal career service. The center's professional staff reports numerous instances where neighborhood aides, who entered the program with an attitude of indifference to middle-class niceties such as punctuality and neatness, have been transformed by their work experiences. In many cases the personalities and personal relationships are now such that it is difficult for an outsider to distinguish the professionals from the aides. Finally, the aide program is a test of the possibilities of creating new types of medical manpower. Success in this effort does not lie within the reach of the center alone, but the character and calibre of its trainees could play a role in the emerging national effort to soften the boundaries and redefine the scope of the separate health professions.

CAN THE POOR PARTICIPATE?

The Spanish Americans, however, are dissatisfied. They claim, accurately, that the aides have been selected not from the poorest of the residents but from among the more flourishing. (The health center was committed to taking on "graduates" of a Denver University training program that included some not-very-disadvantaged residents, including the wife of one state senator.) The Spanish Americans want jobs assigned solely on the basis of need, not on the basis of qualifications or apparent potential. They feel that, without their intervention, the aides would not have been included in the center's employee-benefit plans, and would have been generally less well treated. The center's staff feels it won a major victory in getting the local civil service to accept its graduates without preliminary testing; the Spanish Americans resent the fact that center trainees will still be placed at the bottom of the civil service scale. They are also less than

enthusiastic about the part of the center's training program—the medical assistant trainees—that involves preparation for para-medical functions not yet accepted by the medical profession. In this sense, the individual trainees are admittedly being used experimentally; the Spanish Americans want the poor to be able to advance personally. At the same time, they fear that health center jobs are being used to "buy off" potential neighborhood leaders who might otherwise continue to press the city for more reforms. Each side contends that the other is seeking to use the jobs as a form of neighborhood patronage, or for professional or political advancement.

The unrest in the relations between the health center staff and its neighborhood advisory board is focused not so much on the content of particular decisions but on who makes them. It appears that the staff of the center honestly wanted advice: they wanted to know what hours would be convenient, how people felt about paying, what facilities were most needed. They wanted assistance in spreading word of the center around the neighborhood and in running a ceremonial open house. They did not want to share their authority or to include the poor in substantive policy-making decisions.

The health center is by no means the only poverty agency that has run into this difficulty. Apart from a handful of student activists organizing in the nation's ghettos, few people have been able to make the jump from benevolence to respect in dealing with the poor. The result is that institutions beginning as efforts to mobilize the poor on their own behalf are constantly threatened with slipping back into an older style of charity, where "we" are trying to "do something" for "them." At the moment, the Spanish Americans on the advisory board seem to have been somewhat neutralized by a minor revolt of Negro representatives who do not share their militance. The present advisers, chiefly Negro women, are relatively passive, seemingly content to plan dinner parties and write letters of thanks to various benefactors, to stay in a subservient place and in the good graces of the professionals. The domination of the board by these elements leaves the center less connected with an important part of its constituency than it perhaps ought to be. The situation may be changed by neighborhood elections to a new poverty board to be held in August, but, if weak representation continues, one of the major bulwarks against turning the center back into something remote and alien from the neighborhood will be gone.

The future of the neighborhood health centers is uncertain. Their cost per patient at this stage is extremely high. (The center is being funded at over $1.5 million a year.) There is a question about OEO's priorities on a national basis. With increasingly limited funds at its disposal, how much should it spend on health? The question of priorities is also important locally, and is becoming an issue in the rising medical society opposition to the health center in Denver. The people in the Curtis Park–Arapahoe area now have access to good, convenient medical care; the rest of Denver's poor are still making the trip to Denver General. The exclusive servicing of a defined population is important for research purposes. It is also obviously inequitable and may even be inhumane. What is a sensible allocation of medical resources? Would it be more fair to use the money, as the medical society would like, to rehabilitate Denver General to provide slightly more care for all the people? Or do the experimental aspects of the health center justify the inequalities it inevitably involves? Finally, there is a question of medical politics. The health centers have passed into existence almost unnoticed. Now everyone knows they are there, and pressures—not only from organized medicine, but from Washington health agencies less than eager for the competition—are certain to increase. At this stage the most that can be said for sure is that while the pleasantness of the neighborhood health centers is now established, their practicality and permanence remain to be proved.

HEALTH BIBLIOGRAPHY

I.   DEFINITIONS AND MAGNITUDES

   U.S. Public Health Service, *Medical Care, Health Status and Family Income*, 1964, U.S. Government. Summary statistics and descriptions of a variety of health measures.

II. ANALYTIC PERSPECTIVES

   A.   General

   Herman Somers and Anne Somers, *Doctors, Patients and Health Insurance*, 1961, Brookings. Important survey of American health care system.
   Fred Anderson, "The Growing Pains of Medical Care," *The New Republic*, January 17, 24, and 31, 1970. Lucid, intelligent analysis of general causes of recent crisis in medical care.
   The American Health System: Power, Profits, and Politics, a Health-PAC Book, prepared by Barbara and John Ehrenreich, 1970, Random House. A radical analysis of health care system, and its increasing domination by large hospital empires and large corporations.

   B.   The Demand for Health Services

   Herbert Klarman, *The Economics of Health*, 1965, Columbia University Press, pp. 20–73. Survey of issues in understanding demand for health.
   Victor R. Fuchs, "The Contribution of Health Services to the American Economy," *Milbank Memorial Fund Quarterly*, October, 1966. Description of role of health in economy and the demand for its benefits.

Selma J. Mushkin, "Health as an Investment," *Journal of Political Economy*, October, 1962, Special Supplement, pp. 129–157. Analysis of demand for health as an investment in human capital, in more productive workers.

Richard Auster *et al.*, "The Production of Health: An Exploratory Study," *Journal of Human Resources*, Fall, 1969, pp. 411–436. An attempt to separate benefits of health services from effects of other economic and environmental factors.

C.   The Supply of Health Services

Victor R. Fuchs, "The Basic Forces Influencing Costs of Medical Care," *Report of the National Conference on Medical Costs*, 1967, U.S. Government. Summary analysis.

Herbert Klarman, *The Economics of Health, op. cit.*, pp. 74–125. Includes chapters on personnel and hospital service supply.

Rashi Fein, *The Doctor Shortage: An Economic Diagnosis*, 1967, Brookings. Surveys the various bottlenecks in the supply of physicians.

Martin Feldstein, "The Rising Price of Physicians' Services," *Review of Economics and Statistics*, May, 1970. Econometric analysis of recent rapid increases.

D.   Financing Health Care

Health Insurance Institution, *Sourcebook of Health Insurance Data* (227 Park Ave., New York, N.Y. 10017). Basic figures on kinds and sources of insurance.

Herman Somers and Anne Somers, *Medicare and the Hospitals*, 1967, Brookings. Basic summary of the relationships between aid for the poor and the institutional structure of the system.

Eugene Feingold, *Medicare: Policy and Politics*, 1966, Chandler. Another useful study.

7 Housing

Editor's Introduction

The shortage of housing is so real . . . that families may actually begin a squatters' movement in order to find a place to live. It has not come to living in autos yet, but it could happen here.

—Cleveland public housing official

People are looking all over for good homes and we have thousands of these empty ones around.

—Detroit buildings official[1]

In early 1970, a *New York Times* reporter was describing an area near the center of Washington, D.C.:[2]

On a winter afternoon, the area seems to be a ghost town occupied by children at play. This scene of premature decay and abandonment provides visual evidence of a trend that is evident in large cities across the country.

While the nation is undergoing the most critical housing shortage since World War II, structurally sound dwellings in the inner cities are being abandoned in increasing numbers to vandalism and demolition.

The juxtaposition of the housing shortage and abandoned buildings reflected the paradoxical allocation of resources in the housing sector. Fancy homes were being built in the suburbs, but the central cities were decaying. Rows of houses stood vacant while thousands of families searched for decent housing.

The causes of this imbalance were complex, but the problem reflected a simple phenomenon. The private sector was not building housing in central cities. In particular, it was neither building nor renovating any low-cost housing. Apparently, corporate investment was ignoring the low-cost housing market because it could not profit from low-cost units. Experience with government efforts to construct housing for the poor had also been disappointing. The volume of public housing construction fell consistently below projected Congressional goals.

The public and the government seemed increasingly to be turning to a final solution to the paradox: large subsidies to stimulate private investment in low-cost housing. If industry couldn't receive enough profit from construction of housing for the poor, the government apparently decided, then the public should provide a large enough subsidy to satisfy corporate profitability criteria.[3] As one government-commissioned report concluded: "The root of the problem in housing America's poor is the gap between the price that private enterprise must receive and the price the poor can afford. . . . The economic gap separating millions of deprived families from adequate housing can only be bridged by government subsidies."[4]

I have intended this chapter directly to question the validity of that new direction in public policy; from the radical perspective, it derives from invalid premises about the housing market. The introduction has four sections: a discussion of problem definitions and magnitudes; a summary of liberal and conservative views; an outline of the radical approach to the problem; and an introduction to the readings.

[1] Quoted in *The New York Times,* June 4, 1970, and February 9, 1970, respectively.
[2] *The New York Times,* February 9, 1970.
[3] As, for instance, in the celebrated program sponsored by federal housing chief George Romney, "Operation Breakthrough," which promised large subsidies for prefabricated homes.
[4] *A Decent Home,* The Report of the President's Commission on Urban Housing (Washington: U.S. Government Printing Office, 1968), p. 47.

THE DIMENSIONS OF THE PROBLEM

The urban housing crisis has two principal *physical* or *structural* dimensions. First, many Americans live in housing of miserable quality, defined by *absolute* standards. Second, many Americans suffer *relatively* desperate housing problems, as a result principally of their race.

On the first level, we conventionally use three measures of the *absolute* quality of housing:

—Housing is considered substandard if its basic structure is physically dilapidated or if it lacks basic plumbing facilities.[5] By government standards, roughly 6.9 million American households lived in substandard housing in 1970.[6]

—Housing is considered overcrowded if it provides less than one room per person for its occupants. By this hardly luxurious criterion, a family of three requires at least a living room, a kitchen and one bedroom to satisfy its space demands. Roughly 6 million families lived in overcrowded housing in 1970, about one third of them in substandard housing.[7]

—Families are expected to pay no more than 25 percent of their total income for housing. If the cost of their housing exceeds that percentage of family income, it is considered too expensive. At least 11 million households paid more than 25 percent of their income for housing in 1970; we do not know how many of them lived either in substandard or overcrowded units.[8]

Thus, to sum up the three definitions of absolute housing quality, a minimum of 11 million households—or one sixth of all households in the country—could not find adequate housing in 1970 by one or more of these criteria.[9] And of these poorly housed families, at least half lived in metropolitan areas, primarily in central cities.[10]

At the second level, some Americans suffer *relatively* severe housing problems. Blacks in central cities face these "relative" problems most frequently. As a result of racial discrimination in the housing market, blacks suffer two kinds of relative housing problems:

—For the same quality of housing, blacks pay more on the average than do whites. In an analysis of the St. Louis housing market, for instance, two economists concluded that blacks must pay roughly 5 to 10 percent more than whites for the same quality of housing.[11]

—For the same price, blacks invariably get housing of lower quality than do whites. In 1960, for instance, 57.1 percent of black central city residents paying between $50 and $79 for one- or two-room apartments were living in substandard units. Only 24.6 percent of whites in the same city/rent/room class were living in substandard units.[12]

Finally, the urban housing crisis has a single but critical *nonphysical* dimension. Increasingly in many urban areas, the character of housing and neighborhoods is becoming hopelessly standardized. Housing tends more and more to appear in environments which serve only the simple physical need for shelter, but which ignore other important human needs—the need for variety, the need for pleasant surroundings, the need for various, unexpected and intimate human contact.[13] In the suburbs, tract homes proliferate, spreading conformity, homogeneity and com-

---

[5] See U.S. Bureau of the Census, *Measuring the Quality of Housing. . .* , Working Paper No. 25 (Washington: 1967).

[6] Based on estimates in Anthony Downs, "Moving toward Realistic Housing Goals," in Kermit Gordon, ed., *Agenda for the Nation* (Washington: Brookings, 1968), p. 143.

[7] Based on an extrapolation of trends between 1950 and 1960. See Bernard Frieden, "Housing and National Urban Goals: Old Policies and New Realities," in James Q. Wilson, ed., *Metropolitan Enigma* (Cambridge: Harvard University Press, 1968), p. 167; and Downs, *op. cit.*, p. 143.

[8] Based on estimates in *A Decent Home, op. cit.*, pp. 42–43; and Downs, *op. cit.*, pp. 143–144.

[9] This minimum presumes that all those paying more than 25 percent are exactly the same families who live in substandard and/or overcrowded units. This presumption is obviously absurd, but it does provide a minimum estimate.

[10] The estimates for metropolitan areas derive from the same sources as in footnote 8. In all, to replace currently inadequate housing and to meet all new housing needs (for new household units and other demands) by 1980, we would have to build 26 million units, or 2.6 million a year. At its highest, private construction of housing reached 1.6 million units a year during the 1960's. See Downs, *op. cit.*, and *A Decent Home, op. cit.*

[11] John Kain and John Quigley, "Housing Market Discrimination, Homeownership and Savings Behavior," Discussion Paper No. 58, Program on Regional and Urban Economics, Harvard University, 1970.

[12] Chester Rapkin, "Price Discrimination Against Negroes in the Rental Housing Market," in Kain, ed., *Race and Poverty* (Englewood Cliffs, N.J.: Prentice-Hall, 1969), p. 119.

[13] For varied statements of this basic criticism, see Jane Jacobs, *The Life and Death of Great American*

partmentalized living. In the central cities, high-rise luxury apartments and huge prison-like public housing abound, replacing older, more various environments. For many Americans, the physical quality of housing has improved but the strength of community has been fractured.[14]

THE LIBERAL AND CONSERVATIVE VIEWS

Among most liberal and conservative analysts of the urban housing market, one finds a surprising degree of consensus about the *range* of causes of current housing problems. Experts tend to agree less about the *relative importance* of those forces. Four principal perspectives dominate explanations of housing problems; most disagreements about policy and the wisdom of current programs evolve from the implications of these four perspectives.

1. Most basically, nearly everyone agrees that current levels of housing construction costs make it impossible for builders to profit from the construction of housing cheap enough for poor families without some kinds of government subsidies. Several important factors seem to explain the level of these costs and their recent rapid rate of increase.[15]

—The power of the building trades unions has both limited the supply of labor and has pushed up the level of wages in the construction industry.

—The building industry has always been one of the least concentrated industries in the economy. This low level of concentration has had two important effects. First, firms are apparently so small that they cannot realize economies of scale in construction. Second, they cannot afford the development of radically new cost-saving technologies.

—Because housing construction is so capital-intensive, its costs vary directly with the cost of capital (and therefore with the rate of interest) in the economy. For several years now, rates of interest have been kept at extremely high levels to try to reduce the rate of inflation.

2. Analysts of housing focus on the operation of what they call the "filtering" or "turnover" process.[16] Typically, in this view, low-cost housing becomes available indirectly through the housing market as a result of new high-cost construction and the impact of that new construction. Older stock is said to "trickle down" through the income scale, "turning over" rapidly enough to satisfy lower-income families before it deteriorates.[17] This perspective provides an essential link in the formulation of many housing policy recommendations. If costs prohibit the private construction of new low-cost housing, then one way the private sector can increase the supply of housing for the poor comes through its construction of new high-cost units and the operation of the filtering process. As one economist put it recently:[18]

The turnover process does make sound housing available to income groups which cannot afford new construction. It is this process that is largely responsible for the fact that, in 1960, a majority of families at the lowest income levels were living in standard housing.

3. Many view the operations of the housing market from the perspective of "location

Cities (N.Y.: New American Library, 1961), and Richard Sennett, *The Uses of Disorder* (N.Y.: Knopf, 1970).

[14] Herbert Gans has traced the process, first describing the destruction of a rich, varied urban community in Boston, *The Urban Villagers* (N.Y.: The Free Press, 1962), and then very sympathetically describing a rather more standardized suburban working-class community, *The Levittowners* (N.Y.: Pantheon, 1967).

[15] For a good discussion of the building industry, see Downs, *op. cit.*

[16] For the best discussion of this process, see William Grigsby, *Housing Markets and Public Policy* (Philadelphia: University of Pennsylvania Press, 1963).

[17] Essentially, the filtering process works in the following way: new construction of high-cost housing increases the supply and thereby lowers the relative price of high-cost housing; many relatively higher-income families move out of their older housing into the new stock. This in turn decreases the demand for their older housing segment of the market (with supply constant), lowering the relative prices of that sector. With lower relative prices, this stock is now within reach of families with slightly lower income. These families move out of their relatively lower-quality houses, thereby lowering demand and consequently relative prices for their old houses. This in turn opens those houses to the pocketbooks of still lower-income families. And so on down to the lowest-quality houses and the poorest families.

[18] Irving H. Welfeld, "Toward a New Federal Housing Policy," *The Public Interest*, No. 19, Spring, 1970, p. 34.

theory" and its implications for changes in residential location.[19] According to this set of theories, the location of industry in metropolitan areas determines the location of residential housing. With everything else equal, workers will try to live as close to their jobs as they can in order to minimize transportation costs. Since the turn of the century—and especially since World War II—industry has been moving out of the central cities into the suburbs.[20] As jobs have decentralized, demand for land in the central cities has declined and demand for suburban locations has increased. In the face of sharply reduced demand, relatively older central city housing stock has deteriorated rapidly. And large business interests in the central cities, trying to protect the value of their land holdings, encourage the demolition of old decaying residential housing, hoping for and investing in new luxury units or new office space.[21]

As a result of this process, those who live predominantly in the central city, and especially those blacks who are trapped there because of housing market discrimination, must contend with dilapidated housing. Their incomes—and therefore their effective demand for housing—cannot sustain the prices necessary to spur renovation of the stock.

4. Finally, everyone admits that pure racial discrimination exists in the housing market, that its effects are widespread, and that it explains many of the housing problems of blacks in the cities. Few can agree, however, on a satisfactory explanation of housing segregation. One writer who has studied the problem extensively concludes: "Until we know how and why segregation exists on its current scale and what its social impacts are, we can accomplish little in healing the breach between the two societies. . . ."[22] In any case, segregation continues. Since World War II, it has been increasing in many Northern cities. If we cannot adequately explain its mechanisms, we must nevertheless try to deal with its consequences.

By any possible standard, the federal government has totally failed to solve our urban housing problems. In 1949 Congress declared the urgent goal "of a decent home and a suitable living environment for every American family." As the figures on housing problems cited above should testify, it has not come close to its objective. Arguments about the failures of past policy and the priorities for future policy usually center around four related questions:[23]

—Should we rely on the filtering process indirectly to provide low-cost housing while we concentrate on increasing the rate of new construction of high-cost units? Or should we also increase the rate of direct construction of low-cost units?

—If we build low-cost units directly, should the government build the units or should the private sector be provided with subsidies to build them?

—In the case of either answer to either question, what emphasis should be placed on new construction, and what emphasis should we put on renovation of the older housing stock, in our efforts either to speed the turnover process or directly to increase the supply of low-cost housing?

—Finally, should we accept the facts of housing market segregation, building low-cost housing primarily in central city ghettos, or should we try to break the cycle of increasing segregation by building low-cost housing in the suburbs?

Answers (or combinations of answers) to these questions vary widely. Many, as Bernard Frieden argues in this chapter, assert that we should pursue a more diversified set of strategies, opening a wider set of alternative housing choices. At the same time, certain elements of priority appear in the liberal and conservative literature on housing policy, and it seems important to highlight those areas.

In answer to the first question, many agree that it would be most efficient to rely principally on the turnover process. This argument contends that costs of new construction render direct provision of low-cost units inefficient, that the turnover process does reach the poorest families, and

---

[19] For a good discussion of these forces, see John Meyer, John Kain, and Martin Wohl, *The Urban Transportation Problem* (Cambridge: Harvard University Press, 1965), Chapters 2–3, pp. 9–55.
[20] See Kain, "The Distribution and Movement of Jobs and Industry," in Wilson, ed., *Metropolitan Enigma, op. cit.*
[21] For an interesting history of the way this process evolves, see Edgar Hoover and Raymond Vernon, *Anatomy of a Metropolis* (Garden City: Doubleday Anchor, 1961).
[22] Anthony Pascal, "The Analysis of Residential Segregation," in J. P. Crecine, ed., *Financing the Metropolis* (N.Y.: Sage Publications, 1970).
[23] See Downs, *op. cit.*, for a good summary.

that those who still must pay more than 25 percent of their incomes can receive general income maintenance or specific rent supplements.[24]

In answer to the second question, nearly everyone argues that we should rely on the private sector because recent history has proved that the public sector cannot build low-cost housing efficiently. This set of historical contentions includes the following components: First, that the failure of public housing programs to produce a sufficiently high volume of construction can be attributed to the inefficiency of government bureaucracy and the difficulty of public construction in effecting technological innovation;[25] second, that the public urban renewal program, through which the government has provided some subsidies to private industry for reconstruction of central cities, has failed to increase the stock of low-cost housing because the government subsidies were not substantial enough to build housing cheap enough for the poor;[26] and third, that only the private sector—and especially large corporations—have the capacity to apply management expertise, technological wizardry and appropriate economies of scale to the reduction of housing costs.[27]

In answer to the third question, many argue that both new construction and renovation are needed. But since so many new units are necessary to solve our housing problems, renovation is regarded as too slow a process, affecting too few units, to warrant high priority.

Finally, in answer to the fourth question, most agree that it would be ideal if we could build low-cost housing in the suburbs because blacks could then choose to live closer to suburban employment sites. Disagreements about the importance of effecting suburban construction evolve from differing views of its political feasibility and of the positive value of preserving the integrity and political power of black communities in central city ghettos.[28]

THE RADICAL VIEW

The radical analysis of urban housing problems consists of two fairly simple arguments. Radicals contend first of all that trends in the structure of American social and economic institutions are making it increasingly unlikely that absolute and relative physical housing problems can be solved within the context of those institutions. They also argue that the structure of those institutions makes it virtually impossible that housing in this country will provide *both* adequate physical shelter *and* an enriching community environment for everyone. I have summarized the two arguments in order.

Radicals agree with many of the liberal and conservative analyses of absolute housing problems. They argue especially that the structure of the housing industry and the necessary rates of profit in that industry make it virtually impossible for industry directly to construct low-cost housing. Further, radicals suggest that several trends in this country have reinforced that impossibility. First, the intensified quest by all large corporations for stability and security of investment opportunities has made low-cost housing construction increasingly unattractive compared to other kinds of investments.[29] Low-income populations move constantly, and low-income areas change their characters rapidly. Since large-scale housing investments must be amortized

---

[24] For one of the strongest statements of this argument, see Welfeld, *op. cit.* He concludes euphorically, "Through these means it is possible to create a harmony of political interests and an economically efficient system," p. 43.

[25] See the references in the selection by Lawrence Friedman in this chapter.

[26] For the strongest statement of the case against urban renewal, see Martin Anderson, *The Federal Bulldozer* (Cambridge: MIT Press, 1964), and for arguments about the program, see J. Q. Wilson, ed., *Urban Renewal: The Record and the Controversy* (Cambridge: MIT Press, 1966).

[27] In *A Decent Home, op. cit.,* this argument is made extensively.

[28] In one strong statement on the problem, Kain and Persky have argued that all the inefficiencies engendered throughout the metropolitan market by the continued presence of the ghetto require that we try to dissolve it even if the costs are high. "Alternatives to the Gilded Ghetto," *The Public Interest,* No. 14, Winter, 1969. In another apposite view, Piven and Cloward argue that the objective of integrating housing in the suburbs has so aroused opposition to public housing that it has vitiated the program; at least by building in the ghetto, they argue, we can get some housing built. "Desegregated Housing: Who Pays for the Reformers' Ideal?" in Kain, ed., *Race and Poverty, op. cit.*

[29] For statements of the intensity of this quest, see Paul Baran and Paul Sweezy, *Monopoly Capital* (N.Y.: Monthly Review Press, 1966), or J. K. Galbraith, *The New Industrial State* (Boston: Houghton-Mifflin, 1967).

over long periods of time in order to return a stable and competitive rate of profit, the viability of investment in low-income housing may be threatened by sudden movements of low-income populations or sudden shifts in the demand for low-income housing. Second, the long-run shifts in the political structure of metropolitan areas have also undercut possibilities for new low-income housing. On the one hand, with substantial metropolitan decentralization (from central cities to suburbs), many relatively affluent citizens have been able to incorporate their own homogeneous, protected suburban enclaves, escaping from the jurisdiction of central city governments.[30] It is often in the interests of these affluent communities to establish protective zoning ordinances, in order to keep out low-income families with heavy requirements for public services.[31] As the metropolitan areas have become increasingly balkanized, those urban governments with the greatest wealth have screened out low-income units, while those governments with the greatest concentrations of low-income families have lost the tax base on which they could afford public construction of low-income housing. And central city financial interests have found it increasingly important to preserve the value of their central city land holdings (in the face of suburbanization and declining demand for central city space) by tearing down low-income housing and replacing it with high-rise luxury apartments (in order to attract wealthy families back to central city areas).[32] All of these developments seem to lessen the possibilities that private or public construction of low-income housing will increase in the normal course of events.

Liberals and conservatives tend to reply to those arguments by citing the importance of the "turnover" process. They insist that none of these trends precludes the provision of decent housing to the poor as an indirect result of new housing construction for higher-income families. Radicals reply with two arguments. First, most evidence seems to suggest that the black poor do not benefit very much from the "turnover" process, that the persistence of segregated housing markets prevents the normal filtering of higher-quality housing in the white market into the lower-income black market. In the most recent study of the filtering process, Lansing, Clifton, and Morgan provide especially strong evidence of this market separation.[33] Since the black poor constitute an increasing percentage of those living in substandard housing in cities, one has less and less faith that the turnover process can solve the absolute (or relative) housing problems of the urban poor. Second, as public pressure increases in the United States against overt and explicit racial discrimination, the functional economic importance of housing segregation increases.[34] For instance, the schools play an important economic role in channeling blacks into lower-class jobs and in preparing blacks for lower-class status. In the South, the school system could perform this function through the preservation of legally segregated schools. As a result of the civil rights movement, legal segregation in education is no longer possible. But Northern schools perform the same functions as long as housing segregation solidifies the *de facto* segregation of schools. And as the importance of racism increases (as a means of preserving capitalist surplus), the importance of *de facto* housing segregation as the least explicit form of discrimination increases simultaneously. One can expect fewer and fewer private and public efforts to desegregate the housing market over time.[35]

All of these points suggest that radically increased efforts by the government to provide better housing for the poor constitute the only avenue toward solution of absolute and relative housing problems. But the radical theory of the State, summarized in Chapter One, implies that the

[30] For the beginning of the process, see Robert Woods, *1400 Governments* (N.Y.: Doubleday, 1961).
[31] On some of this political economy, see the two-part article by James O'Connor, "The Fiscal Crisis of the State," *Socialist Revolution,* January–February, 1970, and March–April, 1970.
[32] For a history of one such effort, see the selection by Beagle *et al.* below.
[33] See their book, *New Homes and Poor People* (Michigan: Survey Research Center, 1970), and the concluding chapter from it among the readings below.
[34] See the chapters on education and employment in this book for some other comments on the increasing importance of racism, especially the introduction to the employment chapter.
[35] Indeed, informed liberal opinion seems quite willing to accept the new ghetto demands for community control, as it relaxes pressure on integration. In August, 1970, George Romney, Secretary of Housing and Urban Development, clarified this development by refusing to withhold housing funds from suburban communities which have zoning ordinances prohibiting the construction of low-income housing; a presidential task force had recommended withholding funds but Romney rejected their advice. (*The New York Times,* August 27, 1970.) Note that this aid cut-off would simply have replicated the procedures used to enforce school desegregation in the South.

government will not directly aid the poor (unless such assistance becomes necessary to help stabilize the system). Liberals and conservatives tend to reply that the government has already provided substantial housing assistance to the poor, and that the radical argument must therefore be considered absurd. Look at all the government housing programs, they say—at urban renewal, public housing, public subsidies of low-income housing, and so on.[36]

In fact, radicals reply, government housing programs have never been used to help the poor. One should look at program effects, radicals argue, not program intentions, in order most accurately to judge the possibilities for effective public action. In the case of housing, the evidence on the effects of housing programs seems clear. Contrary to liberal and conservative claims, the two principal government housing programs in the last twenty years—public housing and urban renewal—have failed to improve housing for the poor not because they were run by entangled, inefficient, cumbersome bureaucratic organizations. They failed because dominant institutions never intended that those programs should provide housing for the poor. The urban renewal program has been dedicated to the preservation of central city land values; it has sought to accomplish this by ripping down slum housing and constructing new luxury and middle-income housing.[37] In many cities, critics have given urban renewal a more accurate name: the "Negro removal" program.

Equally, the public housing program was never intended to provide housing for the poor.[38] It was initiated during the Depression to provide low-cost housing for the temporarily indigent middle class, and to provide a counter-cyclical category of direct federal expenditure. Since World War II, the white middle and working classes have been able to find their own housing, and the Cold War has established the defense budget as the principal fiscal tool for stabilization. Congress has never appropriated enough money to make public housing work, local public housing authorities have not even spent what little money the federal government has authorized, and those to whom our institutions have given control over public housing have no intention of redirecting the program in order dramatically to improve its contribution to the low-income housing stock in urban areas. Hartman and Carr conclude from their survey of local public housing authorities:[39]

> Our survey has shown that the men and women who make basic public housing policy at the local level are in no sense representative of the client group the programs are intended to serve. A substantial proportion of the commissioners do not favor adding to the stock of publicly subsidized housing, nor use of newer forms of public housing, nor many of the "liberalization" trends, including increased tenant participation. . . . [The authority] inserts, at a critical level of internal decision-making, an intervening layer of part-time, lay commissioners who act as a brake on the program by failing to keep abreast of new trends and techniques and by representing a microcosm of middle-class, white views about the poor, their housing, and the responsibilities of government.

Those authorities reflect the real balance of institutional power in this country and, despite the profusion of good intentions at the federal level, will continue to block public construction of low-income housing until the balance of power shifts.

Suppose, despite all these barriers, that the government was suddenly forced, *mirabile dictu*, radically to increase its efforts to provide low-cost housing. Even if that happened, which radicals strenuously doubt, it seems nearly certain that the housing product would be imprisoning and oppressive, that physically adequate structures would barely compensate for the inhumanity of the design, environment, and community surrounding those structures. This seems certain if the housing were constructed either directly by the government or indirectly by private industry with the help of government subsidy.

[36] See the selection on Federal Housing Programs by the President's Committee on Urban Housing among the readings below.
[37] For basic statistical evidence, see Martin Anderson, *The Federal Bulldozer, op. cit.* For the debate about urban renewal, see James Q. Wilson, ed., *Urban Renewal: The Record and the Controversy, op. cit.*
[38] See the selection by Friedman among the readings below.
[39] Chester Hartman and Gregg Carr, "Housing Authorities Reconsidered," *Journal of the American Institute of Planners*, January, 1969, pp. 18–19.

Government housing would almost inevitably consist of tall, standardized, prison-like structures completely isolated from other communities and other facilities. This has been true in the past, and seems more likely to be true in the future.[40] With the balkanization of suburban governments and corporate attempts to revive central cities, pressures have consolidated against the government to keep the poor out of sight because they depress property values. Furthermore, because of the depletion of the treasuries of most large central cities, governments would have to build the most inexpensive, land-intensive housing possible in order both to save money and to minimize the land subtracted from the private property tax base.

Privately constructed low-cost housing, if it materialized on a large scale, seems even more likely to ignore community needs for housing conducive to, rather than oppressive of, human development. In order to attract private industry into the low-cost housing field, it seems apparent that we shall have to provide large financial incentives for research and development in housing construction technology; the current state of construction technology simply does not permit profitable construction of low-cost housing even with substantial government subsidy. Given the power of large corporations, their apparent interest in attracting government subsidy for research and development, and the current state of public and government opinion about the housing market, it seems almost certain that these R&D subsidies would go to very large corporations.[41] And it seems probable that large corporations will be interested in low-cost housing development only if they can be guaranteed extremely stable, extremely large investment possibilities. To protect their investments, they will probably insist on subsidy arrangements with the government similar to those the government has provided defense firms—cost-plus or cost over-run contracts through which the firm cannot possibly suffer a loss. Finally, large corporations will undoubtedly seek to "de-localize" the housing market, developing standardized, nationally marketable housing designs to permit mass production and prefabrication. All of these probabilities suggest that privately constructed low-cost housing would be provided by an emergent "housing-industrial complex"—a concentration of housing construction in the hands of a few large corporations, subsidized by the government, building on extremely large scales and providing housing designed according to abstract, cost-saving, "de-localized" criteria. The consequent housing would bear almost no relationship to the communities for which it was built, and communities would be able to play little or no role in its planning, design, and construction. Housing policies would be determined by corporate profitability criteria and by corporate requirements for guaranteed investment outlets, not, as one might vainly hope, by publicly determined standards of quality, accessibility, beauty, suitability, or community.

What is the alternative? There are no alternatives, the radical argument suggests, in the context of current social and economic institutions. In another context, it should be simple enough to involve people in the planning and design of housing suited for individual communities—to build housing affording variety, community, interaction, and a certain intimacy. It should also be simple enough to provide housing for all, regardless of ability to pay, according to need. If society didn't spend so much money on war, space, obsolescent cars, useless luxury goods, and pure waste, there could be plenty of money for decent, human, relevant housing supportive of community development.

THE READINGS

The first four readings provide some Impressions, Definitions and Magnitudes. The short selection from Joseph Lyford's book, *The Airtight Cage*, illustrates the failure of both landlords and the public bureaucracies to respond to human needs for decent housing. The selection from the Report of the National Commission on Civil Disorders sketches the dimensions of housing

[40] One needs only to look around for evidence of this. Two particularly striking examples are the rows of high, drab structures along State Street on the South Side in Chicago, and the Columbia Point Development off in the middle of nowhere in Boston. For the classic description of the political process which produces this kind of housing and its isolation, see Edward Banfield and Martin Meyerson, *Politics, Planning and the Public Interest* (Glencoe, Ill.: The Free Press, 1955).
[41] This has been true of George Romney's first attempt at enticing private industry into large-scale development of low-income housing, the program called "Operation Breakthrough." First design awards were announced for the program in 1970.

problems in central cities. The first selection from the report of the President's Committee on Urban Housing provides some estimates of total American housing needs, of the magnitudes of absolute housing problems. And the second selection from the same report describes the plethora of federal housing programs, candidly admitting that they do not suffice to provide housing for the truly poor.

The group of analytic readings amplify some of the points of the radical argument, though less directly than the readings in some other chapters. In searching for suitable selections for this volume, I found it most difficult to find pieces on housing which helped elaborate the basic radical approach. Nonetheless, these selections seem helpful in underscoring some of the points of the radical view.

The article by Frieden provides a basic discussion of the character of the housing industry and the limitations of the turnover process in providing housing for many of the poor. His article helps illustrate some of the basic characteristics of the private market which lead radicals to argue that the private market itself will not provide an adequate supply of low-income housing. The conclusion of the book by Lansing, Clifton, and Morgan summarizes the most recent statistical evidence to support that argument. Although filtering has helped improve the quality of housing available to some white low-income families, it has been dramatically less effective in increasing the supply of standard housing to poor blacks.

The final three articles provide a useful perspective on possibilities for an improvement in either public or private provision of low-income housing. One critical point of the radical argument is that the structure of the housing industry requires that greatly increased private provision of low-cost housing could come only from large corporations. George Sternlieb implies one substantial problem with that source. In the concluding chapter of his book, *The Tenement Landlord,* he summarizes one of the clearest findings from his study of slum housing in Newark; quite clearly, he discovered that resident owners always provided better quality housing than absentee owners. If housing becomes even more thoroughly dominated by absentee large corporations, one can hardly expect an increased sense of owner responsibility for the community.

Finally, the pieces by Friedman and by Beagle, Haber, and Wellman illustrate the reasons for the failure of the two main government programs theoretically intended to provide housing for the poor. Friedman's article sketches the history of the public housing program and clearly establishes that its intention was never to provide decent housing for the permanent poor. The piece by Beagle *et al.* illustrates for one city the same conclusion about the urban renewal program. In San Francisco, at least, urban renewal was intended to serve the interests of powerful financial interests with large downtown land holdings.

THE AIRTIGHT CAGE

Joseph P. Lyford

This brief story describes the dedicated but ultimately futile efforts of one
New York City tenant to obtain adequate housing for his family. It illustrates
the striking indifference of both landlords and government bureaucracies.
José Rodriguez had to battle both and, despite his tenacity, he lost.

The episode comes from Lyford's book about an urban renewal area on the
Upper West Side in Manhattan, *The Airtight Cage*. Lyford lived in the
area while he was writing the book. He has been a staff member of the
Center for the Study of Democratic Institutions.

José Rodriguez . . . is one of those unin-
fluential citizens whose fate helps illustrate
the nature of man's relationship to his government in the twentieth century. The Rodriguez family's personal education about the
democratic system began in earnest when
José, his wife Christine, and their two young
children moved into a rooming house in the
West Nineties and acquired a notoriously
callous landlord. The Rodriguezes liked their
new location because it was just across the
street from a new elementary school, and
only a couple of blocks from a junior high
school. Local authorities also had reason to
be pleased with the advent of the Rodriguezes. Although both parents were employed, they took an interest in local affairs.
On several occasions Rodriguez helped out
with special events at public schools and
hospitals, and both children quickly made an
excellent impression on their teachers.

Rodriguez's income and that of his wife,
who worked in a laundry, enabled them to
pay on time each month their $110 rent for
the new place, which consisted of two and
a half rooms on the basement floor. It became apparent soon after they moved in that
they were not getting anywhere near their
money's worth. The apartment, no better and
no worse than hundreds of decomposed compounds which flourished under the city's so-
called rent control program, was badly in
need of painting and plastering. Holes in
the floor were covered by carpet or card-
board, and a large opening under the kitchen
sink produced frequent visits from rats in
the basement. Rodriguez also found that the
toilet bowl was coming loose and water ran
over the bathroom floor. The apartment was
also overrun with cockroaches. Rodriguez
asked for exterminator service, to which he
was entitled. The landlord refused it. Nor
did the landlord pay for a stove and kitchen
sink which Rodriguez had bought for the
kitchen, although the original equipment had
been so decayed as to be unusable.

When Rodriguez found that he could not
get his landlord to clean the filthy hallways
or get rid of the vermin, he phoned the Department of Health until a department official told him curtly to buy himself a can of
insecticide and stop bothering the department. Next he complained to the office of
Area Services North, a local agency of the
Housing and Redevelopment Board, which
was charged with seeing that private landlords in the urban renewal area maintained
their buildings properly and kept them free
of code violations. Rodriguez's experience
with Area Services North was typical; nothing happened.

So he wrote to Chairman Mollen [of the
New York City Housing and Redevelopment
Board] himself. When the chairman also refused to do anything about the complaint,
Rodriguez decided to write to the then candidate for the U.S. Senate, Robert Kennedy.
The letter described the family's living conditions and declared that city agencies entrusted with the enforcement of health and
building codes had failed to cooperate with
the tenants.

SOURCE: The Airtight Cage *by Joseph P. Lyford,*
pp. 308–312. Copyright © 1966 by Joseph P.
Lyford. Reprinted by permission of Harper &
Row, Publishers, Inc.

"How much can a human being take?" Rodriguez concluded. "Please, Mr. Kennedy, help us."

A week or so later, he received an answer.

"I was shocked to hear of your plight," wrote Kennedy, "and I am certainly going to do everything I can to help you and your fellow tenants." What Kennedy meant by "help" was that he had referred Rodriguez's letter to Chairman Mollen, "who has assured me that he will have your situation thoroughly investigated."

Five weeks later, Rodriguez received a letter from Mollen describing the results of the "thorough investigation" the chairman had promised Mr. Kennedy.

"A check, both at our office and with the Department of Buildings, revealed that certain violations existed on said premises." Mollen also wrote that the attorney for the landlord had stated that several violations had been removed and that other violations existed because of Rodriguez's continued refusal to allow repairmen to enter his apartment.

Chairman Mollen then proceeded to give the back of his hand to the family Rodriguez. "In your complaint to Senator-elect Kennedy you stated that various city agencies involved in code enforcement had neglected to cooperate with the tenants. I am certain that if you cooperate the city will do all it can to see that conditions are improved."

At no time during Mollen's "investigation" did any representative of the Housing and Redevelopment Board or of any code-enforcement agency take the trouble to talk to Rodriguez or to look at his apartment to see if, in fact, any violations had been removed. Nor was Rodriguez ever given an opportunity to respond to the charges—which were untrue—that he had refused entry to any workman hired by the landlord. By his own admission Chairman Mollen's sole source of information was the landlord's attorney. Apparently no city official had the time to make an on-the-spot investigation. However, shortly before he wrote to Rodriguez, Chairman Mollen attended a tree-planting ceremony a few blocks from the apartment, at which occasion his photograph was taken for the Spanish newspaper *El Diario*.

Such rebuffs as Mollen's letter dealt the Rodriguez family a double blow. Not only did it mean they could expect little help from the authorities, but it also was the signal to the landlord that he could harass them with impunity. This landlord was not accustomed to having his tenants complain, and he decided to get rid of the troublemakers as quickly as possible. Until their arrival he had operated the building and another even more decrepit one on the same street in defiance of all manner of fire, occupancy, building, and health regulations without any protest from his tenants. Most of them were Puerto Ricans desperate for a place to live, who were jammed into these buildings in violation of occupancy regulations; any complaints about their treatment would have meant their immediate eviction. A measure of the landlord's control over the tenants was the fact that he even distributed their mail. There were no regulation mailboxes in the Rodriguezes' house: the postman dropped the mail into the slot of a padlocked box to which the landlord had the only key. Rodriguez protested to the U.S. Post Office, but the postal authorities did nothing about it.

For nearly a year the landlord carried out a campaign of harassment to drive the Rodriguez family out of the house. He served several eviction notices, and on more than six different occasions he appeared at the door of their apartment with summonses charging Rodriguez with assault, theft, disorderly behavior, nonpayment of rent, or threats of violence. On most of these occasions, he was accompanied by a policeman who had been told by the landlord that Rodriguez was dangerous. To answer each summons or notice of eviction, Rodriguez had to take the better part of a day to find a lawyer, prepare a defense, call witnesses, and travel downtown to criminal court or the agency where a hearing was to be held. The summonses forced him to absent himself from his union hiring hall, thereby losing a chance at any employment opportunity which might turn up that day.

The truth of the landlord's charges can be judged by the fact that in some cases he did not even appear to press his complaint, and in all cases the charges against Rodriguez were dismissed. But, although he lost each time, the landlord succeeded in irritating and worrying the family, keeping it in a constant state of insecurity, using up Rodriguez's time, causing him expense, and interfering with his employment.

In the opinion of this observer, Rodriguez

won his rounds in court in spite of the judicial procedure because he could speak English (although with a heavy accent), because he kept his temper both in and out of court, in spite of considerable provocation in both places, and because he kept a complete file of documents bearing on his case. Finally, he had some friends who were occasionally able to get him a lawyer without charge. Had he lacked any of these assets, it is difficult to say whether he would be a free man today. The proceedings in court had very little resemblance to the administration of justice as it is discussed in bar association meetings. Rodriguez was merely one of a long line of people—largely Negroes and Puerto Ricans—who were handled on an assembly-line basis by an overworked, harried judge who sometimes did not appear to understand the charges. There would be a "Now what's this all about?"; then, after a few moments of confused argument, the magistrate would berate both plaintiff and defendant, tell them to stop picking on each other, and threaten them both with jail if they ever appeared before him again. Or he might just postpone things by granting the landlord an adjournment, thereby prolonging Rodriguez's discomfort a little longer.

On one occasion when Rodriguez took the offensive and filed charges against the landlord for failing to render services and correct violations, the head of a city agency appeared as a witness for the landlord himself, appealing to the judge to postpone a decision on the case until her agency had had time to make an inspection of the Rodriguez apartment—a plea which came months after Rodriguez had vainly appealed to her agency and to her boss, Chairman Mollen, for just such an inspection. When the inspection was finally held, the two inspectors became angry at Rodriguez for having invited one of his friends to be present as a witness, and Rodriguez was never allowed to see the report of the inspection.

The conclusion to the harassment of Rodriguez could have been predicted. For one thing, Rodriguez began to run out of lawyers. Friendly attorneys were willing to help on a one-shot basis, but when the next summons was served they were always too busy. Rodriguez appealed to local civil rights groups, to Puerto Rican organizations, to the FDR-Woodrow Wilson Democratic Club, and got promises of help, but the help never materialized.

One night Rodriguez was arrested and arraigned in the 24th Precinct police station, charged by the landlord with assault. This case was also thrown out of court, but it was Rodriguez's last victory. During a summer rainstorm a few weeks later, a marshal knocked at the Rodriguez door with a court order evicting the family for nonpayment of rent. The order had been signed without Rodriguez's ever having had a hearing on the charges, which were false. So the Rodriguez family and all its belongings were moved out onto the sidewalk, and all a handful of friendly neighbors could do was to cover the furniture with plastic to keep it dry. Then the Rodriguezes were transported to a fifth-floor walkup apartment in a frightful city-owned building a block or so away.

HOUSING PROBLEMS IN CENTRAL CITIES

The National Advisory Commission on Civil Disorders

The following excerpt provides an interesting series of figures on the range and intensity of housing problems in central cities, especially in black ghettos. The figures support the conclusion that, for many in the central cities, "the goal of a decent home and suitable environment is as far distant as ever." The selection comes from the "Riot Commission Report," published in 1968.

The passage of the National Housing Act in 1934 signalled a new federal commitment to provide housing for the nation's citizens. Fifteen years later Congress made the commitment explicit in the Housing Act of 1949, establishing as a national goal the realization of "a decent home and suitable environment for every American family."

Today, after more than three decades of fragmented and grossly under-funded federal housing programs, decent housing remains a chronic problem for the disadvantaged urban household. Fifty-six percent of the country's nonwhite families live in central cities today, and of these, nearly two-thirds live in neighborhoods marked by substandard[1] housing and general urban blight. For these citizens, condemned by segregation and poverty to live in the decaying slums of our central cities, the goal of a decent home and suitable environment is as far distant as ever.

During the decade of the 1950's, when vast numbers of Negroes were migrating to the cities, only 4 million of the 16.8 million new housing units constructed throughout the nation were built in the central cities. These additions were counterbalanced by the loss of 1.5 million central-city units through demolition and other means. The result was that the number of nonwhites living in substandard housing increased from 1.4 to 1.8 million, even though the number of substandard units declined.

SOURCE: *Report of the National Advisory Commission on Civil Disorders, 1968.*

[1] The Department of Housing and Urban Development classifies substandard housing as that housing reported by the United States Census Bureau as (1) sound but lacking full plumbing, (2) deteriorating and lacking full plumbing, or (3) dilapidated.

Statistics available for the period since 1960 indicate that the trend is continuing. There has been virtually no decline in the number of occupied dilapidated units in metropolitan areas, and surveys in New York City and Watts actually show an increase in the number of such units. These statistics have led the Department of Housing and Urban Development to conclude that while the trend in the country as a whole is toward less substandard housing, "There are individual neighborhoods and areas within many cities where the housing situation continues to deteriorate."[2]

Inadequate housing is not limited to Negroes. Even in the central cities the problem affects two and a half times as many white as nonwhite households. Nationally, over 4 million of the nearly 6 million occupied substandard units in 1966 were occupied by whites.

It is also true that Negro housing in large cities is significantly better than that in most rural areas—especially in the South. Good quality housing has become available to Negro city dwellers at an increasing rate since the mid-1950's when the postwar housing shortage ended in most metropolitan areas.

Nevertheless, in the Negro ghetto, grossly inadequate housing continues to be a critical problem.

SUBSTANDARD, OLD, AND OVERCROWDED STRUCTURES

Nationwide, 25 percent of all nonwhites living in central cities occupied substandard units in 1960 compared to 8 percent of all

[2] Hearings before the Subcommittee on Executive Reorganization of the Committee on Government Operations, United States Senate, 89th Congress, 2nd session, August 16, 1966, p. 148.

whites. Preliminary Census Bureau data indicate that by 1966, the figures had dropped to 16 and 5 percent respectively. However, if "deteriorating" units and units with serious housing code violations are added, the percentage of nonwhites living in inadequate housing in 1966 becomes much greater.

In 14 of the largest U.S. cities, the proportions of all nonwhite housing units classified as deteriorating, dilapidated, or lacking full plumbing in 1960 (the latest date for which figures are available), were as follows:

NONWHITE HOUSING IN 14 CITIES

City	Percentage of Nonwhite Occupied Housing Units Classified Deteriorating or Dilapidated, 1960	Percentage of Nonwhite Occupied Housing Units Classified Deteriorating, Dilapidated, or Sound but Without Full Plumbing, 1960
New York	33.8%	42.4%
Chicago	32.1%	42.8%
Los Angeles	14.7%	18.1%
Philadelphia	28.6%	32.0%
Detroit	27.9%	30.1%
Baltimore	30.5%	31.7%
Houston	30.1%	36.7%
Cleveland	29.9%	33.9%
Washington, D.C.	15.2%	20.8%
St. Louis	40.3%	51.6%
San Francisco	21.3%	34.0%
Dallas	41.3%	45.9%
New Orleans	44.3%	56.9%
Pittsburgh	49.1%	58.9%

SOURCE: U.S. Department of Commerce, Bureau of the Census.

Conditions were far worse than these city-wide averages in many specific disadvantaged neighborhoods. For example, a study of housing in Newark, New Jersey, before the 1967 disorders, showed the following situation in certain predominantly Negro neighborhoods as of 1960:

PERCENTAGE OF HOUSING UNITS DILAPIDATED OR DETERIORATED
IN SELECTED AREAS OF NEWARK, 1960

Area Number	Population	Percentage Nonwhite	Percentage of All Housing Units Dilapidated or Deteriorating
1	25,300	75.5%	91.0%
2	48,200	64.5%	63.8%
3A	48,300	74.8%	43.1%

SOURCE: George Sternlieb, The Tenement Landlord (New Brunswick, N.J.: Rutgers, 1966), pp. 238–241.

These three areas contained 30 percent of the total population of Newark in 1960, and 62 percent of its nonwhite population.

The Commission carried out special analyses of 1960 housing conditions in three cities, concentrating on all Census Tracts with 1960 median incomes of under $3,000 for both families and individuals. It also analyzed housing conditions in Watts. The results showed that the vast majority of people living in the poorest areas of these cities were Negroes, and that a high proportion lived in inadequate housing:

Item	Detroit	Washington, D.C.	· Memphis	Watts Area of Los Angeles
Total population of study area	162,375	97,084	150,827	49,074
Percentage of study area nonwhite	67.5%	74.5%	74.0%	87.3%
Percentage of housing units in study area:				
—Substandard by HUD definition	32.7%	23.9%	35.0%	10.5%
—Dilapidated, deteriorating or sound but lacking full plumbing	53.1%	37.3%	46.5%	29.1%

SOURCE: U.S. Department of Commerce, Bureau of the Census.

Negroes, on the average, also occupy much older housing than whites. In each of ten metropolitan areas analyzed by the Commission, substantially higher percentages of nonwhites than whites occupied units built prior to 1939.

PERCENTAGE OF WHITE AND NONWHITE OCCUPIED HOUSING UNITS BUILT PRIOR TO 1939 IN SELECTED METROPOLITAN AREAS

Metropolitan Area	White Occupied Units	Nonwhite Occupied Units
Cleveland	33.2	90.6
Dallas	31.9	52.7
Detroit	46.2	86.1
Kansas City	54.4	89.9
Los Angeles— Long Beach	36.6	62.4
New Orleans	52.9	62.2
Philadelphia	62.0	90.8
Saint Louis	57.9	84.7
San Francisco— Oakland	51.3	67.6
Washington, D.C.	31.9	64.9

SOURCE: U.S. Department of Commerce, Bureau of the Census.

Finally, Negro housing units are far more likely to be overcrowded than those occupied by whites. In U.S. metropolitan areas in 1960, 25 percent of all nonwhite units were overcrowded by the standard measure (that is, they contained 1.01 or more persons per room). Only 8 percent of all white-occupied units were in this category. Moreover, 11 percent of all nonwhite-occupied units were seriously overcrowded (1.51 or more persons

per room), compared with 2 percent for white-occupied units. The figures were as follows in the ten metropolitan areas analyzed by the Commission.

PERCENTAGE OF WHITE AND NONWHITE OCCUPIED UNITS WITH 1.01 OR MORE PERSONS PER ROOM IN SELECTED METROPOLITAN AREAS

Metropolitan Area	White Occupied Units	Nonwhite Occupied Units
Cleveland	6.9	19.3
Dallas	9.3	28.8
Detroit	8.6	17.5
Kansas City	8.7	18.0
Los Angeles— Long Beach	8.0	17.4
New Orleans	12.0	36.1
Philadelphia	4.9	16.3
Saint Louis	11.8	28.0
San Francisco— Oakland	6.0	19.7
Washington, D.C.	6.2	22.6

SOURCE: U.S. Department of Commerce, Bureau of the Census.

HIGHER RENTS FOR POORER HOUSING

Negroes in large cities are often forced to pay the same rents as whites and receive less for their money, or pay higher rents for the same accommodations.

The first type of discriminatory effect— paying the same amount but receiving less— is illustrated by data from the 1960 Census for Chicago and Detroit.

In certain Chicago census tracts, both

whites and nonwhites paid median rents of $88, and the proportions paying various specific rents below that median were almost identical. But the units rented by nonwhites were typically:

—Smaller (the median number of rooms was 3.35 for nonwhites versus 3.95 for whites).

—In worse condition (30.7 percent of all nonwhite units were deteriorated or dilapidated units versus 11.6 percent for whites).

—Occupied by more people (the median household size was 3.53 for nonwhites versus 2.88 for whites).

—More likely to be overcrowded (27.4 percent of nonwhite units had 1.01 or more persons per room versus 7.9 percent for whites).

In Detroit, whites paid a median rental of $77 as compared to $76 among nonwhites. Yet 27.0 percent of nonwhite units were deteriorating or dilapidated, as compared to only 10.3 percent of all white units.

The second type of discriminatory effect —paying more for similar housing—is illustrated by data from a study of housing conditions in disadvantaged neighborhoods in Newark, New Jersey. In four areas of that city (including the three areas cited previously), nonwhites with housing essentially similar to that of whites paid rents that were from 8.1 percent to 16.8 percent higher. Though the typically larger size of nonwhite households, with consequent harder wear and tear, may partially justify the difference in rental, the study found that nonwhites were paying a definite "color tax" of apparently well over 10 percent on housing. This condition prevails in most racial ghettos.

The combination of high rents and low incomes forces many Negroes to pay an excessively high proportion of their income for housing. This is shown dramatically by the following chart, showing the percentage of renter households paying over 35 percent of their incomes for rent in ten metropolitan areas:

PERCENTAGES OF WHITE AND NONWHITE OCCUPIED UNITS WITH HOUSEHOLDS PAYING 35 PERCENT OR MORE OF THEIR INCOME FOR RENT IN SELECTED METROPOLITAN AREAS

Metropolitan Area	White Occupied Units	Nonwhite Occupied Units
Cleveland	8.6	33.8
Dallas	19.2	33.8
Detroit	21.2	40.5
Kansas City	20.2	40.0
Los Angeles— Long Beach	23.4	28.4
New Orleans	16.6	30.5
Philadelphia	19.3	32.1
Saint Louis	18.5	36.7
San Francisco— Oakland	21.2	25.1
Washington, D.C.	18.5	28.3

SOURCE: U.S. Department of Commerce, Bureau of the Census.

The high proportion of income that must go for rent leaves less money in such households for other expenses. Undoubtedly, this hardship is a major reason many Negro households regard housing as one of their worst problems.

AMERICAN HOUSING NEEDS

The President's Committee on Urban Housing

This set of analyses and tables provides some further evidence on magnitudes of housing problems in the United States. Based on work done for the special committee on urban housing, the selection includes some of the most recent available estimates of housing needs. Given our avowed goal of providing a decent home for everyone, the selection outlines the enormity of fulfilling that objective.

The selection comes from the report of the President's Committee on Urban Housing, *A Decent Home,* published in 1968.

—How many American families are too poor to afford the market rate price for adequate housing? Are their numbers increasing or declining?

—How many existing homes are unfit for occupancy by the Nation's standard of living?

—How many homes must be built to meet the growing needs of the total population?

When this Committee received its charge from the President in June 1967, reliable statistics for answering such questions were so difficult to obtain that TEMPO, General Electric's Center for Advanced Studies, was commissioned to make an in-depth computerized study of current and future U.S. housing construction and subsidy requirements. In addition the Committee reviewed an independent study by Robert Gladstone and Associates prepared for a Committee member. . . .

26 MILLION NEW OR REHABILITATED HOUSING UNITS

TEMPO began by analyzing National population trends reflected in the 1950 and 1960 U.S. Censuses and then projected to 1978 the Nation's urban and rural population growth, new household formation, and racial characteristics. The basic trends can be seen in Table 1. With these projections determined, TEMPO next analyzed the fate of today's 66 million housing units over the next decade: how many will be lost by demolition, destruction and merger? How many will

SOURCE: *The President's Committee on Urban Housing, "American Housing Needs," from* A Decent Home, *1968.*

deteriorate? How many must be demolished or rehabilitated if all substandard housing is to be eliminated by 1978?

By coupling the population trends (Table 1) with the projected fate of existing housing, TEMPO produced estimates of total gross construction needs, both to accommodate the growing population and for replacement or rehabilitation of all substandard units.

TEMPO's findings on construction needs can be found in Table 2.

TEMPO found our Nation must build and rehabilitate 26 million houses and apartments in the next decade to provide for all the new households forming, to allow enough vacancies for our increasingly mobile population, to replace houses destroyed or demolished, and to eliminate all substandard housing. Gladstone, using a different approach emphasizing market analysis, estimates 10-year construction needs at a comparable level. [Table 3 presents a detailed breakdown of projected substandard units.]

The total figure of 26 million presents two major challenges to the Nation:

—Greatly expanded production for families who can afford adequate housing without government assistance.

—Measures to relieve the severe shortage of adequate housing for the poor.

The latter, a more immediate social problem and the primary subject of the Committee's work, is set in the context of the former. The housing market and the housing industry are all of a piece with each of the several parts affecting the others. Finding and producing housing for the urban poor is made more difficult if more resources must also be devoted to provide added housing for the

TABLE 1
POPULATION AND HOUSEHOLD CHARACTERISTICS OF THE UNITED STATES
AND PERCENTAGES OF SELECTED POPULATION CLASSES—
1950, 1960, 1966, 1968, 1978

	1950	1960	1966	1968	1978
Population (millions):					
Total	151.3	178.5	194.1	201.8	235.2
White	135.1	158.1	170.8	177.3	204.3
Nonwhite	16.2	20.4	23.3	24.5	30.9
Central City:					
White	45.5	47.5	46.6	46.1	44.9
Nonwhite	6.3	10.3	12.8	13.5	18.8
Households (millions):					
Total	42.9	53.0	58.9	60.9	74.3
White	39.0	47.9	53.0	54.8	66.3
Nonwhite	3.9	5.1	5.9	6.1	8.0
Percentages of U.S. population:					
Inside SMSA:*					
White[1]	59	62	64	64	65
Nonwhite[2]	56	64	68	70	77
Central City:					
White[1]	34	30	27	26	22
Nonwhite[2]	43	51	55	55	61
Nonwhite as percent of total Central City	12	18	22	23	30

* Standard Metropolitan Statistical Area.
[1] Relative to the total United States white population.
[2] Relative to the total United States nonwhite population.

SOURCE: GE TEMPO, *United States Housing Needs: 1968–1978.*

TABLE 2
U.S. HOUSING CONSTRUCTION NEEDS—
1968 TO 1978 (MILLIONS OF UNITS)

Construction of new standard units:	
Units for new households	13.4
Replacement of net removals of standard units	3.0
Allowance for vacancies	1.6
Subtotal	18.0
Replacement or rehabilitation of substandard units:	
Units becoming substandard during 1968–78	2.0
Replacement of net removals	2.0
Other substandard units in the inventory in 1966	4.7
Subtotal	8.7
Total Construction Needs	26.7

SOURCE: GE TEMPO, *United States Housing Needs: 1968–1978.*

TABLE 3
OCCUPIED SUBSTANDARD HOUSING
UNITS—1950 TO 1978 (THOUSANDS
OF UNITS)

Category	1950	1960	1966[1]	1978[1]
Total units	15,256	9,007	6,727	4,300
By location:				
Inside SMSA	5,426	2,761	2,088	2,150
Outside SMSA	9,830	6,246	4,639	2,150
Percent inside SMSA	35	31	30	50
By condition:				
DILAP[2]	3,708	3,083	2,663	1,900
NDIP[3]	11,548	5,924	4,064	2,400

[1] TEMPO projections.
[2] DILAP means "dilapidated with adequate plumbing."
[3] NDIP means "not dilapidated with inadequate plumbing."

SOURCE: GE TEMPO, *United States Housing Needs: 1968–1978.*

total population. If the housing needs of middle-income citizens are not met, then it will be impossible to meet the housing needs of the great mass of the poor.

To meet this projected total need for the coming decade there must be a vast increase of the Nation's housing production. The average of 2.6 million new and rehabilitated units required for each of the 10 years, in order to meet this objective, compares with the current annual rate of 1.5 million new housing units per year. Recently the Nation has produced only about 50,000 subsidized units a year—in 10 years at that rate, only half a million. Production of both subsidized and unsubsidized housing must clearly be expanded to rid the cities of substandard housing by 1978.

SIX TO EIGHT MILLION UNITS FOR THE POOR

Over the next 10 years, assuming that current economic trends and National policies continue without marked change, the number of American households unable to afford decent housing will remain almost constant. . . . TEMPO, besides calculating the housing construction levels required to eliminate substandard housing in the next decade, also carried out the complementary task of projecting the number of families who are, and will be, unable to afford adequate housing without government assistance. Its estimates on these "noneffective demand households" are shown in Table 4.

The number of house-poor families will decline only slightly in the coming decade, if help is not forthcoming. One family in eight is now house-poor, and only slow improvement is in sight. Massive government assistance is essential not only to enable these families to afford adequate quarters, but also to make the production target of 26 million units feasible as an economic matter. We estimate that six to eight million families must be receiving housing assistance by 1978, if all Americans are to be living in decent housing by that time.

When Does a Family Need a Subsidy?

To speak of millions of families who "cannot afford decent housing" implies a standard of what is reasonable or fair for a family to pay for shelter.

TEMPO found that (1) the average relation of housing expenditures to income for the U.S. total population is about 15 percent but (2) that white families earning between $4,000 to $5,000 a year spend an average of 20 percent of their income for housing. It employed this 20 percent figure to reach its estimate and projection of families unable to afford standard housing without some form of subsidy. Gladstone, on the other hand, applied the Federal rent supplement program's criterion, under which a family must allocate 25 percent of their gross monthly income for shelter costs. In many European countries, the percentage of income paid by families in subsidized housing is considerably smaller than either figure. . . .

A Look at These Nearly Eight Million Needy Families

One may divide the families requiring housing subsidies into two broad income groups:

—Those below the Federal government's poverty line (called "low income" for purposes of Federal housing programs), and

TABLE 4
UNITED STATES NONEFFECTIVE DEMAND HOUSEHOLDS (IN MILLIONS)

	White households			Nonwhite households			
Year	Inside SMSA	Outside SMSA	Total	Inside SMSA	Outside SMSA	Total	Total households
1960	3.6	2.5	6.1	1.0	1.2	2.2	8 3
1968	3.4	2.2	5.6	1.0	1.2	2.2	7.8
1978	3.4	1.9	5.3	1.1	1.1	2.2	7.5

SOURCE: GE TEMPO, *United States Housing Needs: 1968–1978.*

—Those above the poverty line but who would still have to pay more than 20 to 25 percent of their income for decent housing in the absence of a subsidy (called "moderate income" for purposes of Federal housing programs).

Economic characteristics. Among low- and moderate-income families requiring a subsidy, the greatest need, perhaps not surprisingly, is that of the poorest of the poor. What is surprising is that their needs have not received priority.

Table 5 presents TEMPO's projection of the income distribution of households in metropolitan areas in 1978. The table suggests that while the percentage of urban families earning less than $4,000 a year will decline from 31 percent in 1960 to 22 percent in 1978, their absolute numbers will *increase* slightly. Even in 1978, almost half of the urban families with incomes under $4,000 will be earning less than $2,000.

Racial characteristics. About 70 percent of the six to eight million families unable to afford housing will be white, and about 30 percent will be nonwhite. The nationwide proportionate need among nonwhites will be almost three times more acute than among the white majority. In 1978, one in every four nonwhite families will need housing assistance, compared to only one in every 12

TABLE 6
DISTRIBUTION OF NONEFFECTIVE DEMAND HOUSEHOLDS BY WHITE AND NONWHITE HEAD, INSIDE ALL SMSAs— 1960, 1968, 1978

Year	White head		Nonwhite head	
	Thousands	Percent[1]	Thousands	Percent[2]
1960	3,612	11.8	1,017	29.2
1968	3,374	9.6	989	23.4
1978	3,380	7.7	1,132	18.3

[1] Relative to all white families in SMSAs.
[2] Relative to all nonwhite families in SMSAs.

SOURCE: GE TEMPO, *United States Housing Needs: 1968–1978.*

white families. Also in 1978, as Table 6 shows, 18 percent of all *urban* nonwhite families will require some form of housing subsidy, compared to only about 8 percent

TABLE 7
PERCENTAGE OF WHITE AND NONWHITE HOUSEHOLDS IN SPECIFIC INCOME GROUPS OCCUPYING SUBSTANDARD HOUSING, INSIDE AND OUTSIDE SMSAs—1960

Household characteristics (dollars in thousands)	Inside SMSAs		Outside SMSAs	
	White (percent)	Non-white (percent)	White (percent)	Non-white (percent)
Annual income:[1]				
Under 2.0	21	45	45	87
2.0 to 2.9	15	35	33	77
3.0 to 3.9	12	28	25	65
4.0 to 4.9	9	21	18	56
5.0 to 5.9	6	16	13	49
6.0 to 6.9	4	14	10	43
7.0 to 9.9	2	9	7	36
Over 10.0	1	7	4	31
All incomes	7	28	23	77

[1] Income is for the calendar year 1959, and is limited to that received by the primary family or primary individual.

SOURCE: GE TEMPO, *United States Housing Needs: 1968–1978.*

TABLE 5
INCOME DISTRIBUTION OF HOUSEHOLDS INSIDE ALL SMSAs, 1960 AND 1978

Annual income ($1,000)	1960 Households in—		1978 Households in—	
	Thousands	Percent	Thousands	Percent
Less than 2.0	5,014	14.7	5,246	10.5
2.0 to 2.9	2,541	7.5	2,960	5.9
3.0 to 3.9	2,932	8.6	2,824	5.6
4.0 to 4.9	3,482	10.2	3,072	6.1
5.0 to 5.9	4,015	11.8	3,285	6.6
6.0 to 6.9	3,557	10.5	3,640	7.1
7.0 to 9.9	6,930	20.4	8,685	17.3
10.0 or more	5,538	16.3	20,434	40.7
Total	34,009	100.0	50,145	100.0

SOURCE: Derived from GE TEMPO, *United States Housing Needs: 1968–1978.*

of all urban white families. [Table 7 presents more detailed figures.]

The nonwhite family must pay an economic penalty because of racial discrimination. "Nonwhites," TEMPO concluded after amassing data on National housing cost patterns, "must earn approximately one-third more annual income than whites, irrespective of household size, to assure [themselves of] standard housing." . . .

Geographic characteristics. The six to eight million families in need of housing assistance live in rural America as well as in what the President called "the corroded core of the American city."

According to TEMPO, only about 56 percent of today's house-poor families live in metropolitan areas with populations of 50,000 or more (Standard Metropolitan Statistical Areas). TEMPO's projections indicate that subsidy requirements in these areas will increase to 60 percent of total requirements by 1978, however, because the numbers of needy urban dwellers will remain relatively constant while the numbers of their rural counterparts will decline. . . . About one-eighth of the house-poor families in 1978 will be nonwhite households living in the central cities.

This report emphasizes urban housing needs. It is not our intention, however, to minimize or ignore the sizable housing problems of rural America for both needs are tightly related. A recurring factor in the life of urban slums has been a steady trek of rural poor—black and white—from the countryside to the nation's big industrial cities.

The elderly. One of the largest and neediest groups among the poor are the elderly—couples, widowers, bachelors, widows —living on social security, meager savings, a pension, or welfare. TEMPO projects that nearly half of the 3.4 million white urban households needing housing assistance in 1978 will be headed by a person aged 65 or older. These older Americans make up a much larger part of the American poor than is the impression sometimes given by the current literature on poverty. In 1960, 77 percent of all persons over 65 who lived alone had incomes of less than $2,000— making them one of the largest of all the subgroups of the poor.

FEDERAL HOUSING PROGRAMS

The President's Committee on Urban Housing

These excerpts outline the features of major federal housing programs designed to provide housing for the poor. The selection makes clear that policy is tending more and more toward subsidy to private industry for low-cost housing construction and that even the most recent subsidy programs do not provide sufficient subsidy to induce housing for the truly poor.

Like the preceding selection, this comes from *A Decent Home.* This selection has been heavily excerpted; many small administrative and operational details about each program have been deleted.

There are a great many Federal housing programs. Most are administered by HUD, but the Veterans Administration, the Farmers Home Administration, and the Department of Defense all have significant housing programs of their own. Many of the HUD programs, like the traditional mortgage insurance programs of FHA, do not involve the subsidization of housing costs. The major HUD housing subsidy programs are outlined below. . . .

SOURCE: *The President's Committee on Urban Housing, "Federal Housing Programs," from* A Decent Home, *1968.*

PUBLIC HOUSING

Although the layman may refer to all Government-assisted housing as "public housing," the term is used by housing professionals only to denote the specific program begun in 1937. The Public Housing program, as it has traditionally operated, places responsibility for development, ownership, and management of subsidized rental projects in the hands of independent local government agencies called housing authorities. A local housing authority cannot receive Federal assistance without the approval of both its local government and the Housing Assistance Administration, a subdivision of the Department of Housing and Urban Development. Some state laws go further and require local government approval of specific sites. Some jurisdictions, like the entire states of California and Texas, require that the Federal contract to support Public Housing projects be approved by local voters in referenda. Although practically all large cities have established housing authorities, many small jurisdictions, particularly suburban ones, do not participate in the program. For example, in 1967 less than half of the localities with populations between 25,000 and 50,000 had housing authorities. . . .

Rents in Public Housing are lowered through a number of subsidies, both Federal and local. The cost of project development is financed with long-term tax-exempt local bonds. This tax exemption lowers direct debt retirement costs. The Federal Government makes annual contributions to the local housing authority which cover all costs of retiring the bonds. The Federal Government is also authorized to pay a local authority an additional $120 per year for the benefit of each family which is elderly, displaced, extremely poor, or contains four or more children. Lastly, public housing projects do not pay normal local real estate taxes but instead pay lower amounts in-lieu-of-taxes.

Because of these substantial subsidies, admission to public housing projects is restricted to families whose incomes are below limits established by the local housing authority under statutory Federal guidelines. At the end of 1964 the median income limit for admission for a family of two adults and two children, in localities within urbanized areas, was $4,000. The highest limit ($5,760) was in New York City. The median income of all families admitted to Public Housing in recent years has been roughly $2,500. The median rent for all public housing units is approximately $45. Roughly one-half of all public housing units are occupied by Negro tenants and one-third by elderly persons. Given the inadequate coverage and size of welfare payments, there are still millions of families who are too poor to live in public housing projects. Even those who live there may have to commit a disproportionate share of their incomes to pay the low rents. . . .

In 1967, the Public Housing program included some 650,000 units which housed almost 2.4 million persons. This figure dwarfs production totals under the other programs described below, principally because Public Housing was the only housing subsidy program in the United States until the last decade. Table 1 presents production figures for all Public Housing programs between 1939 and 1967. Production has been rather erratic, at least until recent years; the highest production peaks were reached in 1941 and 1952–53.

202 AND 221(d)(3) BELOW MARKET INTEREST RATE PROGRAMS

These two low-interest loan programs, although differing in details, use the same subsidy technique and are best analyzed to-

TABLE 1
LOW-RENT PUBLIC HOUSING UNITS
COMPLETED, ACQUIRED, OR LEASED
FOR CALENDAR YEARS 1939–67

Year	Units	Year	Units
1939	4,960	1954	44,293
1940	34,308	1955	20,899
1941	61,065	1956	11,993
1942	36,172	1957	10,513
1943	24,296	1958	15,472
1944	3,269	1959	21,939
1945	2,080	1960	16,401
1946	1,925	1961	20,965
1947	466	1962	28,682
1948	1,348	1963	27,327
1949	547	1964	24,488
1950	1,255	1965	30,769
1951	10,246	1966	31,483
1952	58,258	1967	38,756
1953	58,214		

SOURCE: Housing Assistance Administration.

gether. The 202 program begun in 1959 is administered by the Housing Assistance Administration which is also responsible for Public Housing. The subsidy used is a direct loan from HUD to sponsoring nonprofit corporations, originally at an interest rate based on the outstanding Federal debt and since 1965 at a flat 3 percent interest rate. Profit-motivated sponsors are not permitted to own these projects; only elderly or handicapped persons may live in 202 projects. Current income limits for tenant eligibility are the lesser of: (1) $4,500 per year for single persons, and $5,400 per year for two person families; or (2) 80 percent of the appropriate 221(d)(3) BMIR limits. Under this program, HUD also provides the interim financing needed for construction, again at a 3 percent rate of interest. The permanent loans may have a term of up to 50 years and can cover up to 100 percent of the costs of a project. Projects built under 202 are *not* restricted to jurisdictions which have HUD-approved Workable Programs.

The 221(d)(3) Below Market Interest Rate program (221(d)(3)BMIR), a considerably broader program than 202 in terms of eligible sponsors and eligible tenants, was begun in 1961. FNMA is now authorized to purchase 221(d)(3) mortgages bearing interest rates of 3 percent. . . .

Table 2 presents projections of the rent levels achievable in Detroit with the 221(d) (3) BMIR, Public Housing and Rent Supplement programs and compares them with those achievable in nonsubsidized housing represented by the Section 207 program. It also indicates the incomes needed to support the required rents for 20 and 25 percent rent-income ratios. While this table is based only on Detroit cost data and contains some assumptions which may not be generally applicable, it does serve to illustrate that housing cannot be generally built for rents which low-income groups can be expected to pay without subsidies at least as great as those provided by the Rent Supplement program.

As of June 1967, 62,000 units of 221(d) (3) BMIR housing had been completed or were under construction. Roughly one-half

TABLE 2

AVERAGE OR MINIMUM REQUIRED RENTALS ON NEWLY CONSTRUCTED ONE- AND TWO-BEDROOM APARTMENTS UNDER DIFFERENT FEDERAL HOUSING PROGRAMS AND THE REQUIRED FAMILY INCOME IMPLIED AT SPECIFIED RENT-INCOME RATIOS*

| | | | Required income at rent-income ratios of 20 or 25 percent for families occupying— | | | |
| | Required annual (monthly) rentals on units with— | | One bedroom | | Two bedrooms | |
Program	One bedroom	Two bedrooms	20 percent	25 percent	20 percent	25 percent
207 average (no subsidy)	$2,270 ($189)	$2,719 ($227)	$11,350	$9,080	$13,595	$10,876
Public Housing average	905 (75)	1,161 (97)	4,525	3,620	5,805	4,644
Rent Supplement minimum	472 (39)	540 (45)	2,360	1,888	2,700	2,160
236 minimum	1,472 (123)	1,763 (147)	7,360	5,888	8,815	7,052
221(d)(3)BMIR average	1,664 (139)	1,993 (166)	8,320	6,656	9,965	7,972

* The calculations apply to Detroit in 1967 and cities with similar cost levels. Within the group of cities with more than 2 million inhabitants, Detroit had the lowest dwelling construction cost limits for Public Housing in 1966. They were at the same level as those in Dallas (population 1.1 million in 1960). Development cost limits in all other cases except the Rent Supplement program (RS) were assumed to be equal to those specified for 221(d)(3) BMIR. These were $14,150 for one-bedroom and $16,950 for a two-bedroom dwelling unit. No rent supplement projects have been completed in Detroit by 1967.

SOURCE: Von Furstenberg and Moskof: *Federally Assisted Rental Housing Programs: Which Income Groups Have They Served or Whom Can They Be Expected to Serve?*

of these units had been built by profit-motivated developers and about one-half by non-profit and cooperative sponsors. . . .

RENT SUPPLEMENT

The Rent Supplement program was offered by the Administration in 1965 as a substitute for 221(d)(3) BMIR. Under the rent supplement technique, the tenant family pays 25 percent of its income toward rent, while the Federal Government pays directly to the landlord the difference between economic rent levels and the tenant's contribution. This approach has the advantages of keying the amount of subsidy to the tenant's need and of spreading the cost to the Federal Government over a long period. In its deliberations on the Housing Act of 1965, Congress did not accept the Administration's recommendation that the Rent Supplement program be aimed at moderate-income families as well as low-income families. Instead, it adopted the Rent Supplement program only after restricting eligibility for supplements to families whose incomes on admission are below the eligibility limits for Public Housing in the same locality. In addition, Congress continued the 221(d)(3) program instead of substituting the Rent Supplement program for it as the Administration had recommended.

In essence, the Rent Supplement program attempts to shift the responsibility for building and operating low-rent housing projects from the local housing authorities (relied on in the Public Housing program) to private groups, both profit-motivated and nonprofit. After receiving approval of a proposed project from FHA (which administers the program), the private housing owner finances his project with a private mortgage at the market interest rate. On completion of construction, the housing owner rents units in the project to any family he chooses. However, not all tenants in a project are eligible for supplements. To be eligible, a family must have a low income (one below limits established by the Secretary of HUD which themselves must be below the limit for admission to Public Housing in that area), have few assets, and be a member of one of the following deserving groups: elderly, handicapped, displaced by Government action or natural disaster, or now living in substandard housing. As mentioned, these eligible tenants pay 25 percent of their income toward rents and the Federal Government pays any remainder directly to the landlord. Tenants who are not eligible for supplements pay the entire rent themselves. As a tenant's income rises, his supplement is reduced. For this reason, a family whose income rises substantially after admission to a Rent Supplement project is not required to leave it.

Congress passed the Rent Supplement program by the smallest of margins in 1965 and has since limited its implementation in a number of ways. The program has received few appropriations; in fact it has barely survived attacks during the appropriations stage. To mollify Congressional pressures HUD has been forced to impose regulations on the program which have made it increasingly unworkable. One regulation requires that in no instance may a tenant receive a supplement which exceeds 70 percent of the fair market rental of the unit. Other regulations which have proved to be very damaging to the program establish specific dollar limits on construction costs and on maximum fair market rentals. These low maximums inhibit production and force those who do build to produce rather austere projects. Still other regulations flatly prohibit even some of the limited amenities allowed in 221(d)(3) BMIR projects. . . .

The basic rent supplement approach, emphasizing flexible subsidies as well as private ownership, private financing, and private management, has many advantages. As Table 2 illustrates, this program can reach rather low income levels. If Congressional limits were removed, this program could serve the full range of families in need and could be used effectively by private business.

SECTION 236 RENTAL HOUSING PROGRAM

The new 236 program, part of the Housing Act of 1968, is designed to replace eventually both the 202 and 221(d)(3) programs. Like the Rent Supplement program, it relies on private developers—both nonprofit and profit-oriented—or rental or cooperative housing. The subsidy technique is similar to that used in the Rent Supplement program: tenants pay 25 percent of their income toward rent, and the Federal Government pays a supplement which makes up the difference between a tenant's payment and market rents. There is, however, a crucial difference. The maximum Federal payment on a unit lowers the rent to the level which would be achieved had the project been financed with a 1 percent mortgage. Thus, the primary difference between 236 and the Rent Supplement program is that the subsidy under 236 is not as deep.

The maximum Federal subsidy to a tenant per month will be about $50 to $60. This is not enough to reach the poorest families. To be eligible, a family's income (less $300 per child) must not exceed 135 percent of the limits for admission to Public Housing projects. Thus, 236 will serve primarily families whose incomes range between $4,000 and $6,500 per year. Table 2 indicates that in high cost areas, such as Detroit, tenant incomes must be higher unless families chose to allocate more than 25 percent of gross income to housing. To alleviate this problem partially, 20 percent of the units of a 236 project can be occupied by tenants receiving Rent Supplement payments and who thus might have lower incomes. . . .

HOMEOWNERSHIP PROGRAM— SECTION 235

The Homeownership program contained in the Housing Act of 1968 is a major landmark in the history of Federal housing legislation. Prior to its enactment, all major housing subsidy programs were limited to rental units, with cooperative housing units permitted in a few instances.

Assistance under the new Homeownership program generally will be restricted to new or substantially rehabilitated units. Private homebuilders will plan the housing and have it approved by FHA for inclusion in the program prior to the beginning of construction. When built, the houses will be sold to eligible buyers who will finance their purchases with FHA-insured market rate mortgages from private lenders. The subsidy technique used is similar to that in the Section 236 rental program. The Federal Government contracts to pay part of the homebuyer's mortgage payments. The maximum Govern-

ment subsidy reduces the homebuyer's payment to that which he would owe if his purchase had been financed with a mortgage bearing an interest rate of 1 percent. Translated into dollars, the maximum subsidy will be about $40 to $70 a month, depending on the value of the house and the market interest rate. The actual amount of the subsidy may be somewhat less, depending on the income of the family buying the house. All families must devote at least 20 percent of their income to paying off the mortgage. (This figure of 20 percent is lower than the 25 percent used under the rental programs because the homebuyer must bear all utility charges, maintenance, and repair expenses himself.) As family income rises, the Federal payments due to the lender consequently will be gradually reduced and eventually eliminated. Because the maximum Federal subsidy is limited, the program will not be of much help to families with very low incomes. However, it will provide assistance to those in the broad range of incomes between $3,000 and $7,000 a year. . . .

This brief description of the major Federal housing programs reveals that a striking acceleration in the innovation of new programs has occurred in the last decade and particularly in the last five years. Even the conventional Public Housing program, the only Federal housing subsidy program in existence between 1937 and 1959, has been rejuvenated with recent innovations. The basic trends in policy developments are:

—Increased reliance on private development, private financing, private ownership, and private management of subsidized housing;

—Greater subsidization of homeownership (and membership in cooperatives or condominiums) and less exclusive emphasis on rental buildings;

—Less reliance on low interest loans and greater reliance on periodic Federal subsidies;

—Less emphasis on particularized programs . . . in favor of broadly applicable programs; and

—More emphasis on subsidy programs for families somewhat above the very lowest income levels.

URBAN HOUSING: OLD POLICIES AND NEW REALITIES

Bernard J. Frieden

The following selection provides an excellent general perspective on the performance of the private housing market. Although not a radical himself, Frieden summarizes the essential dynamics of the turnover process in the housing market and questions its capacity to provide suitable low-cost housing for the poor.

The selection is part of a longer article by Frieden, called "Housing and National Urban Goals: Old Policies and New Realities," which appeared in James Q. Wilson, ed., *The Metropolitan Enigma,* published in hard cover in 1968 and in paperback in 1970. Frieden revised his article slightly for the later paperback edition; this selection incorporates the revisions. In the longer original article, this selection was preceded by a section on housing goals and housing trends during the 1950's, and followed by a section on "diversifying housing strategies."

Frieden is professor of city planning at MIT and a member of the Harvard-MIT Joint Center for Urban Studies. He has written *The Future of Old Neighborhoods* (1964) and numerous articles.

The experience of the 1950's shows considerable progress in improving housing welfare in the United States, but the performance of the housing market was unimpressive in some important respects. In urban areas, the improvement that did take place was not sufficient to cope with the growing numbers of black families, and in the country at large an increasing number of families at all economic levels were forced to spend more than a reasonable share of their income for rent in order to better their housing conditions. Despite these qualifications, the trends of the 1950's have provided grounds for optimism about the future. William Grigsby has concluded his careful study of changes in the 1950's with a prediction that substandard housing in the United States will be eliminated by 1980.[1]

SOURCE: *Bernard J. Frieden, "Housing and National Urban Goals: Old Policies and New Realities," from The Metropolitan Enigma. Reprinted by permission of the publishers from James Q. Wilson, ed.,* The Metropolitan Enigma, *Cambridge, Mass.: Harvard University Press. Copyright © 1968 by the President and Fellows of Harvard College; 1967 by The Chamber of Commerce of the United States of America.*

[1] William Grigsby, *Housing Markets and Public Policy* (Philadelphia: University of Pennsylvania Press, 1963), p. 322.

Frank Kristof, in the study of New York City . . . indicates that New York's housing needs can be met within the normal functioning of the housing market (including the continued use of public policy in support of this goal) by 1980.[2] In a subsequent study for the National Commission on Urban Problems (Douglas Commission), Kristof applied the same concept of housing needs to the country at large and concluded that the rate of progress of the 1950's has continued into the early 1960's and can reasonably be expected to continue in the decades ahead. Kristof's projections, which assume no significant increase in the federal role in housing, show a steady reduction from 20.5 million units needed in 1950 (to replace substandard housing, end overcrowding, and provide a 5 percent vacancy reserve of sound housing) to 5.7 million units needed by 1990.[3]

If these expectations are reasonable, they still pose the question of whether reaching

[2] Frank S. Kristof, "Housing Policy Goals and the Turnover of Housing," *Journal of the American Institute of Planners,* 31 (August, 1965).

[3] Frank S. Kristof, *Urban Housing Needs Through the 1980's: An Analysis and Projection* (Washington: National Commission on Urban Problems, Research Report No. 10, 1968).

the national housing goal by the 1980's is an acceptable rate of progress. There is widespread dissatisfaction with housing conditions now, particularly among Negroes and low-income groups. The prospect of waiting another twenty years to reach the goal of the Housing Act of 1949 will not evoke great enthusiasm in the slums. Further, the definition of substandard housing that enters into these projections is a minimal one, based on Census categories that do not include such factors as central heating, adequacy of light and air, blighted surroundings, or violations of local housing codes. In addition, our notion of what constitutes acceptable housing will continue to reflect constantly rising expectations. By the 1980's, much of the old housing that meets today's concept of minimum standards will be considered obsolete in size, layout, or appearance. In this sense, postponing the replacement of today's inadequate housing until then means that large numbers of people will continue indefinitely to live in conditions that they and the rest of society consider unacceptable.

Whether the rate of housing improvement can be accelerated depends upon many circumstances, including some that are independent of housing policies. The close connection between low incomes and inadequate housing has already been stressed. The elimination of poverty in the United States would go a long way toward eliminating substandard living conditions. Short of this goal, rising incomes for those who are now poor will be essential to maintain—if not increase—the rate of progress that was achieved in the 1950's. But aside from a general growth of income or the provision of a guaranteed annual income, the operation of the housing market will have much to do with future rates of improvement. The market mechanisms that contributed to improvement in the 1950's will not necessarily operate the same way in the future. A closer look at the components of housing change is helpful in assessing future prospects.

A high volume of new housing construction has been one of the main forces of improvement. Total housing production between 1950 and 1959 (excluding farm units) averaged slightly more than 1.5 million units started per year.[4] This new construction more

than kept pace with population growth, and triggered a series of changes in the rest of the housing supply. Two thirds of the new home building took place inside metropolitan areas, mostly in the suburbs. Millions of middle-income families moved from the central cities to new suburban developments, leaving behind a large stock of vacant housing. These vacancies freed the tight housing situation of the late 1940's and made it possible for other families to move out of crowded or unsatisfactory quarters. The turnover of existing housing was sufficient to provide living space for new migrants arriving in the cities as well as older city residents and newly formed families. In most large cities, the movement out to suburbia was greater than population growth resulting from migration plus natural increase. With this decline of central city population, crowding was eased considerably in the dense slum neighborhoods. Crowding was also reduced within the dwelling units: large households, in which grown children lived together with their parents and other relatives, split up to live in separate quarters. Since the population pressure was easing, many small units were merged to form larger apartments. Each wave of movement freed some housing that became available to others. Accompanying this turnover of housing was the impressive amount of renovation noted earlier. Housing that formerly lacked plumbing facilities or bathrooms or needed repairs was put in sound condition.

The indirect effects set in motion by new construction emerged very clearly from a pilot study of housing turnover in New York City.[5] In the study sample, 64 new units gave rise to a chain of turnover involving 90 additional units. At each successive link in the chain, families with lower incomes moved into turnover units, improving the space or quality of their housing and in a few cases moving from a substandard to a standard unit. Most families increased their rent bill as a result of the move, though the new median rent generally remained about one fifth of family income. This turnover process is not necessarily the same as "filtering," a concept that implies a drop in the cost of old housing as a result of vacancies triggered by new construction. Nevertheless, the turnover

[4] U.S. Department of Commerce, *Construction Statistics, 1915–1964* (Washington: Government Printing Office, 1966), pp. 17–18.

[5] Frank S. Kristof, "Housing Policy Goals," pp. 241–242.

of existing housing is a means of supplying additional sound housing for income groups unable to afford the price of new construction. Turnover can involve higher rent-income ratios for the movers, as indicated in the New York study and in the national data cited earlier. The widespread effectiveness of the turnover process in providing sound housing for lower-income groups can be seen in the fact that even at the lowest income levels in 1960 . . . , a majority of families were living in standard housing.

Turnover is thus the basic process by which low-income groups improve their housing in the cities. It also has special significance as the way in which Negroes find places to live. Between 1950 and 1960, the nonwhite population grew from 9 million to 13.2 million in metropolitan areas, with more than 80 percent of this increase occurring in the central cities. Living space for this growing population came almost entirely from older housing formerly occupied by white people. Only a small proportion of Negroes who need housing manage to buy or rent new housing, or move into newly built public housing. Between 1950 and 1959, almost a million metropolitan housing units went from white to nonwhite occupancy; fewer than 100,000 went from non-white to white occupancy during the same period. Thus in 1959, as many as 30 percent of all nonwhite families in metropolitan areas were living in housing where white families had lived in 1950.[6]

Successful operation of the turnover process depends upon three major factors: a high volume of new construction, a low volume of demolition of existing units, and adequate maintenance and upgrading of older housing. During the 1950's all these factors interacted to produce a substantial improvement in housing in urban areas and in the country at large. Within metropolitan areas, 9.8 million new units were built and only 1.0 million were lost through demolition and another 700,000 through such means as fire and flood; 1.8 million dwellings were upgraded from substandard to standard condition and 600,000 were downgraded from standard to substandard.[7]

These same components of housing

change do not look as promising for the late 1960's and beyond. An increased volume of new construction is needed to keep pace with population growth and mobility, to offset demolitions and losses at the 1950's rate, to continue progress in eliminating substandard and overcrowded conditions, and to allow for a reasonable vacancy reserve. Current estimates, prepared by both governmental and private studies, are that at least 2 million new units per year are needed now and 2.5 million within a few years.[8] Actual production remained at about 1.5 million units a year through 1965 but dropped to 1.2 million in 1966 and has remained at this level through most of 1967. Further, the rate of housing demolition in urban areas will increase substantially in the late 1960's and 1970's. The acceleration of urban renewal and of highway construction alone is expected to result in 100,000 demolitions a year, mostly in urban areas.[9] The total effect may be to double the yearly demolition of 100,000 units in metropolitan areas in the 1950's, when urban renewal and federally aided highway construction were just getting under way. Nor is demolition limited to substandard housing: in the 1950's, more than 40 percent of the units demolished in metropolitan areas were in sound condition with all plumbing facilities.

The third major component—renovation of substandard housing—is more difficult to anticipate. Home repairs and improvements constitute a major industry in the United States. By 1967, outlays for maintenance, repairs, and replacements approached $11 billion per year.[10] We do not know, how-

[6] U.S. Census of Housing: 1960, vol. IV, Components of Inventory Change, Final Report HC(4), pt. 1A-1, table 2.
[7] Ibid., pp. 21–24.

[8] U.S. Congress, House, Committee on Banking and Currency, Subcommittee on Housing, Hearings, Demonstration Cities, Housing and Urban Development, and Urban Mass Transit, 89th Cong., 2nd sess., 1966, pp. 66, 246; U.S. National Commission on Technology, Automation, and Economic Progress, Technology and the American Economy, vol. 1 (Washington: Government Printing Office, 1966), p. 87; Charles Abrams, The City Is the Frontier (New York: Harper and Row, 1965), p. 277.
[9] U.S. Congress, House, Study of Compensation and Assistance for Persons Affected by Real Property Acquisition in Federal and Federally Assisted Programs, printed for use of the Committee on Public Works, 88th Cong., 2nd sess., 1964, p. 258; Alvin L. Schorr, Slums and Social Insecurity, p. 61.
[10] U.S. Department of Housing and Urban Development, Housing and Urban Development Trends, 22 (May 1969), p. 29.

ever, what proportion of the total is spent on improving substandard housing. Almost two thirds of the expenditures were for owner-occupied single-family houses,[11] and a large part of the remainder was undoubtedly for maintaining and improving rental housing already in sound condition. There is some evidence to suggest that the high rate of renovation in the 1950's has already taken care of many of the easy jobs and that property owners will be slower to renovate the remaining substandard housing that is in poorer condition.[12] One careful analysis of the hardcore slums of Newark, New Jersey, has found disturbing signs that most slum owners have little interest in property improvements, regardless of market conditions, tax policies, or the availability of financing. When the demand for tenement apartments is very strong, the landlord sees no need to improve his property; when the demand is weak, he does not improve because he fears for his investment.[13]

Thus the current outlook is for a slowing of the rate of housing improvement that occurred in the 1950's. In the 1950's, we built more than enough new housing to keep pace with new household formation, we demolished relatively little old housing, and we renovated a large number of substandard units. In the 1960's, new construction appears to be falling behind the needs created by urban population growth and housing losses, the volume of demolition is increasing, and the prospects for maintaining a high level of renovation are uncertain.

PROBLEMS WITH THE TURNOVER PROCESS

Among possible strategies for meeting the national housing goal, one approach would be to accelerate the forces that operated successfully in the 1950's. Policies could aim at stimulating a higher volume of new construction, more rapid turnover of existing units, and greater investment in maintenance and renovation of low-cost housing. But exclusive reliance on this turnover process creates other problems and leads to some bewildering dilemmas for public policy.

Urban growth in the United States has been pushing outward from the core of the central city, with new housing added in a series of rings wrapping around the central city and encompassing more and more suburban territory. Each ring of development tends to contain housing built at about the same time. Thus the old housing that middle-income families will abandon when they move to new quarters is generally concentrated in the inner part of the metropolitan area. Some years ago, these areas of declining middle-class occupancy constituted only a small part of the central city just beyond the downtown business district. By the 1950's, with more housing considered obsolescent, and with a larger number of middle-income people able to move to newer housing, the area of declining middle-class occupancy blanketed very large parts of the central cities and even a number of the oldest suburbs just beyond the city boundary. With low-income people relying almost entirely on older housing abandoned by more affluent groups, it was inevitable that the economic and racial composition of the central cities and some adjoining suburbs would undergo drastic changes.

As a result, the same process that brought about a striking improvement in national housing conditions yielded a plentiful harvest of acute social and economic problems in the central cities. The combination of new suburban development and housing turnover in the older cities led to a massive dispersal of the population along racial and economic lines. By the late 1950's, the suburbs had succeeded in attracting a concentration of white, young, middle- and upper-income families with children and the central cities were left with higher proportions of the elderly, broken families, Negroes, low-income workers, and the unemployed. These social and economic disparities between central cities and suburbs do not hold true throughout the country, but they do apply to virtually all the large metropolitan areas and to urban areas of all sizes in the Northeast.[14]

The consequences have been severe, both for the people involved and for city govern-

[11] *Ibid.,* p. 30.
[12] William Grigsby, *Housing Markets,* p. 269.
[13] George Sternlieb, *The Tenement Landlord* (New Brunswick, N.J.: Rutgers-The State University, Urban Studies Center, 1966).

[14] For documentation and analysis of central city-suburban differences, see U.S. Advisory Commission on Intergovernmental Relations, *Metropolitan Social and Economic Disparities: Implications for Intergovernmental Relations in Central Cities and Suburbs* (Washington, D.C.: ACIR, 1965).

ments. One result has been a growing social and cultural isolation of the poor from the rest of society. In neighborhoods where the poor are concentrated, models of success are few and unemployment among youth is sometimes so prevalent that it becomes the normal pattern. It is difficult to judge just how significant this type of isolation is for the poor, and social science evidence is by no means definitive. Other effects of the same social separation are more direct. Workers in the central cities are increasingly cut off from blue-collar jobs in expanding suburban industrial centers, and manufacturing and related lines of employment continue to decline in the central cities. Transportation is difficult to the new industrial parks, and central city workers are not sufficiently in touch with suburban firms to learn about job opportunities.

For Negroes, these problems are intensified. Even many of those who can afford to move to new housing in suburbia are blocked by discrimination or hostility and are forced to stay in central city ghettos. One recent analysis of 1960 data makes it clear that white families with low and moderate incomes are finding their way to the suburbs, but black families in the same income brackets are not. Richard Langendorf carried out calculations for eleven large metropolitan areas to test where Negro families would be living if, at every income level, an identical proportion of Negroes and whites were homeowners and an identical proportion of Negroes and whites in both homeowner and tenant categories lived in the suburbs. Under these assumptions, which imply that household income is the key determinant of where people live, the proportion of Negroes in the suburbs would increase substantially. For all eleven areas combined, 16 percent of nonwhites actually lived in the suburbs in 1960; under the new assumptions this figure would rise to 40 percent. The number of suburban nonwhites in New York, Los Angeles, Pittsburgh, and St. Louis would double; in Washington and Baltimore it would more than triple; in Detroit it would increase four times; and in Cleveland it would increase about twenty times.[15]

Where people live has much to do with

the quality of public services available to them, and this connection leads to one of the most fundamental problems posed by current urban development: the gap between local needs and local resources. Disadvantaged groups in the central cities are highly dependent upon public services. They need a variety of educational programs for both children and adults; they have special needs for health and welfare assistance, recreation facilities, and police and fire protection. Central cities face high service demands, but many of their prosperous taxpayers have left and their commerce and industry are also moving to the suburbs. The cities have been struggling to cope with this gap between service needs and local tax resources. One strategy has been to press for greater state and federal assistance; the recent proliferation of federal aid programs for the cities is a direct consequence. Another typical city strategy has been to develop urban renewal programs intended to win back (or hold onto) middle-income families, retail stores, and industrial firms. Despite the increase in federal aid and the more limited effects of renewal programs, public services in the cities have had to be held far below the levels that are needed to enable disadvantaged groups to compete with others on equal terms.

In this sense, it is fair to say that our solution to the national housing problem has been creating a national urban problem. Federal housing policies seem to be at odds with other federal objectives. Some programs—chiefly FHA mortgage insurance, federal aid for highways that facilitate suburban growth, and aid for suburban water and sewer systems—accelerate the pace of new housing construction in the suburbs and the turnover of central city housing. Others—principally urban renewal and aid for mass transit—aim at reviving the central cities and stemming the flight to the suburbs. Urban renewal in turn depletes the supply of low-cost housing and thus slows the turnover effects stimulated by national housing policy. The programs that favor suburban growth promote population dispersal along racial and economic lines, setting the stage for race segregation between central cities and suburbs, which runs counter to civil rights goals. This same dispersal handicaps the central cities in their efforts to provide adequate services for low-income groups, countering other na-

[15] Richard Langendorf, "Residential Desegregation Potential," *Journal of the American Institute of Planners*, 35 (March, 1969), pp. 90–95.

tional goals of eliminating poverty and providing equality of educational opportunity.

Continued dependence upon the turnover process to accommodate low-income groups is also producing open social and racial conflict in many central city neighborhoods. In the 1950's, the growing black population of the central cities was able to take over a great deal of housing left behind by mobile white families who chose to move to suburbs. Even in the 1950's, however, this turnover process failed to reduce the number of urban Negro families living in substandard and overcrowded housing. The continued growth of Negro population in the cities means that many Negro families have nowhere to go but into whatever vacancies turn up in white areas. But as the more mobile white families have departed, a core of deeply rooted people have remained in old neighborhoods—people who cannot afford to move to the suburbs or who want to stay where they are. Many established ethnic neighborhoods remain in the central cities, where people are tied to friends, family, churches, clubs, and other loyalties that develop in a close-knit community. Often they are fearful of invasions by Negroes or other newcomers. Some neighborhoods have tried to stabilize the situation by supporting urban renewal programs designed to remove pockets of low-cost housing and price out potential invaders. Others express their fears in a white backlash reaction, with open hostility to Negro newcomers and the threat of violence just below the surface.

The time has come to diversify our mechanisms for meeting the housing needs of low-income groups. The turnover system is working, but it is producing too many objectionable by-products. These by-products in turn have generated new policies that will interfere with the future turnover of old housing. In particular, many central cities have found their changing population composition unacceptable and have developed urban renewal programs to stabilize existing neighborhoods or to attract back middle-income families—both of which will sacrifice low-income housing needs in order to diversify the city's population.[16]

Still another reason for supplementing the turnover process with other approaches lies in the nature of national housing goals. The goal of a decent home and a suitable environment for every family is too limited for the needs of urban life today. In our spreading metropolitan areas, mobility is a prerequisite for equal opportunity. Families need to be able to move to keep up with changing work locations, to have access to specialized services or institutions, and to have some measure of freedom in choosing a desired type of housing or type of community. Most middle-income families now enjoy this freedom of movement through the operation of the housing market, though many middle-income Negroes still do not. Most low-income families have very limited freedom of movement: the turnover process restricts their choice to areas where old housing is concentrated. A more adequate statement of national housing goals would go beyond decent shelter and surroundings, and would include diversity of choice in housing and freedom of movement throughout metropolitan areas. New strategies are needed to achieve this more complex goal.[17]

[16] See Bernard J. Frieden, "Toward Equality of Urban Opportunity," *Journal of the American Institute of Planners*, 31 (November 1965), 320–330.
[17] See *ibid.*

NEW HOMES AND POOR PEOPLE

John Lansing, Charles Wade Clifton, and James N. Morgan

The following selection is the concluding chapter of a book which studies
the real effects of the "turnover" process. Through survey techniques, the
authors trace the effectiveness of new housing construction in "trickling down"
to improved housing for the poor. Though the authors are not radical, they
support the fundamental radical criticism of the efficacy of the private market
in providing standard housing for the poor, providing empirical evidence
for some of the general conclusions in Frieden's article above. In particular,
the authors conclude from their surveys that new construction does open
up some new housing for some white poor, but that blacks benefit much less.

Their conclusions are especially important because many experts are
tending to place increasing weight on the construction of new housing and
the "turnover" process as a general solution for the housing problems of the
poor. In a recent article, Irving H. Welfeld presented a strong statement
of this case ("Toward a New Federal Housing Policy," *The Public Interest*,
Spring, 1970). Welfeld argued that direct construction of new housing for
the poor was too costly and too politically unpopular. Relying on the
effectiveness of the "turnover" process, he urged that "the question of housing
production must be divorced from the question of housing assistance to low
income families." On the one hand, he said, the government should provide
subsidies to increase the rate of construction of middle-income units. On
the other hand, the government should increase income subsidies to poor
families to allow them to move into units trickling down from the older
middle-income market. He concluded: "The effect, hopefully, would be to
increase housing turnover and thereby free a sizeable portion of the existing
housing stock for (subsidized) poor families."

The conclusions of the following selection should induce some skepticism
about the potential for this approach. The authors are associated with the
Survey Research Center at the University of Michigan.

The purpose of this project has been to
trace the indirect effects of the construction
of new homes. These indirect consequences
are of interest from an analytic point of view
for understanding of the working of the housing market, and from a policy point of view
for assessing the probable effect on the housing of the poor of measures which affect the
total market for housing but do not directly
affect poor families.

Do the poor benefit from new construction? It is proposed here that they benefit
either if they move into new housing or if
they occupy any positions in the sequences

of moves begun by new construction. If they
move, they benefit! This view is consistent
with the conventional economic argument
that people voluntarily enter into a transaction only if they expect to be better off as a
result. The survey data confirm that most
people who move do like their new housing
better. . . . Even people who do not like
their new quarters may benefit by being in
an improved location, for example, closer to
employment.

How many poor people benefit from new
construction in a given period, then, depends
on the volume of new construction, the length
of the sequences of moves begun by the
new construction, and the proportion who
are poor at each position in the sequences.
There are well-known statistical series on the
volume of new construction. This project was

SOURCE: *John Lansing, Charles Wade Clifton,
and James N. Morgan, New Homes and Poor
People. Used by permission of Survey Research
Center, Institute for Social Research, the University of Michigan.*

designed to yield estimates of the other two magnitudes. There has been some difficulty in estimating the average length of the sequences of moves owing to the problem of non-response in interviewing. The longer a sequence, the greater the probability that it will not be followed to its logical end. Also, some dwellings may be left vacant indefinitely before they are finally re-occupied or removed from the stock of housing. As a result of these factors the survey result is subject to some margin of uncertainty, but the most reasonable estimate of the average length of sequences of moves works out to 3.5 positions. That is, on the average for every 1000 new homes about 3500 families are able to move. This estimate cannot be checked directly against any non-survey estimate of the same magnitude. It is reasonable, however, in the light of what is known about the total number of families in the population who move in any one year and the total number of events which initiate sequences of moves, including, in addition to new construction, deaths and other factors which cause vacancies.

The proportion of families who are poor at each position in the sequences of moves is here estimated at .04 at position one, .06 at position two, and .14 at positions three, four, etc. Combining this information with the information on the length of sequences, we have an estimate that about 333 people will be poor out of the 3545 people who move as a result of the construction of 1000 new dwellings. That is, about 9.4 percent of the movers will be poor. The definition of poverty used here is that a family is poor if its income is less than $1000 plus $500 per capita for each member of the family.

Another approach to the definition of poverty is to count as poor all families below $3000 in 1965 income. In the metropolitan areas included in this study 13 percent of all families had incomes below $3000. At positions three and above in the sequences of moves about 14 percent or more of the families had incomes below $3000.

These results indicate that poor people do benefit indirectly from new construction. We can be even more optimistic when we note that roughly half of all sequences of moves are initiated by deaths, the subdivision of existing structures, emigration, and the like. Poor people presumably benefit also from these sequences. Indeed, since new dwellings are ordinarily expensive one would expect the poor to occupy a larger proportion of the positions in sequences of moves otherwise initiated.

We should not conclude from this analysis that the poor are well-provided (or ill-provided) with housing. Nor should we conclude that the price of housing is or is not reasonable. We *can* conclude that the poor are indirectly affected by the construction of new housing even if they do not occupy the new dwellings.

This conclusion, however, applies to the poor collectively. It is necessary to ask a further question: is the housing market segmented? If it is segmented, then there may be parts of the population who benefit from new construction less than in proportion to their numbers.

The housing market, one might suggest, may be segmented by age or stage in the family life cycle. It is certainly true that housing appropriate for a very small family is not appropriate for a very large one. But the evidence in this study is that people of quite different stages in the life cycle often succeed each other in the same housing unit. In view of that fact, it is hard to see how housing could be scarce for one age group and plentiful for another. To put the same point in a different way, quarters which differ in number of rooms must be quite close substitutes.

One might also suggest that the housing market is segmented by social status. If the education of the head of a family is taken as a proxy for its status, the evidence is that housing shifts frequently from people of one status level to people of another.

Segregation by race, however, is another matter. It is well known that the income of Negroes is less than that of whites. The question at issue is whether Negroes are disadvantaged in the housing market to a greater extent than is implied by their lower incomes. The evidence is that they are indeed disadvantaged.

First, it may be asked, do Negroes move into new homes in the same proportion that one would expect on the basis of their incomes? The finding is that they do not. In fact, Negroes comprise about six-tenths of the number of occupants of new dwellings which one would predict on the basis of their incomes.

Second, Negroes in the low income group

can benefit from new construction if they are able to move into a home which has been left vacant by a white family. "Trickle-down" can work if property changes from Negro to white occupancy. Such transitions do occur, but they are infrequent.

The result of these two factors is that Negroes do not benefit from new construction to the extent that their incomes would lead one to expect. We estimate that the proportion which Negroes represent of families in the sequences of moves begun by new construction is about .70 of what would be predicted on the basis of the incomes of all families in the sequences and the proportion which Negroes form of each income group in the metropolitan areas being studied.

We cannot attribute to racial discrimination the difference between .70 and 1.00. Negroes are at an economic disadvantage because of their low assets as well as their low incomes. The extent of their disadvantage in assets is indicated by the fact that their average net worth is less than a fifth of that for the population as a whole. Young Negro families are likely to be unable to obtain gifts or loans from their parents to finance the down payment on a home as well as limited in their own resources. We have not attempted to separate this factor from direct racial discrimination in housing.

The findings about Negroes have various implications which may be suggested although they are not developed here systematically. They have geographical implications. New homes tend to be built on the edges of urban areas, so that the oldest part of the housing stock is near the center and the newer parts are located at increasing distances from the center. One would expect low income groups to occupy the older part of the housing supply near the center and to move outward both as their economic position improves and as the supply of housing ages. For Negroes this process seems to work imperfectly. It has implications for the supply of housing available to members of low-income groups who are not subject to the same disadvantages as Negroes in the housing market. To the extent that Negroes are kept out of the market for aging housing the supply of aging houses available to others is larger than it would be otherwise.

Throughout this report we have stressed the problems of the housing of the poor. The same data can also be used to consider the importance of sequences of moves for people in the moderate income group, say, $3,000 to $6,000. The conclusion that poor people benefit indirectly from new construction applies even more strongly to those of moderate income. Those in this group made up about 19 percent of all families in the metropolitan areas studied in 1965. Although they were only 17 percent of those at position one in the sequences, they were three out of ten of those at positions two and above.

In brief, the results of the study lead to two main conclusions concerning housing policy. First, as far as low income whites are concerned, any policy which increases the total supply of housing will be beneficial. The working of the market for housing is such that the poor will benefit from any actions which increase the supply in the total market. There is a natural tendency for someone who is concerned with the provision of housing for the poor to take a direct approach. To provide housing for people, hand them the key to the door of a home! The evidence in this research is that the direct approach is not the only approach which will be effective. The housing market (for whites) operates as a single market. Any policy which shifts either the demand curve or the supply curve in the market will affect the price in the total market.

Second, Negroes are in what amounts to a partially separate market. Measures which influence the housing market as a whole, and in particular, measures which increase the supply of housing in the market as a whole, influence the market for housing for Negroes only in an attenuated form. The provision of housing for Negroes at the level which their present incomes justify will require either direct provision of more new housing units for Negro occupancy or measures which facilitate the transition of existing houses from white to Negro occupancy. It is not possible as matters now stand to rely on the sequences of moves resulting from new construction for the provision of housing for the Negro poor.

We have not attempted in this study to review the choices of policy which have been proposed or tried as methods of improving the supply of housing to the poor. Such a review has been undertaken recently by Rothenberg.[1] It seems to be recognized in-

[1] Jerome Rothenberg, *Economic Evaluation of Urban Renewal*, Brookings, 1967.

creasingly that no single method is sufficient: a mix of programs is needed. It may be helpful, however, to state here explicitly some of the implications of this research for policies now being developed and applied.

One group of policies is intended to influence the supply of housing. One approach is to offer long-term loans at below market rates of interest. While interest rates are no doubt important, for many low-income people, and especially Negroes, a major obstacle to becoming home owners is the down payment requirements even when incomes may be adequate to cover monthly payments.

A second group of policies is intended to influence demand. Two methods are urged: programs to provide money which is earmarked for housing, as in rental allowances, and general subsidies to the poor, as in the negative income tax. This research shows that for Negroes these policies in themselves will not be adequate. Negroes are at a substantial disadvantage in the housing market in addition to that which results from low income.

THE TENEMENT LANDLORD

George Sternlieb

This selection is the concluding chapter of Sternlieb's book by the same title. In it, he summarizes the evidence of his surveys of Newark slum housing. He concludes especially that resident ownership plays a critical role in the maintenance of decent housing. Houses owned by absentee landlords were uniformly in worse condition than those owned by community residents. His conclusions have important implications for the recent tendency of public policy toward increasing subsidy to large corporations for low-cost housing construction. Large corporations will be more "absentee" than anyone.

Sternlieb is a professor of city planning at Rutgers, and recently completed a large study of the effects of rent control on housing in New York.

The entangled mesh of ownership patterns, of changes in the form and function of the older city and the folkways of its inhabitants, the great migration patterns which have dominated the demographic considerations in and about the United States metropolitan areas, the rising standards of expectation, all provide the matrix within which the data presented in our earlier chapters have taken form. Any efforts at improving attitudes toward slum maintenance and rehabilitation must in turn take this matrix into account, or prove unsuccessful.

The present market situation is one of virtual stagnation in the hard-core slum areas. The combination of risk, decreasing profitability, and loss of potential for capital gains has substantially restricted the kinds of pro-

SOURCE: *George Sternlieb*, The Tenement Landlord (*Rutgers University Press, 1966*).

fessional owners who are willing to invest in slum properties. It takes a highly insensitive individual to become a professional nonresident owner of slum property, in the light of present societal attitudes. This is not an individual who is easily influenced to invest his money unless an appropriate return can be secured. Given the relative weakness of the slum apartment market, a weakness which has been aided in Newark's case by substantial amounts of public housing, as well as the shifts out of the central city . . . , the professional landlord has been faced with the choice of basically two alternatives: to stand pat and not increase his investment, or to attempt to improve his parcel in order to secure higher rentals.

The pattern that was observed in the course of this study indicates that the choice substantially has been the former. The observer cannot fail to be struck by the "heads you win, tails we lose" nature of this phenomenon. When the apartment market is very strong the landlord need not improve; when the apartment market is very weak the landlord fears for his investment and does not improve. What can municipal authorities use to break this impasse? Code enforcement is the usual reply. Code enforcement, however, must be, as will be noted later in more detail, accompanied by financing help and tax reassurance. Without this accompaniment it will merely lead to wholesale evasion and corruption. Before pursuing these matters in more detail, it is essential that the basic question be resolved—what the city, as a reflection of society, is or should be doing with slums and their occupants.

WHAT IS, OR SHOULD BE, THE CITIES' ATTITUDE TOWARD SLUMS AND SLUM DWELLERS?

If this writer may be permitted a gross oversimplification, the problem of the slums is one both of plumbing and morale. It has largely been viewed in the past as consisting solely of plumbing. This is not to denigrate the former; but the provision of appropriate housing amenities is certainly an essential step toward improving the outlook and aspiration level of slum dwellers. However, the morale problem cannot be cured merely by providing physical amenities. The relatively limited success of public housing bears testimony on this point.

Government policy towards the slums must have as its primary aim the improvement of the aspiration level and capacity for goal realization of the slums' inhabitants. Tax policy, code enforcement, financing aid, and municipal services; all of these must be viewed within the context of the overall objective.

The community must face the realities of the slum situation fairly, without self-deception or romanticism, and at the same time move for change. A review of slum conditions as they exist is in order.

1. In Newark, as in many of other Northern industrial cities, the overwhelming majority of hard-core slum area residents are Negroes. The whites, who continue to decrease in number, are typically an elderly remnant of earlier immigration.

2. There is little evidence of a substantial return of the white middle class to the slum areas of the city.

3. A substantial proportion of slum tenements are owned by absentee white owners. These owners are not merely absentees from the slums per se, they are also absentees, at least as residents, from the city in which they own property.

4. The factor of ownership is the single most basic variable which accounts for variations in the maintenance of slum properties. Good parcel maintenance typically is a function of resident ownership.

5. Dependent upon major programs of land clearance for purposes of urban renewal and/or highway construction, a population vacuum will develop in the slums. The tidal wave of Southern Negro migration has slowed down and is substantially bypassing some of the Northern cities which were its traditional goals.[1] With virtual stability in the Puerto Rican population size, there is no new depressed group on the horizon to fill the older slums.

6. While this population decrease makes the problem of relocation much simpler, it also tends to limit the landlords' capacity and will to improve parcels.

7. Given a substantial dependence upon land taxes in the face of increased demands upon the municipality for services, taxes have become a major inhibitor of entrepreneurial activity in the central city. Both in terms of their impact, and in terms of the uncertainty which surround their administration, current municipal tax policies are leading to further degeneration of the slums.

8. The relationship of client and patron, which plays a dominant role in the dealings between government, both municipal and federal, and the poor population of the slums, is deleterious to the morale of the individuals concerned.

Within these parameters are there policies which would improve present slum conditions, both in terms of buildings and of people? Over the past year a whole armory of enabling legislation has been passed by

[1] The nonwhite population of the United States is continuing to leave the South, but the outflow has been slowed considerably. Out-migration of Negroes from the South has averaged little more than seventy thousand per year in the period from 1960 to 1963, or only half that of the 1950 to 1960 period. This is based on a study done by the Metropolitan Life Insurance Company, see MLIC, *Statistical Bulletin*, April 1965, p. 3.

Congress. Local authorities have been given the essential weapons for the fight against blight and for better housing conditions. The Housing and Urban Development Act of 1965 is indicative of the growing sophistication of government policies in rehabilitation. From a direct loan program, which provides long-term 3 percent loans, to the rehabilitation grant procedure under section 115 of Title I of the 1964 act, and to the demolition grant and aid to code enforcement divisions, a vast armory has been supplied to local authority.[2]

It should be stressed that the enabling legislation mentioned above is strictly that —enabling legislation. It remains for local authority to take the initiative in implementing programs which will take advantage of this legislation. There are certain to be many difficulties on the road to implementing this legislation. There is no new legislation that does not require some degree of experience in its utilization. Certainly, however, the community is better armed for rehabilitation than has ever before been the case.

The discussion which follows will focus first on the development of resident landlords, and the ancillary elements which this will require, such as guidance and financing arrangements, as well as tax policy. From this the discussion turns to the question of municipal services and the problem of the hard-core slum and code enforcement.

BOOSTING THE PROPORTION OF RESIDENT LANDLORDS IN SLUM TENEMENTS

. . . [T]here is no question of the significance of landlord residence, particularly of single-parcel landlords, as insurance of proper maintenance of slum tenements. Given the priority accorded by multiple-parcel owners to tenant problems as an inhibitor, . . . the lack of feeling on this score by resident landlords, coupled with their good record in maintenance, is most significant. It is the resident landlord, and only the resident landlord, who is in a position to properly screen and supervise his tenantry. No one-shot wave of maintenance and paint up–sweep up campaigns can provide the day-to-day maintenance which is required in slum areas.

[2] See H.H.F.A., Local Public Agency Letters 340, 341, 342, 343, 345, & 349 [Washington, 1965].

Given the relatively small size of Newark tenement units, and others like them, this can only be accomplished by a resident landlord. The record of these landlords, as we have indicated, is such as to inspire confidence in their future behavior on this score.

By making it feasible for more residents to become owners, we further encourage the development of local leadership which is so sorely lacking in most slums. The role of resident owners as guides and creators of life patterns for the youth of the slums to follow is clearly evident.[3]

How could this type of development be stimulated? There are several prime requirements. The first of these, obviously, is financing help. In Exhibit 1 is presented a table which indicates cash flow requirements as a function of mortgage term and interest rates. As can be noted in the Exhibit, the term of mortgages is much more significant from a cash flow point of view than are interest rates. For example, a mortgage at 6 percent which is written for a fifteen-year period imposes a smaller cash flow burden than an equivalent size mortgage for a ten-year period at 3.5 percent. Given the dearth of available financing, which is currently the case in the slums, there is obviously no alternative but to provide something in the way of long-term FHA guaranteed mortgages for slum tenement purchases by residents. The analogy with the early Homestead Act springs readily to mind. In that case, government lands were provided at relatively reasonable rates and with liberal financing to those who would live on them. The same thing must be done in the slums. The 1965 Housing Act is a beginning on the road.

With this must be coupled inexpensive fire and liability insurance for resident owners in slum areas. The expense and difficulty of securing these necessities is rising rapidly and it strikes hardest upon the poor landlord who has limited leverage with an underwriter.

Financing, however, is merely one of the several steps which is required. Earlier in this work reference was made to the storm window syndrome. This is merely one symptom of the frequent victimization of relatively

[3] Given the lack of a masculine image, which has been commented on as a not unfamiliar shortcoming of family upbringing among the poor, the significance of a resident owner peer unter pares to slum youth as a potential goal setter is clear-cut.

EXHIBIT 1
MONTHLY LEVEL PAYMENTS REQUIRED TO AMORTIZE $1,000
OVER VARIOUS TERMS AND AT VARIOUS INTEREST RATES

Interest Rate (Percent)	Term (in years)						
	10	15	20	25	30	35	40
6.0	$11.10	$8.44	$7.16	$6.44	$6.00	$5.70	$5.50
5.5	10.85	8.17	6.88	6.14	5.68	5.37	5.16
5.0	10.61	7.91	6.60	5.85	5.37	5.05	4.82
4.5	10.36	7.65	6.33	5.56	5.07	4.73	4.50
4.0	10.12	7.40	6.06	5.28	4.77	4.43	4.18
3.5	9.89	7.15	5.80	5.01	4.49	4.13	3.87

SOURCE: Ernest M. Fisher, *Urban Real Estate Markets: Characteristics and Financing* (N. Y. C.: National Bureau of Economic Research, 1951), p. 71.

innocent new resident buyers of slum tenements by a variety of home improvement services. The pride of these people in ownership makes them easy marks for "pay later" operators. The point raised by a money lender interviewed in the course of this study should be kept in sight here. He pointed to the fact that commonly when he has to repossess a parcel, the typical cause is that the owner has burdened the parcel with two or more home improvement loans. Just as the Agriculture Department provides a variety of advisory services for the farmer, so the city and/or the Federal Government must provide equivalent advisory services for the new home owner in the slum areas. These advisors must be competent not merely in home improvements, but also in financing and appraising parcels. It would seem entirely possible that among the ranks of senior savings and loan people, as well as within the ranks of the present FHA personnel, such individuals could be found. Technical competence, however, must be linked with a basic sympathy with the aspiration level of the new owner and with none of the *deus ex machina* attitude that so often exists in government relations with the poor.

The question of tax policy is a most significant one on this score, as it is in terms of the general problem of slums. It may well behoove the city to continue its policy of full assessment based upon market values. Obviously, where broad-based taxation is available on a basis other than land, it may reduce

some of the strain. Reassessment policy, however, must be more clearly defined than is presently the case. The landlord should have no reason to fear city reassessment merely because of painting the outside of his house.

It is essential that the city not merely adopt a more reasonable attitude toward taxation, but also *sell* the facts of this attitude to those who may be influenced by misconceptions as to its reality. In addition, in the long run it may very well pay the city to provide the equivalent of homestead rebates for resident landlords. This is a format (which will be recognized by those readers who are familiar, for example, with tax policy in a city such as Miami Beach) in which the homesteader, i.e. the resident landlord, receives either a reduction or a rebate in his real estate taxes. This might well be coupled with a stipulation that the rebate be employed in the improvement of the parcel in question. The area of uncertainty and suspicion which surrounds current taxing procedures must be clarified. Its existence clearly inhibits improvements. Once again the reader may wish to review the data presented in Chapter 11 [of *The Tenement Landlord*] which indicates the fears of landlords on municipal tax policy. *This fear has been justified frequently in fact because of the financial bind of a municipality dependent on realty taxes in the face of expanding needs and a static base. In these circumstances, pressure on the landlord's pocket is a constant. While, as has been indicated, tax relief in itself will not generate improvement—it is an essential step toward fostering it. Alternative means of financing municipal needs, therefore, must be found.*

MUNICIPAL SERVICES

There seems to be ample evidence that the level of municipal services required by the slum areas is higher than that required by nonslum equivalent areas. At the same time there is reason to believe that the actual delivery level of these services is reversed with poorer areas being slighted. The comments of a Negro owner on this subject are most apropos.

[Parcel #330 was purchased in 1935.] You know the neighborhood has really changed terribly since we moved in here. At first it was mostly German and Jewish, and the police in the city took care of things. No trucks parked overnight in the streets and no noise or anything like that. Now there is mostly Negro and they don't seem to come any more. If you complain they want to put you in jail.—Many of the owners here would like to stay, but the neighborhood is run down so that most of them sell just to get away. Since Negroes have become predominant, the city has allowed things that they would not allow when I just first moved here.

One should notice that the parcel was very well maintained. The owner commented that he was sure that continued municipal surveillance would have saved the neighborhood regardless of who moved in. The backyard of this parcel, which has a very handsome garden, looks out upon a sea of debris. The owners complain that they have had to screen their back porches to keep the rats out. Another Negro landlord made the following comment:

When I went to complain to the police department about overnight truck parking and teenage hoodlums on the block, the cops made me feel like a criminal. I was glad to go home and kind of hide myself behind the door.

These comments mirror attitudes which are most common among current resident landlords.

Every effort must be made by the city to provide an optimum level of services within the slums. Such functions as police protection, street lighting, parking restrictions, garbage collection, and a host of others could be named here. Not least among these is the question of educational facilities. While this is a subject whose depth is beyond the scope of this study, it cannot be omitted. Without substantial efforts on all of these fronts, the efforts at rehabilitating the slums must falter.

THE FUTURE OF THE HARD-CORE SLUM

As has been noted in the section on "Who Owns the Slums," there are clear-cut indications that new resident buyers are unwilling to move into an area which is as far gone as is Area 1. The dominance of large-scale absentee landlordism in that area is a tribute to the fact that they are the only landlords who are willing to invest in such problem situations. One can seriously question the potential of such an area for rehabilitation. Given the relatively loose housing market, which presently exists in center-city Newark, the bulldozer approach to such hard-core areas would seem to be the only answer. This should not wait upon redevelopers. The existence of such hard-core blight (it should be recalled that the area in question has less than 25 percent sound housing on the basis of the 1960 Census) can only serve to drag down the neighborhoods peripheral to it.

The loss of tax revenue to the municipality through this process of demolition must be accepted as surgery essential to preserve the surrounding areas from the spread of deep-seated blight. Obviously, the scale of this blight will require considerable discretion on the part of municipal authorities on the phasing and speed of demolition. Given the present functioning of the market, as has been indicated earlier, private enterprise cannot be depended on to remove buildings which are no longer usable. Again, new urban renewal legislation to ease this process was adopted in 1965; it must be vigorously utilized.

There is some question whether a change in tax policy to encourage demolition might not be in order. The needs of the city for more open space, the potential of already assembled and cleared substantial size tracts in encouraging further development, must be depended upon to generate future use for the areas in question. The maintenance of the hard-core blight areas, given the facts of alternative housing availability, cannot be justified upon tax income reasons alone.

CODE ENFORCEMENT

Parallel with all of the suggestions above is the requirement that code enforcement be made much more rigorous. But prior to this, there is required a much more adequate definition of just what the code should be. For example, the requirement of central heat is observed least in some of the better housing areas in Area 3. It is not uncommon, particularly among members of earlier immigrant groups, that cold-water flats with suitable decentralized heating facilities are preferred to those whose heat supply is subject to the administration of the landlord and of the vagaries of the heating system. *Adequate insect and rodent control, plumbing that works, paint, and general cleanliness may be much more significant to the inhabitants of a tenement both physically and spiritually than the existence of central heat or plaster walls.* Whether the studs used in a repair are 16 inches on center or are 20 inches on center may be completely irrevelant to a tenant. A building which is completely satisfactory on the basis of existing codes, may be completely unsatisfactory in terms of its effect upon its occupants.

Code enforcement, therefore, must require a much more subjective approach than has previously been the case. This is particularly the case with those buildings in the hands of landlords who cannot afford repairs. In these cases, it may be necessary to work out a long-term plan of rehabilitating the parcel in question, with major emphasis being given to the paint and cleanliness functions, those most easily encompassed by "sweat equity." Good maintenance and resident landlordism are much more significant than mechanical adherence to a mechanical code. With the legality of multiple housing codes clarified, the city has a new avenue of creative action.

The responsibility of social workers to appreciate the fact that the loose housing market does enable them to move their clients "up" into better quarters is clear, though far from universally acted on. At least one of the major owners interviewed for this study is upgrading his parcels for welfare tenants whose housing allowances have been "opened up" slightly and who have alert social workers as guides.

NO FALSE ROMANTICISM!

The self-help capacity of the poor is limited. Some resident landlords are elderly, others are uneducated, and some lack an appropriate aspiration level. The fact remains, however, that as a group, they are presently the best landlords in the slums, and provide probably the major hope for better maintenance in the future. It will require a talented and understanding guidance operation to help generate landlord enthusiasm while restraining over-expenditure. The problems here should not be underestimated. It is essential if this operation is to be truly successful, particularly from a morale standpoint, and also from the standpoint of securing *long-run* improvement, that the advisory service be a guide and an inspiration, not a directorate.

The present and future strains on the municipalities' budget, coupled with limited increases in revenue, will make it most difficult to pay for the services which are required. The alternative, however, of increasing degeneration is all too clear-cut. From a fiscal point of view, the program outlined above is a most burdensome one; this point should not be evaded. There is no other answer, however, from the city's point of view.

Tax policy must be directed toward aiding the good landlord, and penalizing those owners who do not properly maintain their properties. A tax policy based on sales value, as shown in Chapter 11, can easily have the reverse effect. The potential of homestead exemption, of rigorous code enforcement, and of self-help stimulating devices, must be rigorously exploited.

REHABILITATION AND RENT INCREASES

There is a well-founded fear on the part of the tenantry that rehabilitation leads to rent increases. This must be accepted as a fact of the market. Although tax policy can somewhat relieve this factor, particularly when coupled with more adequate financing, this fact should be faced. *The potential of rent subsidies for the underincomed with* which to pay better rents is quite clear here. *There is no substitute for this approach. This is not to underestimate the value of code enforcement—but rather to add a carrot to the stick. There is more positive achievement by making rehabilitation profitable than in attempting to secure it through punitive measures.* The reward in terms of the aspiration level and general morale of the slum dweller will, I think, outweigh the cost. This is particularly true when the cost/benefits are contrasted with those of institutionalized public housing.

The key to improving the slums from a "people" point of view is the creation of a resident responsible middle class within those areas—not a middle class which while physically in the area does not belong to it, as is the case with the efforts to create new middle class housing within slum areas cleared by urban renewal. This has no organic unity with the tenements per se, and can only provide frustration rather than leadership and emulation. These goals can best be accomplished and living conditions within the slum areas most enhanced by increasing the number of owner residents of slum tenements. This will require a highly coordinated effort in terms of tax policy, financing help, code enforcement, and advisory services. The rewards of a succesful program are very great. The costs of present policies are equally evident.

PUBLIC HOUSING AND THE POOR

Lawrence M. Friedman

The following discussion provides a critically important historical perspective on the federal public housing program. The program has been generally abandoned and has failed to provide very much housing for the poor, as Friedman notes, because it was never intended to serve the housing needs of the poor. Given this history, it seems much more difficult to argue that public housing has failed to meet an objective it never intended to achieve.

The selection represents the first portion of a longer article, "Public Housing and the Poor: An Overview." Friedman is a professor of law at the University of Wisconsin Law School.

Public housing became a reality in the United States only in the days of the New Deal.[*] There were some gingerly steps toward public housing during the First World War, and a few more in the states in the Twenties, but a serious, living program had to wait for the days of the great depression.[1] The major piece of federal legislation on housing was the Wagner-Steagall Act of 1937[2] which, despite a gloss of amendments, remains on the statute books today, hardly altered in its basic design. On September 1,

SOURCE: *Lawrence M. Friedman, "Public Housing and the Poor: An Overview,"* California Law Review, 54, 642–649 (1966). *Copyright © 1966, California Law Review, Inc. Reprinted by permission.*

[*] Some of the material on which this paper is based was gathered in the course of interviews. Some individuals who were interviewed would prefer not to be quoted directly. Some of the information supplied must be treated as confidential. Consequently, supporting authorities for some statements have been omitted.

[1] On the forerunners of the Wagner-Steagall Act, see Fisher, *Twenty Years of Public Housing* (1959); a good short account is Riesenfeld & Eastlund, "Public Aid to Housing and Land Redevelopment," 34 *Minn. L. Rev.* 610 (1950). On the Wagner-Steagall Act itself, see McDonnell, *The Wagner Housing Act: A Case Study of the Legislative Process* (1957).

[2] 50 Stat. 888 (1937), as amended, 42 U.S.C. §§ 1401–30 (1964), as amended, 42 U.S.C. §§ 1402–21b (Supp. I, 1965).

1937, President Roosevelt signed the bill[3] which was to begin a "new era in the economic and social life of America."[4] Hopes ran high in the early years of the program. The wall of resistance to federally supported housing had been breached. A "real start" would be made "at last" toward "wiping out . . . city slums."[5] The states passed enabling legislation, local housing authorities were formed, and the flow of cash into public housing began in earnest. "In city after city," wrote Nathan Straus in 1939, "the sound of the wrecker's hammer is heard, sites are being cleared, the excavators are at work, and the superstructures are going up . . . . [By] next summer . . . five thousand families will be moving from the slums into new and decent homes."[6] In the years since then, public housing has become a familiar aspect of the urban landscape. By the end of 1965 every state had some public housing units in planning or operation,[7] and more than 2,100,000 people lived in low-rent public housing.[8] In New York City more than half a million people lived in public housing units built with the aid of federal, state, or city money.[9] The overwhelming majority of these units were products of the federal program. New York City had more public housing than any other city; but every major city and a host of minor ones ran more or less substantial programs of their own.[10] As of October

1964, 26,175 people lived in public housing in Detroit, Michigan; Duluth, Minnesota, at the end of 1964, operated three hundred units divided into three separate projects.[11] Whatever else these figures signified, they meant that vast tracts of slum wasteland had been cleared and that millions of people over the last thirty years had been rehoused in units which met at least minimum sanitary and spatial standards.

But to judge by some newspaper and magazine accounts—and even by the words of housing experts—the public housing program had betrayed its fond expectations. In 1937 Catherine Bauer, a highly respected expert on housing, praised the Wagner-Steagall Act as "progressive legislation"—a hopeful first step toward the goal of good housing for all.[12] Twenty years later, in 1957, Miss Bauer returned to the subject in an article in *Architectural Forum*. The title was significant: "The Dreary Deadlock of Public Housing."[13] She found little to praise in the program as it had evolved. Rather, she saw rigidity and paternalism in management, crudity and segregation in project design, and a deplorable fragmentation of over-all housing policy. In the following issue of the magazine, eleven housing experts commented on her article and made suggestions for change.[14] Not one of the eleven disagreed with her general thesis: that the public housing movement was stagnant; that politically the program was at a standstill; that existing projects were badly conceived and perhaps did more harm than good; and that the whole program needed radical reformation. This was the twentieth anniversary of the Wagner-Steagall Act.

It was a bad time for the image of public housing. Harrison Salisbury, Russian correspondent for *The New York Times*, came home to write his reactions to the domestic scene. What he saw in New York's housing projects profoundly shocked him—for example, the "stench of stale urine that per-

---

[3] *N.Y. Times,* Sept. 3, 1937, p. 1, col. 3.
[4] Letter from Franklin D. Roosevelt to Nathan Straus, Administrator of the United States Housing Authority, March 17, 1938, quoted in Straus & Wegg, *Housing Comes of Age* 189 (1938).
[5] *N.Y. Times,* Sept. 3, 1937, p. 16, col. 3.
[6] Straus, "Housing—A National Achievement," *Atlantic Monthly,* Feb. 1939, pp. 204, 210.
[7] As of the end of 1963, Utah, Wyoming, and Iowa had no units of public housing. *Housing and Home Finance Agency, Annual Report* 306 n.1 (1963). Iowa since has passed enabling legislation. *Iowa Code Ann.* § 403A (Supp. 1964). At the end of 1964, every state had one or more local public housing authorities, except Oklahoma and this state had two projects federally owned and operated. *Housing and Home Finance Agency, Annual Report* 235, 239, Tables IV-1, IV-3 (1964).
[8] *Id.* at 235.
[9] New York City Housing Authority, Project Statistics 26, Dec. 31, 1964.
[10] Every city of more than one million population ran a public housing authority aided housing program, and 89% (42 out of 47) of the cities of more than a quarter million and less than a million. Sixty-three percent of the cities with more than fifty thousand and less than two hundred

fifty thousand had programs. *Housing and Home Finance Agency, Annual Report* 240 (1964).
[11] Information supplied by the respective housing authorities.
[12] "Now, at Last: Housing," *The New Republic,* Sept. 8, 1937, pp. 119, 121.
[13] Bauer, "The Dreary Deadlock of Public Housing," *Architectural Forum,* May 1957, p. 140.
[14] "The Dreary Deadlock of Public Housing—How to Break It," *Architectural Forum,* June 1957, p. 139.

vades the elevators" in Fort Greene Houses, Brooklyn.[15] He had other things to report about the "new ghettos," as he called them. They were "human cesspools worse than those of yesterday."[16] Fort Greene and similar projects were "monsters, devouring their residents, polluting the areas about them, spewing out a social excrescence which infects the whole of our society."[17] The slums themselves had rarely felt such a tongue-lashing.

Salisbury's conclusions were published in book form and widely read. They were by no means the last such attack on public housing. Readers of the *Chicago Daily News*, in April 1965, were invited to share a sense of wrath and dismay toward public housing. A sensational series of articles excoriated the Robert R. Taylor homes, Chicago's "$70 Million Ghetto." Taylor was the "world's biggest and most jam-packed housing development," an "all-Negro city within a city," a "civic monument to misery, bungling and a hellish way of life," a " 'death trap,' a concentration camp." Its tenants—who sometimes called their home "the Congo Hilton" —lived in misery, "grappling with violence and vandalism, fear and suspicion, teen-age terror and adult chaos, rage, resentment, official regimenting."[18] In the same year, a tenant of the Syracuse Housing Authority described her home as "nothing but a prison camp." In Syracuse, under the impetus of the war against poverty, the Negro poor organized to do battle with those they identified as their oppressors. Prominent among these oppressors were officials of the local housing authority. To judge by the outcry, public housing in Syracuse was also worse than the slums.[19]

Public housing does not totally lack defenders, but they have spoken softly of late. It is hard to think of any prominent housing figure outside of government who defends the program as it is. Politically, the program has little appeal. Appropriations for additional units have been grudgingly voted in

Congress; time and time again requests have been scaled down. What is perhaps more significant, authorizations have often gone begging because local government agencies have not been interested in applying for federal grants—authorized units have "washed away."[20] This is perhaps the darkest symptom of all: A program must be genuinely unpopular if free federal money is spurned. The unpopularity of public housing need not be left to oblique inference. In scores of cities and small towns, public housing has been put to the test by the voters. Where it is legally possible, opponents have demanded referenda on the question. In a distressing number of cases, bond issues to finance the program have failed or public housing has been voted out of town.[21]

Where does the trouble lie? Is it in the conception, the shape of the public housing program? Is it in its mode of administration? Perhaps the problems lie in both. The indictment is clear: Public housing, ostensibly designed to clear the slums and to alleviate the sufferings of the poor, has failed to do either. We turn now to the facts.

CONCEPTION AND DESIGN

The public housing law is one of a vaguely defined group of statutes called "social" or "welfare" legislation.

It would be a mistake to suppose (if anyone did) that the Wagner-Steagall Act[22] arose solely out of a gradual persuasion of decent-minded people that the slums were odious, crowded, and evil, and that the federal government had a duty to relieve the sufferings of the poor. The social and economic conditions in the slums provided the opportunity, the background, and much of the emotive power of the law. Yet reformers had long dreamed in vain of public housing. And the slums were surely no worse than they had been in the nineteenth century, though possibly they were larger.

In 1937 the country was suffering from a

[15] Salisbury, *The Shook-Up Generation* 74 (1958).
[16] *Id.* at 75.
[17] *Id.* at 77.
[18] *Chicago Daily News*, April 10, 1965, p. 1, col. 1.
[19] The tenant quotes are from *The Tenants Report, Public Housing: Syracuse Style, This Is the Way It Is*, 1965. Materials on the Syracuse movement were supplied to me by Professor Warren C. Haggstrom of Syracuse University.

[20] Seligman, "The Enduring Slums," in *The Exploding Metropolis* 92, 105 (1958).
[21] *E.g.*, in elections in April and June 1961, Rapid City, South Dakota, and Marin County, California, turned down low-rent proposals. 18 *J. of Housing* 289 (1961).
[22] 50 Stat. 888 (1937), as amended, 42 U.S.C. §§ 1401–30 (1964), as amended, 42 U.S.C. §§ 1402–21b (Supp. I, 1965).

deep and dangerous depression. Fully one-quarter of the work force was unemployed during the worst days of the depression. In the spring of 1933, thirteen to fifteen million were unemployed.[23] Millions of families were barely making a living. The number of "poor people" in the country had been vastly increased; indeed, many of the "poor people" were formerly members of the middle class, who had enjoyed prosperity in the twenties. They retained their middle-class culture and their outlook, their articulateness, their habit of expressing their desires at the polls. There were, therefore, millions of candidates for public housing who did not belong (as later was true) to the class of the "problem poor"; rather they were members of what we might call the submerged middle class. The attractiveness of public housing was enormously enhanced because the potential clientele was itself enormous, composed of millions of relatively articulate citizens, angry and dispirited at their unjust descent into poverty. Public housing was not supported by the dregs of society; a discontented army of men and women of high demands and high expectations stood ready to insist on decent housing from government or at least stood ready to approve and defend it. The political climate was receptive to federal planning and federal housing—not so much as a matter of radical ideology, but out of a demand for positive programs to eliminate the "undeserved" privations of the unaccustomed poor.

Moreover, business was stagnant in the thirties. Programs of social welfare and relief were tested by their ability to create new jobs and prime the business pump as much as by their inherent welfare virtues. Public works programs were exceedingly popular for this reason.[24] A vast federal program of house building naturally received the enthusiastic support of manufacturers of building supplies and workers in the building trades. The normal opposition to "socialized" housing made its appearance in debate,[25] but it was weak and somewhat muted. Nonetheless, business support for the act was conditioned upon the act being so structured as to avoid any actual government competition with business. Homes would be built only for those who could not possibly afford to buy

them on their own. A clear wall must separate the public and private sector. This too was only partly ideological. Government, it was felt, should not cut into the markets of private industry; it must stimulate fresh demand and make fresh jobs—otherwise the effect of the program on the economy would be wasted.

During the depression, the volume of private housing construction was very low. In 1925, 900,000 housing units were constructed; in 1934, only 60,000.[26] Yet in one sense no housing shortage developed. During much of the depression, plenty of apartments stood vacant.[27] People who were poor doubled up with relatives, lived in "Hoovervilles" and shanties, returned to rural areas, and in general failed to consume the housing supply. Rents were extremely low. The high vacancy rate posed a potential danger for the program. If public construction increased the housing supply during a period in which many dwellings stood vacant, rents would decrease still more and vacancies would increase. In a decade willing to kill baby pigs and impose acreage controls on farmers, one could hardly expect to see government flooding the housing market with new units. And in fact, the Wagner-Steagall Act was careful to avoid the problem of oversupply. No units were to be built without destroying "dwellings . . . substantially equal in number to the number of newly constructed dwellings provided by the project."[28] This provision—the so-called "equivalent elimination" provision[29]—killed two birds with one stone. It neutralized potential opposition from landlords and the housing industry by removing the danger of oversupply; at the same time, by making slum clearance a part of the law, it appealed to those whose desire for public housing stemmed from their loathing of the slums and slum conditions. The Wagner-Steagall Act was thus shaped by the force of concrete social conditions; what emerged was a program geared to the needs of the submerged middle class, tied to slum clearance, and

23 Brown, *Public Relief* 1929–1939, at 65 (1940).
24 Mitchell, *Depression Decade* 314–38 (1947).
25 *E.g.*, 81 *Cong. Rec.* 8079 (1937) (remarks of Senator Walsh).

26 Brookings Institution, *The Recovery Problem in the United States* 183–84 (1936).
27 *Id.* at 184–85.
28 50 Stat. 891 (1937), as amended, 42 U.S.C. § 1410(a) (1964), as amended, 42 U.S.C. § 1410(a) (Supp. I, 1965).
29 Robinson & Altman, "Equivalent Elimination Agreements in Public Housing Projects," 22 *B.U.L. Rev.* 375, 376 (1942).

purged of any element of possible competition with business.[30]

Constitutional difficulties played a part in determining one of the most notable features of the program—its decentralization. From 1933 on, the Public Works Administration had run its own public housing program.[31] In 1935 a federal district court case held that the federal government had no power under the constitution to clear land and build public housing. It was not proper, said the court, for the federal government "to construct buildings in a state for the purpose of selling or leasing them to private citizens for occupancy as homes."[32] The federal government never appealed this decision. In 1935 the government's prospect of sympathetic treatment by the United States Supreme Court seemed bleak; attempting to overturn the adverse housing decision might risk the whole program of public works. On the other hand, no important legal barriers stood in the way of a decentralized program. Washington could supply money and a certain amount of benign control; title to property and the motive force in condemnation could remain vested in local public agencies. A key New York state decision strengthened this view, distinguishing the federal cases as inapplicable to state power.[33] Moreover, decentralization was politically attractive to those who dreaded further expansion of the "federal octopus."

Financial considerations had an important impact on the design of the housing law. If the federal government had made outright grants to local authorities to build houses, immense amounts of money would have been immediately required. Under the act, however, local authorities were invited to borrow money through bond issues; with the proceeds, they were to acquire sites, clear them, and put up houses. The federal government would enter into "contracts" with local housing authorities, under which the federal government would agree to make annual contributions for a long period of time. The federal government would pay (in essence) enough money for the interest on the bonds and the amortization of the principal. Operating expenses for the housing projects would come out of current rents. In this way, federal contributions would be kept relatively small; housing could be built on the installment plan, and paid for over a period of fifty or sixty years.[34]

Note, too, that the tenants were only partially subsidized. They were not given "free" housing. Each tenant had to pay his rent. Project rents had to be sufficient to pay operating costs—maintenance, administration, and payments in lieu of taxes to local government for fire and police protection and other municipal services.[35] Though the federal act was discreetly silent on the subject, the rent requirement meant that the unemployed and the paupers were not welcome in public housing. They could not pay the rent, any more than in private housing. There are "some people," said Senator Wagner, "who we cannot possibly reach; I mean those who have no means to pay the rent. . . . [O]bviously this bill cannot provide housing for those who cannot pay the rent minus the subsidy allowed."[36] The projects were for poor but honest workers—the members of the submerged middle class, biding their time until the day when they regained their rightful income level. The tenants were not to receive any "charity." The difference between a dole and a subsidy is psychologically powerful, whether or not the distinction is good economics. The working class residents of public housing were not to receive a gift from the government, but their rightful due as citizens. Public housing, arguably, was no more "charitable" than the free land of the

[30] The 1949 act, to make the point crystal clear, provided that no annual contribution contract be entered into unless the local agency demonstrates "that a gap of at least 20 per centum . . . has been left between the upper rental limits for admission to the proposed low-rent housing and the lowest rents at which private enterprise unaided by public subsidy is providing . . . decent . . . housing." 63 Stat. 422 (1949), as amended, 42 U.S.C. § 1415(7)(b)(ii) (1964).

[31] Fisher, *Twenty Years of Public Housing* 82–89 (1959).

[32] United States v. Certain Lands, 9 F. Supp. 137, 141 (W.D. Ky.), aff'd, 78 F.2d 684 (6th Cir.), dismissed, 294 U.S. 735 (1935), 297 U.S. 726 (1936). See also United States v. Certain Lands, 12 F. Supp. 345 (E.D. Mich. 1935).

[33] New York Housing Authority v. Muller, 270 N.Y. 333, 1 N.E.2d 152 (1936).

[34] 50 Stat. 892 (1937), as amended, 42 U.S.C. §§ 1410(b), (c) (1964), as amended, 42 U.S.C. § 1410(c) (Supp. I, 1965).

[35] The so-called "in-lieu" payments. See 63 Stat. 428 (1949), as amended, 42 U.S.C. § 1410(h) (1964), as amended, 42 U.S.C. § 1410(h) (Supp. I, 1965).

[36] 81 *Cong. Rec.* 8099 (Aug. 3, 1937).

Homestead Act of 1862—an earlier form of middle-class subsidy. Decent, sanitary apartments were a stepping-stone to a fee simple cottage—the American dream. Perhaps a radical fringe of housing reformers looked on public housing as something more fundamentally "public"; but the core of support lay in an old and conservative tradition.

If this general analysis is correct, what would happen to public housing if a rising standard of living released the submerged middle class from dependence on government shelter? Public housing would be inherited by the permanent poor. The empty rooms would pass to those who had at first been disdained—the unemployed, "problem" families, those from broken homes. The pro-gram could adapt only with difficulty to its new conditions, because it had been originally designed for a different clientele. To suit the programs to the needs of the new tenant would require fresh legislation; and yet change would be difficult to enact and to implement precisely because the new clientele would be so poor, so powerless, so inarticulate. The political attractiveness of public housing would diminish. Maladaptations to reality in the program would disenchant housing reformers; they would declare the program a failure and abandon it to search out fresh cures for bad housing and slums.

All this is precisely what has happened. . . .

CREATIVE CAPITALISM AND URBAN REDEVELOPMENT

Danny Beagle, Al Haber, and David Wellman

The following selection illustrates the real purposes of urban renewal as it has been manifested in local areas. Rather than aiming to provide housing for the poor, as many originally believed it was intending, the program explicitly aimed in San Francisco to serve the interests of corporate and financial landholders in the city.

The selection comes from an article called "Turf Power and the Tax Man," which appeared in *Leviathan*. The original article had six sections: The Mission Coalition; Creative Capitalism; Regional Government; Rapid Transit: BART: Urban Redevelopment; and The Politics of Resistance. This selection includes the entirety of the second and fifth sections. The fourth section is reprinted in the chapter of this book on transportation.

The first section of the original article discussed the history of a coalition of community-action groups in San Francisco's Mission District which had succeeded in gaining a veto power over planning and development of S.F. Model Cities programs for the Mission area. The group had been built through patient community organizing; it was clear "that the group would use its power, and the money that goes with it, to protect the interests of the community."

The second section, included here, discusses the importance of that power in the light of obvious corporate interest in control over urban development. The section argues that three recent thrusts in San Francisco have been stimulated by its corporate leaders and represent basic elements of their master plan for the area: regional government, urban redevelopment, and rapid transit.

The section on regional government described the long-standing efforts of

SOURCE: *Danny Beagle, Al Haber, and David Wellman, "Turf Power and the Tax Man," in* Leviathan *I, 2.*

business leaders to promote metropolitan government in the Bay Area; they are interested in regional government to rationalize the tax system for metropolitan areas and to consolidate control over relatively administrative government agencies. The evolution of regional government, the authors argue, "will mark the end of even the pretense of popular participation in local government." They quote *Fortune* magazine: "'Businessmen like regional government plans because they are so satisfyingly apolitical.'"

The sixth section argues that radical organization and resistance must strike at corporate control over urban fiscal policy and taxing powers. Without that effort, groups like the Mission Coalition will be gaining veto over empty shells.

The authors have all been active in the Movement in the Bay Area and have written often for activist publications.

CREATIVE CAPITALISM

A major victory seems to have been won [by the Mission Coalition]. But have [San Francisco Mayor] Alioto and those he represents been defeated? The mayor has been described by his Chamber of Commerce as a believer in "creative capitalism"—a ubiquitous description increasingly applied to the new-style administrators who specialize in managing conflict and mangling democracy.

Can creative capitalism actually permit the kind of community self-determination demanded and envisioned by the Mission? Has the city abandoned its plan for Mission renewal? Or is something else going on—where community control becomes a false issue and its victories pyrrhic?

This is no idle question. Community control has become the central unifying demand for almost all insurgent movements now challenging established authority. These are the struggles of the urban crisis: the response of the oppressed to the breakdown in social services—schools, welfare, hospitals, public safety—and to the intolerability of continued private exploitation and public neglect.

The ruling urban groups have made well-publicized and dramatic responses to these struggles and the problems which animate them. Their strategy emerges in layers: first, repression of disorderly elements; second, an attempt to shift more of the financial burden of social administration and reconstruction to the federal government; third, an attempt to humanize necessity by trying to eliminate the least rational forms of exploitation and oppression; and fourth, a tentative exploration of decentralized and neighborhood development experiments, ranging from community boards of education all the way to black capitalism. These urban groups see jobs and income as crucial: the solution lies in continued economic prosperity and growth for the rich while increased opportunity is provided for the poor.

The area of conflict has been defined by the contest between the new-style urban modernizers and the grassroots decolonizers. On the one side are the Aliotos, Lindsays, Cavanaughs and Walter Washingtons of City Hall, closeted with their Ford Foundation advisors, federal paymasters and guideline writers. And on the other side are the *people* —the Mission Coalitions, the Panthers, the Ocean Hill-Brownsville parents, Black Student Unions, citizen police patrols, and economic development corporations built on the militance of an activated grassroots base. Between the two sides is the turf of the underclass community. To be decided, in the battle or in bargaining, is who rules that turf.

American society may be seen in terms of its colonized ghettos and the trials of its oppressed—poor and not so poor. But this is a view of America from the bottom up. And however necessary such an angle of vision may be in the building of democratic opposition, it has limitations in the design of strategy. America is not ruled from the bottom up. To understand the political arena, we must also understand the society as those on top see it, as they have defined the problems and as they have planned to insure that they stay on top.

For the business community, the sufferings and rebellion of the underclass are but a minor part of a much larger problem. For business, the city is only incidentally a place where people live their lives, seeking personal fulfillment and the community of their fellows. It is above all a place of business: banks and board rooms, exclusive clubs and restaurants—a place where goods are produced and exchanged, where markets are structured and divided up, where influence is concentrated and negotiated, and giving purpose to it all, where money is made and the powerful preside.

A great city, which all businessmen want theirs to be, is one which excels in all these activities. For business to be good, of course, there must be a modicum of order. The underclasses, who have no part in the world of money-making, must be kept striving and responsible. The city must be an attractive place: where businessmen will want to locate, where tourists and conventioners will come and spend money, where comforts and aesthetic pleasures are available, and where optimism can be high—free from the distractions of congestion and pollution and the clamors of the dissatisfied. After all, the rulers must believe that they are the beneficent instruments of the general welfare.

San Francisco is clearly a great city: the historic center of California development and Pacific Basin commerce, it is the home of the great corporations and financial institutions of the West. Its bay is not only a great harbor, but an attractive complement to its beautiful hills, lush parks, and mild climate. Its opera and museums and exotic ethnic neighborhoods create the proper aura of high culture and cosmopolitan living. But the responsible citizens of the presiding business world realize that this greatness is in jeopardy.

The San Francisco Bay Area consists of nine counties—San Francisco, San Mateo, Santa Clara, Alameda, Contra Costa, Solano, Napa, Sonoma and Marin—which border San Francisco and San Pablo bays. Over the last twenty years, the area has experienced changes typical of many other metropolitan areas. Industrial growth, population expansion and rapid urbanization have caused the development of a solid ring of urban life around the bay.

Most Bay Area planners and corporate leaders foresee the continuation of these trends. Population will continue its rapid expansion. Somewhere over four million now, it will reach seven million in twenty years. Urbanization will continue, with only narrow strips of agricultural land and certain park areas left as open space. Heavy industry will continue to gravitate toward the cheaper lands of the eastern and northern ends of the bay. Members of the working and middle classes will probably continue to follow their jobs out to the suburbs.

This growth, however, brings serious problems:

Sprawl, congestion, blight and disorder are making the cities inhospitable, if not yet physically unsafe, for business. Corporate leaders are alarmed by the possibility that San Francisco will become a city of the immobile and the transient: ghetto dwellers, old people and, god forbid, hippies. According to present projections, the city will become 40 percent black and chicano by 1980, unless something is done.

Traditional land use patterns—low density, low income housing and obsolete industrial facilities near downtown—preclude needed housing for the well-off downtown work force and depress the potential tax base.

The plethora of governmental units around the bay, each responsive to its own group of entrenched special interests, leads to an intolerable inefficiency in administering the regional economic and social complex.

These problems, too pressing to be left to the politics of popular democracy, have prompted the business leadership of San Francisco to assume the role of social planners and technocratic guardians.

Since the end of World War II, the Bay Area's corporate leadership has interpreted the crisis in terms of the imperatives of business operations and the deficiencies in business-government relations. Sprawl and congestion have made it increasingly difficult to do business in the central city. The cost of schools and other city services has forced up taxes, undermining the comparative advantage of the city and its ability to attract and hold business. If the city were more efficiently run and made more hospitable to business, if non-productive and non-consuming groups were removed, if anachronisms in land use were eliminated; then it would be possible to revitalize and expand the downtown business area and to surround it with the middle and upper income housing needed by the management and white collar groups which staff it. This would automatically produce the economic growth necessary to create jobs and the tax income needed to "take care of" some causes of social disruption. It would also encourage the return of "socially desirable" middle class families to the central city.

Thus, the basic concern of the corporate planners has been to insure San Francisco's continued predominance and growth as the civil service, banking, insurance, real estate, cultural and tourist center of the Bay Area and the West Coast. Corporate planners design and evaluate their specific strategies for dealing with the urban crisis in terms of this orientation. Three major programmatic thrusts follow: regional government, mass transit, and urban redevelopment.

If San Francisco is to grow as the commercial and cultural hub of the Bay Area, the entire region will require a centralized government to rationally determine social priorities, allocate land use, and distribute the tax burden. In the Bay Area, there are now nine counties, over ninety cities, and countless special districts ranging in importance and size from the East Bay bus service district to the Fairfield Mosquito Abatement District. These local units frequently have overlapping and fuzzy jurisdictions which cause enormous expense, duplication and inconvenience for businessmen. Local governments are becoming an increasingly important market for certain types of industries, such as construction, banking and utilities. Even sophisticated defense contractors and systems specialists see the urban market as a prime area for expansion. They prefer to deal with a unified market. For one thing, greater volume means greater profits. For another, a centralized marketplace requires the systems analysis techniques which these companies have developed. The little guy can't compete. He gets a piece of the action only by allying and subordinating himself to the major companies.

San Francisco's corporate leadership also connects the need for regionalization with the prospect of indefinite growth and expansion. According to the research director of the Bay Area Council, a group of senior executives from the area's largest corporations, "We are primarily interested in physical expansion, and administrative streamlining is necessary for this."

Second, there must be an efficient regional transportation network which can funnel suburban white collar people to and from the central city, for shopping and work. Corporate leaders hope that this will facilitate the concentration of economic life and also minimize the congestion which has made urban life unbearable for many middle class people. Regional transportation networks, of course, cannot be set up on a county-by-county basis. They require overall coordinated planning

supervision and resource allocation. San Francisco's guardians echo a group of New York businessmen who recently argued that the cost of transportation "could threaten our competitive position in the nation and the world if complementary functions are too unduly dispersed or if transport is inadequately planned."

Finally, urban renewal will involve both the reconstruction of downtown and residential construction for those middle and upper income people who will staff the growing financial-administrative complex. The black and Latin American ghettos which frequently occupy valuable property close to downtown will, unfortunately, have to be displaced. The expansion of tourist and cultural attractions (such as the Japanese Cultural Center) and the modernization of industrial plant (such as the Port Development Project) are natural adjuncts. That the former destroyed twelve blocks worth of Japanese community and the latter will decimate such "charm" as is left on the waterfront simply reflects the new imperatives. In San Francisco we destroy communities and replace them with Cultural Centers. . . .

URBAN REDEVELOPMENT

The third aspect of the overall corporate strategy, urban renewal and redevelopment, is being handled by another, though overlapping, group of San Francisco businessmen. The Blyth-Zellerbach Committee was formed in the fifties by the late Charles Blyth, a prominent San Francisco stockbroker, and J.D. Zellerbach, heir to an enormous toilet paper fortune and *de facto* owner of Bogalusa, Louisiana. J.D., we are told, "learned about urban redevelopment in private enterprise." He became interested in the field when he was bogged down with an inefficient urban bureaucracy in trying to put together enough land downtown to build his new national headquarters. Thus, from the beginning, urban renewal was closely tied in with the idea of administrative reorganization of local government.

The Blyth-Zellerbach Committee was composed of representatives of Zellerbach, the Bank of America, Bechtel, Pacific Telephone, Pacific Gas and Electric, Standard Oil, Levi Strauss, the American Trust Company, Magnin's (a large downtown retailer) and Matson Navigation. The Committee is chaired today by R. Gwin Follis, retired board chairman of Cal Standard. According to the Chamber of Commerce, the Blyth-Zellerbach Committee is made up of men "who can provide money where it is needed. This group has served as the catalyst for the entire urban renewal effort."

The Committee has always had a close relationship with the official director of development, Redevelopment Agency Executive Director M. Justin Herman. As one of its first acts, the Committee financed the initial studies for San Francisco's first urban renewal project, the Golden Gateway, an upper-middle income development on the waterfront, which replaced an outdated produce market and provided housing for the downtown business class.

In 1960 the Blyth-Zellerbach Committee organized the San Francisco Planning and Urban Renewal Association (SPUR) in order to develop a broader citizens' movement in support of renewal. Since then SPUR has become the Redevelopment Agency's official "Citizens' Advisory Group" on matters concerning renewal. (These citizens keep advising each other!) The Blyth-Zellerbach Committee underwrote SPUR's expenses completely for three years, and now provides fifty percent of its money. Financier Jerd Sullivan provided the link between the two groups, serving for many years as both president of SPUR and as a member of the Blyth-Zellerbach Committee. John Hirten, SPUR's former executive director, provided the link to the BAC, of which he was a trustee.

The dual concern of urban renewal activity in San Francisco was described by a University of California professor recently addressing a SPUR meeting. He argued that "San Francisco is becoming increasingly polarized. There is a real need to attract middle class people with children. Yet we have a responsibility to Negroes." Redevelopment Agency executive Herman suggests that the duality of concern is not quite even-handed. On the problem of slum dwellers, Herman remarked, "Anyone who is thoughtful and sympathetic realizes that there is not just discrimination but also a deficiency [among blacks]. . . . The moral goal is just—to equalize the opportunity. But even if it were theoretically possible to eliminate discrimination, Negroes still don't make enough money to live in San Francisco."

In fact, this is the way it has worked out so far wherever renewal has operated. Six thousand blacks used to live in the first Fillmore renewal area. After redevelopment, which constructed a series of expensive high-rise apartment houses, only three black families were able to move back into the area. Some black middle class families from other areas did move in, but not the poor. They moved on to other ghettos in San Francisco and in other parts of the Bay Area.

In 1964, the Redevelopment Agency began to make its move into adjacent areas in the Fillmore ghetto. Over fourteen thousand people, 70 percent of whom are black, have been and will be affected by this thrust. The basic reason given for the expansion of Fillmore renewal was to protect high land valuations in the first renewal area. As the supply of old and low cost housing decreases, the increased demand for remaining units will press rents up.

The pressure on relocation housing caused by renewal should not be surprising. The intent of the program is not to build low income housing. It is to meet the business, housing and tourism needs of a "greater" San Francisco. These needs are pre-eminently for middle income housing accessible to downtown. Even where there was vacant land, like the Diamond Heights project, or non-residential land, like the Golden Gateway, construction has been exclusively for luxury units. Opportunities to provide for low income relocation were passed by. According to present plans, isolated ghettos, like Hunters Point, far from downtown, may be renewed without permanent displacement of the current population. But on prime land, renewal remains removal. The class bias of the program is not malicious, but simply a reflection of the costs of construction and maintenance (repairs, taxes, debt service, profits) which exceed what a poor family can pay. Urban renewal is not public housing.

HOUSING BIBLIOGRAPHY

I. DEFINITIONS AND MAGNITUDES

President's Committee on Urban Housing, *A Decent Home,* 1968, U.S. Government, pp. 39–54. Good summary of definitions and dimensions.

II. ANALYSIS

A. General Perspectives

Bernard J. Frieden, "Housing and National Urban Goals: Old Policies and New Realities," in James Q. Wilson, ed., *The Metropolitan Enigma,* 1970, Doubleday Anchor paperback. Excellent summary of trends and problems, with slightly pessimistic expectations for future.

Anthony Downs, "Moving Toward Realistic Housing Goals," in Kermit Gordon, ed., *Agenda for the Nation,* 1968, Brookings, pp. 141–176. Urges, in view of problems and their difficulty, that we not be so ambitious in our housing goals over the next decade.

Ira S. Lowry, "Housing," in Anthony Pascal, ed., *Cities in Trouble: An Agenda for Urban Research,* 1968, The Rand Corporation, pp. 4–26. Interesting discussion of external effects of various housing policies.

Dick Netzer, *Economics and Urban Problems,* 1970, Basic Books. Two separate chapters on housing problems.

"Housing," Parts I–II, *Law and Contemporary Problems,* Duke University, Spring-Summer 1967. General summary.

B. Metropolitan Location and Housing Structure

John Meyer, John Kain, and Martin Wohl, *The Urban Transportation Problem,* 1966, Harvard, pp. 24–49. Summary of the impact of changes in metropolitan form on the shape of the housing market. (Cf. also pp. 109–129, 144–169 for empirical evidence of preceding hypotheses.)

William Alonso, "A Theory of the Urban Land Market," *The Regional Science Association Papers and Proceedings,* 1960. Formal theory of location and housing demand. (Presented at greater length in his *Location and Land Use,* 1965, Harvard.)

William Alonso, "The Historical and Structural Theories of Urban Form: Their Implications for Urban Renewal," *Land Economics,* May, 1964. The more practical implications of the theories.

Edgar M. Hoover, "The Evolving Form and Organization of the Metropolis," in Harvey S. Perloff and Lowden Wingo, eds., *Issues in Urban Economics,* 1968, Johns Hopkins, pp. 237–284. More elaborate and more difficult presentation of same ideas.

Richard F. Muth, *Cities and Housing,* 1969, University of Chicago. Extremely difficult, technical analysis of housing market.

C. Filtering and the Housing Stock

William Grigsby, *Housing Markets and Public Policy,* 1963, University of Pennsylvania. Comprehensive analysis of changes in the housing stock. (Especially Chapters 3–4.)

Irving Wellman, "Toward a New Federal Housing Policy," *The Public Interest,* No. 19, Spring, 1970. Application of filtering concepts to present housing policy issues.

John Lansing *et al.*, *New Homes and Poor Families*, 1970, University of Michigan. Empirical evidence on the effectiveness of the filtering process in trickling down new housing through the stock to the poorest families.

D. Residential Segregation: Theory and Reality

Karl Taeuber and Alma Taeuber, *Negroes in Cities*, 1965, Aldine, pp. 1–10, 26–68, and skim remainder. Basic study of extent of residential segregation in American cities.

Eunice and George Grier, "Equality and Beyond: Housing Segregation in the Great Society," in Kenneth Clark and Talcott Parsons, eds., *The Negro American*, 1967, Houghton Mifflin. Useful summary of housing problems among blacks.

George Sternlieb, *The Tenement Landlord*, 1966, Rutgers University. Classic study of effects of segregation in Newark housing market.

Chester Rapkin, "Price Discrimination in the Rental Housing Market," in John F. Kain, ed., *Race and Poverty*, 1969, Prentice-Hall. Specific evidence on the extent of racial discrimination.

Anthony Pascal, "The Analysis of Residential Segregation," in J. P. Crecine, ed., *Financing the Metropolis*, 1970, Sage. Summary of previous theories and suggestion of a new synthetic analysis.

John F. Kain, "Theories of Residential Location and Realities of Race," *Proceedings of the Savings and Residential Finance Association*, 1969. Interesting summary of issues in understanding residential segregation.

Robert A. Haugen and A. James Heins, "A Market Separation Theory of Rent Differentials in Metropolitan Areas," *Quarterly Journal of Economics*, November, 1969. A more institutional analysis of segregation.

Thomas C. Schelling, "Models of Segregation," *The American Economic Review*, May, 1969, pp. 488–493. A game-theoretic approach to segregation, slightly difficult.

III. POLICY ISSUES

A. General Perspectives

Jerome Rothenberg, *Economic Evaluation of Urban Renewal*, 1967, Brookings, especially pp. 201–259. Useful sorting of various policy issues.

William Grigsby, "A General Strategy for Urban Renewal," in James Q. Wilson, ed., *Urban Renewal: The Record and the Controversy*, 1967, MIT Press, pp. 624–662. Useful and sensible summary of issues.

Richard Cloward and Frances Fox Piven, "Desegregated Housing: Who Pays for the Reformers' Ideal?" in Kain, ed., *Race and Poverty*, *op. cit.* Argues that drive for housing integration has undercut efforts to improve housing quality.

B. Urban Renewal

In Wilson, ed., *Urban Renewal, op. cit.*, articles by Davis and Whinston, pp. 50–67; Hartman, 293–335; Fried, 359–379; Anderson, 491–508; Groberg, 508–531; and Smith, pp. 532–536. The swirl of controversy about the failures of urban renewal and the causes of failure.

C. Public Housing

Lawrence Friedman, *The Government and Slum Housing*, 1967, Rand McNally. Useful summary; concludes failures of public housing stem from weak intentions rather than weak performance.

Jewell Bellush and Murray Hausknecht, "Public Housing: The Contexts of Failure," in Bellush and Hausknecht, eds., *Urban Renewal: People, Politics and Plan-*

ning, 1967, Doubleday Anchor, pp. 457–461. Summary of issues.

Chester Hartman and Gregg Carr, "Housing Authorities Reconsidered," *Journal of American Institute of Planners,* January, 1969. Argue that authorities do not try to improve housing for the poor.

D. The Private Housing Industry

A Decent Home, op. cit., Section IV, pp. 113–209. Basic summary of characteristics of home building industry and ways to improve it.

William Wheaton *et al.,* eds., *Urban Housing,* 1966, Free Press, especially pp. 307–313 and 324–331.

8 Transportation

Editor's Introduction

*Today, Americans drive 97 million cars, buses, and trucks. Ten years
from now we'll be operating 120 million vehicles—and the number goes up from
there. In 1967 we drove 960 billion miles. We'll hit a trillion in 1968.
Better roads and highways are vital to our social and economic welfare and
to national defense.*

—Francis C. Turner
Federal highway official[1]

As Americans have become increasingly concerned with ecology and the environment, they
have deflected traditional debate about urban transportation policy. Formerly, advocates argued
primarily about the putative efficiency of different modes of transportation, especially whether
the government should allocate more money for rapid transit or for highways. Now the tone and
level of the debate have altered. Choking in smog, deafened by horns, stalled in traffic, displaced
for highway construction, many citizens are baldly demanding that we replace the automobile
as our principal means of urban transportation. Before, planners discussed the utility of marginal-
cost and peak-load pricing. Now, students picket auto shows and activists sue General Motors.

In its new guise, public concern about urban transportation policies has directly confronted
the loci of power dominating those policies. We now realize that we must reach General Motors
stockholders, anonymous trustees of public transit authorities, and bankers who buy the bonds
with which transit systems are financed. Formerly, the public ignored these sources of power
while planners and academics pursued the traditional illusion that public decisions are made in
the interests of everyone.

In this chapter, I have based the radical analysis of transportation problems on a single important contention—that powerful economic institutions have created and will continue to in-
tensify our urban transportation problems. The obvious implication of that contention is that we
must change those institutions in order to solve the problems.

The first section of this introduction summarizes the dimensions of urban transportation problems, the second section outlines liberal and conservative approaches to those problems, the
third presents the structure of the radical argument, and the fourth sketches the purposes and
contents of the readings.

PROBLEM DEFINITIONS

Americans worry about urban transportation problems on two different levels. First, and quite
directly, the public complains about the comfort, convenience, and cost of available transportation. Second, many worry about the implications for other social activities of the dominant modes
of urban transportation—about their implications for industrial and residential location, housing
costs, pollution and noise, urban form and density, and even the viability of present forms of
metropolitan government.

1. The first problem—the social provision of travel alternatives—involves three separate
issues. All three issues emerge from a single critical phenomenon, the increasing domination by
the automobile of all intra-metropolitan transportation. And there can be little doubt about this
context, as the readings in this chapter show. To pick one from a hundred striking statistics, the

---

[1] Quoted in A. Q. Mowbray, *Road to Ruin* (N.Y.: Lippincott, 1969), p. 229.

city of Los Angeles will have devoted 34 square miles to its freeways by 1980, an area equal to the total size of the city of Miami.[2]

The first issue concerns the range of choice available to citizens in making their travel decisions. More and more in American cities, residents have only one choice of travel mode—the car. Although, as most analysts seem to argue, the public may generally prefer the car, it seems equally clear that they have little opportunity to express other preferences. Jobs are moving out of central cities to the suburbs, to locations accessible only by car. Suburban residential developments have become a dominant pattern, forcing dependence on the automobile even for small errands. And with the dominance of the auto, other problems become inescapable. Auto insurance must be purchased, even though it is expensive and often unreliable. Cars must occasionally be repaired, even though repair services often charge outrageous prices for sloppy work. If someone would prefer to avoid those burdens, his options diminish all the time.

The second issue concerns the simple adequacy, cost, and convenience of transportation available for the most important single transit need, the journey to work. As John Meyer points out in his summary in this chapter, there are four principal groups of people with journey-to-work needs: those remaining few who live and work close together in the central city; those who work in the central city and live in fairly distant locations, especially in the suburbs; those who live and work in the suburbs, engaging in "cross-commutation"; and those who work outside the central city but continue to live inside it, "reverse commuting."

Of those four clusters of journey-to-work needs, the present system of urban transportation seems to satisfy only one with any adequacy. "Cross commuters" living and working in the suburbs typically have enough money to afford cars. They are often able to drive to work rather quickly and conveniently, especially as a result of the recent rush of suburban highway construction.[3] But the other three groups of needs do not seem to be serviced very well.

—Those working and living inside central cities must usually rely on public transit (because they cannot afford cars and/or because inner-city auto travel becomes increasingly burdensome as traffic congests and parking space evaporates). But the quality of public transit in central cities has tended to decline in recent years while the costs of rides have increased.[4]

—Those trying to commute long distances by car into the central city complain of congestion, delay, and inadequate parking facilities. And commuter railroad service has tended to collapse in fits of disrepair and mismanagement.[5]

—Those trying to travel out of the central city to suburban jobs typically find that public transit systems do not serve their needs at all. Most "reverse commuters" are blacks who cannot live near suburban jobs because of housing discrimination or the higher costs of suburban housing. They are often poor, perhaps too poor to afford a car, but they must depend on the car nonetheless. John Meyer and John Kain observe,[6]

> It is therefore not surprising that transit operators serving suburban plants report that low-income workers frequently use transit only when obtaining their jobs and for the first few days or weeks of employment. Once the workers manage to save enough for the down payment on a car, or become acquainted with some fellow workers living near them, they drive to work or join a carpool.

The third major issue in the social provision of travel alternatives concerns the income biases of the present transportation system. As the quality and availability of public transit declines, as public transit fares therefore increase, as the prevalence of automobile travel increases, and as the decentralization of employment makes it more and more difficult to reach suburban jobs without a car, the system becomes increasingly biased against people who are already most disadvantaged: those who are too poor to afford a car, or who work too unstably to find sufficient credit for auto time purchase, or who cannot live in the suburbs because of discrimination and lack of capital.

[2] Cited *ibid.*, p. 12.
[3] Most notably, the Federal Highways Program built circumferential beltways around many large cities, providing transportation around rather than through the congested centers.
[4] For this evidence, see Dick Netzer, *Economics and Urban Problems* (N.Y.: Basic Books, 1970).
[5] Especially commuter railroads around the Eastern seaboard.
[6] Meyer and Kain, "Transportation and Poverty," *The Public Interest*, No. 18, Winter, 1970, p. 79.

2. Recently, many have grown more aware of the sweeping implications of increasing auto dominance for other social activities.

—The automobile accounts for 50 percent of air pollution in the United States.[7] Some other modes of transit would certainly improve air quality: electric-powered cars, for instance, or heavier reliance on group transit.

—Travel by auto has increased the probability of traffic congestion, with its attendant headaches and ugliness. Denser use of traffic modes or a different pattern of industrial and residential location would decrease congestion.

—Automobile accidents constitute the largest single cause of "unnatural" death in the country. Less congestion, more public transit, and fewer high-speed highways would certainly decrease this source of personal harm.

—Increasing reliance on the automobile helps perpetuate the decentralization of employment. Among other things, this accentuates the difficulties of central-city blacks in gaining access to suburban jobs.[8]

—Rapid decentralization also tends to force longer and longer trips between home and work. Economists argue that workers have a choice about travel time, and that longer trips therefore reflect their preferences.[9] John Meyer, in his selection below, also conjectures: "Possibly, too, as one social psychologist has hypothesized, the typical male wage earner considers the time it takes to get between work and home as the only time that is truly his own, without interruption by foreman or wife. It is possible (no one knows) that some commuters are reluctant to reduce this time."[10] But the quality of time spent *en route* varies, needless to say, and the commuters described by Jimmy Breslin in his brief selection in this chapter can hardly cherish their hours in New York subways. At least, workers should have more choice about the length of time they must spend traveling to their jobs.

LIBERAL AND CONSERVATIVE VIEWS

In general, liberals and conservatives analyze transportation problems in the same way they view other problems. They take the institutional context for granted and try to calculate the most "rational" ways for individuals to adjust to that context. In the case of transportation, they presume the present location of industry and housing, the given structure of the auto industry, and the given network of highways. They seek minor adjustments in the system in order to correct some of its deficiencies.

Liberals and conservatives seem to agree on their analyses of the sources of increasing auto dominance, and their interpretations are revealing. They seem to provide two answers. First, they suggest that the automobile (and public provision of highway facilities) has increasingly dominated urban transportation almost inadvertently, as a result of shortsightedness and poor planning. Those in charge of public policy had not really intended some of the developments of the past 20 years. To correct the effects of this shortsightedness, we simply need better analysis and better planning. As Dick Netzer puts it, "At least some of the 'market failure' appears to be accidental rather than intentional."[11]

Second, many argue that the automobile has prevailed because the public has chosen it. In the traditions of economic assumptions about consumer sovereignty, this school contends that most Americans have freely chosen to buy more and more automobiles, and to direct (or permit) their government to build more and more highways because they value the independence,

[7] See the Editor's Supplement in the chapter on environment.
[8] For some evidence of the importance of this phenomenon, see John Kain, "Housing Segregation, Negro Unemployment, and Metropolitan Decentralization," *Quarterly Journal of Economics*, May, 1968, pp. 175–197.
[9] See these basic arguments in John Meyer, John Kain, and Martin Wohl, *The Urban Transportation Problem* (Cambridge: Harvard University Press, 1965), the standard work on urban transportation. Also see some of the selections in George Smerk, ed., *Readings in Transportation Policy* (Bloomington: Indiana University Press, 1968).
[10] See "Urban Transportation: Problems and Perspectives."
[11] Netzer, *op. cit.*, p. 38.

maneuverability, and flexibility of the automobile so highly. Meyer, Kain, and Wohl in their comprehensive survey of *The Urban Transportation Problem,* summarize this view:[12]

Private automobile commutation, by eliminating transfers and supplying greater privacy and schedule flexibility (where car-pooling is limited), is unquestionably a superior economic good in the minds of many urban commuters. Therefore, as income levels have increased, it is hardly surprising that more and more commuters have taken to the automobile. In short, there is considerable evidence that consumers may prefer an "automobile" solution to their urban transportation needs, even if it is a costly solution.

Both of these answers carry clear implications about the chances for redirecting public policy in the future. The first answer suggests that we need simply to carry out our analyses more carefully than we have. If we conclude from them that we need more mass transit to serve the needs of the poor, then we can have it by asking for it. The second implies that the automobile will continue to dominate until the public independently changes its preferences, until it can be convinced to change its preferences, or until the government decides somehow independently to correct for biases in the system by providing special subsidies to alternatives benefiting the poor. In any case, as with other problems, the analyses assume that government policy has reflected and will continue to reflect the preferences of nearly everyone. The fact that the government has emphasized highway construction over mass transit subsidy simply corresponds to consumer preference for the automobile over mass transit.

Further, liberal and conservative analysts usually ignore the social costs and implications of transit alternatives in making their rational calculations about transportation efficiency. They seem to do this for two main reasons. First, they view the pattern of transportation needs as the result of more basic trends in industrial and residential location; affecting these basic trends would involve tinkering with the entire market system, which liberals and conservatives would prefer not to do.[13] Second, they assume that the government is responsible for decisions about social costs. Since the government reflects the will of the people, it will presumably incorporate social costs into its decisions if the people are concerned about those social costs.[14]

THE RADICAL VIEW

The radical analysis of transportation problems provides a perfect example of the general radical contention, as Edwards and MacEwan put it in their selection in Chapter One, that "human needs become subordinated to the needs of the market and capital expansion." Long-run trends in industrial expansion and location have created the current pattern of transportation needs. As a result of those trends, individuals are forced to spend a great deal of time and money in providing for their own transportation. And given their needs, the ways in which the present institutions satisfy those needs serve the interests of the dominant classes in society.

This argument can be separated into several parts.

First, radicals contend that the current pattern of metropolitan form in the United States reflects the long-run evolution of locational preferences among capitalists, that individual citizens have had almost no choice about that basic pattern.[15] At first, manufacturing concentrated in central cities to take advantage of economies of scale and the availability of rail and river transportation. But as firms have conglomerated, internalizing many externalities, and as the truck has become an increasingly viable transportation alternative, manufacturing has tended to move outside the central city to take advantage of lower land costs.[16] This has effectively created new patterns of urban sprawl, without regard to the social implications and costs of that sprawl. Jane Jacobs has argued, for instance, that relatively dense, heterogeneous city neighborhoods provide the most humanly enriching kinds of environment.[17] Whether one agrees with

---

[12] *Op. cit.,* p. 361.
[13] See the arguments in Chapter One above.
[14] See the introduction to Chapter One.
[15] For some of this argument, see André Gorz, *Strategy for Labor* (Boston: Beacon, 1967), Chapter Four.
[16] On the basic patterns, see Leon Moses and Harold Williamson, "The Location of Economic Activity in Cities," *American Economic Review,* May, 1969.
[17] *The Death and Life of Great American Cities* (N.Y.: New American Library, 1961).

her or not, it seems clear that the present form of metropolitan development has been dictated without regard to human needs.

Second, given that pattern of development, radicals argue that the ways in which society has provided for the transportation needs created by changes in metropolitan form have been dictated by the power of a few dominant groups within the capitalist class. The auto industry has consistently pushed private automobile ownership and rapid auto obsolescence in order to maximize automobile sales.[18] As two recent books have dramatically illustrated, the extraordinary proliferation of publicly supported highways in this country has been pushed by a coalition of the auto, oil, and construction industries.[19] And, as several selections in the readings below illustrate, the evolution of mass transit alternatives has been effectively dictated by powerful financial interests—by banks who hold bonds in transit authorities and by business, commercial, and financial interests with substantial holdings in central-city real estate.

More generally, it seems possible to view social decisions about changes in the transportation system in this country as the outcome of two relatively competing interests within the capitalist class. On the one hand, many interests profit from the increasing decentralization of metropolitan areas: those interests directly benefiting from continually increasing use of the automobile (auto, oil, construction, and certain bureaucratic interests), and those manufacturing interests for whom decentralization allows much cheaper land costs in location of their plants. On the other hand, there are those institutions and interests for whom central-city land holdings and investment in building constitute an important part of total assets. For these groups, decentralization decreases the value of central-city land, while central-city urban renewal and mass transit permitting easier commutation into the central city help preserve or even increase the value of their land.[20] For the general public to be able to influence the outcome of this "struggle," it would first have to undercut the direct influence which these interests possess over public decision-making.[21]

Third, in direct application of the radical theory of the State, radicals also argue that public support of transportation inevitably results in the provision of the best services to the rich. Public transportation policies not only derive from the long-run interests of the capitalist class as a whole, in effect, but in supporting those interests the policies also provide the best transportation service to individual members of the class. The bias of public subsidies of auto transportation (through highway construction) toward the rich does not need to be demonstrated, since those subsidies benefit only those groups who are able to afford cars and especially those groups who live in the suburbs. The most important piece of evidence to support this particular radical contention concerns the income biases of mass transit. To read the liberal and conservative literature, one would assume that publicly supported mass transit serves an especially important distributional function because it provides services for the poor who cannot afford automobiles, compensating for the income biases of public highway expenditures. In fact, as wide varieties of evidence have recently revealed, present mass transit facilities favor the non-poor over the poor. Martin Wohl, in his selection among the readings in this chapter, summarizes some of this evidence. Other bits of the evidence are available in scattered places.[22]

If these three specific pieces of the general radical analysis of transportation problems seem valid now, it appears that they are becoming increasingly valid over time.

The influence of business over metropolitan patterns of development seems to be growing, particularly as major corporations continue to merge and conglomerate. More and more, business interests transcend the boundaries not only of cities but of countries, making their calculations on a truly international scale.[23]

---

[18] See some interesting comments on the phenomenon in E. J. Mishan, *The Costs of Economic Growth* (N.Y.: Praeger, 1967), pp. 90–95.

[19] Mowbray, *op. cit.*, and Helen Leavitt, *Superhighway—Superhoax* (N.Y.: Doubleday, 1970).

[20] See the arguments in the selection by Beagle *et al.* in the housing chapter above.

[21] The extent to which this is a struggle depends on the degree to which the two clusters of financial interests are overlapping. If they represent quite different economic interests, they will have to fight over policy. If they represent the same interests, they can distribute policy among both kinds of policy tools. It would probably take some effective research on the interests involved in political lobbying in Congress and the public bureaucracies to answer the question.

[22] See, for instance, Oscar Ornati, *Transportation Needs of the Poor* (N.Y.: Praeger, 1969).

[23] For a general analysis of these trends, see Stephen Hymer, "The Multinational Corporation and the

The power of institutional interests promoting automobile travel seems to be growing as well. In the selection below, A. Q. Mowbray provides a graphic example of the failure of government efforts to overcome the power of auto and highway interests. And oil companies, whose production and capital investments depend heavily on continued auto use, are concentrating their control over all natural fuel resources, in order effectively to block the development of different kinds of fuel.[24]

Finally, there seems to be no prospect that public decisions about the provision of mass transit facilities will benefit the poor any more in the future than they have in the past. During the 1960's, two major new metropolitan mass transit systems were planned, for instance, one in the San Francisco Bay Area and one in Washington, D.C. In both cases, as two selections among the readings below document, the systems will primarily serve the transportation needs of wealthy suburban residents and the business needs of downtown financial interests. The institutional and political forces which dominate the planning of such systems have simply reproduced for the future the income biases of the past.

Could all of this be any different? Doesn't advanced technology require the use of the automobile and the decentralization of cities? What differences in transportation systems would radicals recommend?

Radicals simply argue that social planning should incorporate the full range of human needs in human development. Planning of metropolitan form should reflect human needs for space, air, relaxation, density, human interaction, and variety. Planning should not be dominated by criteria of pure industrial efficiency or technological dynamics. In socialist societies which reflected those priorities, cities would probably be planned in such a way that jobs and housing were mixed closely together, minimizing transportation needs. And to guarantee social equality, all transportation would probably be publicly provided. But radicals do not pretend that one can easily wipe out the present. In modern advanced capitalist societies, automobile transportation has become necessary and a new set of social priorities could not erase that fact. Were there a revolution in the United States tomorrow, short-term transportation planning would have to cope with the automobile whatever its long-run plans. As André Gorz has written of the evolution of cities:[25]

And finally the private automobile becomes a social necessity: urban space is organized in terms of private transportation; public transportation lags farther and farther behind the spread of the suburbs and the increasing distance required to travel to work; the pedestrian or the cyclist becomes a danger to others and himself; athletic and cultural facilities are removed from the city, beyond the reach of the non-motorized suburbanite and often even of the city dweller. The possession of an automobile becomes a basic necessity because the universe is organized in terms of private transportation. This process is halted only with difficulty in the advanced capitalist countries. To the extent that the indispensability of private automobiles has made life unbearable in the large, overpopulated cities where air, light, and space are lacking, motorized escape will continue to be an important—although decreasing—element in the reproduction of labor power, even when priority has returned to city planning, to collective services, and to public transportation.

THE READINGS

The first two readings provide some Impressions, Definitions, and Magnitudes. The article by Jimmy Breslin, written in the angry aftermath of a fare increase in the New York City public transit system, sketches the reality of urban transportation problems for some central-city residents. In a selection from a longer article, John Meyer describes some of the most recent trends in the evolution of urban transportation and sorts through the different kinds of problems in the system.

Law of Uneven Development," in J. N. Bhagwati, ed., *Economics and World Order* (N.Y.: World Law Fund, 1970).
[24] Varieties of reports were available on oil company purchases of natural gas and coal fields, for instance, throughout 1970, as well as their purchases of small power companies. See James Ridgeway, *The Politics of Ecology* (N.Y.: Dutton, 1970).
[25] Gorz, *Strategy for Labor, op. cit.,* p. 88.

The rest of the readings support pieces of the radical analysis. The selections from the book by A. Q. Mowbray provide a description of the power and composition of the interests primarily responsible for the continued and increasing dominance of the automobile and the highway. The other four articles illustrate the pattern of influence over and the income biases prevalent in public decisions about mass transit. Together the four pieces thoroughly illustrate the radical contention that even mass transit alternatives are determined by the power of capitalist interests and serve the individual transit needs of wealthy citizens. Martin Wohl substantiates the general bias of mass transit systems toward the non-poor. The remaining three selections illustrate the forces producing that bias in three cities. Beagle, Haber, and Wellman describe the origins of the San Francisco Bay Area Rapid Transit System in the financial concerns of central-city businessmen. Willard Brittain establishes the biases of the new Washington, D.C., system toward the wealthy suburbs and the powerlessness of black and poor central-city residents to affect that bias. And Theodore Kheel describes the financial interests dominating the policies of one New York "public" transportation authority.

SQUEEZING THE YAHOOS

Jimmy Breslin

Jimmy Breslin describes here his ride on the New York City public transit system in January, 1970, shortly after the fare was raised by the Transit Authority from 20 to 30 cents. Breslin's anger both at the system and at the Authority reflects not only his Irish temper but the manifest reactions of thousands of New Yorkers, who threatened for a short time to refuse paying the increased fare.

Breslin writes regularly for *New York Magazine,* recently wrote a novel, *The Gang that Couldn't Shoot Straight,* and ran for New York City Council President in 1969 on Norman Mailer's ticket.

At 8:05 on a gray Tuesday morning, I stood on the back of a line of 11 people at the bus stop on 210th Street and Linden Boulevard in a part of Queens called Cambria Heights. The area, like almost every-place else in Queens, is something less than its name. The only height in Cambria Heights is a curb. There is a smallish elm tree at the 210th Street bus stop. On this morning, two sparrows rattled the bare branches and chirped into the damp air. The foot of the tree was covered with a clot of dirt-blackened ice. Pepsi-Cola cans and used Kleenex were imbedded in the ice. The bus, bouncing through potholes that looked like shell craters, pulled up. I shuffled with the line, arms held up against the ribs, taking the first of these tense little quarter-steps that brush against your energy so much more than full strides. The great Archie Moore used to boast, "I am still a champion during my old age because only I know the secret of all energy, the way to force a man to *tensionize* himself into exhaustion." Archie's secret was to make the other guy fight with constricted movements, as if he were going to work in the morning in Queens.

When I got on the bus and put my 30 cents into the till, I had the good luck to find one empty strap left. I grabbed it and the bus began to sway and bounce through potholes to the next stop and the stops after that on the way to Jamaica and the subway

SOURCE: *Jimmy Breslin, "Squeezing the Yahoos,"* New York Magazine. *Copyright © 1970 by Jimmy Breslin. Reprinted by permission of the Sterling Lord Agency.*

ride to the city, as people in Queens refer to Manhattan. As there is no way to read a paper while standing on a bus in Queens—my eyes roll around in my head like I'm playing roulette—I looked at the advertising cards. There were only three paid ads out of the 12 inside the bus. Nine of the showcards called for support of job training, of the USO, of the Urban Coalition. Each of the paid ads represented sections of the insanity of our normal living. One card was for an animal cemetery, another proclaimed the somber beauty of a big funeral for a woman's husband, and the last card was placed by a finance company. It showed a happy man handing flowers to his wife. "There's money left over for thoughtful surprises when people like you . . . people who want better things to happen now . . . ask GAC for budget help. Loans up to $1,400."

I remember the day they let loan companies go from a limit of $500 to $850, and Nelson Rockefeller said something about it being all right when he signed the bill. It was one of the worst things to happen to the working people in the state. Now the limit is up to $1,400. A working man who takes a loan of $1,400 from one of these places is almost sure to wind up carrying the loan for the rest of his life. Every time he gets it down to $600 or so, he is going right back in to rehash it and start off with the $1,400. The mere act of paying back a loan of this size, at finance company rates, will keep him borrowing forever. . . .

The anger produced by the loan company ad kept me going through many bus stops. Once, I looked out the window and saw the main entrance to St. Albans Naval Hospital. The brick buildings, with clean snow covering the lawns, seemed almost pleasant. It did not work that way inside the bus. By now, there was a spreading discomfort in the small of the back and I began pulling my shoulder up to relieve it. I asked the fellow next to me for the time. He held out his watch. It was 8:27. If he had told me the time himself, he would have been the only person on this crowded bus to speak during the entire ride. In silence, with diesel fumes starting to thicken in the rear of the bus, the people swayed and bounced for the rest of the trip to Jamaica and the subway.

It was 8:31 when the bus passed Broadway Joe's restaurant on the corner of 168th Street and Jamaica Avenue. The location originally was the home of the Terrace Tavern, site of my first $50 horse bet: on Cosmic Bomb to win the Kentucky Derby (he ran nowhere) and, more recently, the Queens headquarters for the Norman Mailer campaign. Joe Namath better have more luck. I would have laughed to myself about this, but the small of my back was aching now, and the fumes in the bus were making me sick. I pushed out of the bus at the last stop, Hillside Avenue, and took deep swallows of the damp air and then started quarter-stepping my way toward the subway entrance. At 8:35 a.m., body tense, feet shuffling, I pushed onto a filthy, crowded E train and pulled my shoulders up for the ride to the city.

A woman who had been on the bus with me, Mrs. Margaret Steinlein, nodded hello.

"How's the new fare?" I asked her.

"My daughter-in-law lives in Bellerose—it's only 15 minutes away by car, but when she doesn't have the car she takes three buses to come and visit me. They're short bus rides but she still takes three of them. That costs 90 cents one way now. Think if you make the trip with two kids you have to pay for. I mean, you can't do it anymore."

Of course that is the story of the transit fare raise. The buses and subways of this city were meant to bring it together. Particularly the subway. Without the subway, there is no City of New York. The subway is the thing that takes a father and two children from Flatbush to the Hayden Planetarium. It is what a kid rides from the Bronx to Madison Square Garden. One of

the thrills of growing up was to press your forehead against the front window of the train and see the dark tunnel dissolve into white tile and the first sign saying MADISON SQUARE GARDEN flash by. Upstairs was the rodeo, or the Rangers, and you would leave the window and rush to the door and press against it so you would be the first out onto the platform when the train stopped. It took a nickel and then a dime to ride the subway then, and it made Queens close to the Museum of Natural History and Brooklyn close to the Central Park Zoo. But the other week, when the politicians and labor leaders sat down and came up with the 30-cent transit fare, they started to push the city apart. In a family of five, with a workingman's take-home pay, you do not casually tell three of the kids, "Yes, you can go to the zoo if you don't feel like staying here today." Not if you live in Cambria Heights and the round trip costs a total of $6.40. Instead, you might tell them, "Oh, the zoo is too far. Why don't you stay around here today?" Once this process starts, it is not the City of New York anymore. It is just another sprawling place.

I don't think the people who sat in on the transit fare rises really understood this. And I don't think they understood something else: the simple draining act of riding in this subway car I was in from 168th Street station in Jamaica to Fulton Street in downtown Manhattan. The small of the back aches; each time the doors open, more heads push into the car, and directly above the heads comes this movement of air, soot-filled air from the station and the trash baskets and the tracks and the tunnels, and as you breathe it, mucilage forms on the palate. Nobody reads, nobody talks. Everybody just seems to sway on his feet and arch his back and stare numbly at the windows. Once in a while a man pulls his head back from the perfume smell of a woman's hair. That is the closest thing to a sex move I ever saw on the E train during rush hours. The crowding and swaying and thick air is enough to disgust even the worst degenerate. *Hey, lady! Stop rubbing against me—you got me leaning on my heels now and my knees are killing me.*

From 8:35 a.m. until 9:20, I rode this way. There was not even the hint of simple human dignity. The people who use the subways to go to work in the mornings might as well be handcuffed and naked. And at 9:20, one hour and 15 minutes after I got on the bus in Cambria Heights, I was through with the trip and I came upstairs and went into a coffee shop and sat down. I thought about the people who took the ride with me. I was through. They were only starting. Wilted and humiliated, they went into buildings and to a day's work. And at night, there would be another hour-and-15-minute ride, under the same conditions, back to Cambria Heights. In the newspaper, which I was unable even to open until getting to the counter of the coffee shop, I noticed a story about New York City's welfare costs reaching $2 billion a year. I thought about the guy in Cambria Heights who has just put in a day's work, and those two bus-and-subway trips, reading that story at night. Reading it and going berserk. And I thought about all the people I've known in charge of things in Manhattan and Washington and Albany, the ones with chauffeurs and diplomas and known family names, who shake their heads: "These yahoos in Queens, can you tell me how a decent human being can *reach* them? Those right-wingers, hell, they don't care if people starve."

I had a clipping in my pocket and I looked at it over coffee. It was a list of the home addresses of members of the Metropolitan Transit Authority who voted for the 30-cent fare. The chairman was William J. Ronan of 55 East 72nd Street and Ivy Cottage, East Hampton, Long Island. Other members included Leonard Braun, president of the Newport Petroleum Company, Mineola, Long Island. Mr. Braun lives in Halesite, Long Is-

land. And then there were William L. Butcher, chairman of the board, the County Trust Company, White Plains; Eben W. Pyne, senior vice-president, First National City Bank. He lives in Old Westbury, New York. And they said Norman Mailer's 51st State idea was crazy! But forget the geography. There is something much deeper than that. You see, there is something dramatically wrong, a case of terminal cancer, when any group of people sits down and discusses the transit situation in the City of New York and does not come up with something immediate which would help the simple dignity of a human being who lives and works in this city and must undergo the degrading experience of riding in its subways during the rush hours.

Thirty cents is a lot of money to pay for the instrument which makes the city what it is. The late Mike Quill was closest of all to this. "The subways should be free," he always said. But money is just one part of the problem. The other part is the one that the people in charge never seem to think of because the people who get to be in charge of things never really have had to experience it. That is the one-hour-and-15-minute ride from Cambria Heights to a day's work in Manhattan and the one-hour-and-15-minute ride back to Cambria Heights. Not just once, as I did it to write this. But every day, and the days run into each other and become weeks and the weeks turn to months and then years and people spend a lifetime of indignity, and you wonder what it does to them.

URBAN TRANSPORTATION: PROBLEMS AND PERSPECTIVES

John R. Meyer

In this selection from a longer survey article on urban transportation, Meyer sketches the dimensions of current transportation problems. Although other sections of Meyer's original article (not included here) provide elements of conventional policy prescriptions for transportation problems, these excerpts provide a straightforward delineation of the problems. Meyer emphasizes that many aspects of the issue should not cause as much concern as they seem to provoke.

Meyer is professor of economics at Yale University and president of the National Bureau of Economic Research. With John Kain and Martin Wohl, he wrote *The Urban Transportation Problem.*

DEFINITION

Urban transportation can be viewed from many perspectives. For the city planner, urban transportation is a tool for shaping or creating a city with certain desired characteristics. For local businessmen and property owners, urban transportation is a force that creates or modifies real estate values and business potentials. For the engineer, urban transportation is a challenge to design facilities to meet the needs of the community while remaining within budgetary constraints. For the economist, it is a bit of all of these plus a problem in public finance.

To the consumer, however, urban transportation is something rather different. Users, naturally enough, are interested in getting to and from work or school, to and from shopping, to and from homes of friends and family, and to and from the locations of recreational activities—as economically and expeditiously as possible. To the consumer, moreover, satisfactory transportation implies not only economy and speed, but also such factors as comfort, privacy, protection from

bad weather, schedule frequency and flexibility, and a host of other considerations. In short, urban transportation is a consumer good and, like others, is purchased because of intangible as well as tangible considerations. One of the least understood aspects of urban transportation is exactly what value consumers place on each of these considerations in making their choices.[1]

Clearly, then, many different objectives might be served by urban transportation plans or, at least, many people *think* that

[1] Among the better of the few studies available are W. Y. Oi and P. W. Shuldiner, *An Analysis of Urban Travel Demands* (Evanston: Northwestern University Press, 1962); S. L. Warner, *Stochastic Choice of Mode in Urban Travel: A Study in Binary Choice* (Evanston: Northwestern University Press, 1962); and L. N. Moses and H. F. Williamson, Jr., "Value of Time, Choice of Mode, and the Subsidy Issue in Urban Transportation," *Journal of Political Economy,* 71 (June 1963), 247–264. Other sources of detailed information are area transportation studies performed for specific cities or municipalities, e.g., Chicago, Pittsburgh, and Philadelphia. For some suggestive questionnaire information on public attitudes toward different transport modes see the editors of *Fortune, The Exploding Metropolis* (Garden City, N.J.: Doubleday & Company, Inc., 1958), and John B. Lansing, *Residential Location and Urban Mobility: The Second Wave of Interviews* (Ann Arbor: Survey Research Center, University of Michigan, January 1960), as well as two earlier reports in the same series involving the same author.

SOURCE: *John R. Meyer, "Urban Transportation: Problems and Perspectives." Excerpted by permission of the publishers from pp. 42–50, 66–69 of James Q. Wilson, editor, The Metropolitan Enigma, Cambridge, Massachusetts: Harvard University Press. Copyright © 1968 by the President and Fellows of Harvard College; 1967 by the Chamber of Commerce of the United States of America.*

different urban transportation plans might serve a variety of objectives. From the standpoint of analyzing urban transportation problems objectively this impression creates certain difficulties—specifically, that of discerning which goals (or which compromise between different objectives) are to be observed.

For present purposes, let us take the consumer point of view and accept as given present governmental arrangements. This assumption is not to say that this point of view or these arrangements are necessarily optimal.[2] Rather, it is simply an assertion that there seems to be no clearly obvious and feasible alternative. As a corollary, this acceptance of present institutional arrangements also means a heavy emphasis upon quantifiably measuring what current behavioral choices actually are.

THE SETTING AND TRENDS[3]

One of the more striking facts about urban transportation in the United States today is the extent to which it is dominated by the highway. It is reasonably clear that, like it or not, the automobile is here to stay, at least for a while. According to the 1960 Census of Population, about 64 percent of all work trips in United States urban areas were made by auto. Only about 20 percent of all urban area work trips are made by public transit; if one looks only at the central city portions of these urban areas, the public transit figure increases, but only to 26 percent. Indeed, almost half as many people walk to work as use public transit in urban areas.

Of course, the level of public transit usage for work trips varies widely among urban

areas. It is less than 2 percent in some of our smaller cities (for example, Eugene, Oregon, or Bay City, Michigan), well over half in New York City (61 percent), and between one third and one half in several other cities (for example, Chicago, Boston, Washington, New Orleans, and Philadelphia). Thus, transit is also here to stay, at least in our largest cities.

More significantly, approximately 70 percent of all public transit work trips in the United States are made entirely on local streets or highways (mainly using buses but also involving some streetcars). In addition, a third or so of those using rail transit on reserved rights-of-way also use bus or other local street transit for some portion of their work trips. It would appear that well over 70 percent of all public transit used for getting to and from work occurs on urban streets or highways and an even higher portion of public transit usage for all purposes is probably on such facilities (because rail transit is more highly specialized in serving work trips than other transit modes). Rail transit is not only a small fraction of all public transit, it is concentrated in a few areas: roughly one third or a bit more of all rail commuting is done in New York City and environs.

The obvious implication of all this is that popular discussion that assumes that the fundamental urban transportation problem is one of choosing between private auto or rail rapid transit is badly misdirected, especially for cities other than New York City and, possibly, Chicago. At a minimum, such an assumption diverts attention from ways of improving the performance of those modes that account for the vast majority of all transit.

Nor is there any reason to believe that rail transit will become much more widely used in the near future. In large measure the attractiveness of rail as compared to other modes of transit depends on the number of persons demanding transit service in a particular urban corridor during the rush hours; this, in turn, depends on where people work and how densely populated are their residential neighborhoods. As illustrated by the comparative costs shown in Figures 1 and 2, the greater the demand volume and urban density, the lower the cost per passenger trip of transit. Even so, only where

[2] As Senator Claiborne Pell has aptly put it in *Megalopolis Unbound: The Supercity and the Transportation of Tomorrow* (New York, 1966, p. 88): "We must debate our intentions and preferences and, within the limits of our constitutional, democratic system, devise at least a philosophical plan for a future growth on a regional national basis. Only then will the specific local plans for municipal development have coherence and integrity."

[3] Documentation and more detailed presentation of the materials presented in this section can be found in J. Meyer, J. Kain, and M. Wohl, *The Urban Transportation Problem* (Cambridge, Mass.: Harvard University Press, 1965), chaps. 3, 4, and 5.

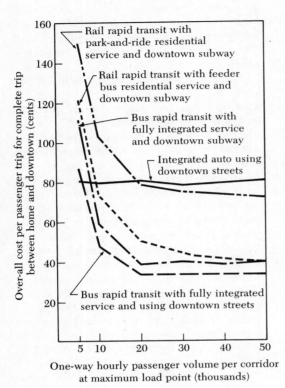

FIGURE 1

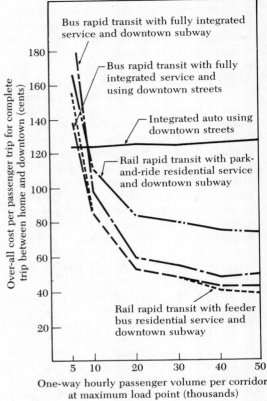

FIGURE 2

there are high-density residential areas (Figure 2) is the cost of rail transit lower than other forms; where densities are medium (Figure 1), buses are generally cheaper. These costs are also dependent on the means employed to get rail commuters to and from their homes and whether subways are used in central business areas. Rail transit improves if subways are used but is disadvantaged if people must drive and park their own cars at the rail station. As for the primary condition necessary to make rail transit economical, high hourly passenger transit volumes per corridor, only Chicago and New York have corridor flows exceeding 25,000 per hour in the United States today. Very few urban corridors in the United States have hourly transit maximums in excess of 10,000 or 15,000 and those generally have rail transit service already.

It is significant that there has been a slow but steady decline in the demands placed upon urban transport systems. These downward trends have been created by a slow decline in employment opportunities in central business districts.[4] Specifically, the number of people requiring service into and out of major central business districts during the morning and (even more important) evening rush hours has for the most part been declining or, at best, remaining steady. The peak demand placed upon the urban transportation system by rush hour entry and egress from central business districts is crucially important because it roughly de-

[4] For further discussion, see John Kain, "The Distribution and Movement of Jobs and Industry," in James Q. Wilson, ed., *The Metropolitan Enigma.*

termines the maximum capacity needs of the urban transportation system; as noted, these, in turn, are fundamentally important in determining the costs of different urban transport modes.

Though rush hour demands have been declining or staying the same, the transport capacity available for meeting these peak demands to and from central business districts has been increasing. For the most part this increase in capacity has been the result of highway construction, particularly of high performance highways with limited access. There has also been a small increase in transit route mileage, though this is often coupled with a reduction in schedule frequencies. Schedule frequency reductions, however, have been mainly in off-peak periods. Since public transit systems have continued to be primarily oriented to serving central business districts, the public transit capacity available for meeting peak hour central business district requirements has tended to remain constant or, in a few cases, to have increased somewhat.

Given this combination of a slowly declining or steady level of peak hour demands plus an increase in available capacity, some slow improvement in the overall performance of urban transportation systems has taken place. Contrary to popular impression, it does not typically take the average commuter longer to travel the same distance in the city today as formerly. On the contrary, the point-to-point travel times required between various centrally located workplaces and residential sites has, on the whole, been reduced in most United States cities in the last ten or fifteen years. During the rush hours, though, these improvements have been relatively small. An urban commuter trip that might have taken twenty-five minutes ten or fifteen years ago probably takes some twenty minutes or so today. The improvement, moreover, is likely to be shared by public transit systems as well as by private automobiles. Better expressways, for example, usually mean that fewer cars use local streets on which the the buses operate, so that the buses (as well as the cars that remain on the local streets) usually experience a three to seven mile per hour improvement in speed whenever a parallel urban expressway is completed nearby. Similarly, any reduction in demands on a rail transit

system (caused, say, by the greater attractiveness of private automobiles on improved highways) usually means that the rail transit system is somewhat less congested during rush hours and can therefore reduce waiting times at major downtown stations and thereby marginally improve its performance speed.

Needless to say, faster rush hour speeds resulting from major improvements in the highway system are only a fraction of the higher speeds now possible during off-peak or non-rush hours. Average speeds of 50 or 60 miles an hour or more are not uncommon experiences on urban expressways during off-peak periods today. These are to be contrasted with speeds rarely in excess of 35 or 40 miles an hour during rush periods today, which, while an improvement on the 30 mile or less speeds of a decade or so ago, are still not fast by modern standards.

Perhaps an even more relevant measure of performance for an urban transportation system is the time required to "decongest" or evacuate central business districts in the evening rush hours. (The evening rush seems more pertinent than the morning, since a higher level of demand is placed upon the system in the evening, apparently because of the addition of shoppers and other travelers to normal commuter demands.) A major problem with this measure is that it is somewhat difficult to define objectively. Roughly speaking, however, it can be represented as the time period during which the capacity of the central portion of the urban transportation system is more or less fully utilized because of outgoing commuters and other travelers. As an approximation, it seems that in most major cities this period has shortened by about 30 to 40 percent in recent years, say, from approximately an hour or so in the late 1940's to approximately 40 minutes today. (These numbers will vary, of course, from city to city.)

Evacuation times for central business districts also make evident another important aspect of urban transportation. It is simply quite unrealistic to speak about the "elimination of congestion" as a major goal for urban transportation planning, at least so long as most businesses choose to close shop at approximately the same hour of the day. To speak of eliminating most congestion in or around major central business districts during the evening rush hour under such circumstances is very much like speaking of eliminating congestion in or around a major football stadium just after the final whistle. To do so would require an inordinately large transport capacity—inordinately large in the sense that the cost of completely eliminating congestion under such circumstances probably would be considered outrageous by most consumers.

THE PROBLEM

If there has been a slow but steady improvement in the performance of urban transportation systems, why do we hear so much discussion of a so-called "urban transportation crisis"? The answer lies in a complex set of considerations of which probably the most important is what might be termed "a failure of anticipations."

This failure of anticipations is in great part a consequence of the uneven rates of improvement in off-peak and peak performances of urban transport systems. Traveling across densely populated urban areas at 50 or 60 miles an hour on a high-performance highway during an off-peak period seems to be an exhilarating experience, and urban commuters, quite humanly, would like to duplicate the experience during the rush hours. The difficulty, of course, is that too many of them wish to do so at one time and thus it becomes impossible without a vast increase in capacity. Whether or not they would be willing to pay the high price is open to debate. There is considerable evidence, though, that if we had a free market in the provision of urban highway commuter facilities, some considerable expansion of such facilities would probably take place.[5]

To put it another way, in our modern affluent society an improvement from 25 to 30 or 35 miles an hour or so in the average performance speed of private transport systems during the rush hours has not satisfied some commuters. This is particularly true since many of them have chosen to give up the improved transport time by living further away from their workplaces. Thus, the average time required to commute from home to

workplace and return has remained more or less constant. People have apparently been willing to incur higher transportation costs in order to achieve a lower cost for a certain quality of housing or yard space. Possibly, too, as one social psychologist has hypothesized, the typical male wage earner considers the time it takes to get between work and home as the only time that is truly his own, without interruption by foreman or wife. It is possible (no one knows) that some commuters are reluctant to reduce this time.

At any rate, more and better public transit seems to have a considerable attraction for many commuters, *not* because they want to use the transit themselves, but because they hope that it will attract *other* auto drivers off the roads. Those remaining could then realize faster speeds and less congestion on the highways. The alternative of trying to provide sufficient highway capacity so that they can commute at 50 miles an hour or so even during the rush hours is likely to be expensive both in terms of direct dollar outlays and in terms of property displacement. Indeed, if we were to go down this "road," some of the wilder claims about paving over our urban areas might actually be realized! . . .

In general, four basically different transportation systems seem to be emerging in most of our metropolitan areas. The demands placed upon these four systems are, in turn, very much a function of the changing industrial and residential location patterns discussed earlier.

The first of these systems might be described as *traditional public transit*. This system serves people employed in central business districts who also reside reasonably close by. In smaller and less dense cities this system's functions are customarily performed by buses, while in our larger, denser, and older cities they may be performed by rail transit. Costs per trip on these systems are customarily quite low. The typical trip is relatively short and takes approximately 15 or 20 minutes to complete. The clientele will be secretaries and other clerical workers employed in banks, offices, stores, and similar activities as well as service workers, very often from minority groups, with jobs in hotels, restaurants, and related activities.

The second system is *long distance commutation*. Its main function is to move people from relatively distant suburban residential

---

[5] H. Mohring, "Urban Highway Investments," in R. Dorfman, ed., *Measuring Benefits of Government Investments* (Washington, D.C.: The Brookings Institution, 1965).

locations to workplaces at the heart of the central business district. The typical trip is a good deal longer than that performed by traditional public transit. The clientele usually has a much higher average income and comes from management or the professions. These systems tend to have very high performance characteristics, so that even though the typical trip is considerably longer than that by traditional transit, the travel time required does not rise proportionally. The costs per trip for these systems also tend to be high, commonly being over one dollar per trip and sometimes as high as three dollars per trip or more. (It should be emphasized that these costs are very often *not* fully paid by the users in the form of assessed charges.) Rail commutation is a very common mode for these trips, especially in our larger and older cities. Operation of a private automobile over high-speed urban expressways is another popular choice for these trips. Occasionally, high-speed express buses may be used.

The third system pertains to *cross-commutation,* designed for commuters who find both their employment and residences in suburban areas. An almost complete cross-section of urban America—blue-collar, clerical, managerial, and professional—is likely to be involved. For the most part these trips are made today by private automobile, although occasionally the bus is used. (Better marketing and design of bus transit might well increase the percentage using public transit for these trips, but the poor finances and, possibly, the traditional conservatism of transit management have tended to prohibit experimentation with new transit services aimed at capturing more of this market.) An important feature of this type of commuter trip is that the demand for it is growing very rapidly and there is every reason to expect that it will continue to grow.

The fourth type of basic urban transportation system might be described as an *inside-out system.* It serves work-trips made by people living in relatively central locations and working in the suburbs. The Negro female domestic working in a suburban home and living in a centrally located ghetto is the archetype; today, however, she is probably increasingly joined by male Negroes because employment opportunities in manufacturing, inter-city transportation, and even wholesaling and retailing are increasingly found at suburban locations, whereas housing opportunities remain restricted to the central ghetto. Furthermore, many white families with two or more workers, at least one of whom is employed in the central business district and one in a suburban workplace, have often found central city residential locations convenient.

The usual technical description of these outbound commuter trips is "reverse commutation," but this suggests that the central city systems described above can adequately serve these outbound commuter trips on their "empty backhauls." However, this is an oversimplification because the origination and destination patterns required for these inside-out trips is often very different from that of downtown-oriented transit. For example, it is unlikely that a Negro male employed in a suburban industry will be adequately served by a simple reversal of a downtown system. The chances of these systems serving the outbound white commuter well are also remote, since he normally does not live as close to the central business district as the minority groups.

The fact that conventional public transit or commuter systems have not served these inside-out trips well has been documented recently by Negro complaints about difficulties in reaching certain employment opportunities. Such complaints were recognized in the McCone report on the Watts riots. These inside-out trips are very often performed by private automobiles, with the cost of the trips being reduced by car-pooling. Some recent public transit experiments financed by the Department of Housing and Urban Development (as in Watts, for example) may eventually reduce this reliance upon private automobiles.

It should be quite clear that since the groups served by these four different basic urban transportation systems are rather different, the incidence of benefits derived from improvements in these systems will vary considerably. For example, improvement of the long-distance, high performance suburb to downtown systems will tend primarily to benefit higher income groups. To the extent that development of these systems is subsidized from public funds, the implicit income transfer probably would be regressive. By contrast, expenditures aimed at improving conventional short-haul central city transit will almost certainly benefit mostly low- to middle-income groups.

It is also clear that future demands placed upon these different systems may vary widely. The need for cross-haul services between suburban residences and workplaces seems to be growing most rapidly, while the demand for conventional public transit seems to be declining. Demands for long-distance commutation seem to be more or less constant or slowly increasing, depending upon the extent to which a particular downtown area houses office and related service activities. Finally, as long as housing opportunities for minority groups are primarily limited to the centrally located ghetto, the demand for "inside-out" commutation is likely to grow.

Thus, in light of anticipated future needs, public policy might well focus attention on the development of cross-haul and inside-out systems. Any such emphasis would depart, of course, from that implicit in the development or subsidization of long-distance rail commuter lines, an all too characteristic emphasis in recent urban transportation planning.

The most neglected aspect of urban transportation planning would seem to be devising means to meet cross-haul or reverse commuter trips via public transit. The need is for experimentation with new and more flexible forms of public transit and the establishment of more public transit routes that traverse *only* suburban and non-central locations. In particular, many cross-haul and reverse commuter trips are almost certainly better served by public transit that does *not* become involved in downtown congestion with all that implies in time losses and increased operating costs. More intensive analysis of basic urban commuter markets and a concomitant improvement in marketing strategies employed by public transit managements would greatly facilitate these developments.[6]

In summary, it must be recognized that cities are constantly undergoing change. There are many reasons for believing that the changes in workplace and residential location being induced by ever-changing manufacturing, bookkeeping, transportation, and communication technologies may result in radically different urban transportation patterns in the near future. Indeed, one of the major failures of many urban public transit systems has been their failure to serve new workplaces in suburban or metropolitan ring locations. If present trends in residential and workplace locations continue, the major unmet urban transportation needs ten or twenty years from now may well be between, within, and across the outer portions of our large metropolitan areas rather than to and from the core.

[6] Lewis M. Schneider, *Marketing Urban Mass Transit: A Comparative Study of Management Strategies* (Boston, 1965), presents several interesting ideas on how these improvements might be implemented.

THE POWER OF HIGHWAY INTERESTS

A. Q. Mowbray

The following selections, from Mowbray's recent book *Road to Ruin*, illustrate the power of vested interests supporting vast and continuing highway construction. Automobiles kill, congest, and pollute, while highways devour, but our ability to move away from automobile transportation is thoroughly circumscribed by the power of the interests described in this selection. The first part of the selection sketches the composition of highway interests, while the second documents a classic instance of the raw application of their power.

SOURCE: *From the book* Road to Ruin *by A. Q. Mowbray. Copyright © 1969, 1968, by A. Q. Mowbray. Reprinted by permission of J. B. Lip-* pincott Company and Bill Berger Associates, Inc. *Copyright © 1969, 1968. Reprinted by permission of the author.*

The highway bulldozer is powered by an alliance of the federal and state governments, guided and stimulated by the lobbying activities of the beneficiary industries. For many years, the highway pork barrel has been nurtured and tended by a happy and compatible establishment comprising the Public Works committees of both houses of Congress, the Federal Highway Administration, the state highway officials, and the lobbyists for the many industries—automobiles, petroleum, construction materials, building contractors, auto clubs, and so on—that benefit from the huge amounts added every year to the barrel. There is considerable mutual back-scratching all along the line.

Cooperation between federal and state officials has always been very close. During the years when the Federal Highway Administration was part of the business-oriented Department of Commerce, the two federal highway administrators, Bertram Tallamy and Rex Whitton, both highway engineers, were past-presidents of the American Association of State Highway Officials. When the Department of Transportation was created in 1966, and the Federal Highway Administration was shifted there, a chink appeared in that relationship: neither the Secretary of Transportation, Alan Boyd, nor the new Highway Administrator, Lowell Bridwell, was a highway engineer, Boyd having been a Florida lawyer and Bridwell an Ohio newspaperman. Advocates of other forms of transportation can now get at least a hearing in the executive branch, but so far the money still goes to highways.

In the legislative branch, or, as former Senator Joseph Clark calls it, the "sapless branch," the devotion to the pavers appears to be undimmed. Billions of dollars each year are generated automatically in the Highway Trust Fund without the need for the Congress to lift a finger to tax anyone. It remains only to deal the money out to the states. The lobbyists for the various highway industries are in faithful, unblinking attendance to ensure that no bottlenecks appear in the pipeline. Members of Congress usually maintain a discreet silence about such things, but, in the fall of 1967, Representative Lionel Van Deerlin, a Democrat from California, burst out in an unaccustomed fit of pique: "For far too long the automobile industry, swaggering through our House office buildings with high-

handed lobbyists—some of them paid up to $100 an hour—has sought to impose auto management's selfish interests over the judgment of the American public." Mr. Deerlin's ire had been aroused by the difficulty that Congress was experiencing in passing legislation to curb air pollution, but one feels confident that the same "high-handed lobbyists" are working just as hard to promote highway construction as they are to soften air-pollution controls.

The automotive industry is only the beginning. Every additional mile of highway means an additional 50,000 gallons of motor fuel consumed each year. We are adding pavement to the land at the rate of about 45,000 miles per year, which means an additional consumption of about $2\frac{1}{4}$ billion gallons of fuel each year. At 4 cents per gallon, that means an increase in the Highway Trust Fund of $90 million per year. In the face of this growth, the petroleum industry cannot be expected to maintain an attitude of cool detachment. Nor can the highway engineers. At least one of them has complained in writing about the proliferation of small foreign cars on our highways. Their fuel consumption is too low to support road-building at the proper rate.

About 90 percent of the new pavement laid each year is topped with asphalt. Since the beginning of the Interstate Highway program, the capacity of the asphalt pavement industry has increased by 132 percent—from 97 million to 225 million tons per year. There are 3,500 asphalt plants in the United States, distributed among 1,800 different companies. Asphalt production has set a new record every year since the Interstate program began, with the single exception of 1967.

The trucking industry also has an interest in better highways. There are now more than 15 million trucks on our roads, carrying 22 percent of all our intercity freight, and carrying 90 percent of our livestock and 63 percent of our produce to market. Nearly ten million persons earn their living in the manufacture, distribution, maintenance, or commercial use of trucks.

The list goes on and on. The statistics are equally impressive for dozens of other industries dependent in one way or another on highway transportation. None of them is reluctant to communicate its faith in the importance of paving to our national economy, in the creed, as one of them puts it, that "as highway transportation grows so grows the nation."

H. E. Humphreys, Jr., says flatly that if "any impediment" is put in the way of the natural growth of highway transport, no city, no farm, no business, no family, no individual will be exempt from the destructive consequences. "The shuttle that weaves the web of our national life," he says, "is auto-mobility." The engineering director of the Keystone Auto Club has wondered out loud how any opposition to highway building could possibly develop in a land where "the automobile has been so long a symbol of our high standard of living."

A recent full-page advertisement in *The Wall Street Journal*, "One of a series presented by Ford Motor Company on behalf of the American Trucking industry to help keep America moving ahead," helped to spread the gospel:

"You find congestion wherever you find people. Always have, even in the horse-and-buggy days.

"Automobiles broke the turn-of-the-century traffic jam. Downtown traffic moved faster, more freely. And because people became mobile they could spread out from the city's heart.

"Now the plot (and the traffic) thickens again. What's the answer? Keep private vehicles out of the central city entirely, as some planners advocate?

"Hardly. Keep cars away and you keep people away. That's how Americans are today.

"Modern highways don't cause congestion, they relieve it. You may complain about expressway traffic in New York or Detroit or Los Angeles. But you get in and out in about two-thirds the time you could a decade ago. And twice as safely.

"We need improved public transportation in many cities, certainly. (Interestingly, more than three-fourths of all transit passengers ride buses using the same highways and streets as passenger cars.)

"But this is even more certain: we also need to complete—and to supplement—our urban highway system so that cars, trucks, and buses can serve the American people more efficiently." . . .

The third corner of the federal-industry-state troika is distributed among the capitals of the fifty states.

The Congressional delegation for each

state is pleased to announce annually an increasing allocation of federal-aid highway money. The governor is pleased to welcome the money and the state highway department is pleased to spend it. Highway construction and maintenance is the largest single activity of the state; it accounts for 70 to 75 percent of all capital expenditures. The remainder takes care of schools, hospitals, public buildings, natural resources, and other miscellaneous needs. The highway department is thus by far the largest distributor of largesse in the state. It wishes to remain so.

The regular, continuing federal-aid highway program provides that half the construction costs will be provided by the federal government. The 41,000-mile Interstate program provides 90 percent federal money. In both of these programs, there is feverish competition among the states to qualify as many projects as possible for federal approval. Therefore, when a route is proposed, one finds its quick approval being urged by the highway department, the governor, the state legislators, and just about everyone else for whom the federal dollar means votes, or on whom a dollar can rub off.

One quirk of the federal highway law can result in the bulldozing of entirely new roads across the landscape, when the improvement of an older route might do the job as well. The 90-percent federal money in the Interstate program is available only for *new* routes. For improvement of older routes, only 50-percent federal money can be had. So, faced with a choice, local officials find it tempting to push through the new road.

Even where federal funds are involved, it is the state that has the primary responsibility to select the route for a new highway, design it, acquire the land for the right-of-way, let the contracts to the road builders, supervise the construction, and thereafter maintain the completed highway. If federal funds are involved, the Bureau of Public Roads must review and approve each step along the way, and the states must meet certain requirements of federal law. These requirements have been tightened several times since 1956, in response to anguished outcries from local communities throughout the country as the combination of heady power and huge influxes of Trust Fund money sent state highway bulldozers slashing indiscriminately across the countryside.

At the time the Trust Fund was set up and

the Interstate system approved, Congress added the requirement that no project would be approved unless the state could show that a public hearing had been held in the community and that the *economic* effects of the proposed highway had been considered. In the debate on this provision, some Senators opposed it on the grounds that it was an intrusion on states' rights. The intrusion is minimal, however, since there is no requirement that the state take any heed of what is said during the hearings. As a result, the usual gambit of the highway department has been to delay holding public hearings until the plans for the highway are so far along that any major change in the route would be economically unfeasible. . . .

The magic formula [for building roads] is known as the Highway Trust Fund. It was invented in 1956, when the nation entered on the greatest spree of highway building in the history of the world, a program that has justifiably been called "the greatest public works program in history." Launched by legislation signed by President Eisenhower in June, 1956, the National System of Interstate and Defense Highways will be a 41,000-mile system of super roads connecting 90 percent of all the cities in the nation over 50,000 population. The system is designed to handle the traffic expected in 1975; and 90 percent of its cost will be paid out of federal funds, only 10 percent by the various states. This program is superimposed upon the regular, continuing federal-aid highway programs, which have built a million miles of roads financed by the states and the federal government on a 50–50 basis.

This ambitious highway measure, passed by a voice vote in the House and an 89–1 roll call in the Senate, projected a total cost for the system at about $40 billion, to be spent over the next thirteen years. (The estimated cost for the program has since increased to something like $55 or $60 billion, and the completion date has crept up by stages from the original target of 1972 to something more like 1975 or 1976.) After much wrangling in Congress about how to pay for this monumental program, a scheme was devised that not only assures a steady flow of funds, but also renders the flow all but immune from the year-to-year whimsies of a fickle legislature. Under this scheme, a Highway Trust Fund was established, into

which pour in an unceasing stream tax money from the sale of gasoline and other motorists' necessities such as spare parts and tires. At the outset one cent of the federal tax on every gallon of gasoline fed the Trust Fund; this has now increased to four cents.

This self-perpetuating fund simply grows —independent of any new authorization by Congress. Each year the Administration doles out the bounty to the states as their highway departments come up with plans that seem reasonable to the Federal Bureau of Public Roads. As the road mileage increases, more cars take to the roads and drive more miles, burning more gallons of gasoline, wearing out more tires, and feeding more money into the inviolate Trust Fund. A perfect closed loop calculated to keep smiles on the faces of the highway builders.

During the decade following enactment of the Interstate Highway Act, all went smoothly. The money poured into the Highway Trust Fund in a golden stream. Engineers across the land drew lines on maps, and the bulldozers followed, in increasing numbers. While each year Washington budget-makers strained to find the money for a thousand crying needs, and Congressional committee rooms echoed to the voices pleading for funds to pour on this or that hurt, the inviolable Highway Trust Fund plowed ahead under its own power, the money pouring into one end and out the other, as though regulated by an immutable law of nature.

The pork-barrel aspects of this gigantic operation gave it apparent immunity from the tug and haul of all other earthly endeavors. "We want more roads," the nation had said, and more roads it was getting. The bill had providentially been paid in advance. It remained only to dole out the largesse year by year.

It took a major land war in Asia and the threat of runaway inflation to cast the first faint shadow of doubt over the operation. In the fall of 1966—with war costs mounting, spending levels rocketing above $100 billion, and heavy federal borrowing pressing prices upward—President Johnson looked about for ways to reduce federal spending without curtailing vital programs. By mischance, his eye fell on the highway program.

Federal grants to the states for highway building had been running along at about $4 billion per year, and highway builders anticipated an allocation of $4.4 billion for fiscal year 1967. On the day before Thanksgiving, however, the Administration announced that the states would receive only $3.3 billion. This was not a cut in allocations, it was simply a "freeze" of money already allocated, a delay in handing it to the states for use.

The announcement had been cagily timed. Election day was safely past, and the long Thanksgiving weekend might provide a cooling-off period for any Congressional or gubernatorial hotheads.

But the President had underestimated the power of the highway lobby. No sooner had the freeze been announced, than White House wires began to buzz with messages from the state capitals expressing the displeasure of the various state highway departments and governors; letters and telegrams from road contractors rained down upon the congressmen, and they, in turn, rose upon the floor of Congress to denounce the President.

"Illegal" and "unwarranted" were some of the terms used to describe the freeze. The chairmen of the Public Works committees of the House and Senate announced angrily that they would hold joint hearings to investigate the cutback in highway funds. Representative George H. Fallon, chairman of the House Committee on Public Works, said "the cutback and freeze makes it impossible to maintain an orderly highway construction program. The failure to do so is not only economically shortsighted but puts us in the highly questionable position of acceding to an action that must spell death and injury to the thousands of people who will be involved in accidents."

Engineering News-Record, the authoritative weekly construction magazine, echoed the life-and-limb argument: "Delayed completion of new highways claims a high price in lives and property lost in traffic accidents, as well as in the economic losses caused by traffic congestion. Individuals and groups concerned with highway construction should do their best to make [their wishes known] to the Administration, and to Congress."

The individuals and groups concerned with highway construction needed no prodding. Their wishes were flowing to Washington in abundance. Robert S. Holmes, president of the politically potent American Road Builders Association, burned the midnight oil preparing testimony for the joint Congressional hearings on the fund freeze.

As general manager of highway construction for U. S. Steel Corp., Mr. Holmes was quick to announce that the freeze would eliminate a half-million tons of steel from highway construction.

Massachusetts Governor John Volpe, himself a one-time road contractor, charged that the President had designs on the frozen highway funds, that he intended to use them for other purposes. This, said Volpe, would be a "misuse of gas tax money" and a "direct violation of the intent of Congress." The full $1.1 billion in frozen funds, he said, should be restored at once.*

On February 13, in a move to take some sting out of the rising storm, Secretary of Transportation Alan Boyd announced that the frozen funds would be released just as soon as economic conditions permitted. But his words were as effective as a meat ball thrown to a hungry lion. Representative Fallon and Senator Jennings Randolph went busily ahead with plans for their joint hearings. The Building Trades Department of the AFL-CIO adopted a resolution demanding restoration of the frozen funds, warning that the slowdown in construction would seriously jeopardize the industry and cause substantial increases in unemployment.

On February 27, Secretary Boyd was up on Capitol Hill testifying at the joint Public Works hearings. He had brought with him a large chunk of rich, red meat to throw to the lions: the Administration had decided to release $175 million of the frozen $1.1 billion immediately, and promised $225 million more before the end of June, which was the end of the fiscal year. Further, he promised that the Administration would release to the states the full $4.4 billion authorized by Congress for the coming fiscal year, starting July 1. As though unwilling to let his transportation secretary get all the credit, Mr. Johnson, back in the White House, made the same announcement, at almost the same moment.

The President said the partial release of funds was prompted by an easing of the inflation threat, but many in Washington saw it as a bending to the will of an irresistible political force. Even so, the lions were still hungry. Senator Randolph said the hearings would continue. Representative William C. Cramer, ranking Republican on the House

---

* [Ed.: Volpe later served as President Nixon's first Secretary of Transportation.]

roads subcommittee, demanded that the President release the entire $1.1 billion. "This is nothing more than a token gesture," he said. "The Administration has converted the federal-aid highway program from a stable program for which advance planning could be undertaken with the assurance of orderly construction financed by an inviolate trust fund to an 'iffy' program which goes up and down like a Yo-Yo depending upon the policies and economic theories of the Administration."

On February 28, President Johnson sent his budget director, Charles L. Schultz, down to the joint Congressional hearings to capitulate. In his testimony, Mr. Schultz hinted broadly that very substantial sums of money would be restored to the highway program within a few weeks. When Representative Fallon asked how good a bet this was, Mr. Schultz smiled and replied that, although he was not a betting man, he would be willing to put a substantial stake on the probability. This satisfied the congressmen. Although several days of hearings still were scheduled, they were abruptly ended.

On March 17, Mr. Johnson made good his promise: he released an additional $350 million. Three months later he released the remainder of the $1.1 billion. Said the President, "Inflationary pressures have subsided." *Engineering News-Record* believed there might be another reason. "Administration officials soon realized they had a tiger by the tail," said the construction weekly. And they loosed their hold on the highway funds "before the aroused beast mauled them severely. . . . Contractors, equipment dealers and manufacturers, material suppliers and others lost no time in complaining to their congressional delegations in no uncertain terms. The clamor come through loud and clear at the White House."

This, the magazine said, should be a lesson to the President and also to his new Secretary of Transportation: "Never underestimate the raw power of the federal-aid highway program. Politically, it contains something of benefit to every member of Congress, something he can show the home folks that he has got for them. Practically, the vested interests with a major stake in the program are strong, vocal and well organized; they pack tremendous clout."

The great highway battle of 1967 ended with a clean victory for the forces of highway construction. By spring it was apparent that, even with the very temporary setback occasioned by the President's imprudent shenanigans, 1967 would be the biggest year the road builders had ever had. The states planned to spend more than $5.2 billion during the year, an estimate that would increase to record-breaking proportions when the unfrozen funds swelled the flood. And 1968 promised to be even better; the President had already stated his intention to release $4.4 billion to the states.

PUBLIC TRANSPORTATION AND INCOME GROUPS

Martin Wohl

Wohl provides striking evidence here that public transportation does not serve the needs of the poor, as many tend to assume, and that it does not somehow compensate for the income bias of public subsidy to highways. In fact, data available suggest that public transit systems also favor upper-income users, joining highways as another example of public support of the rich. The selection represents most of the original article, called "Income Circumstances of Public Transit Users," which appeared in *Traffic Quarterly*.

Wohl has served recently as Director of Transportation Studies at the Urban Institute in Washington, D.C. With John Meyer and John Kain, he wrote *The Urban Transportation Problem*.

SOURCE: *Martin Wohl, "Income Circumstances of Public Transit Users,"* in Traffic Quarterly, *January, 1970. Reprinted by permission of the Eno Foundation for Transportation.*

Public concern is increasingly being shown for the establishment or improvement of public transportation systems to enhance the living and working conditions and the opportunities of urban dwellers, particularly the less-well-to-do and handicapped. Yet in attempting to provide mobility and flexibility —especially for the poor, handicapped, or disadvantaged—and in pressing for massive public transport programs directed to that end, we have utterly failed to examine the results of such programs. More specifically, we have failed to identify the users of the various services and the extent to which they benefit from the services; neither have we identified the extent to which the objectives have been achieved, nor the effects of subsidies and income transfers on the social groups involved.

The purpose of this paper is, first, to delineate the kinds of questions that seem appropriate to a realistic analysis of decisions on providing or improving urban transport services. Emphasis will be placed, not on the overall decision-making process or on aggregate benefit-cost analysis, but on the incidence of the transport costs and benefits and on identifying, where possible, the extent to which particular income or social groups are affected (either adversely or beneficially) by different actions. Second, the few available data on these matters will be recorded and summarized so that inferences may be drawn about income circumstances appropriate to various types of urban transportation services and facilities.

A prime argument in support of continuing publicly supported urban transport services (whether they be publicly or privately owned) is that various immobile groups should be given a transport choice rather than forced to accept expensive private transportation, and that their living and working opportunities should be extended beyond present circumstances and beyond the limitations imposed by their not being able to afford better transportation or housing. Rather than debate whether society should or should not adopt this posture, we should consider the consequences of so doing and look more closely at the alternative actions open to us. That is, *given* the desire to provide more mobility and flexibility—in terms of living and working patterns and opportunities—what are the transport and nontransport alternatives available to us and

what are their effects, in terms of efficiency and distribution?

Among the most important aspects to be considered are the following:

1. As we provide subsidized urban transport services, who will be using and be helped by them and to what extent?

2. How else than by subsidizing transport services can mobility be increased for certain groups?

3. What are the costs, both in aggregate and differential terms, of providing public and private transport choices and different kinds and levels of services?

4. What are the nontransport alternatives (with respect to housing, shopping, business, and employment locations and other conditions) that may increase urban opportunities and reduce the necessity for providing improved transport services?

5. Is it necessary to make a distinction between public and private transport services and to maintain the availability of both public and private choices?

6. Must, or should, public support be restricted to public transport systems, or should it be extended to include private systems?

A little reflection on these and similar questions reveals that, to date, most of them have yet to be seriously raised, much less answered. Further, our data base hardly permits even an approximate analysis and evaluation. To illustrate, consider—albeit briefly—the current Mass Transportation Demonstration project now under way in South Central and East Los Angeles (the so-called Watts project), a project largely sponsored under the HUD Urban Transportation Administration demonstration program. The mission of this project, the bulk of whose funds have been expended to date on the Century Boulevard Line bus operation, is "to determine and test the relationship between a public transportation system and job and other opportunities of low-income groups." Even with this charter, and with the emphasis on low-income groups and with residents in particular, none of the six progress reports has so far included more than fragmentary information on the extent to which the objective has been met, or on income characteristics of the bus riders. In fact, the only glimpse into this aspect of the bus demonstration project is found in data indicating that at most only 50 percent of the bus riders are Watts residents. However, no data were gathered (or at least reported) that would shed light on the income of riders from Watts or other areas.

A second aspect of this project worth noting is that providing Century Boulevard Line bus services required expenditures (to society) of approximately 60 cents per passenger trip, about 35 cents of it covered by federal subsidy from the UTA demonstration program. Two points arise. The first obviously pertains to the matter of income distribution—that is, to the question of who is receiving the subsidy and who is paying it and how they compare socially and financially. The second point concerns operational characteristics of the trips being made on this bus line (e.g., time of day, trip length, etc.) and the possible service alternatives. Could a taxi service, for example, be more closely tailored to serve low-income groups and offered at a cost that is competitive with the relatively expensive bus service?

Or, to take another example: might it not be more reasonable—in terms of helping low-income groups, particularly, to obtain more mobility and to take advantage of a wider range of job and living opportunities —to consider using federal credit backing or loans or subsidies to enable low-income workers to purchase used automobiles, for which they now lack capital or credit backing? Again, the point is that there is no apparent reason why federal subsidies or demonstration projects should not be extended to take account of both public *and* private transport opportunities, instead of being limited to the former, as at present.

A related consideration, as various urban transport services are introduced or improved to increase the mobility and employment opportunities of low-income groups, is that individuals' housing locations can (and in some cases will) shift as they become gainfully employed and stabilize their earning capability. Similarly where they may initially take advantage of, say, improved bus service to gain and hold a job, this employment may in turn —and in a short time—permit them to earn sufficient income to buy and use a private automobile in place of public transport or to join a car pool. (Clearly, evidence and experience gained from the Route 128 study supports such a general conclusion.)[1] Obvi-

ously, this is to argue for flexibility in investigating the use of improved public transport to develop or enhance employment opportunities.

Turning now to the general proposition of public-transport coverage and usage, let us cite some of the "conventional wisdom" and describe the overall characteristics of public vs. private travel. First, it is generally held that the automobile is the symbol of the "rich" traveling public and public transit the symbol of the "poor." This view has encouraged massive support for public transportation (including subsidization of private commuter railroad services available to the public) as a means of helping the poor. However, the little evidence available—placed in aggregate form at this stage of the paper— suggests the fallacy of such a position. For example, the average annual family income of all U.S. workers was $5,660 in 1960, while that of workers using transit was $6,466.[2] While it is difficult to explain fully this differential (and it is likely that the two groups are somewhat incomparable), two things seem worth suggesting. First, the income distribution of transit riders probably tends to be bimodal, with a fairly large concentration of both high-income and low-income riders, while that of auto travelers may be spread more uniformly over the entire income spectrum. Two, the high- and low-income transit riders tend to be separated by types of transit service, with the low-income group making shorter, local bus and subway trips (where this service is available) and the high-income group making longer subway and commuter-railroad trips. Obviously, this "natural" income segregation stems largely from the fact that higher-income families can afford and obtain housing in expensive fringe and suburban communities, as well as afford the extra travel expenses. On the latter point, as one's residence is removed farther from the Central Business District (CBD), the difficulty and expense of getting to and from subway or commuter railroad facilities increase, often requiring that a second family car be available for local collection and distribution. These income differentials and travel patterns —by type of transit service—can be seen to

[1] A. J. Bone and Martin Wohl, "Industrial Development Survey on Massachusetts Route 128," Bulletin 189, Highway Research Board, 1958, Washington, D.C.
[2] From *Fact Book,* The Transit Advertising Association, Inc., December 1963.

TABLE 1
FAMILY INCOME AND TRAVEL CHARACTERISTICS FOR CHICAGO WORKERS USING TRANSIT FOR THE WORK TRIP

Line-Haul Mode	Residential Collection Mode	Family Income	Average Distance to Work (miles)
Commuter Railroad	Auto	$7325	13.5
	Rail	7453	11.1
	Bus	7066	13.8
	All	$7425	13.5
Rapid Transit	Auto	7696	9.2
	Rapid	6456	6.6
	Bus	7003	7.4
	All	$6850	7.2
Suburban Bus	Auto	5956	5.2
	Bus	6904	4.6
	All	$6683	4.6
City Bus	Auto	6405	9.3
	Bus	6766	3.9
	All	$6789	4.0

SOURCE: Abstracted from J. Meyer, J. Kain, and M. Wohl, *The Urban Transportation Problem* (Cambridge: Harvard University Press, 1965), Table 48.

some extent in data for Chicago area workers who use transit for the work trip (Table 1).

Second, one must examine more closely the problems of providing suitable urban transport service for the young and for the elderly or handicapped. While one may expect these two groups to represent an unusually large share of transit riders, the few available data do not seem to bear this out. In Table 2, the percentage of transit riders by age group is placed alongside the percentage of the U.S. population by age group. (Admittedly, one would prefer to compare the transit figures with data on all urban trips made, but these latter data are not reported in the literature.) While inferences are somewhat tenuous, it appears that at present the transportation of the young is largely handled by (parents') chauffeuring or by walking or cycling. With almost 25 percent of U.S. families already owning two or more cars (a

TABLE 2
PERCENTAGE DISTRIBUTION BY AGE GROUP

Age Group	Percentage of Transit Riders in Age Group Shown*	Percentage of U.S. Population in Age Group Shown
Less than 20 years	7.0	38
20 through 39	38.8	26
40 through 59	41.7	23
Over 59	12.5	13

* *Fact Book, op. cit.*

figure that is increasing at about 2 or 3 percent a year) and with only 4 percent of the U.S. population under 20 years of age being licensed drivers, it seems reasonable to expect other services than public transit to be used by the young—even assuming some considerable improvement in these services. Such a conclusion seems particularly inevitable when one looks at aggregate urban patterns and at the absolute and relative increase of suburban vs. central-city living and working.

For the elderly, a different set of problems arises. On the one hand, they may have difficulty affording other than cheap transport service and may require service at different hours and places than do most others requiring or desiring public transit. On the other hand, their age and generally declining physical condition—and mental attitude— probably lead them to want (if not "demand") services of much higher quality than are consistent with the prices they are willing and able to pay. For example, the climbing up stairs, the long walks to or from stations, the long waits, the standing in vehicles, the difficulty in reading signs, the jolting while riding in and emerging from starting and stopping vehicles, and the short time available for loading and unloading public transit vehicles, and so forth—all these elements work to the disadvantage of the elderly and tend to suggest that other public transport services than current bus and rail transit would be more suitable. Perhaps this is to suggest that as this group becomes more affluent, it will tend to shift out of transit and into taxi or private automobile travel.

From the 1963 Census of Transportation some observations can be made about differences among work commuters from different income groups or classes. Some of the more important of these data are shown in Tables 3 through 6. In analyzing these data, however, one should take care to realize that the summaries apply to all commuters—those working and living in the suburbs, those living and working in central cities, and those living in the suburbs but working in the downtown area (which are a small minority, both of urban commuters and of the downtown work force).

Note first that the distance to work for nonwhite and low-income commuters, respectively, tends to be shorter than that for white and higher-income commuters (see

TABLE 3
DISTRIBUTION OF WORK TRIPS BY DISTANCE TO WORK

Percentage of U.S. workers in each group having distance to work shown:*

		1 Mile or Less	2 or 3 Miles	4 or 5 Miles	6 to 10 Miles	11 Miles or More
	By Race					
(a)	White	14	23	14	25	24
	Nonwhite	20	23	16	21	20
	By Family Income					
	Less than $2,000	20	23	15	20	22
	$2,000–3,999	19	24	14	23	20
	$4,000–5,999	14	24	16	24	22
(b)	$6,000–7,499	15	21	14	27	23
	$7,500–9,999	11	22	14	25	28
	$10,000–14,999	10	23	14	23	30
	$15,000 and over	15	19	12	31	23
	Averages					
(c)	All commuters	15	23	14	24	24

* From 1963 Census of Transportation, Passenger Transportation Survey, Home-to-Work Travel.

TABLE 4
DISTRIBUTION OF WORK TRIPS BY TIME TO WORK

Percentage of workers (by race and mode of travel) having times to work shown:*

	Less than 15 min.	15 to 35 min.	36 min. and over	Not Applicable or not Reported
By Race				
(a) White	29	52	15	4
Nonwhite	14	47	28	11
By Mode of Travel				
Driver only	32	54	11	3
(b) Car pools	25	55	19	1
Public transit	4	44	49	3

* *1963 Census of Transportation, op. cit.*

Table 3).[3] Generally, this stems from the fact that whites and higher-income commuters as a group tend to be suburban residents and workers (or suburban residents and downtown workers, but to a lesser extent), while nonwhites and other low-income workers tend to find their residences and work places heavily concentrated in the more central areas. Despite these longer distances for whites and higher-income commuters, we find that the travel times have just the reverse relationship, as shown in Table 4(a). Generally, the radial and intersectorial travel of the suburban workers, while covering longer distances, is made at considerably higher speeds (particularly on a door-to-door basis) than that of central-core workers, who have to fight intown congestion, wait for transit service, and walk to and from transit facilities.

In analyzing these data, it is difficult to gain sufficient perspective to focus intensively on the effects of improved transit service, because of the way in which the data are aggregated. Principally, transit travel is limited to a handful of large metropolitan areas—such as New York, Chicago, Philadelphia, and Boston, which together account for about half of all U.S. transit work trips. In these high-transit-usage cities, transit work trips are confined largely to the downtown or central-core work groups. As a result, some caution is advised in generalizing from data

that aggregate work trips from small and large cities, from low- and high-transit-usage areas, and so forth.

In a sense, this aggregation problem adds to the difficulties of interpreting data such as that shown in Table 5, on the modal choices of different income groups. That is, the percentages represent a blend of cities for which transit ridership, even in the very-high-income group, is quite extensive and cities in which little or no transit service exists or is used; thus, any comparisons are likely to be misleading. Nevertheless, with these limitations, one may intuitively arrive at (or compute, if one desires) the relative family incomes of commuters on the different modes. Again, it may be shown that transit commuters, on the average, come from families with higher incomes than nontransit riders (as a group); it is clear, however, that commuters who drive alone (as a group) have the highest family incomes. However, as will be discussed, situations will arise where usage is considerably greater for the transit mode than the drive-alone mode, even for the highest-income groups.

Percentages of workers living within certain distances of public transportation, or not having access to public transportation, are presented in Table 6. The most important information here pertains to the availability of public transportation.[4] Generally,

[3] For a more intensive analysis of this characteristic, see Meyer, Kain, and Wohl, *op. cit.*, Ch. 7.

[4] "Public transportation was deemed not available if, in the judgment of the respondent, the worker was unable to get from home to work by public

TABLE 5
DISTRIBUTION OF WORK TRIPS BY MODE

Percentage of workers in each income group using the mode shown:*

Family Income†	Percent	Auto Driver Only	Car Pooler	Public Transit	Other Means
Less than $2,000	(7)	36	36	18	10
$2,000–3,999	(14)	47	29	18	6
$4,000–5,999	(24)	59	23	15	3
$6,000–7,499	(16)	57	27	12	4
$7,500–9,999	(16)	63	22	12	3
$10,000–14,999	(12)	60	24	13	3
$15,000 and over	(4)	67	25	6	2

* 1963 Census of Transportation, op. cit.
† The percentages of workers falling within each income group are shown in parentheses; for 7 percent, income was not reported.

TABLE 6
DISTANCE FROM HOME TO PUBLIC TRANSPORTATION

Percentage of U.S. workers living at distance shown from public transportation, or not having such transportation available:*

Family Income	Less than ¼ mile	¼ to ½ mile	Over ½ to 1 mile	Over 1 mile	Public Transit not Available
Less than $2,000	30	9	2	3	56
$2,000–3,999	35	11	2	3	49
$4,000–5,999	39	12	4	4	41
$6,000–7,499	34	14	5	3	44
$7,500–9,999	35	15	4	6	40
$10,000–14,999	32	16	5	9	38
$15,000 and over	31	17	6	5	41

* 1963 Census of Transportation, op. cit.

one may surmise from these data that public transportation is more readily available to the high- than to the low-income groups, particularly the lowest two. When we take into account the ability of low- and high-income groups to afford public or private transportation, as well as information about *presently* available public transport, one might conclude that future improvements or extensions

transportation. This included situations where there was a complete lack of public transportation as well as situations where public transportation was available but could not be used by the worker," 1963 Census of Transportation, op. cit., p. 31.

of public-transportation services should concentrate on lower-income groups, and thus on the central-city and core areas where they generally live and work. Given this conclusion and considering some of the more prominent new rapid-transit systems now being built, including the location of their lines and stations, one must wonder if the wrong markets are not being tapped. The new San Francisco rapid-transit system (BART), for example, will have a total of 75 route miles of line and 37 stations; but less than 8 route miles of line and only eleven stations will be located within the city of San Francisco (the remainder spreading out in three directions within the East Bay suburban communities). By contrast, one should note that three-quarters of the San Francisco-Oakland Standard Metropolitan Statistical Area occupied housing units which have *no* automobile available are within the city of San Francisco,[5] and that roughly 75 percent of City of San Francisco workers live within the central city itself. (Of all U.S. metropolitan area workers who are members of households owning no auto, over 80 percent reside within central cities and only 20 percent reside in the suburbs. Similarly, 80 percent of the nonwhites live within the central cities.) Also noteworthy is the fact that the preponderance of urban poor people—in aggregate for the U.S.—reside in the central cities of our metropolitan areas.[6] Though more will be said about these points in connection with specific illustrations, it seems reasonable to observe that the San Francisco BART situation is little different from that contemplated for the Los Angeles and Atlanta rapid-transit systems and that the bulk of new rapid-transit services are focusing primarily on residential areas housing (principally) other than the urban poor and downtown work group.

Of relevance to the above points, let me also note that, generally, *downtown* workers tend to live within the central city rather than in the suburbs. In Chicago, a city served by a 70-mile rail transit network and an over 400-mile commuter railroad network, about 60 percent of the Central Business District workers live within 8 miles of the CBD, and about 74 percent within 10 miles. Ten miles roughly corresponds to the average distance between downtown Chicago and the Chicago city limits. Thus, we can estimate that only one-quarter of Chicago's downtown workers commute from the suburbs. In Detroit, a city of much less density and having virtually no rail service, the corresponding percentages are 70 and 94 percent; and Detroit's city limits average roughly 8 miles from its CBD. Only 19 percent of the mid-Manhattan (or

CBD) workers live outside New York City, and the great bulk of those fall within high-income groups. New York has about 1,000 miles of commuter railroad to serve its out-of-city commuters. In Washington, D.C., only 20 percent of the downtown workers live more than six miles from downtown and only 5 percent live more than 8 miles from downtown; the six-mile distance is roughly equivalent to that between downtown and the city limits. . . .

[In summary, the evidence on present and proposed mass transit systems suggests five principal conclusions about their relative impacts on different income groups.]

First, neither the line mileage nor the station coverage of the new or proposed rail rapid transit systems or extensions—unlike past traditions for subways and rail transit facilities—will be concentrated (to nearly the same degree) within the central city or urban core areas but will be focused more prominently on the suburbs, a role traditionally followed by suburban commuter railroads.

Second, workers from households not owning automobiles, as well as the urban poor and nonwhites, reside principally within our central cities rather than the suburbs. Similarly, and of perhaps more importance, those people who work downtown and who will best be served by radial-type fixed rail systems focusing on the downtown area tend to live within central cities rather than the suburbs—from 75 to 80 percent of the time, even in our densest cities which are well served by extensive commuter railroad networks. In sum, most proposed transit programs are focused primarily on improving public transportation for long-distance downtown commuters living in the suburbs, a group which at best represents only 5 to 10 percent of the urban populace even today and which will represent considerably less tomorrow. The bulk of funding is focused on extended rail transit to the suburbs where downtown workers most likely to need better facilities do not live, and is not generally focused on serving the poor, aged, or handicapped. The anticipated service will probably be little different or better than that which has been available to the well-to-do suburban commuter for many decades.

Third, those types of public transport facilities which do offer considerable potential for serving either masses of riders or the poor,

[5] E. L. Kanwit, A. Eckartt, and B. Goley, *Selected Statistics by Standard Metropolitan Statistical Areas for Use in Transportation Planning*, U.S. Bureau of Public Roads, 1964.
[6] As of 1964, about 60 percent of the metropolitan areas' poor resided within the central cities. See *Federal Role in Urban Affairs*, Hearings before the Subcommittee on Executive Reorganization of the Committee on Government Operations, U.S. Senate, 1966, Table I.

old, and handicapped and those transport systems which do stand a chance of competing with the automobile (both in terms of service and cost to the user) receive far too little attention. To take two examples: One, work on newer flexible and/or high service types of technologies or operations (such as "dial-a-bus" or dual-mode) seems to receive scant effort rather than the level consistent with their potential. Two, the public taxi—a service regarded by some as "the transit system of the future" because of its higher service features (which increasingly are desired by a society of growing affluence), and because of its immediate high potential both for large masses and for the poor, aged, and handicapped—seems to be excluded from the domain of public transportation services generally considered to be eligible for government study and funding. If, for example, franchise or licensing arrangements for taxicabs could be altered and if funds were available for buying up medallions, assisting cruising cabs to link up with passengers, and devising "pooling" in appropriate instances, such a change could place more cabs on the streets, yield better service, lower costs, and fares, and bring about a consequent increase in ridership. Of course, the difficulties of the aged and handicapped —climbing stairs, getting in and out of doors, managing in quick starting and stopping vehicles, and so forth—suggest that taxi service is more suitable for them than bus or rail service. Also, the origin-destination and route ubiquity of taxis relative to that afforded by other transit is too obvious to dwell on.

Fourth, more attention deserves to be devoted to the problem of providing accessibility to the poor and to the unemployed who are handicapped (particularly in the job search) by lack of auto availability. Obviously, two pertinent possibilities would be: (1) the establishment of low-cost rental car agencies within ghetto areas; and (2) the use of government funds to provide assistance in buying autos (say, low-cost but mechanically sound used ones), either directly as a grant or indirectly in terms of credit backing until the persons are financially able to carry the entire burden.

Finally, concern should be voiced that continued funding and subsidization of commuter railroad and rail rapid transit systems is not likely to help those groups specially designated as needing particular assistance —i.e., the poor, aged, handicapped, and very young. It seems evident that riders now using existing rail rapid transit and suburban commuter railroads—or who will be using these facilities in the future—do not generally fall into any of those four classes. For this reason, subsidization of most types of public transit facilities can hardly be regarded as an efficient or "fair" income transfer or welfare device. One example of a more direct approach would be that implied earlier: simply to open up the taxi market by eliminating franchises and to give taxi "chits" to the poor, handicapped, aged, and very young. Another would be direct or indirect government assistance in buying cars for the poor or unemployed who are handicapped by the lack of auto availability.

RAPID TRANSIT: THE CASE OF BART

Danny Beagle, Al Haber, and David Wellman

Placing one new rapid transit system in its institutional context, the following selection argues that the development of BART, the flashy new subway network in the San Francisco Bay Area, serves the interests primarily of the "creative capitalists" who control downtown San Francisco and hope to preserve the value of their holdings.

The selection comes from an article called "Turf Power and the Tax Man,"

SOURCE: *Danny Beagle, Al Haber, David Wellman, "Turf Power and the Tax Man," from* Leviathan *I, 2.*

originally appearing in *Leviathan*. The article had six sections: The Mission
Coalition; Creative Capitalism; Regional Government; Rapid Transit: BART;
Urban Redevelopment; and The Politics of Resistance. This selection
includes the entirety of the fourth section. The second and fifth sections are
reprinted in the chapter of this book on housing, and the other sections
are summarized in the headnote to that selection.

The authors have all been active in the Movement in the San Francisco Bay
Area and have written frequently for activist publications.

The second element in the [corporate metropolitan] strategy is the creation of a rapid transit network which will connect the central city to the outlying consumer markets and labor pools.

The push for a rapid transit system in the Bay Area began in the early fifties with Carl Wente (chairman of the board of the Bank of America), Kendric Morrish (a Wells Fargo director) and Mortimer Fleishhacker (a Crocker Citizens Bank director connected with both BAC and the Blyth-Zellerbach Committee, a corporate group supporting urban renewal). These men initiated feasibility studies for what was to become the Bay Area Rapid Transit District (BART). In 1962 voters approved an initial bond issue for the construction of a high speed transit system embracing San Francisco, Contra Costa and Alameda counties and, ultimately, San Mateo and Marin.

The first chairman of the BART board of directors was Adrian Falk, a retired vice-president of S&W Fine Foods and past president of the California Chamber of Commerce. According to Falk, BART's basic function was to make possible the centralization of certain executive functions in downtown San Francisco. "It's the only practical way," he told a local newspaperman. "Certain financial, banking, and industrial companies want to be centralized, want to have everyone near each other. They don't want to have to go one day to Oakland, the next day to San Jose, the next day to San Francisco."

The major contributors to the public relations fund during the 1962 bond election were the three downtown banks plus a large number of companies which stood to benefit directly from construction contracts: Westinghouse, Kaiser, Bethlehem, Bechtel and the Downtown Property Owners and Builders. Bank of America's Carl Wente was head of the finance committee.

BART was sold to the electorate as a crusade against the auto lobby. In fact, it ran into little trouble from this direction. The construction of thirty-two additional freeway lanes is projected for this area in the next ten years (there are forty-eight now). From the outset, BART was conceived of more as a commuter railroad than a true public transit system. It makes no pretense at carrying the great bulk of local traffic. Traffic on the Oakland-San Franciso Bay Bridge is still expected to reach the point of absolute capacity by 1975.

BART will have many consequences: first, it will greatly encourage downtown congestion and density. It has already stimulated a substantial building boom. Almost immediately after construction began, the three major banks put up high-rise headquarters buildings downtown, and increasingly the downtown San Francisco landscape is spotted with new BART-oriented construction sites. According to the Chamber of Commerce, a "direct dividend" of BART's construction will be the new "Embarcadero Center," a Rockefeller venture of great ugliness. The Embarcadero Center will involve three high-rise buildings on the waterfront, and gradually plans are being announced for redevelopment of the entire waterfront area.

More important, though, BART will guarantee the growth and renewed prosperity of downtown business. Essentially, it expands many times over the labor market area and the marketing area for goods and services. The "best workers" can be recruited for downtown jobs, choosing from the whole three-county area. And likewise, the richest, most discriminating consumers are given easy access to the prestige retailers of the downtown complex and the professional services in which it specializes.

Also, property values all along the transit route will soar. In Toronto, they increased up to tenfold adjacent to the new subway line. And BART officials expect a comparable rise in their domain. Millions of dollars will be made by the public-spirited businessmen who pushed the plan and then made their services available to construct it. And the taxpayers will be stuck with paying off the bond issues and debts of $2 billion or more. That BART will actually be profitable, that it will contribute significantly to the retirement of its debt, is highly unlikely. BART has already run into financial troubles, spending far more than its initial capitalization. The public is about to pay for these profits, inefficiencies and costs of inflation out of a special hike in the sales tax.

But the problem is not that business will make money off the construction and financing of public services; nor even that business will do a bad job and end up providing uncomfortable, ugly and congested services. The problem is that it serves the rich and is paid for by the poor. By increasing the public debt and tax burden and by raising property values along the route, BART insures an increased squeeze on those least able to pay. Its effect on housing is obvious. Rents will be forced up as tax costs are passed on, and homeowners will be deprived of their property as the costs of ownership increase.

BART doesn't even have the saving grace of helping workers from the black and brown ghettos get to industrial jobs outside the city. The trains do run both ways. But the routes link the central city with the rich suburbs, not the industrial hinterland. And the trains will pass through ghettos only incidentally: Hunters Point is not on the route, and there are no stations in the Oakland ghettos. BART will make little contribution to an anti-poverty policy of connecting poorer workers with jobs and a wider employment area.

"The end result of BART is that San Francisco will be just like Manhattan," according to an influential insurance broker. "It's not a question of whether it's desirable," he continued, "but what's the practical matter. As a practical matter you can't have eighteen different banking and insurance centers. You have to concentrate them with all the various services around them. The people who run these centers want all their services —the people they work with—advertisers, attorneys, accountants—around them. It's a complete part of the way we do business in this country."

METRO: RAPID TRANSIT FOR SUBURBAN WASHINGTON

Willard W. Brittain

This short piece provides another illustration of the class biases of transportation institutions. A new subway was planned and is being constructed, ostensibly to provide special benefits to the poor in the central city. Its benefits in fact accrue disproportionately to the affluent suburbs, while central-city residents pay the largest share of the costs.

The selection was written originally for this volume. It was based on the author's senior essay in economics at Yale College, completed in May, 1970. Brittain is now a student at the Harvard Business School.

It has been recognized that many American cities need radically improved public transit facilities. As automobile traffic increases, downtown congestion and pollution become unbearable. As central city populations become more concentrated with the

SOURCE: *Willard W. Brittain, "Metro: Rapid Transit for Suburban Washington," written for this book.*

poor and the aged—those unable to afford cars—and as employment continues to move to the suburbs, many central city residents find it more and more difficult to travel to the suburban jobs.

Washington, D.C., has been suffering acutely from this syndrome of intra-urban transportation problems. Its central city population is now 70 percent black, much of it poor. Its predominantly white suburbs have been growing rapidly since the 1950's.[1] Employment has been decentralizing at an accelerating pace, and the federal government itself has been joining the exodus in recent years.[2] Increasingly, Washington's central city residents are those most in need of rapid transit. They have the fewest cars, they have to travel farthest to work, and they suffer most from rapidly increasing fares caused by the area's presently inefficient system.

The Washington metropolitan area is finally going to have a rapid transit system. Construction has started on a 98-mile system called Metro, which will extend into suburban counties in Maryland and Virginia.[3] Metro has its own authority, the Washington Metropolitan Area Transit Authority (WMATA), and by the time the system is finished, it will cost roughly $2.5 billion. Along with the new system in San Francisco, Metro has been hailed as the latest panacea for metropolitan transportation problems. It will be modern, cheap, accessible and efficient, its planners say. It has the personal blessing of President Nixon, and many consider it the most masterful plan for the city since L'Enfant's original design. Its economic planners predict that the Washington area, because of its unique characteristics, will benefit more from Metro than other cities have from their own rapid transit systems. In their own "money talks" language, they predict: "For every local dollar invested in the system, approximately $9.40 would be returned in quantifiable benefits by 2020."[4]

With all its attendant fanfare, Metro provides an interesting test of the biases of Washington's political structure. Washington's central city residents, because they need better transportation the most, should receive a disproportionate share of the benefits from the Metro system. Its planners acknowledge this argument; indeed, according to the cost assignments, they contend that the District will clearly benefit most from Metro. But contention does not create reality. In fact, the structure of power in the Washington metropolitan area, and the District's own political powerlessness, is producing a rapid transit system which will principally serve the suburbs. It will assign the District the largest share of its costs and return to District residents the smallest share of the benefits. In doing so, Metro's biases will simply complement those of Washington's other public services.

QUANTIFIABLE BENEFITS

The economic measurements for the Metro system were made by a consulting firm, Development Research Associates.[5] They quantified benefits for the entire system, including the District, the five participating jurisdictions from Virginia and the two participating jurisdictions from Maryland. With their formulae they intended to reflect the distribution of putative benefits from the system in 1990, with the implicit assumption that those who benefit should pay their fair share of the costs. WMATA, however, suggested an allocation formula based on relative populations (weighted 15 percent), relative ridership (15 percent), level of service per jurisdiction (30 percent) and the amount of construction per jurisdiction (40 percent). According to their figures, the relative shares of costs produced by this formula would closely reflect the relative ridership projected for the system and therefore, they argued, represented a reasonable basis for assigning costs. In 1990, the District was expected to have 34.2 percent of Metro riders, Maryland 37.1 percent and Virginia 28.7 percent. The WMATA finally agreed on a similar allocation of costs: the District would bear 37.73 percent of the total costs to the local areas, Maryland 34.35 percent and Virgina 27.91

[1] Between 1950 and 1970 annual population growth averaged 11.1 percent in the Maryland suburbs, 10.9 percent in the Virginia suburbs, and 2 percent in the District.
[2] Retail employment in the Maryland and Virginia suburbs is fast surpassing that in the District. (*Washington Metropolitan Area Statistics,* pp. 56–60.) Federal employment increased between 1960 and 1968 by 39 percent in D.C., 133 percent in the Virginia suburbs, and 78 percent in the Maryland suburbs.
[3] The jurisdictions participating in the Metro project in Virginia are Alexandria City, Arlington County, Fairfax County, Fairfax City, and Falls Church City. In Maryland they are Montgomery County and Prince Georges County. The other participating jurisdiction is the District of Columbia.
[4] This particular ratio is valid if we consider only the local cost of the project. See *Benefits to the Washington Metropolitan Area from the Adopted Regional System* (Washington, D.C.: Development Research Associates, October, 1968), p. 5.

[5] See *Benefits to the Washington Metropolitan Area from the Adopted Regional System, ibid.*

percent. Although the District was expected to have a smaller population than the suburbs by 1990, its large share of the costs was justified by its projected ridership and by its heavy share of construction (on the assumption that construction provides jobs and a boost to the local economy).

At the same time, however, Development Research Associates was suggesting a very different basis on which to estimate benefits from the system. Quite correctly, they argued that the real monetary benefits would accrue from the system in categories like the following: cost savings to those who would ride the system, time savings to those who would ride the system, time savings to commuters who continued to drive but could travel more quickly as a result of less congestion, and parking cost savings to peak period commuters. In calculating their estimate of the 9.4:1 benefit-cost ratio for the entire system, they used a very sophisticated set of calculations developing these categories into an aggregate estimate of the benefits. Table 1 presents their calculations of total benefits from the system for all jurisdictions annually by 1990.

And yet, although they clearly felt that these categories most accurately reflected the potential benefits of the system, they did not try to use these categories to calculate a disaggregated set of benefit estimates *by jurisdiction,* to help in making an equitable allocation of system costs. Nowhere in the proliferation of literature commissioned by the transit authority did any disaggregation of these benefits by jurisdiction appear. Be-

cause I was interested in the real benefits District residents could expect to receive from the system, I used the categories of Table 1, the same formulae and methods for estimation, and developed my own estimates of benefits separately for each jurisdiction. I used separate ridership forecasts, car ownership data, and income figures for each jurisdiction. Making some reasonable assumptions about the value of time to riders in the different jurisdictions, I derived estimates of the absolute dollar and relative benefits annually by 1990 for the separate political units. In the context of cost allocation, the most important estimates were those for the District, the Maryland suburbs as a whole, and the Virginia suburbs as a whole.

Table 2 presents those estimates and compares them to the relative share of costs assigned by the transit authority, based on the much different, much less relevant formula for benefit estimates described above.

It becomes clear from Table 2 why the authority's literature did not present such disaggregated benefit estimates for the system; they document the substantial bias of the system against the District, in favor of the suburbs. The transit authority admitted that they picked the final categories and weights for the cost allocation formula because they were "acceptable" to all the jurisdictions involved. With the right hand they were trying to justify cost allocation on the basis of theoretical equity and objective calculation. With the left they were acknowledging that their decisions were determined by political expediency. As a result the Dis-

TABLE 1
ANNUAL BENEFITS BY 1990 (IN 1968 CONSTANT DOLLARS)

a. Time savings to those who use public transit now and will continue to do so in the new system	$82,920,600
b. Auto drivers and passengers diverted to the Metro system	
1. Time savings to peak period commuters	11,130,000
2. Operating costs savings	11,638,700
3. Parking costs savings to peak period commuters	15,441,100
4. Insurance costs savings to commuters	2,177,700
5. Additional vehicle savings	17,908,400
c. Non-diverted peak period motorists	36,750,000
d. Business community	
1. Trucking industry (time savings and operating costs savings because of less congestion)	4,620,000
2. Suburban employers (they will no longer have to provide parking spaces for those who use the Metro system to get to work)	3,484,000

TABLE 2

	$ Benefits	% of Annual Benefits by 1990	Assigned % of Net Project Costs
D.C.	37,214,000	20%	37.73%
Md.	87,313,840	48%	34.35%
Va.	59,542,560	32%	27.91%

trict residents who need the system most are receiving the fewest benefits at the greatest cost.

Evidently, the District was the victim of coalition politics by the suburban jurisdictions. They had the power and the District had almost none. The District's "mayor" and the city council are appointed by the President subject to Congressional approval. Congress must also approve the District's annual budget. In five of the seven participating suburban jurisdictions referenda were necessary to approve bond issues for their share of Metro costs. In the other two suburban areas the power to issue bonds is in the hands of the city or county council who are elected directly by the residents. In both places rapid transit was an election issue. The only political process open to D.C. residents for expressing their views on Metro was testimony before Congress, since D.C. does not have the power to raise bond issues itself. The testimony could obviously not reflect public opinion with the accuracy of the referenda or mandates in the suburbs. Congressional approval was necessary in order for D.C. to borrow money at 6 percent interest to finance its share of Metro costs. Whether or not D.C. should have a rapid transit system and even how much it should pay for it were questions decided directly by the U.S. Congress—in which the District has no representatives.

The federal government has tax exempt status for property which amounts to 43.3 percent of all taxable property in D.C. The federal government does, however, make a payment to the city which for 1969 amounted to 90 million dollars—approximately 18 percent of D.C.'s total revenue. The District's payments to the transit authority and the debt service payments to the treasury will come out of revenue raised directly by the District government (except as money from

the 18 percent federal share is used for this purpose). To the extent that the District's taxes are regressive, the heaviest relative burden of the city's overpayment for Metro will fall on the poor. In fact, the inherently regressive property tax is the largest source of revenue. The next largest tax is a sales and gross receipts tax, followed by an individual income tax.

NON-QUANTIFIABLE BENEFITS

In order to justify the inequitable allocation of costs among the political jurisdictions one must have much faith in the non-quantifiable benefits of Metro. In particular, poor black residents of the District must have faith in this class of benefits because their incomes and the public services provided to them will be relatively affected the most. "Many of the major, and possibly most important, benefits resulting from the implementation of the regional rail system are those which cannot be measured. Aside from the purely economic impact . . . rapid rail transit will have broad positive implications for the social environment and overall well-being of the Washington area."[6] The non-quantifiable benefits hypothesized by Development Research Associates are:

1. The reduction of air pollution.
2. Improved transportation for the young and aged.
3. The facilitation of decentralization while maintaining downtown viability.
4. The provision of accessibility to employment opportunities for disadvantaged inner-city residents.

There is much doubt about the real significance of these benefits. It is my contention that the downtown area will remain the important hub of the metropolitan area for a long time, but that Metro will not contribute significantly enough to downtown business and employment growth for District revenues to outdistance the fast expanding need for a larger tax base. Supposedly those industries with the need for much face-to-face communication will remain behind. But already insurance companies, financial institutions, and other service industries have large enclaves in the Washington suburbs, providing the attraction of location econo-

[6] Development Research Associates, *Benefits to the Washington Metropolitan Area from the Adopted Regional System, ibid.,* p. 3.

mies to new firms or those about to move. Of course the largest single employer in the city is the federal government. Within the last few years several agencies have moved into the suburbs; community protests were necessary to forestall the planned move of the largest employer of semiskilled workers in the area (the Government Printing Office) to the suburbs.

Metro will enable many already employed central city residents to follow their jobs to the suburbs but increased accessibility alone will not help appreciably in solving the problems of unemployment and underemployment. The job market expansion exists in the suburbs, but the "type of jobs created will not match the skills of the unemployed and the underemployed in the area," according to an independent labor supply and demand study.[7] The heralded reverse commuting services of Metro will provide access for the most part to jobs to be filled by people moving into the Washington area, or by the new

[7] Hammer, Greene, Siler Associates, *Labor Force Supply and Demand in Metropolitan Washington,* Washington, D.C., 1968, pp. 60–61.

influx of people who commute into the SMSA. The real importance of Metro may lie in employment generated by its construction if minority hiring and training practices can be guaranteed. Experiences so far in this aspect of Metro have not been auspicious.

CONCLUSION

Theoretically, Metro could be of real significance for poor black people in the District of Columbia, those most in need of a rapid transit system. This will not be the case, however, as the largest share of the benefits from Metro has been directed to the suburbs by a political structure in which the District of Columbia has virtually no political autonomy. Furthermore, the benefits to be realized by District residents do not align with the costs assigned them by a transit authority dominated by suburban members. The poor residents of the District are being asked to expect the non-quantifiable benefits of Metro to "breathe new life into the District of Columbia"—non-quantifiable benefits which are doubtful at best.

THE PORT AUTHORITY STRANGLES NEW YORK

Theodore W. Kheel

Kheel's piece illustrates one of the mechanisms by which transportation institutions are dominated by the interests and priorities of the rich. In this case, the New York Port Authority has substantial control over the transportation system in New York, and caters to the wishes of its corporate bondholders.

Kheel is a prominent labor mediator and lawyer in New York, who at the time of this article was waging a campaign to have the twenty-cent fare in New York City by extracting a subsidy for subways from the affluent Port Authority. The campaign got nowhere.

A few weeks ago [New York] State Controller Arthur Levitt released the results of an audit he had made of the diverse operations of the Port of New York Authority, the

SOURCE: *Theodore W. Kheel, "How the Port Authority Is Strangling New York,"* New York Magazine, *November 17, 1969. Copyright © 1969 by the New York Magazine Co. Reprinted by permission.*

huge para-governmental agency that runs all the major airports, many of the bridges and tunnels, and much of the sprawling network of marine and motor terminals that serve New York, the busiest port in the world. The Port Authority, Levitt reported, made a lot of money on five of its facilities, lost money on 14 others, and did little more than break even on another six. On total revenues of

$208 million in 1967, according to Levitt's analysis, the Port Authority was able to show a surplus of just $6 million after meeting all its obligations. This 3 percent cushion, one was allowed to infer from the *New York Times'* account of the Levitt audit, was a commendably small margin, a tribute to the Port Authority's disinterested labors on behalf of all of us.

This view of the Port Authority's operations is, to put it charitably, naïve nonsense. In 1967 the authority actually showed a surplus of nearly $82 million. The difference between the money it showed and the money it really made results from a bookkeeping gambit, the purpose of which was to mask the Port Authority's true moneymaking power. Newspaper reports of the Levitt audit were grossly misleading. The Port Authority's willingness to let them stand, uncorrected, was unpardonable chutzpah. But that is what we have been taught to expect of the agency.

Far from being the far-seeing, creative enterprise it was meant to be, the Port Authority today is a dangerously short-sighted and rigidly conservative money machine harnessed to serve, not the broad public interest, but the private visions of an astonishingly narrow, relentlessly opportunistic management. The citizens of New York and New Jersey, acting through their respective legislatures, created the Port Authority in 1921 to coordinate the building of a balanced transportation system to meet the needs of the burgeoning port and the metropolitan area around it. Instead, the Port Authority has betrayed its mandate and has contributed greatly to the massive *imbalance* in ground transportation that is surely strangling Greater New York. It has all but totally ignored commuter railroads. It has preferred to grow huge—and hugely profitable—by catering to motorists. Without even the flimsy justification of acting in the interest of its stockholders—it has none—the Port Authority pursues money, not service, with the arrogance, indifference and contempt for the public welfare characteristic of 19th-century robber barons.

An enormous gap exists between what the Port Authority professes to be and what it really is. Its financial data are reported in such a way as to suggest that the Port Authority is walking—prudently, to be sure—a financial tightrope. In fact, the Port Authority is awesomely profitable; last year the money left over after paying its expenses, as most accountants understand the word, was not 3 percent, but more like 37 percent, of its combined revenues.

The Port Authority began life with high purpose, a little seed money, but no power to levy taxes or pledge state revenues. It was supposed to pay its own way. Indeed it has. In the past 48 years it has spent nearly $2 billion on facilities (worth several times that amount today) and has repaid long-term loans of nearly $1 billion. It has about $1 billion in bonds outstanding today, but it could add another $1 billion to that debt load with ease. Last year it had revenues of $226 million and cleared $89 million after paying operating expenses and debt interest. Operating profit was more than triple its $25 million in amortization charges last year.

Nowhere in its charter or in any state law is it said that everything the Port Authority does must be self-supporting. Nor is it written that the Port Authority must possess the *finest* credit rating in the bond market. Austin J. Tobin, its executive director for 27 years, once said, "Above all else, the people expect their officials to give them prudent and conservative management of public funds." This is disingenuous. Public servants are expected to manage public funds as prudently and conservatively *as their essential purpose permits*. A seemingly unprofitable venture, such as helping mass transportation, might be more genuinely productive than any seemingly self-supporting service the Port Authority has yet turned its hand to—and ultimately could cost us far less.

But we were not aware, during the 1950s and 1960s, of what the Port Authority was up to. We did not see that it had substituted for the will of the people, as expressed in the bi-state compact that created it, the will of the bond market as expressed by the price moneylenders charge for their loans. Today, the Port Authority's transportation policies are made, not by civic planners responding to the needs of the people, but by the bond market.

Because it is a bi-state agency, the Port Authority has been able to play one state against the other and forestall effective control by either. The Port Authority likes to brag that its board of 12 commissioners are accountable to the governors and the state legislatures of New York and New Jersey. In fact, the organization they are entrusted to run seems to run itself, accountable to no one except its own bondholders. The commissioners themselves are scarcely representative of the people in whose name they act. The current board includes four lawyers with banking interests, three stockbrokers, two bankers, one industrialist, and one certified public accountant. The 12th commissioner, and the only strong advocate of mass transit in the bunch, is Dr. William J. Ronan, chairman of the Metropolitan Transportation Authority.

Not surprisingly, Ronan has had little success in opening the Port Authority's closed mind about mass transportation. When it sold $100 million worth of bonds in the money market late last year, the Port Authority's prospectus contained a statement that reassured the money market but should unsettle the rest of us: "The Commissioners serve without remuneration for six-year overlapping terms. They are engaged in business or professional activities apart from their offices as Commissioners. In some cases these involve business or professional connections or relations with persons, firms, or corporations which do business with or are actual or potential users of the facilities of the Authority." Such men are not likely to upset the bond market or their own interests by involving the Port Authority in such financially risky causes as mass transit. The Port Authority has so repudiated mass transportation that its associate counsel, Daniel B. Goldberg, once referred to mass transit as a "disease" to be kept out of its "financial body."

So, while commuter railroads go bankrupt, the Port Authority brags about its matchless credit rating. While subways amass big deficits, the Port Authority boasts that it is self-supporting. In fact, the Port Authority is the unblushing beneficiary of massive assistance, both direct and indirect, from government, from industry and from just about everyone living within the Port District, roughly the area within a 25-mile radius of the Statute of Liberty. The Port Authority does a brisk business getting cars and trucks into and out of the metropolitan area. The strangulating traffic its bridges and tunnels bring, the cost of air pollution, street and road maintenance, crowded courts and hospitals, zooming insurance rates, demands on police and sanitation services—these are someone else's problems, not the Port Authority's. The Port Authority complains that riders on the Hudson tubes, now operated by the authority, receive a subsidy of 31 cents per ride. But a man who drives his own car to work in Manhattan for 50 cents via the Port Authority's Lincoln Tunnel may be indirectly subsidized by as much as five dollars per ride. That is a rough estimate of what it may now be costing, in municipal services and lost time to industry, to cope with New York City's traffic problem.

In its youth the Port Authority thought differently. It considered itself, as it said in its annual report for 1924, the "guide and guardian of the port," seeking to produce "the greatest cooperation of existing agencies, the utmost efficiency and the minimum of cost." In that role, it observed then, "it should not be expected to be self-supporting."

In those days the Port Authority thought highly of rapid transit. In its annual report for 1927, when the George Washington Bridge was being designed, the Port Authority said: "There will also be added later, when needed, a lower deck which will provide for two, four or six lines of rapid transit tracks or bus traffic, as may be required." The Port Authority envisioned rapid transit tracks on its Bayonne and Arthur Kill bridges as well. It was ready to put some of its hard cash into this. In its annual report for 1927 the Port Authority observed that while no provision had been made to finance these bridge transit facilities, "sufficient funds will be available from surplus tolls and charges to provide for this improvement." A disease? No, a prime reason for the Port Authority's existence.

The Port Authority once sounded positively evangelical in talking about the need for an integrated policy and program of transportation for the entire metropolitan area. This is the Port Authority speaking, again in 1927:

The problem of providing adequate passenger transportation for the thousands of daily riders from and within the suburban districts centering about the City of New York is becoming acute. The situation is intensified by the fact that nearly half of these commuters travel within limited rush hour periods, morning and evening, and these daily, periodic

*surges of humanity must flow through
channels that have other intensive
transportation demands . . . .*

*Local transit agencies have been coping
with this problem for several years in the
respective districts . . . . There has existed,
until this time, however, no concerted
attempt to coordinate the interstate and
regional phases of a problem whose solution
can only be attained by the most
comprehensive study and the broadest
lines of planning. It is the lack of interstate
consideration that has been in no small
measure responsible for the unbalanced
development of residential areas in the
different sectors of the port. It is the cause
of congested terminals and crowded trains
of the New York carriers. General relief
can be obtained only through regional
planning of a comprehensive suburban
transit system. (Emphasis added.)*

The very next year, however, the Port
Authority began to discover the money to be
made in serving automobiles. In 1928 it
earned its first operating profit, a modest
$250,000, when the Outerbridge Crossing
and the Goethals Bridge, connecting Staten
Island with New Jersey, were opened to
traffic. In 1931 it bought the Holland Tunnel at cost from New York and New Jersey,
which had jointly built it. The authority
opened the George Washington Bridge in
1931, and the Bayonne Bridge later the
same year. Six years later, it opened the
first tube of the Lincoln Tunnel.

With these, the Port Authority had the
main assets that would in time make it rich.
Drawing a bead on the booming use of private cars and trucks, on air and marine
traffic—on everything but rapid transit—the
Port Authority has substantially increased its
gross revenues and net profits every year
since the end of World War II. Its gross
revenues have roughly doubled every 10
years since 1939. Its net revenues have
grown proportionately.

The Port Authority, it now seems clear,
began to repudiate its vision of a comprehensive, coordinated system of transportation
when it began counting its bridge and tunnel tolls. Once it got going it stopped emphasizing the advantages of true mass transportation in its annual reports. Instead, it
concerned itself with its borrowing capacity

and enhancing its appeal to moneylenders.

The big money began to flow in during
the postwar years as more and more people
turned away from mass transportation and
began using cars not merely for holidays but
to get to work. Providentially in place by
then as executive director of the Port Authority was Austin Tobin. By its own special
lights, Tobin was the ideal executive to drive
the Port Authority into the motor age and
drive advocates of mass transit into despair.

Tobin joined the legal staff of the Port
Authority upon graduation from Fordham
Law School in 1927 and has been with the
Port Authority ever since. For the last 27
years he has been the boss, setting policy
and making decisions. "My own executive
office," Tobin has said, "has the same normal
responsibilities as those of the president of a
private corporation."

Unlike Robert Moses, who had control of
a comparable organization—the Triborough
Bridge and Tunnel Authority—Austin Tobin
has shunned personal publicity. Were it not
for his indifference to celebrity, Tobin might
remind one of J. Edgar Hoover, or perhaps
Air Force General Curtis LeMay—stocky,
decisive, and not easily distracted from what
he presumes to be his job.

What makes Austin Tobin tick? What induces a man with clear gifts and great energy
to put blinders on, to narrow his choices
rather than to expand them? Mere personal
ambition cannot explain it. His annual salary
of $70,000 makes him one of the best-paid
public servants in the country, to be sure,
but Tobin would doubtless have done well
anywhere. Perhaps it is the sense of power
his position gives him—enormous resources
at his command and, through the indifference
of the states, remarkably little restraint on
his use of them.

Under Tobin, the Port Authority has gone
to great lengths to prevent attempts to involve it in the steadily worsening problems
of the commuter railroads that serve New
York. In 1961 New Jersey wanted the Port
Authority to take over the bankrupt Hudson
and Manhattan Railroad. At the time, the
authority was already rich and getting richer
fast.

The threat of being forced to take over a
money-losing railroad really shook up Port
Authority officials. "These proposals," Daniel
Goldberg, Tobin's associate counsel, later re-

called, "made us take a good look at our financial structure to see to what extent, if at all, we were open to this kind of a *financial raid* at the *sacrifice* of the *security* that our *bondholders* had bargained for when they had loaned us hundreds of millions of dollars." (Emphasis added.)

Goldberg's comment is admirably candid. It reveals how very far from its original purpose the Port Authority had strayed. Bondholders had been promised, it appears, that the Port Authority would flatly refuse to take over any "headache," and mass transportation was a headache. Anyone who tried to get the Port Authority to do this was guilty of a "financial raid at the sacrifice of the security that *our* bondholders had bargained for." What about "our" commuters and "our" straphangers? What about the Port Authority's own original bargain to co-ordinate *all* forms of transportation? They did not matter. Bridges and tunnels for motorists produced huge profits. Mass transportation was a losing proposition. The bondholders favored loans to the former but not the latter.

As any business would, under the circumstances, the Port Authority had already taken some measures to protect itself against a "raid." But it was not really secure. Its own ambition had made it vulnerable. In its formative years the authority had borrowed separately for each facility it built. This limited the use it could make of the profits any one facility generated. But later it set up a General Reserve Fund for all bonds and got the right to use surpluses from each facility for other purposes. This move gave the Port Authority considerably more room to flex its muscles. But in time it sought still more flexibility because, as Goldberg once explained, "we looked forward to the enormous postwar horizons that the Port Authority was facing up to. We needed a new financial device where the purposes would be unlimited, where the dollars would be unlimited, and only legality and financial practicability would impose the limits." The Port Authority got that, precisely, in its Consolidated Bond Resolution of 1952, under which it has sold almost 95 percent of all its currently outstanding bonds.

But if the purposes and dollars were unlimited, the Port Authority could indeed absorb the Hudson and Manhattan Railroad.

And, if that were so, why could it not be forced to take over other commuter railroads as well? How to protect itself from this terrible disease, that was the question.

By way of answer, the Port Authority brought off a daring coup. It had already announced its interest in building a World Trade Center, a gigantic real-estate venture it hoped to launch in lower Manhattan. New York State had posed no objections. Only New Jersey, with its troublesome fussing about the Hudson and Manhattan tubes, stood in the way. To get what it wanted, the Port Authority worked out a clever strategy. It agreed to take over the Hudson and Manhattan Railroad, but in return it not only got permission to go ahead with the World Trade Center but also extracted covenants from both New York and New Jersey intended to prevent the states from ever again dragging it into the commuter transit business. The Constitution of the United States, no less, is the instrumentality for this ploy. Article IV says that no state shall impair the obligations of a contract. Thus, because appropriate language was written into the contract with the states under which it took over the tubes, the Port Authority believes it can never again be asked to do anything significant for mass transportation.

Reluctant as it was to get involved, the authority has done a first-rate job with the Hudson tubes since it took over in 1962. Renamed PATH (for Port Authority Trans-Hudson system) and overhauled at a cost of $125 million to date, the line is rapidly improving and passenger revenues are climbing. By the Port Authority's reckoning, PATH ran up operating losses of nearly $10 million last year. Beyond question, the community would be spending a great deal more if PATH had been allowed to die.

Under Tobin's leadership the authority has lost all sense of its original purpose. One evidence of this is the second level of the George Washington Bridge it finally completed in 1962—not for rapid transit, as envisioned back in 1927, but for private cars and trucks.

The clearest sign of the Port Authority's intellectual bankruptcy and arrogant indifference to the real needs of this community is the monstrous real-estate venture it has launched in lower Manhattan. The World Trade Center it is now building will have twin towers rising 110 stories high, taller than the Empire State Building. It will hold more space than the Pentagon. It will cost at least $600 million.

The Port Authority has committed this huge sum—enough, say, to build a new East Side subway in New York—despite the fact that Manhattan is at present experiencing the greatest office-building boom in the history of man. The World Trade Center is rising despite the fact that private builders have demonstrated a unique capacity to build office buildings in Manhattan without government assistance. The real needs of the people in the Port District which private industry *cannot* satisfy include housing, education, community services, medical care, parklands, environmental protection, and, of course, transportation. The only possible reason for the Port Authority's going into the office-building field at this time is simply that it is profitable.

The World Trade Center is a striking example of socialism at its worst—a state agency needlessly and inefficiently intervening in a market already well served by private capital.

Unlike the private outfits now constructing office space, the Port Authority will receive a subsidy of many millions from the federal, state, and city governments to build office space in Manhattan. Here is how the subsidy comes about: The interest the Port Authority pays on its bonds is tax-exempt to the lender. The authority will borrow the money it needs at an annual interest cost many millions of dollars *below* the price private borrowers would pay. Where is the difference coming from? From the federal, state and city governments that would otherwise collect that amount in taxes paid by bondholders. In addition, the Port Authority will pay New York City at least $15 million a year less in real estate taxes than private builders would pay for comparable space. When the World Trade Center is completed in 1972, Washington, Albany and New York may be subsidizing it by a sum approaching $50 million *per year*. This for a commodity easily available from others. This at a time when governments are hard-pressed to find funds for needs that private industry cannot supply. In all conscience the Port Authority should sell the trade center to private investors, thereby boosting tax revenues, and get back to its proper business.

The Port Authority makes money from the federal government another way. It borrows money at low rates in the municipal bond market because its interest payments are tax-exempt. It invests a part of this in United States Government securities as reserves for the bondholders—securities which, because they are not tax-exempt, pay the higher interest. The Port Authority pockets the difference, a pure subsidy from the federal government.

The Port Authority boasts that the World Trade Center will include a handsome new terminal for its PATH trains. But apart from that, it is silent on what it will do about the massive traffic congestion the World Trade Center is certain to create. Who will provide the transportation and other facilities needed to accommodate 50,000 tenants and 80,000 visitors *per day* in an area that is already crippled by overloaded transit facilities? That, the Port Authority blithely assumes, is someone else's problem.

The Port Authority has been generous to the states on occasion—but only when it could see something in it for itself. In 1955, for example, it gave New Jersey—*gave*—$24 million to speed construction of highways leading to its own George Washington Bridge. There is no reason, save not giving a damn, why it could not do something for the millions of commuters in New York and New Jersey who depend on the railroads. But nothing of the sort is in prospect. The Port Authority seems determined to go about its business as usual—arrogant, exploitative and oblivious to its larger responsibility. It has succeeded in tying its own hands through restrictions written into its bonds and its contracts with the states. These restrictions, of course, are not nearly so binding as the Port Authority now likes to think. What lawyers do, lawyers can often undo.

But the hard fact is, it will be difficult to get the Port Authority to change its ways. In a report to Mayor Lindsay . . . I stated that by doubling the tolls for vehicular traffic at all Port Authority crossings, the Port Authority would realize at least $70 million of additional revenues without any additional operating expenses; that these additional revenues would more than double the Port Authority's present borrowing capacity, making it possible for the Port Authority to borrow up to two billion dollars more, and that this could be used to help mass transportation in New York and New Jersey without in any way impairing the Port Authority's commitments to its bondholders, its credit standing, its ability to complete projects under way, and its opportunity to invest in new ventures. The Port Authority refused comment on this, as it had refused to comment on other suggestions I had made on ways the Port Authority could help mass transportation.

Can the Port Authority continue to ignore its mandate? Can it continue to remain unresponsive to the needs of the urban communities in New York and New Jersey in the Port District? It seems determined to do just that. After all, who can stop it?

TRANSPORTATION BIBLIOGRAPHY

I. DEFINITIONS AND MAGNITUDES

Dick Netzer, *Economics and Urban Problems*, 1970, Basic Books, pp. 35–40, 137–165. Simple summary of problems and issues.

John Meyer, "Urban Transportation," in James Q. Wilson, ed., *Metropolitan Enigma*, 1968, Harvard, pp. 41–70. Discusses different perspectives on what the problems are.

II. GENERAL ANALYSIS

George Smerk, ed., *Readings in Urban Transportation*, 1968, University of Indiana. Interesting selection of readings, covering the full range of issues.

George Smerk, *Urban Transportation: The Federal Role*, 1965, Indiana. Useful discussion of policy issues.

John Meyer, John Kain, and Martin Wohl, *The Urban Transportation Problem*, 1966, Harvard. Extremely technical analysis of the problem, and the relative efficiency of alternative modes for improving transportation.

A. Ganz, *Emerging Patterns of Urban Growth and Travel*, 1968, MIT Press. Relationship between form and transportation.

Wilfred Owen, *The Metropolitan Transportation Problem*, 1956, Brookings. Older but excellent study.

Edgar M. Hoover, "Motor Metropolis: Some Observations on Urban Transportation in America," *The Journal of Industrial Economics*, June, 1965.

III. INSTITUTIONAL INFLUENCE

A. Autos and Highways

A. Q. Mowbray, *Road to Ruin*, 1969, Lippincott. Frightening documentation of power of autos and highway interests.

Helen Leavitt, *Superhighway—Superhoax*, 1970, Doubleday. Equally searing account of influence of vested interests in preserving dominance of auto and highway interests.

B. Public Transportation and Income

John Meyer and John Kain, "Transportation and Poverty," *The Public Interest*, No. 18, Winter, 1970. Summary of a conference. Note references to unpublished papers presented at conference, many of which are original treatments of transit problems of the poor.

Martin Wohl, "Users of Urban Transportation Services and Their Income Circumstances," *Traffic Quarterly*, January, 1970. Documents the bias of public transit toward the non-poor.

Oscar Ornati, *Transportation Needs of the Poor*, 1969, Praeger. With special references to New York City, documents the isolation of the poor from major public transit modes.

Alan A. Altshuler, "Transit Subsidies: By Whom, for Whom?" *Journal of the American Institute of Planners*, March, 1969. Discussion of who benefits from public subsidy of transportation.

9 Environment

Editor's Introduction

We simply don't need any more gross national product, any more unnecessary goods and factories. What we do need is a redistribution of existing real wealth, and a reallocation of society's resources. Everyone knows what this redistribution and reallocation should do; the crises of the last ten years have made it all so obvious: The poor must have adequate income, the cities must be rebuilt to fit human requirements, the environment must be de-polluted. . . . We must, in short, junk the business system and its way of life and create revolutionary new institutions to embody new goals—human and environmental.

All this sounds utopian. Well, utopias are relative. More utopian by far than revolution is the idea that the present society, dominated by business, can create lasting, meaningful reforms sufficient, for example, to permit mankind to survive the century.

—The Editors of *Ramparts*[1]

At the beginning of the 1970's, ecology had emerged as America's newest toy. Politicians all supported protection of the environment, foundations provided money for ecological activists, and corporations puffed in advertisements about all their efforts to control pollution. Because everyone seemed quickly to admit the problem and its severity, many assumed that the country could solve it very soon.

We cannot, radicals would argue, solve the problems of the environment within the context of our economic system. Expecting advanced capitalism to protect the environment seems rather like expecting war to eschew violence—the consequence flows tautologically from the institution. Arguments along these lines have been made frequently in recent months, so this introduction can be especially brief. In it, I have summarized the different kinds of environmental problems, sketched liberal and conservative approaches to those problems, and outlined the radical argument that capitalist institutions produce environmental degradation quite inevitably.[2] The final section of the Introduction summarizes the readings which follow.

DEFINITIONS OF THE PROBLEM

Paul Ehrlich and other environmental writers have mastered the art of tragic hyperbole.[3] I cannot compete on their level, so I have avoided doomsday-ism in this summary. A supplement among the readings quite dryly summarizes the sources and extent of prevalent kinds of pollution in urban areas. The supplement documents the enormity of the problems and that's enough said at that level.

Environmental problems have two principal sources in advanced societies, the first institutional and the second technological. Institutionally, certain kinds of pollution inevitably result from the prevalence of decentralized production in a market system. The production of most

---

[1] *Ramparts*, April, 1970, p. 4.

[2] In May, 1970, an international conference of social scientists and engineers met in Japan to discuss problems of the environment. The conference chairman ruled at the beginning of the meetings that the term "environmental degradation" would be the official subject of the conference, and that everyone should communicate by reference to the problem of "E.D." for short. See the interesting diaries of the conference by Wassily Leontief, *The New York Review of Books*, May 23, 1970.

[3] See any of Ehrlich's books, but especially *The Population Bomb*, 1968, and, with Anne Ehrlich, *Population, Resources and Environment*, 1970.

commodities in a market economy involves both internal and external costs of production. A chemical company faces its internal costs of labor and materials, for instance, and imposes external costs on the rest of society by emitting smoke from its chimneys. The chemical company does not have to pay for the smoke damage, so it will ignore those external costs and produce according to its internal cost calculations. To incorporate those external costs into decisions about production, society must either force the company to pay the costs of their externalities or must "internalize" the externalities, centralizing production so that previously external costs now become part of internal calculations.[4]

Technologically, the problems develop for two reasons. First, few productive operations are technologically efficient, preserving energy and resources in the final product. Nearly all productive processes produce waste—in the form of heat, smoke, chemical by-products, dirt, garbage, and so on. As technology becomes more complicated, these wastes often become more pervasive.[5] Second, certain kinds of wastes have unforeseen consequences when they are produced in large quantities. Pollutants in water eventually exceed the capacity of living organisms to dissolve them, for instance. And chemicals in the air ultimately combine to form new kinds of chemicals.[6]

Analyses of environmental problems and prescriptions for possible solutions must therefore encompass both institutional and technological considerations.

LIBERAL AND CONSERVATIVE VIEWS

Liberal and conservative responses to environmental problems flow quite naturally from their faith in the market system and the capacity of the government to serve the "public interest." This general faith is manifested at three levels.

First, on the institutional level, both perspectives presume that the tendency of decentralized units of production to produce pollution can be corrected without any fundamental changes in the organization of production. This presumption involves either of two basic policy recommendations. Liberals tend to favor the former, while conservatives tend to favor the latter.

—Liberals in particular argue that the government can quite adequately regulate pollution, establishing and enforcing pollution standards. The government would stipulate that no more than a certain amount of pollution per unit of production would be permitted, or that a certain absolute level of pollution could not be exceeded by any individual firm. Those who exceeded pollution standards would be prosecuted. The standards would presumably correct pollution, because liberals have faith in our ability to plan and predict the future. The standards would reflect social preferences about levels of pollution, because the government reflects the interests of everyone. Finally, the standards would obviously be enforced fairly, since the government does not tend to favor any particular interests unfairly.[7]

—Conservatives tend rather to favor a non-regulatory, pricing incentive approach to pollution, given their general hesitations about direct government regulation. Orthodox economic analysis provides the analytic basis for the conservative approach. Based on their neoclassical faith in an optimal point of production under strictly competitive assumptions, many economists urge that a fee be imposed on a firm for each marginal unit of pollution; the fee would be equal to the marginal social cost of the pollution. This fee would increase the marginal internal cost of the activity and force the firm to cut back on either production or pollution until marginal cost equaled marginal revenue.[8] A recent article by Larry E. Ruff has argued this approach:[9]

Under such a system, anyone could emit any amount of pollution so long as he pays the price which the PCB [Pollution Control Board] sets to approximate the marginal social cost of

[4] For the best discussion of this kind of analysis, see E. J. Mishan, *The Costs of Economic Growth* (N.Y.: Praeger, 1967).

[5] See especially Robert U. Ayres and Allen V. Kneese, "Pollution and Environmental Quality," in Harvey Perloff, ed., *The Quality of the Urban Environment* (Baltimore: Resources for the Future, 1969).

[6] For more on these and other examples, see the Ehrlichs, *Population, Resources and Environment, op. cit.*

[7] This, generally speaking, has been the approach adopted tentatively by the government so far.

[8] See the selection by Mills, below, and Mishan, *op. cit.*

[9] Larry Ruff, "The Economic Common Sense of Pollution," *The Public Interest*, No. 19, Spring, 1970, p. 79.

pollution. Under this circumstance, private decisions based on self-interest are efficient. If pollution consists of many components, each with its own social cost, there should be different prices for each component. Thus, extremely dangerous materials must have an extremely high price, perhaps stated in terms of "years in jail" rather than "dollars," although a sufficiently high dollar price is essentially the same thing. In principal, the prices should vary with geographical location, season of the year, direction of the wind, and even day of the week, although the cost of too many variations may preclude such fine distinctions.

As Ruff points out, pollution would continue, because no further demands for changes in production would be involved; the system would rely entirely on the force of economic incentive.

Second, on the technological level, both liberal and conservative perspectives suggest that we can easily devise new technologies to dissolve the wastes of old technologies. If a principal source of air pollution is sulphur dioxide from the burning of sulphurous fuel, for instance, then they presume that we can easily develop a device which will capture the SO_2 before it enters the atmosphere, reconvert it to sulphur, and use the sulphur in production. If automobiles produce carbon monoxide, similarly, they presume we can easily develop a device for improving the efficiency of fuel combustion, reducing the waste of that combustion. The perspectives assume further that large corporations have been responsible for developing sophisticated technologies, so they propose to stimulate large corporations to devise anti-pollutant technologies. The government would simply spur them with government subsidies for their research and development costs.

John McDermott has recently dissected this orthodox faith in technology in a brilliant article called "Technology: The Opiate of the Intellectuals."[10] McDermott argues that orthodox intellectuals' faith in technology is becoming a dominant ideology in our society; he calls it the ideology of *laissez innover*, in analogy with the earlier ideology of the marketplace, *laissez faire*.

Technology, in their view, is a self-correcting system. Temporary oversight or "negative externalities" will and should be corrected by technological means. Attempts to restrict the free play of technological innovation are, in the nature of the case, self-defeating. Technological innovation exhibits a distinct tendency to work for the general welfare in the long run. Laissez innover![11]

Third, on the futuristic level, liberals and conservatives share a general faith in our foresight, in our ability to anticipate and measure externalities early enough and well enough to permit their regulation. Now that we worry about such things, they argue, we can foresee adverse side effects and prevent them. This kind of faith implies, for instance, that better planning and foresight could have anticipated traffic congestion and imposed an early tariff on automobile production and distribution in order properly to reflect the social costs of congestion. It implies, to pick another example, that our calculus is precise enough to estimate the cost of a human life, enabling us to impose optimal fees upon air polluting activities to account for their eventual contributions to lung cancer.

In summary, liberals and conservatives respond to environmental problems by accepting the current organization of economic institutions, expecting that technology can facilitate marginal adjustments to industrial externalities, and that we shall survive the current ecological crisis with better planning and the help of our public-interested governments.

THE RADICAL VIEW

The radical view of environmental problems emphasizes that capitalist institutions will continue to produce more and more pollution in the future, regardless of the steps society takes to correct present environmental conditions. As a result, the perspective suggests, the environment

---

[10] *The New York Review of Books,* July 31, 1969.

[11] In response, McDermott argues that technology serves the interests primarily of those in control of social and economic institutions, that *laissez innover* therefore constitutes a conservative ideology, much as *laissez faire* did before. "*Laissez innover* is now the premier ideology of the technological impulse in American society, which is to say, of the institutions which monopolize and profit from advanced technology and of the social classes which find in the free exploitation of *their* technology the most likely guarantee of their power, status, and wealth."

cannot ultimately be protected within the context of those institutions. The analysis builds on several related arguments.

1. Environmental degradation is a natural consequence of the enormously high priority advanced capitalist societies place on economic growth.[12] As standards of living rise, industry will find it increasingly necessary to create products involving high components of waste or high external costs; society will have already been saturated with more durable goods. Ideally, capitalists would like to produce goods which society immediately destroys (like bombs), for industry must then produce the goods again. Short of such immediate disposal, industry prefers rapid obsolescence, so that the demand for automobiles—to pick the most notable example—will not fall off when everyone is able to afford his first car. By most standards, for instance, we would not need supersonic planes to serve our transportation needs, since subsonic planes serve them adequately enough. But if industry requires growth, it eventually becomes necessary to develop supersonic planes, rendering subsonic planes obsolete, as a way of preserving its high rates of capital accumulation. If there is no demand for supersonic planes, industry must create it.

2. In an advanced society with complicated social and technological interactions, it becomes increasingly impossible to anticipate the consequences of technological change. Quantitative change, as Marx put it in another context, suddenly gives way to qualitative change. The diffusion of chemicals in the air, for instance, suddenly produces a synergistic chemical reaction which creates an entirely new chemical.

3. If the first two points are valid, that growth tends increasingly to produce waste and tends increasingly to generate unanticipated technological or ecological reactions, then it becomes increasingly important to slow the rate of economic growth. Ideally, the rate of growth should be sufficient to preserve a relatively decent standard of living for all; beyond that, the furious capitalist quest for capital accumulation should slow its pace. And that poses a single question of overriding importance: Can modern capitalist institutions be induced to slow the rate of economic growth? The answer to that question depends on the answer to two more specific questions: first, are current rates of economic growth necessary and inevitable for corporations in their modern capitalist embodiments; and second, if those rates are necessary, can the corporations be forced by society to accept lower rates of growth and lower rates of accumulation against their wills without a radical change in the social and institutional balance of power?

4. The answer to the first of those two questions, radicals contend, must certainly be that corporations will absolutely and inevitably pursue the highest possible rate of growth. If any individual corporation failed to do so, as Chapter One pointed out, it would jeopardize its competitive position with respect to other corporations. Further, as Herbert Gintis argues in his selection below, a rapid decrease in the rate of economic growth might threaten the aggregate stability of the system itself; the promise of growth and future affluence provides one of the few forceful incentives for workers to continue accepting the conditions of capitalist society. Expecting any different kind of behavior, as Robert Heilbroner says below, is "tantamount to asking a dominant class to acquiesce in the elimination of the very activities that sustain it."[13]

5. Radicals argue strongly that the answer to the second question must also be negative. Applying their general view of the State described in Chapter One, radicals contend that the State serves the interests of the capitalist class and would not force that class to renounce its principal interest. Recent experience with government "regulation" in the environmental area provides some dramatic examples. James Ridgeway describes two such cases.[14] Under the federal water pollution act of 1956, some provisions were established for government action against firms discharging extensive "interstate" pollution. Since the law was passed, Ridgeway reports,

there have been 46 different enforcement actions; four of them have reached a hearing stage, and only one went to court. In practice what happens is that the politicians, bureaucrats and technicians get together at a conference and agree to meet at various dates in the future.

[12] Environmental problems also plague many advanced socialist countries, which have placed equally high emphasis on growth. See the discussion of pollution in Russia in Marshall Goldman, ed., *Controlling Pollution* (Englewood Cliffs, N.J.: Prentice-Hall, 1967).
[13] See "Ecological Armageddon" in the readings.
[14] From Ridgeway, "You Don't Need a Sewerman," *Hard Times*, November 3–10, 1969, p. 3.

Each time they meet, it is agreed that progress has been made. The conference method helps to legitimize pollution by conferring it to death.

The Agricultural Research Service, similarly, has been given considerable enforcement powers over the use of pesticides. If it detects unsafe or ineffective products, "it can always cancel the registration, seize the goods, or ask the Justice Department to prosecute violators." In this case, too, Ridgeway concludes, no prosecution follows:

Despite these broad powers, the ARS did not prosecute one case in 13 years, even though it cited thousands of companies, many of them repeatedly, for violations. Instead the Service writes the chemical companies obsequious notes, pleading with them not to sell crummy and dangerous merchandise. In a few instances it seizes batches of tainted goods at one retail outlet, but leaves them out for sale at all the other outlets.

6. Finally, our capacity to reduce the destructive effects of continual economic growth will be additionally limited by a relatively recent development. As industry has recognized the emerging public concern over ecology, it has moved rapidly to capture that concern in the form of higher profits. As Martin Gellen shows in this chapter, a pollution-industrial complex is evolving. Large corporations are beginning to develop products designed to cut down the pollution they produce. Instead of cutting back on initial production, they will be demanding additional profits for the production of goods to eliminate the by-products of their initial production. They will not only be imposing external costs on society, but will be demanding a profit for removing those external effects. And if our experience with industrial complexes carries any hint of the future, this new complex will inevitably acquire its own independent power, further constraining our freedom to limit the rate of economic growth.

THE READINGS

The first two selections provide Impressions, Definitions, and Magnitudes. Edith Iglauer describes some of the first evidence of the fatal effects of air pollution and presents some gloomy prospects for the future. An Editor's Supplement summarizes most of the important components of environmental degradation and their relative magnitudes.

The final four selections provide a basic set of contrasts between the orthodox and radical approaches to environmental problems. The article by Edwin Mills illustrates the basic viewpoint of liberals and conservatives on the problem of pollution, taking current institutions for granted and viewing the world from a competitive market perspective. Mills himself tends to support the more conservative, market incentive approach over the direct regulatory approach. Robert Heilbroner provides a contrasting view of the problem, emphasizing, as radicals do, the fundamental importance of economic growth in creating environmental problems and the centrality of the issue of our power to slow the rate of growth. The next two pieces illustrate two of the points in the radical argument that growth cannot be slowed in the context of current institutions. Martin Gellen documents the final point above, that a pollution-industrial complex is beginning to develop. As he concludes, "To make an industry out of cleaning up the mess that industry itself makes is a logical extension of corporate capitalism." As the power of that complex develops, it will make it increasingly difficult to slow the rate of growth. Perhaps more important, Herbert Gintis argues that the promise of economic growth provides the most important support of the stability of the capitalist system and makes economic growth absolutely essential to the capitalist class. His arguments provide special amplification of the basic radical contention that corporations will not slow the rate of economic growth on their own.

THE AMBIENT AIR

Edith Iglauer

This short selection describes some of the first instances of tragic air inversions dramatizing the problem of air pollution. The author speculates on the long-run conditions in large metropolitan areas, when suburbanites "will scarcely dare step out into the yard." The selection comes from a longer article which originally appeared in *The New Yorker*.

In urban areas of the Northern Hemisphere during the months from October to February, what are called temperature inversions—in which a layer of cool air is trapped under a layer of warm air—have caused lethal events that are referred to by experts on air pollution as "incidents," "acute episodes," or "disasters," depending on their severity. Each time, a blanket of warm air has for several days imprisoned heavily polluted air over a densely populated surface area, and when the winds have cleared the stagnant air away it has been discovered that there were many more deaths than would normally have been expected. In December, 1930, a heavily industrialized section of the Meuse Valley, in Belgium, had a bad three-day fog during which hundreds of people became ill and sixty died—more than ten times the normal number of deaths. Shortly afterward, during a thick nine-day fog in January, 1931, five hundred and ninety-two people in the Manchester and Salford area of England died—again a large jump in the death rate. But to us in the United States these events seemed remote—until 1948, when, in Donora, Pennsylvania, a small mill town dominated by steel and chemical plants, a four-day fog filled with zinc sulphate and sulphur dioxide, among other pollutants, made almost half the fourteen thousand inhabitants sick. Twenty persons died. Ten years later, Donora residents who had been acutely ill during that episode were found to have a higher rate of sickness and to die at an earlier age than the average for all the townspeople.

The British, who have been complaining about the unpleasant effects of coal smoke since the year 1273, when it was termed "prejudicial to health," were recording air-pollution episodes as far back as 1873, when, during a London fog, two hundred and sixty-eight unexpected deaths from bronchitis were noted. But it was not until a great fog blanketed London in 1952 that the sinister potential of air pollution became fully apparent to everyone. This fog lasted from December 5th to December 8th, and ten days later, when the complete mortality reports had been evaluated, a shocked world learned that there had been an astonishing four thousand more deaths in Greater London during that period than would normally have been expected. During previous temperature inversions over London, the excess mortality had been among the elderly and infants under a year old, but in this disaster the percentage increase in mortality was similar for all age groups. In Donora, victims had not begun dying until the third smoggy day, but in London a number of the unexpected deaths occurred within the first twenty-four hours; then when the air cleared the rate fell abruptly. The statistics indicated that almost all those who died unexpectedly had records of bronchitis, emphysema, or heart trouble, and that people in the last category were most vulnerable. It was small comfort to conjecture that most of the people who died would probably not have lived much longer anyway. Again, in January, 1956, a thousand extra deaths in London were blamed on an extended fog. In that same year, Parliament passed a Clean Air Act, and Britain embarked on an extraordinary program to reduce the burning of soft coal. The effects of the program became apparent in 1962, for, in December of that

SOURCE: *Edith Iglauer, "The Ambient Air,"* in The New Yorker. *Copyright © 1968, The New Yorker Magazine, Inc.*

year, London experienced a severe fog and inversion, and this time seven hundred excess deaths were recorded—still too many, of course, but an improvement over the previous figures. The lower mortality was attributed not only to less smoke but to generally better medical care (including wide use of antibiotics) and to greater public awareness—through newspaper, radio, and television coverage—of what was happening and of how to take precautions during a period of severe air pollution. Those with serious heart or respiratory ailments knew by then that they should stay indoors, that they must not smoke, that they should get plenty of rest, and that they should move slowly in order to decrease the demands on their respiratory systems. Frightening alarms were carefully avoided, yet far more than the normal number of people dropped dead in the streets from heart failure.

New York has the most severe air-pollution problem in the United States, but its air is still not as dirty as that of London, which has the reputation for being the cradle of air pollution. In November, 1953, early in 1963, and over the Thanksgiving weekend in 1966, New York had smog episodes that were bad, but not as deadly as London's. They have been carefully studied by Dr. Leonard Greenburg, who was New York City's first Commissioner of Air Pollution Control and is now Professor of Preventive Medicine at Albert Einstein College of Medicine, where he is working with a group of air-pollution specialists. He has calculated that there were approximately two hundred and twenty excess deaths owing to air pollution in 1953, three hundred to three hundred and fifty in 1963, and one hundred and sixty-eight in 1966. These episodes are a warning that the city's air supply has its limits and must be protected before it becomes so contaminated that the normal prevailing winds cannot disperse the filth. New Yorkers wake on almost every morning to a temperature inversion that usually extends about a thousand feet above the ground and lasts from six to eight o'clock, though even in good weather it is not fully burned away by the sun until about ten. The brilliant red sunsets so much admired in New York and Los Angeles are caused by large particles in the air, most of them produced by incomplete combustion in the generation of heat and power. Meteorologists and air-pollution experts do not enjoy these sunsets, and they get really depressed when they consider how the tendency of our growing population to cluster in relatively small areas will affect the air and climate of the future. They say that in twenty years, when population increases have caused Philadelphia to merge into New York and New York into Boston, so that there will be one long city with no open spaces in between, the wind patterns will change and only people living on the edges of this huge sprawl will get any rural breezes. The fellow at the center will be living on what is called a "heat island"—a phenomenon that is already occurring in a small way in several cities. At street level, New York is now, on the average, from ten to fifteen degrees warmer at night than the Westchester suburbs, owing to the heating of the buildings in winter and the storage of solar heat in the asphalt and concrete in summer. In fifty years, the Westchester suburbanite may be able to grow tropical plants in his yard, but the great mass of air around him may be so polluted that he will scarcely dare step out into the yard.

SOURCES AND EXTENT OF POLLUTION

Editor's Supplement

This supplement summarizes the sources and magnitudes of the three principal kinds of urban pollution: air, water, and solid waste.[1]

AIR POLLUTION

Five principal sources of energy conversion provide five principal kinds of air pollution. The five sources are transportation (especially automobiles), industry, electric power plants, space heating (especially in homes), and refuse disposal incineration. The five principal components of air pollution are carbon monoxide, sulphur oxides, hydro-carbons, nitrogen oxides, and particulate matter.

Of total tons of all forms of air pollution throughout the country in 1965, automobiles were responsible for 60 percent, industry accounted for 17 percent, electric power plants 14 percent, space heating 6 percent, and refuse disposal 3 percent.

Automobile pollution produced mainly carbon monoxide (three fourths of its total tonnage) and hydro-carbons (one seventh).

Industry produced mainly sulphur oxides (almost 40 percent of its total tonnage) and particulate matter (roughly one quarter).

Electric power plants produced mainly sulphur oxides (60 percent of its total tonnage).

Space heating and refuse disposal included all kinds of pollutants in roughly equal proportions.

Of all pollutants, carbon monoxide accounted for roughly one half of total tonnage, sulphur oxides for slightly more than 15 percent, and the rest for smaller shares.

Pollution levels and components varied widely around the country. Automobiles accounted for 80 percent of air pollution in Los Angeles in 1965, for instance, but much less than 50 percent in New York City.[2]

One cannot isolate the extent to which the different chemical components of air pollution are responsible for different kinds of deleterious health effects. Indeed, one can barely measure the extent to which differentially higher levels of air pollution cause higher rates of disease. The four kinds of disease which seem statistically associated with higher levels of air pollution to the greatest degree are bronchitis, lung cancer, cardiovascular disease, and total respiratory disease.[3] According to a recent survey of health effects of air pollution, a 50 percent reduction in average air pollution levels in the United States would save $2 billion in annual costs associated with morbidity and mortality, or 4.5 percent of total costs associated with morbidity and mortality each year.[4]

WATER POLLUTION

There are eight main sources of water pollution: organic sewage, the most important and most tractable; infectious agents, like typhoid, which have been basically eliminated; plant nutrients, which come from sewage and fertilizer wash-off, producing algal growth on or near water surfaces; organic chemicals, like insecticides, pesticides, and detergents—these proliferate and are difficult chemically to break down; inorganic chemicals, like sludges and chemical residues—these are miscellaneous and not especially serious; land sediments from erosion; radioactive substances; and waste heat from electric power plants and industry.[5]

[1] Except where otherwise noted, the source for this supplement was *The New York Times*, April 20, 1970, p. 33.
[2] Roger Revelle, "Pollution and Cities," in James Q. Wilson, ed., *Metropolitan Enigma* (Cambridge: Harvard University Press, 1968), p. 98.
[3] Lester B. Lave and Eugene P. Seskin, "Air Pollution and Human Health," *Science*, August 21, 1970.
[4] *Ibid.*, p. 730.
[5] Revelle, *op. cit.*, pp. 107–120.

President Johnson said in 1967 that "every major river system in the country is polluted. . . . Every second, about 2 million gallons of sewage and other fluid waste pour into the nation's waterways."

Roger Revelle estimates that it would cost roughly 5 billion dollars per year over 15 years to construct enough treatment facilities to control water pollution.[6]

SOLID WASTE POLLUTION

Solid waste pollution has the consequence especially of requiring more and more land for dumping space—it thus constitutes a principal source of "land pollution."

Every person in the country, on the average, generates about 7 pounds of trash a day. That adds up to 3.5 billion tons of waste a year. Much of it is agricultural crop and animal waste; only 360 million tons is urban waste. Of that urban waste, miscellaneous paper typically accounts for 25 percent; newspapers for 14 percent; garbage for 12 percent; glass, ceramics, and stone for 10 percent; grass and dirt for 10 percent, and so on.

About 73 percent of garbage is dumped openly on land, 15 percent is incinerated, 8 percent is used in sanitary landfill, 3 percent is salvaged, and 1 percent is used in composting.

[6] *Ibid.*, p. 132.

ECONOMIC INCENTIVES IN AIR POLLUTION CONTROL

Edwin S. Mills

This selection provides a fairly straightforward illustration of the conventional liberal and conservative approach to pollution problems. Building from orthodox economic analysis, Mills urges a system of tax incentives to stimulate private control of pollution.

The piece originally appeared in Harold Wolozin, ed., *The Economics of Air Pollution*. Mills is a professor of economics at Johns Hopkins University.

Smoke is one of the classic examples of external diseconomies mentioned in the writings of Alfred Marshall and his followers. Generations of college instructors have used this form of air pollution as an illustration to help their students to understand conditions under which competitive markets will or will not allocate resources efficiently. By now, the theoretical problems have been explored with the sharpest tools available to economists. The consensus among economists on the basic issue is overwhelming, and I suspect one would be hard-pressed to find a proposition that commands more widespread agreement among economists than the following: The discharge of pollutants into the atmosphere imposes on some members of society costs which are inadequately imputed to the sources of the pollution by free markets, resulting in more pollution than would be desirable from the point of view of society as a whole.

In spite of the widespread agreement on the fundamental issues regarding externalities such as air pollution, there have been remarkably few attempts in the scholarly literature to carry the analysis beyond this point. Most writers have been content to point out that the free market will misallocate resources in this respect, and to conclude that this justifies intervention. But what sort of intervention? There are many kinds, and some are clearly preferable to others.

Too often we use the imperfect working of a free market to justify *any* kind of intervention. This is really an anomalous situation. After all, markets are man-made institutions, and they can be designed in many ways. When an economist concludes that a free market is working badly—giving the wrong signals, so to speak—he should also ask how the market may be restructured so that it will give the right signals.

Thus, in the case of air pollution, acceptance of the proposition stated above leads most people to think entirely in terms of direct regulation—permits, registration, licenses, enforcement of standards and so on. I submit that this is rather like abandoning a car because it has a flat tire. Of course, in some cases the car may be working so badly that the presence of a flat tire makes it rational to abandon it, and correspondingly the inadequacies of some market mechanisms may make abandonment desirable. Nevertheless, I submit that the more logical procedure is to ask how a badly functioning market may be restructured to preserve the clear advantages of free and decentralized decision-making, but to remedy its defects. Only when there appears to be no feasible way of structuring a market so that it will give participants the right signals, should it be given up in favor of direct regulation.

It is easy to state the principle by which the socially desirable amount of pollution abatement should be determined: *Any given pollution level should be reached by the least costly combination of means available; the level of pollution should be achieved at which the cost of a further reduction would exceed the benefits.*

To clothe the bare bones of this principle with the flesh of substance is a very tall order indeed. In principle, if every relevant number were known, an edict could be issued to each polluter specifying the amount by which he was to reduce his discharge of pollutants and the means by which he was to do so. In fact, we are even farther from having the right numbers for air pollution than we are from having those for water pollution.

In this situation, I suggest that any scheme for abatement should be consistent with the following principles:

1. It should permit decision-making to be as decentralized as possible. Other things being equal, a rule that discharges must be reduced by a certain amount is preferable to a rule that particular devices be installed, since the former permits alternatives to be considered that may be cheaper than the devices specified in the latter.

2. It should be experimental and flexible. As experience with abatement schemes accumulates, we will gain information about benefits and costs of abatement. We will then revise our ideas about the desirable amount and methods of abatement. Control schemes will have to be revised accordingly.

3. It should be coupled with careful economic research on benefits and costs of air-pollution abatement. Without benefit-cost calculations, we cannot determine the desirable amount of abatement. We can, however, conjecture with confidence that more abatement is desirable than is provided by existing controls. Therefore, our present ignorance of benefits and costs should not be used as an excuse for doing nothing. I would place great emphasis on doing the appropriate research as part of any control scheme. A well-designed scheme will provide information (e.g., on the costs of a variety of control devices) that is relevant to the benefit-cost calculations.

MEANS OF CONTROL

We are not in a position to evaluate a variety of schemes that are in use or have been proposed to control or abate air pollution. It will be useful to classify methods of control according to the categories employed by Kneese in his discussion of water pollution:

1. *Direct Regulation.* In this category, I include licenses, permits, compulsory standards, zoning, registration, and equity litigation.

2. *Payments.* In this category I include not only direct payments or subsidies, but also reductions in collections that would otherwise be made. Examples are subsidization of particular control devices, forgiveness of local property taxes on pollution-control equipment, accelerated depreciation on control equipment, payments for decreases in the discharge of pollutants, and tax credits for investment in control equipment.

3. *Charges.* This category includes schedules of charges or fees for the discharge of different amounts of specified pollutants and excise or other taxes on specific sources of pollution (such as coal).

My objection to direct regulation should be clear by now. It is too rigid and inflexible, and loses the advantages of decentralized decision-making. For example, a rule that factories limit their discharges of pollutants to certain levels would be less desirable than a system of effluent fees that achieved the same overall reduction in pollution, in that the latter would permit each firm to make the adjustment to the extent and in the manner that best suited its own situation. Direct restrictions are usually cumbersome to administer, and rarely achieve more than the grossest form of control. In spite of the fact that almost all of our present control programs fall into this category, they should be tried only after all others have been found unworkable.

Thus, first consideration ought to be given to control schemes under the second and third categories.

Many of the specific schemes under these two categories are undesirable in that they involve charges or payments for the wrong thing. If it is desired to reduce air pollution, then the charge or payment should depend on the amount of pollutants discharged and not on an activity that is directly or indirectly related to the discharge of pollutants. For example, an excise tax on coal is less desirable than a tax on the discharge of pollutants resulting from burning coal because the former distorts resource use in favor of other fuels and against devices to remove pollutants from stack gases after burning coal. As a second example, a payment to firms for decreasing the discharge of pollutants is better than a tax credit for investment in pollution-control devices because the latter introduces a bias against other means of reducing the discharge of pollutants, such as the burning of nonpolluting fuels. Thus, many control schemes can be eliminated on the principle that more efficient control can normally be obtained by incentives that depend on the variable it is desired to influence rather than by incentives that depend on a related variable.

Many of the specific schemes under *Payments* can be eliminated on the grounds that they propose to subsidize the purchase of devices that neither add to revenues nor reduce costs. Thus, if a pollution-control device neither helps to produce salable products nor reduces production costs, a firm really receives very little incentive to buy the device even if the government offers to pay half the cost. All that such subsidy schemes accomplish is to reduce somewhat the resistance to direct controls. Of course, some control devices may help to recover wastes that can be made into salable products. Although there are isolated examples of the recovery of valuable wastes in the process of air-pollution control, it is hard to know whether such possibilities are extensive. A careful survey of this subject would be interesting. However, the key point is that, to the extent that waste recovery is desirable, firms receive the appropriate incentive to recover wastes by the use of fees or payments that are related to the discharge of effluents. Therefore, even the possibility of waste recovery does not justify subsidization of devices to recover wastes.

The foregoing analysis creates a presumption in favor of schemes under which either payments are made for reducing the discharge of pollutants or charges are made for the amount of pollutants discharged. The basic condition for optimum resource allocation can in principle be satisfied by either scheme, since under either scheme just enough incentive can be provided so that the marginal cost of further abatement approximates the marginal benefits of further abatement. There are, however, three reasons for believing that charges are preferable to subsidies:

1. There is no natural "origin" for payments. In principle, the payment should be for a reduction in the discharge of pollutants below what it would have been without the payment. Estimation of this magnitude would be difficult and the recipient of the subsidy would have an obvious incentive to exaggerate the amount of pollutants he would have discharged without the subsidy. The establishment of a new factory would raise a particularly difficult problem. The trouble is precisely that which agricultural policy meets when it tries to pay farmers to reduce their crops. Jokes about farmers deciding to double the amount of corn not produced this year capture the essence of the problem.

2. Payments violate feelings of equity which many people have on this subject. People feel that if polluting the air is a cost of producing certain products, then the consumers who benefit ought to pay this cost just as they ought to pay the costs of labor and other inputs needed in production.

3. If the tax system is used to make the payments, e.g., by permitting a credit against tax liability for reduced discharge of pollutants, a "gimmick" is introduced into the tax system which, other things being equal, it is better to avoid. Whether or not the tax system is used to make the payments, the money must be raised at least partly by higher taxes than otherwise for some taxpayers. Since most of our taxes are not neutral, resource misallocation may result.

I feel that the above analysis creates at least a strong presumption for the use of discharge or effluent fees as a means of air-pollution abatement.

Briefly, the proposal is that air-pollution control authorities be created with responsibility to evaluate a variety of abatement schemes, to estimate benefits and costs, to render technical assistance, to levy charges for the discharge of effluents, and to adopt other means of abatement.

Serious problems of air pollution are found mostly in urban areas of substantial size. Within an urban area, air pollution is no respecter of political boundaries, and an authority's jurisdiction should be defined by the boundaries of a metropolitan air shed. Although difficult to identify precisely, such air sheds would roughly coincide with Standard Metropolitan Statistical Areas. Except in a few cases, such as the Chicago-Gary and the New York-northern New Jersey areas, jurisdiction could be confined to a single metropolitan area. In a number of instances, the authority would have to be interstate. In many large metropolitan areas, the authority would have to be the joint creation of several local governments. There would presumably be participation by state governments and by the federal government at least to the extent of encouragement and financial support.

Each authority would have broad responsibility for dealing with air pollution in its metropolitan air shed. It would institute discharge fees and would be mainly financed by such fees. It would have the responsibility of estimating benefits and costs of air-pollution abatement, and of setting fees accordingly. It would have to identify major pollutants in its area and set fees appropriate to each significant pollutant. The authority could also provide technical advice and help concerning methods of abatement.

Although there would be great uncertainty as to the appropriate level of fees at first, this should not prevent their use. They should be set conservatively while study was in progress, and data on the responses of firms to modest fees would be valuable in making benefit-cost calculations. Given present uncertainties, a certain amount of flexible experimentation with fees would be desirable.

Questions will necessarily arise as to just what kinds and sources of pollutants would come under the jurisdiction of the proposed authority. I do not pretend to have answers to all such questions. Presumably, standard charges could be set for all major pollutants, with provision for variation in each metropolitan air shed to meet local conditions. It is clear that provision should be made for the possibility of varying the charge for a particular pollutant from air shed to air shed. The harm done by the discharge of a ton of sulfur dioxide will vary from place to place, depending on meteorological and other factors. It is probably less harmful in Omaha than in Los Angeles. It is important that charges reflect these differences, so that locational decisions will be appropriately affected.

Consideration would also have to be given to the appropriate temporal pattern of charges. In most cities, pollution is much more serious in summer than at other times. Charges that were in effect only during summer months might induce a quite different set of adjustments than charges that were in effect at all times.

No one should pretend that the administration of an effective air-pollution control scheme will be simple or cheap. Measurement and monitoring of discharges are necessary under any control scheme and can be expensive and technically difficult. Likewise, whatever the control scheme, finding the optimum degree of abatement requires the calculation of benefits and costs; these calculations are conceptually difficult and demanding.

The point that needs to be emphasized strongly is that the cost of administering a control scheme based on effluent fees will be less than the cost of administering any other scheme of equal effectiveness. An effluent-fee system, like ordinary price systems, is largely self-administering.

This point is important and is worth stating in detail. First, consider an effluent-fee system. Suppose a schedule of fees has been set. Then firms will gradually learn the rate of effluent discharge that is most profitable. Meanwhile, the enforcement agency will need to sample the firm's effluent to ensure that the firm is paying the fee for the amount actually discharged. However, once the firm has found the most profitable rate of effluent discharge, and this is known to the enforcing agency, the firm will have no incentive to discharge any amount of effluent other than the one for which it is paying. At this point the system becomes self-administering and the enforcement agency need only collect bills. Second, consider a regulatory scheme under which the permissible discharge is set at the level that actually re-

sulted under the effluent-fee scheme. Then the firm has a continuing incentive because of its advantage on the cost side to exceed the permissible discharge rate so as to increase production. Monitoring by the enforcement agency therefore continues to be necessary.

Of course, under either a regulatory or an effluent-fee scheme, a change in conditions will require the search for a new "equilibrium." Neither system can be self-enforcing until the new equilibrium has been found. The point is that the effluent-fee system becomes self-enforcing at that point, whereas the regulatory system does not.

ECOLOGICAL ARMAGEDDON

Robert Heilbroner

Heilbroner provides a general perspective within which to view environmental problems. He emphasizes that we must slow the rate of economic growth in the long run in order to control environmental degradation, and poses the most important question of the radical analysis—whether economic growth can be slowed in the context of capitalist institutions. He hedges his final answer; more radical analysts would not.

Heilbroner teaches economics at the New School for Social Research, and has written many books on a wide variety of economic subjects.

Ecology has become the Thing. There are ecological politics, ecological jokes, ecological bookstores, advertisements, seminars, teach-ins, buttons. The automobile, symbol of ecological abuse, has been tried, sentenced to death, and formally executed in at least two universities (replete with burial of one victim). Publishing companies are fattening on books on the sonic boom, poisons in the things we eat, perils loose in the garden, the dangers of breathing. The *Saturday Review* has appended a regular monthly Ecological Supplement. In short, the ecological issue has assumed the dimensions of a vast popular fad, for which one can predict with reason-

SOURCE: *Robert Heilbroner, "Ecological Armageddon," in* The New York Review of Books, *May 23, 1970. Reprinted with permission. Copyright © 1970 The New York Review.*

able assurance the trajectory of all such fads —a period of intense general involvement, followed by growing boredom and gradual extinction, save for a die-hard remnant of the faithful.

This would be a tragedy, for I have slowly become convinced during the last twelve months that the ecological issue is not only of primary and lasting importance, but that it may indeed constitute the most dangerous and difficult challenge that humanity has ever faced. Since these are very large statements, let me attempt to substantiate them by drawing freely on the best single descriptive and analytic treatment of the subject that I have yet seen, *Population, Resources, Environment* by Paul and Anne Ehrlich of Stanford University. Rather than resort to the bothersome procedure of endlessly citing their arguments in quotation marks, I shall take the liberty of reproducing their case in a rather free paraphrase, as if it were my own, until we reach the end of the basic argument, after which I shall make clear some conclusions that I believe lie implicit in their work.

Ultimately, the ecological crisis represents our belated awakening to the fact that we live on what Kenneth Boulding has called, in the perfect phrase, our Spaceship Earth. As in all spaceships, sustained life requires that a meticulous balance be maintained between the capability of the vehicle to support life and the demands made by the inhabitants of the craft. Until quite recently, those demands have been well within the capability of the ship, in its ability both to supply the physical and chemical requirements for continued existence and to absorb the waste products of the voyagers. This is not to say that the earth has been generous—short rations have been the lot of mankind for most of its history— nor is it to deny the recurrent advent of local ecological crises—witness the destruction of whole areas like the erstwhile granaries of North Africa. But famines have passed and there have always been new areas to move to. The idea that the earth as a whole was overtaxed is one that is new to our time.

For it is only in our time that we are reaching the limit of earthly carrying capacity, not on a local but on a global basis. Indeed, as will soon become clear, we are well past that capacity, provided that the level of resource intake and waste output represented by the average American or European is taken as a standard to be achieved by all humanity. To put it bluntly, if we take as the price of a first-class ticket the resource requirements of those passengers who travel in the Northern Hemisphere of the Spaceship, we have now reached a point at which the steerage is condemned to live forever—or at least within the horizon of the technology presently visible—at a second-class level; or a point at which a considerable change in living habits must be imposed on first class if the ship is ever to be converted to a one-class cruise.

This strain on the carrying capacity of the vessel results from the contemporary confluence of three distinct developments, each of which places tremendous or even unmanageable strains on the life-carrying capability of the planet and all of which together simply overload it. The first of these is the enormous strain imposed by the sheer burgeoning of population. The statistics of population growth are by now very well known: the earth's passenger list is growing at a rate that will give us some four billion humans by 1975, and that threatens to give us eight billion by 2010. I say "threatens," since it is likely that the inability of the earth to carry so large a group will result in an actual population somewhat smaller than this, especially in the steerage, where the growth is most rapid and the available resources least plentiful.

We shall return to the population problem later. But meanwhile a second strain is placed on the earth by the simple cumulative effect of *existing* technology (combustion engines, the main industrial processes, present-day agricultural techniques, etc.). This strain is localized mainly in the first-class portions of the vessel where each new arrival on board is rapidly given a standard complement of capital equipment and where the rate of physical and chemical resource transformation per capita steadily mounts. The strain consists of the limited ability of the soil, the water, and the atmosphere of these favored regions to absorb the outpourings of these fast-growing industrial processes.

The most dramatic instance of this limited absorptive power is the rise in the carbon dioxide content of the air due to the steady growth of (largely industrial) combustion. By the year 2000, it seems beyond dispute that the CO_2 content of the air will have doubled, raising the heat-trapping properties of the atmosphere. This so-called greenhouse effect has been predicted to raise mean global temperatures sufficiently to bring catastrophic potential consequences. One possibility is a sequence of climatic changes resulting from a melting of the Arctic ice floes that would result in the advent of a new Ice Age; another is the slumping of the Antarctic ice cap into the sea with a consequent tidal wave that could wipe out a substantial portion of mankind and raise the sea level by 60 to 100 feet.

These are all "iffy" scenarios whose present significance may be limited to alerting us to the immensity of the ecological problem; happily they are of sufficient uncertainty not to cause us immediate worry (it is lucky they are, because it is extremely unlikely that all the massed technological and human energy on earth could arrest such changes once they began). Much closer to home is the burden placed on the earth's carrying capacity by the sheer requirements of a spreading industrial activity for the fuel and mineral resources needed to maintain the going rate of output per person in the first-class cabins. To raise the existing (not the anticipated) population of the earth to American standards would require the annual extraction of 75 times as much iron, 100 times as much copper, 200 times as much lead, and 250 times as much tin as we now take from the earth. Only the known reserves of iron allow us to entertain such fantastic rates of mineral exploitation (and the capital investment needed to bring about such mining operations is in itself staggering to contemplate). All the other requirements exceed by far all known or reasonably anticipated ore reserves. And, to repeat, we have taken into account only today's level of population: to equip the prospective passengers of the year 2010 with this amount of basic raw material would require a doubling of all the above figures.

I will revert later to the consequences of this prospect. First, however, let us pay attention to the third source of overload, this one traceable to the special environment-destroying potential of newly developed technologies. Of these the most important—and if it should ever come to full-scale war, of course the most lethal—is the threat posed by nuclear radiation. I shall not elaborate on this well-known (although not well-believed) danger, pausing to point out only that a nuclear holocaust would in all likelihood exert its principal effect in the Northern Hemisphere. The survivors in the South would be severely hampered in their efforts at reconstruction not only because most of the easily available resources of the world have already been used up, but because most of the technological know-how would have perished along with the populations up North.

But the threats of new technology are by no means limited to the specter of nuclear devastation. There is, immediately at hand, the known devastation of the new chemical pesticides that have now entered more or less irreversibly into the living tissue of the world's population. Most mothers' milk in the United States today—I now quote the Ehr-lichs verbatim—"contains so much DDT that it would be declared illegal in interstate commerce if it were sold as cow's milk"; and the DDT intake of infants around the world is twice the daily allowable maximum set by the World Health Organization. We are already, in other words, being exposed to heavy dosages of chemicals whose effects we know to be dangerous, with what ultimate results we shall have to wait nervously to discover. (There is food for thought in the archaeological evidence that one factor in the decline of Rome was the systematic poisoning of upper-class Romans from the lead with which they lined their wine containers.)

But the threat is not limited to pesticides. Barry Commoner predicts an agricultural crisis in the United States within fifty years from the action of our fertilizers, which will either ultimately destroy soil fertility or lead to pollution of the national water supply. At another corner of the new technology, the SST threatens not only to shake us with its boom, but to affect the amount of cloud cover (and climate) by its contrails. And I have not even mentioned the standard pollution problems of smoke, industrial effluents into lake and rivers, or solid wastes. Suffice it to report that a 1968 UNESCO Conference concluded that man has only about twenty years to go before the planet starts to become uninhabitable because of air pollution alone. Of course "starts to" is imprecise; I am reminded of a cartoon of an industrialist looking at his billowing smoke-stacks, in front of which a forlorn figure is holding up a placard that says: "We have only 35 years to go." The caption reads, "Boy, that shook me up for a minute. I thought it said 3 to 5 years."

I have left until last the grimmest and gravest threat of all, speaking now on behalf of the steerage. This is the looming inability of the great green earth to bring forth sufficient food to maintain life, even at the miserable threshold of subsistence at which it is now endured by perhaps a third of the world's population. The problem here is the very strong likelihood that population growth will inexorably outpace whatever improvements in fertility and productivity we will be able to apply to the earth's mantle (including the watery fringes of the ocean where sea "farming" is at least technically imaginable).

Here the race is basically between two forces: on the one hand, those that give promise that the rate of population increase can be curbed (if not totally halted); and on the other, those that give promise of increasing the amount of sustenance we can wring from the soil. . . .

I have no doubt that one can fault bits and pieces of the Ehrlichs' analysis, and there is a note of determined pessimism in their work that leads me to suspect (or at least hope) that there is somewhat more time for adaptation than they suggest. Yet I do not see how their basic conclusion can be denied. Beginning within our lifetimes and rising rapidly to crisis proportions in our children's, humankind faces a challenge comparable to none in its history, with the possible exception of the forced migration of the Ice Age. It is with the responses to this crisis that I wish to end this essay, for telling and courageous as the Ehrlichs' analysis is, I do not believe that even they have fully faced up to the implications that their own findings present.

The first of these I have already stated: it is the clear conclusion that the underdeveloped countries can *never* hope to achieve parity with the developed countries. Given our present and prospective technology, there are simply not enough resources to permit a "Western" rate of industrial exploitation to be expanded to a population of four billion —much less eight billion—persons. It may well be that most of the population in the underdeveloped world has no ambition to reach Western standards—indeed, does not even know that such a thing as "development" is on the agenda. But the elites of these nations, for all their rhetorical rejection of Western (and especially American) styles of life, do tend to picture a Western standard as the ultimate end of their activities. As it becomes clear that such an objective is impossible, a profound reorientation of views must take place within the underdeveloped nations.

What such a reorientation will be it is impossible to say. For the near future, the outlook for the most population-oppressed areas will be a continuous battle against food shortages, coupled with the permanent impairment of the intelligence of much of the surviving population due to protein deficiencies in childhood. This pressure of population may lead to aggressive searches for *Lebensraum;* or, as I have frequently written, may culminate in revolutions of desperation.

In the long run, of course, there is the possibility of considerable growth (although nothing resembling the attainment of a Western standard of consumption). But no quick substantial improvement in their condition seems feasible within the next generation at least. The visions of Sir Charles Snow or the Soviet academician Sakharov for a gigantic transfer of wealth from the rich nations to the poor (20 percent of GNP is proposed) are simply fantasies. Since much of GNP is spatially nontransferable or inappropriate, such a huge levy against GNP would imply shipments of up to 50 percent of much movable output. How this enormous flood of goods would be transported, allocated, absorbed, or maintained—*not to mention relinquished by the donor countries*—is nowhere analyzed by the proponents of such vast aid.

The implications of the ecological crisis for the advanced nations are not any less severe, although they are of a different kind. For it is clear that free industrial growth is just as disastrous for the Western nations as free population growth for those of the East and South. The worship in the West of a growing Gross National Product must be recognized as not only a deceptive but a very dangerous avatar; Kenneth Boulding has begun a campaign, in which I shall join him, to label this statistical monster Gross National Cost.

The necessity to bring our economic activities into a sustainable relationship with the resource capabilities and waste absorption properties of the world will pose two problems for the West. On the simpler level, a whole series of technological problems must be met. Fume-free transportation must be developed on land and air. The cult of disposability must be replaced by that of reusability. Population stability must be attained through tax and other inducements, both to conserve resources and to preserve reasonable population densities. Many of these problems will tax our ingenuity, technical and socio-political, but the main problem they pose is not whether, but *how soon* they can be solved.

But there is another, deeper question that the developed nations face—at least those that have capitalist economies. This problem can be stated as a crucial test as to who was right—John Stuart Mill or Karl Marx. Mill maintained, in his famous *Principles of Economics,* that the terminus of capitalist evolution would be a stationary state, in which the return to capital had fallen to insignificance, and a redistributive tax system would be able to capture any flows of income to the holders of scarce resources, such as land. In effect, he prophesied the transformation of capitalism, in an environment of abundance, into a balanced economy, in which the capitalist, both as the generator of change and as the main claimant on the surplus generated by change, would in effect undergo a painless euthanasia.

The Marxian view is of course quite the opposite. The very essence of capitalism, according to Marx, is expansion—which is to say, the capitalist, as a historical "type," finds his *raison d'être* in the insatiable search for additional money-wealth gained through the constant growth of the economic system. The idea of a "stationary" capitalism is, in Marxian eyes, a contradiction in terms, on a logical par with a democratic aristocracy or an industrial feudalism.

Is the Millian or the Marxian view correct? I do not think that we can yet say. Some economic growth is certainly compatible with a stabilized rate of resource use and disposal, for growth could take the form of the expenditure of additional labor on the improvement (aesthetic or technical) of the national environment. Indeed, insofar as education or cultural activity are forms of national output that require little resource use and result in little waste product, national output could be indefinitely expanded through these and similar activities. But there is no doubt that the main avenue of traditional capitalist accumulation would have to be considerably constrained; that net investment in mining and manufacturing would effectively cease; that the rate and kind of technological change would need to be supervised and probably greatly reduced; and that as a consequence, the flow of profits would almost certainly fall.

Is this imaginable within a capitalist setting—that is, in a nation in which the business ideology permeates the views of nearly all groups and classes, and establishes the bounds of what is possible and natural, and

what is not? Ordinarily I do not see how such a question could be answered in any way but negatively, for it is tantamount to asking a dominant class to acquiesce in the elimination of the very activities that sustain it. But this is an extraordinary challenge that may evoke an extraordinary response. Like the challenge posed by war, the ecological crisis affects all classes, and therefore may be sufficient to induce sociological changes that would be unthinkable in ordinary circumstances. The capitalist and managerial classes may see— perhaps even more clearly than the consuming masses—the nature and nearness of the ecological crisis, and may recognize that their only salvation (as human beings, let alone privileged human beings) is an occupational migration into governmental or other posts of power, or they may come to accept a smaller share of the national surplus supply simply because they recognize that there is no alternative. When the enemy is nature, in other words, rather than another social class, it is at least imaginable that adjustments could be made that would be impossible in ordinary circumstances.[1]

There is, however, one last possibility to which I must also call attention. It is the possibility that the ecological crisis will simply result in the decline or even destruction of Western civilization, and of the hegemony of the scientific-technological view that has achieved so much and cost us so dearly. Great challenges do not always bring great responses, especially when those responses must be sustained over long periods of time and require dramatic changes in life styles and attitudes. Even educated men today are able to deny the reality of the crisis they face: there is wild talk of farming the seas, of transporting men to the planets, of unspecified "miracles" of technology that will avert disaster. Glib as they are, however, at least these suggestions have a certain responsibility when compared to another and much more worrisome response: *Je m'en fiche.* Can

[1] Let me add a warning that it is not only capitalists who must make an unprecedented ideological adjustment. Socialists must also come to terms with the abandonment of the goal of industrial superabundance on which their vision of a transformed society rests. The stationary equilibrium imposed by the constraints of ecology requires at the very least a reformulation of the kind of economic society toward which socialism sets its course.

we really persuade the citizens of the Western world, who are just now entering the
heady atmosphere of a high consumption
way of life, that conservation, stability, fru-
gality, and a deep concern for the distant
future must now take priority over the personal indulgence for which they have been
culturally prepared and which they are about
to experience for the first time? Not the least
danger of the ecological crisis, as I see it, is
that tens and hundreds of millions will shrug
their shoulders at the prospects ahead
("What has posterity ever done for us?"),
and that the increasingly visible approach of
ecological Armageddon will bring not re-
pentance but Saturnalia.

Yet I cannot end this essay on such a note.
For it seems to me that the ecological en-
thusiasts may be right when they speak of
the deteriorating environment as providing
the *possibility* for a new political rallying
ground. If a new New Deal, capable of engaging both the efforts and the beliefs of this
nation, is the last great hope to which we
cling in the face of what seems otherwise to
be an inevitable gradual worsening and
coarsening of our style of life, it is possible
that a determined effort to arrest the ecological decay might prove to be its underlying
theme. Such an issue, immediate in the experience of all, carries an appeal that might
allow vast improvements to be worked in the
American environment, both urban and industrial. I cannot estimate the likelihood of
such a political awakening, dependent as
these matters are on the dice of personality
and the outcome of events at home and
abroad. But however slim the possibility of
bringing such a change, it does at least make
the ecological crisis, unquestionably the
gravest long-run threat of our times, potentially the source of its greatest short-term
promise.

THE MAKING OF A POLLUTION-INDUSTRIAL COMPLEX

Martin Gellen

As in other areas, an industrial complex is forming. This time, it is forming to
profit from society's concern about pollution. Its growth and emergent power
will drastically constrain the number of alternatives society can consider
in seeking to curb pollution. It tends to ensure that rapid economic growth will
continue, and that we shall simply allow corporations to profit from cleaning
up their own mess.

The article originally appeared in a special issue of *Ramparts* on the
environment. Gellen is an associate of the Bay Area Institute for Policy Studies
and is doing organizing around environmental issues.

In January of [1970] Coca-Cola Company announced its purchase of Aqua-Chem,
a leading manufacturer of water treatment
equipment and desalination systems. "The
acquisition will permit Coca-Cola to enter
the mainstream of environmental control systems," declared a spokesman for the company. Perhaps the people at Coke have seen

SOURCE: *Martin Gellen, "The Making of a Pollution-Industrial Complex," in* Ramparts, *May,
1970. Copyright © Ramparts Magazine, Inc.,
1970. By permission of the editors.*

the handwriting on the wall and realize that
their livelihood depends on having clean
water to make brown. But whatever the precise reasoning, the marriage of Coke and
Aqua-Chem is just one among a rash of similiar developments on Wall Street where pollution control has emerged as one of the
hottest growth industries of the '70s. As
Forbes magazine put it in a recent cover
story, there's "cash in all that trash."

Since the beginning of December 1969,
despite a market engaged in a remarkably

stubborn downward spiral, stock issues of companies with substantial interests in pollution control have made price advances of often better than 50 percent. For instance, Research-Cottrell, Inc., the largest of the corporations devoted entirely to environmental systems, has quadrupled its sales in five years. For the pollution control industry as a whole, the average annual growth rate for the next five years is expected to climb to better than 20 percent, which is almost three times that of most manufacturing groups.

Lester Krellenstein, an engineer and pollution control promoter for the brokerage firm of H. Hentz and Company, believes that President Nixon's appointment of a Council of Environmental Quality triggered the heavy buying. According to Krellenstein, "A great deal of money is going to be made in this business." Present estimates of the potential market start at $25 billion.

But of all the developments in the fledgling industry, by far the most instructive is the corporate integration of polluters and controllers. About two dozen pollution control companies are subsidiaries or divisions of the largest corporations and polluters in the United States. Represented among this latter group are Dow Chemical Co., Monsanto Chemical, W. R. Grace, Du Pont, Merck, Nalco, Union Carbide, General Electric, Westinghouse, Combustion Engineering, Honeywell, Beckman Instruments, Alcoa, Universal Oil Products, North American Rockwell, and many others. Although these super-corporations currently make less in sales from pollution control than do smaller firms like Research-Cottrell and Wheelabrator, their superior access to capital, resources, markets, management skills and political power will invariably be translated into a superior competitive position as the ecology movement flowers and the control industry grows.

The pollution control industry is really an extension of both the technological capabilities and the marketing patterns of the capital goods sector of the economy. Most of the companies involved in pollution control are not only polluters themselves but are the same firms which supply the chemicals, machines, plant fuels and parts for even bigger polluters, such as General Motors, U.S. Steel, Boeing, Standard Oil, Philco-Ford, American Can Co. and Consolidated Edison. For many of these firms, pollution control is merely one aspect of a program of "environmental diversification," which is generally accompanied by heavy investment and aggressive acquisition programs.

Koppers, for instance, is an engineering and construction firm that designs municipal sewage plants as well as air and water purification systems. Among its many specialties in pollution abatement is the production of gas removal devices for electric utilities, steel plants, coke plants and foundries. At the same time, however, Koppers is one of the world's leading builders of steelmaking equipment and is responsible for designing over 25 percent of all basic steelmaking facilities in the U.S., as well as half of the present domestic coke plants in operation. Thus it gets the business coming and going. Since 80 percent of the coke plants in the nation will require modernization in the '70s, and the steel industry expects to increase its overall capacity by 50 percent, Koppers can expect good profits designing the pollution control systems needed to curb the pollution caused by all the new coke ovens, steel furnaces and foundries which it will construct.

It is the chemical industry, however, that best illustrates the consequences of the incest between the pollution control business and the industrial polluters. First, the chemical industry is in the enviable position of reaping sizable profits by attempting to clean up rivers and lakes (at public expense) which they have profitably polluted in the first place. To facilitate this, practically every major chemical company in the U.S. has established a pollution abatement division or is in the process of doing so. Dow Chemical, for example, produces a wide variety of products and services for water pollution abatement, including measuring instruments, specialty treatment chemicals, and a special biological filter medium called SURF-PAC. The company designs, engineers, builds and services waste water treatment plants and is currently supervising municipal sewage plants in Cleveland and working on waste disposal problems for lumber companies in Pensacola, Florida, and West Nyack, New York. All of these projects are funded by the Federal Water Pollution Control Administration (FWPCA).

Thus, the chemical industry—which ranks

second in production of polluted waste water and generates close to 50 percent of the biological oxygen demand in industrial water before treatment—has, at the same time, established a dominant position in the water pollution control business.

A second consequence of placing the "control" of pollution in the hands of big business is that the official abatement levels will inevitably be set low enough to protect industry's power to pollute and therefore its ability to keep costs down and revenues high. According to a recent study by the FWPCA, if the chemical industry were to reduce its pollution of water to zero, the costs involved would amount to almost $2.7 billion per year. This would cut profits almost by half.

Fortunately for the chemical industry, the present abatement target is only 75 percent reduction in water pollution through "secondary treatment" methods which will clean up the solids but leave the phosphates, nitrogen compounds and a host of other poisonous substances which secondary treatment can't possibly catch.

Of course, it is precisely the profit incentive as the criterion of what shall and shall not be produced that makes it impossible to stop the proliferation and profusion of poisons in even the most obvious places. Thus, the chemical industry has polluted the housewife's food package not only through the unintended absorption of pesticide residues, but also through innumerable colorings, additives (like the cyclamates) and preservatives designed to increase food purchases and consumption, in order to buoy up sagging sales curves. The package itself, which is a sales boosting device par excellence, can be both the most polluting and dangerous feature of all. As a *pièce de résistance* the chemical industry produces the nonbiodegradable plastic container, which comes in all sizes, shapes and colors, and, if made from polyvinyl plastic, like Dow's Saran-Wrap, can be deadly in the most literal sense of the word. When Saran-Wrap is accumulated as trash and burned, it produces phosgene gas—a poison gas used in World War I and currently stockpiled by the Department of Defense. Exposure for only a short duration to 50 parts of phosgene per million parts of air will cause death. The chemical industry currently makes approximately five billion pounds of polyvinyl plastic per year and out-

put is expected to rise by seven percent this year alone.

Another consequence of business control of cleaning up the environment is cost to the public. Most municipal water treatment plants in large urban areas are currently constructed to handle an excess capacity frequently 100 percent greater than the volume of waste actually produced by their resident populations. Much of this surplus capacity is used by big business (especially the chemical industry) to dispose of its wastes. Although industries are charged for this use, it is the consumers and taxpayers, through federal grants and state bonds, who bear the cost of construction and maintenance of the treatment facilities. Thus the public pays the polluters to construct the treatment facilities necessitated by the polluters in the first place.

Thus pollution control, developed as a complementary industry, is a way to insure that the favorable balance between cost, sales and profits can be maintained and business can continue as usual—indeed, better than usual, for pollution control means new investment outlets, new income and new profits; the more waste, the better. Pollution control as conceived by the pollution control industry is merely an extension of the same pattern of profit-seeking exploitation and market economics which is at the root of the environmental crisis itself.

The most salient fact about the crisis that now threatens to overwhelm us is that it is first and foremost a product of the so-called free-enterprise system. "American business," as *Fortune* admits, "since it organizes and channels a high proportion of the total action of this society, has been and still is deeply implicated in depredations against the environment." It is not technology per se, but the way technology is employed (its organization and channeling) that creates the problems. Take, for example, the automobile. What logic determined man's use, as his central mode of transportation, of a device which threw concrete highways across the plains, cut up the forests, poisoned the atmosphere, congested the cities and created the sprawling conurbations that have smothered the land? Was it safe? Computed as fatalities per mile, the death rate for cars is 25 times that for trains and 10 times that for planes. Was it efficient? A traffic study made in 1907 shows that horse-drawn vehicles in New York moved at an average speed of 11.5 miles per hour. Today, automobiles crawl at the average daytime rate of six miles per hour.

At the beginning of the '60s it was estimated that in a single day, motor vehicles burned about seven million gallons of gasoline and in the process produced enough carbon monoxide to pollute the air to a depth of 400 feet over an area of 681 square miles. One-third of the entire land area of Los Angeles (two-thirds of the downtown section) had been absorbed by cars and trucks and the facilities to service them. The area was so congested that plans were laid to spend another $7.5 billion over the next decade on highway construction. The highway program would cost $10,000 per family, while during the same period only $3090 per family would be spent in Los Angeles County for schools, hospitals, parks, water supply, recreation and all other facilities. And Los Angeles is no worse in this respect than other city or urban areas. New York is now spending $100 million per mile to construct a crosstown highway. But in the peak hours, 87.6 percent of the people entering the central business district come by public transport (71 percent by subway).

Is there any rationality in all this? There is. But it is a private rationality. The essence of the private property system is that social technology and production are privately or corporately organized and channeled through the market. Thus, in launching his new product, Henry Ford had only private costs to reckon (i.e., the costs to him in labor, materials, etc.). The individual consumer who bought the car had only to reckon his personal preferences versus the purchase price. The question of who would pay the costs of roads, of restructuring cities and organizing the flow of traffic, was taken care of by Ford, the rubber industry, the glass industry, the concrete industry and related interests getting together and twisting the arm of the government. They saw to it that the public would pay for solving the problems created by the new machine.

The costs of pollution are borne by our lungs and in individual cleaning bills; the costs of lack of safety are paid in individual hospital bills and individual deaths. Suppose Ford had been forced from the outset to reckon the social costs (at least the ones that could be quantified) and to put that in the price of his autos. At that price, people would have bought trains as their mass transportation, or more reasonably, they would have been forced to structure their cities and communities in a way which would have enabled them to walk to virtually all of the places necessary.

The problems created by the market system are thus like original sin: their implications keep spreading and diversifying. Now, when the demand for cars shows signs of being saturated, the market strategists get to work and—by changing models, manipulating consumers and planning the obsolescence of their product—generate the need for more and more cars, ad infinitum. The waste in resources is staggering (it has been estimated that style changes in autos alone cost $4 billion annually) and the increase in pollution incalculable.

The pollution control industry itself reflects this irrationality in production for profit. It, too, is a growth industry. It, too, depends for its existence on society's capacity to make waste. The production of steel, copper, aluminum, asbestos and beryllium components for air pollution systems and sewage plants will probably create more air pollution and kill more rivers. The waste involved in the production of all the specialty chemicals and biological agents needed for water treatment alone is staggering. Moreover, the waste in resources required to operate $100 billion worth of control systems will certainly not reduce the despoliation of the environment.

Instead of reorganizing the productive system for social ends, thereby eliminating the problem of waste production and distribution at its source, pollution control under business auspices amounts to no more than rationalizing and improving waste production by making it less ugly, less harmful, less objectionable, and more pleasant for everybody. The object of this kind of pollution control is to make pollution "functional" in society, to institutionalize it, to change it into a necessary and regular part of the everyday world. There is no more effective way to do that than to make it possible for a whole industry to make money out of it. To the military-industrial complex, we can now add an eco-pollution-industrial complex, with a vested interest in continuing economic growth and environmental malaise.

The philosophical justifications for this "solution" are already well developed. As President Nixon's science adviser, Dr. Lee A. DuBridge, puts it, "Let's face it—waste products are a fact of life we have to recognize. . . . Clearly, the U.S. will be producing more waste in the future—not less." The purpose of pollution control, DuBridge explains, is simply to "determine reasonable levels of pollution consistent with good health." Such a logic simultaneously justifies the political economy of waste, effectively de-politicizes the issues of the environment, and defines the problem of pollution in terms of technological solutions and bureaucratic directives. As such it is the normal logic of a society whose business, as Coolidge once said, is business.

Following every failure of the business system in a major social area, the government has stepped in to create a new social-industrial complex, passing the costs of rehabilitation and correction on to the tax-paying public, and reserving the benefits for the corporations. Like the defense suppliers and the educational-manpower conglomerates, the pollution control industry now enjoys the good fortune of being legislated into success. Lavish profits will come from ready-made markets bolstered by special laws controlling pollution levels of factories, special tax write-offs for the industrial buyers of abatement equipment, and plenty of R&D money for the pollution controllers themselves. As government outlays on abatement grow, so will the profits accruing to the pollution control industry. With Uncle Sam posing as Mr. Clean, the crisis of the environment can't help being profitable.

At the National Executives Conference on Water Pollution Abatement, convened last fall by the Department of the Interior in order to "bring the environmental programs of business and government into close alignment," John Gillis, president of Monsanto Chemical Co., led the business executives in calling for immediate federal financial aid in the form of quick tax write-offs and investment credits. The Tax Reform Bill passed by Congress early this winter answered the call. While abolishing the 7 percent investment credit, Congress instituted a special five-year amortization allowance for pollution control equipment, which will actually allow a lot of corporations somewhat larger tax deduc-

tions than did the investment credit. In addition, some 22 states also offer such subsidies for installation of pollution control equipment. California, for example, provides for a special five-year write-off, while Connecticut gives anti-polluters a 5 percent tax credit.

With the prospects of rising R&D expenditures by the federal government, everyone is getting into the act. Anaconda and Alcoa have recently established environmental divisions. Esso Research has started a five-year planning study to determine the National Air Pollution Control Administration (NAPCA) needs in the area of nitrogen oxide emission control. The presence of aerospace corporations and other major defense contractors like Dow, G.E. and Westinghouse on the federal pollution control payroll is of course more than mere coincidence. Currently, the aerospace industry receives about 25 percent of all the research contracts awarded by NAPCA. Aerojet-General, Avco Industries, Bendix Corporation and Litton Industries are some of the more prominent newcomers to the field. For Litton, Bendix and Aerojet-General, pollution control is a spin-off from their government-sponsored programs for development of biological weapons. Aerojet-General has also received over a million dollars in contracts from the Federal Water Pollution Control Administration for control of toxic agents in water supplies.

After riot control, pollution control is another area in which North American Rockwell, builder of Apollo and one of the country's biggest defense contractors, expects to make "important social contributions as well as profits," according to Robert T. Chambers, chairman of Envirotech, which is NAR's new pollution abatement subsidiary. Envirotech will market some of the measuring devices which NAR has developed through work for FWPCA, NAPCA, the Defense Department's chemical and biological warfare programs, and the space program. Just to keep it all in the family, President Nixon is reportedly planning to place the coordination of pollution control R&D programs under the aegis of the National Aeronautics and Space Administration instead of setting up a special agency for this purpose.

Nixon is also arranging to whip up a little business for investment bankers. As a part of Nixon's $10 billion program for municipal sewage plant construction, state and local governments will finance their $6 billion share of the deal through tax-exempt bonds. The President will also establish an Environmental Funding Authority to buy up any of the bonds which the locals can't sell. The EFA will probably handle a good number of them, since the municipal and state government bond markets are currently glutted. Its own funds would come from the sale of bonds at the even higher non-municipal rates. The Treasury Department (headed by banker David Kennedy) would make up the difference between the interest the EFA would receive on local bonds and what it would have to pay out on its own. In other words, the taxpayers would once again pay the bill.

Thus, pollution control programs illustrate the ways in which government promotes the welfare of business at the expense of the tax-paying public. The non-taxpaying poor will also suffer. It's all a matter of priorities. More federal spending for pollution control will mean less for the war on poverty. "Ul-timately," pontificates *The Wall Street Journal*, "preservation of the environment may have to take absolute priority over social stability and welfare."

The crisis of the environment must be viewed in terms of a paradox central to modern society. The mobilization of the productive energies of society and the physical forces of nature for the purpose of accumulating profits or enhancing private power and privilege now conflicts directly with the universal dependence of men upon nature for the means of their common survival. A society whose principal ends and incentives are monetary and expansionist inevitably produces material and cultural impoverishment —in part precisely because of the abundance of profitable goods. To make an industry out of cleaning up the mess that industry itself makes is a logical extension of corporate capitalism. What is needed, however, is not an extension of what is already bad, but its transformation into something better.

THE DIALECTICS OF ECONOMIC GROWTH

Herbert Gintis

The author provides some compelling arguments that continued economic growth is necessary for the stability of the capitalist system. As Chapter One noted, individual corporations will inevitably seek to grow as rapidly as they can, for fear of losing to competitors. Perhaps more important, growth is of fundamental importance to the capitalist class as a whole, because the promise of future affluence provides one of the few incentives for workers to tolerate their conditions in capitalist societies. Growth also dialectically undercuts the stability of the system, as Gintis concludes, by providing so much affluence that many become materially satisfied and ultimately establish other priorities which capitalism cannot meet.

The selection comes from a longer article, "New Working Class and Revolutionary Youth," which presents the general case that revolutionary attitudes among youth pose a fundamental challenge to the capitalist system. This selection served to elaborate the interrelationships between economic growth and rising revolutionary consciousness. The article appeared in *Socialist Revolution* and *The Review of Radical Political Economics*.

Gintis is a lecturer at Harvard University and a research associate of the Center for Educational Policy Research.

SOURCE: *Herbert Gintis, "New Working Class and Revolutionary Youth,"* in Socialist Revolution, *May–June, 1970. Reprinted by permission of Socialist Revolution.*

The *virtue* of capitalism is its ability to generate vast and ever increasing quantities of goods and services, through the economic rationalization of social institutions. If the system is to be accepted, individuals must view the generation of goods and services as an *ultimate* virtue. Thus socialization of the individual, socialization occurring through family, church, communications media, and schools, centers around the instilling of *material goal orientations*. In a parallel manner, that workers, students, and community members accept a situation in which the overriding majority of social decisions are made without regard to other than material considerations, requires that socialization *suppress* the development of any non-material goals in the individual.

The expectation that increasing material consumption is the path to happiness has probably always lurked in the background of the individual's "decision" to submit to and even participate in his own alienation. Since this expectation seems never to be filled in the *present*, the justification of economic rationality has thereby, and predictably, turned to the prospects of *economic growth* as the path toward social welfare. Indeed, the historic stability of American capitalism has depended not on the *level* of material welfare it has provided, but on the rate at which it has *expanded* production and successfully thrown crumbs to the dispossessed.

To avoid collapse, America must expand. This economic imperative has become part of the national creed; it is an ideology so deeply imbedded that it affects almost every aspect of social life. But it is a *rational* ideology; indeed, economic growth has been the traditional and effective buffer to social schism and conflict. Be they black vs. white, poor vs. rich, worker vs. capitalist, the struggle over the distribution of material product is fought on capitalism's home ground. For in the context of economic growth, such struggle becomes a game in which all may win and none need lose—when the "size of the pie" is rapidly increasing, the struggle over the apportioning of the pieces is perforce attenuated. Capitalist hegemony is secured in palming off the ideology which equates "success" with consumption-oriented security.

Further, economic growth is the very *catalyst* for the acceptance of the ideology glorifying individual consumption activities.

The development of materially oriented, economically rational "homo economicus" requires that the individual *submit to* and *consciously accept the legitimacy of* basic socializing institutions, such as schools and advertising media. To *operate*, such institutions must be considered *legitimate,* and for all the emphasis on the "internalization" of social values found in bourgeois sociology, it remains that an individual, as a member of a social class, and insofar as his actions become subject to internal evaluation and review, will accept the channeling of his aspirations in "socially approved" directions *only insofar as* he experiences this channeling as contributory to, or at least compatible with, his own welfare, and generalizing from this, the welfare of his social class. In many ways this acceptance is subjected continually to the test of experience, and becomes more an empirical than a value judgment. The individual is led to believe that by restricting the demands he makes on society to individual material economic demands, he will be happy. Quite simply, is this true or false? The importance of economic growth in this context is that *it introduces a crucial element of incomplete knowledge,* rendering the individual less able to put these questions to the test, and hence reinforcing the position of the conscious instruments of socialization provided by the system.

Let me illustrate this with some examples. First the total situation: Am I happy with my life, having effectively rejected all social goals other than my material well-being? No. But then I am not materially secure, and since I can expect my income to rise in the future, and my children's incomes to be double mine, I may as well accept the system.[1] The assumption here is that someone with double his income must be happy, everything else being equal, and this is indeed what he is told. But he has incomplete knowledge in that he does not know whether it is in fact true, and has no way of testing it.

Am I happy with my community? No, because my community serves no function other than representing the mute and sterile physical environment within which my fam-

[1] In the U.S., real family incomes double every 25 to 30 years (that is, incomes after taking account of inflation). While a worker may not know this fact in this form, he sees the alternatives posed in terms of his children's educational and occupational opportunities.

ily is located. However, when my income rises, I will be able to move to a community with a better physical environment, or at least my children will. Indeed a worker is told that he will be happier in such an "improved" community, and even if this is only a possibility, it must be weighed against the vast expenditure in effort involved in attempting to create an active functioning community with the power to make important economic and social decisions. Again economic growth leads to incomplete knowledge and the acceptance of socialized norms.

Am I happy with my work? No. Am I happy with my education? No. As for the intrinsic value of all these activities, the individual may well feel at a loss for something positive to say, except that it is possible, and indeed it is drummed into him that it is inevitable, that they will lead to security in individual consumption, the "sufficient condition" of personal welfare. Such expectations of future rewards remind one of the role of religion in an earlier period as an "opiate" of the working class. "There'll be pie, bye and bye, in that glorious Land in the Sky" mocks Joe Hill, and the radical organizer in him cries out, "It's a lie!" And so it is a lie in our day too, yet a lie to which most have turned an attentive ear. Break capitalism? Reorganize our communities to reflect the true economic and social needs and aspiration of its members? Take over the factories and offices? Organize work around the needs of workers as human beings and the needs of the communities to which they are responsible? Wrest the schools from the service of capital that they may serve as places where human beings grow rather than factories for the production of machine surrogates? All these, directives issuing from the activities men enter into in their daily lives, are countermanded by the "pie in the sky," the expectation of security from economic growth.

We may sum up the role of economic growth in equilibrating capitalism as follows:

(a) Capitalism does not provide the social institutions for the derivation of welfare from non-individual consumption activities. The lack of functioning communities, solidary and non-alienating work environments, etc., renders consumption activities the only *feasible* path to personal well-being. Thus, consumptive goal orientations become plausible.

(b) Because of economic growth, individuals cannot *refute* the proposition that consumptive goal orientation actually makes people happy—the individual experience of the *present* cannot be projected into the *future*.

(c) Thus individuals submit to socialization which actually produces integrated *Homo Economicus*. This is most obvious in the case of schools, where a youth "puts up with the classroom shit" because of the rewards in the form of higher income, and as a result, becomes the type of individual who derives welfare *only from* higher income.

(d) Hence, the system becomes rational in the eyes of the socialized individual: he has underdeveloped capacities for individual fulfillment other than through material consumption, and society provides no other outlets for activity than consumption activity.

(e) Struggle for class welfare centers around the division of material product, a struggle which capitalism can easily handle.

(f) The system remains stable and grows, thus recreating the preconditions of (a) and (b).

Hence there is an important *logical* element in the structure of the internalization of norms, and a concomitant *empirical* element subject to possible verification. Namely, the internalization of individual consumption orientation fails to be a "self-fulfilling prophecy" in that however fully internalized, it *need not lead to individual welfare*: the belief that consumption activity is the source of welfare is *independent* in large measure from the individual's goal orientations, and empirically refutable.

The falseness of the "individual consumption doctrine" has of course always been a part of radical Marxism, and few of us can forget the burning phrases of the early manuscripts:

Everything the economist takes from you in the way of life and humanity, he restores to you in the form of money and wealth. And everything you are unable to do, your money can do for you. . . . Thus all passions and activities must be submerged in avarice. . . .

An enforced increase of wages . . . would therefore be nothing but better payment for the slave, and would not win either for the worker or for labor their human status or dignity. Indeed, even the quality of wages . . . only transforms the relationship of the present-day worker to his labor the relationship of all men to labor. Society is then conceived as an abstract capitalist.

. . . [E]conomic growth, the "virtue" of capitalism, the force in terms of which the system is justified and stabilized, *is itself subject to a self-negating dialectic.* If capitalist society justifies itself by "delivering the goods," to use a phrase of Herbert Marcuse, its very deliverance undercuts its justification; for it is inevitable that once satisfied in this direction, individuals will thereby make other demands on their social system, and such demands cannot be satisfied by an economically rationalized order, by a society wherein "all social value is reduced to exchange value."

The basic "contradiction" that capitalism faces, then, is the following: economic growth is a prerequisite to social stability; yet men have essentially satisfiable material needs, satisfiable in the sense that further increase in material goods and services plays a minor part in securing their welfare independent of whether they *think* it will, or not; economic growth leads to the capacity for the satisfaction of these needs; hence economic growth, the prerequisite for *stability,* leads to *instability.*

There are two ways in which American capitalism has succeeded to date in handling this basic contradiction, this dialectic of economic growth. First, it has used the control of communications media ever more forcefully to emphasize the *expectational* justification of the system: if you are not well off, you will be later and your children will be even more so, because of economic growth. Secondly, it has used *fundamental irrationalities of production* to increase the *mass* of goods and services *without contributing* to their ability to satisfy human needs. . . .

The radical position vis-à-vis this mechanism I think should be clear. Capitalist economies *grow,* but they do not satisfy men's *needs* because the growth is *irrational.* Irrationalities occur through destruction of residential areas; irrationalities occur through the vast destruction of goods and services in the military-industrial-space complex; irrationalities occur through enforced obsolescence of commodities, style changes, and the culturally enforced norms of conspicuous consumption; irrationalities occur through the insufficient supply of important public services, such as medical, child care, transportation, natural recreational areas. The *expectation* of future welfare through growth is unwarranted, because these irrationalities must increase—*the original contradiction of economic growth reappears in more immediate and critical form in the irrationalities of production and destruction of commodities* —and they must increase because the continuance of capitalism is *inconsistent* with the full material satisfaction of needs. Further economic growth will render the truth of this argument ever more manifest, and in fact the "experience of irrationality" will fall daily closer to the experience of the worker. . . . Lastly, economic growth allows us to say that the real material needs of individuals can be satisfied *today* through the reorganization of the economy along rational lines, along lines compatible with the elimination of alienation from work, community, and self. We might then look to a *tomorrow* in which technology, rather than developing around the needs of profit and capital, develops around the needs of individuals liberated in individual and social activity.

ENVIRONMENT BIBLIOGRAPHY

I. DEFINITIONS AND MAGNITUDES

New York Times, April 20, 1970, p. 33. A full-page supplement with summaries and figures of all the different major sources and effects of pollution.

Congressional Quarterly, "Fact Sheet: Urban Pollution," May 23, 1969, pp. 817–822. Another useful summary of dimensions and figures.

U.S. Department of Health, Education, and Welfare, *Toward a Social Report,* 1969, U.S. Government, pp. 27–34. A third useful summary of definitions and trends.

Marshall I. Goldman and Robert Shoop, "What Is Pollution?" in Marshall I. Goldman, ed., *Controlling Pollution: The Economics of a Cleaner America*, 1967, Prentice-Hall, pp. 59–70. Short discussion of the different kinds of pollution and how we measure them.

II. ANALYSIS

A. General Perspectives

Robert Heilbroner, "Ecological Armageddon," in *New York Review of Books*, April 23, 1970. Superb general summary of issues.

Kenneth Boulding, "The Spaceship Earth," in Garrett de Bell, *The Environmental Handbook*, 1970, Ballantine. View of the earth as a closed system.

Roger Revelle, "Pollution and Cities," in James Q. Wilson, ed., *The Metropolitan Enigma*, 1968, Harvard, pp. 91–133. Useful analysis of kinds of pollution and their causes, though without taking any positions on priorities of causes.

Robert U. Ayres and Allen V. Kneese, "Pollution and Environmental Quality," in Harvey Perloff, ed., *The Quality of the Urban Environment*, 1969. Resources for the Future, pp. 35–74. More difficult analysis, concentrating on the systematic balance of resource use and waste generation.

Roger Revelle and Hans H. Landsberg, "Introduction," in Revelle and Landsberg, eds., *America's Changing Environment*, 1970, Houghton Mifflin, pp. ix–xxxvii. Another fairly useful summary of issues, again without taking a position.

B. Perspectives of Marginal Economic Analysis

Jon Breslaw, "Economics and Ecosystems," in de Bell, ed., *The Environmental Handbook, op. cit.*, pp. 102–112. Simple statement of the implications of marginal analysis for understanding pollution.

Larry Ruff, "The Economic Common Sense of Pollution," *The Public Interest*, No. 19, Spring, 1970, pp. 69–85. A slightly more assertive statement that marginal analysis allows us to understand and solve all our pollution problems.

R. H. Coase, "The Problem of Social Cost," *Journal of Law and Economics*, March, 1965. A slightly more technical statement of the marginal framework and its implications for external diseconomies like pollution.

Francis M. Bator, "The Anatomy of Market Failure," *Quarterly Journal of Economics*, August, 1958. Very technical, dense but extremely comprehensive survey of how marginal, competitive models of neoclassical economics can break down.

E. J. Mishan, *The Costs of Economic Growth*, 1967, Praeger, pp. 45–108. Brilliant discussion of the way in which economists discuss external costs (as in the above selections), showing how that discussion depends on institutional arrangements in society and how the implications of the analysis carry profoundly distributional biases. Extremely important book.

John H. Dales, *Pollution, Property and Prices*, 1968, University of Toronto. Excellent discussion of relationship of property values to prices in the economic analysis.

C. Relationship to Economic Growth

E. J. Mishan, *The Costs of Economic Growth, op. cit.*, entire. Questions the devotion of economists to increasing the rate of economic growth, suggesting the likelihood of more growth bringing more pollution.

Paul and Anne Ehrlich, *Population, Resources, Environment*, 1970, W. H. Freeman. Alarming discussion of all the ways in which continuing economic and population growth threaten the environment and our lives.

Murray Bookchin, "Toward an Ecological Solution," *Ramparts*, May, 1970. The necessity of placing ecological priorities over that of growth.

Henry Jarrett, *Environmental Quality in a Growing Economy*, 1966, Johns Hopkins. More conventional, more sanguine analysis than the above.

D.   The Effects and Implications of Technology

John McDermott, "Technology: The Opiate of the Intellectuals," *New York Review of Books*, July 31, 1969. Brilliant exposition and critique of the liberal faith in the neutrality of technology, of what McDermott characterizes as a new ideology of "*laissez innover.*"

George M. Woodwell, "Science and the Gross National Pollution," *Ramparts*, May, 1970. The role of science in affecting pollution.

Don Price, *The Scientific Estate*, 1965, Harvard. Useful general account of the role of scientists in affecting public policy.

Jacques Ellul, *The Technological Society*, 1964, Knopf. Classic statement of the independent dynamic role technology plays in modern society.

III.   TECHNICAL SOLUTIONS

A.   Air Pollution

Harold Wolozin, ed., *The Economics of Air Pollution*, 1966, W. W. Norton, especially the articles by Kneese, Crocker, and Ridker (in addition to the Mills piece included in this book of readings).

Azriel Teller, "Air-Pollution Abatement: Economic Rationality and Reality," in Revelle and Landsberg, eds., *op. cit.*

Restoring the Quality of Our Environment, Report of the Environmental Pollution Panel, President's Science Advisory Committee, 1966, U.S. Government. Excellent technical discussion of policy measures.

B.   Water Pollution

Marshall I. Goldman, ed., *Controlling Pollution*, *op. cit.*, articles by Kneese, Cook, Thackrey, and Edson.

Allen Kneese, *Water Pollution*, 1962, Resources for the Future. Very useful summary.

Allen Kneese, *The Economics of Regional Water Quality Management*, 1964, Johns Hopkins. Especially his discussion of the Ruhr valley water control system in Germany, the most successful attempt at curing water pollution in the world.

Ted Willrich and N. Hines, *Water Pollution Control and Abatement*, 1965, Iowa University. Good technical summary.

C.   Waste Management and Land Pollution

Waste Management and Control, Report to the Federal Council for Science and Technology by Committee on Pollution of the National Academy of Science, 1966, National Research Council of the National Academy of Science. Comprehensive intelligent report on variety of solutions.

D.   The Politics of Technical Solutions

James Ridgeway, *The Politics of Ecology*, 1970, Dutton. Comprehensive survey by muckraking journalist of the poverty of government efforts at control.

Gene Marine, "The California Water Plan: The Most Expensive Faucet in the World," *Ramparts*, May, 1970. Interesting account of politics behind mammoth California water boondoggle.

Katherine Barkley and Steve Weissman, "The Eco-Establishment," *Ramparts*, May, 1970. The powers governing the ways we fight pollution.

Brenn Stilley, "The SST," in de Bell, ed., *op. cit.*, pp. 177–181. The politics of the supersonic transport plane.

5 6 7 8 9 10   9-403